KU-112-429

Exam 70-547: *PRO: Designing and Developing Web-Based Applications Using the Microsoft .NET Framework*

Objective	Location in Book
Envisioning and Designing an Application	
Evaluate the technical feasibility of an application design concept.	
▪ Evaluate the proof of concept.	Chapter 1, Lesson 2
▪ Recommend the best technologies for the features and goals of the application.	Chapter 1, Lesson 1
▪ Weigh implementation considerations.	Chapter 1, Lesson 1
▪ Investigate existing solutions for similar business problems.	Chapter 1, Lesson 1
Create a proof-of-concept prototype.	
▪ Evaluate the risks associated with ASP.NET 2.0 technology or implementation.	Chapter 1, Lesson 2
▪ Validate that the proposed technology can be used in the application.	Chapter 1, Lesson 2
▪ Demonstrate to stakeholders that the proposed solution will address their needs.	Chapter 1, Lesson 2
Evaluate the technical specifications for an application to ensure that the business requirements are met.	
▪ Translate the functional specification into developer terminology, such as pseudo code and UML diagrams.	Chapter 2, Lesson 3
▪ Suggest component type and layer.	Chapter 2, Lesson 2
Evaluate the design of a database.	
▪ Recommend a database schema.	Chapter 8, Lesson 1
▪ Identify the stored procedures that are required for an application.	Chapter 8, Lesson 1
Evaluate the logical design of an application.	
▪ Evaluate the logical design for performance.	Chapter 3, Lesson 1
▪ Evaluate the logical design for maintainability.	Chapter 3, Lesson 1
▪ Evaluate the logical design for extensibility.	Chapter 3, Lesson 1
▪ Evaluate the logical design for scalability.	Chapter 3, Lesson 1
▪ Evaluate the logical design for availability	Chapter 3, Lesson 1
▪ Evaluate the logical design for security.	Chapter 3, Lesson 1
▪ Evaluate the logical design against use cases.	Chapter 3, Lesson 1
▪ Evaluate the logical design for recoverability.	Chapter 3, Lesson 1
▪ Evaluate the logical design for data integrity.	Chapter 3, Lesson 1
Evaluate the physical design of an application. Considerations include the design of the project structure, the number of files, the number of assemblies, and the location of these resources on the server.	
▪ Evaluate the physical design for performance.	Chapter 3, Lesson 2
▪ Evaluate the physical design for maintainability.	Chapter 3, Lesson 2
▪ Evaluate how the physical location of files affects the extensibility of the application.	Chapter 3, Lesson 2
▪ Evaluate the physical design for scalability.	Chapter 3, Lesson 2
▪ Evaluate the physical design for availability	Chapter 3, Lesson 2
▪ Evaluate the physical design for security.	Chapter 3, Lesson 2
▪ Evaluate the physical design for recoverability.	Chapter 3, Lesson 2
▪ Evaluate the physical design for data integrity.	Chapter 3, Lesson 2
Designing and Developing a User Interface	
Choose an appropriate layout for the visual interface.	
▪ Decide the content flow across pages.	Chapter 4, Lesson 1
▪ Evaluate user navigation needs.	Chapter 4, Lesson 1
▪ Identify the goal of the page.	Chapter 4, Lesson 1
▪ Ensure the congruency and consistency of the user experience throughout the application.	Chapter 4, Lesson 1
Evaluate a strategy for implementing a common layout throughout the UI.	
▪ Suggest when to use style sheets, master pages, Web parts, custom controls, scripting, and user controls.	Chapter 4, Lesson 2
▪ Suggest an applicable UI standard based on the intended client environment. Considerations include chosen operating systems, technologies, and browser types.	Chapter 4, Lesson 2
Choose an appropriate control based on design specifications.	
▪ Evaluate the type of data that must be captured or displayed.	Chapter 5, Lesson 2
▪ Evaluate available controls. Considerations include standard .NET Framework controls and custom, internally developed, and third-party controls.	Chapter 5, Lesson 1
▪ Evaluate how available controls are implemented in previous and ongoing projects or applications.	Chapter 5, Lesson 2
▪ Evaluate the user demographic. Considerations include localization concerns.	Chapter 5, Lesson 2
▪ Evaluate the user environment. Considerations include screen size and browser type and version.	Chapter 5, Lesson 2
Choose an appropriate data validation method at the UI layer.	
▪ Choose a validation method based on the data type provided.	Chapter 6, Lesson 1
▪ Decide how to report the feedback. Considerations include callbacks, exceptions, and writing to an event log.	Chapter 6, Lesson 1
▪ Identify the source of invalid data.	Chapter 6, Lesson 1
▪ Identify the cause of an invalid entry.	Chapter 6, Lesson 1
▪ Evaluate whether invalid data can be prevented.	Chapter 6, Lesson 1
▪ Evaluate whether an exception must be thrown.	Chapter 6, Lesson 1
▪ Evaluate whether an exception must be logged.	Chapter 6, Lesson 1
▪ Evaluate whether visual feedback, such as a message box or color, is required.	Chapter 6, Lesson 2
Choose appropriate user assistance and application status feedback techniques.	
▪ Design a user assistance mechanism.	Chapter 6, Lesson 2
▪ Choose an appropriate application status feedback technique based on available control types.	Chapter 6, Lesson 2
▪ Choose an appropriate application status feedback technique to support accessibility.	Chapter 6, Lesson 2
▪ Design an application status feedback mechanism.	Chapter 6, Lesson 2
Choose an appropriate mechanism to deliver multimedia data from an application.	
▪ Evaluate available multimedia delivery mechanisms. Considerations include bandwidth problems, file formats, frames per second, and streaming types.	Chapter 7, Lesson 1
▪ Design a multimedia delivery mechanism.	Chapter 7, Lesson 1
Designing and Developing a Component	
Establish the required characteristics of a component.	
▪ Decide when to create a single component or multiple components.	Chapter 8, Lesson 1
▪ Decide in which tier of the application a component should be located.	Chapter 8, Lesson 1
▪ Decide which type of object to build.	Chapter 8, Lesson 1
Create the high-level design of a component.	
▪ Establish the life cycle of a component.	Chapter 8, Lesson 2
▪ Decide whether to use established design patterns for the component.	Chapter 8, Lesson 2
▪ Decide whether to create a prototype for the component.	Chapter 8, Lesson 2
▪ Document the design of a component by using pseudo code, class diagrams, sequence diagrams, activity diagrams, and state diagrams.	Chapter 8, Lesson 2
▪ Evaluate tradeoff decisions. Considerations include security vs. performance, performance vs. maintainability, and so on.	Chapter 8, Lesson 2
Develop the public API of a component.	
▪ Decide the types of clients that can consume a component.	Chapter 8, Lesson 3
▪ Establish the required component interfaces.	Chapter 8, Lesson 3
▪ Decide whether to require constructor input.	Chapter 8, Lesson 3

Exam objectives: The exam objectives listed here are current as of this book's publication date. Exam objectives are subject to change at any time without prior notice and at Microsoft's sole discretion. Please visit the Microsoft Learning Web site for the most current listing of exam objectives: *http://www.microsoft.com/learning/mcp/*.

Microsoft

MCPD Self-Paced Training Kit: Designing and Developing Web-Based Applications Using the Microsoft® .NET Framework

Mike Snell, Bruce Johnson, Brian C. Lanham, and Sara Morgan of GrandMasters, with Shawn Wildermuth

PUBLISHED BY
Microsoft Press
A Division of Microsoft Corporation
One Microsoft Way
Redmond, Washington 98052-6399
Copyright © 2003 by GrandMasters, LLC; Shawn Wildermuth; and Microsoft Corporation

All rights reserved. No part of the contents of this book may be reproduced or transmitted in any form or by any means without the written permission of the publisher.

Library of Congress Control Number: 2006938197

Printed and bound in the United States of America.

1 2 3 4 5 6 7 8 9 QWT 2 1 0 9 8 7

Distributed in Canada by H.B. Fenn and Company Ltd.

A CIP catalogue record for this book is available from the British Library.

Microsoft Press books are available through booksellers and distributors worldwide. For further information about international editions, contact your local Microsoft Corporation office or contact Microsoft Press International directly at fax (425) 936-7329. Visit our Web site at www.microsoft.com/mspress. Send comments to tkinput@microsoft.com.

Microsoft, Microsoft Press, Active Directory, ActiveX, BizTalk, Developer Studio, Excel, InfoPath, IntelliSense, Internet Explorer, MSDN, MSN, Outlook, PowerPoint, SharePoint, SQL Server, Visio, Visual Basic, Visual C#, Visual C++, Visual Studio, Windows, Windows Live, Windows Media, Windows Mobile, and Windows Server are either registered trademarks or trademarks of Microsoft Corporation in the United States and/or other countries. Other product and company names mentioned herein may be the trademarks of their respective owners.

The example companies, organizations, products, domain names, e-mail addresses, logos, people, places, and events depicted herein are fictitious. No association with any real company, organization, product, domain name, e-mail address, logo, person, place, or event is intended or should be inferred.

This book expresses the author's views and opinions. The information contained in this book is provided without any express, statutory, or implied warranties. Neither the authors, Microsoft Corporation, nor its resellers, or distributors will be held liable for any damages caused or alleged to be caused either directly or indirectly by this book.

Acquisitions Editor: Ken Jones
Developmental Editor: Maureen Zimmerman
Project Editor: Maria Gargiulo and Laura Sackerman
Technical Editor: Bob Hogan
Copy Editor: Kerin Foley
Editorial Production: nSight
Indexer: Jack Lewis
SubAsy Part No. X13-30472
Body Part No. X13-30466

Dedication

I would like to thank my wife, Carrie, my daughter, Allie, and my son, Ben, for their patience and understanding while I took on another long nights-and-weekends project.

–Mike Snell

I'd like to thank my wife, Alisa, and my four children, Kyle, Cameron, Gillian, and Curtis, for their love and support. While they might not have written any of the words directly, they certainly helped create an environment where I could get my ideas down on paper. It may be the first time that my kids have seen their names in a book, but I strongly suspect that it won't be the last. Not that I'm sure to be authoring more books in the future, but that they will be.

–Bruce Johnson

To Kurt, Robin, Sam, Brian, and everyone else who believed in me...when I didn't.

–Brian C. Lanham

For Steve

–Sara Morgan

To Chris Sells, my friend and mentor

–Shawn Wildermuth

For my kids, Nashly, Abbi, and London

–Shannon Horn

A huge thanks to Ken Jones, Maureen Zimmerman, and everyone else at Microsoft for their work during this project. I would also like to thank my wife, Mariya, for her support. She is my big help and always had good advice for those times when I said, "I have no idea how I am going to create the next batch of practice items." Thanks also to my son, Anthony, who was patient when he asked me, "Dad, when are you going to finish your work?" And thanks to my little Sophie, who always gives me energy and cheers me up.

–Val Mazur

For my angel, Belina, and for my family–Tim, Jerri, and Greta–who have always been there for me. I love you all so much

–Murray Gordon

About the Authors

Mike Snell

Mike Snell has more than 15 years of experience as a software architect and consultant. He has led a number of enterprise-level projects, building client solutions on the Microsoft platform. He has delivered training and mentoring to hundreds of developers. Currently, Mike runs the Microsoft Consulting Practice at CEI (*www.ceiamerica.com*) in Pittsburgh, Pennsylvania. There, with his team of consulting architects, he helps CEI's diverse client base build mission-critical software.

Mike is recognized as a Microsoft Regional Director, a Microsoft Certified Solution Developer (MCSD), and a Project Management Professional (PMP). His co-authoring credits include *MCPD Self-Paced Training Kit (Exam 70-548): Designing and Developing Windows-Based Applications Using the Microsoft .NET Framework* (Microsoft Press, 2007) and *Microsoft Visual Studio 2005 Unleashed* (Sams, 2006).

Bruce Johnson

Bruce Johnson is a partner at ObjectSharp Consulting and is a 25-year veteran of the computer industry. The first half of his career was spent working in the trenches—otherwise known as the UNIX field. The last 14 years he has spent on projects at the leading edge of Windows technology—from C++ through the myriad versions of Visual Basic and ASP, up to the present incarnations in .NET 3.0. Bruce's experience includes creating commercial Web applications, implementing Web services in a financial institution, and building Windows Forms applications.

As well as having fun with system design and development, Bruce has given more than 200 presentations at conferences and user groups throughout North America. He has written columns and articles for numerous magazines and attempts to write regular posts on his blog at *www.objectsharp.com/blogs/bruce*. He guarantees that his activity on this blog will increase after this book is published.

Brian C. Lanham

After serving as a nuclear-qualified electrician for six years in the United States Navy, Brian C. Lanham pursued a computer science degree at Pennsylvania State University. During that time, Brian developed C applications for UNIX and DOS. He then moved on to Microsoft Windows and Web applications. Although he has dabbled in Java, .NET is his platform of choice. Brian currently lives in the Roanoke, Virginia, area. He can be reached at *codesailor@gmail.com*.

Sara Morgan

Sara Morgan, MCSD, MCDBA, is an independent author and consultant based in Baton Rouge, Louisiana. She specializes in developing leading-edge Web-based applications using Microsoft technologies. Since graduating from Louisiana State University with a degree in quantitative business analysis, she has been developing software for a variety of industries, including a not-for-profit hospital, a financial company offering mortgages, a major retailer, a software company that writes legislative software, and an application service provider.

Sara has written articles for *MSDN Magazine, Enterprise Development, .NET Development, Visual Studio Magazine* and DevX.com. Sara's articles about enhanced computing and her latest research efforts can be found at *www.custsolutions.net.*

Shawn Wildermuth

Shawn Wildermuth is a Microsoft C# MVP and is the founder of Wildermuth Consulting Services, LLC, a company that delivers software and training solutions in the Atlanta, Georgia, area. Shawn goes by the moniker "The ADO Guy" and can be contacted through his Web site at *http://adoguy.com.*

A member of the INETA Speaker Bureau, Shawn has spoken at several national conferences. He is the author of the book *Pragmatic ADO.NET* (Addison-Wesley, 2002) and coauthor of *MCTS Self-Paced Training Kit (Exam 70-536): Microsoft .NET Framework 2.0–Application Development Foundation* (Microsoft Press, 2006). He has written articles for a variety of magazines and a number of Web sites, including MSDN, DevSource, InformIT, Windows IT Pro, Server-Side, WindowsDevCenter, and Intel's Rich Client Series. Shawn has enjoyed building data-driven software for more than 20 years.

Shannon Horn

Shannon Horn delivers training for companies such as Microsoft and AppDev and has been a featured speaker on training videos with Learn-Key. He has also worked with large corporate clients on projects using .NET and Web technologies. Shannon is currently pursuing his third-degree black belt in tae kwon do; he plays electric bass guitar and lives for his kids. You can find out more about him by visiting *http://shannonhorn.spaces.live.com/.*

Mark Blomsma

Mark Blomsma is a Microsoft MVP in Visual C#, a software architect, and owner of Develop-One (*www.develop-one.com*) in Maine. He is a frequent speaker at .NET User Groups and has written articles for a variety of magazines such as *.NET Magazine* and *SDN Magazine*. He specializes in Microsoft .NET technology, enterprise application development, application integration, and software renovation. Visit his blog at *http://blog.develop-one.com*.

Val Mazur

Val Mazur, a Microsoft MVP for Visual Developer and Visual Basic, has been developing applications since 1985. Currently working as a .NET developer for a software company in Toronto, Canada, Val specializes in data access technologies. He is a contributor to Microsoft KnowledgeBase articles related to data access, a moderator for the ".NET Framework Data Access and Storage" and "SQL Server Data Access" MSDN forums, and the author of a number of publicly available .NET components that work with Microsoft Excel files (*http://xport.mvps.org*). Contact Val at *vmazur@mvps.org*.

Murray Gordon

Murray Gordon is the Director of Technology at Cambar Solutions (*www.cambarsolutions.com*) in Charleston, South Carolina, a consultation services and custom supply chain software company to many of the world's largest distribution companies. His vision is to transform rigid, heavily customized IT environments into flexible, adaptive environments that are competitive with contemporary enterprise solutions. Murray has led consulting engagements for development, implementation, operation, and support of mission-critical systems in food, health care, petroleum, finance, manufacturing, and retail sales. He has been an active contributor to the evolution of distributed computing architectures since 1994.

Murray is a frequent speaker at events such as Microsoft Code Camps and .NET User Groups. He is the president of the Greater Charleston .NET User Group (*www.gcnug.org*) in Charleston, South Carolina. You can check out his blog at *http://www.geekswithblogs.com/murraybgordon*.

Contents at a Glance

Table of Contents

What do you think of this book? We want to hear from you!

Microsoft is interested in hearing your feedback so we can continually improve our books and learning resources for you. To participate in a brief online survey, please visit:

www.microsoft.com/learning/booksurvey/

What do you think of this book? We want to hear from you!

Microsoft is interested in hearing your feedback so we can continually improve our books and learning resources for you. To participate in a brief online survey, please visit:

www.microsoft.com/learning/booksurvey/

Introduction

This training kit is designed for developers who plan to take Microsoft Certified Professional Developer (MCPD) Exam 70-547: Designing and Developing Web-Based Applications Using the Microsoft .NET Framework. Developers who work on medium or large-scale development projects will also benefit from the content in this training kit.

We assume that before you begin using this kit, you are familiar with creating Web applications using Microsoft Visual Studio 2005 and ASP.NET 2.0. You should also have a working knowledge of Microsoft Visual Basic or C#. You should have worked on a team throughout the software development life cycle, and you should be familiar with technical envisioning and planning, design and development, and stabilizing and releasing software.

By using this training kit, you'll learn how to do the following:

- Envision and design an application
- Design and develop a user interface
- Design and develop a component
- Design and develop an application framework
- Test and stabilize an application
- Deploy and support an application

Hardware Requirements

The following hardware is required to complete the lab exercises:

- Computer with a 600-MHz or faster processor (1 GHz recommended)
- 192 MB of RAM or more (512 MB recommended)
- 2 GB of available hard disk space
- DVD-ROM drive
- 1,024 x 768 or higher resolution display with 256 colors
- Keyboard and Microsoft mouse or compatible pointing device

Software Requirements

The following software is required to complete the practice exercises:

- One of the following operating systems:
    - ❑ Microsoft Windows 2000 with Service Pack 4
    - ❑ Windows XP with Service Pack 2
    - ❑ Windows XP Professional, x64 Editions (WOW)
    - ❑ Windows Server 2003 with Service Pack 1
    - ❑ Windows Server 2003, x64 Editions (WOW)
    - ❑ Windows Server 2003 R2
    - ❑ Windows Server 2003 R2, x64 Editions (WOW)
    - ❑ Windows Vista
- Visual Studio 2005 (A 90-day evaluation edition of Visual Studio 2005 Professional Edition is included on DVD with this book.)
- Microsoft SQL Server 2005 Express Edition running on your computer. (This can be installed as part of Visual Studio.)

IMPORTANT   Visual Studio Team Suite

To complete the lab exercises for Chapter 15, Lesson 1, you will need to have Microsoft Visual Studio 2005 Team Edition for Software Developers installed on your computer. This is available as part of Visual Studio 2005 Team Suite. You can download a free 180-day trial version of Visual Studio 2005 Team Suite from http://www.microsoft.com/downloads /details.aspx?FamilyId=5677DDC4-5035-401F-95C3-CC6F46F6D8F7&displaylang=en. You will need to uninstall Visual Studio 2005 Professional to install Visual Studio Team Suite on the same computer.

To complete the lab exercises for Chapter 15, Lesson 1, you will need:

- ❑ 256 MB of RAM or more
- ❑ 3.3 GB available disk space to download Visual Studio Team Suite
- ❑ 2 GB available disk space to install Visual Studio Team Suite
- ❑ One of the following operating systems:
    - ● Microsoft Windows 2000 with Service Pack 4
    - ● Windows XP with Service Pack 2
    - ● Windows Server 2003 with Service Pack 1
    - ● Windows Vista

Using the CD and DVD

A companion CD and an evaluation software DVD are included with this training kit. The companion CD contains the following:

- **Practice tests**   You can reinforce your understanding of the exam content by using electronic practice tests that you customize to meet your needs from the pool of Lesson Review questions in this book, or you can practice for the 70-547 certification exam by using tests created from a pool of 275 realistic exam questions. These questions give you many different practice exams to ensure that you're prepared to take the real thing.
- **Code**   Many chapters in this book include code and sample files associated with the lab exercises at the end of every lesson. Each exercise has a project or solution you can use to start the exercise and a version of the completed exercise for your review. To install the code and sample files on your hard disk, run Setup.exe in the Code folder on the companion CD. The default installation folder is \My Documents\Microsoft Press\ MCPD Self-Paced Training Kit Exam 70-547.
- **An eBook**   An electronic version (eBook) of this book is included for times when you don't want to carry the printed book with you. The eBook is in Portable Document Format (PDF), and you can view it by using Adobe Acrobat or Adobe Acrobat Reader.

The evaluation software DVD contains a 90-day evaluation edition of Visual Studio 2005 Professional Edition in case you want to use it with this book.

How to Install the Practice Tests

To install the practice test software from the companion CD on your hard disk, do the following:

1. Insert the companion CD into your CD drive and accept the license agreement. A CD menu appears.

   NOTE   If the CD menu doesn't appear

   If the CD menu or the license agreement doesn't appear, AutoRun might be disabled on your computer. Refer to the Readme.txt file on the CD-ROM for alternate installation instructions.

2. Click the Practice Tests item and follow the instructions on the screen.

How to Use the Practice Tests

To start the practice test software, follow these steps:

1. Click Start | All Programs | Microsoft Press Training Kit Exam Prep. A window appears that shows all the Microsoft Press training kit exam prep suites installed on your computer.
2. Double-click the lesson review or practice test you want to use.

NOTE   Lesson reviews vs. practice tests

Select the (70-547) Designing and Developing Web-Based Applications Using the Microsoft .NET Framework *lesson review* to use the questions from the "Lesson Review" sections of this book. Select the (70-547) Designing and Developing Web-Based Applications Using the Microsoft .NET Framework *practice test* to use a pool of 275 questions similar to those in the 70-547 certification exam.

Lesson Review Options

When you start a lesson review, the Custom Mode dialog box appears so that you can configure your test. You can click OK to accept the defaults, or you can customize the number of questions you want, how the practice test software works, which exam objectives you want the questions to relate to, and whether you want your lesson review to be timed. If you're retaking a test, you can select whether you want to see all the questions again or only those questions you missed or didn't answer.

After you click OK, your lesson review starts.

- To take the test, answer the questions and use the Next, Previous, and Go To buttons to move from question to question.
- After you answer an individual question, if you want to see which answers are correct—along with an explanation of each correct answer—click Explanation.
- If you'd rather wait until the end of the test to see how you did, answer all the questions and then click Score Test. You'll see a summary of the exam objectives you chose and the percentage of questions you answered correctly overall and per objective. You can print a copy of your test, review your answers, or retake the test.

Practice Test Options

When you start a practice test, you choose whether to take the test in Certification Mode, Study Mode, or Custom Mode.

- **Certification Mode**   Closely resembles the experience of taking a certification exam. The test has a set number of questions, it's timed, and you can't pause and restart the timer
- **Study Mode**   Creates an untimed test in which you can review the correct answers and the explanations after you answer each question
- **Custom Mode**   Gives you full control over the test options so that you can customize them as you like

In all modes, the user interface you see when taking the test is essentially the same but with different options enabled or disabled, depending on the mode. The main options are discussed in the previous section, "Lesson Review Options."

When you review your answer to an individual practice test question, a "References" section lists where in the training kit you can find the information that relates to that question and provides links to other sources of information. After you click Test Results to score your entire practice test, you can click the Learning Plan tab to see a list of references for every objective.

How to Uninstall the Practice Tests

To uninstall the practice test software for a training kit, use the Add Or Remove Programs option in Windows Control Panel.

Microsoft Certified Professional Program

The Microsoft certifications provide the best method to prove your command of current Microsoft products and technologies. The exams and corresponding certifications are developed to validate your mastery of critical competencies as you design and develop, or implement and support, solutions with Microsoft products and technologies. Computer professionals who become Microsoft-certified are recognized as experts and are sought after industry-wide. Certification brings a variety of benefits to the individual and to employers and organizations.

MORE INFO   All the Microsoft certifications

For a full list of Microsoft certifications, go to *www.microsoft.com/learning/mcp/default.asp.*

Technical Support

Every effort has been made to ensure the accuracy of this book and the contents of the companion CD. If you have comments, questions, or ideas regarding this book or the companion CD, please send them to Microsoft Press by using either of the following methods:

E-mail: tkinput@microsoft.com

Postal Mail:

Microsoft Press
Attn: MCPD Self-Paced Training Kit (Exam 70-547): Designing and Developing Web-Based Applications Using the Microsoft .NET Framework, *Editor*
One Microsoft Way
Redmond, WA 98052–6399

For additional support information regarding this book and the CD-ROM (including answers to commonly asked questions about installation and use), visit the Microsoft Press Technical Support Web site at *www.microsoft.com/learning/support/books/*. To connect directly to the Microsoft Knowledge Base and enter a query, visit *http://support.microsoft.com/search/*. For support information regarding Microsoft software, please visit *http://support.microsoft.com*.

Evaluation Edition Software Support

The 90-day evaluation edition provided with this training kit is not the full retail product and is provided only for the purposes of training and evaluation. Microsoft and Microsoft Technical Support do not support this evaluation edition.

Information about any issues relating to the use of this evaluation edition with this training kit is posted to the Support section of the Microsoft Press Web site at *www.microsoft.com /learning/support/books/*. For information about ordering the full version of any Microsoft software, please call Microsoft Sales at (800) 426-9400 or visit the Microsoft Web site at *www.microsoft.com*.

Chapter 1
Application Requirements and Design

It is important to understand the vision for a given application. The vision is usually defined by the project stakeholders and management. They have the budget; it is their business problem you will be trying to solve. Your job is to translate their vision into tangible software. This is no easy task.

Application architects and developers are often asked to help the business analysts build a consensus on the vision and define the goals, as well as a full set of requirements, for the application. Once you have these items in hand, you can begin the process of recommending, evaluating, and refining a design for the application.

This chapter looks at how you should evaluate an application's vision, goals, and requirements and propose a solution based on this information. This includes recommending technologies, defining a design, and then vetting your recommendations through the creation of a prototype. You also need to be in a position to demonstrate the feasibility of the project (and your design) to the visionaries and stakeholders. Ultimately, it will be their confidence in your proposed solution that determines whether a project is funded and moves from vision to implementation.

Exam objectives in this chapter:

- Evaluate the technical feasibility of an application design concept.
  - Evaluate the proof of concept.
  - Recommend the best technologies for the features and goals of the application.
  - Weigh implementation considerations.
  - Investigate existing solutions for similar business problems.
- Create a proof-of-concept prototype.
  - Evaluate the risks associated with ASP.NET 2.0 technology or implementation.
  - Validate that the proposed technology can be used in the application.
  - Demonstrate to stakeholders that the proposed solution will address their needs.

Lessons in this chapter:

Before You Begin

To complete the lessons in this chapter, you should be familiar with object-oriented development concepts. In addition, you should be comfortable with all of the following tasks:

- Reviewing goals and requirements for a Microsoft ASP.NET application
- Detailing the functional specifications for an ASP.NET application
- Identifying how Microsoft .NET Framework architectures and related technologies solve specific business problems
- Creating ASP.NET Web-based solutions
- Developing Web-based applications with Microsoft Visual Studio 2005 using Microsoft Visual Basic or C#
- Reading and working with class diagrams and other technical models

---

Real World

Mike Snell

Use cases are not requirements. I have seen many attempts to skip requirements in favor of use cases. A use case, however, is meant to describe a set of tasks a user performs to reach a common goal or to get some work done. A requirement (and the specifications that go with requirements) is used to define scope for the application. If used correctly, use cases have different goals and serve different purposes. I put this to the test on a couple of new projects that were being scoped by my team. One had a set of requirements but lacked use cases. The other had use cases but lacked requirements. Both had project managers that were adamant about the project being sufficiently defined. Neither, in my opinion, was correct.

To demonstrate this, I took a section of the project with requirements and wrote three different use cases. Each use case covered the same requirements three different ways. I did something similar with the project that had only use cases. The requirements upon which the use cases were based were left open to interpretation. I was able to define a lot of the high-level requirements from the use case, but I was left to make up the detailed requirements (and I missed some key requirements).

This simple test was not meant to prove that requirements are better than use cases or vice versa. Instead, it demonstrated that the project was better served when there was a line drawn between the two. Requirements serve one purpose, and use cases serve another.

In both situations, the project managers realized that both requirements and use cases were warranted to help clarify what was being developed. You can start with either, but you should build the missing item. This will give you confidence that you understand the full set of requirements upon which you must deliver and will allow you to see the project from the user's perspective.

Lesson 1: Evaluating Requirements and Proposing a Design

Reaching a common understanding among the developers, the business, and the users is the principal goal of application requirements. Nearly all enterprise applications built by professionals define and document requirements. How those requirements are documented, agreed upon, and managed often differs from one project to the next.

As an example, the MSF (Microsoft Solutions Framework) for Agile Software Development defines a work item for what it calls QOS (quality-of-service) requirements. This allows for defining requirements around performance, load, availability, stress, accessibility, serviceability, and maintainability. The same methodology includes another work item called a *scenario*. A scenario is MSF language for Agile's term for use case. It is meant to define a path of user activity through the system to reach a specific goal. Together, these items represent the user view (scenarios) and the nonfunctional view (QOS) of the system.

Consider another example. MSF for Capability Maturity Model Integration (CMMI) defines a work item called a *requirement*. The requirement work item has a number of subtypes. These include scenario, quality of service, safety, security, functional, operational, and interface. This methodology groups all requirements together but then allows them to be subgrouped by user requirements (scenarios), nonfunctional requirements (QOS, safety, security), or functional requirements (functional, operational, and interface).

These two examples are simply the beginning. The definition of software requirements has been discussed, debated, and written about for many years. There are many good books dedicated solely to the subject of requirements. There are also many standards and methodologies that take a slightly different perspective on software requirements. The intent here is not to change the way you write requirements. Enough is common among these methods to make them all viable. Rather, this chapter will establish a simple baseline for talking about requirements, and it will then discuss how you evaluate requirements and recommend solutions based on those requirements.

MORE INFO Microsoft Solutions Framework (MSF)

The Microsoft Solutions Framework is a software development process. There are two processes: Agile and CMMI. Microsoft has worked to build these two into Visual Studio Team Systems. They have also documented process guidance around both. For more information, you can view the respective Web sites for these processes at *http://msdn.microsoft.com/vstudio/teamsystem/msf /msfcmmi/default.aspx* and *http://msdn.microsoft.com/vstudio/teamsystem/msf/msfagile/*.

> **After this lesson, you will be able to:**
> - Recognize poor requirements and propose improvements.
> - Evaluate a set of application requirements for completeness and feasibility.
> - Recommend technologies based on a set of requirements.
> - Investigate and evaluate existing alternatives to your recommendations.
> - Define a high-level application design based on requirements and recommendations.
> - Determine whether an application's design is feasible and practical.
>
> **Estimated lesson time: 40 minutes**

What Makes a Good Set of Application Requirements?

A good requirement set includes requirements that are defined from multiple perspectives. This makes a lot of sense. All projects have multiple influences. The business (or executive sponsorship) has a set of objectives and goals for the application. Users define specific tasks they need to accomplish. Developers and testers need to know what specific features will be required to make this application a success. There are also requirements necessary for supporting and maintaining the application, for performance and scalability, and more. The goal is to define enough of these requirements to ensure the project's success.

This chapter will define four types of requirements: business, user, functional, and quality of service. Together, these categories represent the perspectives necessary to define the requirements for the vast majority of applications. They provide a common understanding from the business perspective to the developer perspective. They also allow the quality assurance team to ensure that the application stays focused and on track. Let's take a look at each requirement category in further detail.

Business Requirements

A *business requirement* defines what the business believes to be important for the success of the project. The business typically comprises management or stakeholders who are funding the project. They often define requirements in terms of vision or goals for the application. However, these goals need to be turned into real, tangible requirements.

For example, consider a business requirement that states, "The new version should allow us to sell the application to new markets." This is a great goal for the system. It helps justify the expense of the development in that it will open up new sales channels and markets and, hence, increase revenues and profits. However, this goal needs to be translated into a real business requirement. Real, high-level business requirements derived from this goal might look like the following:

- The system must include metadata support for all named concepts. This will allow companies in different markets to rename these concepts based on their terminology.
- The system must implement an open standard for the exchange of sales data. This will allow all markets to interoperate with the application.
- The application must support the definition of feature packs for specific markets. A feature pack is a set of features that can be turned on or off as a group (think add-in). The application's core should not be dependent on features inside a given feature pack.

You can see that these are tangible requirements tied to a goal for the application: to support multiple markets. It is also important to note that these are *high-level requirements*—that is, requirements without detailed specifications. That is okay. The requirements can be kept and tracked at a high level. An application architect will have to translate requirements into specifications and design. The specifications and design should not, however, alter, add to, or detract from the requirements.

User Requirements

User requirements are the tasks the users must be able to accomplish to meet the objectives of their jobs. Most developers are accustomed to receiving or documenting user requirements. This typically involves sitting with users and discussing exactly what the developer does (or needs to do) to help the users. The following are all high-level user requirements:

- A customer service representative must be able to place an order for a customer.
- A user must be able to query to find the available inventory and determine the number of units of a given product that are currently in stock.
- A user must be able to view his or her order history in a list. He or she must be able to select an order from the list and view its details.

These are all high-level user requirements. They lack use-case definition and specifications. The first question a business analyst might ask, for example, is "How?" How does a customer service representative place an order for a customer? The user will then typically detail a number of steps that are involved in this process. These steps represent the use case for "customer rep places order for customer." This use case helps clarify the requirement. In addition, an architect should define the specifications for the given requirement. Developers need to know what constitutes an order, what fields are required, what rules will be processed, and so on.

Functional Requirements

Functional requirements or *functional specifications* are the features the developers must build to satisfy the other requirements. These requirements are typically defined in great detail to help developers understand exactly what it is they need to develop. The functional requirements are typically written by a technical lead or architect. They are not the requirements of the users or business.

A functional requirement, for example, might be to create an ASP.NET Web page for managing a customer's profile. The functional requirement should include the name of the page, the controls used on the page, the input validation rules, the security rules for the page, the classes that should be called to support the page's functionality, and so on.

As you can see, functional requirements can be very detailed. It is often better to do functional design rather than to write functional requirements. This allows you to take advantage of application models, tools such as Visual Studio, and some code to define the functionality of the system. Developers often understand these items better. In addition, it saves you the time of documenting these items in two different places (document and code models).

Quality-of-Service Requirements

Quality-of-service (QOS) requirements define the contractual, or nonfunctional, requirements for the system. QOS requirements do not typically represent specific user problems. Rather, they define the requirements around things such as performance, scalability, and standards. These requirements should not be overlooked. They need to be defined and considered when doing application architecture and development. The following are examples of QOS requirements:

- All customer-facing page requests in the site should return to the user within five seconds over a standard high-speed Internet connection.
- The system should scale, in single-server scenarios (see server specifications), to 25 concurrent users and 400 active users with standard think times.
- The system should use Microsoft Windows integrated security to secure pages and identify users.

You can see that QOS requirements are very important. They further define what the application must support from a nonfunctional perspective. You must get this information at the beginning of the project to make wise decisions about how you recommend and implement technologies for a given business problem.

Exam Tip   Pay close attention to the exact requirements for any given question on the exam. You need to satisfy all of the requirements listed in the question and only those requirements. Do not assume anything; pay close attention to exactly what is written.

Use Cases Versus Requirements

Use cases and requirements are not the same thing. A use case is a Unified Modeling Language (UML) model meant to describe a set of user steps that accomplish a task. Requirements define what must be created to satisfy the needs of the user. Together, they provide a good view of how the user sees the system. However, you should be wary if you encounter attempts to do away with one in favor of the other.

When this happens, the most common scenario is that use cases supplant requirements. This is sometimes even successful. These situations are almost always highly agile, involve the client on a day-to-day basis, have small teams, and do not involve a geographically distributed work force. If this is your environment, you might be able to take advantage of use cases in lieu of requirements. Avoid, however, cluttering your use cases with a ton of specification details to the point that you can't find the use case anymore. For more traditional environments, consider starting with either requirements or use cases and building the missing item. You typically need both to be successful.

Requirements and use cases have two different goals. Requirements define what needs to be created for the system to be successful. They are useful for defining scope and determining whether you have met objectives. Requirements are often traced all the way through the implementation process. Project managers and testers create requirements traceability matrices that define how a requirement is realized through the system.

Use cases, on the other hand, are meant to define a set of steps to reach a common user goal. Use cases are more about the process by which a user reaches a requirement. They help architects, developers, and testers understand how people work and how the system should accommodate their activities. They are not, if written correctly, requirements.

Evaluating the Requirements for the Application

When you are presented with a set of requirements, you need to be able to evaluate them and determine whether they are complete, feasible, and sufficient. The categories of requirements that must be present to make a complete set—business, user, functional, and QOS—have already been discussed. Next you must determine whether they are sufficiently well-documented. The following represent criteria, or questions, that you can use to determine whether the requirements are sufficient.

- **Requirement perspectives**   Are all requirement perspectives considered? Do you have definitions for the business, user, and QOS requirements? Can you derive the functional requirements and design from this set of requirements?

- **Unambiguous**   Does each requirement define a specific, actionable scope item? Can each requirement be acted upon? Make sure that there are no soft requirements. Eliminate from the requirements phrases such as "The application should be easy to use." This is a goal. A requirement would indicate something like "The application should implement a task pane of common user actions from a given feature."

- **Complete**   Are the requirements complete? You need to identify missing elements in the requirements. You should also indicate where further clarification of one or more requirements is warranted. Perhaps, for example, some requirements need further fleshing out through use cases. If you are having trouble understanding a requirement or designing to it, then it is not complete.

- **Necessary**   Are all the requirements actually necessary to satisfy the goals of the application? This is the opposite of complete. Sometimes business analysts, developers, and architects can add things into the system that are not really required. Watch for unnecessary additions to the project through overzealous requirement definitions.
- **Feasible**   Are the requirements, as they are documented, really feasible? Review the requirements against known constraints such as budget, timeline, and technology. It is better to raise red flags during the requirements definition phase than to wait until the project is already over budget.

Thinking of your requirements in these terms will make everyone's job much easier. A good set of requirements will lead to good architecture, good testing, and high user acceptance.

Recommending the Best Technologies for the Application

There is a big difference between defining application architecture and recommending technologies for an application. These tasks often become intermingled and are confused with one another. One should not be a substitute for another. Architects and developers should be asked to look at the requirements for a system and make technology recommendations. These technology recommendations, in conjunction with the requirements, will drive much of the application's architecture. Therefore, obtain technology recommendations prior to considering application architecture.

The decision to recommend one technology over another should be driven solely by the requirements. A developer should evaluate the requirements and choose the right technologies to fit. However, in all practicality, these decisions sometimes have more to do with what is available than with what is best. If you are faced with this dilemma, factor it directly into your decision process. Make it a requirement to use as much existing hardware and software as you can. If this is validated and justified, then you can respect the requirement.

Next, you will look at how you might recommend certain technologies over others based solely on the user, business, and QOS requirements rather than on what is available or convenient. Of course, to make recommendations, you must have some familiarity with certain technologies and know how those technologies can be brought to bear for a given solution.

An ASP.NET Web application can be broken down into a core set of application layers or components. These items make up the bulk of your technology recommendation opportunities. It makes sense to review the layers and components that define an ASP.NET application. The following list describes each of these items, defines the options that are available, and provides a decision tree that will help lead you toward recommending one technology over another.

Client

The *client* represents how your application will be presented to the users. The client is the users' interface into the application. It is what they see and use every time they work with the application. The following list represents some of the many ASP.NET client technology options available to you.

- **Standard browser-based client**   Represents the standard client enabled through a Web browser. These clients are typically targeting the widest audience with a single solution.

  Multibrowser compliance is often a principal driver when recommending this type of client.

- **AJAX-enabled client**   Represents a browser-based client that takes advantage of Java-Script to enable Windows-like features through a browser (think Microsoft Outlook Web Access). This provides users with a highly interactive (and much more usable) experience inside a browser.

  When you recommend this solution, you are typically trying to combine the ubiquity of the Web browser with a high degree of usability. You might sacrifice some browser compatibility, however, or choose to write multiple, down-level versions of the application.

- **Smart Client**   Represents a client that is deployed through a Web browser but runs as a Windows application on the client's computer. Smart Clients provide a high degree of user interactivity but still work with a Web server to use the pervasiveness of the Internet.

  Recommend this solution when you need to build a Web-based application with a very high degree of user interactivity, and you can control the client's operating system. This solution is dependent on Windows and the .NET Framework being deployed on a user's desktop.

- **Microsoft Office Client**   Represents a client that is built with Microsoft Office Word, Excel, or Outlook as the principal user interface (UI). You might still call back to a Web server through Web services to exchange data. However, users use the familiar paradigm of Office to complete their work.

  Recommend an Office client when you are building applications that take advantage of the capabilities of Office (such as spreadsheet or contact management). You also need to ensure that the target version of Office is deployed on each user's desktop.

- **Windows Mobile**   Represents clients that are enabled through handheld devices running the Microsoft Windows Mobile operating system.

  You would recommend this solution when users are highly mobile and need access to information over their handheld devices.

Third-Party Controls

Third-party controls represent developer controls not shipped by Microsoft or embedded in Visual Studio 2005. You will want to explore the controls that are available to you to weigh build-versus-buy decisions. For example, if your application requires that you integrate with a credit card processor, you should explore the many components available for you to do so. In most scenarios, third-party controls can eliminate risk, reduce costs, and increase delivery time. Some of the many control categories that are available include charting, scheduling, navigation, UI styling, licensing, reporting, integration, and spreadsheets and data grids.

Application Server

The *application server* represents the server that you will recommend to run your ASP.NET server code. Typically, architects and developers recommend the software but not many of the hardware specifications. When recommending an application server for an ASP.NET solution, you should consider the version of Microsoft Internet Information Services (IIS) required, the version of the .NET Framework you need to target, and the security constraints of the application.

Application Libraries

An *application library* is a set of components (and, many times, source code) that you can download and use in your solution. An application library typically encapsulates a set of features that is common to many applications. For example, the Microsoft Enterprise Library provides features for caching, error management, configuration, and more. You need to review your application's requirements and determine whether these libraries can be used to help ensure best practices and higher quality.

Similar to application libraries are application frameworks. A *framework* is a set of base classes and components that abstracts many of the architectural "plumbing" away from the developer. Frameworks try to offer a cohesive solution to many architectural problems. These typically include managing state among application layers, physically distributing the layers of an application, handling plumbing, and more.

Security

You must be able to recommend security technologies that you can use to meet the security requirements of the application. For example, you need to determine whether you should implement forms-based security or Windows security in your application. This is typically dependent on the user base. If your users are a set of Internet users, then forms-based might be your only option. If, however, you are writing for a corporate audience, it might be best to integrate your solution with Active Directory directory service. Other security recommendations might include how you store and encrypt data, how you connect to that data, and so on.

Data Storage

Data storage represents how your application will store and access its data. There are many options available to you. Let the requirements of the application lead you toward the best solution. The following list represents some of the options that might be available to you:

- **File-based storage**   This means storing your data in files in the application's file system. File-based solutions typically involve storing data as XML.

  You would recommend this only on small applications where a database solution is not available or warranted.

- **Microsoft SQL Server 2005 Express Edition**   SQL Express is a free database solution available from Microsoft. It provides a starting point for creating small project databases. It also provides a file-based solution for independent software vendors (ISVs) that are considering embedding SQL in their application.

  Consider this option when you are constrained by costs; you can limit yourself to a single CPU, a single gig of random access memory (RAM), and a 4 gigabyte (GB) database size; and do not require many of the advanced features of a full database solution.

- **SQL Server Everywhere Edition**   SQL Everywhere (also called SQL Mobile) provides a small, lightweight, highly functional database for handheld devices.

  Recommend this option when you are building mobile solutions that store and retrieve data locally to the handheld device.

- **SQL Server editions and options**   The SQL Server family includes Standard and Enterprise Editions and offers features such as reporting services, analysis services, data mining, notification, and more. If you encounter these requirements, you need to be aware of how these services can help.

- **Other data storage**   There are a number of other options available to you for your ASP.NET solutions. You might, for example, have a requirement to retrieve your data from an *Oracle* database or a DB2. In either case, you can recommend the right .NET Framework data provider to do so.

MORE INFO   SQL Server Editions

There are many editions of SQL Server—one to fit every need. For a good overview of what is available, view "SQL Server 2005 Features Comparison" at *http://www.microsoft.com/sql/prodinfo /features/compare-features.mspx.* This provides an item-by-item comparison of features.

This should give you a good overview of what to expect when recommending technologies for ASP.NET solutions. Your task should be to focus on the requirements: review them, and make recommendations based solely upon them. You should not, for example, be recommending a SQL Express database for an enterprise application with hundreds of concurrent users.

> ## Quick Check
> 1. Name the common types, or categories, of requirements.
> 2. What is a quality-of-service (QOS) requirement?
> 3. What are the characteristics of a good requirement?
>
> ### Quick Check Answers
> 1. Requirements should be seen from multiple perspectives. These include business, user, functional, and quality-of-service perspectives.
> 2. A QOS requirement defines a contractual requirement that the system must meet. These requirements are often used to define scalability, performance, and other nonfunctional requirements.
> 3. A good requirement should be unambiguous, complete, necessary, and feasible.

Investigating Existing Solutions for Similar Business Problems

When making your technology recommendations, it is wise to consider existing solutions to similar business problems. Rather than building from scratch, you can sometimes buy an existing bit of software, a product, or a third-party component, or use one of these that might already be available to you. This can save you valuable design, development, and test cycles. For example, you might look at software that has already been written within your organization. Often, this software can be componentized to support multiple applications. If you resist the urge to reinvent, you keep the development team focused on just the features that make your application unique. The following are some common technologies to consider when making alternate recommendations for your ASP.NET solutions.

- **Corporate assets**   You should always look internally first. Many companies have spent a lot of money solving the same problem multiple times. You might find that you can take some existing code, turn it into a component, and use it for multiple applications.
- **Third-party components**   As discussed, there are some great third-party components available at a low cost in terms of creating reports, charts, and other features.
- **Microsoft Windows SharePoint Services**   This software provides a set of services for creating collaborative portal solutions. You can use .NET Framework 2.0 to build Web Parts and Web Part pages for Windows SharePoint Services (WSS). This can be a great solution for companies looking to create internal collaborative solutions.
- **Microsoft Commerce Server**   This software provides a platform for building business applications that center on e-commerce. Commerce Server 2007 has been written to work specifically with ASP.NET 2.0, BizTalk Server, SQL Server, SQL Server Reporting Services, and others. Consider this option when recommending e-commerce applications.

- **Microsoft BizTalk Server**   This software provides a solution for managing business process and integration. BizTalk Server 2006 allows integration with Visual Studio 2005. It also provides adapters for key applications in the industry. Consider recommending this solution when you have a lot of system integration around key business processes.
- **Microsoft Host Integration Server**   This software provides a server product for integrating with IBM mainframes. This includes connecting with data sources, messaging, and security. Consider recommending this when you have to build an application that has a high degree of interoperability with IBM mainframes.

Creating a High-Level Application Design

You have your application requirements. You have evaluated these requirements and confirmed that they are good. You then put together a technology recommendation based on the requirements. Your next step is to define a model for the application's high-level design. This design should help document and explain the application you intend to create. It must, therefore, define the technologies that you intend to use and indicate how these technologies will be connected.

How you model your application design is not as important as just modeling it. There are many tools that will allow you to define an application design. You can create boxes and arrows in Microsoft Office Visio, or you can use Visual Studio 2005 Team Architect. The latter provides the Application Diagram for defining applications, their connectivity, and their configuration. You might not have this tool available to you, but it makes for a good model of what should be in your high-level application design. Let's take a look.

Visual Studio Team Architect Application Diagram

You add items to your application diagram using the Toolbox in Visual Studio 2005. Figure 1-1 shows the Visual Studio Toolbox. Notice that you can drag application types from the Toolbox onto the designer. This allows you to indicate which technologies you are recommending for a given solution. You can define Windows applications, ASP.NET Web Services, ASP.NET Applications, and more. In addition, there are a number of endpoints that you can attach to an application. These endpoints are used by an architect to configure which applications communicate and through what means. Let's look at an example.

Figure 1-2 provides a sample application diagram. Notice that the application is defined as having three UIs. It defines an Office application for sales reports (SalesMetrics), a browser-based application for customers (CustomerInterface), and a Windows Smart Client for the customer relationship management (CRM) administration application (CrmAdminDesk). The diagram also defines a couple of Web services (CrmServices and ReportingServices) and two databases (ReportDb and CustomersAndOrders).

Figure 1-1 The Visual Studio Toolbox

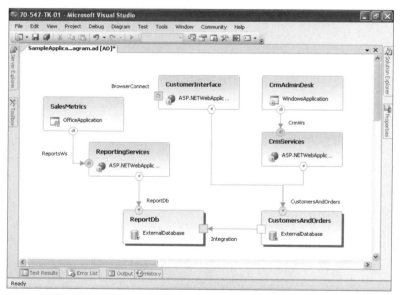

Figure 1-2 The Application diagram

You can configure the settings and constraints required for each application on the diagram. Think of this as your application configuration plan. For example, the Reporting Services Web application might define constraints on the application server's operating system and version of the .NET Framework. Figure 1-3 shows the Setting and Constraints dialog box in Visual Studio for this application. Notice that you define these parameters through the interface.

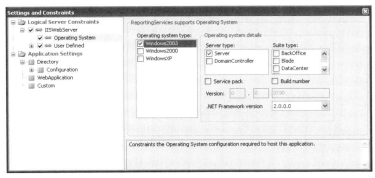

Figure 1-3   The Settings and Constraints dialog box

Defining the application's requirements, making your technology recommendation, and creating a high-level design are the necessary risk-aversion steps to begin your project. You will use this information to define a prototype, refine your design, and begin creating detailed specifications and an application architecture. You will learn the prototyping process in the next lesson.

MORE INFO   Creating detailed design

You will cover the process of creating physical models, including layers, class, activity, and sequence, for developers in Chapter 2, "Decompose Specifications for Developers."

Lab: Evaluate Requirements and Propose a Design

In this lab, you will evaluate a list of application requirements. You will then use these requirements to make design and technology choices and propose an application design.

▶ **Exercise: Review Requirements and Recommend Technologies**

For this exercise, review the following set of application requirements. You will then perform the following steps to arrive at a set of recommendations for the application. The following are key requirements for the application:

- R1: The application should be accessible to our distributed, traveling sales force. This workforce uses a variety of Internet connections and also often needs to work when disconnected.

- R2: Our inside sales team will also use the application. The team members, along with their managers, will enter customer data and manage their orders.

- R3: The system needs to support up to 100 concurrent users.

- R4: Users should not have to log on to the application. It needs to recognize their network logon name and password.
- R5: The application should integrate with the inventory system. When an order is requested, an inventory check should be done. When an order is placed, the inventory system needs to be notified.
- R6: The application needs to send order-extract files to the order-processing system.
- R7: The application should report sales data to upper management. They would like to see the report as a set of graphical elements on a dashboard. They would like to be able to drill into this data and do further analysis.

Now that you have the application requirements, follow these steps to arrive at a set of recommendations:

1. Review the application requirements and determine which client technology you should implement based on the specifics in the requirements.
   - ❑ R1 indicates that you should consider a Smart Client to support disconnected scenarios. You might also consider creating a mobile application.
   - ❑ R2 does not dictate a UI. However, if the team is totally internal, a Smart Client solution would work well for them, too.
   - ❑ R7 indicates that you should consider a Web-based solution or, perhaps, Microsoft Office Excel.

2. Determine a data storage mechanism for the application.
   - ❑ R1 indicates that you might need to consider a local storage option. This could be isolated storage, or you could consider SQL Everywhere on the mobile device or desktop.
   - ❑ R3 indicates a large enough workforce that you will want to support a SQL Server standard back-end. It might synch with the mobile clients.

3. What additional technologies (outside of ASP.NET) should you consider for this solution? Consider cost-effective products that satisfy some of these requirements.
   - ❑ R5 indicates that integration around a couple of business processes is necessary. Explore the potential of using BizTalk Server to aid in this effort.
   - ❑ R6 indicates sending data extracts. Again, BizTalk might be warranted. Also, consider SQL Server Integration Services (SSIS).
   - ❑ R7 opens up the possibility of using WSS and SQL Reporting Services. The former could be used to deliver the dashboard-like features. The latter could deliver the reports. You might also consider using SQL Analysis Services to help with the drill-down of the reporting.

Lesson Summary

- Application requirements should be defined from multiple perspectives. This includes the business or executive sponsorship, the users, the developers (functional), and the quality of service (nonfunctional).

- Your functional requirements or functional specifications are better off defined through application modeling tools. You should not have to document this once on paper and again in the models.

- A good requirement should be unambiguous, measurable, and actionable. It should neither read like a goal nor be left open to interpretation.

- Verify that all your requirements are necessary to the success of the system. Those that are not should be set aside.

- It is important that developers and architects make recommendations that match the real requirements. They should not recommend technologies only because they are cool or available. Rather, they should perform careful analysis and make proper recommendations.

- Always review your recommendations against existing solutions. There might be an off-the-shelf product or an internal company asset that you can use.

- Start the process of validating your recommendations by creating a high-level application design. This should include your recommendations in terms of technologies, how these technologies integrate to form a solution, and any configuration parameters and constraints of these items.

Lesson Review

You can use the following questions to test your knowledge of the information in Lesson 1, "Evaluating Requirements and Proposing a Design." The questions are also available on the companion CD if you prefer to review them in electronic form.

NOTE Answers

Answers to these questions and explanations of why each answer choice is right or wrong are located in the "Answers" section at the end of the book.

1. You have been given the requirement "The application should log all system failures and generate a support ticket to ensure proper follow-up and response." This is an example of what type of requirement?

    A. Business requirement

    B. Quality-of-service requirement

    C. User requirement

    D. Functional requirement

2. Requirements are useful for which of the following? (Choose all that apply.)

    A. Allowing testers to confirm if the implemented application is acceptable

    B. Defining the process a user will perform to accomplish a given task

    C. Defining a common understanding of scope among the business, users, and project team

    D. Determining which technologies should be used for the application

3. Given the following requirements, which client technology would you recommend?

    ❑ Users expect a highly interactive experience. They should not have to wait for multiple seconds between requests.

    ❑ The application must work on Microsoft Windows, Unix, and Macintosh computers.

    ❑ The users should be able to run the application only from their corporate computers.

    A. Standard browser-based client

    B. AJAX-enabled client

    C. Mobile client

    D. Smart Client

4. Given the following requirements, which data storage technology would you recommend?

    ❑ Users should be able to work with the application when they are not connected to the Internet.

    ❑ The application's data is retrieved and aggregated from multiple sources on a monthly basis. After the updated data is posted, users should receive it.

    ❑ The application should have a small footprint on the user's computer or device.

    A. SQL Enterprise

    B. SQL Express

    C. SQL Everywhere (Mobile)

    D. SQL Standard

Lesson 2: Creating a Proof-of-Concept Prototype to Refine an Application's Design

Assuming that you have good application requirements and that you have created technology recommendations and a high-level design for your project, you are ready to start the design and move straight to coding, right? In some cases, this might be true. However, for larger applications, and in cases in which some of the requirements and recommendations are still undefined, it can be a great risk-reduction step to create a prototype.

In this lesson, you will look at how you might create a prototype to answer questions from the requirements and the technology recommendations. You will look at how you can use this prototype to help increase stakeholders' confidence in the project and reduce many risks associated with it. A prototype is often the step needed to get project stakeholders to approve your project.

After this lesson, you will be able to:

- Choose the type of prototype required for your specific situation.
- Explain the difference between a mockup and a proof of concept.
- Evaluate high-level design decisions through a prototype.
- Evaluate the effectiveness of your prototype.
- Demonstrate the feasibility of the project to stakeholders through the prototype.

Estimated lesson time: 20 minutes

Real World

Mike Snell

In the haste to get a project going, get developers coding, and "stop wasting time" with meetings and reviews, teams often skip the prototype step altogether. What I have observed, however, is that if you do not create a prototype (as with most projects), you end up refactoring design decisions much more frequently and to a greater extent through the first few releases of the project. There simply is no substitute for doing some of the work and seeing the results. No matter how good you are, an application on paper is not an application.

> If you defer the prototype, you'd better plan for the refactoring. I often run into projects for which no one took the time to create a prototype, and the project plan still assumes a smooth release of features. This is never the case. In addition, developers hate to get working and be consistently bombarded with changes to the way things should work. Do not discount this disruption; it costs money and time and often sets the wrong tone for the start of a project.
>
> What I've learned is that prototypes are essential. It seems obvious now: a concept is just that. You need to prove the concept. You can take the prudent approach and plan for developing the concept at the beginning, or you can risk having to work through the concepts as part of the critical path. This can make for a very shaky first release. I believe you're much better off if you work through these concepts during an initial prototype phase. This gives you a sense of control and starts the project running smoothly.

What Constitutes a Good Prototype?

A good prototype answers the questions left open from the requirements and technology recommendations. The problem is that, often, these questions are not explicitly asked: they are just unresolved. This is what you call a gap. There might be a gap between what a user defines as a requirement or scenario and what he or she really wants to see. There might be a gap between what a developer has defined for the application architect and what the project stakeholders understand. There might be a gap between a new architecture that an architect has read about and is proposing and what is truly required. These gaps exist regardless of whether they are defined. A prototype is meant to reduce the overall project risk by closing some of these gaps.

Mockups and Proof-of-Concept Prototypes

There are many types of prototypes. Some projects create UI prototypes. Others might prototype an architecture consideration. Still others might look at the feasibility of using a specific technology such as BizTalk Server or Commerce Server. In fact, every project has different needs regarding a prototype. However, for your purposes, these prototypes can be classified into two principal groups: mockups and proof of concept.

A *mockup* is meant to verify the requirements and use cases through the creation of a number of key screens in the system. Mockups are also called *horizontal prototypes* because they take a single, horizontal picture of the application. They do not go deeply (or vertically) into the other layers of the application such as the business objects and the database layers. Mockups are a great way to determine whether the requirements are complete and understood. They also help validate the use cases, the navigational structure, and some of the logical interactions of the application.

Mockups do have shortcomings. They do not help you prove any of the architecture concepts for the system. They also do not validate the technology decisions. Mockups, however, are a great tool for moving from paper to something more tangible. Users often have different opinions when they see something as a picture versus as a bunch of text in a document. Mockups are also useful for defining how the application will look and behave. This removes ambiguity from the implementation and builds early consensus on what will be delivered.

A *proof-of-concept prototype* is meant to validate the requirements and confirm the technology recommendations and high-level design. A proof-of-concept prototype is also called a *vertical prototype* because it looks at the application across the entire stack (UI, services, business objects, and database). Proof-of-concept prototypes have also been called *reference architectures* because they provide a reference for the development team on just how the system should work from top to bottom. This removes ambiguity, creates a standard, and eliminates a lot of risk.

You create a proof-of-concept prototype by choosing a key requirement of the application and then building it out through each layer of the design. It makes more sense to prove out a riskier requirement than to work with a well-known requirement. The latter might be easy, but it lacks the risk reduction you are looking for with a proof of concept.

The Prototyping Process

There are many ways to create mockup-style prototypes. You can use Visual Studio to create screens that connect to dummy data and wire up the navigation. You can also use drawing tools such as Visio to simply lay up images that represent the mockup. You may even decide to draw the screens on a whiteboard, index cards, or even sticky notes. The process for creating mockups should, however, involve the user. It should be highly interactive because it really is just an extension of the requirements.

A proof-of-concept prototype should, of course, be created with Visual Studio and any other tools you are trying to review. You can often get developer or trial editions of the software for this purpose. If you intend to evaluate, for instance, the feasibility of creating a Smart Client UI, use Visual Studio and an application server to define a UI. You can see that these types of prototypes are a lot more involved than a mockup. However, their purpose is not only to validate key requirements but also to confirm design decisions.

Creating a Prototype to Evaluate Key Design Decisions

You must make many key design decisions when recommending an ASP.NET solution. These, like all design decisions, come with a certain amount of risk. The risks are usually related to the feasibility of the technology to satisfy all of the requirements and the developer's solid grasp of just how that technology works. The following are all risks that you should consider reducing when proposing ASP.NET solutions. Each of these risks can be mitigated through the creation of a proof-of-concept prototype.

Confirm a Server-Side Versus a Client-Side Experience

If your requirements state that you need to support multiple browsers on multiple machines and you might not rely on client-side JavaScript, then you should consider prototyping this experience. This might involve creating server-side controls that demonstrate to the users how the system will react as they use it.

For example, if you need to have all controls on a page validated prior to continuing, you might choose to validate only when the user hits a button on the page (and not when he or she loses focus on a control). This will reduce the number of round-trips to the server but might reduce the overall usability of the solution.

Conversely, if you are required to create a highly interactive user experience inside a browser, you might also wish to prove this out. You can create client-side controls that emit JavaScript. These client-side controls should react to user activity prior to hitting the server. The prototype can help you evaluate how much effort will be required to create this type of experience. You might also decide to evaluate third-party controls that already support this type of client-side interactivity.

Confirm the Application Container

The application container is the shell that houses the application and provides base services. In a Smart Client scenario, this is understood to be a master form with navigation, status indicator, and base functionality such as undo, cut, copy, paste, auto-update, and so on. In a browser application, this might include your master pages, style sheets, themes and skins, the navigation, and any shared controls that you intend to create.

The time to define this container is in the prototype phase. This allows the technical leaders of the application to set this very key decision on how developers will add forms or pages to the system. This also eliminates ambiguity around this key factor. Finally, defining the application container through the prototype gives users a better understanding of how the system will operate as a whole. You will not implement everything that that container defines, but users can see it there and understand how it will work.

Define User Interface Elements to Confirm Requirements

The prototype also helps you understand your scope. Work to understand the many screens that will be required for your application and try to list each of these screens and categorize them by screen type. A screen type helps you group similar screens. The following are some screen types you might consider:

- **Data entry form**   This represents a page in which you are requesting that the user enter data for the application.
- **Data list form**   This is a page that displays a list of data. This list may require paging, sorting, filtering, and so on.
- **Wizard**   You might have a set of pages that work together as a wizard to capture user data.
- **Report**   You might have a number of report pages in the system. These reports might allow for filtering of the data through parameters or viewing the data graphically.

When you define the screens and group them, consider their complexity also. Complexity of the screen can be defined in terms of its functionality (read versus write, and so on), the number of elements on the screen, the user interactivity, and the access to and from the screen. Having this complexity for each screen will help you better understand the overall scope of your project.

Next, create a working prototype of at least one of each screen type. This will ensure that screen type is understood by users and by the developers of the system. Having a set of implemented screen types will also add to the overall reference architecture for the development team.

Finally, you might wish to define how the actual UI appears and behaves as part of the prototype phase. This step usually involves creating designs and working with the users to validate those designs. Having these designs decided at the outset will help set standards for the application.

Evaluate Web Service Recommendations

If you intend to recommend Web services as part of your design, you need to evaluate their effectiveness. A prototype can help in this regard. When creating the proof of concept, consider all of the following with respect to Web services:

- How will users be connected to the services?
- How will the application behave when there is no connection or the connection is slow? Are the results acceptable to the users, or do you have to consider design alternatives?
- How will you manage transaction reliability and ensure no data loss? Will all calls to the Web service be synchronous?
- How will you manage concurrency issues? Will the last user to save overwrite someone else's changes unknowingly?
- How will you manage the security for the Web services? How do you intend to authenticate and authorize the callers to the service?

Evaluate Your Proposed Security Model

Your security model should be part of the prototype. This will provide insight into what is required to support the security requirements. When you define a prototype, consider all of the following with respect to security:

- **Feasibility**   Be sure that what you are proposing is feasible. If, for instance, you are proposing that each user authenticate through an Active Directory account, you need to make sure all users have such accounts or that they can be created. You also need to make sure all the target browsers support this type of authentication.
- **Authentication**   Confirm your choice for user authentication. Will you need to implement forms-based authentication in an Internet scenario, or will you require Windows authentication?
- **Authorization**   Confirm your authorization strategy. You might need to filter data based on a user's access rights. You might even need to control this on a field-by-field basis in a business object.
- **Access rights to resources**   Define how you intend to access key resources in the application. Are there files that need to be checked against an access control list (ACL)? How should the database connection string be stored securely?
- **Connectivity between resources**   Validate the feasibility of your proposed high-level design. This might be less of a prototype task and require some discussions with your infrastructure team. For instance, there might be firewall rules that prevent some of your communication decisions.

Evaluate Third-Party Applications or Controls

Unless you are very familiar with your third-party control or application recommendations, these represent an important factor to consider in the prototype. In fact, any technology that is not familiar should be prototyped. If, for example, you intend to use Windows Workflow Services for the first time, you need to validate your assumptions through a proof of concept. Some third-party control categories you should consider prototyping and evaluating include:

- **General UI**   You might be using these to create unique UI elements and navigation constructs.
- **Grid control**   You might require a specialized data grid control to manage report-like or spreadsheet-like features.
- **Licensing**   You might need to control licensing for your application or control.
- **Charts and reports**   You might have a requirement to create charts and graphs for the reporting or dashboard features.
- **Data transformation and exchange**   You might use a tool or controls to handle data import or transformation or to generate export files.

Evaluate Proposed Data Access and Storage Methods

A proof of concept is also a good time to evaluate your recommendations around data access and storage. If, for example, you are proposing SQL Everywhere be loaded on personal digital assistants (PDAs) and other mobile devices to support offline and synchronization requirements, and you have never done so, you need to prototype. Again, this will help you evaluate your decision in terms of feasibility, practicality, and level of effort.

Evaluate Your State Management Decisions

ASP.NET applications must manage state effectively. State is how data is moved and persisted throughout the layers of an application. When it comes to state management, there are a number of factors to validate. Some of these include the following:

- **Shared state**   Do users have to be able to share application state such as in an auction system?
- **State persistence**   Can state be maintained on the user's desktop (cookies)? The application server? Will a stateless load balancer be required? Should state be moved to a state server to increase scalability?
- **Saving state**   How will state move from memory to being at rest (the database)?
- **Caching**   How much application state can be cached? What are the ramifications of the caching strategy in terms of reading old data, updating the cache, and consuming server resources?

Confirm and Refine the Recommended Architecture

Your prototype is also the chance to refine your architecture recommendations. If, for example, you are proposing creating a framework for the application, then now is the time to validate the feasibility of that framework. One functional requirement might be to eliminate the need for developers to manage saving and retrieving object data, for example. This type of framework needs to be reviewed and validated through a proof of concept.

You might also try to prove out how you will partition the layers of the application. A good reference architecture will demonstrate to a developer how his or her code should behave and where it should be located. For example, if you create for the application a user interactivity layer that should be used to house UI code, then you should prototype only the code that goes into this layer and how the controls of the UI might interact with this code. Prototypes are often as much about validating proposed architectures as they are about evaluating or demonstrating recommended technologies.

> ## Quick Check
> 1. What is the primary purpose of creating a prototype?
> 2. What is the difference between a mockup and a proof-of-concept prototype?
> 3. What is meant by the term *reference architecture*?
>
> ## Quick Check Answers
> 1. A good prototype answers the questions left open from the requirements and technology recommendations.
> 2. Mockups are a horizontal view of the application at the UI level. A proof of concept takes a vertical slice of the application and implements it across the layers.
> 3. A reference architecture is an implementation of the architecture across the application layers. For example, this might include an ASP.NET Web page, a set of business objects, the data access methods, and the data storage solution—all for a single feature.

Demonstrating the Feasibility of the Design

You need to evaluate and prove the effectiveness of the prototype. Remember that your intent is to better understand and establish the application requirements and design recommendations. The prototype is meant to build confidence and foster a sense of mutual understanding among users, stakeholders, and the developers—before it's too late.

Go into the prototype phase expecting to find issues with the requirements and design. Do not be afraid to make changes to your assumptions, your design, or your requirements. That is the point. You need to find conflicts between documented requirements and what is practical and feasible. For this reason, spend some time evaluating the effectiveness of your prototype. Consider all of the following factors:

- **Missing or poor requirements**   Did you identify requirements that were incomplete or ambiguous? Were there areas that required additional clarification or use cases?
- **Design challenges**   What portions of the application will present additional design challenges? Identify areas that will need more focus. Also, consider whether you need to extend the prototype session to complete this effort.
- **Technology recommendations**   Are there different recommendations that you would make based on the prototype? Did your recommendations satisfy everything you had hoped they would?
- **Level of effort**   The prototype should help you understand how much effort will be required to build the application. Take a look at what was required for the reference architecture. Now make sure that you have enough time built into the project based on this effort (obviously adjusted for the skills of the team).

■ **Usability**   A good gauge of the prototype is whether it seems natural to the users or they require training to work with the screens. If they lean toward the latter, then you need to keep working.

Finally, you need to take what you've learned from the prototype and put together a presentation for the stakeholders. This will help formally communicate what you've learned and accomplished during the prototype phase. These demos will help the stakeholders release budget to get the project to the next level.

Lab: Create a Proof-of-Concept Prototype

The best way to ensure your understanding of this material is to create an actual proof-of-concept prototype. You can use this lab as an aid for creating a prototype for your next project.

▶ **Exercise: Create a Prototype for Your Project**

Use this exercise as a guide for creating a project prototype. If you don't have a new project, consider each item in the exercise relative to your last (or your current) project. If you were not able to create a prototype for this project, ask yourself, "What risks might I have eliminated if I had created a prototype?" or, "How would things have gone more smoothly if we had started with a prototype?"

1. Read through the application requirements and use cases. Identify the screens that might be required to satisfy the application. List each screen and the primary functionality of the screen. Look for similarities between the screens. Use these similarities to define screen types or groupings.

2. Identify areas of the requirements that seem gray or incomplete. Match these areas to the screen types you identified in the previous task. Create a UI mockup for each of these screens. Review the mockups with the users and get their feedback.

3. Review your proposed architecture with the development team. Find out what questions they have. Do they understand it the same way you understand it? Create a reference implementation of the architecture through the layers. Review this reference architecture with the team and find out whether they now have a better understanding.

4. Confirm the key design decisions you made for the application through the prototype. This might include verifying your security model, understanding how you will use Web services, or validating your data management technique. You should choose to validate any items that seem risky or not fully understood.

5. Update the requirements, recommendations, and design based on the prototype. Be sure to track changes. Review how many changes resulted from the prototype.

6. Try to create an accurate estimate of the time it will take to complete the project. Can you get other developers to agree to these estimates? Do you feel the estimates are accurate and complete? If not, what would make them more accurate and complete?

7. Document the lessons that the prototype taught you. Put them together in a presentation. This should include your original assumptions, the evaluation, and the revised assumptions as a result of the prototype effort. In addition, add the key screens and other items to the presentation. Take this presentation to the stakeholders and get their feedback.

Lesson Summary

- A prototype is meant to fill in the gaps that remain between the paper definition and the reality of implementation.
- You can define UI mockups to validate the UI and navigation of the system.
- A proof-of-concept prototype takes a vertical slice of the application and implements it across the layers. This is also called a reference architecture.
- You should use the target technologies to create the proof of concept. There are developer evaluation versions of nearly all technologies you might recommend.
- An ASP.NET prototype should confirm the recommended client, the application container, the UI elements (or screen types), the use of Web services, your security model, the third-party controls you've recommended, the proposed data access and storage methods, your state management decisions, and your overall high-level design.
- Review your prototype and confirm its effectiveness. You need to be comfortable making changes based on your prototype: that is the intent. You also should use the prototype to demonstrate the feasibility of the project to stakeholders.

Lesson Review

You can use the following questions to test your knowledge of the information in Lesson 2, "Creating a Proof-of-Concept Prototype to Refine an Application's Design." The questions are also available on the companion CD if you prefer to review them in electronic form.

NOTE   Answers

Answers to these questions and explanations of why each answer choice is right or wrong are located in the "Answers" section at the end of the book.

---

1. Review the following questions, which you need to answer with your prototype. Based on these questions, what type of prototype should you create?
   - How will users be led through the search, review, and purchase process?
   - How will the user identify the features and actions of the system without extensive training?
   - What are the common types of screens required for the application?

      A. Vertical prototype

      B. Mockup prototype

      C. Proof-of-concept prototype

      D. Reference architecture prototype

2. You need to confirm the estimates for your project. Which of the following prototype steps should you take? (Choose all that apply.)

      A. Create a reference architecture.

      B. Define the screens, their types, and their complexities.

      C. Create a working prototype of each unique element defined by the application.

      D. Update the requirements based on the findings from your prototype.

3. Which of the following should you consider when evaluating your proposed security model? (Choose all that apply.)

      A. User authentication mechanism

      B. User authorization methods

      C. Resources control

      D. Connectivity

4. You need to evaluate the effectiveness of your prototype. Which of the following might lead you to believe your prototype was effective? (Choose all that apply.)

      A. A number of gaps were identified in the requirements.

      B. The use cases were validated as correct and sufficient.

      C. Certain areas of the application were exposed as requiring additional focus in terms of design.

      D. The new technologies that were recommended worked just as expected.

Chapter Review

To further practice and reinforce the skills you learned in this chapter, you can complete the following tasks:

- Review the chapter summary.
- Review the list of key terms introduced in this chapter.
- Complete the case scenario. This scenario sets up a real-world situation involving the topics of this chapter and asks you to create a solution.
- Complete the suggested practices.
- Take a practice test.

Chapter Summary

- Look at the requirements of your application from multiple perspectives, including those of the user, the business, the developers (functional requirements), and the quality-of-service (or nonfunctional) requirements.
- A requirement should be clear, measurable, and actionable.
- Developers should use application modeling tools to define functional requirements (also called specifications), and these requirements should neither be described too much nor too little in the documentation.
- Developers need to be able to look at a set of requirements, perform careful analysis, and make appropriate technology recommendations based solely on those requirements. You should not recommend too much or too little.
- Don't always assume a build-it stance to satisfy requirements. Consider how an off-the-shelf product or internal asset might decrease time to market and reduce overall risk.
- Validate requirements by creating an application prototype. The prototype can fill in the gap that exists between the paper definition of the requirements and what actually works.
- Mockups and proof of concept are two common forms of application prototypes. A mockup helps validate the UI and navigation of the system. A proof-of-concept prototype takes a vertical slice of the application and implements it across the layers. This helps eliminate risks in the design and gives the developers a reference on which to model their work.

- Create an ASP.NET prototype to confirm the recommended client technology, the application container, the UI elements (or screen types), the use of Web services, your security model, the third-party controls you've recommended, the proposed data access and storage methods, your state management decisions, and your overall high-level design.

- Evaluate your prototype to make sure that it not only effectively demonstrates that you can create simple UI elements to satisfy basic requirements but also that it targets the risky, or unknown, elements in the system. The point of a prototype is to assess what changes to the requirements and recommendations might be necessary.

Key Terms

Do you know what these key terms mean? You can check your answers by looking up the terms in the glossary at the end of the book.

- application library
- application server
- business requirement
- client
- data storage
- framework
- functional requirement
- functional specification
- horizontal prototype
- mockup
- proof-of-concept prototype
- quality-of-service (QOS) requirement
- reference architecture
- third-party control
- use case
- user requirements
- vertical prototype

Case Scenario

In the following case scenario, you will apply what you've learned about evaluating requirements, recommending technologies, and creating a prototype. You can find answers to these questions in the "Answers" section at the end of this book.

Case Scenario: Evaluate Requirements and Propose an Application Design

You are a senior developer at a large media organization that sells and tracks advertising for its clients. This organization has gone through a number of recent mergers and acquisitions. It was determined that there are many pockets of information within the company and a lot of duplicated effort. Each pocket, or group, has its own way of doing things. An initiative has been started to define an application that allows the groups within the company to work together to define and promote best practices.

Interviews

You attend a meeting to brainstorm on the high-level requirements for the system. This meeting includes key project stakeholders, user representatives, and IT staff. It is co-facilitated by the lead business analyst and you. The following statements were made during the meeting.

- **Sales manager** "We need to establish best practices around the submission of proposals, the rates we charge, the services we offer, the steps required, supporting documents, personnel involved along with approvers, and so forth. We need to collect this information in the form of documents, discussions, and tasks that help define best practices. We then need to formalize this content and create a best-practice guidance area for our highly distributed sales team. This guidance should include templates, tasks, contacts, examples, and instructions. The guidance also needs to be categorized by the types of services we offer and the type of client that is buying the service."

  "My team is really busy. They cannot be expected to look for new information around process guidance. Instead, they need to be alerted through e-mail about content that is pertinent to them."

  "The application should be fast. I would expect to see all pages return in less than five seconds."

- **Art Department manager** "We are constantly looking for prior versions of art work files. It would be nice to have a place to store prior versions and show history such as the user, the client who requested art, and the date. This history is an asset to the company. It needs to be treated as such in terms of security and backup. Users should also be able to search for these items."

  "We have a fairly high turnover between the three art department groups. This application should reduce the training time for new hires."

- **Operations manager** "We need a clean user interface. The application should be easy to use and approachable. We want users to feel empowered and thus return to the site to get more information."

  "We would like to see a best-practice team developed. This team would collaborate on a given best practice. When they are finished, the best practice should be submitted for review and approval. No best practice should be defined (or changed) without the approval of the appropriate department manager."

"It would be nice to consolidate our sales reports. This will get the company on the same page. Right now, we have to go to three different systems to get report data and then manually consolidate that information. We then send it out in a stock format. Each group then creates its flavor of the report from the data."

■ **HR manager**   "We will need to establish a common set of guidance, forms, and instructions for the company. These include corporate benefits, hiring practices, job postings, and more. We need to consolidate this information across departments, agree to it, publish it to the user, and then keep it updated for the company. I see a private area where teams discuss this information and then a public area where users go to get the latest updates."

"We need to publish the organizational structure of the company. This includes the executive management all the way down and through the departments. This will help people recognize whom they should contact for what service. It would be nice to have pictures and contact details associated with each person in the system."

"It would be nice if users could update their own information in the system. This will help keep the data from getting old. New users should be created by HR."

■ **IT manager**   "We no longer have a single corporate standard Web browser. Instead, we need to support Microsoft Internet Explorer, Firefox, and Safari."

"We estimate that over 1,500 internal users would participate in the process of searching and reviewing best practices. All of these users have corporate accounts in Active Directory. This application should expect no more than 100 concurrent users."

■ **Development manager**   "We have just created Web services that allow access to the reporting data. You can get this data as XML from a call to the Web services at *http:/ /contoso/reports/reportservic.asmx*. There are three Web service methods: *GetSalesEast()*, *GetSalesWest()*, *GetInternationalSales()*."

"We are considering using the .NET Framework 2.0 for the application. The development team has little experience with this technology. They have written classic ASP and some .NET Framework 1.x stuff. It would be nice if they had some examples to follow."

Questions

While thinking about the preceding statements, answer the following questions.

1. What are the user requirements of the system?
2. What are the business requirements of the system?
3. What are the QOS (or nonfunctional) requirements of the system?
4. Which requirements represent functional requirements of the system?

5. Which requirements need more detail to make them unambiguous and more actionable?

6. What client solution would you recommend for the application?

7. What security model would you recommend for the application?

8. What third-party tools should you consider for the application?

9. What data storage mechanism might you recommend for the application?

10. What areas of the application seem as though they require additional research through prototyping?

Suggested Practices

To help you successfully master the exam objectives presented in this chapter, complete the following tasks.

Evaluate Requirements and Propose a Design

For this task, consider completing both practices. If you do not have an application with which to work, consider an application that you have used recently. These practices will give you a better feel for your understanding of the material.

- **Practice 1**   Spend some time with your business analysts to define application requirements. Work with users to elicit these requirements. Try documenting the requirements and then presenting them back to the users. Refine them based on their feedback. Evaluate these requirements to confirm that they are unambiguous and can be measured.

- **Practice 2**   Take a look at the requirements you created in Practice 1 and consider which technologies you would recommend based on these requirements. Alternatively, find an older set of requirements. Look at these with a fresh pair of eyes. How would you solve these requirements given today's tools and technologies?

Create a Proof-of-Concept Prototype to Refine an Application's Design

This task should be common to most senior-level developers. If, however, you have not participated in this process with users, you should strongly consider completing Practice 1. Practice 2 should help you understand how a technology model answers a few questions but presents more. Only a prototype can answer many of these questions.

- **Practice 1**   Work with users to define a UI. Use index cards or a large whiteboard. Ask the users to describe a scenario in which they would use the application and how they would use it. Then draw out how the UI will enable this scenario. This should help you understand expectations, navigation concerns, and interactivity.

■ **Practice 2**   Define a simple, high-level application design. Document a set of assumptions for the design. Present this design to a small group of developers in a meeting. Listen to how these developers expect to implement the system. List their concerns; try not to elaborate on your design. Now, review the list and consider how these questions might be answered through a prototype.

Take a Practice Test

The practice tests on this book's companion CD offer many options. For example, you can test yourself on just one exam objective, or you can test yourself on all the 70-547 certification exam content. You can set up the test so that it closely simulates the experience of taking a certification exam, or you can set it up in study mode so that you can look at the correct answers and explanations after you answer each question.

MORE INFO   Practice tests

For details about all the practice test options available, see the "How to Use the Practice Tests" section in this book's Introduction.

Chapter 2
Decompose Specifications for Developers

Bridging the considerable gap between a set of documented requirements and a complete, physical application design is no small task. You need to review requirements and use cases. You then use these to define your logical model (the relationships and constraints of your domain). Finally, you apply that information against your technology recommendations and target architecture to create developer specifications. The result of this last step will be the creation of a physical model. A physical model defines the system in terms that can be implemented by developers, who use these models and specifications to write code. The users and testers will then review the implementation results against the requirements, use cases, and logical model to ensure that there were no gaps in the design process.

This chapter covers how to move from requirements and use cases to a physical application model. It first discusses how to use application requirements to progress to a logical model for the application. It then covers how to apply your proposed design of the logical model to drive the physical models for developers. (See Chapter 1, "Application Requirements and Design.") Developers then use this information to write their code.

Exam objectives in this chapter:
- Evaluate the technical specifications for an application to ensure that the business requirements are met.
  - Translate the functional specification into developer terminology, such as pseudo-code and Unified Modeling Language (UML) diagrams.
  - Suggest component type and layer.

Lessons in this chapter:

Before You Begin

To complete the lessons in this chapter, you should be familiar with developing Web-based applications with Microsoft Visual Studio 2005 using Microsoft Visual Basic or C#. In addition, you should be comfortable with all of the following:

- Reviewing requirements and use cases for a Microsoft ASP.NET application
- Detailing the functional specifications for an ASP.NET application
- Knowing how Microsoft .NET Framework architectures and related technologies solve specific business problems
- Creating ASP.NET Web-based solutions
- Working with object-oriented development concepts
- Reading and working with UML (class diagrams and other physical models)

Real World

Mike Snell

When interviewing developers over the years, I've often asked the question, "How do you get from the requirements document to functional specifications that developers can use to write code?" I usually get a puzzled look, and receive answers like, "I take the requirements and I write the functional specifications." This tells me that these developers are used to taking requirements, breaking them down in their heads, making assumptions, and then writing specifications. This is a big leap to take.

The point is that most developers (or application architects, for that matter) do not have a methodical approach to decomposing requirements into design. I have often hired these same developers, and they are always happy to see a detailed process to bridge this gap. They often say to me, "Yeah, I was doing almost the same thing in my head. I just wasn't writing it down or sharing it with anybody." But as they build bigger and bigger systems, the need to follow a standard, methodical approach is significantly heightened.

Lesson 1: Create a Logical Model

It is important to discover the logical objects, relationships, and attributes that you are modeling with software. After all, the software is meant to solve real business problems for real people. The items that your software will represent are considered logical because they either exist, or are thought to exist, as real and actual concepts. For example, the concept of a patient being given a prescription by a doctor is a tangible, logical set of objects and relationships.

Your logical model should not change once you have agreement on it—that is, unless the real-world concepts on which it is based change. This is unlike technical specifications and design that may be affected by technology and other constraints. For example, if you change architectures, you may decide to model your objects differently. However, your logical model, because it represents logical concepts, will not change. In this way, the logical model gives everyone on the team (users, business analysts, architects, developers, and so on) an understanding of the system from a logical viewpoint. This viewpoint, which is easier to read and understand, is also more approachable than the technical physical models.

This lesson describes how Object Role Modeling (ORM) works and how to create and read ORM diagrams. After learning the basics of ORM, you will then look at how you can use this tool to document your understanding of the application's requirements in the form of logical relationships.

After this lesson, you will be able to:
- Determine the principal objects (entities) in your system based on the requirements and use cases.
- Determine the logical relationships between objects.
- Determine the attributes (properties, fields) of an object.

Estimated lesson time: 20 minutes

Object Role Modeling (ORM)

An *object role modeling diagram* represents the real-world concepts that define or influence your software. An ORM diagram includes the primary objects (also called entities) in the system, the relationships between those objects, and the attributes (and even attribute values) that define those objects. You use the ORM notation to create this logical representation between objects. Other tools for representing these relationships are entity-relationship (ER) diagrams, which are primarily associated with databases, and class diagrams, which are associated with physical, object-oriented development. ORM diagrams, on the other hand, offer a purely logical modeling tool for users, business analysts, and developers.

You create ORM diagrams by decomposing the user requirements and use cases for your application and pulling out the objects, relationships, and attributes. You will see this process later in the lesson. First, however, you should look at how to model this information and how to understand the ORM notation.

The ORM Notation

The ORM notation offers a number of shapes and connectors to define your logical model. However, for the most part, you can simplify your approach to the notation by understanding a few primary concepts. This discussion is distilled down to these primary concepts. Once you have a grasp of these items, you can represent 95 percent or more of your models. These primary concepts include object (or entity), relationship (or fact), and cardinality.

ORM Objects

In ORM diagrams, each object is represented by an oval containing the name of that object. Remember, these are logical models. Therefore, *ORM objects* are any nouns in the requirements or use case. They do not have to be full-blown, physical objects or primary entities. Rather, they represent the logical things that make up the system. For example, consider the following simple use case about an application:

1. A customer searches through the trip schedule to find a trip.
2. The customer then enters payment details (credit card number, name on card, security code, and expiration date) and books the trip.
3. The system creates a reservation for the customer.

   In this use case, *customer*, *trip schedule*, *trip*, *payment details*, and *reservation* would all be considered objects. This might seem obvious. However, *credit card number*, *credit card name*, *credit card security code*, and *credit card expiration date* are also objects in ORM terms. Figure 2-1 shows these items as objects on an ORM diagram.

MORE INFO   Visio and ORM

Microsoft Office Visio provides an ORM diagramming tool. If you have Microsoft Office System Standard Edition, you can create an ORM diagram. This is simply a drag-and-drop diagram. If you have Visio for Enterprise Architects, which ships with Microsoft MSDN Premium, you can create an *ORM source model*. This is an advanced ORM tool that provides a Fact Editor that makes defining objects and relationships much easier. You can also validate your assumptions through examples. Both diagrams are in the Visio database category because they seem to relate to building logical database models. However, an ORM should not be thought of as simply a database tool.

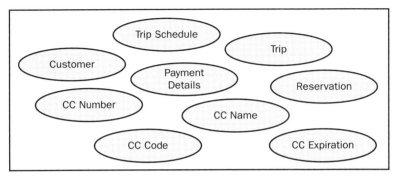

Figure 2-1   Objects on an ORM diagram

ORM Relationship

An *ORM relationship* defines how two or more objects are related to one another. In an ORM, a relationship between objects is represented as a line connecting the objects. Along this line will be a rectangle divided into segments based on the number of objects in the relationship. This is typically two segments because most often, you are modeling relationships between two objects (called a binary relationship). However, if you are modeling a relationship that exists among three objects (called a ternary relationship), you need to define all three relationships.

Look at some examples. Consider the previous simple use case and the objects derived from it. The use case defines relationships between each of the objects. These relationships are represented in Figure 2-2. Notice that there is a ternary relationship among customer, trip, and reservation. Both trip and customer come together to form a reservation.

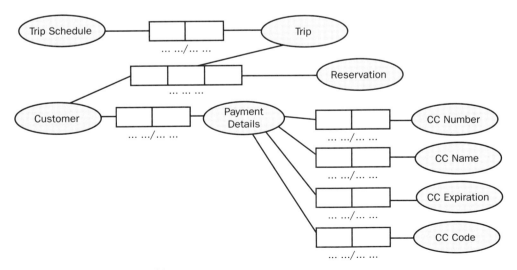

Figure 2-2   ORM relationships

ORM Facts

Your diagram is still missing, among other things, the facts that define the relationship. A fact indicates how two (or more) items are related. This is also called the *fact model* for your application. Facts don't change. They represent how objects really relate to one another.

In an ORM diagram, you define facts by adding text beneath the relationship shape. Notice that in Figure 2-2, there are ellipses (...) on either side of a slash (/) under each relationship shape. You define the relationship by replacing each ellipsis with text. The slash indicates how you read the relationship. The text on the left side of the slash reads from left to right. The text on the right side of the slash defines the inverse of the relationship. Figure 2-3 shows the model with the facts defined. You read the first fact as "Trip Schedule has Trip" and the inverse as "Trip is in Trip Schedule."

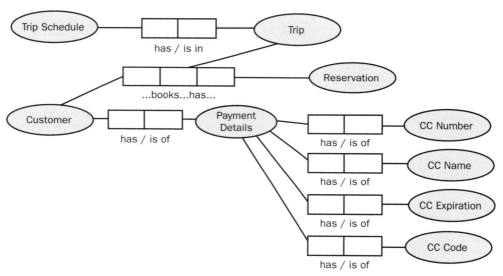

Figure 2-3   ORM relationship facts

ORM Constraints

Constraints are the final missing piece of the model. *ORM constraints* define how the objects participate in the relationship. This includes defining which objects are mandatory and the multiplicity of the relationship. Mandatory objects in a relationship are indicated by a closed (or filled) circle attached to either end of the connection. This closed circle indicates that the given object is mandatory in the relationship. That is, the related object does not exist without this object.

Multiplicity indicates whether two objects relate to one another as one-to-one, one-to-many, or many-to-many. Multiplicity is indicated with a series of arrows over the relationship shape. Figure 2-4 shows the multiplicity options for ORM relationships.

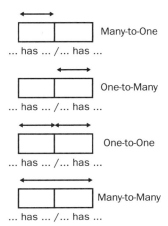

Figure 2-4 ORM relationship multiplicity

Figure 2-5 shows these constraints applied to the sample diagram. For example, you can now read the first relationship (between Trip Schedule and Trip) as "Each Trip Schedule has zero or more trips, and some trips are in more than one schedule." This gives you a very good understanding of your system in terms of objects and the facts that exist between those objects.

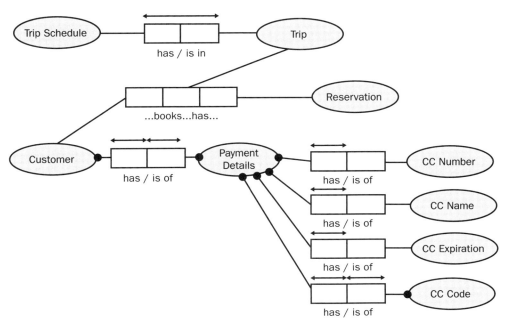

Figure 2-5 The ORM with constraints applied

Driving ORM Diagrams from Requirements and Use Cases

You saw in the previous example that you were able to define an ORM from a simple use case. Most use cases and requirements are much more detailed than this simple example. You will want to go over these requirements and use cases line by line and pull out the objects and facts. The objects are easy to find because they are represented by nouns. The relationships (or facts) are the verb phrases that indicate a connection between objects.

When you first start your ORM, the objects and facts will come quickly and easily. After you read further, however, you will identify fewer and fewer new objects and fewer new facts. Instead, you might find that you need to rethink or refactor the way you are looking at certain items. Look at each statement in the specifications and determine whether the statements found therein are supported by your ORM. If they are not, either the statement must change or the ORM must change. Once these items are aligned, you should have a solid understanding of how the items in your software relate.

Quick Check

1. What is the primary purpose of a logical model of your requirements and use cases?
2. How do you read the relationship between two objects?

Quick Check Answers

1. A logical model defines the facts in the domain for which you are building software. Creating a logical model of your requirements will both validate the requirements and provide a solid understanding of the domain.
2. The relationship is read from left to right using the text on the left side of the slash under the relationship shape. The inverse relationship is read using the text on the opposite side of the slash.

Using the ORM Diagrams to Identify Objects, Properties, Methods, Entities, and Fields

Your ORM is a logical view of your objects and relationships. As you continue the design process, you will use the logical model (ORM diagrams and logical architecture) along with your technology recommendations to drive physical models. Your logical models should not change. However, when you apply these logical models to your target technology, you will make decisions that might confuse and even contradict your logical model. This is OK because you need to make tradeoffs when moving to the physical model.

Lesson 3, "Create Physical Application Models for Developers," covers the process of creating the physical model in more detail. The basic concept, however, is that you find in the ORM the items that have the most relationships. The diagram tends to be most interesting when read from the perspective of these items, such as customer or trip in the previous example. These will become your primary database entities and the classes in your application. The items that relate to these primary entities will sometimes become sub-entities themselves (with their own definitions), or they may become database fields and object properties. The relationships will form the basis for your database-stored procedures and your application methods.

Lab: Create a Logical Model

In this lab, you will review a number of high-level application requirements and a simple use case. You will use this information to define the logical objects in the domain and their relationships to one another. You will do so in the context of an ORM diagram.

▶ **Exercise 1: Review Requirements and Define a Logical Model**

In this exercise, review the following application requirements and simple use case. Then, perform the steps to determine the objects and facts in this domain. First, consider the following application requirements:

- R1: The application should be accessible to any person with an Internet connection.
- R2: The system needs to support up to 250 active customers booking trips.
- R3: Customers must register with the site to book a trip.
- R4: Customers must be able to check a trip for availability.
- R5: Customers can book a trip by selecting a trip type, entering a date, selecting a time, and making a deposit.
- R6: A customer's booking should reserve a trip. Another customer should not be able to book the same trip with the same guide for the same day and time window.

Review the use case for this application, in which a customer books a trip.

1. User navigates to the home page of the resort's Web site.
2. Customer selects the "add an excursion" option when booking a resort reservation.
3. The system presents a list of available trip types and related pricing based on the season associated with the trip dates. Trip types might include kayaking, snorkeling, and sailing.
4. Registered customer selects a trip type, enters a date for the trip, and selects a time.
5. System checks the trip to ensure its availability.
6. System asks the user to make a deposit to make the reservation.
7. Customer enters payment details for the deposit (credit card number, name, security code, and expiration) and indicates to the system to finish the booking.
8. System reserves the trip (guide, duration, and date) for the customer.

Now perform the following lab steps to identify the objects in the domain as defined in the preceding requirements and use case.

1. Identify the objects in the domain. Go through the requirements and use case and pull out all of the nouns. Review those nouns and determine whether any two represent the same thing. Refactor (rewrite) the requirements and use case to use a single representation of each noun.

    For example, *user*, *customer*, *person*, *active customer*, and *registered customer* are all the same thing. *Reservation* and *booking* are the same. *Trip* and *excursion* are also the same.

2. Use Visio to create an ORM diagram. Add the nouns as objects on the diagram.

    Your objects should include the following: *customer, application, connection, system, site, trip, trip type, trip date, trip time, deposit, resort, reservation, guide, home page, pricing, trip availability, payment details, credit card number, credit card name, credit card security code, credit card expiration.*

3. Review the list of objects. Remove any objects that you know are not relevant to your logical model.

    These might include *application, connection, system, site, home page.*

4. Define the facts in the system. Go back through each requirement and each line of the use case. Read the phrases that indicate or imply a relationship. Try to model each fact, indicating both the left-to-right relationship and the inverse.

    Your fact database should include the following facts (and their inversions):

    ❑ Trip has Duration / Duration defines Trip
    ❑ Payment Details has CC Security Code / CC Security Code is of Payment Details
    ❑ Payment Details has CC Name / CC Name is of Payment Details
    ❑ Payment Details has CC Card Expiration / CC Card Expiration is of Payment Details
    ❑ Payment Details has CC Number / CC Number is of Payment Details
    ❑ Customer has Payment Details / Payment Details is of Customer
    ❑ Customer makes Deposit / Deposit is of Customer
    ❑ Trip has Pricing / Pricing defines Trip
    ❑ Trip has Guide / Guide defines Trip
    ❑ Customer makes Reservation / Reservation is of Customer
    ❑ Reservation has Trip / Trip defines Reservation
    ❑ Trip has Trip Time / Trip Time defines Trip
    ❑ Trip has Date / Date defines Trip
    ❑ Trip has Trip Type / Trip Type defines Trip
    ❑ Trip has Trip Availability / Trip Availability defines Trip
    ❑ Customer books Trip / Trip booked by Customer

5. Define the constraints on your facts. Verify each fact against the requirements and use case, considering any constraints that apply to the fact. This should include determining which ends of the relationship are mandatory and the multiplicity of the relationship. Once finished, lay out your facts on an ORM diagram. Your diagram should look like the one in Figure 2-6.

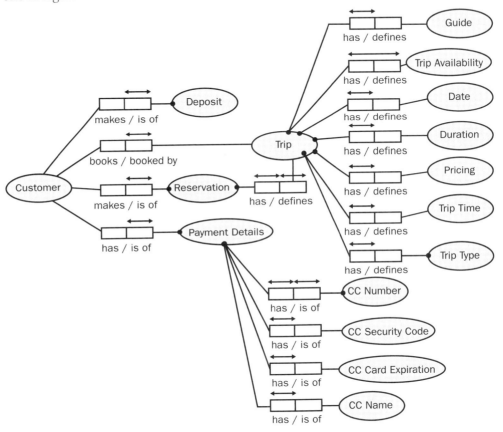

Figure 2-6   The facts in an ORM diagram

Lesson Summary

- A logical model is important (and is called a logical model) because your software represents real and actual concepts. These concepts do not typically change. You need to have a solid grasp of these concepts to make sure your software meets the demands of these real-world concepts.

- An object role modeling (ORM) diagram is used to model the logical objects in your software. This includes the relationships between those objects and the constraints that should be put on those relationships.

- An ORM diagram should be thought of as a purely logical view of your objects. It should not represent your classes or your database. You can use your ORM diagrams to drive toward your database and class diagrams. However, this typically means tradeoffs to support the technology. The ORM diagrams do not require such tradeoffs. Instead, they should stay faithful to the logical concepts your software represents.

- The ORM notation uses an oval to represent an object, a line with a relationship box to represent a relationship, and arrows over the box to represent multiplicity. You can write out the relationship as text under the relationship shape on the diagram.

Lesson Review

You can use the following questions to test your knowledge of the information in Lesson 1, "Create a Logical Model." The questions are also available on the companion CD if you prefer to review them in electronic form.

NOTE   Answers

Answers to these questions and explanations of why each answer choice is right or wrong are located in the "Answers" section at the end of the book.

---

1. Consider the following statement about your application: "A buyer checks products against store inventories. If inventories are reduced below the inventory threshold, the buyer must purchase replenishments from one or more vendors." Which of the following represents the logical objects defined in this statement?

    A. Buyer, Product, Inventory, Replenishment, Vendor

    B. User, Product, Vendor, Store

    C. Buyer, Product, Store, Inventory, Inventory Threshold, Replenishment, Vendor

    D. Inventory Check, Purchase Replenishments

2. Consider the following statement about an application: "A customer places an order for one or more books." How would you model the relationships to the *Order* object?

    A. Unary: Order has Order Customer, Order has Order Book

    B. Binary: Customer places Order, Book defines Order

    C. Ternary: Order has Customer, Customer buys Book, Book defines Order

    D. Binary: Order placed by Customer, Order defined by Book

3. Consider the following statement about an application: "An employee reports to a supervisor." How would you write this fact and the inverse of this fact? (Choose all that apply.)

   A. Employee reports to Supervisor

   B. Supervisor has Reports

   C. Supervisor manages Employee

   D. Employee is a Supervisor

4. Consider the following fact, read from left to right: "Shipping Slip has Ship-to Address." What constraints would you attach to this relationship?

   A. Closed circle on Shipping Slip, an arrow over the left side of the relationship shape.

   B. Closed circle on Ship-to Address, an arrow over the right side of the relationship shape.

   C. No circles, an arrow over the left side, and another arrow over the right side of the relationship shape.

   D. Closed circle on Shipping Slip and a single long arrow that covers both the left and right sides of the relationship.

Lesson 2: Define Application Layers

A logical architecture helps developers understand how a system is put together, how it works, and how they should add code to it. Logical architectures are not required to make your application work; instead, they are simply a means of explaining how it works. It is very difficult for most developers to simply look at code, or even walk through code, and get a feel for exactly how the application works. Therefore, it can be helpful to define a logical understanding of the layers, components, and communication paths in your system. This also helps architects design the system.

This lesson looks at how you can create and use logical architecture models. You will first look at defining the layers of your application. You will then learn about creating a component model. Finally, you will examine how you can describe the communication between the layers and components.

After this lesson, you will be able to:

- Define the logical layers of your application and indicate what code should go into each layer.
- Indicate the communication paths and protocols between the layers in your system.
- Create a logical architecture to define your application.

Estimated lesson time: 20 minutes

Define the Layers of Your Application

The logical layers of your system represent how you plan to divide your code into logical pieces or groups. For example, a three-tier system might define a user interface (UI), business objects, and database layer. These are considered logical layers because the code is divided logically by what it represents. Physically, the code libraries themselves may run in the same process. In this case, layers are combined for technical tradeoffs (or physical reasons). As an example, think of an ASP.NET application that defines a set of business objects in the App_Code directory. These objects run in the same process as the UI classes run. However, the code is logically separated; UI code goes in the UI layer, and business object code goes in the business object layer.

What Does It Mean to Have Application Layers?

Application layers can be thought of as similar to application tiers. The term *tiers* was preferred for a time because applications were being built as two-tier and three-tier designs. Tiers include the UI, middle tier, and database tier. A two-tier application is a UI working with a database. A three-tier application adds a middle tier to manage the business objects and rules in the system. This abstraction allows for the innovation (or replacement) of the UI or database code without rewriting the "guts" of the business logic.

This last concept—the ability to abstract portions of an application so that they can evolve independently—pushed application architectures toward *n-tier* (an application with more than the three basic tiers). For example, a database tier can be split among a database abstraction layer for the business objects, a database utility (or helper) layer, stored procedures, and the database itself. The UI tier might be split between the strict UI code (events and layout operations) and the code that calls the middle tier. The middle tier itself can also be split. All of these splits can be referred to as application layers. You can assign a name to each layer and the system will be easier to understand.

Layers provide a clean, logical way to look at an application. Application layers are typically organized from top to bottom. The top is where the user activity happens. The bottom is where the data is stored when at rest. Your application *state*, the data that moves from the database to the UI, is passed through the layers (from top to bottom and back again). Each layer in the middle represents a view of the state in your application or a service that works on that state. For example, the UI translates state for display to the user. The business layer works on state and applies business rules to it. The database layer knows how to save state to the database. To gain a logical understanding of a system, you must define the layers and how state is passed between them (the communication paths). Of course, that presents your high-level, logical architecture. You still need to group features into components and define component models.

Layers of ASP.NET Applications

An ASP.NET application can be divided into a number of different logical layers. Your decision on which layers to enforce is typically dependent on your quality-of-service (QOS) requirements. For example, if your application is a quick, possibly throwaway system with low scalability and maintainability concerns, you might choose to implement only a couple of layers (UI and database). If, on the other hand, you are optimizing your architecture for varied physical deployments, high scalability, multiple UIs (Web, Mobile, Reports, and so on), and a high degree of reuse, then you will opt to abstract your application into many more logical layers—you might even create a framework.

Most enterprise-level ASP.NET applications written today employ some version of the three primary layers: UI, middle tier, and database. Each of these layers might then be split into additional layers. The following list presents each of these layers and some of their common splits. Any combination of these layers may make up an ASP.NET application.

User Interface The UI layer provides users with a window to the application. This layer is typically responsible for getting data from the middle tier and displaying it to the user. It is also responsible for controlling how a user interacts with that data. This includes data entry, validation, creating new elements, search, and so on. The UI layer is also in charge of getting the user's modifications back to the middle tier for processing. The UI layer is often a layer by itself but is sometimes split into one or more of the following additional layers:

- **Presentation (or user experience)**   This layer defines only the presentation portion of the UI. It is the portion responsible for laying out the UI. This is the markup code in your .aspx, .ascx, .css, and .html files. ASP.NET does a good job of abstracting this code if you use the code-behind model. The single-file model, however, combines the presentation and UI code.

- **User interface code**   This layer is where developers place the code to interact with the UI. It is required and automatic with the ASP.NET code-behind model. The layer includes code to respond to events such as loading a page or clicking a button.

- **Business logic interaction code**   You might create this layer if you do not wish to tie the code that interacts with your business layer (middle tier) to the UI code. This can be helpful if you are planning to replace your UI. For example, you might create a browser-based client today but plan to move to Extensible Application Markup Language (XAML), a Windows Client, or something else.

Middle Tier   The middle tier is where you house your business logic. This is often just referred to as the business layer. However, this tier typically includes a lot more than just business logic. It might include components for handling caching, logging, error management, and so on. You might use the enterprise library (or similar code) in this tier. The middle tier typically runs on an application server such as Microsoft Windows Server and Internet Information Services (IIS). However, you can create your own middle tiers (using things such as Microsoft Windows services and sockets). The middle tier is sometimes split into one or more of the following additional layers:

- **Business layer (or business services)**   This layer is where you put your domain objects and their business rules. You might be writing stateless components that work with Enterprise Services, real object-oriented business objects, or simple data transfer objects with processing services. In any case, most applications define a business layer. This isolates the business logic so it is reusable, remains stable (because UIs get rewritten), is easier to change, and so on.

- **Application layer (or application services)**   This layer represents the plumbing that makes your application work. This plumbing typically satisfies QOS (or non-functional) requirements such as the application being required to log errors or cache data for performance. You want to keep this code isolated from your business logic. Sometimes, this code is put into a framework. You can also consider the Microsoft Enterprise Library for .NET Framework as part of the application layer.

- **Database layer (or database services)**   This layer abstracts the retrieval and storage of data in your database. This code is sometimes combined with the business layer. However, this tight coupling can make the code harder to understand, more brittle to change, and less reusable. The database abstraction layer is often part of the database layer. However, it typically runs not on the database but on the middle tier. That is why it is discussed here.

Database Layer The database layer represents how you manage the data in your application. For most enterprise applications, this means a relational database such as Microsoft SQL Server. The database layer is responsible for the saving, retrieval, and integrity of your data. The database tier is sometimes split into one or more of the following additional layers:

- **Database layer** See the "Middle Tier" section of this chapter.
- **Stored procedures** This layer represents the SQL or managed code used to select, insert, update, and delete data in the database. It also includes any database-defined functions you might create.
- **Integration services** This layer represents how the database works with other data sources for integration purposes. In SQL Server, this is SQL Server Integration Services (SSIS) or the earlier Data Transformation Services (DTS).
- **Database tables, log, and indexes** This layer represents the actual data in the system, the log of activity, and the indexes used by the database software.

Quick Check

1. What is the purpose of logical application layers?
2. What is the intent of creating multiple (three or more) application layers?

Quick Check Answers

1. Logical application layers help developers and architects understand how a system works and where to write their code.
2. You abstract code into a layer to mitigate risk. You might be trying to increase reuse; you might be worried about layers changing independently; you might be trying to increase scalability; or you might be trying to isolate developers. The decision to create more than two layers typically revolves around support QOS requirements.

Define Communication Between Layers

The application layers define the logical abstractions you intend for the code in the system. You will need to consider how you intend to deploy these logical layers in a physical environment. The environment might constrain your deployment options, or you might have other concerns. For example, you might not be allowed to have a Web server that is open to the Internet and communicates directly with a database server. In this case, you might have to deploy your business logic layer on a Web server and your database layer code on another server behind the firewall. Clearly, it is important to be aware of these issues when defining your layers. (Imagine if you coupled the layers in the prior example and did not find out about this constraint until it came time to deploy the project!)

Another deployment issue you need to consider is the communication paths and protocols between the layers. As you saw in Chapter 1, you can use tools such as Visual Studio Team Architect to set these constraints, indicate the communication paths, and define the ports in terms of security and protocol. For your logical architecture, you could decide to simply indicate the layers in the system and their intent and then draw arrows between the layers that communicate. On each arrow, you might indicate the intended communication, such as Hyper Text Transfer Protocol (HTTP), Transmission Control Protocol/Internet Protocol (TCP/IP), Simple Object Access Protocol (SOAP), and so on. Figure 2-7 shows an example of a logical architecture.

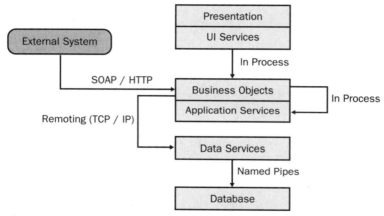

Figure 2-7   An application-layer diagram (logical architecture)

This diagram shows the logical layers of the application. Notice that, based on deployment constraints, the UI code (presentation and UI services), the business object layer, and the application services layer will all execute in the same process. There is also an external system that will connect to some of the business logic via a Web service. The database services code will be deployed on a different server. Therefore, the communication to this server is through remoting. Finally, the database services code will be the only layer communicating directly with the database; it will do so across named pipes.

Lab: Define Logical Application Layers

In this lab, you will define the logical layers of an application. You will start by reviewing a number of design goals and some functional requirements and then use this information to propose the logical layers of a solution architecture. You will also add physical constraints to those layers in terms of communication paths and deployment options.

▶ **Exercise: Review Design Goals and Define Logical Application Layers**

In this exercise, review the following design goals and some functional requirements. Then follow the steps to determine the application layers and communication paths. Following are the design goals with which you will be working:

- G1: The application should be accessible to any employee on the corporate network with a Web browser.
- G2: The UI should be easy to deploy and update.
- G3: The business processing rules should be extracted into their own set of classes and methods. For now, these rules are only part of this application.
- G4: The database access code will be created by a database developer rather than by each module's developer. All data access should be encapsulated in a common area.
- G5: All common application functions should be grouped together. We are considering using Microsoft Enterprise Library for .NET Framework or something similar to provide these services to the various layers of the application.
- G6: We are targeting the existing application server for the deployment of this application.
- G7: We plan to use the relational database to manage the data and data transactions in the system. This database is accessible from the application server via TCP/IP.

Now that you have reviewed the design goals, perform the following lab steps to determine the application layers and communication paths:

1. Determine the UI layers you would define.

   G1 indicates that this is a browser-based application; this means ASP.NET Web forms and user controls. G2 indicates easy deployment and updating. For this reason, you might suggest using a single-file model for the Web forms and user controls (as opposed to code-behind). These facts might lead you to a single layer for the UI. This layer would combine both presentation and the code to interact with the business objects.

2. Determine the layers you would define for the middle tier.

   G3 indicates that the business rules should be abstracted into their own layer. G5 indicates that there are common services for the entire application. These facts should lead you to recommend both a business logic layer and an application services layer.

3. Determine the layers you would define for the data tier.

   G4 indicates that a single, separate developer will be working on data access methods. This should warrant a separate layer for the database services.

4. Draw the recommended layers on a diagram. Figure 2-8 shows a representation.

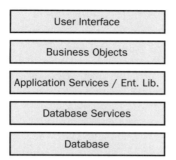

Figure 2-8 The proposed application layers

5. Determine the communication paths between the layers.

   The design goals indicate that the UI layer should interact with only the business objects. It should not call the other services directly. The business objects layer should work with the application services layer. It also works with the database services to store and retrieve data. The database layer should work with the application services layer and the database.

6. Determine the physical processes that will execute each layer in the system.

   The UI, business objects, application services, and database services can all run on the same computer and in process. G6 indicates an application server for this. The database server is another computer. The application server should connect to this through TCP/IP. Figure 2-9 shows a representation of your final, logical, layered architecture.

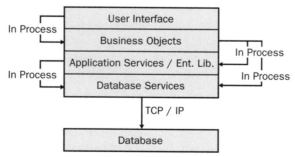

Figure 2-9 The completed logical application layers

Lesson Summary

- You define the logical layers of your application to help developers and architects understand how your system works and where their code logically fits.
- A logical architecture indicates the layers in the system and the communication paths between those layers.

■ You abstract code into layers to help mitigate risk and increase reusability. You might also have design goals that you are satisfying with the logical layers in your application.

■ An ASP.NET application is usually split among the UI layers (presentation and form interaction code), the middle tier (business logic and application services), and the database tier (database abstraction code and the database itself).

Lesson Review

You can use the following questions to test your knowledge of the information in Lesson 2, "Define Application Layers." The questions are also available on the companion CD if you prefer to review them in electronic form.

NOTE Answers

Answers to these questions and explanations of why each answer choice is right or wrong are located in the "Answers" section at the end of the book.

---

1. Which of the following are benefits of defining application layers? (Choose all that apply.)

   A. Increase code reuse

   B. Make your code more understandable

   C. Indicate the library (.dll) that code should go into

   D. Make your code more maintainable

2. You have decided to create a presentation layer for your UI. Which of the following code items belong in this layer? (Choose all that apply).

   A. Extensible HTML (XHTML)

   B. .aspx files written as a single-file model

   C. .aspx files written as a code-behind model

   D. Code-behind files

3. You are writing an application that has the following constraints:
    - ❑ The application needs to be written in a very short time frame.
    - ❑ The application will not be reused. The company is already working on a replacement. However, that will take longer to develop.
    - ❑ The application should support approximately 10 users.
    - ❑ The application will be accessed via a Web browser.
    - ❑ The application logic is not very complex.
    - ❑ The application will be deployed on a single server (IIS and SQL Server).

    Considering these constraints, what application layers would you recommend?

    A. Presentation $\rightarrow$ User Activity $\rightarrow$ Business Objects $\rightarrow$ Database
    B. User Interface $\rightarrow$ Business Services $\rightarrow$ Database
    C. User Interface $\rightarrow$ Database
    D. User Interface $\rightarrow$ Application Services $\rightarrow$ Database

Lesson 3: Create Physical Application Models for Developers

The physical models for an application indicate how developers should build a system. These are technical models using a technical notation such as Unified Modeling Language (UML) or the Visual Studio Class Designer. The models use the information from the requirements, logical models (ORM diagrams), high-level architecture, and application layers to define the components, classes, methods, and messaging between objects.

This lesson looks at how you can define components from the modules, sub-modules, and layers in your application. It then looks at building class models based on the domain you defined in the ORM diagrams. Next, you will examine the purpose of some additional UML models (sequence, collaboration, and activity) that help you understand your system better. Finally, explore how you can use pseudocode to help developers better understand your intent.

MORE INFO   The Unified Modeling Language

Neither this lesson nor this training kit is meant to be a definitive primer on UML. There are many good books out there that tackle that subject. Rather, this lesson offers a basic overview of UML models as they relate to physical models for developers. It will not cover the intricacies of the notation, nor will it cover all of the many models. If you are totally unfamiliar with UML, consider some additional training on this subject. For an overview of UML, visit *http://www.uml.org/*.

> **After this lesson, you will be able to:**
> - Understand the purpose of a component diagram.
> - Understand the purpose of a class diagram.
> - Understand the purpose of an activity diagram.
> - Understand the purpose of sequence and collaboration diagrams.
> - Create pseudocode to aid developers.
>
> **Estimated lesson time: 35 minutes**

Real World

Mike Snell

I have worked in many environments in which architects want nothing to do with the structured notation of UML. Typically, these architects feel the notation is too complex or the effort is not warranted. Of course, they still need to create application models to help developers. Sometimes, this has meant simple boxes and arrows; other times, I have seen the contents of a sequence diagram written out as long sections of text.

I have also seen the opposite (although this is rarer): environments that require every UML model for every object, method, interaction, activity, state, deployment, and so on. These teams typically produce more documents than code.

For my own teams, when I am in charge, I take a practical approach. I suggest we use the pieces of UML when they make sense. If we are having a hard time understanding how objects communicate, we create a sequence diagram. If we have a complex method, I suggest an activity diagram. These are not required, but they are often useful. We have also been using the Visual Studio Class Designer to create our physical class diagrams. This saves us time, too, in that we do not have to stub out the code.

Create a Component Diagram

A *component diagram* is used to indicate the components (or code packages) that you will create for your application. A *component* is made up of logically related classes grouped together in a single deployable unit. You can think of a component as a .dll, control, or Web service. Component diagrams are useful for indicating physical dependencies and physical deployment (in conjunction with a deployment diagram). This section looks at how you determine the components in your system and how you create a component diagram.

Defining Application Components

When working through your requirements, use cases, and logical model, you also work to group functionality logically. For example, consider the requirements and use cases for a sales management system. You will want to group the requirements into modules like sales person, accounts, supervisor, order, forecast, and so on. You then might break these modules into submodules and define the set of features within each module and sub-module.

Follow a similar technique for the code elements of your application. Group the code into physical components that will be used to indicate which library contains a given set of code. These components may follow the same lines as your application layers, or they may follow your modules or even features. For example, if you follow your application layers, you might have a UserInterface component, a BusinessObjects component, and so on. Or you might decide to break out some of these layers into multiple components. You could create a Sales-Person component, an Order component, or something else. Each of these might contain business logic for a given module. However, this physical distribution could be based on the choice to encapsulate each module of the application.

Create a Component Diagram

You create a component diagram by adding components to the diagram and then setting their dependencies. Figure 2-10 shows an example of a component diagram. The components are represented by the rectangles that include the two smaller rectangles on their left. Notice that each component name is preceded with text, indicating its logical layer, and then two colons. This text represents the components package. A UML package is a logical grouping of components, classes, and other objects. Here, you are using packages to group components by logical layers. For example, the SalesMgmtUI component is inside the *User Interface* package.

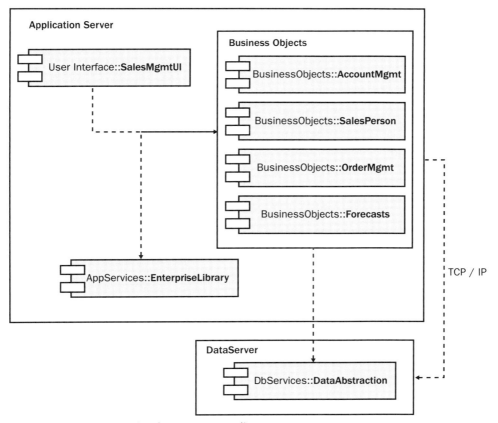

Figure 2-10   An example of a component diagram

The outer boxes that surround the components are called nodes. A UML node indicates a deployment container. This is typically a physical piece of hardware. For example, the business objects, UI, and application services are all on the *Application Server* node. This node would be a Windows Server running IIS. You can also use the node concept to group the business objects. This cuts down on the arrows required to indicate all the dependencies in the diagram.

Create a Class Diagram

A *class diagram* defines the structure of the classes (methods and properties) and the relationship between those classes. A class diagram defines the specification of the system. The classes in the model are static representations. The model is not meant to show how these classes interact, nor does it show the classes as objects. Rather, it shows the definition of the classes, how they are related, and how they are defined in terms of one another (and in terms of object-oriented design).

The UML defines a model for creating class diagrams. This model represents a notation for methods, properties, inheritance, associations, data types, and so on. The notation is meant to be "technology agnostic." It is focused on object-oriented concepts and not on a particular technology such as .NET Framework or Java. Visual Studio 2005, however, provides a class diagramming tool. This tool is not meant to follow the UML notation. However, it too defines classes, properties, methods, enumerations, inheritance, dependencies, and so on.

The principal benefit of using Visual Studio is that it is a "live" model. It represents a two-way synchronization with your code and your diagram. If you build your class models in Visual Studio, you get the code stubbed out as well. If you change your code, the model gets updated. Therefore, as code is modified, your model is automatically updated. For this section, you will leave the UML and just learn about designing classes with the Class Designer.

Define Classes for Your Application

The classes in your application should derive from your solution architecture (or framework) and your business domain. The solution architecture classes you define are dependent on that architecture. For example, if you intend to create a central class for handling the logging of errors, you create a class called *Logger* or something similar. If you want a base class for managing object security, you create that as part of your framework. The same is true for other framework-like classes, such as a database helper class or a cache management class.

The business domain classes also need to respect your solution architecture. If, for example, your architecture dictates that each class knows how to save and create itself from the database, you need to design your business classes accordingly. Perhaps you would create a common interface, for example. As another example, if you are using a pattern like data transfer object (DTO) to create your business model, you need to create simple domain classes with only fields or properties, and then create a set of domain services to work with these classes. The point is that how you define your business domain classes is dependent on the technical constraints of your overall solution architecture.

The makeup of your business domain itself should be defined based on your logical model. The *business domain* refers to the classes you will define, which classes are made up of other objects (inheritance and encapsulation), and the properties of your classes. If you look back at your ORM diagrams, you will find your primary entities. These are the principal objects that link to a lot of other objects in the model. These objects can be thought of as the "perspective" objects. That is, they are the objects that you most typically start with, and you examine the relationships from their perspective. They are usually easy to pick out. For example, a *SalesPerson* or *Account* object in a sales management application will end up with a lot of links and be considered important from that point of view. They also participate heavily in the feature set, modules, sub-modules, requirements, and use cases. The other objects in your ORM are sometimes bit players in the domain. At other times, they end up as simply properties, or even values of properties, of a class.

To create your business domain (class diagram), look through your ORM diagrams and pick out the domain objects and their properties. You then need to apply the physical constraints of your technology choices and the constraints of your solution architecture to the class diagram. The result should be a domain model that stays true to your logical model and supports your technology choices.

Create a Class Diagram

The Class Designer in Visual Studio provides a notation that should be easy to pick up for those accustomed to working with UML. The notation represents classes as rectangles. These rectangles (like UML classes) are split into multiple sections (usually two). The top grouping in the class contains the properties of the object; the bottom contains the methods. The notation also allows for the display of things such as fields and nested types. Figure 2-11 shows a sample class diagram for illustration purposes.

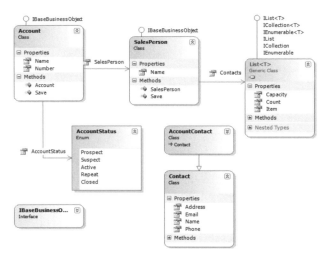

Figure 2-11   A sample class diagram

The Visual Studio 2005 Class Designer gives a visual representation of a number of object-oriented elements. These elements include all of the following:

- **Class**   A class is represented as a rectangle with properties and methods. In Figure 2-11, *Account*, *SalesPerson*, *List*, *AccountContact*, and *Contact* are all classes.

- **Interface**   An interface is represented like a class but has a different color (green). In Figure 2-11, *IBaseBusinessObject* is an interface.

- **Implement interface**   The interfaces that a class implements are represented with the lollipop icon extending from the top of the object. For example, *Account* in Figure 2-11 implements *IBaseBusinessObject*.

- **Association/Aggregation**   A property that is of a specific type in your domain is indicated by an arrow with the property name on the line of the arrow. *AccountStatus* is an example from Figure 2-11.

- **Inheritance**   A class that inherits another class is indicated with the open-ended arrow head (similar to UML). In Figure 2-11, *AccountContact* inherits *Contact*.

- **Enumeration**   An enumeration is indicated as a rectangle that is not rounded off (like the classes are). Figure 2-11 has the enumeration *AccountStatus*.

- **Other items**   The notation allows you to see a number of additional items, including *Abstract Class*, *Struct*, *Delegate*, and a *Comment*. You can also show members of the .NET Framework. (Notice that Figure 2-11 shows *IList<T>* from the *Generic* namespace.) In addition, you can modify the model to show data types and parameters.

Exam Tip

Pay close attention to the modeling defined in this lesson when you study for the exam. All the items mentioned here may appear in one form or another throughout the exam. You should have a good understanding of how to read these models.

Create a Sequence Diagram

A *sequence diagram* shows object interaction during execution (or run time). The model demonstrates the lifetime of these objects and shows the message exchange between them. Object-oriented programming results in a lot of small objects interacting with one another. The objects call each other through a sequence (or chronology) to get work done for the application. The many objects making many calls to each other can make it difficult to understand how they come together to form a complete solution. A sequence diagram is meant to illustrate and clarify just how these objects talk to one another to form a specific solution.

The UML notation dictates how you create sequence diagrams. Objects are listed as rectangles at the top of the diagram with lifelines extending from them. An object *lifeline* is an indication of how long an object will live before it is disposed of or made ready for garbage collection. The objects themselves are described in the rectangle that sits atop this lifeline. The description that goes in the rectangle is meant to describe an instance of the class. For this reason, you typically write the description as *an Object* or *the Object*, where the object is the name of the class or variable representing the class.

Figure 2-12 shows a sample sequence diagram. In this example, *EditContactUI, Contact, ContactService,* and *ContactDb* are all objects. This example is meant to show how these objects work together to support the use case "edit customer." The design has a UI form (*EditContactUI*), a domain object (*Contact*), a Web service for managing the domain object (*ContactService*), and a database abstraction class for the object (*ContactDb*).

Notice the long rectangles that extend along the lifeline of each object. These rectangles indicate when an object is created and when it goes out of scope. For example, the *ContactDb* object is created twice by the *ContactService* during this process.

The messages that pass between objects are indicated by the arrows from one lifeline to another. These messages are meant to be read from top to bottom and left to right (as a sequence). Each message represents a method call, property call, or return value. For example, the *GetContact* message represents a call to the *GetContact* method of the *ContactService* object. The calls to the *Contact.Name, Contact.Email,* and related properties are also depicted. Return calls are shown as a dashed arrow; *return confirmation* is an example. All the messages depicted in Figure 2-12 are synchronous. You can also indicate asynchronous messages by using an arrow that has only its lower half.

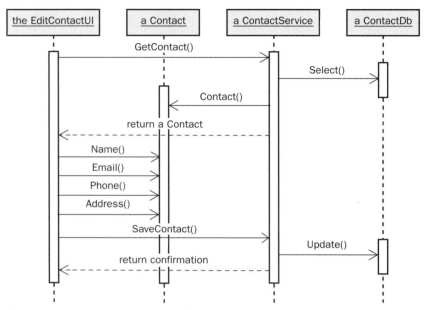

Figure 2-12 A sample sequence diagram

Collaboration Diagram

A collaboration diagram shows the same type of interaction between objects as does a sequence diagram. However, the collaboration diagram allows you to lay out the objects in any way you like. The actual sequence is dictated by numbered messages (and not by the model's constraints). Figure 2-13 shows the same sequence diagram shown in Figure 2-12 as a collaboration diagram.

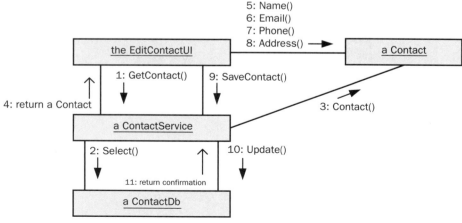

Figure 2-13 A sample collaboration diagram

Quick Check

1. What is the definition of a component? What is the purpose of a component diagram?
2. What is the purpose of a class diagram?
3. When would you use a sequence diagram versus a collaboration diagram?

Quick Check Answers

1. A group of logically related classes and methods make up a component. A component diagram shows how components work with one another to form a solution and how they are deployed in a physical environment (onto nodes).

2. A class diagram provides static specifications for developers to implement and to help them understand how the classes are structured. It does not provide information about how the class works. It simply alludes to this type of information.

3. You create a sequence diagram to depict the logical sequence between objects across their lifeline. A collaboration diagram does not show an object's lifeline, and the sequence of events is determined only by numbered messages. However, the collaboration diagram allows you to lay out the objects in any spatial order.

Create an Activity Diagram

The UML defines the activity diagram as an answer for flow-charting and workflow definition. An *activity diagram* allows you to indicate activities that happen one after another and in parallel. For this reason, the activity diagram is sometimes used to model workflow and the business process associated with use cases. However, the principal intent of an activity diagram is to be a physical model that helps developers understand complex algorithms and application methods. This is the purpose of the model that this lesson will discuss.

Figure 2-14 shows a sample activity diagram of a constructor for the fictitious *Contact* class. The closed black circle indicates the start of the method. The arrows indicate the processing flow. Each rounded rectangle indicates an activity in the method. You can see that the example starts with the *Get Contact Details* activity and moves from one activity to another. You can think of these activities as markers in your method (or even commented sections). These are the things the method must do.

The activity diagram allows you to indicate branches or decisions that must be made in the code. These are represented by the diamonds. The control that comes off of each side of the branch is guarded. That is, it must be labeled as a Boolean condition that must be met for the code to flow in that direction. The first branch in the example is a decision about whether the application is online. If it is online, the control moves to *Check Cache*. If not, the control moves to *Pull from Cache*.

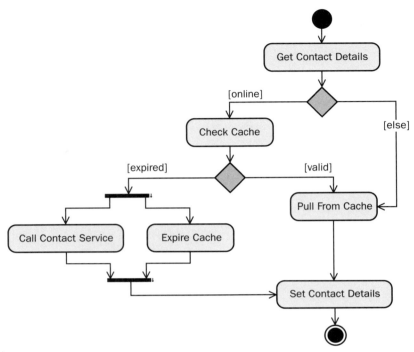

Figure 2-14 A sample activity diagram

The activity diagram also allows you to indicate parallel processing (or multithreading). You do so with a fork. The *fork* indicates that two processes are happening at once. In the example, both *Call Contact Service* and *Expire Cache* are forked and in parallel. Once any parallel processing is complete, it is *joined*. The diagram shows a join for the two items executing in parallel. Finally, once the processing is complete, you use a black circle with an outer ring to indicate the completion of the activity.

Create Pseudocode

An effective developer model that is often overlooked is pseudocode. *Pseudocode* is not a diagram or a model; it is text that is written as you would write code. It does not follow a specific language or notation. It does, however, offer developers who prefer to see code, or are more used to code than to models, a code-like view of a method. It can also be an easier and faster way to express concepts for architects and designers who are not used to writing up a lot of diagrams and might also prefer code.

Pseudocode is what you make it. Strive to mimic some of the structure of your chosen language just to help your developers read it. If, for example, you use C#, you might put curly braces in your pseudocode. If you use Visual Basic, consider using *end* statements. However, the pseudocode will not compile, will make strange assumptions that code should not make, will take shortcuts, and so on. It is not meant to be real code. The following is an example of some pseudocode for the method defined in Figure 2-14.

```
' VB
Public New
  If Application.Online
    GetCache()
    If Cache.Expired
      New Thread.execute (call ContactService)
      Cache.Exipre
      Thread.wait for completion
    Else
      GetCache(me)
    End
  Else
    GetCache(me)
  End
  Me.Name = contact.name() ... set all properties
End
```

```
// C#
public Contact() {
  If Application.Online {
    GetCache()
    If Cache.Expired
      New Thread.execute (call ContactService)
      Cache.Exipre
      Thread.wait for completion
  } else {
    GetCache(me)
  } else {
    GetCache(me)
  }
  Me.Name = contact.name() ... set all properties
}
```

Lab: Create Physical Models

In this lab, you will work to define a few physical models for an application. You will first work to create a class diagram. You will then define object interaction diagrams (both collaboration and sequence).

▶ **Exercise 1: Review Object Relationships and Define a Class Diagram**

In this exercise, you will first review a few architectural goals for an ASP.NET application. You will then look at an ORM diagram (Figure 2-15) that depicts a portion of the site that enables a customer to book a particular excursion on his or her vacation. You will then work with the design goals and the ORM to define the business services layer. Finally, you will specify the business domain, using a class diagram.

Architecture Goals

- All business logic should be encapsulated into a separate business domain layer.
- Each business object should know how to save, update, load, and delete itself.

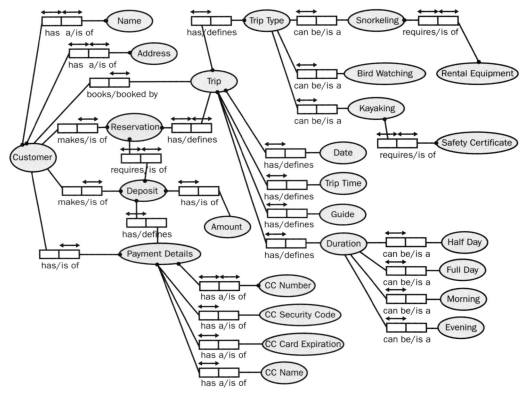

Figure 2-15   The book excursion ORM

The following steps will lead you through this exercise.

1. Use Visual Studio 2005 to create a new ASP.NET Web site (File | New | Web Site). You can call this site whatever you like; you can pick either Visual Basic or C# as the primary language.

2. Add a class diagram to the site: In Solution Explorer, right-click the site, select Add New Item, select Class Diagram, and then click Add. You can name this diagram whatever you like. When Visual Studio prompts you, confirm that you wish to add the diagram to the App_Code directory.

3. Determine the primary objects in the system by reviewing the ORM (Figure 2-15) to determine which objects have many links. Add a class to the diagram for each primary object you chose. Figure 2-16 shows an example.

Figure 2-16   The primary objects from the ORM

4. Determine the objects from the ORM that represent simple properties of your domain objects. These are objects from the ORM that did not end up as primary objects, are not relationships, and are not considered values of properties. Add these properties to each class in the model, using the Class Details window. (Right-click a class and choose Class Details.) Figure 2-17 shows an example of added properties.

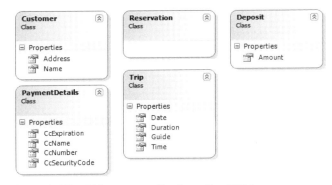

Figure 2-17   Object properties from the ORM

5. Determine the association relationships between the classes. These relationships represent properties that link the objects together. You define these relationships using the *Association* tool from the Class Designer Toolbox. After selecting the *Association* tool, click and drag from the class that has the association to the class that is the association to form the arrows. Figure 2-18 shows the class diagram with the associations. The Class Designer *Association* tool is very similar to the Visio *Connector Tool*.

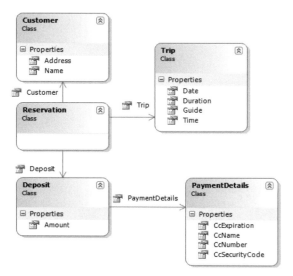

Figure 2-18   Association relationships

6. Determine the enumerations you wish to define based on the model. These are items that define a property in terms of values. You create an enumeration using the *Enum* tool in the Toolbox. Figure 2-19 shows an example.

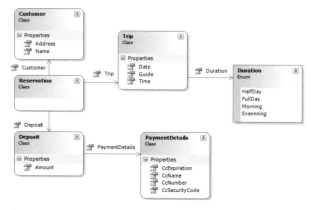

Figure 2-19   Enumerations added to the model

7. Determine which objects represent base classes and which should implement inheritance. The ORM model indicates a trip type. This could be thought of as an enumeration. However, some of the types have their own values. Therefore, you should consider creating an inheritance structure. You do so by adding the new classes to the model, one for each trip type. You then drag the *Inheritance* tool from the child class to the base class. Figure 2-20 shows an example.

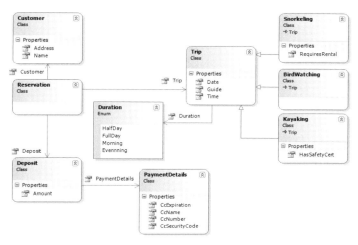

Figure 2-20   Inheritance added to the model

8. Determine any interfaces you wish to define for the system. The architecture goals indicate that each business object needs to save, load, update, and delete itself. Therefore, you might consider implementing a common interface for your business objects. You do so by adding an *Interface* object from the Toolbox. You then indicate the methods and any properties that are part of this interface. You can then use the *Inheritance* tool to indicate which objects implement this interface. Figure 2-21 shows the class model with the *IBusinessObject* interface.

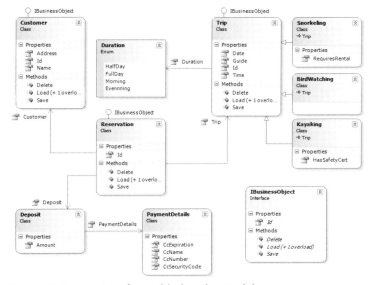

Figure 2-21   An interface added to the model

▶ **Exercise 2: Create an Interaction (Sequence) Diagram**

In this exercise, you will review a use case that describes a customer booking a trip. You will then use this use case, along with a description of the classes in your system, to create a sequence diagram. The sequence diagram is meant to describe how the physical model realizes the use case.

MORE INFO   Visio for Enterprise Architects

This lab assumes that you are using Visio for Enterprise Architects. If you do not have this, you can still use a drawing tool to draw a sequence diagram that mimics the lab. For information on how to obtain Visio for Enterprise Architects, visit *http://msdn2.microsoft.com/en-us/library/ms182014.aspx*.

Book Trip Use Case

Precondition: The user has searched for and selected a trip. He or she has logged on to the system and is now a registered customer.

1. This customer indicates that he or she wishes to book the selected trip.
2. The system generates a reservation ticket for the customer and holds the trip.
3. The system takes the customer to the BookTrip page of the site.
4. The customer enters a deposit for the trip as part of the reservation.
5. The system books the trip and generates a confirmation number on the reservation ticket.
6. The confirmation number is sent back to the customer for his or her records.

Book Trip Architecture Model

■ *Customer*: A class that represents a customer in the system.
■ BookTrip.aspx: A page in the system that allows a customer to enter a deposit for the selected trip.
■ *Reservation*: A class that represents a customer's trip.
■ *BookingService*: A class that contains methods for booking a trip, retrieving a trip, integrating with other systems (deposit), and saving to the local database (reservation).

The following steps will lead you through this exercise.

1. Open Visio and create a new UML Model Diagram (File | New | Software | UML Model Diagram).
2. Add the classes to the model. In the Model Explorer, right-click Top Package and choose New | Class. Name each class and click OK. Add the following classes from the architecture model: *Customer, BookTrip, Reservation, BookingService*.

3. Define methods for each class. For this exercise, you will simply define the methods you intend to use for the sequence diagram. If you had created your class diagram previously, you would use the full class description as an input into the sequence diagram.

   You add a method to a class in Visio by right-clicking the class in the Model Explorer and choosing New | Operation. This opens up the UML Operation Properties dialog box. You can use this dialog box to name your operation and indicate its return type, its visibility, and any parameters that are required. You add parameters by clicking the Parameters category on the left side of the dialog box.

   Create the following operations along with their parameters:

   ```
   BookingService.GetReservationTicket(customer as Customer)
   BookingService.BookTrip(reservation as Reservation)
   Customer.Load(id as int)
   Reservation.Load(customer as Customer)
   Reservation.SetDepositDetails(ccNumber as string,
     ccExpMonth as int, ccExpYear as int)
   ```

4. Add a sequence diagram to the UML model. Right-click Top Package in the Model Explorer and choose New | Sequence Diagram.

5. From the UML Sequence shapes section, drag an Object Lifeline shape onto the diagram for each primary object in the interaction. Double-click each object to define its instance. Select a class from the model as the *Classifier*. Indicate an instance name in the *Name* field.

   You should have an object lifeline (in this order) for *a BookTripUI, a Customer, a Reservation,* and *the BookingService.*

6. Align the tops of each object lifeline. Extend each lifeline down about half of the page.

7. Add an activation (long rectangle) to the lifeline of each of your objects. You will use this activation to indicate when the object is created and when it is disposed of.

8. Begin connecting your objects, using messages. Each message is defined by a method on the object that is being called. For example, the first message you should create will be from *BookTripUI* to *Customer.* The message should be the *Load(id)* method. Review the use case and the architecture model and continue to connect objects. Your final sequence diagram should resemble Figure 2-22.

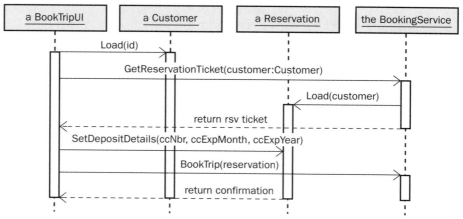

Figure 2-22   The completed sequence diagram

Lesson Summary

- A component is a group of logically related classes and methods.

- A component diagram represents the components in your system and shows how they work with one another to form a solution. You can show the deployment of components onto nodes. A node typically represents a piece of hardware (such as a server).

- A class diagram illustrates the static specification of classes. This includes methods, properties, fields, and so on. It also shows relationships such as inheritance and encapsulation. The Visual Studio 2005 Class Designer allows you to model classes, structs, enumerations, interfaces, and abstract classes.

- You define the classes in your system, called the business domain, using the logical model (ORM diagrams) and the technological constraints of your solution architecture. The ORM diagrams help define the primary objects in your business domain. These objects link to a lot of other objects in the model. The objects to which they link might end up as properties, property values, or other objects.

- A sequence diagram depicts the messages between objects over a sequence of events. The sequence diagram typically shows multiple objects across a use case.

- A collaboration diagram shows the sequence of events between objects as numbered messages. The collaboration diagram is a lot like a sequence diagram; however, it allows you to show the objects in any spatial layout.

■ An activity diagram indicates the activities in an algorithm or methods that happen one after another and in parallel. An activity diagram is like a flow chart.

■ Pseudocode is code-like text that is written to show a code-like view of a method. Pseudocode helps developers who prefer to see code to understand a complex algorithm or method.

Lesson Review

You can use the following questions to test your knowledge of the information in Lesson 3, "Create Physical Application Models for Developers." The questions are also available on the companion CD if you prefer to review them in electronic form.

NOTE   Answers

Answers to these questions and explanations of why each answer choice is right or wrong are located in the "Answers" section at the end of the book.

1. You have been instructed to define the physical specification for developers. Which model would you use?
   A. Component diagram
   B. Collaboration diagram
   C. Pseudocode
   D. Class diagram

2. Which of the following are differences between a sequence diagram and a collaboration diagram? (Choose all that apply.)
   A. A sequence diagram shows message calls over time. A collaboration diagram shows asynchronous messaging.
   B. A sequence diagram uses the model to illustrate sequence and order. A collaboration diagram illustrates this through numbered messages.
   C. A sequence diagram has object lifelines and shows when objects are created and destroyed. A collaboration diagram does not show this information.
   D. A sequence diagram enforces the layout of objects across the top of the page. A collaboration diagram allows you to lay out objects in any spatial manner you choose.

3. Which of the following are good uses for an activity diagram? (Choose all that apply).
   A. Defining class interactions and groupings
   B. Modeling complex algorithms
   C. Showing a sequence of business events or workflows
   D. Modeling multithreaded methods

4. Which of the following are true statements with respect to a component diagram? (Choose all that apply).

    A. A component diagram has a node that represents physical hardware.

    B. A component diagram allows you to indicate the communication protocols between servers.

    C. A component diagram can show the logical layers of the application.

    D. A component diagram illustrates which objects reference each other.

Chapter Review

To further practice and reinforce the skills you learned in this chapter, you can complete the following tasks:

- Review the chapter summary.
- Review the list of key terms introduced in this chapter.
- Complete the case scenario. This scenario sets up real-world situations involving the topics of this chapter and asks you to create a solution.
- Complete the suggested practices.
- Take a practice test.

Chapter Summary

- A logical software model is designed to represent real and actual concepts from your business domain. The logical model should change only if these concepts change. You can model this domain using Object Role Modeling (ORM) diagrams.
- A logical architecture (think layers or tiers) indicates how your system logically works and in which layer developers need to put their code. This model also shows the communication paths between the layers. Layers mitigate risk and increase reusability. Most enterprise-level ASP.NET applications define layers for the UI, the middle tier, and the database tier.
- Developers rely on physical models to help them understand how to implement code with respect to the requirements and design. Physical models include component, class, sequence, collaboration, and activity diagrams. A component diagram shows the logical grouping of classes as components and the relationships between these components. A class diagram defines the static specification of the classes in your domain. A sequence diagram depicts messages between objects over time (left to right, top-down). A collaboration diagram shows the object call sequence as numbered messages between objects. An activity diagram illustrates workflow or the activities in a complex algorithm. Finally, pseudocode is text written to look like code. It can be used to show a code-like view of a method to help developers understand complex operations.

Key Terms

Do you know what these key terms mean? You can check your answers by looking up the terms in the glossary at the end of the book.

- activity diagram
- business domain
- class diagram

- collaboration diagram
- component
- component diagram
- layers
- multiplicity
- node
- object role modeling (ORM)
- pseudocode
- sequence diagram
- state (or application state)

Case Scenario

In the following case scenario, you will apply what you've learned about decomposing specifications for developers. You can find answers to these questions in the "Answers" section at the end of this book.

Case Scenario: Evaluate User Inputs and Create Physical Models

You are a senior developer for a company looking to build a time-tracking application. Employee time is budgeted against internal company projects. Each department has a number of project codes with which employees bill time. The new system should help the company understand how it is spending resources on specific initiatives. You have been assigned the task of implementing the approval process for submitted time sheets. You have been given a use case and design goals for review.

Use Case: Approve Pending Time Sheet

Precondition: The user has logged on to the system. The system has recognized the user as part of the Supervisor group. The supervisor has selected the menu option Approve Pending Time Sheets.

1. The system displays a list of pending time sheets to the supervisor. Time sheets are ordered first by time period and then by actual submittal date and time.
2. The supervisor selects a time sheet from the list to review and approve.
3. The system displays the employee's time entered against each day in the given time period and for each billing code (project) in the system. The system also displays the budgeted versus actual rate for each billing code for the employee.
4. The supervisor looks for any irregularities with the time sheet.
5. If no issues are found with the timesheet, the supervisor indicates Approve.

Post-condition: The system has marked the selected time sheet's status as approved. The time sheet is locked and cannot be edited or have its status changed unless an administrator moves the status to reopen.

Alternate Case: Reject Time Sheet

Precondition: The use case follows the Approve Pending Time Sheet case through Step 4.

1. The supervisor finds irregularities with the time sheet and indicates that the time sheet should be rejected.
2. The system asks the supervisor to provide a reason for rejection.
3. The system sends a notification to the employee, whose time sheet was rejected, asking him or her to make modifications and re-submit.

Post-condition: The system has marked the selected time sheet's status as rejected. The time sheet is open for editing by the employee and requires re-submission.

Design Goals/Functional Requirements

- The time sheet application may have multiple UIs. Users want to be able to enter time in Microsoft SharePoint, in Web applications, and on their phone. The time sheet business rules will be the same regardless of the UI.
- Supervisors should be able to approve time sheets from a Web application or a mobile device.
- The application should take advantage of the Enterprise Library for .NET Framework to provide a set of base services.
- The Web server will not be able to access the database server directly, due to security concerns.

Questions

While thinking about the preceding specifications (use case and design goals), answer the following questions.

1. How would you model the domain of the use case, using an ORM diagram?
2. What would a logical architecture model (application layers) look like for this specification?
3. What would a high-level class diagram look like for this specification?
4. How would you create a sequence diagram to describe the object interaction concerning the approval portion of the use case?

Suggested Practices

To help you successfully master the exam objectives presented in this chapter, complete the following tasks.

Create a Logical Model

Many developers have never created ORM diagrams. However, such diagrams make a great approach to defining a logical model based on requirements and user scenarios. Consider practicing this task to make sure you get experience in creating ORM diagrams. This will help you master this objective.

- **Practice 1** Review requirements and use cases of (preferably) a new system that has just been designed or an older system that you might have worked on. Use this information to define an ORM diagram using Visio. Review this logical representation with a business analyst or user who provided input into the use cases. Determine whether the use case really intended the results of the ORM.

- **Practice 2** Use the ORM you created for Practice 1. Compare it to the domain model (classes or database) that was defined for the system. Determine why tradeoffs were made with respect to the ORM diagrams. Consider whether these were mistakes or the technology dictated an alternate solution. Consider how that might affect the understanding of the system without the ORM diagrams.

Create a Logical Architecture

This task should be familiar to most senior-level developers, who often think of systems in terms of layers. If, however, this is not your experience, you can use this task to better master this objective.

- **Practice 1** Look back at a few existing projects you've worked on. Try to describe the layers of the application. If you cannot describe them, then try to trace the code. Is the code spread out in multiple places across the application or was there a disciplined effort to contain the code?

- **Practice 2** Using the layers you created as part of Practice 1, try to find justification for these layers within the non-functional requirements and design goals.

Create Physical Application Models for Developers

Class modeling is where application design and coding meet. If you've never created class models (or are unfamiliar with the Visual Studio 2005 Class Designer), Practice 1 will provide a good overview of how to use class modeling to help you better structure your code. In addition, if you need more work with UML, perform the following practices to create key UML diagrams.

- **Practice 1** Use Visual Studio 2005 to create a class diagram (or model an existing set of classes). Use the tool to add new methods, properties, and classes to your application.
- **Practice 2** Create a sequence diagram to describe how a feature of your application works. Pick a feature that you've implemented. Start with its use case and see how well you can describe the messages between your objects without looking at the code. Then compare the sequence diagram to the implemented code.
- **Practice 3** Convert your sequence diagram from Practice 2 into a collaboration diagram.
- **Practice 4** Consider the next method you intend to write. Draw an activity diagram to describe the method before you write it. Determine whether this helped you understand the method before you wrote the code.

Take a Practice Test

The practice tests on this book's companion CD offer many options. For example, you can test yourself on just one exam objective, or you can test yourself on all the 70-547 certification exam content. You can set up the test so that it closely simulates the experience of taking a certification exam, or you can set it up in study mode so that you can look at the correct answers and explanations after you answer each question.

MORE INFO   **Practice tests**

For details about all the practice test options available, see the "How to Use the Practice Tests" section in this book's Introduction.

Chapter 3
Design Evaluation

Evaluating your design before you start building the Web-based application will give you the chance to find mistakes, problems, and omissions before they become expensive to fix. Providing speed, scalability, and robustness to your design is key to any successful Web development project.

Exam objectives in this chapter:
- Evaluate the logical design of an application.
  - ❑ Evaluate the logical design for performance.
  - ❑ Evaluate the logical design for maintainability.
  - ❑ Evaluate the logical design for extensibility.
  - ❑ Evaluate the logical design for scalability.
  - ❑ Evaluate the logical design for availability.
  - ❑ Evaluate the logical design for security.
  - ❑ Evaluate the logical design against use cases.
  - ❑ Evaluate the logical design for recoverability.
  - ❑ Evaluate the logical design for data integrity.
- Evaluate the physical design of an application. Considerations include the design of the project structure, the number of files, the number of assemblies, and the location of these resources on the server.
  - ❑ Evaluate the physical design for performance.
  - ❑ Evaluate the physical design for maintainability.
  - ❑ Evaluate how the physical location of files affects the extensibility of the application.
  - ❑ Evaluate the physical design for scalability.
  - ❑ Evaluate the physical design for availability.
  - ❑ Evaluate the physical design for security.
  - ❑ Evaluate the physical design for recoverability.
  - ❑ Evaluate the physical design for data integrity.

Lessons in this chapter:

Before You Begin

To complete the lessons in this chapter, you should be familiar with Microsoft Visual Basic or C# and be comfortable with the following tasks:

■ Successful completion of all lessons in Chapter 1, "Application Requirements and Design," and Chapter 2, "Decompose Specifications for Developers"

■ Using Microsoft SQL Server Management Studio to attach databases

■ Familiarity with the Database Designer of SQL Server Management Studio

---

Real World

Shawn Wildermuth

Too many times in my professional life, I have watched a well-meaning development team take the time to create a solid design, then immediately jump into implementation instead of reviewing that design for flaws. In almost all those cases there has been schedule pressure to start producing something that either management or a client could actually see working. This is a critical flaw in a project's life cycle. Reviewing and changing a design allows you to fix assumptions and problems before they become expensive to correct. Taking time to do a review is almost always worth the extra time.

Lesson 1: Evaluating the Logical Design

In developing a design for a Web site or other Web-based solution, creating a logical design is one of the steps that will help formulate your ideas. You learned how to create a logical design in Chapter 2. Once this logical design is complete, and before you move forward with building the Web application, you will need to evaluate the logical design to make sure it meets both the requirements and the generally accepted design criteria.

After this lesson, you will be able to:
- ■ Evaluate a logical design for standard design criteria.

Estimated lesson time: 10 minutes

Evaluation of the Logical Design

In Chapter 2, you worked from use cases to a logical design of your system. Once you have a logical design for a proposed system, you must evaluate the design based on a set of standard evaluation criteria. In general, this means evaluating the design for performance, maintainability, extensibility, scalability, availability, recovery, data integrity, and use-case correctness. You can usually group these evaluations into run-time evaluation (performance, scalability, availability, recoverability, and security); architectural evaluation (maintainability and extensibility); and requirements evaluation (business use case).

Performance Evaluation

Although the logical design of a system is high-level, there are performance considerations that can be evaluated. The two types of evaluation you need to conduct are reviews of the system tiers and of abstraction layers.

As you review the logical design, ensure that it is not over-designed into too many tiers. Typically, designing a Web application into three logical tiers is sufficient. Creating additional logical tiers is usually an indication of a poor design unless there is a very well thought out reason for the additional tiers.

Make sure that there are very specific reasons to "abstract out" particular parts of the design. In particular, look for extraneous and unnecessary levels of abstraction that can affect performance by forcing the flow of data across too many objects. By removing extraneous levels of abstraction, you can ensure that the design has a high level of performance.

The level at which you can do a performance evaluation of the logical design is typically limited to finding redundancies. The level of detail required to determine other performance problems is just not available in the logical design.

Scalability Evaluation

The logical design review is also the place where you should be evaluating the design for *scalability*. Scalability simply refers to the ability to adapt to the increasing load of the Web site as the number of users increases. This means allowing your application to work well within a Web farm and with load balancers. Although it is true that the logical design does not attempt to place different parts of the system into its physical or machine structure, there are several keys to ensuring that the design is scalable.

When reviewing scalability, you should review how state is handled in the logical design. For a typical Web application, you will store some state for users across multiple Web requests. Ensure that your objects can handle being serialized so they can live with any scalability concerns. Serialization usually means that they support the .NET Serialization (for example, supporting *ISerializable*). Serialization is important because, in a Web application, how objects are cached or communicated can be very different based on a myriad of different configuration options.

Your project might start as a simple single Web server installation in which serialization never occurs. But by supporting it, your application can move to Web farm session state, sticky load-balancing sessions, and other mechanisms without changing your objects. Evaluating the scalability of the logical design allows you to fix scalability problems before they become expensive to fix.

Availability and Recoverability Evaluation

Your logical design should also take into account the availability and recoverability of your project. High availability is the characteristic of a design that allows for failover and recovery from catastrophic failures. This includes failover ability, reliable transactions, data synchronization, and disaster preparedness. Because the logical design is a fairly high-level view of the design, not all of these availability concerns can be dealt with at the logical level. Instead, ensure that your entities can deal with availability solutions.

Your entities will be able to handle high-availability solutions in several ways:

- They will use reliable transactions such as database transactions; Microsoft Message Queuing (MSMQ) transactional messaging; or distributed transactions such as Enterprise Services or Distributed Transaction Coordinator (DTC) transactions.
- They will be able to deal with catastrophic failure by supporting reconstruction of corrupted files and configurations to save data outside a transaction.
- They will allow for failover to different hosting centers in case of catastrophic failure inside or outside your hosting center.

Security Evaluation

The Internet can be a dangerous place for which to develop software. When you expose your Web site to visitors from the Internet, you are increasing the surface area of a wide range of potential attacks including scripting, SQL injection, spoofing, brute force authentication, and other Web attacks. In addition, your project could also be vulnerable to network attacks such as denial of service (DoS), machine break-ins, and port sniffing.

With this in mind, be sure to evaluate your logical design for security. The logical design does not include information about how your Web application will be hosted, so you do not need to evaluate the design based on typical security issues such as firewalls, and the like.

However, what you should pay attention to in reviewing the logical design is how it will handle authentication and authorization. Depending on your particular requirements, you might use anonymous, forms-based, Microsoft Windows, or a custom authentication solution. The important thing is that you choose an authentication scheme that will scale up with your Web site's usage. This usually means using anonymous authentication for Web sites that are only publicly available. Anonymous authentication means there will be no way to log on to your Web application.

In contrast, Windows authentication can be used when you are using an existing Windows authentication subsystem, such as over an intranet or virtual private network (VPN). Windows authentication should never be used for publicly available Web applications. Typically, creating a Windows user for each user who logs on to a Web site just does not scale. In addition, giving logged-on users a Windows identity can open up security holes because those users could now have access to resources inside your organization that you do not want them to have. In most situations, forms-based authentication is the right decision because it scales out well to large numbers of users and does not grant any unintended network rights.

Depending on whether you need to work with mobile and lightweight clients, you will need to review the cookie-less authentication requirements of your application. If you extend forms-based authentication, you must be careful how the authentication cookies are handled so that you do not inadvertently remove the support for cookie-less authentication.

Authorization to different parts of your Web application is equally fraught with peril. Usually, using role-based security to allow or deny users to different parts of your application is the right approach. This is done in the configuration of a Microsoft ASP.NET application by using configuration settings. Alternatively, you can use URL-based authorization, but this should be avoided in most situations because maintaining correct access control lists (ACLs) on the underlying file system for a Web site becomes particularly problematic with changes across a Web farm.

MORE INFO   ASP.NET authentication and authorization

For more information on ASP.NET authentication and authorization, refer to "Managing Users by Using Membership" at Microsoft Developer Network (MSDN) Online on the Microsoft Web site at *http://msdn2.microsoft.com/en-us/library/tw292whz.aspx.*

To tie into the authorization and authentication models, you must evaluate how the ASP.NET membership application programming interfaces (APIs) are going to be used. Generally, the membership system in ASP.NET is the right approach even if you are working with external authentication credentials. You could build your own system to handle the membership information, but by leveraging the membership APIs, you can streamline the amount of code the authentication system uses.

Finally, you must ensure that your logical design protects you against certain types of security attacks that do not require intrusion into your network. The most important to review against are SQL-injection attacks. SQL-injection attacks are possible if you are building SQL statements on the fly. You can protect against SQL-injection attacks by using either stored procedures or parameterized queries when talking to the database. By using stored procedures or parameterized queries, you can ensure that any data inserted into a SQL statement is treated as data and not evaluated as part of the statement.

MORE INFO   SQL injection

For more information on SQL injection, see the MSDN Magazine article "Data Points," by John Papa, on the Microsoft Web site at *http://msdn.microsoft.com/msdnmag/issues/05/05/DataPoints/.*

The last part of the security evaluation is to determine how much (if any) code access security (CAS) to use in your application. Code access security allows you to prevent the managed code from using certain types of code. This allows you to protect the code from attempting to perform certain types of operations. For example, if your application is using a middle tier to access the database and get data and is then handing it to your user interface code (as should be done), then the code in the user interface will not need direct access to the ADO.NET managed providers. Therefore, reducing the user interface code's permissions to use the Microsoft SQL Server managed provider or the OLE DB managed provider will protect you from inadvertent use of the database.

MORE INFO   Code Access Security

For more information on CAS, see the MSDN Library: Patterns and Practices article "How To: Use Code Access Security in ASP.NET 2.0" on the Microsoft Web site at *http://msdn.microsoft.com/library /en-us/dnpag2/html /PAGHT000017.asp.*

Quick Check

1. How should you use Windows Authentication in a Web-based application?
2. How do you prevent SQL injection attacks?
3. What should you do to prevent your .NET assemblies from being compromised by intruders in a publicly available Web site?

Quick Check Answers

1. Windows Authentication should not be used in publicly available Web sites. For intranet Web sites, access to Windows Authentication-enabled Web sites should be protected by using a VPN.
2. Using stored procedures or parameterized queries will prevent SQL injection attacks. Avoiding using ad hoc SQL statements will also prevent SQL injection attacks.
3. You should sign your assemblies with strong names to ensure that intruders cannot inject dangerous code into your projects.

Maintainability Evaluation

Ninety cents out of every development dollar are used to maintain—not build—a system. That makes the maintainability of a system crucial to its long-term success. Evaluation for maintainability starts here in the logical design.

The maintainability in the logical design is based on segmenting elements of the logical design into a specific tier of the design. Specifically, each element of the logical design should belong to one (and only one) tier of logical design. The most common problem with a logical design in the realm of maintainability is in entities that cross the data/user interface boundary. For example, if you have an entity in the logical design that is meant to store data about a customer, that same component should not also know how to expose itself as a Web control. Separating those pieces of functionality will ensure that changes to the user interface remain separate from changes to the data layer. Mingling user interface and data tiers inevitably creates code that becomes harder to maintain.

Extensibility Evaluation

It is important to assess view extensibility in your design from two distinct perspectives: Can I extend other components, and are my components extensible?

Evaluate the logical design and determine which entities in your design can be built on top of other components. Usually, this means determining what classes to extend from the Microsoft .NET Framework itself. Look also at what classes you could use in your own code on which to build these new objects. For example, in a customer entity in the logical design, you might have a common base class that does data access for your entity objects. On the other hand, you might derive those classes from a class in the .NET Framework (for example, the *Component* class) to get built-in behaviors.

It is important to look for ways to reuse existing code to complete your design instead of building everything from scratch. Using components from inside the .NET Framework as well as in any existing code base will improve the quality of your project. (That is, old code usually means better code.) This also decreases development costs.

In your logical design, also look for ways to ensure that the code you write is extensible. One of the reasons we write object-oriented code is to allow code reuse. The more of your design that can be reused, the better the investment in the technology you are going to make.

Data Integrity Evaluation

Your logical design should also imply how the data that the Web application will work with remains integral during the full life cycle of the application. This means that you will need to ensure that not only does the database have a full set of schema (including primary keys, foreign keys, and data constraints) but that the client code determines the correct type of data concurrency to use for your application.

The decision that you make about what type of concurrency to use—optimistic versus pessimistic—will affect the overall safety and performance of your data tier. *Optimistic concurrency* implies that data will not have changed between the time of retrieving data and saving changes. During that time, if data has changed, you will need to determine the best way of handling those changes. Optimistic concurrency generally performs better because there are fewer database locks and logical locks on the data, so more clients can access data concurrently. However, using optimistic concurrency increases the chance that data will change between updates.

Alternatively, choosing *pessimistic concurrency* ensures that the data that a client is changing cannot change during the time that the client is working with that data. In all but the most severe case, optimistic concurrency is the right decision because it scales out better and performs well.

Business Use Case Evaluation

Also at the point of the logical design review, you will need to review the business use cases to ensure that what you have designed continues to meet those needs. You might assume that, because the design was spawned from the use cases, this evaluation is not necessary, but that is wrong. Much like a conversation that is communicated across a room and changed by each listener, it is very common and easy to make assumptions about what the use cases are in a design. In this review of the use cases against the design, you will almost always find inconsistencies (or ambiguities) that need to be addressed.

Lesson Summary

- Evaluating a logical design for run-time attributes such as performance, scalability, availability, recoverability, security, and data integrity will ensure that the logical design is best suited to fulfill the requirements.

- Evaluating a logical design for architectural issues such as maintainability and extensibility will ensure that the Web application can efficiently mature as a product.

- Evaluating a logical design for completeness against the business use cases will ensure that it meets or exceeds the real reason the Web application is being written.

Lesson Review

You can use the following questions to test your knowledge of the information in Lesson 1, "Evaluating the Logical Design." The questions are also available on the companion CD if you prefer to review them in electronic form.

NOTE Answers

Answers to these questions and explanations of why each answer choice is right or wrong are located in the "Answers" section at the end of the book.

1. When is Windows authentication acceptable to use as your Web application's authentication method?
   - **A.** For publicly available Web sites without any log-in functionality
   - **B.** For Web sites available only within an intranet or VPN (behind a firewall)
   - **C.** For publicly available Web sites with log-in functionality
   - **D.** For publicly available Web sites that are only for users within an enterprise

2. What types of database access methods should be used to avoid SQL injection attacks? (Choose all that apply.)
   - **A.** Dynamically created SQL statements
   - **B.** Stored procedures
   - **C.** Parameterized queries
   - **D.** Dynamically created SQL statements with error checking

3. To how many different logical tiers can each component in your design belong?
   - **A.** One.
   - **B.** Two.
   - **C.** As many as required.
   - **D.** Components should not be tied to a specific tier of the design.

Lesson 2: Evaluating the Physical Design

Once you have completed the evaluation of the logical design, the physical design is next. This evaluation will entail reviewing the concrete details of how the Web project will be constructed, in terms of both physical layout on disk and separation within a network.

After this lesson, you will be able to:
■ Evaluate the physical design of your Web application against standard design criteria.
Estimated lesson time: 10 minutes

Evaluation of the Physical Design

The physical design of a Web project includes how the project is going to look when deployed and ready for use. The big difference between this evaluation and the evaluation of the logical design is that the physical design will have more concrete details. This includes Web site layout (for example, how the project will exist physically on the Web server) as well as the network topology of what code and data will exist on what type of machine.

As with the logical design, the evaluation of the physical design is broken up into a series of evaluation categories. These include performance, maintainability, extensibility, scalability, availability, and security evaluations.

Performance Evaluation

The performance evaluation of the physical design starts with a review of the different aspects of the physical design. These aspects include content, network, and database implementations. Each of these design aspects can adversely or positively affect the final performance of the Web application.

As you evaluate the content of your Web application, compare the physical makeup of the Web site with the actual requirements. This usually entails determining the performance requirements for clients based on bandwidth. Some Web projects require a broadband connection, and there is little concern for the actual size of a page (and the files associated with a page). If you are creating a generally consumable Web application, you will still need to be concerned about total page sizes because narrowband (for example, dial-up Internet) users still comprise a sizable piece of the overall Internet user base. This means you should review the sizes of the generated pages and any images used. In addition, look at the size of *ViewState* on ASP.NET pages to see if there are ways to decrease its overall size. It is common to find that controls that have no need for *ViewState* are still using it to store their state. Review the layout semantics and ensure that they meet the requirements for the project. Layout semantics are typically how cascading style sheets (CSS) are used, whether themes are supported, and whether frames are used. In general, use the same layout semantics across the application.

Next, review the network implementation of the project. How the data tier is implemented in the physical design can greatly affect Web application performance. To determine whether access to the tier is helping or hurting performance, look at how the middle tier is implemented. There are no hard and fast rules for achieving the right implementation, but separating your data tier into a separate class of machine in the physical design is not always necessary. Typically, if the middle tier will tax the Web servers by using a lot of memory or processor cycles, you would choose to separate the user interface tier and the middle tier into separate machines. Because of the added expense of remotely accessing the data across machine boundaries, it is often more economical, in terms of performance, to keep the middle tier on the same machine as the Web server.

Finally, you need to review the database implementation to ensure that it is performing adequately. As part of your performance evaluation, check the database operations to make sure that they are performing as expected (both in isolation and under load testing). If this evaluation finds fault, there are many solutions to tuning the database, but they are too numerous to explain in this training kit.

Scalability Evaluation

The scalability evaluation of the physical design is much like the logical scalability evaluation: you need to determine whether the system can adapt to handling higher-sized loads. This is done by reviewing the physical design to make sure that all components (custom components written for the project as well as first-party and third-party components used in the project) are compatible with moving from a single Web server to a Web farm. This usually entails ensuring that all components that store state can be stored in longer-term caches and sessions that are used in Web farm scenarios. Review the design for what kinds of objects are stored as state and make sure that they support serialization into nonlocal session state (for example, State Server or SQL Server).

Next, make sure that your application can handle working behind load-balancing solutions, in which requests to the Web server might or might not be served by the same Web server. Your Web application needs to know what load-balancing solutions, if any, you are using to determine how to set up the session state for your application.

Availability and Recoverability Evaluation

In reviewing the availability of your Web application, you will need to determine what level of availability is required. For example, if you are running a public-facing application, it becomes very important to handle failover to different machines, and even data centers, if you have a catastrophic failure (for example, hardware failure, interruption of Internet access, and so on). Alternatively, if you are building a small internal application, then availability is not crucial to your success. Ensure that your physical design takes into account the actual availability requirements at this time. This includes more than just making sure the deployment strategy takes this into account; it should also include support for ensuring that backup databases and Web servers are available with the correct version of the code and data. There are different strategies, but usually you will want to use a failover clustered database server for local availability. Remote availability (failover to separate data centers) requires more elaborate planning that might include mirroring, replication, or log shipping to ensure that the database in the remote location has the most current version of the data.

The flip side of availability is recoverability. Even if you do not need to support failover to new machines, data centers, and so on, you will likely need to support recovering from a failure. This means you need a strategy for backing up any data in the system. This includes database data, event data (for example, MSMQ and event logs), and any other transient data that is crucial to your business.

Security Evaluation

When you evaluate your physical design for security, the goal is to make the code that you are ultimately deploying as secure as possible. This means that first you should determine what code (if any) should be strongly named (for example, signed) when you deploy it. In general, to ensure that when code is run, it can be verified as having been created by your company, sign all assemblies that you are deploying. The idea here is to disallow injected code from being run on your Web site.

Next, review the directory structure of the Web site to ensure that, when deployed, the individual files will be accessible through a Web request. In addition, you will want to review the role-based security of the Web application to ensure that only the correct users have access to the required portions of a Web site. This is often the biggest hole in the security of a deployed Web application. This hole can be mitigated by a formal review of the directory structure and of which roles are allowed and where.

You will also want to ensure that any forms-based authentication or membership options that you are using are consistent with your security policy. This means that if you expect strong passwords, you should make sure the membership provider requires one. If you allow only resetting of passwords and not retrieval of passwords, ensure that the membership provider is set up to disallow retrieval.

> **Real World**
>
> *Shawn Wildermuth*
>
> Designing an ASP.NET Web application and ensuring that it is secure can, depending on your user base, be a daunting task. I worked for one particular company where we sold a subscription to our data. Users were issued usernames and could set their passwords. In doing a security review after a break-in, we found that 80 percent of the users to the system used the same password (the name of the company). The users did not store personal information in our system, but they used their credentials to access information we had gathered. Therefore, our users did not have a vested interest in creating secure passwords. We changed our password policy and required stronger passwords. We also added timeouts for failed logins, which prevented brute force password breaches.

Maintainability Evaluation

In reviewing the maintainability of the physical design, pay attention to the common-sense approach of the code base. This means that components should use common directory structures and should have directory structures of the project mirror namespace usage as much as possible. The key to maintainability is making the code base easy to navigate.

Extensibility Evaluation

The physical makeup of any Web application can really affect how extensible it is. In general, your review of the extensibility should include a review of what Web controls, Web parts, and other components are written as part of the project. Where possible, the location of these Web controls, Web parts, and components should be as centrally located as possible so they can be used in multiple Web applications if possible. Writing the same control for different Web applications is just tedious. Alternatively, copying components from one project to the other breaks the ability for each application that uses a particular component to get the benefits of bug fixes and improvements to the control.

Data Integrity Evaluation

Finally, evaluate the data integrity of your physical design. Unlike your evaluation of the logical design, this evaluation should include review of the user interface down to the database. Data constraints included in the database schema will ensure that the data stays consistent, but you should also include that same constraint higher in the code to reduce the need to go to the database just to find a data inconsistency. For example, if you have in the database a check constraint to make sure that social security numbers are nine digits, your user interface should have validation of that fact. That way, if an invalid social security number is entered, it is reported to the user to fix rather than making him wait for the data to be sent to the database just to receive a failure message.

Lesson Summary

- Ensuring that the deployed application meets the full requirements of a project should be part of evaluating the physical design.
- This physical design evaluation will review the performance, scalability, availability, recoverability, security, maintainability, extensibility, and data integrity of the designed system.

Lesson Review

You can use the following questions to test your knowledge of the information in Lesson 2, "Evaluating the Physical Design." The questions are also available on the companion CD if you prefer to review them in electronic form.

NOTE Answers

Answers to these questions and explanations of why each answer choice is right or wrong are located in the "Answers" section at the end of the book.

---

1. When reviewing the performance of Web page requests, which of the following do you need to review? (Choose all that apply.)

   A. *ViewState* usage

   B. The number of controls per page

   C. Image size

   D. Session state use

2. Where should you enforce data integrity constraints? (Choose all that apply.)

   A. In the user interface

   B. In the data tier

   C. In the database

   D. In XML Schema

3. Should you strongly name (for example, sign) all of your assemblies for a publicly available Web site?

   A. Yes

   B. No

Chapter Review

To further practice and reinforce the skills you learned in this chapter, you can complete the following tasks:

- Review the chapter summary.
- Review the list of key terms introduced in this chapter.
- Complete the case scenarios. These scenarios set up real-world situations involving the topics of this chapter and ask you to create a solution.
- Complete the suggested practices.
- Take a practice test.

Chapter Summary

- Taking the time to evaluate the logical design of your Web application will help refine your design as well as ensure that the code written from the design is exactly what is required for the project.
- Performing a review of the physical design will ensure that your design is going to meet the requirements as well as perform well once deployed.

Key Terms

Do you know what these key terms mean? You can check your answers by looking up the terms in the glossary at the end of the book.

- logical design
- optimistic concurrency
- pessimistic concurrency
- physical design

Case Scenarios

In the following case scenarios, you will apply what you've learned about evaluating logical and physical designs. You can find answers to these questions in the "Answers" section at the end of this book.

Case Scenario 1: Review the Logical Design for a CRM Application

You work for a small company that needs a customer relationship management (CRM) application. You will need to create a system that can hold common CRM data about customers, sales people, and orders.

Interviews

The engineering manager was interviewed, and his statement follows.

■ **Engineering manager**   "We will be creating a new CRM application. We need to evaluate the logical design that our design team has created to describe the different elements."

Questions

Answer the following questions for the design team.

1. How will you review the design for business case completeness?
2. How are you going to handle a maintainability review of the design?

Case Scenario 2: Review the Physical Design for a CRM Application

As in Case Scenario 1, you still work for a small company that needs to build a CRM. You will continue your design evaluation by reviewing the physical design.

Interviews

The engineering manager was interviewed, and his statement follows.

■ **Engineering manager**   "We will be creating a new CRM application. Our design team has created a physical design of the different elements as they will exist on specific machine types. We need to review this design."

Questions

Answer the following questions for the design team.

1. How will you evaluate the security of the physical design?
2. How will you evaluate the extensibility of the physical design?

Suggested Practices

To successfully master the objectives covered in this chapter, complete the following tasks.

Evaluate a Logical Design

For this task, you should complete at least Practice 1. You can do Practice 2 for a more in-depth understanding of logical design evaluation.

- **Practice 1**   Evaluate the logical design from Chapter 2 based on the criteria in Lesson 1, "Evaluating the Logical Design" of Chapter 3.
- **Practice 2**   Create a set of recommendations based on your review of the logical design.

Evaluate a Physical Design

For this task, you should complete at least Practice 1. Practice 2 offers a more in-depth understanding of physical design evaluation.

- **Practice 1**   Evaluate the physical design from Chapter 2 based on the criteria in Lesson 2, "Evaluating the Physical Design," of Chapter 3.
- **Practice 2**   Create a set of recommendations based on your review of the physical design.

Take a Practice Test

The practice tests on this book's companion CD offer many options. For example, you can test yourself on just one exam objective, or you can test yourself on all of the 70-547 certification exam content. You can set up the test so that it closely simulates the experience of taking a certification exam, or you can set it up in study mode so that you can look at the correct answers and explanations after you answer each question.

MORE INFO   Practice tests

For details about all the practice test options available, see the "How to Use the Practice Tests" section in this book's Introduction.

Chapter 4
Creating a User Interface

In this chapter, you'll learn how to use ASP.NET controls to create a user interface (UI) for a multi-page Web forms application. You'll learn about different styles of Web forms, how to choose controls based on the tasks you want to perform, how to validate data fields, and how to navigate among Web forms in your application. You'll also learn how to create your own controls and how to implement a consistently familiar appearance across your Web forms applications.

Exam objectives in this chapter:
- Choose an appropriate layout for the visual interface.
  - Decide the content flow across pages.
  - Evaluate user navigation needs.
  - Identify the goal of the page.
  - Ensure the congruency and consistency of the user experience throughout the application.
- Evaluate a strategy for implementing a common layout throughout the UI.
  - Suggest when to use style sheets, master pages, Web parts, custom controls, scripting, and user controls.
  - Suggest an applicable UI standard based on the intended client environment. Considerations include chosen operating systems, technologies, and browser types.

Lessons in this chapter:

Before You Begin

To complete the lessons in this chapter, you should be familiar with Microsoft Visual Basic or C# and comfortable with the following tasks:

■ Creating an ASP.NET Web page in Microsoft Visual Studio 2005.

Real World

Brian C. Lanham

My first college professor told me, "You can write the slickest application in the world but, if it isn't usable, no one will use it." This point was emphasized by a situation wherein users of an application I wrote were more impressed by the colors displayed in the application than in some of the (really neat, I thought!) features that the application provided.

Users should be able to start using your applications quickly and easily. Depending on the type of application, you might have a very broad range of user types. E-commerce applications, for example, reach more types of people than do intranet applications. Creating a UI that provides consistency is difficult. ASP.NET 2.0 makes the task much easier. New features and controls, such as themes, master pages, and menus, are just some examples of how to improve the usability of your Web application quickly.

Lesson 1: Choosing an Appropriate Layout for the Visual Interface

The UI is arguably the most important aspect of your Web forms application. It is the means by which users access your application. Therefore, users' opinion of the application is a function of how quickly and easily they adapt to the UI. Also, users should not have to re-learn the UI every time the application is updated. To further complicate matters, different application types require different UIs. For example, an e-commerce application requires items such as a shopping cart and a checkout wizard, which are not applicable to a personal Web site with a photo album. All of these factors combine, requiring you to plan the UI layout carefully and strategically, and adhere to the layout guidelines and decisions as closely as possible. This lesson reviews techniques for choosing appropriate Web site layout and navigation. These are critical to promoting a consistent user experience and, more importantly, ensuring that users can find their way back to a known location (such as Home).

After this lesson, you will be able to:
- Provide users with appropriate navigational aids such as menus and breadcrumbs.
- Appropriately control navigation behavior between multiple pages.
- Apply styles to navigation elements to improve usability.
- Provide users with a site map of your application.

Estimated lesson time: 90 minutes

Determining a Content Flow Across Pages

Because of the stateless nature of Web applications, it is sometimes difficult to determine an appropriate course of action based on user action ahead of time. Users may choose an item from a menu, select a link, or click a button on a page. Because of this, your Web forms application needs to anticipate multiple feedback scenarios.

Despite all of this, your Web forms application needs to avoid surprising the user. No action the user takes should result in an unanticipated reaction. There might be times, however, when the application must alter its progression to satisfy some combination of user input. In this section, you will explore some techniques for handling content flow across pages in situations in which the flow is not necessarily linear.

Cross-Page Posting

ASP.NET supports same-page posting by default. In this scenario, user actions such as clicking a button result in the page posting back to its server version. For example, if a user requests Page.aspx and clicks a button, the page posts back to Page.aspx on the Web server.

ASP.NET 2.0 introduces new capabilities whereby pages can post to pages other than themselves. Although powerful, this capability potentially introduces additional complexities. You might already be familiar with the *Server.Transfer* method, which will be covered later in this lesson. Cross-page posting differs from *Server.Transfer* in that posting is initiated from the client.

You create a cross-page posting by setting the *PostBackUrl* property defined by the *IButtonControl* interface, from which *Button*, *ImageButton*, and *LinkButton* inherit. If the *PostBackUrl* property is set, ASP.NET will post the page to the specified form. In addition, ASP.NET will also post, to the specified page, values from the input controls on the posting page.

To use cross-posted pages, ASP.NET defines the *PreviousPage* property on the *Page* object. This property gives you access to the page, if any, that posted to the current page. Following is an example of using the *PreviousPage* property:

```vb
' VB
Protected Sub page_load(ByVal sender As Object, ByVal e As EventArgs)
        If PreviousPage IsNot Nothing Then
            Response.Write("Posted from " & PreviousPage.Header.Title)
        End If
    End Sub[/code]
```

```csharp
// C#
    protected void Page_Load(object sender, EventArgs e)
    {

        if (PreviousPage != null)
            Response.Write("Posted from " + PreviousPage.Header.Title);
    }
```

Cross-page posting can result in a tight coupling between pages. This means that changes in one page can require you to make changes in other pages. The more pages you couple, the more change points you create. Although you usually want to avoid tightly coupling your components, there are situations when it is necessary. The cross-page posting model provides support for coupling pages.

You can force the recipient page to accept postings from only specified pages by using the *@ PreviousPageType* directive. This directive defines two mutually exclusive attributes: *TypeName* and *VirtualPath*. The *TypeName* attribute specifies the data type, which is the class name, of the acceptable previous page. The *VirtualPath* attribute specifies the path to the file that generates the type. If you use both attributes at the same time, the directive fails.

```
<%@ PreviousPageType VirtualPath="~/Default.aspx" %>
```

```
<%@ PreviousPageType TypeName="PostingPage" %>
```

Another, less strict, technique is to check the type of the previous page on the postback. The following code sample demonstrates determining the type of the previous page at run time.

```vb
' VB
    Protected Sub Page_Load(ByVal sender As Object, ByVal e As EventArgs)
        If PreviousPage IsNot Nothing Then
            If PreviousPage.GetType.ToString.Equals("PostingPage") Then
                ' Do some action.
            Else
                ' Do some other action.
            End If
        End If
    End Sub
```

```csharp
// C#
    protected void Page_Load(object sender, EventArgs e)
    {
        if (PreviousPage != null)
        {
            if (PreviousPage.GetType.ToString.Equals (" FromPage")
            {
                // Do some action.
            }
            else
            {
                // Do some other action.
            }
        }
    }
```

Using the *PreviousPage* object, you can access the *Page* properties. If you want to access specific items from the previous page, you can cast the previous page to a specific type. For example, suppose you create a Web form called PostingPage.aspx and you want to cross-post from that page to a page called ReceivingPage.aspx. The type of the *PreviousPage* property is *System.Web.UI.Page*. Therefore, to access any custom properties and methods on the posting page explicitly, you can cast it to a specific type.

There are a few restrictions to this technique. First, note that the controls are declared as protected members. Therefore, to access controls on the posting page, you must use the *Find-Control* method. Second, because of the ASP.NET 2.0 compilation model, you must explicitly reference the posting page in the receiving page to cast to that type. This is accomplished by using the @ *Reference* directive. The following example demonstrates these techniques.

Establish the reference to the posting page on the receiving page by using the @ *Reference* directive as shown here:

```
<%@ Reference Page="~/PostingPage.aspx" %>
```

In the *Page_Load* event handler, cast the posting page into the appropriate type and use the *FindControl* method to reference a text box on the posting form.

```vb
' VB
Protected Sub page_load(ByVal sender As Object, ByVal e As EventArgs)
    Dim PostPage As PostingPage
    Dim UserName As String
    Dim txtSomeField As TextBox

    ' 1) Cast the posting page to a strong type for reference.
    PostPage = DirectCast(Me.PreviousPage, PostingPage)

    ' 2) Reference a custom property on the posting page.
    UserName = PostPage.UserName

    ' 3) Use the FindControl (...) method to reference a control on the posting page.
    txtSomeField = DirectCast(PostPage.FindControl("txtFieldName"), TextBox)
End Sub
```

```csharp
// C#
protected void Page_Load(object sender, EventArgs e)
{
    PostingPage postPage;
    String userName;
    TextBox txtSomeField;

    // 1) Cast the posting page to a strong type for reference.
    postPage = PostingPage(this.PreviousPage);

    // 2) Reference a custom property on the posting page.
    userName = postPage.UserName;

    // 3) Use the FindControl (...) method to reference a control on the posting page.
    txtSomeField = TextBox(postPage.FindControl("txtFieldName"));
}
```

Using *Server.Transfer*

Another technique for navigating from one page to another is to use the *Transfer* method of the *Server* object. Like cross-page posting, calling *Server.Transfer ()* passes along page information, such as input field values, to the recipient page.

If you want to determine whether the current page was posted from another page's post-back or from a *Server.Transfer ()* call, you can use the *IsCrossPagePostBack* property of the *PreviousPage* object. If *Server.Transfer ()* is used, the *IsCrossPagePostBack* property is *False*. If, on the other hand, a cross-page posting occurred, the property value is *True*.

Cross-Page Posting and Validation

If you are using validation controls to verify user input, cross-page posting might cause problems. If, for example, your Web forms application is serving pages to older browsers or browsers with JavaScript support disabled, client-side validation will not occur. In these situations, you are relying, then, on the server to validate the controls. If using *Server.Transfer ()*, you can still rely on the server-side validation. This is because you must explicitly call *Server.Transfer ()* and, therefore, you have an opportunity to verify page validity. However, in a cross-page posting scenario, server validation still occurs, but the server is redirected to a new page and the validation problems are, essentially, ignored.

To provide some assistance in this scenario, ASP.NET gives you the *IsValid* method of the *PreviousPage* object. Using this technique, you can determine whether the previous page is valid and take appropriate action. Note, however, that if you return users to the previous page, all of their input is lost because the *ViewState* no longer contains information for the previous page. Here is a code sample:

```vb
' VB
    Protected Sub page_load(ByVal sender As Object, ByVal e As EventArgs)
        If PreviousPage IsNot Nothing Then
            If PreviousPage.IsValid Then
                ' Continue working.
            Else
                ' Return to the previous page or show an error page.
            End If
        End If
    End Sub
```

```csharp
// C#
    protected void Page_Load(object sender, EventArgs e)
    {
        if (PreviousPage != null)
        {
            if (PreviousPage.IsValid == true)
            {
                // Continue working.
            }
            else
            {
                // Return to the previous page or show an error page.
            }
        }
    }
```

Exam Tip   Validation of user input is always a requirement, so don't forget that the *Page_Load* event of the original page will *not* be executed; therefore, no server-side validation occurs *unless* you specifically code for it using *IsValid*.

Quick Check

1. How is cross-page posting similar to and different from *Server.Transfer* and automatic postback to the original page?
2. What are some potentially negative impacts of using cross-page posting?

Quick Check Answers

1. Cross-page posting is similar to *Server.Transfer* in that it provides a means of executing server-side code. Cross-page posting differs from automatic postback in that the execution transfers to the code-behind (class) of a page other than the page that the browser currently displays. Cross-page posting occurs from the browser, whereas *Server.Transfer* occurs from server-side code.

2. Cross-page posting can create tightly coupled pages whereby changing one page might result in a required change to another page. Also, cross-page posting can make validation more difficult because the code-behind of the page displayed by the browser is not executed prior to transferring to another page. Validation controls will be executed client-side, but the corresponding server-side validation of these controls does not occur. In addition, accessing control from the original page becomes more difficult because these controls are now contained in a container one level deeper in the control hierarchy of the page.

Evaluating User Navigation Needs

ASP.NET 2.0 provides an extensive suite of Web controls. The toolbox includes navigation controls to help you provide users with a consistent means of moving around in your Web forms application. The new controls are also helpful to you as a developer in that they are data-driven. This allows you to provide consistency as your site grows and minimizes code changes required to support changes to the site structure. In this section, you will explore the new navigation controls.

Using the Menu Controls

Menus are relatively common Web site elements that have been missing from the ASP.NET toolbox until ASP.NET 2.0. The new ASP.NET 2.0 *Menu* control allows you to add a menu to your Web forms application quickly and to populate the menu through bound data or manually using *MenuItem* controls.

Each instance of the *Menu* control consists of a collection of *MenuItem* objects. The *MenuItem* object, in turn, contains a collection of *MenuItem* objects as well.

Populating Menus and Menu Templates

MenuItem objects can be added to a menu declaratively and programmatically. The following example shows declarative menu creation.

```
<form id="form1" runat="server">
    <div style="text-align:left">
    <asp:Menu runat="server" ID="mnuMain" Orientation="Horizontal" StaticMenuItemStyle-
HorizontalPadding="5px">
        <Items>
            <asp:MenuItem Text="Home" NavigateUrl="~/default.aspx"/>
            <asp:MenuItem Text="Reports" NavigateUrl="reporthome.aspx">
                <asp:MenuItem Text="Sales YTD" NavigateUrl="reports.aspx?id=1" />
                <asp:MenuItem Text="Sales by Region" NavigateUrl="reports.aspx?id=2" />
            </asp:MenuItem>
            <asp:MenuItem Text="Change Password" NavigateUrl="changepassword.aspx"/>
            <asp:MenuItem Text="Logout" NavigateUrl="logout.aspx" />
        </Items>
    </asp:Menu>
    </div>
</form>
```

Notice that in this code, the Reports menu item contains other menu items. The ASP.NET *Menu* control automatically interprets nested menu items and provides expansion and contraction capabilities. Figure 4-1 shows the output from the preceding code.

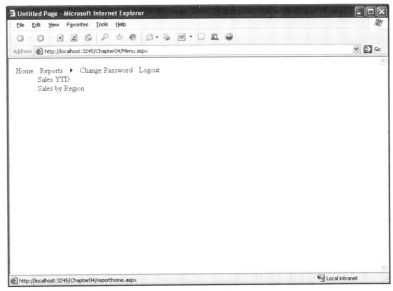

Figure 4-1   A sample *Menu* control in action

The same menu may be created programmatically as well. The following code shows how to create the preceding menu on the *Page_Load* event.

```vb
' VB
    Protected Sub Page_Load(ByVal sender As Object, ByVal e As EventArgs) Handles Me.Load

        Dim mnuReports As MenuItem

        ' Configure the menu.
        mnuMain.Orientation = Orientation.Horizontal
        mnuMain.StaticMenuItemStyle.HorizontalPadding = New Unit(5.0, UnitType.Pixel)


        ' Add menu items.
        mnuMain.Items.Add(New MenuItem("Home", String.Empty, String.Empty, "default.aspx"))

        mnuReports = New MenuItem("Reports", String.Empty, String.Empty, "reportshome.aspx")
        mnuReports.ChildItems.Add(New MenuItem("Sales YTD", String.Empty, String.Empty,
"reports.aspx?id=2"))
        mnuReports.ChildItems.Add(New MenuItem("Sales by Region", String.Empty, String.Empty,
"reports.aspx?id=2"))

        mnuMain.Items.Add(mnuReports)
        mnuMain.Items.Add(New MenuItem("Change Password", String.Empty, String.Empty,
"changepassword.aspx"))
        mnuMain.Items.Add(New MenuItem("Logout", String.Empty, String.Empty, "logout.aspx"))

    End Sub
```

```csharp
// C#
    protected void Page_Load(object sender, EventArgs e)
    {
        MenuItem mnuReports;

        // Configure the menu.
        mnuMain.Orientation = Orientation.Horizontal;
        mnuMain.StaticMenuItemStyle.HorizontalPadding = new Unit(5.0, UnitType.Pixel);

        // Add menu items.
        mnuMain.Items.Add(new MenuItem("Home", String.Empty, String.Empty, "default.aspx"));

        mnuReports = new MenuItem("Reports", String.Empty, String.Empty, "reportshome.aspx");
        mnuReports.ChildItems.Add(new MenuItem("Sales YTD", String.Empty, String.Empty,
"reports.aspx?id=2"));
        mnuReports.ChildItems.Add(new MenuItem("Sales by Region", String.Empty, String.Empty,
"reports.aspx?id=2"));

        mnuMain.Items.Add(mnuReports);
        mnuMain.Items.Add(new MenuItem("Change Password", String.Empty, String.Empty,
"changepassword.aspx"));
        mnuMain.Items.Add(new MenuItem("Logout", String.Empty, String.Empty, "logout.aspx"));
    }
```

In addition to declarative and programmatic population, *Menu* controls may be data-bound However, menus rely on hierarchical data, so they cannot be bound directly to relational data sources. Instead, the data source must be hierarchical. The preferred data-binding technique is to bind to an *XmlDataSource* object or some other hierarchical source. In this situation, you must set the *DataSourceID* property to the ID of the data source control. The *Menu* control automatically binds to the specified control. Alternatively, and a less preferred technique, you can bind a menu to an *XmlDocument*, in which case you must set the *DataSource* property of the *Menu* control and explicitly call the *DataBind* method.

When binding to a data source where each data item contains multiple properties (such as an *XML* element with several attributes), a menu item displays the value returned by the *ToString* method of the data item by default. In the case of an *XML* element, the menu item displays the element name. You can bind a menu item to a specific data item property by using the *Data-Bindings* collection to specify menu item bindings. The *DataBindings* collection contains *Menu-ItemBinding* objects that define the relationship between a data item and the menu item to which it is binding. You can specify the criteria for binding and the data item property to display in the node.

Despite the intrinsic capabilities of the *Menu* control, there might be situations in which you need to display relational data in the hierarchical format of a menu. In this case, you can follow the previously described technique of programmatically building the menu based on the relational data. If, for example, you want to provide users with the ability to quickly find employees in your organization by department, you can bind the menu to a relational database containing your employees' information, including their respective departments. Following is an example of data-binding a menu.

```vb
' VB
Private Sub BindData ()
      Dim ds As DataSet
       Dim mnuItemDept As MenuItem
       Dim mnuItemEmp As MenuItem
       Dim EmployeeRows As DataRow()

       For Each row As DataRow In ds.Tables.Item("Department").Rows

           ' Create a menu item for the department.
       mnuItemDept = New MenuItem(row.Item("DepartmentName").ToString, _
row.Item("DepartmentID").ToString)

           mnuMain.Items.Add(mnuItemDept)

           ' Obtain the records for the employees in the current department.
           EmployeeRows = row.GetChildRows(ds.Relations.Item("relDepartmentEmployee"))

           ' Process each employee record and add a corresponding menu item.
           For Each childRow As DataRow In EmployeeRows
```

```
                    mnuItemEmp = New MenuItem(childRow.Item("EmployeeName").ToString, _
                                              childRow.Item("EmployeeID").ToString)

                    mnuItemDept.ChildItems.Add(mnuItemEmp)

            Next

        Next
End Sub
```

```
// C#
    private void bindData()
    {
        DataSet ds;
        MenuItem mnuItemDept;
        MenuItem mnuItemEmp;
        DataRow[] EmployeeRows;

        foreach (DataRow row in ds.Tables.Item("Department").Rows)
        {

            // Create a menu item for the department.
            mnuItemDept = new MenuItem(row.Item("DepartmentName").ToString,
                                      row.Item("DepartmentID").ToString);

            mnuMain.Items.Add(mnuItemDept);

            // Obtain the records for the employees in the current department.
            EmployeeRows = row.GetChildRows(ds.Relations.Item("relDepartmentEmployee"));

            // Process each employee record and add a corresponding menu item.
            foreach (DataRow childRow in EmployeeRows)
            {
                mnuItemEmp = new MenuItem(childRow.Item("EmployeeName").ToString,
                                          childRow.Item("EmployeeID").ToString);

                mnuItemDept.ChildItems.Add(mnuItemEmp);

            }
        }
    }
```

In the preceding examples, the menu items have a defined *NavigateUrl* property. This instructs the *Menu* control to produce a hyperlink on the client. When the user chooses one of these options, the browser navigates directly to that page. There are situations, however, in which you might want to perform some processing before redirecting the user. In these situations, you can leave the *NavigateUrl* property blank and trap the *MenuItemClick* event of the *Menu* control. Continuing the preceding example, suppose you want to display only detailed employee information to users in the Managers role. For users who are not in the Managers role, you would show only summary information for the selected employee. The following code shows a *MenuItemClick* event handler that performs this action.

```vb
' VB
    Protected Sub mnuMain_MenuItemClick(ByVal sender As Object, ByVal e As
System.Web.UI.WebControls.MenuEventArgs) Handles mnuMain.MenuItemClick

        If HttpContext.Current.User.IsInRole("Managers") Then
            ' Transfer to a detail page.
          Server.Transfer ("employeedetail.aspx?id=" & mnumain.SelectedItem.Value.ToString)
        Else
            'Redirect to a summary page.
          Server.Transfer ("employeesummary.aspx?id=" & mnumain.SelectedItem.Value.ToString)
        End If
    End Sub
```

```csharp
// C#
    protected void mnuMain_MenuItemClick(object sender, MenuEventArgs e)
    {
        if (HttpContext.Current.User.IsInRole("Managers"))
        {
          // Transfer to a detail page.
          Server.Transfer("employeedetail.aspx?id=" & mnumain.SelectedItem.Value.ToString);
        }
        {
          // Redirect to a summary page.
          Server.Transfer("employeesummary.aspx?id=" & mnumain.SelectedItem.Value.ToString);
        }
    }
```

Styling Menus

Menu controls provide a very robust and granular-style application programming interface (API). At first, the extensive control you have over the menu appearance might seem excessive. However, if you consider how much users rely on menus and how often they are used, you will quickly appreciate the ease and flexibility with which you can program the *Menu* control. Some of the more common general style settings include the following:

- **Orientation**   Menu controls may be displayed either horizontally or vertically, depending on how you set this property. The default is vertical.
- *StaticDisplayLevels*   The property determines the number of menu levels displayed all the time. The default is 1.

Menu and *MenuItem* control styles are grouped into four distinct categories. Each category applies to a static and a dynamic menu component. The static style settings apply to static menus, whereas the dynamic settings apply to menus that appear when the user causes submenus to expand. In addition, you can control styles at certain levels. Consider, for example, a menu with the ***StaticDisplayLevels*** property set to 2. You can give your users visual cues of menu groups by controlling how the different levels of the menu are displayed. These are controlled through the *LevelMenuItemStyles*, *LevelSubMenuStyles*, and *LevelSelectedStyles* properties.

You can also control the settings for selected menu items and for items over which the mouse cursor is hovering. Note the difference between selecting and hovering over a menu item. The **SelectedStyle* styles apply to menu items that *have been clicked* by the user. These styles are appropriate, for example, for showing a user what he or she selected and where he or she is in the menu. The **HoverStyle* properties apply to those menu items over which the mouse cursor is currently hovering.

Menu Templates   If you require further control over the rendering of menu items, you can use templates. Menu item templates are set via the *StaticMenuItemStyle* and *DynamicMenuItem-Style* properties. Interestingly enough, the *Menu* control always binds to a *MenuItem* object. Therefore, the template you create must extract its value from the *Text* property of the *Menu-Item* object.

MORE INFO   **Extending the Menu control**

The *Menu* control is a very flexible control and can be extended in many ways. For more information, see the Microsoft Developer Network (MSDN) Library article "ASP.NET Menu Control Overview" at *http://msdn2.microsoft.com/en-us/library/ecs0x9w5.aspx*.

Quick Check

1. List and briefly describe the most commonly used properties of the *Menu* control.
2. List and briefly describe some of the most commonly used properties of the *Menu-Item* object.

Quick Check Answers

1. Some of the most commonly used *Menu* properties include:
   - ❑ *DataSource*   Provides access to setting or retrieving the object from which the data-bound control retrieves its list of data items (inherited from *BaseDataBoundControl*).
   - ❑ *DynamicMenuStyle*   Gets a reference to the *MenuItemStyle* object that allows you to set the appearance of a dynamic menu (one of many properties that can be set when using dynamic menus).
   - ❑ *Orientation*   Provides access to setting or retrieving the direction in which to render the *Menu* control; default is vertical.

❑ *Item*   Retrieves a *MenuItemCollection* object that contains all menu items in the *Menu* control.

❑ *StaticDisplayLevels*   Provides access to setting or retrieving the number of menu levels to display in a static menu; default is 1.

❑ *StaticMenuStyle*   Retrieves a reference to the *MenuItemStyle* object that allows you to set the appearance of a static menu (one of many properties that can be set when using dynamic menus).

2. Some of the most commonly used *MenuItem* properties include:

❑ *ChildItems*   Retrieves a *MenuItemCollection* object that contains the submenu items of the current menu item.

❑ *Depth*   Reveals the level at which a menu item is displayed.

❑ *ImageUrl*   Provides access to setting or retrieving the URL to an image that is displayed next to the text in a menu item.

❑ *NavigateUrl*   Provides access to setting or retrieving the URL to which to navigate when the menu item is clicked.

❑ *Parent*   Gets the parent menu item of the current menu item.

❑ *Text*   Provides access to setting or retrieving the text displayed for the menu item in a *Menu* control.

TreeView Control

Web developers have long awaited a *TreeView* control, and ASP.NET 2.0 finally satisfies that need. Like the *Menu* control, the *TreeView* control may be created declaratively, programmatically, or through data binding. However, unlike the *Menu* control, the *TreeView* control can be bound to relational data sources as well as hierarchical data sources.

The *TreeView* class consists of a collection of *TreeNode* objects accessed via the *Item* property. The *TreeNode* class, in turn, consists of a *ChildNodes* property containing a collection of *TreeNode* objects. Also, like the *MenuItem* class, the *TreeNode* class supports a *NavigateUrl* property. If set, the user's browser is directed to the specified URL. This behavior is called navigation mode. The alternate mode, selection mode, is the default behavior for the *TreeNode* class. When a user clicks a node in selection mode, the page posts back to itself and fires the *SelectedNodeChanged* event.

TreeView controls are prolific in Microsoft Windows applications and are increasingly common in Web forms applications. As more and more data is rendered through tree views, they become unwieldy. This is why the ASP.NET 2.0 *TreeView* class provides a feature called

PopulateOnDemand. The on-demand population feature is a powerful tool, giving you incredible control over the user experience. Here's how it works: If you want to populate a tree view in an on-demand fashion, set the *PopulateOnDemand* property of any or all *TreeNode* objects to *True.* This instructs the *TreeView* control to defer loading the particular node until the user clicks that node. In addition, the *PopulateOnDemand* property is available on all nodes at any depth in the tree.

One of the immediate drawbacks of this feature is that the user must endure a postback and subsequent page refresh for every node populated on demand. To mitigate this, the *TreeNode* control includes an additional property called *PopulateNodesFromClient.* If set to *True,* the *TreeView* performs a client-side callback to retrieve the data. If set to *False,* or if the *TreeView* detects that the browser does not support client-side callbacks, the page posts back, and the browser refreshes. The default setting for *PopulateNodesFromClient* is *True.*

Whether the page is posted back to the server or a client-side callback occurs, the *TreeNodePopulate* event is fired. Suppose you are building a student class registration application for a large university, and you need to display a tree view consisting of the colleges, departments, and courses available. The following code shows how you can accomplish this using the *PopulateOnDemand* feature.

```vb
' VB
Protected WithEvents tvwMain As System.Web.UI.WebControls.TreeView
Protected Sub Page_Load(ByVal sender As Object, ByVal e As EventArgs) Handles Me.Load

If Not Page.IsPostback Then
        ' Assume you have a method to load the DataSet with
        ' colleges, departments, and courses.
        Dim dsColleges As DataSet = GetColleges ()
        For Each row As DataRow In GetColleges.Rows

            ' Create a node with the ID for future reference.
            Dim CollegeNode As New TreeNode(row.Item("CollegeName").ToString, _
                                        row.Item("CollegeID").ToString)

            ' Load the current node on demand.
            CollegeNode.PopulateOnDemand = True

            ' Setting this property ensures that the node is
            ' initially collapsed and, as such, does not fire
            ' the TreeNodePopulate event immediately.
            CollegeNode.Collapse()

            tvwMain.Nodes.Add(CollegeNode)
        Next
End If
    End Sub


Protected Sub tvwMain_TreeNodePopulate(ByVal sender As Object, ByVal e As
System.Web.UI.WebControls.TreeNodeEventArgs) Handles tvwMain.TreeNodePopulate
```

```vb
        ' Check the depth to determine what is selected.
        Select Case e.Node.Depth
            Case 0 ' College - Load Departments
                For Each row As DataRow In GetDepartments(e.Node.Value).Rows

                    Dim DeptNode As New TreeNode(row.Item("DeptName").ToString, _
                                                row.Item("DeptID").ToString)

                    ' Load the current node on demand.
                    DeptNode.PopulateOnDemand = True

                    ' Setting this property ensures that the node is
                    ' initially collapsed and, as such, does not fire
                    ' the TreeNodePopulate event immediately.
                    DeptNode.Collapse()

                    e.Node.ChildNodes.Add(DeptNode)

                Next

            Case 1 ' Department - Load Courses

                For Each row As DataRow In GetCourses(e.Node.Value).Rows

                    Dim CourseNode As New TreeNode(row.Item("CourseName").ToString, _
                                                row.Item("CourseID").ToString)

                    ' Load the current node on demand.
                    CourseNode.PopulateOnDemand = True

                    ' Setting this property ensures that the node is
                    ' initially collapsed and, as such, does not fire
                    ' the TreeNodePopulate event immediately.
                    CourseNode.Collapse()

                    e.Node.ChildNodes.Add(CourseNode)

                Next

            Case 2 ' Course - Do nothing, this is the leaf.

            Case Else

        End Select

    End Sub

    // C#
    protected void Page_Load(object sender, EventArgs e)
    {
if (!Page.IsPostback) {

        // Assume you have a method to load the DataSet with
```

```
        // colleges, departments, and courses.
        DataSet dsColleges = GetColleges ();
        foreach (DataRow row in getColleges.Rows)
        {
            // Create a node with the ID for future reference.
            TreeNode CollegeNode = new TreeNode (row.Item ("CollegeName").ToString,
                                           row.Item ("CollegeID").ToString);

            // Load the current node on demand.
            CollegeNode.PopulateOnDemand = true;

            // Setting this property ensures that the node is
            // initially collapsed and, as such, does not fire
            // the TreeNodePopulate event immediately.
            CollegeNode.Collapse();

            tvwMain.Nodes.Add(CollegeNode);
        }
    }
}

    protected void tvwMain_TreeNodePopulate(Object sender ,
System.Web.UI.WebControls.TreeNodeEventArgs e)
    {
        // Check the depth to determine what is selected.
        switch (e.Node.Depth)
        {
        case 0: // College - Load Departments
            foreach (DataRow row in GetDepartments (e.Node.Value).Rows)
            {
                TreeNode DeptNode = new TreeNode (row.ItemArray ("DeptName").ToString,
                                            row.ItemArray ("DeptID").ToString);
                // Load the current node on demand.
                DeptNode.PopulateOnDemand = true;

                // Setting this property ensures that the node is
                // initially collapsed and, as such, does not fire
                // the TreeNodePopulate event immediately.
                DeptNode.Collapse();

                e.Node.ChildNodes.Add(DeptNode);
            }
            break;

        case 1: // Department - Load Courses

            foreach (DataRow row in GetCourses (e.Node.Value).Rows)
            {
                TreeNode CourseNode = new TreeNode (row.ItemArray ("CourseName").ToString,
                                            row.ItemArray ("CourseID").ToString);

                // Load the current node on demand.
```

```
            CourseNode.PopulateOnDemand = true;

            // Setting this property ensures that the node is
            // initially collapsed and, as such, does not fire
            // the TreeNodePopulate event immediately.
            CourseNode.Collapse();

            e.Node.ChildNodes.Add(CourseNode);
        }
        break;

    case 2: // Course - Do nothing, this is the leaf.
        break;

    default:
        break;
    }
}
```

Styling *TreeView* Controls

As with the *Menu* control, the *TreeView* control offers very granular control over styles. Also, like the *Menu* control, the *TreeView* control allows you to control styles at various levels in the tree. Because the *TreeView* control does not (theoretically) limit the number of levels, level styles are applied through the use of a *LevelStyles* collection. Using this collection, the *TreeView* itself infers the level to which the style is applied based on its index in the collection. For example, the style at index zero is applied to the root; the style at index one is applied to the level just below the root, and so on. You must include an empty style placeholder if you want to skip a level. *Style* properties are applied in the following order of precedence:

1. *NodeStyle*
2. *RootNodeStyle*, *ParentNodeStyle*, and *LeafNodeStyle*. Also, if the *LevelStyles* collection is defined, it is applied at this time. The styles defined in the *LevelStyles* collection override other node style properties.
3. *SelectedNodeStyle*
4. *HoverNodeStyle*

MORE INFO   Extending the *TreeView* control

The *TreeView* control is very extensible and provides many options for customizing its behavior and appearance. For more information, see the MSDN Library article "*TreeView* Web Server Control Overview," at *http://msdn2.microsoft.com/en-us/library/e8z5184w.aspx*.

Quick Check

1. List and briefly describe some of the most commonly used properties of the *Tree-View* control.

2. List and briefly describe some of the most commonly used properties of the *Tree-Node* object.

Quick Check Answers

1. Some of the most commonly used *TreeView* properties include:

    ❑ *DataSource*   Enables setting or retrieving the object from which the data-bound control retrieves its list of data items (inherited from *BaseDataBound-Control*).

    ❑ *ExpandDepth*   Enables setting or retrieving the number of levels that are expanded when a *TreeView* control is displayed for the first time.

    ❑ *LevelStyles*   Retrieves a collection of *Style* objects that represent the node styles at the individual levels of the tree.

    ❑ *Nodes*   Retrieves a collection of *TreeNode* objects that represent the root nodes in the *TreeView* control.

2. Some of the most commonly used *TreeNode* properties include:

    ❑ *ChildNode*   Enables retrieving a *TreeNodeCollection* collection that contains the first-level child nodes of the current node.

    ❑ *NavigateUrl*   Enables setting or retrieving the URL to which to navigate when the node is clicked.

    ❑ *Parent*   Retrieves the parent node of the current node.

    ❑ *PopulateOnDemand*   Enables setting or retrieving a value that indicates whether the node is populated dynamically.

    ❑ *SelectAction*   Enables setting or retrieving the event or events to raise when a node is selected.

    ❑ *Text*   Enables setting or retrieving the text displayed for the node in the *Tree-View* control.

Site Maps

Most Web users are familiar with the concept of a site map, and ASP.NET 2.0 provides a site map Web control. This new control gives you a quick means of providing a site map for your site. In addition, the new site map control can take adavantage of the the new ASP.NET provider model. This allows you to expose quickly and easily maintain a site map for your Web forms application, using the intrinsic site map providers or by creating your own provider to supply site map data.

Site maps require the collaboration of several objects to function effectively. The site map is defined in a file called Web.sitemap by default, which is stored in the root of the virtual directory. It is important that this file have a .sitemap extension and be stored in the root of the virtual directory because the XmlSiteMapProvider looks specifically for it. The XmlSiteMapProvider is the default site map provider that ships with ASP.NET 2.0. The XmlSiteMapProvider parses the site map file and creates the *SiteMap* object from it. The *SiteMap* object is then available to the *SiteMapDataSource* object for use in other controls.

The site map file, Web.sitemap, is an XML file consisting of a *<siteMap>* element with nested *<siteMapNode>* elements. You can nest as many levels as needed. Each node should have a title, description, and URL. Note that no two nodes can have the same URL. This is because the XmlSiteMapProvider uses the URL as a unique key when building the *SiteMap* object. An interesting note, however, is that you do not have to specify a URL at all. If you omit the URL value, the node is rendered as text and not as a link. The following Web.sitemap file shows a sample site map. Notice how the *Security* node omits a URL value although the *ChangePassword* node is still defined.

```
<?xml version="1.0" encoding="utf-8" ?>
<siteMap xmlns="http://schemas.microsoft.com/AspNet/SiteMap-File-1.0" >
    <siteMapNode url="~/Reports/reportshome.aspx" title="Reports"  description="Reports">
        <siteMapNode url="~/Reports/report.aspx?id=1" title="Sales YTD"  description="Sales
YTD" />
        <siteMapNode url="~/Reports/report.aspx?id=2" title="Sales by Region"
description="Sales by Region" />
<siteMapNode url="" title="Security" Description="Security Pages">
<siteMapNode url="~changepassword.aspx" title="Change Password" description="Change
Password"/>
</siteMapNode>
</siteMapNode>
</siteMap>
```

Binding the preceding site map to a control is extremely simple. Recall that the XmlSiteMap-Provider automatically detects the site map by file name and location. You simply place a *SiteMapDataSource* object on the page and then set it as the data source for a control. The following code shows how to use a *TreeView* control to accomplish this.

```
<asp:TreeView runat="server" ID="tvwSiteMap" datasourceid="SiteMapDataSource1">
</asp:TreeView>
<asp:SiteMapDataSource ID="SiteMapDataSource1" runat="server" />[/
```

Figure 4-2 shows the output of the preceding site map and code. Notice that the *Security* node is not a link, but the *ChangePassword* item is one.

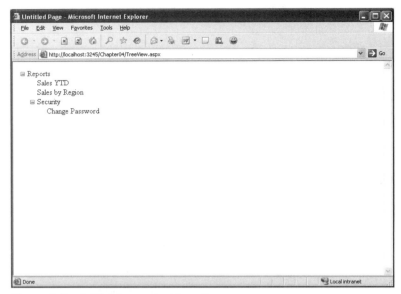

Figure 4-2   A *SiteMap* control in action

MORE INFO   **Extending the SiteMap control**

The *SiteMap* control is powerful yet easy to use. You can customize the display of the control to provide breadcrumbs as well as a hierarchical view of the site. For more information about the control, see the MSDN Library article "Walkthrough: Adding Site Navigation to a Web Site" at *http://msdn2.microsoft.com/en-US/library/w6ws38fw.aspx*.

Site Map Path

Unlike buildings and other physical locations that your users visit, your Web site offers no spatial context. As a result, users can easily get lost, so it is important to provide them with the ability to determine quickly where they are in your site. However, navigating away from the current page to the site map and back is not the best means to accomplish this. To solve this problem, most contemporary sites use the concept of breadcrumbs, which are delimited links shown horizontally at the top of Web pages. The breadcrumbs links show the hierarchy of pages from the current page to the site root or home page. ASP.NET 2.0 provides the *SiteMapPath* control, which provides breadcrumbs functionality. Although the *SiteMapPath* control works with your site map data, if you use it on a page that is not represented in your site map, the control will not be displayed. Figure 4-3 shows a sample *SiteMapPath* control as it is rendered.

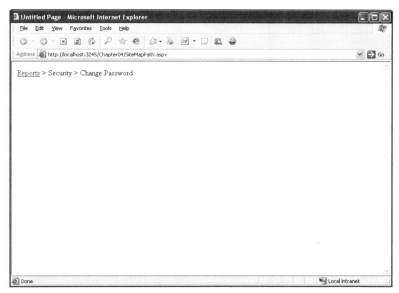

Figure 4-3 A *SiteMapPath* control in action

Placing a *SiteMapPath* control on your path is all that is required for it to display. However, as with other controls, the *SiteMapPath* control is extremely customizable in terms of both styles and how it is programmed.

Exam Tip The navigation controls are new to ASP.NET 2.0, so know the differences between the controls well enough to be able to choose the one that meets the requirements best.

Identifying the Goal of the Page

Despite the cross-page posting capabilities of ASP.NET 2.0, strive to create discrete pages that accomplish a single task by invoking a single system action. Using this technique minimizes the chances of confusing users. Also, it reduces page coupling and thereby eases maintaining and extending your Web forms application.

Another important consideration is to restrict the amount of work accomplished by a page. Because pages typically post back to the server, there is a delay between user submission and system feedback. To minimize the adverse impact of the delay on users, you might be tempted to cram as much functionality into a page as possible.

Ensuring Congruency and Consistency in the User Experience

Although most of the controls discussed thus far fall into the category of rich controls, which provide an enhanced user experience, users will spend as much time with other controls. You must give the other controls as much attention to detail as you give to the rich controls. For example, avoid using buttons on some pages and links on others.

Another important factor is surprise. As users become accustomed to your site, they will develop certain expectations. Your site should avoid surprising the user and should instead promote and support their expectations. For example, you do not want to include a Save button that on some pages, when clicked, redirects the user to a different page, but on other pages does not redirect the user at all. Like features should behave in the same manner. This promotes consistency and minimizes user surprise.

Lab: Consistency and Navigation

In this lab, you will walk through the steps of modifying an existing Web site to add user navigation and improve layout. This lab consists of two distinct exercises. Exercise 1, "Promote Consistency," gives you the opportunity to create consistency through master pages and themes. Exercise 2, "Add Site Navigation," adds to the solution by providing some navigation options.

▶ **Exercise 1: Promote Consistency**

This exercise will show you how to promote consistency across your Web site through the use of master pages and themes. This exercise demonstrates modifying existing pages to take advantage of the newly created themes and master pages.

1. In Visual Studio, start a new Web site. Click File | New | Web Site, and then select ASP.NET Web Site.

2. Add the following Web forms to the site. The reason for adding so many forms will become apparent in Exercise 2.

   a. Ch04_Intro.aspx

   b. Ch04_MasterPage_Intro.aspx

   c. Ch04_MasterPage_Terms.aspx

   d. Ch04_TreeView_Intro.aspx

   e. Ch04_TreeView_Terms.aspx

3. To each of the _Intro forms, add some descriptive text. Use the text to introduce that page and the pages that are children of that page hierarchically.

4. To each of the _Terms forms, add a *GridView* control with the ID GridTerms. Then add code in the code-behind file to generate terms for the grid. The following code samples show the code used to generate the terms. Typically, this information is read from a database.

```vb
' VB
   Protected Sub Page_Load(ByVal sender As Object, ByVal e As System.EventArgs) Handles
Me.Load
       Dim dt As New DataTable("Terms")

       dt.Columns.Add("Term", Type.GetType("System.String"))
       dt.Columns.Add("Definition", Type.GetType("System.String"))

       Dim row1 As DataRow = dt.NewRow()
       row1("Term") = "Term 1"
       row1("Definition") = "Definition 1"
       dt.Rows.Add(row1)

       Dim row2 As DataRow = dt.NewRow()
       row2("Term") = "Term 2"
       row2("Definition") = "Definiton 2"
       dt.Rows.Add(row2)

       Dim row3 As DataRow = dt.NewRow()
       row3("Term") = "Term 3"
       row3("Definition") = "Definition 3"
       dt.Rows.Add(row3)

       Dim row4 As DataRow = dt.NewRow()
       row4("Term") = "Term 4"
       row4("Definition") = "Definiton 4"
       dt.Rows.Add(row4)

       Me.GridTerms.DataSource = dt
       Me.GridTerms.DataBind()
   End Sub
```

```csharp
// C#
   protected void Page_Load(object sender, EventArgs e)
   {
       DataTable dt = new DataTable ("Terms");

       dt.Columns.Add("Term", Type.GetType("System.String"));
       dt.Columns.Add("Definition", Type.GetType("System.String"));

       DataRow row1 = dt.NewRow ();
       row1("Term") = "Term 1";
       row1("Definition") = "Definition 1";
       dt.Rows.Add(row1);

       DataRow row2 = dt.NewRow ();
       row2("Term") = "Term 2";
       row2("Definition") = "Definiton 2";
       dt.Rows.Add(row2);

       DataRow row3 = dt.NewRow ();
       row3("Term") = "Term 3";
```

```
                row3("Definition") = "Definition 3";
                dt.Rows.Add(row3);

                DataRow row4 = dt.NewRow ();
                row4("Term") = "Term 4";
                row4("Definition") = "Definiton 4";
                dt.Rows.Add(row4);

                Me.GridTerms.DataSource = dt;
                Me.GridTerms.DataBind();
        }
```

5. Build the solution and view the _Terms pages in the browser. You can see that the forms have no colors or styles. You can also quickly realize that maintaining consistency among these pages will fast become cumbersome.

6. Improve consistency by first adding some common styling using a theme. Right-click the Web site name and choose Add ASP.NET Folder Theme. Accept the default name of Theme1.

7. Add both a skin file and a style sheet to the theme. Right-click the Theme1 folder and choose Add New Item. Select Skin File and choose the name SkinFile.skin. Repeat for the style sheet, choosing the name StyleSheet.css.

8. Open the skin file and add elements related to *GridView* controls. The following code sample shows the entry in the skin file.

```
<asp:GridView runat="server">
            <HeaderStyle Font-Bold="True" ForeColor="Blue" />
            <AlternatingRowStyle BackColor="Gainsboro" />
</asp:GridView>
9. Open the style sheet file and add styles according to the following sample.
body {
}
.paratext
{
font-family:Courier New;
color:Blue;
}

h3
{
color:Green;
font-size:large;
font-family:Comic Sans MS
}
```

9. Modify the existing pages to take advantage of the theme. Open each .aspx file in turn and select the Design view. In the Properties window, choose DOCUMENT from the pick list. Set the Theme property to Theme1. Save the file.

10. Rebuild the site and view the terms pages in a browser window. Notice how the *GridView* controls are styled according to the theme.

In preparation for adding navigation, you will now provide another level of consistency to your site through master pages.

11. Right-click the site and choose New Folder. Create a folder named **masterpages**. Right-click the folder and choose Add New Item. Add a master page called **Ch04_master.master**. You will add controls to the master page in the next exercise.

12. Set the master page for the existing pages. Open each existing .aspx file in turn and select the Source view. Modify the *@Page* element by adding the following attribute: *MasterPageFile="~/masterpages/Ch04_master.master*.

▶ **Exercise 2: Add Site Navigation**

This exercise extends Exercise 1 to add navigation to the existing applications. You will add both a *TreeView* control and a *SiteMapPath* control to the pages using the master page. You will use a site map to provide navigation data to the navigation controls.

1. Add a site map file to the Web site. Right-click the Web site and choose Add New Item. Select a site map called Web.sitemap. Modify the site map file to include the pages in the site. When complete, the site map file should look as follows.

```xml
<?xml version="1.0" encoding="utf-8" ?>
<siteMap xmlns="http://schemas.microsoft.com/AspNet/SiteMap-File-1.0" >
<siteMapNode url="Ch04_Intro.aspx" title="Chapter 4"  description="">
<siteMapNode url="" title="Master Pages"  description="">
<siteMapNode url="Ch04_MasterPage_Intro.aspx" title="Master Page Intro"  description=""
/>
<siteMapNode url="Ch04_MasterPage_Terms.aspx" title="Master Page Terms"  description=""
/>
</siteMapNode>
<siteMapNode url="" title="Tree View"  description="">
<siteMapNode url="Ch04_TreeView_Intro.aspx" title="Tree View Intro"  description="" />
<siteMapNode url="Ch04_TreeView_Terms.aspx" title="Tree View Terms"  description="" />
</siteMapNode>
</siteMapNode>
</siteMap>
```

2. Modify the master page to include the navigation controls. Add a *SiteMapDataProvider* control to the master page and accept the default name.

3. Add a *TreeView* control and accept the default name. Modify the *TreeView* control so that its data source is the SiteMapDataProvider.

4. Add a *SiteMapPath* control and accept the default name.

5. Modify the existing pages to accept the master page. Perform the following steps on each page.

   a. Remove all leading and trailing HTML tags, including <html>, <head>, <body>, and <form> tags. Leave the *@Page* directive and the content you added such as controls and text.

   b. Create a *Content* control around your custom content. When complete, the following sample demonstrates how the code for one of your pages should look. Note that this sample is for a _Terms page, but other pages will have a similar appearance. Note also that this sample does *not* include the *@Page* directive, which is required.

```
<asp:Content ID="Content1" ContentPlaceHolderID="ContentPlaceHolder1" runat="server">
    <h3> MasterPage Terms
    </h3>
    <span class="termgrid">
    <asp:GridView ID="GridTerms" runat="server">
    </asp:GridView>
    </span>
</asp:Content>
```

6. Build the site. View a page in the browser to see how the *SiteMapPath* and *TreeView* controls display the appropriate site hierarchy.

Lesson Summary

- Cross-page posting is new in ASP.NET 2.0 and allows the page to post back to a page of choice, although not necessarily the originating page. This transfer to a page is done on the client side.
- The new *PreviousPage* and *IsCrossPagePostBack* properties support cross-page posting.
- Navigation controls are new to ASP.NET. These include the *Menu* control, the *TreeView* control, and site map controls. In addition, the *TreeView* control can also be used for navigation. All of these controls use hierarchical data.
- The navigation controls are extensible.

Lesson Review

You can use the following questions to test your knowledge of the information in Lesson 1: "Choosing an Appropriate Layout for the Visual Interface." The questions are also available on the companion CD if you prefer to review them in electronic form.

NOTE   Answers

Answers to these questions and explanations of why each answer choice is right or wrong are located in the "Answers" section at the end of the book.

1. Which of the following files provides the organization of your Web application and is used by the *SiteMapPath* control?

   A. Web.config

   B. Web.sitemap

   C. Sitemap.config

   D. Sitemap.xml

2. Given a Web page named MyPage, which of the following directives forces your page to accept postings only from a Web page PageA?

   A. *<%@ PreviousPageType VirtualPath="~/PageA.aspx" %>*

   B. *<%@ PreviousPageType TypeName="PageA" %>*

   C. Both *<%@ PreviousPageType VirtualPath="~/PageA.aspx" %>* and *<%@ PreviousPageType TypeName="PageA" %>* are required.

   D. Either *<%@ PreviousPageType VirtualPath="~/PageA.aspx" %>* or *<%@ PreviousPageType TypeName="PageA" %>* is required.

3. Which of the following Web controls does not provide navigation functionality?

   A. *Menu*

   B. *SiteMapPath*

   C. *Panel*

   D. *TreeView*

Lesson 2: Implementing a Common UI Layout

Previous versions of ASP.NET provided never-before-seen improvements upon the ability to create reusable Web pages and to remove the challenges of providing a common layout while working with teams of developers. ASP.NET 2.0 further extends these capabilities through several new techniques, including master pages, themes, and Web Parts. In this lesson, you will learn how to use these new techniques to create consistent UI layouts for your Web forms applications quickly. In addition, you'll learn how to provide personalization features for users of your applications. Finally, you'll gain the ability to improve extensibility through reusable components.

After this lesson, you will be able to:
- Decrease development time by using master pages for common UI elements.
- Improve usability by providing a consistent layout with themes.
- Apply styles to navigation elements to improve usability.
- Appropriately choose between style sheets and skins.
- Learn about Web Parts and how to use them in your Web applications.

Estimated lesson time: 45 minutes

Establishing Common UI Elements: Master Pages, Themes, and Web Parts

Providing consistency is one of the most challenging and important aspects of developing a good UI and providing a rich user experience. ASP.NET 2.0 provides several robust techniques for establishing and maintaining a consistent UI throughout your Web application. This section will discuss techniques for building a consistent UI by using ASP.NET 2.0 capabilities.

Master Pages

Since ASP.NET has provided inheritance for Web forms applications, developers have taken advantage of it by creating base pages from which other application Web forms inherit. Although this technique gives a consistent layout, it is not intuitive to establish because the base page is not created graphically. ASP.NET 2.0 solves the problem through a technique called *master pages*.

A master page is an ASP.NET file of the extension .master with a predefined layout that can include static text, HTML elements, and server controls. The master page is identified by the *@ Master* directive instead of by the *@ Page* directive. The *@ Master* directive can contain most of the same attributes as the *@ Control* directive. In addition, the master page consists of top-level HTML elements for a page such as the *html*, *head*, and *form* elements.

Master pages work by combining the static content and controls with *replaceable content place-holders*. These are composed of the new *ContentPlaceHolder* control and are used to define specific regions where content specific to an individual page will appear. The replaceable content itself is, therefore, defined in the content pages. The following code shows a master page definition, including content placeholder controls.

```
<%@ Master Language="VB" CodeFile="General.master.vb" Inherits="_General" %>
<!DOCTYPE html PUBLIC "-//W3C//DTD XHTML 1.0 Transitional//EN" "http://www.w3.org/TR/xhtml1/
DTD/xhtml1-transitional.dtd">

<html xmlns="http://www.w3.org/1999/xhtml" >
<head runat="server">
    <title>Default</title>
</head>
<body>
    <form id="frmMaster" runat="server">
        <asp:ContentPlaceHolder ID="cpLeftNav" runat="server">
      </asp:ContentPlaceHolder>
            <asp:ContentPlaceHolder ID="cpContent" runat="server">
            </asp:ContentPlaceHolder>
    </form>
</body>
</html>
```

Content Pages

Once the master page is created, you can use it on your Web forms application's content pages. To set a content page to use a master page, use the *MasterPageFile* attribute of the *@ Page* directive. Once you reference the appropriate master file, you can map the replaceable content to the appropriate content placeholder controls. Replaceable content regions are mapped to placeholders via the new *Content* control. When you set the *ContentPlaceHolderID* attribute, Visual Studio provides a Microsoft IntelliSense pop-up menu of available content placeholders in the associated master page. The following code shows a content page with *Content* controls added.

```
<%@ Page Language="VB" AutoEventWireup="false" CodeFile="Default.aspx.vb" Inherits="_Default"
Theme="Default" MasterPageFile="masterpages/General.master" %>

<asp:Content ID="contentLeft" runat="server" ContentPlaceHolderID="cpLeftNav">

</asp:Content>

<asp:Content ID="contentBody" runat="server" ContentPlaceHolderID="cpContent">
</asp:Content>
```

Now that the content controls are added and mapped to the placeholders, you are free to add the replaceable content appropriate to the page. The *Content* control is a container and, as such, can contain other controls. For example, you can insert instances of the new *GridView* and *SqlDataSourceControl* controls.

Quick Check

1. What intrinsic control is located on a master page to provide a content area for content pages?
2. What intrinsic control is located on a content page and provides an association with a *ContentPlaceHolder* control from a master page?

Quick Check Answers

1. A *ContentPlaceHolder* control defines a relative region for content in a master page and renders all *Text*, *Markup*, and *Server* controls from a related *Content* control found in a content page.
2. A *Content* control is a container for the content and controls of a content page. A *Content* control is used only with a master page that defines a corresponding *ContentPlaceHolder* control.

Master Page Behavior

It is important to understand how the ASP.NET run time processes master pages so that you can effectively respond to events and provide a rich, congruent user experience. Once you associate a content page with a master page by setting the *MasterPageFile* attribute on the @ *Page* directive, the ASP.NET run time handles merging the master page with the requested content page. Once merged, the resulting conglomerate page behaves much like a stand-alone content page. The following list outlines the high-level behavioral steps of master pages.

1. Master page behavior is initiated when a user requests a content page by typing the URL of the page.
2. When the page is fetched by the ASP.NET run time, the @ *Page* directive is read to determine whether the page is associated with a master page. If it is, the master page file is read as well. If this is the first time the pages are requested, compilation occurs.
3. The master page's content is updated. For example, controls are bound to data sources, look ups occur, and other dynamic content is processed.
4. The master page content becomes part of the content page content. In this sense, the master page acts much like a user control. However, once the master page is merged, the content page's content is contained within the content placeholders of the master page. Figure 4-4 shows the high-level tree hierarchy.

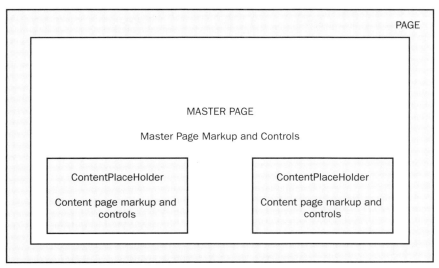

Figure 4-4   Master page hierarchy

5. The content of the content page's *Content* controls is updated and merged into the corresponding *ContentPlaceHolder* controls. Recall that at this point, the *ContentPlaceHolder* controls are already part of the content page's control tree.

6. The resulting merged page is rendered to the browser.

Exam Tip   Master pages can contain master pages. This helps meet the requirements of each department adhering to a specific UI yet still adhering to the corporate or company overall standard.

Paths for Master Pages and Content Pages   Master pages are intended to be applied to a range of content pages throughout your Web forms application. As such, it is very likely that the master page files will be in different folders than the content page files. In fact, Microsoft recommends creating a separate folder for all master page files. One of the side effects of this is that resources referenced by the content page might be in a different relative location than the same resources referenced by a master page. Furthermore, the ASP.NET run time executes the requested page in the content page's file path, not in the file path of the master page.

Consider a situation wherein you have a relative path to an image in the master page file. The *ImageUrl* property is set relative to the master page file. When the content page is processed, the associated master page image may not appear if the relative path to the image is incorrect *for the content page.*

ASP.NET resolves this problem by dynamically modifying URLs of properties that reference external resources. The limitation here is that for the ASP.NET run time to apply the resolution, the control must be a server control. Recall that a server control is any control that specifies the *runat=server* attribute. In the scenario of the image file referenced in the master page, you can place a *runat=server* attribute on the *img* element. This instructs ASP.NET to run the image element on the server. As a result, ASP.NET will dynamically update the *ImageUrl* property to a path relative to the content page.

Note, again, that the ASP.NET run time cannot modify URLs on elements that are not server controls. Therefore, in general, when working with master pages, you should use server controls, even for elements that do not require server code. Using server controls on master pages improves maintainability and makes it easier to move files into different folder structures in the future.

Themes

Web-based computing has become a fact of life. Internet users range from software professionals to grandparents and grandchildren. Because of this, there is a level of expectation regarding available functionality as well as general familiarity. Users don't want to re-learn the Web for every new application they use. Building professional applications requires not just stable, robust functionality but also a professional appearance and familiar behavior.

Cascading style sheets (CSS) have long been the de facto tool for providing consistent colors, fonts, and positioning to Web applications. Style sheets, however, are limited to a fixed set of attributes. ASP.NET 2.0 extends the capabilities of style sheets using a new feature called *themes*.

App_Themes Folder and Skin Files   ASP.NET 2.0 defines several new special-purpose folders for Web sites. Among them is the *App_Themes* folder, which is used to contain all themes defined for a Web site. The *App_Themes* folder is created automatically by Visual Studio when you choose the Theme option from the Add ASP.NET Folder context menu, available when you right-click your Web site project in Solution Explorer. If you create the folder manually, note that it must reside in the top-level directory of the Web forms application. When you add themes with Visual Studio, they are placed in the *App_Themes* folder for you. Themes can consist of skins and style sheets.

A *skin* is a file with the .skin extension that contains property settings that define how controls are rendered. Skins can be applied to all instances of a particular type of control or to all controls of a type. For example, you can specify that all *GridView* controls in your Web forms application use a subtle color difference for alternating rows. This property can be set in a skin file, and ASP.NET does the work of applying the setting for you.

Skins offer a greater range of establishing, controlling, and maintaining UI settings than do style sheets. This is because skin files allow you to specify settings for many more properties than do style sheets. The skin file control elements do not need to completely define the controls they represent. Instead, you need only set the attributes you want to standardize. The only exception to this is the *runat=server* attribute, which is required. Additionally, the *id=* attribute is not allowed in a skin file.

Each theme can consist of multiple skin files. For example, you can have separate skin files for each type of control.

Suppose that you want to ensure that all *GridView* controls in your Web forms application use an alternating row color. Also suppose that you want only those *TextBox* controls used to capture form data to adhere to a predefined length. The following sample from a skin file shows how you can accomplish these tasks using a skin.

```
<asp:GridView runat="server">
    <AlternatingRowStyle BackColor="Gainsboro"/>
</asp:GridView>
<asp:TextBox runat="server" SkinID="skinDataField" Width="266px"/>[/code]
```

Based on the skin file settings shown here, no additional work is required to apply the alternating row color to *GridView* control instances. To apply the appropriate skin to *TextBox* control instances, you need to set the *SkinID* attribute on those *TextBox* elements.

Applying Themes at Design Time   Now that you have a skin file, you need to apply it to one or more Web pages. There are several ways to apply skin information to your Web page. It is interesting to note that themes cannot be applied to master pages. Instead, themes must be applied to pages individually, using the *Theme* property.

Once you specify the theme for the current page, global skin settings, such as the alternating row color you created previously, are applied for you. However, you need to set the skin identifiers to individual controls. You accomplish this by specifying the *SkinID* attribute on the control element. If no global skin setting is available for a given control, and no skin identifier is specified, then the control is rendered without any skin settings. Figure 4-5 shows three *TextBox* control instances rendered with several skin settings.

```
<asp:Button runat="server" ID="btnOne" Text="A Skin" SkinID="skinButtonBoldText" />

<asp:Button runat="server" ID="btnTwo" Text="Another Skin" SkinID="skinButtonBoldItalicText"
/>
<asp:Button runat="server" ID="btnThree" Text="No Skin"/>

<asp:Button runat="server" Font-Bold="True" SkinID="skinButtonBoldText"/>
<asp:Button runat="server" Font-Bold="True" Font-Italic="True"
SkinID="skinButtonBoldItalicText"/>
```

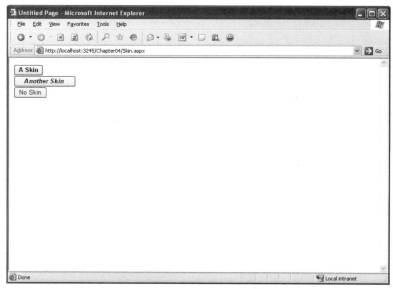

Figure 4-5   Applying skin settings

Another way to apply themes is by using the configuration file. Suppose that you want to apply your theme globally to every Web form in the application. Simply set the *Theme* attribute on the *Pages* element to the appropriate theme for each page in the application.

Cascading Style Sheets   Although skins are incredibly powerful, style sheets are still a viable option for applying thematic colors and fonts to a Web forms application. There might be several reasons for using a style sheet. For example, you might want to apply styles to elements that do not have a corresponding server control. Also, you might have an existing, well-defined style sheet, and you do not want to invest the effort in migrating to a skin file. Regardless of your reasoning, there are a few things you need to consider when using style sheets in themes.

ASP.NET automatically searches the theme folder for files with a .css extension and applies those files to the page. However, to accomplish this task, ASP.NET must insert a *LINK* element in the *HEAD* element of the Web page. This requires that the *HEAD* element of the page run as a server control. To make this happen, set the *runat=server* attribute in the *HEAD* element.

You can use as many style sheets as you want in a theme. Once the style sheet is associated with a page, you can apply the styles to controls using the *CssClass* property of the control.

MORE INFO   **More about cascading style sheets**

For more information about using style sheets, visit World Wide Web Consortium (W3C) at *http://www.w3.org/Style/CSS/*.

Theme Hierarchy   Themes can easily become complicated, especially if a theme consists of multiple skin files and multiple style sheets as well as images and resource files. When a theme is applied, its settings are merged with the local page settings to produce the final look of the page. If a control setting is defined both in the theme and on the page, the theme settings are applied last, effectively overriding the local page settings. Only one theme at a time may be applied to a page. This prevents you from having to wonder which theme setting is applied last in a multiple-theme situation.

***Theme* Property vs. *StyleSheetTheme* Property**   You might be wondering how themes work in conjunction with style sheets. If, for example, a skin file defines attributes for a button control, and a style sheet defines attributes for the same control, how do you know which one is actually applied? More important, you may want to override the default behavior if possible.

The creators of ASP.NET 2.0 anticipated this and created the *StyleSheetTheme* property to help you. When the *StyleSheetTheme* property is set, local page settings override settings defined in the theme when the setting is applied in both places. You might notice that this is how cascading style sheets work, thus the name of this property.

Use this option with caution, especially if you are maintaining an existing Web forms application. Overriding the theme settings might violate the consistency of the UI and can lead to confusion and frustration among users.

Quick Check

1. List the elements that are contained within a single theme.
2. Which elements are required in a theme?

Quick Check Answers

1. The elements that are contained within a single theme are:
   - ❑ Skin(s): A skin file has the file name extension .skin and contains property settings for individual controls such as *Button*, *Label*, *TextBox*, or *Calendar*. Control skin settings are like the control markup itself but contain only the properties you want to set as part of the theme.
   - ❑ Cascading style sheets (CSS): If a .css file is placed in the theme directory, the style sheet is applied automatically as part of the theme.
   - ❑ Images.
   - ❑ Other resources.
2. At a minimum, a theme will contain one skin file.

Dynamically Applying Themes and Using Multiple Themes   Personalization can be a valuable feature in drawing return visitors to your site. Portal sites such as MSN provide personalization capabilities. ASP.NET 2.0 gives you the ability to allow users to personalize their experience while visiting your Web forms application. You have the ability to apply an entire theme or apply elements of a theme at run time.

To apply a theme programmatically, you need to override the page's *PreInit* event handler. In fact, a compilation exception is thrown if you try to set the *Theme* property after the *PreInit* event. Suppose you have a page that allows users to choose a theme. You can set the selected theme in a session variable or in a database (or both). You can apply the theme from the session variable, as shown in the following code.

```vb
' VB
    Protected Sub Page_PreInit(ByVal sender As Object, ByVal e As System.EventArgs) Handles
Me.PreInit

        Me.Theme = Session.Item("currentTheme").ToString

    End Sub
```

```csharp
// C#
    protected void Page_PreInit(Object sender, EventArgs e)
    {
        this.Theme = Session("currentTheme").ToString;
    }
```

An interesting side effect of setting the theme in the *PreInit* event handler is that this event is fired *before* the controls are loaded. This means that you cannot directly allow users to set the theme on a page and have that theme applied to that page immediately.

In addition to programmatically setting the theme of a page, you can also set the style sheet for the page. This is accomplished in exactly the same way and has the same side effects. You must set this property in the *PreInit* event.

Suppose that you want to apply a skin to a particular control without applying the entire theme to the page. This, too, can be accomplished programmatically. As with setting a theme at run time, you need to override the *PreInit* event handler on the page. To apply the skin, set the *SkinID* property of the target control, as shown in the following code.

```vb
' VB
    Protected Sub Page_PreInit(ByVal sender As Object, ByVal e As System.EventArgs) Handles
Me.PreInit

        Me.ddlTheme.SkinID = "skinDDL"

    End Sub
```

```csharp
// C#
    protected void Page_PreInit(Object sender, EventArgs e)
    {
        this.ddlTheme.SkinID = "skinDDL";
    }
```

Web Parts

Themes provide a robust mechanism whereby you can build a consistent appearance and behavior for your Web forms application. They also give you an opportunity to allow users to personalize their experiences by choosing their own themes. This adds a lot of value to your application. However, personalization through themes is restricted to mostly the color schemes and images available in a particular theme.

The logical next step to personalization is allowing users to personalize the content and placement of controls on pages in your Web forms application. ASP.NET 2.0 provides robust support for creating and hosting Web Parts.

The three primary components to a complete Web Part deployment are *Web Parts UI* controls, which rely on UI structural components, which, in turn, rely on personalization. Personalization is the foundational component, and it offers not only the ability for users to personalize their experience; it also persists their settings permanently. The UI structural components provide services that all Web Parts need. These services coordinate Web Parts on a page, tracking individual Web Parts, managing Web Part zones, supporting the different display modes for the Web Parts, and tracking communications among Web Parts.

The *Web Parts UI* controls are the Web Parts. They inherit from the *WebPart* class. You can create your own Web Parts or use existing Web Parts provided by third parties. Also, ASP.NET 2.0 provides an extensive set of controls available for use in Web Part applications. You can use them as is or inherit from them and extend their functionality.

Creating and Using Web Parts   The Web Parts infrastructure is extremely robust. You can drag and drop existing Web Parts from the Visual Studio 2005 toolbox into your Web forms application. Also, you can use any existing Web server control, custom control, or user control as a *Web Part* control.

MORE INFO   Web Parts and Web Part pages

Web Parts and Web Part pages are almost a technology unto themselves. You can get started learning more about Web Parts by visiting the MSDN Web site at *http://msdn2.microsoft.com/en-us /library/hhy9ewf1.aspx*.

Lesson Summary

- There are many techniques available for providing a consistent UI. First, gain an understanding of the requirements and then choose an appropriate technique or several techniques.
- Master pages consist of a template-type page referenced by content pages; content placeholders provide the developer with a means of customization.
- Themes consist of skins and CSS. The skin provides a means of establishing, controlling, and maintaining UI settings.

Lesson Review

You can use the following questions to test your knowledge of the information in Lesson 2: "Implementing a Common UI Layout." The questions are also available on the companion CD if you prefer to review them in electronic form.

NOTE   Answers

Answers to these questions and explanations of why each answer choice is right or wrong are located in the "Answers" section at the end of the book.

---

1. Which control should be used to provide a uniform layout across all pages within a Web application?
   A. Web Part
   B. CSS
   C. Themes
   D. Master pages

2. Which of the following is not part of an ASP.NET 2.0 theme?
   A. Content placeholder
   B. CSS
   C. Image
   D. Skin

3. You have been asked to apply alternating colors to all *GridView* controls in a multi-page Web application. Which of the following techniques requires the least amount of code?

   A. Create a skin for the *GridView* control without a *SkinID* attribute.

   B. Create a skin for the *GridView* control with a *SkinID* attribute.

   C. Use the *RowStyle* and *AlternatingRowStyle* properties.

   D. Use the *CssClass* property.

4. Which event should be used to apply a theme programmatically to a Web page?

   A. *PreInit*

   B. *Init*

   C. *Load*

   D. *PreRender*

Chapter Review

To further practice and reinforce the skills you learned in this chapter, you can complete the following tasks:

- Review the chapter summary.
- Review the list of key terms introduced in this chapter.
- Complete the case scenarios. These scenarios set up real-world situations involving the topics of this chapter and ask you to create a solution.
- Complete the suggested practices.
- Take a practice test.

Chapter Summary

- The new hierarchical controls, including the *Menu*, *SiteMap*, and *TreeView* controls, can read from XML files, giving you increased flexibility and providing users with consistent, secure navigational elements.
- The *SiteMapPath* control can be used in a breadcrumbs-style fashion or in a traditional pop-out menu fashion to provide site-wide navigation as well as location identification.
- *Skins* allow you to extend the capabilities of style sheets by exposing server-side properties of controls, giving you additional ability to develop a consistent UI layout quickly.
- You can use master pages and themes to promote a consistent user experience and to increase development speed.
- Web Parts give you the ability to provide customization features more quickly, which leads to improved user efficiency.

Key Terms

Do you know what these key terms mean? You can check your answers by looking up the terms in the glossary at the end of the book.

- content page
- content placeholders
- master pages
- skin file
- themes
- Web Parts

Case Scenarios

In the following case scenarios, you will apply what you've learned about creating a Web application UI. You can find answers to these questions in the "Answers" section at the end of this book.

Case Scenario 1: Build an Intranet Application

You have been asked to create an intranet application that enables multiple departments to maintain human resources data. You need to create a consistent appearance and behavior in this application even though some data elements might differ among departments.

1. How would you create a consistent layout across the pages in the application?
2. The Web offers no spatial orientation. What are some ways you can provide users with feedback about where they are, relative to the root page of the application? How would you provide them with a single point of reference to view the entire site layout?
3. How would you implement a requirement that each department-specific page have its own color and image scheme?

Case Scenario 2: Provide Personalized Experiences

You are asked to modify an intranet application and provide users with the ability to customize their individual experiences. You want to provide users with the ability to customize their color choices. You also want to provide users with the ability to choose what features appear on their pages.

1. What aspects of ASP.NET 2.0 would you use to provide users with the ability to customize the features that are available to them?
2. What ASP.NET 2.0 aspects can you use to allow individuals to customize the appearance and behavior of their experience in your application?

Suggested Practices

To help you successfully master the exam objectives presented in this chapter, complete the following tasks.

Choose an Appropriate Layout for the Visual Interface

These tasks will help you learn more about the hierarchical data controls. Complete both practices to gain more experience with the *Menu*, *SiteMap*, and *TreeView* controls.

- **Practice 1**   Create a page with the *Menu*, *SiteMap*, and *SiteMapPath* controls. Use the site map XML file to populate the *SiteMap* controls. Use a separate XML file to populate the menu control.
- **Practice 2**   Create a page with the *TreeView* control and populate the control from an XML source.

Evaluate a Strategy for Implementing a Common Layout Throughout the UI

This task helps you learn more about themes and master pages. You should complete at least Practices 1, 2, and 3 to gain experience with master pages and themes.

- **Practice 1**   Create a theme for your Web application. Experiment with using both style sheets and skin files in this theme.
- **Practice 2**   Create a master page for your Web application. Create content pages that use the master page.
- **Practice 3**   Write a content page that reads from controls on the master page. This will give you an understanding of how to reference master page elements in content pages.
- **Practice 4**   Create an additional theme for your Web application. Use the new theme and the existing theme to learn about switching between themes.

Take a Practice Test

The practice tests on this book's companion CD offer many options. For example, you can test yourself on just one exam objective, or you can test yourself on all the 70-547 certification exam content. You can set up the test so that it closely simulates the experience of taking a certification exam, or you can set it up in study mode so that you can look at the correct answers and explanations after you answer each question.

MORE INFO   **Practice tests**

For details about all the practice test options available, see the "How to Use the Practice Tests" section in this book's Introduction.

Chapter 5
Creating and Choosing Controls

In this chapter, you will learn how to evaluate the needs of your applications in terms of displaying information to the user. You will review some of the controls in ASP.NET 2.0 and their capabilities. Knowing the capabilities of the controls available in the toolbox helps you make better choices for creating a robust user experience. This chapter will also teach you how to build your own controls in situations in which existing intrinsic controls don't quite satisfy all your needs. The chapter closes with a lab in which you create a control.

Exam objectives in this chapter:
- Choose an appropriate control based on design specifications.
    - Evaluate the type of data that must be captured or displayed.
    - Evaluate available controls. Considerations include standard .NET Framework controls as well as custom, internally developed, and third-party controls.
    - Evaluate how available controls are implemented in previous and ongoing projects or applications.
    - Evaluate the user demographic. Considerations include localization concerns.
    - Evaluate the user environment. Considerations include screen size and browser type and version.

Lessons in this chapter:

Before You Begin

To complete the lessons in this chapter, you should be familiar with Microsoft Visual Basic or C# and be comfortable with the following task:

■   Creating an ASP.NET Web page in Microsoft Visual Studio 2005

Real World

Brian C. Lanham

There are so many options available to us when building Web applications. It is often just as challenging to choose *how* to implement a site as it is to actually implement the site. What has worked best for me over the years is to start simply and add robustness later. Let your users experience the basic functionality of your application before you start adding bells and whistles. You might spend time and money building or buying and integrating a whiz-bang control that users don't even use. Learn what is available to you out of the box first. Build on that functionality later.

Lesson 1: Web User Controls and Custom Web Controls

Custom Web controls and user controls combine other controls into a single container that is, in turn, used as a single control on a Web page. These controls provide a convenient mechanism for creating reusable visual components for your Web forms application. User controls differ from custom Web controls in that user controls reside in the current Web application, whereas custom Web controls are compiled into a separate assembly. In this lesson, you will explore user controls and custom Web controls and create your own user control.

After this lesson, you will be able to:

■ Understand the differences between custom Web controls and user controls and when to use each appropriately.

■ Create reusable Web components with user controls.

Estimated lesson time: 45 minutes

Web User Controls

Web user controls (or just user controls) combine one Web server or HTML control or more so that they can be used as a single control. This enables you to combine related graphical elements and improves reuse. It also gives you a quick and easy way to improve consistency throughout your application. There are many ways to employ user controls in your Web forms applications. Perhaps you want to display a stock ticker on pages or to request feedback for site content. Instead of copying the code to multiple pages to enable visitors to provide feedback, you can create a user control to encapsulate the necessary functionality. During the lab portion of this lesson, you will create such a user control.

User controls are very similar to Web pages. First, they have an HTML portion and a source code portion. User controls inherit from the *Sytem.Web.UI.UserControl* class, and the files have an .ascx extension. User controls are also created in much the same way as Web pages. When adding a user control to your Web site, you can add controls to it through drag and drop, using the toolbox. Alternatively, you can use the Microsoft IntelliSense feature provided in the HTML source view and declaratively create the graphical elements of the user control.

Using User Controls

When a user control is ready for use, there are two ways to place it on your pages. The most direct means of making a user control available to a page is through the *@ Register* directive. This directive informs the Web page where the user control's source code is and how it is referenced on the page. Following is an *@ Register* directive for a sample user control:

```
<%@ Register Src="WebUserControl.ascx" TagName="WebUserControl" TagPrefix="uc1" %>
```

The @ *Register* directive does not actually place the user control on the Web page. You can do that declaratively by using the values in the *TagPrefix* and *TagName* attributes of the directive. However, you need only one @ *Register* directive regardless of the number of user control instances placed on the page. In this example, you place the user control on the page declaratively as follows.

```
<uc1:WebUserControl runat="server" ID="ucFeedback" />
```

The *Src* attribute of the directive indicates not only the file name but also the relative location of the source file. In the preceding example, the user control is in the root folder of the Web site. Note that you must specify the relative path to the user control for the page to find it; otherwise, an exception will occur if you attempt to use the control on your page. Therefore, it is common to place most user controls in a single sub-folder of the virtual directory root folder.

There is a quicker way to reference a user control on your page. While in Visual Studio, switch the page to Design View. Then, highlight the user control file (the .ascx file) in Solution Explorer and drag it to the page. Drop it in the desired location. Visual Studio 2005 creates the correct @ *Register* directive for you and supplies the user control declaration. The @ *Register* directive is created only once, even if you place multiple instances of the user control on your page.

User Control Life Cycle

If you are going to take full advantage of the power of user controls, you need to understand how user controls interact with the hosting page. When a Web page is accessed for the first time (or the first time following a change), the HTML portion of the page is compiled into a class that inherits from the class defined in the code-behind file. The resulting class is responsible for creating the control hierarchy of the page. Once the control hierarchy is created, the page is rendered by recursively calling the *RenderControl (HtmlTextWriter)* method for each control in the hierarchy. Even though the page is compiled only once (or once as changed), the control hierarchy is created each time the page is requested. User controls work in almost the same way.

One significant difference between intrinsic controls and user controls is that when the user control is added to the page's control hierarchy, the control's *InitializeAsUserControl (Page)* method is invoked. This method is used to allow the user control to create its own control hierarchy and to give it a reference to the page that contains it. This method ensures that user controls that are created declaratively are initialized properly.

Note that user controls can, in turn, contain other user controls and so on continuously. Even so, the user control life cycle behaves in the fashion described here for each layer of controls.

MORE INFO   ASP.NET page life cycle

Learn more about the ASP.NET page life cycle on the Microsoft Web site at *http://msdn2.microsoft.com /en-us/library/ms178472.aspx.*

Custom Web Controls

Unlike Web user controls, custom Web controls are compiled into a distinct assembly. In this way, developers don't need to worry about copying code from one project to the next. Instead, they can simply reference the dynamic link library (.dll) file containing the controls. In fact, custom Web controls can be strongly named and registered with the global assembly cache (GAC) so they can be used without the need to move the .dll files with the application.

Exam Tip   Both Web user and custom Web controls can be dropped onto a Web page. Keep in mind that custom Web controls are compiled assemblies, and their use is like that of any other compiled assembly. The assembly might be stored in the bin, the GAC, and so on.

Lab: User Controls

In this lab, you'll create a user control to enable site visitors to rate content. Let's assume that visitors can offer five ratings, ranging from total dislike to total adoration. Let's also assume that the system must save the information in a relational database and associate the rating with the content unique identifier. Given these requirements, you can see that you can create a user control with a drop-down list. You also see, however, that you will need to reference the hosting page in the user control to obtain the content unique identifier.

▶ **Exercise 1: Create the User Control**

In this exercise, you will create the user control.

1. In Visual Studio, in your Web Site project, add a Web user control to your Web forms application by clicking Website | Add New Item. The Add New Item dialog box appears.
2. Select Web User Control from the list.
3. In the Name field, specify an appropriate name such as **VisitorRatingControl.ascx**. Ensure that the Place code in separate file check box is selected.
4. Click Add. The Add New Item dialog box disappears, and the user control is part of your Web forms application. Visual Studio 2005 opens the user control in Source View. If you did not select the Place code in separate file check box, Visual Studio 2005 inserts a <script> tag to contain your server-side code, such as event handlers.

5. Insert a *DropDownList* control and a *Button* control into your user control. Your source view should look like this:

```
<%@ Control Language="VB" AutoEventWireup="false"
CodeFile="VisitorRatingControl.ascx.vb" Inherits="VisitorRatingControl" %>
<asp:DropDownList runat="server" ID="ddlRating">
    <asp:ListItem Text="I hate it!" Value="-2" />
    <asp:ListItem Text="I don't like it much." Value="-1" />
    <asp:ListItem Text="I'm apathetic." Value="0" />
    <asp:ListItem Text="I like it." Value="1" />
    <asp:ListItem Text="I LOVE IT!" Value="2" />
</asp:DropDownList> <asp:Button runat="server" ID="btnSave" Text="Save"/>
```

6. Switch to Design View and double-click the Save button. This causes Visual Studio 2005 to open the code-behind file and create an event handler for the button's click event.

▶ **Exercise 2: Obtaining the Value of the Control**

In this exercise, you will modify the user control to accept user input and store it in a database.

1. Write code to find the content unique identifier control and obtain its content. Assume the control is a label control that is hidden and is given the identifier *hdnContentID*.

2. Write code to update the database.

```
' VB
    Protected Sub btnSave_Click(ByVal sender As Object, ByVal e As System.EventArgs)
Handles btnSave.Click

        Dim ctrl As Label

        ctrl = DirectCast(Me.Page.FindControl("hdnContentID"), Label)

        Dim sql As String = "INSERT INTO Rating (ContentID, RatingID) VALUES" & _
                            " (@ControlID, @RatingID)"

        Dim cmd As SqlClient.SqlCommand
        cmd.Parameters.Add(New SqlClient.SqlParameter("ContentID", ctrl.Text))
        cmd.Parameters.Add (new SqlClient.SqlParameter ("RatingID",
me.ddlRating.SelectedValue)

        ' Insert Code to Connect, Write Record, and Disconnect.

    End Sub

// C#
    protected void Page_Load(object sender, EventArgs e)
    {
    }
    protected void btnSave_Click(object sender, EventArgs e)
    {
        Label ctrl;
        ctrl = (label) Me.Page.FindControl("hdnContentID");
        string sql = "INSERT INTO Rating (ContentID, RatingID) VALUES" & _ ;
        " (@ControlID, @RatingID)";
```

```
          SqlClient.SqlCommand cmd;
          cmd.Parameters.Add(new SqlClient.SqlParameter("ContentID", ctrl.Text));
          cmd.Parameters.Add (new SqlClient.SqlParameter ("RatingID",
  me.ddlRating.SelectedValue);
          // Insert Code to Connect, Write Record, and Disconnect.
      }
```

▶ **Exercise 3: Apply the User Control to a Page**

In this exercise, you will add your newly created user control to a page.

1. Open a page in Design View.
2. Add a *Label* control and give it an ID value of *hdnContentID*.
3. Drag the user control from the Solution Explorer and drop it on the page.

The completed code examples, in both Visual Basic and C#, are available in the Code folder on the companion CD.

Lesson Summary

■ Custom Web controls and Web user controls each combine the capabilities of other controls into a single, reusable unit.

■ Custom Web controls are appropriate for building a single, reusable graphical component for distribution throughout your entire enterprise and are created as separate assemblies.

■ Web user controls are useful when building reusable components for a few projects. They are created as part of an existing Web site and are generally available for that Web site only.

Lesson Review

You can use the following questions to test your knowledge of the information in Lesson 1, "Web User Controls and Custom Web Controls." The questions are also available on the companion CD if you prefer to review them in electronic form.

NOTE Answers

Answers to these questions and explanations of why each answer choice is right or wrong are located in the "Answers" section at the end of the book.

---

1. You have been asked to create a control that will display the company stock symbol and opening and closing price of the prior day. This control will be included in every future Web application developed for this company. Which type of control should you choose?

   A. Web Part

   B. Custom Web control

   C. User control

   D. Server control

2. Which of the following statements, related to using a Web user control named *MyUser-Control* on a page, is NOT true?

   A. Register *MyUserControl* each time that the control will be used on the page, using a different *TagName* attribute for each instance.

   B. Register *MyUserControl* once with each page that will be using the control, regardless of the number of times *MyUserControl* will be used on the page.

   C. Copy the source code of the *MyUserControl* into the Web project.

   D. Place *MyUserControl* on the page at the desired location.

3. Which of the following statements is NOT true in describing the differences between Web user controls and Web custom controls?

   A. The source code for user controls is included in the project but not for custom Web controls.

   B. Both custom Web controls and user controls can use drag and drop in the Visual Studio design view.

   C. Custom Web controls cannot be extended.

   D. Custom Web controls may be stored in the GAC.

Lesson 2: Choosing Appropriate Controls

The ASP.NET server controls include a wide range of features. Given the robustness of the ASP.NET server controls, you might wonder why HTML controls exist and when to use them. You might also wonder how to choose appropriate controls for a given situation. In this lesson, you'll learn some techniques for choosing appropriate controls and examine some situations in which you might choose HTML controls over ASP.NET server controls. This lesson will also discuss some of the new controls available in ASP.NET 2.0.

After this lesson, you will be able to:

- Understand how to analyze the needs of your application to choose appropriate controls effectively.
- Evaluate the capabilities of existing controls to determine whether they are an appropriate solution to a particular development problem.
- Understand the capabilities of some of the new data-bound controls in ASP.NET 2.0, including *GridView*, *DetailsView*, *FormView*, and *MultiView*.

Estimated lesson time: 90 minutes

Analyzing the Data

Most Web forms applications deal with data, usually in relatively large amounts. As such, data analysis should be your first step in choosing appropriate controls. Often, developers become comfortable with the capabilities of one or two controls and like to reuse them in every situation. Although this might be appropriate 80 percent of the time, there are situations in which other controls would be more appropriate. Before jumping to a control choice, consider the following points about your data.

- **What data is displayed?** Many situations require you to show several fields with relatively small amounts of information. However, some situations require you to show few fields, each containing more information. When evaluating controls in this context, consider the level of effort associated with customizing the controls' display properties.

- **How much data is available?** Determine whether you will display all of the data requested at one time or paginate the data. Furthermore, when dealing with larger amounts of data, users might need supplemental features to help them locate specific data items. For example, you might need to provide sorting and filtering capabilities to enhance the usability of the data page. When evaluating controls in this context, consider the capabilities of the controls to paginate, filter, and sort the data.

- **How often will the data be requested?** Although the request could entail a lot of data, it might be requested infrequently. The contrary is true as well. A different request might entail little data but occur often. When evaluating controls in this context, consider the ability of the controls to pull data from either a data source or a cache or both.

■ **What is the data source?** Data sources vary widely in contemporary Web forms applications. XML files, relational databases, and directory servers can all provide data for a single application. Some controls work more easily than others with non-relational data. When evaluating controls in this context, consider the level of effort required to transform the data, if necessary, into a control-friendly format.

Evaluating the Capabilities of Existing Controls

Before searching for a software solution to a problem, you should always check whether someone else has solved that problem already. Now that you've analyzed your data needs, you can evaluate the existing data controls to determine whether any of them satisfies your needs.

Typically, even the most robust controls will require customization. Most controls will require some extension to satisfy your needs fully. While evaluating controls, look for controls that satisfy *most* of your needs. In this case, you have a base of functionality that you can extend.

Exam Tip When choosing a control, be certain that you know all of the requirements, including items such as whether the control will be reused, whether it can be extended, and whether the functionality needs to be or can be restricted. Try first to choose the simplest solution that requires the least amount of enhancement.

Using New Data-Bound Controls

Earlier versions of ASP.NET revolutionized data display through data-bound controls such as the *DataGrid*. Although these controls are still available, ASP.NET 2.0 takes data display to the next level. In this section, you will learn about the controls available for data display and when to use them.

GridView Control

The *GridView* control is the new flagship control of ASP.NET for displaying data in a tabular format. If you are familiar with the *DataGrid* control, you will be pleased to know that the *GridView* control offers several improvements.

First, the *GridView* control provides improved design-time capabilities. Tasks requiring coding with the *DataGrid*, such as adding, sorting and paging, are automated with the *GridView*, and require no coding. Furthermore, *GridView* controls offer improved data binding. Whereas the *DataGrid* requires you to write code for insert, update, and delete operations, the *GridView* control eliminates the need. This allows you to provide basic create, retrieve, update, and delete (CRUD) features with virtually no coding.

Several other *GridView* features also improve upon the functionality of the *DataGrid*. The *GridView* offers an expanded event model that gives more granular control over *GridView* data-binding and rendering operations. The *GridView* also exposes more column types than the *DataGrid*. You can use the additional column types to provide a more robust user experience.

The *GridView* is clearly useful for displaying information in a tabular format and for providing capabilities to filter, sort, and paginate the data. Another advancement that the *GridView* offers is the ability to bind to multiple sources of data. For example, you can bind the *GridView* to an XML file for display. As with the *DataGrid*, you can also bind the *GridView* to object data sources such as collections and arrays. Consider using the *GridView* any time you need to display many records, many columns, or both.

DetailsView Control

Whereas the *GridView* control potentially displays many records at once, the new *DetailsView* control displays one record at a time. Like other data-bound controls, the *DetailsView* control can be associated with a data source. By default, the *DetailsView* control displays each field in its own row, but the control provides robust customization options. The *DetailsView* control is an excellent option for rendering a master-detail view of data.

FormView Control

The new *FormView* control is very similar to the *DetailsView* control in that it is used to display a single record. The difference, however, is that the *FormView* control does not provide a default layout for the data. Instead, the *FormView* control requires you to create templates for rendering the data. The *FormView* control is useful in situations in which you need to display an individual record, yet a field-per-row layout is insufficient.

MultiView and *View* Controls

The *MultiView* control acts as a container for one or more *View* controls. In turn, you use *View* controls to contain other controls, literal content, and other Web page elements. The *MultiView* control enables you to provide multiple views of related yet different elements quickly.

Suppose, for example, that you need to provide the user with a wizard-style interface for completing a registration. The *MultiView* control, combined with other view controls showing the individual registration elements, is very useful in this scenario.

The new ASP.NET 2.0 data controls provide robust features, further improving the speed and efficiency with which your Web applications can be built.

Exam Tip   Be sure you understand the basic features of each new control and when each is applicable in your Web application.

Quick Check

- Name the four new controls in the .NET Framework 2.0 for displaying bound data. Identify whether the control displays information for multiple or single records.

Quick Check Answer

- *GridView*—Multiple records
- *DetailsView*—Single record
- *FormView*—Single record
- *MultiView*—Single record

Selecting or Creating Controls   After evaluating the capabilities of the intrinsic controls, you select an appropriate control.

Although the intrinsic ASP.NET controls are very robust, you might need some feature that simply isn't provided out of the box. Typically, however, you don't need to create a control from scratch. In fact, many custom controls are made from combining two or more intrinsic controls into a single control. This technique works equally well for both user controls and custom Web controls.

MORE INFO   Custom Web server controls

Both self-authored and commercial off-the-shelf controls are custom Web server controls. Learn more about custom Web server controls on the Microsoft Web site at *http://msdn2.microsoft.com /en-us/library/ms178357(vs.80).aspx*.

MORE INFO   Web server controls

The MSDN Library provides information about the ASP.NET Web server controls and can help you choose the best control based on the requirements. Learn more about Web server controls on the Microsoft Web site at *http://msdn.microsoft.com/library/default.asp?url=/library/en-us/cpgenref/html /cpconaspsyntaxforwebcontrols.asp*.

Globalization, Multiple Browsers, and Accessibility

The world is growing ever smaller as more and more people access the Internet with high-bandwidth connections. If your Web forms application is available on the Internet, there is literally no way to know who might access it or from where. In some cases, you might not be concerned with users outside of a target group. However, in most cases, you need to be aware that users from many potential cultures are visiting your site. Here are some guidelines to consider when planning for an unknown base of users.

■ **Avoid flashiness**   Many users have accessibility needs related to computer use. For example, users who are visually impaired often use screen readers to inform them of the content of Web pages. Users who are hard of hearing might not have the ability to hear audio content at all. Finally, it is estimated that 30 percent of the male population is color blind. Given this information, it is important that you provide a sound site layout and use *Alt* attributes for graphics, that you avoid unnecessary flashiness on your site, and that you use colors subtly. Never rely solely on one means of providing information. For example, rather than relying solely on colors to make items stand out, use a combination of colors and font weight; provide appropriate cues; and remove inappropriate cues.

■ **Multiple cultures**   People from many different cultures are consuming information in many different ways, and they all might have access to your site. Some cultures read right to left whereas others read left to right. Page translators can change the amount of space occupied by your data, thereby altering the layout of your pages. Furthermore, you must understand the user interface (UI) Culture settings, which affect the language used, and the Culture settings related to dates, money, and so on.

MORE INFO   **Encoding and localization**

Learn more about encoding and localization on the Microsoft Web site at *http://msdn2.microsoft.com/en-us/library/h6270d0z.aspx*.

Exam Tip   Know when to use *CurrentCulture* versus *CurrentUICulture*. *CurrentCulture* is used for business logic such as date formatting and string formatting. *CurrentUICulture* is used for setting UI differences such as string values of labels.

■ **Varying browsers**   Many new features in Web application development take advantage of the capabilities of contemporary browsers. Not all users, however, have the latest technology on their desktops. Additionally, compared to PC browsers, browsers in mobile devices have limited capability. You need to decide early in the development process whether and how your Web forms application will support earlier browsers and mobile browsers.

MORE INFO   **Windows Mobile Developer Center**

Do not expect to see much on mobile development on this exam. However, if you would like to explore further, MSDN has a center for mobile development at *http://msdn.microsoft.com/mobility/*.

■ **Low-bandwidth connections**   Many people are still using dial-up connections. This is not restricted to older systems. Many users are surfing the Web with their mobile phones and portable data assistants. Clearly, how you manage data display drives your ability to serve information to users with low-bandwidth connections.

Lesson Summary

- When choosing a control, be sure that you have all the requirements.
- Analyze the data before selecting a control. Consider the volume and type of data as well as the frequency of access.
- If possible, start with an existing control and extend or restrict the control as needed.
- Localization is the process of designing a system for use in multiple cultures. The *CurrentUICulture* control is used to provide multi-language features such as string values. The *CurrentCulture* property provides executable features such as string comparison and sorting.

Lesson Review

You can use the following questions to test your knowledge of the information in Lesson 2, "Choosing Appropriate Controls." The questions are also available on the companion CD if you prefer to review them in electronic form.

NOTE   Answers

Answers to these questions and explanations of why each answer choice is right or wrong are located in the "Answers" section at the end of the book.

---

1. You have been asked to choose a control to display a subset of invoices. Which of the following considerations should you NOT include in choosing the control?
   A. What is the type of the data source?
   B. How often will the data be requested?
   C. Who will be requesting the data?
   D. How much data is available?

2. What types of controls are available to you for ASP.NET 2.0 Web pages? (Choose all that apply.)
   A. Intrinsic Web server controls
   B. Custom Web controls
   C. HTML server controls
   D. User controls

3.   You are writing an e-commerce Web-based application that will be used world-wide. A requirement states that the currency of the user must be supported. Which of the following addresses this requirement?

   A.   Globalization

   B.   Localization

   C.   *CurrentCulture*

   D.   *CurrentUICulture*

4.   You are writing an e-commerce Web-based application with a requirement that multiple browsers, including mobile device browsers, must be supported. Which of the following layout elements is most appropriate for addressing this requirement?

   A.   *Table*

   B.   *GridView*

   C.   *DataGrid*

   D.   *MultiView*

5.   You are designing a Web page that will display a single customer record. The customer record contains multiple addresses. A requirement states that each address must display the city, state, and ZIP code on a single line. Which control will meet this requirement?

   A.   *DataGrid*

   B.   *GridView*

   C.   *FormView*

   D.   *DetailsView*

Chapter Review

To further practice and reinforce the skills you learned in this chapter, you can complete the following tasks:

- Review the chapter summary.
- Review the list of key terms introduced in this chapter.
- Complete the case scenarios. These scenarios set up real-world situations involving the topics of this chapter and ask you to create a solution.
- Complete the suggested practices.
- Take a practice test.

Chapter Summary

- You can create user controls to provide reusable functionality within an application. Custom Web controls enable you to create reusable components for the entire enterprise.
- Consider various aspects of the user-based requirements when designing your layout. Account for globalization, different cultures, accessibility, and user demographics.
- When choosing controls, consider the data to be displayed, the amount of data available, request frequency, and data source.
- When deciding which controls to use for various situations, remember the *GridView*, *DetailsView*, *FormView*, and *MultiView* controls as potentially offering various views on the same data source.

Key Terms

Do you know what these key terms mean? You can check your answers by looking up the terms in the glossary at the end of the book.

- custom Web server control
- user control

Case Scenarios

In the following case scenarios, you will apply what you've learned about choosing appropriate controls for given requirements. You can find answers to these questions in the "Answers" section at the end of this book.

Case Scenario 1: Choosing an Appropriate Control

You have been asked to create a Web application for your corporate intranet. Your application provides portal capabilities so that every page in your application shows summary information of user work tasks by status. The summary display is shown in a footer and provides links so that users can quickly access their task lists and update tasks as necessary.

1. How can you create the summary information in the footer of each page?
2. When users click a link in the summary information portion of the page footer, they are redirected to a page showing a listing of their tasks. You want them to have access to multiple views based on status. Which intrinsic control can you use to accomplish this?
3. Users must provide detailed information when updating tasks. Which controls provide capabilities for users to update individual tasks?

Case Scenario 2: Expanding Your E-Commerce Site

You have been asked to ensure that the company's new e-commerce application is available to users in Europe, Asia, Africa, and the United States.

1. What intrinsic control helps you provide localized text for your application?
2. How will you manage localized settings for dates and currency?

Suggested Practices

To help you successfully master the exam objectives presented in this chapter, complete the following tasks.

Choose an Appropriate Control Based on Design Specifications

Complete these tasks to learn about using different controls and how they are appropriate for different situations. These tasks also help you learn how to handle multiple browsers.

- **Practice 1**   Create a Web page that uses *GridView* and *DataGrid* controls to learn differences between them.
- **Practice 2**   Write a page that changes its output based on browser type.

Take a Practice Test

The practice tests on this book's companion CD offer many options. For example, you can test yourself on just one exam objective, or you can test yourself on all the 70-547 certification exam content. You can set up the test so that it closely simulates the experience of taking a certification exam, or you can set it up in study mode so that you can look at the correct answers and explanations after you answer each question.

MORE INFO   Practice tests

For details about all the practice test options available, see the "How to Use the Practice Tests" section in this book's Introduction.

Chapter 6
Data Validation

As the old adage goes, bad data is worse than no data. ASP.NET 2.0 offers a wide variety of ways to capture user input. This translates to many opportunities for users to provide bad data. In this chapter, you will learn about the support that ASP.NET provides to you for performing data validation. You will also learn about appropriate and inappropriate ways to promote good data (and, thereby, avoid bad data) by communicating with users. This chapter closes with a lab that demonstrates appropriate guidance combined with data validation techniques.

Exam objectives in this chapter:

- Choose an appropriate data validation method at the user interface (UI) layer.
  - ❑ Choose a validation method based on the data type provided.
  - ❑ Decide how to report the feedback. Considerations include callbacks, exceptions, and writing to an event log.
  - ❑ Identify the source of invalid data.
  - ❑ Identify the cause of an invalid entry.
  - ❑ Evaluate whether invalid data can be prevented.
  - ❑ Evaluate whether an exception must be thrown.
  - ❑ Evaluate whether an exception must be logged.
  - ❑ Evaluate whether visual feedback, such as a message box or color, is required.
- Choose appropriate user assistance and application status feedback techniques.
  - ❑ Choose an appropriate application status feedback technique based on available control types.
  - ❑ Design a user assistance mechanism.
  - ❑ Choose an appropriate application status feedback technique to support accessibility.
  - ❑ Design an application status feedback mechanism.

Lessons in this chapter:

Before You Begin

To complete the lessons in this chapter, you should be familiar with Microsoft Visual Basic or C# and be comfortable with the following task:

■ Creating an ASP.NET Web page in Microsoft Visual Studio 2005

Real World

Brian C. Lanham

This story is true. I was an intern at my first software development job. Fortunately, as an intern who was still in college, I knew it all. To prove it, I quickly wrote a command-line application in C. The purpose of this utility was to perform some straightforward batch operation based on command-line parameters. Being the all-knowing intern I was, I quickly tore through this utility application and produced something I was very proud of.

Upon completion, the application was ready for testing—not that it needed it. Such a simple utility (written by the infallible) was a waste of time and effort for a full-time tester. Besides, what were they going to test? Well, I learned exactly what they were going to test about 30 seconds after I submitted it for testing. *30 seconds!* I couldn't believe it. Surely the tester was calling to tell me what a great job I had done.

As it turns out, the application I wrote worked perfectly—if the command-line parameters were exactly what were expected. I had tested functionality only. I hadn't bothered to test for, or program for, situations in which the input is wrong. That one lesson occurred over ten years ago, yet it still is quite clear in my mind. I learned the importance of building validation into the input portion of my software.

Lesson 1: Validating Data

Often, bad data doesn't affect your organization until someone tries to report against it or some business intelligence project uncovers the presence of inconsistencies. If bad data is discovered in these circumstances, correcting it is an overwhelming (read "expensive"), if not impossible, task. There could be millions of records with inconsistent and erroneous information. All these instances will skew your reports and make your business intelligence efforts more ambiguous.

So that you can avoid *correcting* bad data, you must validate data at the time of entry and, thereby, *prevent* bad data from getting into your systems. This lesson is about validating data for Web applications. Web browsers do not always provide the most robust environment, and sometimes users (not to mention input from malcontents such as hackers) can submit ambiguous, erroneous, or outright strange information. Luckily for us, ASP.NET 2.0 provides some excellent support for performing data *validation*. In this lesson, you will learn about choosing an appropriate data validation technique and then how to implement that technique using the intrinsic ASP.NET 2.0 data validation controls.

> **After this lesson, you will be able to:**
> - Effectively use the intrinsic ASP.NET validation controls.
> - Choose an appropriate validation technique for your ASP.NET application.
> - Implement an exception-handling strategy for your ASP.NET application.
>
> **Estimated lesson time: 45 minutes**

Choosing an Appropriate Data Validation Technique

In a multi-tier architecture, the input source is not restricted to the UI and presentation layers. Data can come from many different sources such as other internal systems, other external systems, and other components of the same system. In this situation, it is not sufficient to rely solely on the presentation layer for validation. Figure 6-1 shows a typical multi-tier architecture.

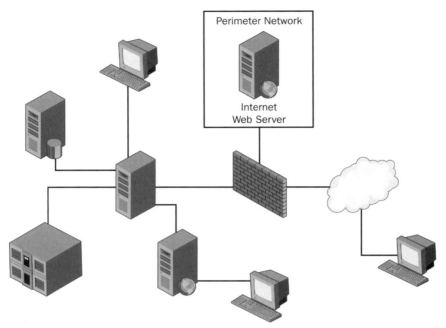

Figure 6-1   A typical multi-tier architecture

On the other hand, if your application receives its input exclusively from the UI, then you can rely solely on the UI to validate the input data. In this lesson, you will be concerned with validating data provided via a Web-based UI. Therefore, you will focus on validating data submitted through a Web browser to a Web application.

Using ASP.NET 2.0 Validation Controls

It should be no surprise that ASP.NET provides a solid base of validation controls. You can use these flexible controls out of the box or build on them through inheritance to create your own validation controls. In this section, you will learn about the available controls and appropriate times to use them.

All ASP.NET validation controls have some common properties with which you should be familiar. The following listing describes the common properties among validation controls.

- **_ControlToValidate_**   This property is used to indicate which control the validation control is to validate.

■ **Display** This property provides three possible values. Setting the property to None pre-vents the control from being displayed inline. Use this setting in conjunction with the *ValidationSummary* control, discussed later. The Static setting renders the validation con-trol inline with other controls. This means that blank space is occupied by the control when it is not showing a message. Use the Dynamic setting when you want to avoid the control occupying blank space.

■ **EnableClientScript** Not every browser supports JavaScript, and even browsers support-ing it might have it disabled. However, for those browsers that support JavaScript, the validation controls can perform client-side validation as well as server-side validation. Client-side validation does not require a postback for validation to occur, resulting in a richer user experience. Note that client-side validation should be used *only* to provide a richer user experience and not as a replacement for server-side validation.

■ **Enabled** This property determines whether the validation control actually performs validation.

■ **ErrorMessage** This property is generally associated with the *ValidationSummary* control.

■ **ForeColor** Use this property to set the color of the inline error message when validation fails.

NOTE **Do not rely solely on colors and fonts to report errors**

It is a common mistake among new Web developers to rely exclusively on attributes such as color to draw attention to errors. However, there are several good reasons for providing mul-tiple visual aids to indicate errors. Changing the color or the font size will likely not reach your entire audience. Much of the population is colorblind. There are also users who are visually impaired and who use screen readers. A best practice is to use additional cues to indicate problems, so you are using several attributes in combination. For example, placing an asterisk or an exclamation point next to a field that is experiencing a data validation issue draws attention to that field. This is true for users who are visually impaired as well because screen readers will identify those fields as the screen is read.

■ **IsValid** This property is used to evaluate whether validation fails.

■ **SetFocusOnError** Setting this property to True causes the focus to be set to the control identified in the *ControlToValidate* property if validation fails.

■ **Text** The *Enabled* property determines whether the validation control actually per-forms validation. The *Text* property is generally associated with the inline message—the message displayed at the location of the validation control.

■ **ValidationGroup** Validation groups are new to .NET 2.0. This property is used to asso-ciate the current validation control with a specific validation group. Validation groups are discussed in more detail later in this chapter.

Now that you have been introduced to the common attributes of validation controls, you can dig deeper into specific facets of each validation control. The next section provides detailed information about each type of validation control. Note that you can use validation controls in combination. For example, you can use *RequiredFieldValidator* and *RegularExpressionValidator* controls on the *TextBox* control for capturing an e-mail address. Keep this in mind as you learn about each control.

Exam Tip   The ASP.NET validation controls perform validation to both the client side and the server side (provided the browser supports client-side JavaScript, and it is enabled). This is the only type of ASP.NET server control that generates client-side script.

***RequiredFieldValidator* Control**   The *RequiredFieldValidator* control is used to ensure that fields that must be populated with data are, indeed, populated with data. This control can be used with virtually any data entry controls, such as *TextBox*, *DropDownList*, and *CheckBox*. The *RequiredFieldValidator* control works by comparing the selected value of the control specified in the *ControlToValidate* property against an initial value that you specify. If you do not specify an initial value, an empty string is assumed.

This initial value against which comparisons are made is established using the *InitialValue* property. The default value is an empty string. However, you can set it to any value you like. Suppose, for example, you want to provide some assistance to users specifying dates by pre-filling the date field with MM/DD/YYYY. In this situation, you can set the *InitialValue* property of the associated *RequiredFieldValidator* control. This means that the user is still required to specify a value and cannot rely on the initial default value that you provide for guidance.

***RangeValidator* Control**   Situations in which a value must fall within a certain range, rather than merely being specified, call for the *RangeValidator* control. This control allows you to ensure that a specified value is within acceptable limits, using a combination of properties including *MaximumValue* and *MinimumValue*. If either of these properties is blank, the control assumes no maximum or minimum (depending on which is blank).

The *RangeValidator* control allows you to validate the ranges of various data types. You are not restricted to numeric types. In fact, the *RangeValidator* control supports range validation of any data type described by the *ValidationDataType* enumeration. These include *Currency*, *Date*, *Double*, *Integer*, and *String*.

Here is a final note regarding this control. If the value of the control identified by the *Control-ToValidate* property is blank, that control passes range validation. Therefore, if you want to validate value ranges *and* ensure that a value is provided, you need to use both the *RangeValidator* and *RequiredFieldValidator* controls.

RegularExpressionValidator Control   *Regular expressions* are an extremely powerful means of quickly parsing text. Regular expressions use an extensive pattern-matching notation to provide searching, replacing, and other text operations quickly and efficiently. The pattern-matching capabilities of regular expressions are of particular interest when using the *RegularExpressionValidator* control.

MORE INFO   Regular expressions

Regular expressions are a discipline all by themselves. Even a rudimentary discussion of regular expressions is beyond the scope of this chapter. However, if you are interested in learning more about regular expressions, the Internet is replete with reference material. For example, MSDN is an excellent resource for learning about regular expressions in the context of the .NET Framework. You can get started at *http://msdn.microsoft.com/library/default.asp?url=/library/en-us /cpguide/html/cpconregularexpressionsaslanguage.asp*.

Regular-expression validation is generally used to ensure that specified data matches a predetermined pattern. For example, all e-mail addresses follow a common pattern. The regular expression used for comparison is specified with the *ValidationExpression* property. This property can contain any valid regular expression. Relying once again on the example of validating an e-mail address, you can use the following regular expression.

```
\w+([-+.]\w+)*@\w+([-.]\w+)*\.\w+([-.]\w+)*
```

It is pretty obvious that the regular expression syntax is quite cryptic. Fortunately, there are libraries of regular expressions available. In fact, the *RegularExpressionValidator* control has some predefined regular expressions (including e-mail address). You can always, of course, write your own regular expressions for validation. Suppose, for example, you have a custom purchase order number format. You can use a regular expression to validate data in the purchase order number field against the pattern you define.

Do not be turned off by the cryptic nature of regular-expression syntax. It is a powerful and extremely useful validation control, and you might find yourself using it in many situations.

MORE INFO   Regular-expression library

You do not need to write your own regular expressions. Many libraries exist, such as RegExLib, at *http://regexlib.com*.

CompareValidator Control   Sometimes you need to compare the value in one field to that of another field instead of to some preset value, range, or pattern. In these situations, you can use the *CompareValidator* control. Like other validation controls, this control uses a *ControlToValidate* property. In addition, it adds a *ControlToCompare* property. This property gives you the ability to specify another control against which the value of the control in the *ControlToValidate* property is compared.

If you want to compare the control's value against a constant value, you can use the *ValueTo-Compare* property instead of the *ControlToCompare* property. If you set both properties, the *ControlToCompare* property takes precedence over the *ValueToCompare* property.

The default comparison operator for the *CompareValidator* control is equality. However, this is programmable through the *Operator* property. Valid operators are defined by the *Validation-CompareOperator* enumeration and include *Equal*, *NotEqual*, *GreaterThan*, *GreaterThanEqual*, *LessThan*, *LessThanEqual*, and *DataTypeCheck*. The *DataTypeCheck* operator is the only unary operator among them. It is used to determine whether the data in the control identified by the *ControlToValidate* property is of a certain type. In fact, if you set the *ControlToCompare* and *ValueToCompare* properties, they are ignored if the operator type is set to *DataTypeCheck*. The *DataTypeCheck* operator uses the value of the *Type* property as a base for determining the acceptable data type. The *Type* property is set based on the *ValidationDataType* enumeration as described in the *RangeValidator* control previously mentioned.

***CustomValidator* Control**   The controls described up to this point generally focus on validating one or two fields based on specific, bounded parameters. Typical requirements, however, usually fall outside the capabilities of the intrinsic controls. In anticipation of this, the creators of ASP.NET made the *CustomValidator* control. The *CustomValidator* control provides you with an opportunity to create custom validation logic for situations requiring complex business rules validation.

Like other validation controls, the *CustomValidator* control exposes common properties such as *ControlToValidate*, *Display*, *ErrorMessage*, *Text*, and *ValidationGroup*. Also like other validation controls, the *CustomValidator* control supports both server-side and client-side validation. To associate custom server logic with the control, you must override the *ServerValidate* event. One of the parameters of the event handler for this event is an object of type *ServerValidate-EventArgs*. Based on the results of the custom validation logic, you can set the *IsValid* property of the *ServerValidateEventArgs* object. For client-side validation, you must create a JavaScript function and reference that function using the *ClientValidationFunction* property of the *Custom-Validator* control.

Using the *ValidationSummary* Control and the *ValidationGroup* Control

In addition to identifying specific fields with data entry problems, it is often useful to provide users with a summary of validation problems on a form. You can use the *ValidationSummary* control to provide that summary information to users. The *ValidationSummary* control is used to display the *ErrorMessage* property values from validation controls on the page when controls being validated are invalid.

Using the *ValidationSummary* control can improve usability by minimizing distracting and confusing text and by drawing the user's attention to a single location. Displaying specific data validation problems next to each field can consume a lot of screen real estate. In addition, it can cause shifts in screen layout, which leads to confusion. Using a *ValidationSummary* control concentrates more verbose information in a single location. More succinct and direct guidance can be associated with individual fields. Good examples of this include placing asterisks or exclamation points next to fields with validation problems.

Sometimes a single Web page might consist of more than one "logical" form. For example, an e-commerce site's checkout process can be a single page, but each step in the process provides information used in future steps. In these situations, it is important to perform validation but only on one subset of the page's controls at a time. The new *ValidationGroup* property in ASP.NET 2.0 offers a solution for these situations. The *ValidationGroup* property is used to associate related validation controls.

MORE INFO   Validation groups

Explore more information about validation groups, including code samples and using validation groups with the *GridView* and *DetailsView* controls, at *http://msdn2.microsoft.com/en-us/library /ms178312.aspx*.

Validation control grouping has many advantages. First, it improves performance by instructing ASP.NET to perform validation on controls associated with a particular group. To accomplish this, ASP.NET 2.0 adds a *ValidationGroup* property to other controls that can cause postbacks such as buttons. This means that you can associate a Save button with a particular validation group. The *Page* class's *Validate* method is overloaded to accept a validation group name as an input parameter. When all of this is connected, the button instructs the page to perform server-side validation on only those controls in the specified group.

Another advantage of validation control is that it affords you the ability to restrict the information that is presented in a *ValidationSummary* control. Clearing the *ValidationGroup* property of the *ValidationSummary* control effectively associates the summary control with validation controls that also have a non-specified *ValidationGroup* property. Alternatively, specifying a value for the *ValidationGroup* property associates the *ValidationSummary* control with validation controls in the same group.

Exam Tip   The *ValidationSummary.ValidationGroup* property is new in the .NET Framework 2.0. This property provides a means of validating groups (or categories) of input controls.

> **Quick Check**
>
> ■ Name and briefly describe the five ASP.NET validation controls.
>
> **Quick Check Answer**
>
> ■ **CompareValidator**   Compares a user value against a constant, another control, or a specific datatype.
> ■ **CustomValidator**   Verifies a user entry against custom code written by a developer. (Values can be derived at run time.)
> ■ **RangeValidator**   Verifies that a user entry is between an upper and a lower bound, using numbers, alphabetic characters, and dates.
> ■ **RegularExpressionValidator**   Verifies that a user entry matches a pattern defined by a regular expression such as e-mail address or telephone number.
> ■ **RequiredFieldValidator**   Verifies that a user enters a value.

Lesson Summary

■ Each ASP.NET validation control uses a set of common properties, including *ControlTo-Validate*, *Display*, *EnableClientScript*, *Enabled*, *ErrorMessage*, *ForeColor*, *IsValid*, *SetFocus-OnError*, *Text*, and *ValidationGroup*.

■ Validation controls can perform client-side validation if the browser supports and enables JavaScript. This provides a richer user experience because the page does not need to post back to the server to perform validation. However, do not rely solely on client-side validation. Use client-side validation *only* for improving the user experience.

■ ASP.NET offers the following intrinsic validation controls: *RequiredFieldValidator*, *RangeValidator*, *RegularExpressionValidator*, *CompareValidator*, *CustomValidator*, and *ValidationSummary*.

■ The *ValidationGroup* property allows you to associate logically related controls on complex forms.

Lesson Review

You can use the following questions to test your knowledge of the information in Lesson 1, "Validating Data." The questions are also available on the companion CD if you prefer to review them in electronic form.

NOTE Answers

Answers to these questions and explanations of why each answer choice is right or wrong are located in the "Answers" section at the end of the book.

---

1. You are designing a Web application for a public library. One of the Web pages provides a visitor with the ability to request that a book that is currently in stock be placed on hold. The required input includes the visitor's library card number. For each book desired, the author and ISBN are required. Research of the ISBN numbering system reveals that the number consists of 10 digits and is divided into four parts separated by hyphens or spaces. The parts are group identifier, publisher prefix, title identifier, and check digit. The number of digits in each of the first three parts of the ISBN varies. The check digit is always a single digit. The group identifier represents a country, area, or language region. The U.S. region is identified by multiple ranges of numbers. It is possible that additional number ranges will be added for the U.S. region in the future. All books located at this library will be from the U.S. region. Which ASP.NET validation controls should you use to meet the requirements of the ISBN number? (Choose all that apply.)

   A. *RequiredFieldValidator*

   B. *RangeValidator*

   C. *CompareValidator*

   D. *CustomValidator*

2. You are designing a Web application for a public library. One of the Web pages provides a visitor with the ability to request that a book that is currently in stock be placed on hold. The required input includes the visitor's library card number. The library card number will be validated against information maintained in a Microsoft SQL Server database. Which of the following ASP.NET validation controls could be used to meet the validation requirements of the library card number?

   A. *RequiredFieldValidator*

   B. *RangeValidator*

   C. *RegularExpressionValidator*

   D. *CompareValidator*

3. You are designing a Web application that contains many controls that accept user input. Because the application will be used by thousands of people, you must consider scalability in providing user feedback to invalid data entered. Which of the following techniques provides the best performance?

   A. Throw an exception.

   B. Display an error message to the user.

   C. Log the error to an event log.

   D. Raise an event.

Lesson 2: Providing User Assistance

It is usually not sufficient to simply validate data entry. You must also guide users so that they can correct mistakes quickly and avoid data entry errors in the future. In this lesson, you will learn about appropriate and effective means of assisting users in correcting data validation issues and, hopefully, preventing them as well.

> **After this lesson, you will be able to:**
> - Provide appropriate and effective assistance mechanisms that allow users to iden-tify and correct validation issues quickly and easily.
> - Provide guidance to users in an effort to minimize the occurrences of validation issues.
>
> **Estimated lesson time: 90 minutes**

Designing and Implementing a User Assistance Mechanism

There are several good techniques for assisting users in correct data entry. In this section, you will review some of these techniques. You will also review appropriate situations for using each technique as well as some pitfalls of using them.

Using the *Wizard* Control

ASP.NET 2.0 offers a new control called the *Wizard* control. The *Wizard* control can be useful in scenarios when you need to collect relatively large amounts of complex information from users before proceeding. In this type of situation, the *Wizard* control can provide users with guidance among related steps in a multi-step information-gathering process.

The *Wizard* control uses the concept of steps to control operations. Steps are generally one of three types: beginning, intermediate, or completion steps. You can add other controls to each step as needed to collect input. This includes custom user controls and third-party Web server controls. In this sense, the *Wizard* control can give users a multi-page feel.

Although the *Wizard* control typically is used for linear navigation, it does allow for jumping to remote steps at will. Nonlinear navigation in the *Wizard* control is accomplished by using the sidebar. Figures 6-2 through 6-5 show a rudimentary order-processing workflow implemented with a *Wizard* control. Notice in the figures how the sidebar can be used to navigate directly to a step and how it remains synchronized with the current step.

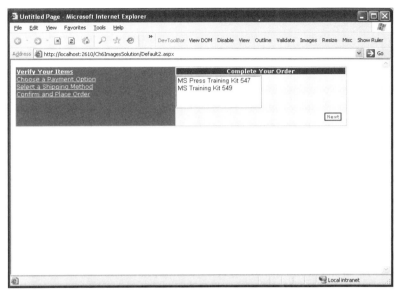

Figure 6-2   *Wizard* control – step 1

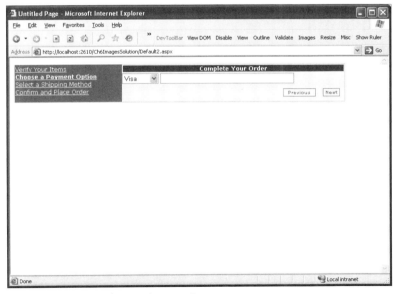

Figure 6-3   *Wizard* control – step 2

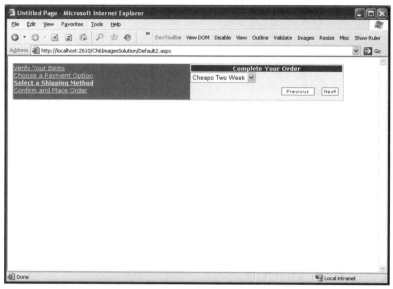

Figure 6-4   *Wizard* control – step 3

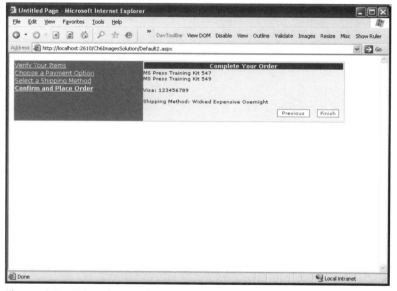

Figure 6-5   *Wizard* control – step 4

Like other controls, the *Wizard* control offers additional customization capabilities. One of the more useful features is the ability to use templates in *Wizard* control steps. The *Wizard* control recognizes templates for the starting step, the finishing step, the completed step, and the steps in between (acknowledged as a single template). Like other controls, you can customize specific views of the *Wizard* control as the user progresses through various steps.

Navigation can be complicated by the need for data validation. Allowing users to jump around in a *Wizard* control might cause problems if you are counting on a more serial flow through the steps. Like other ASP.NET controls, the *Wizard* control exposes a robust event model, providing you with opportunities for handling various navigation actions. By default, the *Wizard* control recognizes click events for Next and Previous buttons as well as sidebar buttons. The *Wizard* control also fires events when the Finish and Cancel buttons are clicked. The Finish button appears in the last step.

The click event handlers provide an object of type *WizardNavigationEventArgs*. This type exposes useful information such as the current and next steps' indexes. It also exposes a property, *DisplayCancelButton*, which allows you to invoke the *DisplayCancelButton* event by setting the property to *True*. Using the event argument information, you have complete programmatic control over the operation of the *Wizard* control.

Suppose your *Wizard* control has a step that relies on information in another step. As such, you need to prevent users from navigating to the dependent step until the required information is available. You can accomplish this by handling the *SideBarButtonClick* event for the *Wizard* control. The following code samples show the event handler processing to redirect the user to the appropriate step in the *Wizard* control.

```vb
' VB
    Protected Sub Wizard1_SideBarButtonClick _
    (ByVal sender As Object, ByVal e As _
    System.Web.UI.WebControls.WizardNavigationEventArgs) _
 Handles Wizard1.SideBarButtonClick
        Dim ddl As DropDownList

        ddl = DirectCast(Me.Wizard1.FindControl("ddlPayType"), DropDownList)

        If ddl.SelectedIndex <= 0I Then
            Me.Wizard1.ActiveStepIndex = 1I
        End If


    End Sub
```

```csharp
// C#
    protected void Wizard1_SideBarButtonClick(object sender, WizardNavigationEventArgs e)
    {
        DropDownList ddl;
```

```
    ddl = (DropDownList)Wizard1.FindControl ("ddlPayType")

    if (ddl.SelectedIndex <= 0)
        Wizard1.ActiveStepIndex= 1;

}
```

This section provided you with an introduction to the *Wizard* control. This control can be useful when dealing with relatively complex data collection scenarios. It is fairly simple to use, yet provides the robust feature set to which you are accustomed in ASP.NET 2.0. However, the *Wizard* control does not address all situations. Instead, it should be used in conjunction with other user assistance mechanisms. The next sections outline some additional user assistance techniques.

Quick Check

- What components make up the ASP.NET *Wizard* control?

Quick Check Answer

- *Navigation*   Displays required buttons for a particular step
- *Header area*   Displays custom information for a particular step
- *Sidebar area*   Links to other steps in the control

Using Suggestions, Samples, and Formats

An increasingly common technique is to provide suggestions to users *before* they specify data. This technique is especially useful in scenarios involving complex data elements—for example, if a data entry form has interrelated data fields, provide users with some advance notice regarding the relationships among fields and acceptable values for related fields.

This technique can be useful in more subtle ways as well. You can suggest data entry formats with hints. Date fields are good examples of the benefits of this technique. Instead of forcing the user to guess how the date must be formatted, you can provide a sample next to the field. This has the advantage of removing the guesswork and minimizing user frustration because less time is required for data entry.

Using Field and Summary Messages

Placing hints and samples with every field is not necessary. In fact, too much help can be a hindrance. However, when an error occurs, you want to provide the user with some guidance. One problem with identifying problems only at individual fields is that the user might overlook the identifier. Imagine, for example, a relatively lengthy form in which the user must scroll. The user might overlook a problem in a single field if the only indication is an asterisk next to the field.

This is not to say, however, that you should avoid indicating problematic fields individually. In these situations, you need to supplement identifying the individual problematic field with a summary of data entry problems. This technique can provide two important benefits. First, the user is immediately aware that there is a problem with the data he or she provided. Second, the summary information gives him or her guidance on where to look in the form for the specific fields with issues. The *ValidationSummary* control, described in Lesson 1, "Validating Data," is an excellent choice for implementing this technique.

Exam Tip   You can use the validation controls along with the *ValidationSummary* control. One common technique is to display an asterisk by each invalid input control and display more detailed messages in the *ValidationSummary* control. For each validation control, set the *Text* property to "*" and the *ErrorMessage* property to "the detail message text."

Handling and Reporting Exceptions

Exceptions occur as a natural part of data processing. The occurrence of an exception does not necessarily mean that something went wrong with the software system or the underlying infrastructure. It could mean that the information provided is wrong or that a user keyed incorrect input. However, regardless of the source of the exception, it is important to report exception information to the user appropriately. The following list provides guidelines to help you properly manage exception handling and reporting.

- **Write exceptions to a log**   IT departments have many motivating factors for keeping detailed records of the goings-on in technology systems. Some requirements are legal whereas others are related to security. Regardless of the motivation, writing exceptions to a log is a beneficial practice. The log gives you an opportunity to see how the system is being used, the types of information being supplied by the users, and, of course, exceptions that occur.

- **Do not use *MessageBox* displays**   The *MessageBox* control is a WinForms component. Therefore, it is displayed on the host system. In the context of Web applications, the host system is the Web server. Therefore, if you use a *MessageBox*, it is displayed on the Web server. This requires someone to acknowledge the *MessageBox* before the Web application proceeds. Instead of using the *MessageBox*, use JavaScript alerts or display custom pop-up windows in your Web application.

- **Trap exceptions in the presentation layer**   Most users, even technically savvy and experienced users, will not understand the exception messages and stack trace information displayed when a Web application encounters an unhandled exception. You should avoid throwing exceptions while in the presentation layer. Instead, trap exceptions in the presentation layer and display friendly messages to the users.

- **Selectively inform the user**   Do not inundate the user with information. When an exception occurs, provide a succinct, accurate, and informative message. It is not necessary to tell him or her everything. However, what you tell the user must be appropriate and useful. As an example, avoid telling him or her of every possible cause for an exception. Instead, display the exact cause of the exception. If you cannot determine the exact cause, do not speculate wildly.

Hindrance Mechanisms to Avoid

Sometimes your best intentions can cause more problems than they solve. The following list outlines some common user assistance mechanisms that are actually unhelpful. As such, avoid using these techniques.

- **Underlining**   For better or worse, the Web was born with lines under links. This means that using underlining to report exception conditions can confuse users. Therefore, avoid using underlining for anything other than hyperlinks.
- **Colors (especially red!)**   Approximately 30 percent of the male population is colorblind. These users will simply not notice color changes. Not only that, but many Web users are visually impaired or completely blind. Screen readers and other assistance devices might not indicate color changes. In general, avoid using colors to indicate problems.
- **Font size changes**   Users like to have control over their environment. It is generally considered poor design to force a font size on users. This is especially true when reporting errors. The user might have adjusted to the font sizes you specify. If you specify relative sizes, the change might be imperceptible to some users.
- **Lengthy technical jargon**   I have yet to meet a user who knows what "Object variable or With block variable not set" means. Even more cryptic to non-programmers are .NET stack traces. Displaying this information not only confuses users, it can frustrate them. If you can describe the exception in lay terms, do so; otherwise, simply indicate that a problem occurred.

Lab: Assisting Users and Validating Data

In this lab, you will walk through the steps of adding validation controls to a page and providing user guidance and assistance. This lab consists of two distinct exercises. Exercise 1, "Validate User Registration Information," includes steps for adding controls to validate user registration information. Exercise 2, "Provide User Feedback and Guidance," extends the results of Exercise 1 by including some additional direction for the user.

▶ **Exercise 1: Validate User Registration Information**

This exercise shows you the typical steps associated with validating a variety of input types, demonstrates the operation of various validation controls, and shows how validation controls are used in combination. This exercise formats the layout of the page using an HTML table that is constructed using the HTML Source view. Each row of the table contains an input control. The table consists of three columns. The left column houses a description of the field. The right column houses the control used to collect the information. The middle column provides spacing between the two outer columns.

1. In Visual Studio, start a new Web site. Click File | New | Web Site, and then select ASP.NET Web Site.

2. The following information is collected for registration: First Name, Last Name, E-mail Address, and E-mail Address Confirmation. Add one *TextBox* control for each of these fields in the right column of the table. Place descriptive text in the left column. The result should resemble Figure 6-6.

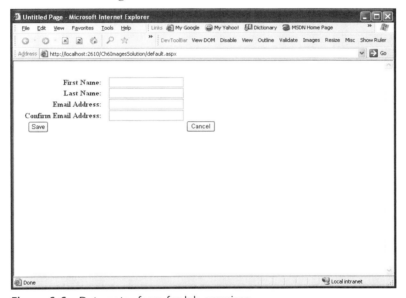

Figure 6-6 Data entry form for lab exercises

The following HTML Source view outputs are used to generate the screenshot shown in the preceding figure.

```
' VB
<%@ Page Language="VB" AutoEventWireup="false"
CodeFile="Default.aspx.vb" Inherits="_Default" %>

<!DOCTYPE html PUBLIC "-//W3C//DTD XHTML 1.0 Transitional//EN"
"http://www.w3.org/TR/xhtml1/DTD/xhtml1-transitional.dtd">

<html xmlns="http://www.w3.org/1999/xhtml" >
<head runat="server">
    <title>Untitled Page</title>
</head>
<body>
```

```
<form id="form1" runat="server">
<div>
    <table width="100%" cellpadding="0" cellspacing="0" border="0">
        <tr>
            <td style="width:49%; text-align:right">
                <strong>First Name:</strong>
            </td>
            <td style="width:2%">
                 
            </td>
            <td style="width:49%; text-align:left">
                <asp:TextBox ID="txtFirstName" runat="server" />
            </td>
        </tr>
        <tr>
            <td style="width:49%; text-align:right">
                <strong>Last Name:</strong>
            </td>
            <td style="width:2%">
                 
            </td>
            <td style="width:49%; text-align:left">
                <asp:TextBox ID="txtLastName" runat="server" />
            </td>
        </tr>
        <tr>
            <td style="width:49%; text-align:right">
                <strong>Email Address:</strong>
            </td>
            <td style="width:2%">
                 
            </td>
            <td style="width:49%; text-align:left">
                <asp:TextBox ID="txtEmail" runat="server" />
            </td>
        </tr>
        <tr>
            <td style="width:49%; text-align:right">
                <strong>Confirm Email Address:</strong>
            </td>
            <td style="width:2%">
                 
            </td>
            <td style="width:49%; text-align:left">
                <asp:TextBox ID="txtEmailConfirm" runat="server" />
            </td>
        </tr>
        <tr>
            <td style="width:49%; text-align:center">
                <asp:Button ID="btnSave" runat="server" Text="Save" />
            </td>
            <td style="width:2%">
                 
```

```
                    </td>
                    <td style="width:49%; text-align:center">
                        <asp:Button ID="btnCancel" runat="server" Text="Cancel"
                        CausesValidation="False" />
                    </td>
                </tr>
            </table>
        </div>
        </form>
</body>
</html>

// C#
<%@ Page Language="C#" AutoEventWireup="true"  CodeFile="Default.aspx.cs"
Inherits="_Default" %>

<!DOCTYPE html PUBLIC "-//W3C//DTD XHTML 1.0 Transitional//EN"
"http://www.w3.org/TR/xhtml1/DTD/xhtml1-transitional.dtd">

<html xmlns="http://www.w3.org/1999/xhtml" >
<head runat="server">
    <title>Untitled Page</title>
</head>
<body>
    <form id="form1" runat="server">
    <div>
        <table width="100%" cellpadding="0" cellspacing="0" border="0">
            <tr>
                <td style="width:49%; text-align:right">
                    <strong>First Name:</strong>
                </td>
                <td style="width:2%">
                     
                </td>
                <td style="width:49%; text-align:left">
                    <asp:TextBox ID="txtFirstName" runat="server" />
                </td>
            </tr>
            <tr>
                <td style="width:49%; text-align:right">
                    <strong>Last Name:</strong>
                </td>
                <td style="width:2%">
                     
                </td>
                <td style="width:49%; text-align:left">
                    <asp:TextBox ID="txtLastName" runat="server" />
                </td>
            </tr>
            <tr>
                <td style="width:49%; text-align:right">
                    <strong>Email Address:</strong>
                </td>
            </tr>
```

```
                <td style="width:2%">
                     
                </td>
                <td style="width:49%; text-align:left">
                    <asp:TextBox ID="txtEmail" runat="server" />
                </td>
            </tr>
            <tr>
                <td style="width:49%; text-align:right">
                    <strong>Confirm Email Address:</strong>
                </td>
                <td style="width:2%">
                     
                </td>
                <td style="width:49%; text-align:left">
                    <asp:TextBox ID="txtEmailConfirm" runat="server" />
                </td>
            </tr>
            <tr>
                <td style="width:49%; text-align:center">
                    <asp:Button ID="btnSave" runat="server" Text="Save" />
                </td>
                <td style="width:2%">
                     
                </td>
                <td style="width:49%; text-align:center">
                    <asp:Button ID="btnCancel" runat="server" Text="Cancel"
                    CausesValidation="False" />
                </td>
            </tr>
        </table>
    </div>
    </form>
</body>
</html>
```

3. Add validation controls.

    Each field is required. Therefore, add a *RequiredFieldValidator* control for each *TextBox* control. The location of the validation controls on the page should be relatively close to the control being validated. The following code example shows a sample *Required-FieldValidator* for the e-mail confirmation field. You must set the *ID* and *ControlToValidate* properties appropriately. Also, be sure to have an appropriate *ErrorMessage* property setting.

    ```
    <asp:RequiredFieldValidator ID="rfvEmailConfirm" runat="server"
    Display="Dynamic" ControlToValidate="txtEmailConfirm"
    ErrorMessage="You Must Provide a Confirmation Email Address." />
    ```

    The e-mail address fields must be in a proper e-mail address format. Fortunately, Visual Studio provides a regular expression for validating Internet e-mail addresses.

Add a *RegularExpressionValidator* control for each e-mail address field. Set the *ValidationExpress* property of each to the following regular expression:

```
"\w+([-+.']\w+)*@\w+([-.]\w+)*\.\w+([-.]\w+)*"
```

Finally, the e-mail address and confirmation e-mail address fields must have identical content. To ensure this, you can use the *CompareValidator* control. The *CompareValidator* control has a couple of additional properties you must set. The *ControlToCompare* property should reference the control to which the *ControlToValidate* control value is compared. Also, you must specify the type of comparison to make. In this case, you want to ensure equality, so set the *Operator* property to Equal. The following sample shows the control declaration.

```
<asp:CompareValidator ID="cmpEmail" runat="Server" Display="Dynamic"
ControlToValidate="txtEmail" ControlToCompare="txtE-mailConfirm"
Operator="Equal" ErrorMessage="Email and Confirmation Email must match." />
```

4. Add a final row to the table for the Save and Cancel buttons. Add an ASP.NET button to the left column and another to the right. Note the *CausesValidation* property of each button. You do not want the Cancel button to invoke any validation, so set its *CausesValidation* property to False. Ensure that the *CausesValidation* property for the Save button is set to True.

This completes the exercise. Your HTML Source view should look similar to the following samples.

```
' VB
<%@ Page Language="VB" AutoEventWireup="false"
CodeFile="Default.aspx.vb" Inherits="_Default" %>

<!DOCTYPE html PUBLIC "-//W3C//DTD XHTML 1.0 Transitional//EN"
"http://www.w3.org/TR/xhtml1/DTD/xhtml1-transitional.dtd">

<html xmlns="http://www.w3.org/1999/xhtml" >
<head runat="server">
    <title>Untitled Page</title>
</head>
<body>
    <form id="form1" runat="server">
    <div>
        <table width="100%" cellpadding="0" cellspacing="0" border="0">
            <tr>
                <td style="width:23%; text-align:right">
                    <strong>First Name:</strong>
                </td>
                <td style="width:2%">
                     
                </td>
                <td style="width:75%; text-align:left">
                    <asp:TextBox ID="txtFirstName" runat="server" />
                    <asp:RequiredFieldValidator ID="rfvFirstName"
```

```
runat="server" Display="Dynamic" ControlToValidate="txtFirstName"
ErrorMessage="First Name is Required." />
                </td>
            </tr>
            <tr>
                <td style="width:23%; text-align:right">
                    <strong>Last Name:</strong>
                </td>
                <td style="width:2%">
                     
                </td>
                <td style="width:75%; text-align:left">
                    <asp:TextBox ID="txtLastName" runat="server" />
                    <asp:RequiredFieldValidator ID="rfvLastName"
runat="server" Display="Dynamic" ControlToValidate="txtLastName"
ErrorMessage="Last Name is Required." />
                </td>
            </tr>
            <tr>
                <td style="width:23%; text-align:right">
                    <strong>Email Address:</strong>
                </td>
                <td style="width:2%">
                     
                </td>
                <td style="width:75%; text-align:left">
                    <asp:TextBox ID="txtEmail" runat="server" />
                    <asp:RequiredFieldValidator ID="rfvEmail"
runat="server" Display="Dynamic" ControlToValidate="txtEmail"
ErrorMessage="Email Address is Required." />
                    <asp:RegularExpressionValidator ID="reEmail"
runat="Server" Display="Dynamic" ControlToValidate="txtEmail"
ErrorMessage="Email Address Format is Invalid."
ValidationExpression="\w+([-+.']\w+)*@\w+([-.]\w+)*\.\w+([-.]\w+)*" />
                </td>
            </tr>
            <tr>
                <td style="width:23%; text-align:right">
                    <strong>Confirm Email Address:</strong>
                </td>
                <td style="width:2%">
                     
                </td>
                <td style="width:75%; text-align:left">
                    <asp:TextBox ID="txtEmailConfirm" runat="server" />
                    <asp:RequiredFieldValidator ID="rfvEmailConfirm"
runat="server" Display="Dynamic" ControlToValidate="txtEmailConfirm"
ErrorMessage="You Must Provide a Confirmation Email Address." />
                    <asp:RegularExpressionValidator ID="reEmailConfirm"
runat="Server" Display="Dynamic" ControlToValidate="txtEmailConfirm"
ErrorMessage="Confirmation Email Address Format is Invalid."
ValidationExpression="\w+([-+.']\w+)*@\w+([-.]\w+)*\.\w+([-.]\w+)*" />
                    <asp:CompareValidator ID="cmpEmail" runat="Server"
```

```
Display="Dynamic" ControlToValidate="txtEmail"
ControlToCompare="txtEmailConfirm" Operator="Equal"
ErrorMessage="Email and Confirmation Email must match." />
                    </td>
                </tr>
            </table>
            <table width="100%" cellpadding="0" cellspacing="0" border="0">
                <tr>
                    <td style="width:49%; text-align:center">
                        <asp:Button ID="btnSave" runat="server" Text="Save" />
                    </td>
                    <td style="width:2%">
                         
                    </td>
                    <td style="width:49%; text-align:center">
                        <asp:Button ID="btnCancel" runat="server" Text="Cancel"
                        CausesValidation="False" />
                    </td>
                </tr>
            </table>
        </div>
        </form>
</body>
</html>

// C#
<%@ Page Language="C#" AutoEventWireup="true"
CodeFile="Default.aspx.cs" Inherits="_Default" %>

<!DOCTYPE html PUBLIC "-//W3C//DTD XHTML 1.0 Transitional//EN"
"http://www.w3.org/TR/xhtml1/DTD/xhtml1-transitional.dtd">

<html xmlns="http://www.w3.org/1999/xhtml" >
<head runat="server">
    <title>Untitled Page</title>
</head>
<body>
    <form id="form1" runat="server">
        <table width="100%" cellpadding="0" cellspacing="0" border="0">
            <tr>
                <td style="width:23%; text-align:right">
                    <strong>First Name:</strong>
                </td>
                <td style="width:2%">
                     
                </td>
                <td style="width:75%; text-align:left">
                    <asp:TextBox ID="txtFirstName" runat="server" />
                    <asp:RequiredFieldValidator ID="rfvFirstName"
                    runat="server" Display="Dynamic"ControlToValidate=
                    "txtFirstName"ErrorMessage=
                    "First Name is Required" />
                </td>
```

```
        </tr>
        <tr>
            <td style="width:23%; text-align:right">
                <strong>Last Name:</strong>
            </td>
            <td style="width:2%">
                 
            </td>
            <td style="width:75%; text-align:left">
                <asp:TextBox ID="txtLastName" runat="server" />
                <asp:RequiredFieldValidator ID="rfvLastName"
                runat="server" Display="Dynamic" ControlToValidate=
                "txtLastName" ErrorMessage="Last Name is Required." />
            </td>
        </tr>
        <tr>
            <td style="width:23%; text-align:right">
                <strong>Email Address:</strong>
            </td>
            <td style="width:2%">
                 
            </td>
            <td style="width:75%; text-align:left">
                <asp:TextBox ID="txtEmail" runat="server" />
                <asp:RequiredFieldValidator ID="rfvEmail"
runat="server" Display="Dynamic" ControlToValidate="txtEmail"
ErrorMessage="Email Address is Required." />
                <asp:RegularExpressionValidator ID="reEmail"
runat="Server" Display="Dynamic" ControlToValidate="txtEmail"
ErrorMessage="Email Address Format is Invalid."
ValidationExpression="\w+([-+.']\w+)*@\w+([-.]\w+)*\.\w+([-.]\w+)*" />
            </td>
        </tr>
        <tr>
            <td style="width:23%; text-align:right">
                <strong>Confirm Email Address:</strong>
            </td>
            <td style="width:2%">
                 
            </td>
            <td style="width:75%; text-align:left">
                <asp:TextBox ID="txtEmailConfirm" runat="server" />
                <asp:RequiredFieldValidator ID="rfvEmailConfirm"
runat="server" Display="Dynamic" ControlToValidate="txtEmailConfirm"
ErrorMessage="You Must Provide a Confirmation Email Address." />
                <asp:RegularExpressionValidator ID="reEmailConfirm"
runat="Server" Display="Dynamic" ControlToValidate="txtEmailConfirm"
ErrorMessage="Confirmation Email Address Format is Invalid."
ValidationExpression="\w+([-+.']\w+)*@\w+([-.]\w+)*\.\w+([-.]\w+)*" />
                <asp:CompareValidator ID="cmpEmail" runat="Server"
Display="Dynamic" ControlToValidate="txtEmail"ControlToCompare=
"txtEmailConfirm" Operator="Equal" ErrorMessage="Email and Confirmation
Email must match." />
```

```
                </td>
            </tr>
        </table>
        <table width="100%" cellpadding="0" cellspacing="0" border="0">
            <tr>
                <td style="width:49%; text-align:center">
                    <asp:Button ID="btnSave" runat="server" Text="Save" />
                </td>
                <td style="width:2%">
                     
                </td>
                <td style="width:49%; text-align:center">
                    <asp:Button ID="btnCancel" runat="server" Text="Cancel"
                    CausesValidation="False" />
                </td>
            </tr>
        </table>
    </form>
</body>
</html>
```

Figure 6-7 shows a sample of the output after validation occurs.

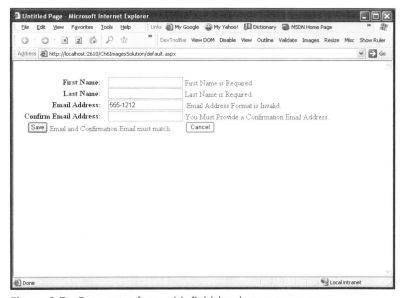

Figure 6-7 Data entry form with field-level error messages

▶ **Exercise 2: Provide User Feedback and Guidance**

This exercise extends Exercise 1 to improve the feedback and guidance provided to the users. The error messages shown in Figure 6-7 are confusing, and they overlap. You can use some of the other validation controls provided by ASP.NET to improve feedback and guidance.

1. Add a *ValidationSummary* control to the top of the page. Note that the *HeaderText* property allows you to use HTML markup to improve the text layout and make it more readable. Set properties as follows:

```
DisplayMode = "BulletList"
HeaderText = "There were some problems with the data you provided.<br>The
following list shows details of the errors.<br><br>(* = Required Field)"
```

2. Recall that when a *ValidationSummary* control is used, it retrieves validation messages from the *ErrorMessage* property of the validation controls. Therefore, you need to modify the validation controls and set the *Text* property. For each validation control, set the *Text* property to "*".

3. Guide the user about appropriate e-mail formats. For the two *RegularExpression* validation controls, set the *Text* property to username@domain.com (janedoe@somedomain.org).

4. It is sufficient to include the results of the comparison validation in the summary. Therefore, to prevent a comparison validation message from displaying outside the summary, set the *Display* property of the *CompareValidator* control to None.

This completes the exercise. Your HTML Source view should look similar to the following samples.

The completed code examples, in both Visual Basic and C#, are available on Chapter06 \Lesson 2\Exercise 1 folder on the companion CD.

```
' VB
<%@ Page Language="VB" AutoEventWireup="false"
CodeFile="Default.aspx.vb" Inherits="_Default" %>

<!DOCTYPE html PUBLIC "-//W3C//DTD XHTML 1.0 Transitional//EN"
"http://www.w3.org/TR/xhtml1/DTD/xhtml1-transitional.dtd">

<html xmlns="http://www.w3.org/1999/xhtml" >
<head runat="server">
    <title>Untitled Page</title>
</head>
<body>
    <form id="form1" runat="server">
    <div>
        <asp:ValidationSummary ID="valSummary" runat="Server"
DisplayMode="BulletList" HeaderText="There were some problems with the data
you provided.<br>The following list shows details of the errors.<br><br>(*
= Required Field)" />
        <table width="100%" cellpadding="0" cellspacing="0" border="0">
            <tr>
                <td style="width:23%; text-align:right">
                    <strong>First Name:</strong>
                </td>
                <td style="width:2%">
                     
```

```
            </td>
            <td style="width:75%; text-align:left">
                <asp:TextBox ID="txtFirstName" runat="server" />
                <asp:RequiredFieldValidator ID="rfvFirstName"
                runat="server" Display="Dynamic"ControlToValidate=
                "txtFirstName"Text="*" ErrorMessage="First Name is
                Required." />
            </td>
        </tr>
        <tr>
            <td style="width:23%; text-align:right">
                <strong>Last Name:</strong>
            </td>
            <td style="width:2%">
                 
            </td>
            <td style="width:75%; text-align:left">
                <asp:TextBox ID="txtLastName" runat="server" />
                <asp:RequiredFieldValidator ID="rfvLastName"
                runat="server" Display="Dynamic" ControlToValidate=
                "txtLastName"Text="*" ErrorMessage="Last Name is
                Required." />
            </td>
        </tr>
        <tr>
            <td style="width:23%; text-align:right">
                <strong>Email Address:</strong>
            </td>
            <td style="width:2%">
                 
            </td>
            <td style="width:75%; text-align:left">
                <asp:TextBox ID="txtEmail" runat="server" />
                <asp:RequiredFieldValidator ID="rfvEmail"
                runat="server" Display="Dynamic" ControlToValidate=
                "txtEmail"Text="*" ErrorMessage="Email Address is
                Required." />
                <asp:RegularExpressionValidator ID="reEmail"
                runat="Server" Display="Dynamic" ControlToValidate=
                "txtEmail"Text="(janedoe@somedomain.org)" ErrorMessage=
                "Email Address Formatis Invalid." ValidationExpression=
                "\w+([-+.']\w+)*@\w+([-.]\w+)*\.\w+([-.]\w+)*" />
            </td>
        </tr>
        <tr>
            <td style="width:23%; text-align:right">
                <strong>Confirm Email Address:</strong>
            </td>
            <td style="width:2%">
                 
            </td>
            <td style="width:75%; text-align:left">
                <asp:TextBox ID="txtEmailConfirm" runat="server" />
```

```
                            <asp:RequiredFieldValidator ID="rfvEmailConfirm"
                            runat="server" Display="Dynamic" ControlToValidate=
                            "txtEmailConfirm"Text="*" ErrorMessage="You Must
                            Provide a Confirmation Email Address."
                            />
                            <asp:RegularExpressionValidator ID="reEmailConfirm"
                            runat="Server" Display="Dynamic" ControlToValidate=
                            "txtEmailConfirm" Text="(janedoe@somedomain.org)"
                            ErrorMessage="Confirmation Email Address Format is
                            Invalid." ValidationExpression=
                            "\w+([-+.']\w+)*@\w+([-.]\w+)*\.\w+([-.]\w+)*" />
                            <asp:CompareValidator ID="cmpEmail" runat="Server"
                            Display="None" ControlToValidate="txtEmail"
                            ControlToCompare="txtEmailConfirm" Operator="Equal"
                            ErrorMessage="Email and Confirmation Email must match."
                            />
                        </td>
                    </tr>
                </table>
                <table width="100%" cellpadding="0" cellspacing="0" border="0">
                    <tr>
                        <td style="width:49%; text-align:center">
                            <asp:Button ID="btnSave" runat="server" Text="Save" />
                        </td>
                        <td style="width:2%">
                             
                        </td>
                        <td style="width:49%; text-align:center">
                            <asp:Button ID="btnCancel" runat="server"
                            Text="Cancel" CausesValidation="False" />
                        </td>
                    </tr>
                </table>
            </div>
            </form>
        </body>
        </html>


// C#
<%@ Page Language="C#" AutoEventWireup="true"
CodeFile="Default.aspx.cs" Inherits="_Default" %>

<!DOCTYPE html PUBLIC "-//W3C//DTD XHTML 1.0 Transitional//EN"
"http://www.w3.org/TR/xhtml1/DTD/xhtml1-transitional.dtd">

<html xmlns="http://www.w3.org/1999/xhtml" >
<head runat="server">
    <title>Untitled Page</title>
</head>
<body>
    <form id="form1" runat="server">
        <asp:ValidationSummary ID="valSummary" runat="Server"
        DisplayMode="BulletList" HeaderText="There were some problems with
```

```
the data you provided.<br>The following list shows details of the
errors.<br><br>(* = Required Field)" />
<table width="100%" cellpadding="0" cellspacing="0" border="0">
    <tr>
        <td style="width:23%; text-align:right">
            <strong>First Name:</strong>
        </td>
        <td style="width:2%">
             
        </td>
        <td style="width:75%; text-align:left">
            <asp:TextBox ID="txtFirstName" runat="server" />
            <asp:RequiredFieldValidator ID="rfvFirstName"
            runat="server" Display="Dynamic" ControlToValidate=
            "txtFirstName" Text="*" ErrorMessage="First Name is
            Required." />
        </td>
    </tr>
    <tr>
        <td style="width:23%; text-align:right">
            <strong>Last Name:</strong>
        </td>
        <td style="width:2%">
             
        </td>
        <td style="width:75%; text-align:left">
            <asp:TextBox ID="txtLastName" runat="server" />
            <asp:RequiredFieldValidator ID="rfvLastName"
            runat="server" Display="Dynamic" ControlToValidate=
            "txtLastName" Text="*" ErrorMessage="Last Name is
             Required." />
        </td>
    </tr>
    <tr>
        <td style="width:23%; text-align:right">
            <strong>Email Address:</strong>
        </td>
        <td style="width:2%">
             
        </td>
        <td style="width:75%; text-align:left">
            <asp:TextBox ID="txtEmail" runat="server" />
            <asp:RequiredFieldValidator ID="rfvEmail"runat="server"
            Display="Dynamic" ControlToValidate="txtEmail" Text="*"
            ErrorMessage="Email Address is Required." />
            <asp:RegularExpressionValidator ID="reEmail"runat=
            "Server" Display="Dynamic" ControlToValidate="txtEmail"
            Text="(janedoe@somedomain.org)" ErrorMessage="Email
            Address Format is Invalid."ValidationExpression=
            "\w+([-+.']\w+)*@\w+([-.]\w+)*\.\w+([-.]\w+)*" />
        </td>
    </tr>
    <tr>
```

```
                    <td style="width:23%; text-align:right">
                        <strong>Confirm Email Address:</strong>
                    </td>
                    <td style="width:2%">
                         
                    </td>
                    <td style="width:75%; text-align:left">
                        <asp:TextBox ID="txtEmailConfirm" runat="server" />
                        <asp:RequiredFieldValidator ID="rfvEmailConfirm"
                        runat="server" Display="Dynamic" ControlToValidate=
                        "txtEmailConfirm"Text="*" ErrorMessage="You Must
                        Provide a ConfirmationEmail Address." />
                        <asp:RegularExpressionValidator ID="reEmailConfirm"
                        runat="Server" Display="Dynamic"ControlToValidate=
                        "txtEmailConfirm" Text="(janedoe@somedomain.org)"
                        ErrorMessage="Confirmation Email Address Format is
                        Invalid." ValidationExpression=
                        "\w+([-+.']\w+)*@\w+([-.]\w+)*\.\w+([-.]\w+)*" />
                        <asp:CompareValidator ID="cmpEmail" runat="Server"
                        Display="None" ControlToValidate="txtEmail"
                        ControlToCompare="txtEmailConfirm" Operator="Equal"
                        ErrorMessage="Email and Confirmation Email must match."
                        />
                    </td>
                </tr>
            </table>
            <table width="100%" cellpadding="0" cellspacing="0" border="0">
                <tr>
                    <td style="width:49%; text-align:center">
                        <asp:Button ID="btnSave" runat="server" Text="Save" />
                    </td>
                    <td style="width:2%">
                         
                    </td>
                    <td style="width:49%; text-align:center">
                        <asp:Button ID="btnCancel" runat="server"
                        Text="Cancel" CausesValidation="False" />
                    </td>
                </tr>
            </table>
        </form>
</body>
</html>
```

Figure 6-8 shows a sample of the output after validation occurs.

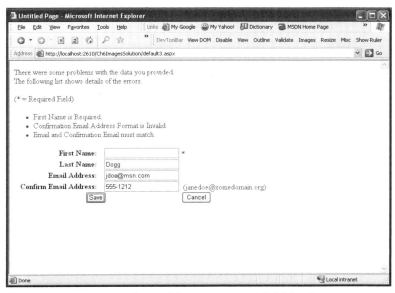

Figure 6-8   Data entry form with summary and field-level error messages

Lesson Summary

- ASP.NET 2.0 introduces the *Wizard* control. This control can be beneficial in guiding users through relatively complex data collection pages.

- You can provide guidance before users provide information. You can, for example, place sample data next to the field. This will help users determine more quickly which format is required.

- You can summarize validation problems in a single location and then use identifiers, such as asterisks, for each field. This reduces clutter and improves readability.

- Rather than reporting every detail to the users, be selective in what information they receive to avoid frustrating them with cryptic error messages.

- Consider the diversity of your audience. Do not rely solely on colors; avoid using red on green; do not use underlining except for hyperlinks; and do not force font sizes.

Lesson Review

You can use the following questions to test your knowledge of the information in Lesson 2, "Providing User Assistance." The questions are also available on the companion CD if you prefer to review them in electronic form.

NOTE **Answers**

Answers to these questions and explanations of why each answer choice is right or wrong are located in the "Answers" section at the end of the book.

---

1. You have added a *Wizard* control to a Web page used to capture membership information for a Penn State fan club. The visual design requirements call for the Nittany Lion logo and the text "Go PSU" to appear on each step of the wizard. Which of the following *Wizard* control properties should be used to create the desired result?

    A. *HeaderTemplate*

    B. *HeaderText*

    C. Both the *HeaderTemplate* and *HeaderText*

    D. *Text*

2. You are designing a Web page. You have been asked to include multiple means of providing assistance to the users of the page. Which of the following is not appropriate?

    A. Context-sensitive help

    B. Tooltips

    C. Red text

    D. Status bar

3. You are adding validation to a Web page. The page has several user input controls. You add a *ValidationSummary* control to the bottom of the page. There is a textbox on the page named *txtName*. You add a *RequiredFieldValidator* control to the page to the right of the *txtName* control and name this control *rfvName*. You set properties of the *rfvName* as follows: *ErrorMessage = Name is required, Text = Enter a name, Display = Dynamic*, and *ControlToValidate = txtName*. Which of the following describes what will be displayed if the user fails to enter a value in the *txtName* control?

    A. *Name is required* is displayed to the right of the *txtName* textbox, and *Enter a name* is displayed in the *ValidationSummary* control.

    B. *Enter a name* is displayed to the right of the *txtName* textbox, and *Name is required* is displayed in the *ValidationSummary* control.

    C. *Name is required* is displayed to the left of the *txtName* textbox, and no text is displayed in the *ValidationSummary* control.

    D. No text is displayed to the right of the *txtName* textbox, and *Name is required* is displayed in the *ValidationSummary* control.

Chapter Review

To further practice and reinforce the skills you learned in this chapter, you can complete the following tasks:

- Review the chapter summary.
- Review the list of key terms introduced in this chapter.
- Complete the case scenarios. These scenarios set up real-world situations involving the topics of this chapter and ask you to create a solution.
- Complete the suggested practices.
- Take a practice test.

Chapter Summary

- Data validation is an absolutely essential aspect of almost every software system. Following the idea that bad data is worse than no data, assume that data provided to the system is inaccurate and always check it.
- ASP.NET 2.0 offers a powerful set of intrinsic validation controls. Additionally, the *CustomValidator* control enables you to create a custom validator to suit your specific needs. The validation controls can be used in combination to provide a complete range of validation capabilities.
- The ASP.NET 2.0 *Wizard* control offers a robust solution for guiding users through complex data entry forms.
- Avoid cluttering your pages with excessive information, cryptic messages, and varying font sizes and colors, all of which lead to confusion and frustration.

Key Terms

Do you know what these key terms mean? You can check your answers by looking up the terms in the glossary at the end of the book.

- regular expression
- validation
- wizard

Case Scenarios

In the following case scenarios, you will apply what you've learned about data validation and validation controls. You can find answers to these questions in the "Answers" section at the end of this book.

Case Scenario 1: Providing User Guidance

You have been asked to create a set of checkout pages for an e-commerce site. The checkout process consists of four steps, including, in this order, verifying purchased items, choosing a payment method, choosing a shipment method, and confirming the purchase. The payment step, which requires a credit card payment, includes fields for collecting a credit card number, an expiration month and year, and the name on the card. The shipping step includes a field for choosing the shipment method from a list of predefined options.

1. What ASP.NET 2.0 control is appropriate for guiding the user through the checkout process?
2. What validation controls can be used to validate the credit card number field data?
3. What validation is required for the shipment method step?

Case Scenario 2: Performing User Input Validation

You are building an intranet application for your organization. Company employees will register for the application. The registration process requires them to specify their e-mail address, first and last name, and phone extension. In addition, they will specify a user name and password for the application. The user name cannot already be in use. The password must adhere to the corporate security standards for password formatting. Because the password field will display in dots as the user types, a password confirmation field is also required.

1. Which validation controls do you use to validate the password, and why?
2. How will you ensure that the user name specified is not already in use?
3. How will you validate the phone extension?

Suggested Practices

To help you successfully master the exam objectives presented in this chapter, complete the following tasks.

Choose an Appropriate Mechanism to Validate Data

Complete these tasks to learn about data validation in Web applications. The first practice gives you opportunities to perform straightforward, single-control validation. In the second practice, you will perform validation among multiple controls. You should complete both practices.

■ **Practice 1**   Create a Web page that provides an input form for users to register with your site. The page should include input controls for user name, first name, last name, password, password confirmation, and birth date. Use appropriate validators to ensure that each field has data. Use validation controls to ensure that the password supplied meets the cipher strength requirements. Validate the specified birth date to ensure that it is formatted properly.

■ **Practice 2**   Using the page created in Practice 1, add validation controls to ensure that the password and password confirmation fields match. Using the birth date, create a custom validation control that determines the age of the registrant and ensures that he or she is at least 18 years old.

Choose Appropriate User Assistance and Application Status Feedback Techniques

Complete these tasks to learn more about assisting users and offering feedback. The first practice gives you an opportunity to exercise the *Wizard* control. The second practice extends the first and allows you to practice using the validation summarization techniques.

■ **Practice 1**   Create a Web page that uses a *Wizard* control to guide users through multiple data entry forms. Place validation controls on each page of the wizard, using the *ValidationGroup* property to ensure that validation occurs on the current *Wizard* elements only.

■ **Practice 2**   Using the page created in Practice 1, add a *ValidationSummary* control that displays validation problems from each step in the *Wizard*. This will give users a summary of all problems with data entry while still allowing them to move among the steps.

Take a Practice Test

The practice tests on this book's companion CD offer many options. For example, you can test yourself on just one exam objective, or you can test yourself on all the 70-547 certification exam content. You can set up the test so that it closely simulates the experience of taking a certification exam, or you can set it up in study mode so that you can look at the correct answers and explanations after you answer each question.

MORE INFO   **Practice tests**

For details about all the practice test options available, see the "How to Use the Practice Tests" section in this book's Introduction.

Chapter 7
Delivering Multimedia

The Internet has extended beyond a mechanism for delivering text. To be competitive, you need to draw visitors to your site and keep them returning regularly. However, as the Internet continues to grow, people have ever-decreasing time to spend on your Web site. Therefore, you need a means to deliver information to them so they can consume it at their own speed, when they choose. Podcasts are an excellent example of this. Instead of reading a transcript of an interview, you can download a podcast to your MP3 player and listen at your convenience. Delivering multimedia in your Web applications is moving past the nice-to-have status. In this chapter, you will learn about delivering multimedia from your ASP.NET Web applications.

Exam objectives in this chapter:
- Choose an appropriate mechanism to deliver multimedia data from an application.
    - Evaluate available multimedia delivery mechanisms. Considerations include bandwidth problems, file formats, frames per second, and streaming types.
    - Design a multimedia delivery mechanism.

Lessons in this chapter:

Before You Begin

To complete the lessons in this chapter, you should be familiar with Microsoft Visual Basic or C# and be comfortable with the following tasks:

- Creating an ASP.NET Web page in Microsoft Visual Studio 2005
- Writing client-side script for Web pages

Real World

Brian C. Lanham

If you think that delivering multimedia through the Web is just for news and entertainment sites, think again. There are many situations that make multimedia delivery a valuable and appropriate delivery mechanism. Users who are visually impaired, for example, can take advantage of having content delivered as streaming audio. Instruction manuals are another example. It is often difficult to use a two-dimensional image to effectively describe a three-dimensional task. Streaming video provides a viable alternative to text-based how-to guides. Creating multimedia is relatively inexpensive; however, the return on that investment can be significant.

Lesson 1: Delivering Multimedia

Delivering multimedia through your Web applications can be a relatively easy task. A lot of technology is in place to assist you in adding multimedia to your Web sites. In fact, many desktop applications ship with the ability to produce interactive multimedia content. You only have to place the content produced by the application on a Web server. However, as with most technologies, it's not that simple.

There are many factors to consider when delivering multimedia. Although it might be technologically straightforward for you to deliver the content, it might not be an appropriate business decision. You must consider the culture and environment of the users, the environment from which you serve the media, and, of course, how the media is produced. In this lesson, you will learn how to add multimedia to your Web applications. You will also discover different formats and techniques for delivering multimedia content. Equally important, you will learn to account for many of the varying factors that are beyond your control before you choose to deliver the media..

> **After this lesson, you will be able to:**
> - Deliver multimedia through a custom ASP.NET Web application that you develop.
> - Objectively consider the factors affecting multimedia delivery and decide whether multimedia is appropriate.
>
> **Estimated lesson time: 45 minutes**

Multimedia Delivery Mechanisms and Considerations

There are two primary means of delivering multimedia through your Web application. You can provide the media file for download (via a hyperlink, for example). If visitors want to view the content of the multimedia file, they can download it to their desktop and play it through a client-side media viewer such as Microsoft Windows Media Player. This technique gives the users the option to download and view the content. Giving users options helps put them in control. More important, users with slower connections or users who are traveling might benefit from the ability to download media and play it back at a more convenient time. You can also embed the media in a Web page. This technique also uses Windows Media Player. In this case, the multimedia is embedded in the Web page, and an external application is not launched. In either case, consider several factors before choosing whether and how to deliver multimedia.

MORE INFO   Windows Media Player SDK

The Windows Media Player Software Development Kit (SDK) documents programming technologies that you can use to extend the capabilities of Windows Media Player and Windows Media Player Mobile. Find more information on Microsoft Developer Network (MSDN) at *http: //www.microsoft.com/windows/windowsmedia/player/windowsmobile/default.aspx*

Considerations for Delivering Multimedia

Do not just blindly start sending multimedia content through your Web applications. As with any technology project, plan carefully for including multimedia in your application. The following list describes several points to consider when weighing the decision to deliver multimedia.

- **Data center bandwidth**   Remember that delivering multimedia places a burden on your servers and your network, adversely affecting performance. Other servers and applications can be affected as well. If, for example, the network is busy delivering multimedia, other network-intensive jobs might fail or run poorly.

- **Storage**   In addition to run-time performance issues, multimedia files can adversely affect the data center by consuming excessive storage. Multimedia files are generally larger than other types of files. Consider the growth rate and life span of your multimedia library before implementing a multimedia solution.

- **Client environment**   Not every file format is supported on every desktop. Consider the client environment when planning multimedia delivery. In doing so, you might need to make concessions. For example, you might not be able to reach every market with your media because you plan to support only a limited set of file formats. As such, do not rely on multimedia as the exclusive delivery mechanism for your content.

- **Client connectivity**   Of course, delivering multimedia consumes quite a bit of bandwidth. Naturally, dial-up users (and there are still some, believe it or not) will have a radically different experience than will high-speed users. Remember that your multimedia content simply will not reach all users.

- **Frames per second**   Digital video technology is similar to analog video in that motion is produced by quickly displaying sequential images. The fluidity of the video output is a function of the number of frames or images captured in a given amount of time. More images per unit time results in smoother video, while fewer images per unit time results in less fluid, "jerky" videos. The rate at which the frames are displayed is called the frame rate and is generally measured in frames per second. Real-time video is approximately 30 frames per second. However, each frame is an image, so the closer a video file is to being real-time, the larger it is. Therefore, the frame rate or frames per second must be considered when evaluating delivery of multimedia video content.

Formats and Codecs

Another factor of delivering multimedia is choosing an appropriate format. The following section will discuss streaming and non-streaming media. However, for now, understand that streaming media allows playback to begin before the entire file is downloaded, whereas non-streaming media requires the entire file to be downloaded before beginning playback.

Recall that multimedia can be video and audio or audio only. Therefore, you need to know something about media formats so you can choose appropriate formats for a given task. For example, video formats carry audio as well, but you don't need to use them if you are sending audio only. A codec (enCOder/DECoder) is an algorithm for compressing and decompressing large files. Together, file formats and codecs offer a range of possibilities for delivering multimedia. It is sufficient to be aware of some common formats of codecs and multimedia, as shown in Table 7-1.

Table 7-1 Common Multimedia Formats

Format Types and Formats	Descriptions
Non-Streaming Audio Formats	These represent audio-only formats that must be downloaded completely before playback can begin.
Waveform (.wav)	
Sound (.snd)	
Unix audio (.au)	
Audio interchange file format (.aif, .aiff, .aifc)	
Non-Streaming Video Formats	
Audio-Video Interleaved (.avi)	The Audio-Video Interleaved format is a non-streaming format. Although this format provides both audio and video, it must be downloaded completely before playback occurs.
Streaming Audio Formats	These formats represent audio-only formats that may be streamed. That is, playback of audio files of these formats can begin before the entire file is downloaded.
Moving Pictures Experts Group standard 1, Layer 1, 2, 3 (.mpa, .mp2, .mp3)	
Windows Media Audio (.wma)	
Streaming Video Formats	These formats represent multimedia files offering both audio and video capabilities. Playback can begin as they are streaming, before the entire file is downloaded.
Moving Pictures Experts Group standard 1 (.mpg, .mpeg, .mpv, .mpe)	
Windows Media Video (.wmv)	

Exam Tip Given a requirement that the user must be able to access video or sound media files, know which formats are audio (such as .wma and .wav) and which are video (such as .mpv and .avi).

> **Quick Check**
>
> ■ Describe the difference between streaming and non-streaming formats.
>
> **Quick Check Answer**
>
> ■ Streaming formats allow playback to begin before the entire file is downloaded; non-streaming formats require the entire file to be downloaded before playback begins.

Designing a Multimedia Delivery Mechanism

There are two basic choices to make when designing your multimedia delivery mechanism. First, decide whether you will deliver in a streaming format, a non-streaming format, or both. Second, choose whether you will embed the media viewer in the browser. This section will discuss both of these choices.

Streaming versus Non-Streaming

The two basic delivery techniques for sending the multimedia data to the client are streaming and non-streaming. Streaming media is audio and video media that can be sent to the client in pieces and played back without the entire media file being present. Non-streaming media requires the entire file contents to be present for playback to begin. There are benefits and consequences to each.

Streaming media allows the user to start consuming the media sooner than he or she could with non-streaming media. In addition, the user is accessing a portion of the media while the remaining media is downloading. This technique generally improves the overall experience for users with high-speed Internet connections. However, it should not be used over low-speed connections. This is because media players try to improve the experience by collecting some subset of the total media file before playing the subset. The process of collecting the subset, called *buffering*, essentially divides the entire media file into smaller pieces as a function of time. For example, a 60-second media file can be downloaded in ten-second increments. The purpose of this is to provide a smoother playback experience by buffering content ahead of time. The idea is that the rest of the content can continue to download while playback is proceeding. The problem, of course, is that over slower connections (such as dial-up), the playback rate vastly exceeds the download rate.

Non-streaming media requires users to download the media file entirely before playback. This allows them to download the media to their desktop, laptop, or mobile device and play it back at a later, perhaps more convenient, time. Non-streaming media is also appropriate for users with low-speed connections because they can begin downloading the media and continue with other tasks until the download completes.

You can provide both forms of media to potentially capture a broader range of users. However, depending on your target audience, you might need to maintain multiple file formats for each set of content. This is because not every format supports streaming. Therefore, if you want to offer both streaming and non-streaming options to your users, you might need to create duplicate media files with one file supporting non-streaming and another supporting streaming playback. In addition, you can double or even triple your storage and bandwidth requirements by providing both formats.

Exam Tip   Given a requirement that the user must be able to access media files without having to download the files, remember that "streaming" does not require downloading. In addition, know which formats stream (such as .wma and .wmv) and which do not stream (such as .wav and .avi).

Embedded versus External Media Playback

ASP.NET provides you with two basic mechanisms for performing multimedia playback. First, you can embed the Windows Media Player control in a Web page. Alternatively, you can instruct the browser to invoke the media player externally. This section will review each of these techniques, including considerations for using them.

Embedding the Windows Media Player control in a Web page gives you complete control over how the user interacts with the media. The Windows Media Player provides an ActiveX control that is embedded in the page using the HTML *<OBJECT>* element. Using the control's Component Object Model (COM) interface, you can program the player to provide custom functionality. You can, for example, use the user interface (UI) provided or write your own. Windows Media Player is programmable ahead of time or on the client, using client-side script. Of course, this means that the user must allow client-side scripts to execute.

Embedding the media in the page is useful in scenarios in which the media complements text or other information on the page. It is also useful if you want to restrict the ability to download the media. Another useful application of embedded media is when you want the media to play back without user action. For example, suppose you want to play background music while the user reads the content. Figure 7-1 shows a Web page with an embedded media player.

Like embedded multimedia, externally played multimedia is often appropriate. If you want the user to be able to control the playback, then using the external media player is appropriate. If you do not want to disturb the page layout, you can provide multimedia externally and maintain the structure of the page.

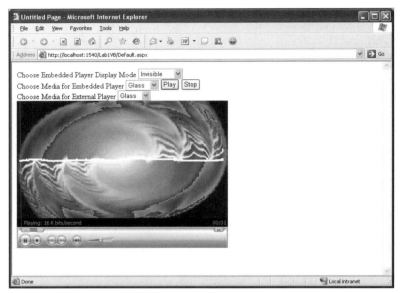

Figure 7-1   Web Page with embedded Windows Media Player

Lab 1: Delivering Multimedia

In this lab, you will use the Windows Media Player control to add multimedia to a Web application that you create. Specifically, you will create a page to deliver a simulated podcast. Note that the Windows Media Player control is a COM component that is actually invoked on the client. This means that the client must have Windows Media Player installed for this to work. If you encounter a problem completing an exercise, the completed files are available in the Code folder on the companion CD.

NOTE   Windows Media Player SDK

This lab will use the sample media files provided by the Windows Media Player SDK. You can download the Windows Media Player SDK at *http://www.microsoft.com/windows/windowsmedia /player/windowsmobile/default.aspx*. You can use any media files you choose for this exercise, but if you want to follow along exactly, you must download and install the SDK with the sample media files.

▶ **Exercise 1: Adding the Windows Media Player to Your Page**

In this exercise, you will add the Windows Media Player control to a page that you create. Recall that the Windows Media Player control is a COM component that runs on the client. Therefore, you will be programming the client browser.

  1. In Visual Studio 2005, create a new Web site by clicking File | New | Web Site, and add a page to it.

2. Open the HTML Source view for the page. Within the body of the page, declare the media player control using the *<OBJECT>* HTML element. The *CLASSID* attribute of the element indicates the globally unique identifier (GUID) of the media player control. Here is how the element should look:

```
<OBJECT ID="Player1" height="480" width="640"
    CLASSID="CLSID:6BF52A52-394A-11d3-B153-00C04F79FAA6">
</OBJECT>
```

3. Add client-side buttons to allow users to control playback. Create a Play button and a Stop button. Remember that these are client-side buttons, not ASP.NET server-side buttons. As such, you will use the *<INPUT>* HTML element to declare the buttons. The following sample shows the buttons' declarations.

```
<INPUT TYPE="BUTTON" NAME="BtnPlay" VALUE="Play" OnClick="StartPlayer()"/>
<INPUT TYPE="BUTTON" NAME="BtnStop" VALUE="Stop" OnClick="StopPlayer()"/>
```

4. Write the client-side script functions called by the click events of the buttons. For this exercise, you will hard-code the media file to play.

```
<script type="text/javascript" language=javascript  >
<!--
function StartPlayer ()
{
    this.document.Player1.URL = "house.wma";
}

function StopPlayer ()
{
    this.document.Player1.controls.stop();
}
-->
</SCRIPT>
```

5. Run the page and invoke playback. Your HTML Source view should look like the following code.

```
' VB
<%@ Page Language="VB" AutoEventWireup="false" CodeFile="Default.aspx.vb"
Inherits="_Default" %>

<!DOCTYPE html PUBLIC "-//W3C//DTD XHTML 1.0 Transitional//EN" "http://www.w3.org/TR/
xhtml1/DTD/xhtml1-transitional.dtd">

<html xmlns="http://www.w3.org/1999/xhtml" >
<head runat="server">
    <title>Untitled Page</title>
</head>
<body>
    <form id="form1" runat="server">
        <INPUT TYPE="BUTTON" NAME="BtnPlay" VALUE="Play" OnClick="StartPlayer()"/>
        <INPUT TYPE="BUTTON" NAME="BtnStop" VALUE="Stop" OnClick="StopPlayer()"/>
        <br />
```

```
            <OBJECT ID="Player1" height="480" width="640"
                CLASSID="CLSID:6BF52A52-394A-11d3-B153-00C04F79FAA6">
            </OBJECT>
        </form>

    <script type="text/javascript" language=javascript  >
    <!--

    function StartPlayer ()
    {
        this.document.Player1.URL = "house.wma";
    }

    function StopPlayer ()
    {
        this.document.Player1.controls.stop();
    }

    -->
    </script>
    </body>
    </html>
```

```
// C#
<%@ Page Language="CS" AutoEventWireup="false" CodeFile="Default.aspx.cs"
Inherits="_Default" %>

<!DOCTYPE html PUBLIC "-//W3C//DTD XHTML 1.0 Transitional//EN" "http://www.w3.org/TR/
xhtml1/DTD/xhtml1-transitional.dtd">

<html xmlns="http://www.w3.org/1999/xhtml" >
<head runat="server">
    <title>Untitled Page</title>
</head>
<body>
    <form id="form1" runat="server">
        <INPUT TYPE="BUTTON" NAME="BtnPlay" VALUE="Play" OnClick="StartPlayer()"/>
        <INPUT TYPE="BUTTON" NAME="BtnStop" VALUE="Stop" OnClick="StopPlayer()"/>
        <br />
        <OBJECT ID="Player1" height="480" width="640"
            CLASSID="CLSID:6BF52A52-394A-11d3-B153-00C04F79FAA6">
        </OBJECT>
    </form>

<script type="text/javascript" language=javascript  >
<!--

function StartPlayer ()
{
    this.document.Player1.URL = "house.wma";
}

function StopPlayer ()
```

```
    {
        this.document.Player1.controls.stop();
    }

    -->
</script>
</body>
</html>
```

▶ **Exercise 2: Give the User Control Over the Player**

In this exercise, you will enhance the page that you created in Exercise 1 to give the user more control over the behavior and display of the page.

1. Add a client-side pick list to your page, using the HTML *<SELECT>* element. This pick list will enable users to control how the player is displayed. Here is the code for the pick list:

```
        <select id="selUIMode" langugae="javascript"
onchange="this.document.Player1.uiMode = selUIMode.value;">
                <option value="invisible">Invisible</option>
                <option value="none">None</option>
                <option value="mini">Mini Player</option>
                <option value="full">Full Player</option>
        </select>
```

2. Add the sample media files to your solution. The media files are located in the SDK installation folder in a sub-folder called media. In Visual Studio, under Solution Explorer, use the Add Existing Item option to select and include the files in your Web site.

3. Use a similar technique to enable users to choose the media to play. In this case, the list of available media will be hard-coded in the page. However, you can easily imagine a server-side solution for generating the list of available media. Here is the code for the pick list:

```
        <select id="selMedia" langugae="javascript" onchange="this.document.Player1.URL
= selMedia.value;">
                <option value="glass.wmv">Glass (movie)</option>
                <option value="house.wma">House</option>
                <option value="jeanne.wma">Jeanne</option>
                <option value="laure.wma">Laure</option>
        </select>
```

Your final code should look like the following:

```
' VB
<%@ Page Language="VB" AutoEventWireup="false" CodeFile="Default.aspx.vb"
Inherits="_Default" %>

<!DOCTYPE html PUBLIC "-//W3C//DTD XHTML 1.0 Transitional//EN" "http://www.w3.org/TR/
xhtml1/DTD/xhtml1-transitional.dtd">

<html xmlns="http://www.w3.org/1999/xhtml" >
<head runat="server">
    <title>Untitled Page</title>
```

```
</head>
<body>
    <form id="form1" runat="server">
        <select id="selUIMode" langugae="javascript"
onchange="this.document.Player1.uiMode = selUIMode.value;">
            <option value="invisible">Invisible</option>
            <option value="none">None</option>
            <option value="mini">Mini Player</option>
            <option value="full">Full Player</option>
        </select>
        <select id="selMedia" langugae="javascript" onchange="this.document.Player1.URL
= selMedia.value;">
            <option value="glass.wmv">Glass (movie)</option>
            <option value="house.wma">House</option>
            <option value="jeanne.wma">Jeanne</option>
            <option value="laure.wma">Laure</option>
        </select>
        <INPUT TYPE="BUTTON" NAME="BtnPlay" VALUE="Play" OnClick="StartPlayer()"/>
        <INPUT TYPE="BUTTON" NAME="BtnStop" VALUE="Stop" OnClick="StopPlayer()"/>
        <br />
        <OBJECT ID="Player1" height="480" width="640"
            CLASSID="CLSID:6BF52A52-394A-11d3-B153-00C04F79FAA6">
        </OBJECT>
    </form>

<script type="text/javascript" language=javascript  >
<!--

function StartPlayer ()
{
    this.document.Player1.URL = "house.wma";
}

function StopPlayer ()
{
    this.document.Player1.controls.stop();
}

-->
</script>
</body>
</html>

// C#
<%@ Page Language="CS" AutoEventWireup="false"  CodeFile="Default.aspx.cs"
Inherits="_Default" %>

<!DOCTYPE html PUBLIC "-//W3C//DTD XHTML 1.0 Transitional//EN" "http://www.w3.org/TR/
xhtml1/DTD/xhtml1-transitional.dtd">

<html xmlns="http://www.w3.org/1999/xhtml" >
<head runat="server">
    <title>Untitled Page</title>
```

```
</head>
<body>
    <form id="form1" runat="server">
        <select id="selUIMode" langugae="javascript"
onchange="this.document.Player1.uiMode = selUIMode.value;">
            <option value="invisible">Invisible</option>
            <option value="none">None</option>
            <option value="mini">Mini Player</option>
            <option value="full">Full Player</option>
        </select>
        <select id="selMedia" langugae="javascript" onchange="this.document.Player1.URL
= selMedia.value;">
            <option value="glass.wmv">Glass (movie)</option>
            <option value="house.wma">House</option>
            <option value="jeanne.wma">Jeanne</option>
            <option value="laure.wma">Laure</option>
        </select>
        <INPUT TYPE="BUTTON" NAME="BtnPlay" VALUE="Play" OnClick="StartPlayer()"/>
        <INPUT TYPE="BUTTON" NAME="BtnStop" VALUE="Stop" OnClick="StopPlayer()"/>
        <br />
        <OBJECT ID="Player1" height="480" width="640"
            CLASSID="CLSID:6BF52A52-394A-11d3-B153-00C04F79FAA6">
        </OBJECT>
    </form>

<script type="text/javascript" language=javascript  >
<!--

function StartPlayer ()
{
    this.document.Player1.URL = "house.wma";
}

function StopPlayer ()
{
    this.document.Player1.controls.stop();
}

-->
</script>
</body>
</html>
```

▶ **Exercise 3: Invoke Player with the External Player**

In this exercise, you will enhance the page, enabling users to choose the embedded player or the external player.

1. Add a client-side pick list to your page, using the HTML *<SELECT>* element. This pick list will enable users to choose media for playback in the external player.

2. Modify the *OnChange* event JavaScript to redirect the page to the media file as a URL. Microsoft Internet Explorer invokes the external player (based on custom user settings) to start playback. Here is the pick list code:

```
<select id="selLocation" langugae="javascript"
onchange="this.document.location.replace (selLocation.value);">
        <option value="glass.wmv">Glass</option>
        <option value="house.wma">House</option>
        <option value="jeanne.wma">Jeanne</option>
        <option value="laure.wma">Laure</option>
</select>
```

Here is the final code for the lab:

```
' VB
<%@ Page Language="CS" AutoEventWireup="false" CodeFile="Default.aspx.cs"
Inherits="_Default" %>

<!DOCTYPE html PUBLIC "-//W3C//DTD XHTML 1.0 Transitional//EN" "http://www.w3.org/TR/
xhtml1/DTD/xhtml1-transitional.dtd">

<html xmlns="http://www.w3.org/1999/xhtml" >
<head runat="server">
    <title>Untitled Page</title>
</head>
<body>
    <form id="form1" runat="server">
        Choose Embedded Player Display Mode
        <select id="selUIMode" langugae="javascript"
onchange="this.document.Player1.uiMode = selUIMode.value;">
            <option value="invisible">Invisible</option>
            <option value="none">None</option>
            <option value="mini">Mini Player</option>
            <option value="full">Full Player</option>
        </select>
        <br />
        Choose Media for Embedded Player
        <select id="selMedia" langugae="javascript" onchange="this.document.Player1.URL
= selMedia.value;">
            <option value="glass.wmv">Glass</option>
            <option value="house.wma">House</option>
            <option value="jeanne.wma">Jeanne</option>
            <option value="laure.wma">Laure</option>
        </select>
        <INPUT TYPE="BUTTON" NAME="BtnPlay" VALUE="Play" OnClick="StartPlayer()"/>
        <INPUT TYPE="BUTTON" NAME="BtnStop" VALUE="Stop" OnClick="StopPlayer()"/>
        <br />
        Choose Media for External Player
        <select id="selLocation" langugae="javascript"
onchange="this.document.location.replace (selLocation.value);">
            <option value="glass.wmv">Glass</option>
            <option value="house.wma">House</option>
            <option value="jeanne.wma">Jeanne</option>
```

```
                <option value="laure.wma">Laure</option>
        </select>
        <br />
        <OBJECT ID="Player1" height="480" width="640"
            CLASSID="CLSID:6BF52A52-394A-11d3-B153-00C04F79FAA6">
        </OBJECT>
    </form>

<script type="text/javascript" language=javascript  >
<!--

function StartPlayer ()
{
    this.document.Player1.URL = "house.wma";
}

function StopPlayer ()
{
    this.document.Player1.controls.stop();
}

-->
</script>
</body>
</html>
```

// C#
```
<%@ Page Language="CS" AutoEventWireup="false" CodeFile="Default.aspx.cs"
Inherits="_Default" %>

<!DOCTYPE html PUBLIC "-//W3C//DTD XHTML 1.0 Transitional//EN" "http://www.w3.org/TR/
xhtml1/DTD/xhtml1-transitional.dtd">

<html xmlns="http://www.w3.org/1999/xhtml" >
<head runat="server">
    <title>Untitled Page</title>
</head>
<body>
    <form id="form1" runat="server">
        Choose Embedded Player Display Mode
        <select id="selUIMode" langugae="javascript"
onchange="this.document.Player1.uiMode = selUIMode.value;">
            <option value="invisible">Invisible</option>
            <option value="none">None</option>
            <option value="mini">Mini Player</option>
            <option value="full">Full Player</option>
        </select>
        <br />
        Choose Media for Embedded Player
        <select id="selMedia" langugae="javascript" onchange="this.document.Player1.URL
= selMedia.value;">
            <option value="glass.wmv">Glass</option>
            <option value="house.wma">House</option>
```

```
                    <option value="jeanne.wma">Jeanne</option>
                    <option value="laure.wma">Laure</option>
                </select>
                <INPUT TYPE="BUTTON" NAME="BtnPlay" VALUE="Play" OnClick="StartPlayer()"/>
                <INPUT TYPE="BUTTON" NAME="BtnStop" VALUE="Stop" OnClick="StopPlayer()"/>
                <br />
                Choose Media for External Player
                <select id="selLocation" langugae="javascript"
    onchange="this.document.location.replace (selLocation.value);">
                    <option value="glass.wmv">Glass</option>
                    <option value="house.wma">House</option>
                    <option value="jeanne.wma">Jeanne</option>
                    <option value="laure.wma">Laure</option>
                </select>
                <br />
                <OBJECT ID="Player1" height="480" width="640"
                    CLASSID="CLSID:6BF52A52-394A-11d3-B153-00C04F79FAA6">
                </OBJECT>
            </form>

    <script type="text/javascript" language=javascript  >
    <!--

    function StartPlayer ()
    {
        this.document.Player1.URL = "house.wma";
    }

    function StopPlayer ()
    {
        this.document.Player1.controls.stop();
    }

    -->
    </script>
    </body>
    </html>
```

Lesson Summary

- You must consider the network usage and storage capacity of your data center before choosing a multimedia delivery mechanism. You must also consider the client environment and connectivity because this will affect the availability of your multimedia content to site visitors.

- Multimedia consists of both audio and video (with audio) files. Choose an appropriate delivery format to minimize bandwidth.

- Multimedia can be delivered to the client as a stream or as an entire file. Streaming content allows playback to begin before the entire file is downloaded. Non-streaming content requires the entire file to be downloaded before beginning playback.
- You can deliver multimedia in a browser-embedded Windows Media Player control or by using the external Windows Media Player application.

Lesson Review

You can use the following questions to test your knowledge of the information in Lesson 1, "Delivering Multimedia." The questions are also available on the companion CD if you prefer to review them in electronic form.

NOTE Answers

Answers to these questions and explanations of why each answer choice is right or wrong are located in the "Answers" section at the end of the book.

---

1. You are designing a Web application for the training company, Contoso, Ltd. One of the requirements is to play training videos inside the Web browser. In addition, the student must be prevented from creating a copy of the video. Which of the following options meets the requirements?

    A. Store the video file on the Contoso Web server. Inside the Web page, provide a hyperlink to the video file.

    B. Store the video file on the Contoso Web server. Embed a Microsoft Windows Media control in the Web page and then connect to the video file.

    C. Store the video file on the Contoso Web Server. Provide a hyperlink inside the Web page to open a Windows Media Player as a separate application.

    D. Store the video file on a separate Web server.

2. You are designing a Web application for the Contoso, Ltd training company. One of the requirements is to play training videos inside the Web browser. In addition, the student must be able to start viewing the video as quickly as possible. Which of the following file formats meet the requirements?

    A. Windows Media Video (.wmv)

    B. Windows Media Audio (.wma)

    C. Waveform Audio (.wav)

    D. Audio-Video Interleaved (.avi)

3. You are designing a Web application for the Contoso, Ltd training company. One of the requirements is to play training videos inside the Web browser. You create a new Web page in Microsoft Visual Studio. Which of the following must you do to add a Windows Media Player to your page? Choose all that apply.

    A. Ensure that the client has the Windows Media Player installed.

    B. Add a Windows Media Player control to the page by dragging a server control from the Toolbox.

    C. Add a Windows Media Player control to the page using the <OBJECT> HTML element.

    D. Add a CLASSID attribute to the <OBJECT> element.

Chapter Review

To further practice and reinforce the skills you learned in this chapter, you can complete the following tasks:

- Review the chapter summary.
- Review the list of key terms introduced in this chapter.
- Complete the case scenario. This scenario sets up a real-world situation involving the topics of this chapter and asks you to create a solution.
- Complete the suggested practices.
- Take a practice test.

Chapter Summary

- Before choosing a multimedia delivery mechanism, you must consider the network usage of your data center, the storage capacity of your data center, the client environment, and client connectivity.
- Multimedia consists of both audio and video (with audio) files. Consider bandwidth when choosing an appropriate delivery format and when choosing whether to deliver multimedia to the client as a stream or as an entire file.

Key Terms

Do you know what these key terms mean? You can check your answers by looking up the terms in the glossary at the end of the book.

- buffering
- codec
- compression
- streaming
- Windows Media file

Case Scenario

In the following case scenario, you will apply what you've learned about delivering multimedia in Web applications. You can find answers to these questions in the "Answers" section at the end of this book.

Case Scenario: Add Instructional Videos to a Web Site

You are the lead developer for a chain of home improvement superstores. You have been asked to modify the company's Web site to provide audio and video multimedia for how-to pages. You are told that you can assume multimedia consumers will be using Windows Media Player. You are also told that some consumers might want to download the media for playback at a more convenient time.

1. What delivery mechanisms should you choose?

2. Based on your response to Question 1, what formats will you support?

Suggested Practices

To help you successfully master the exam objectives presented in this chapter, complete the following tasks.

Choose an Appropriate Mechanism to Deliver Multimedia

Complete these tasks to learn more about delivering multimedia in Web applications. You should complete both practices.

- **Practice 1** Create a Web page that provides streaming media content using an embedded Windows Media Player control.
- **Practice 2** Create a Web page that provides both a link to another page with an embedded control and a link for downloading content.

Take a Practice Test

The practice tests on this book's companion CD offer many options. For example, you can test yourself on just one exam objective, or you can test yourself on all the 70-547 certification exam content. You can set up the test so that it closely simulates the experience of taking a certification exam, or you can set it up in study mode so that you can look at the correct answers and explanations after you answer each question.

MORE INFO   Practice tests

For details about all the practice test options available, see the "How to Use the Practice Tests" section in this book's Introduction.

Chapter 8
Component Design

As you develop a Web-based system, it will become apparent that many different pieces of functionality need to be created. In keeping with standard best practices, you should keep your data and business logic separated from the user interface. This is where components come in.

Exam objectives in this chapter:
- Evaluate the design of a database.
  - Recommend a database schema.
  - Identify the stored procedures that are required for an application.
- Establish the required characteristics of a component.
  - Decide when to create a single component or multiple components.
  - Decide in which tier of the application a component should be located.
  - Decide which type of object to build.
- Create the high-level design of a component.
  - Establish the life cycle of a component.
  - Decide if there are established design patterns for the component.
  - Decide whether to create a prototype for the component.
  - Capture the design of a component.
  - Evaluate trade-off decisions.
- Develop the public application programming interface (API) of a component.
  - Decide the types of clients that can consume a component.
  - Establish the required component interfaces.
  - Decide whether to require constructor input.

Lessons in this chapter:

Before You Begin

To complete the lessons in this chapter, you should be familiar with Microsoft Visual Basic or C# and be comfortable with the following tasks:

- Using Microsoft Visio to create Unified Modeling Language (UML) diagrams
- Using Microsoft Visual Studio 2005 to create class diagrams

---

Real World

Shawn Wildermuth

Designing components is one of the most important tasks of any professional developer. The key to any design is experience. You cannot learn design from this or any book. It's a matter of designing components, reviewing them with other people, and finding out what mistakes you have made . . . rinse and repeat. The most important part of that process is that you review the design with *other people*. Software development is a collaborative process.

Lesson 1: Database Design

Before you can deliver data to the user, you will need a good design for storing it. Storing your data in a database requires that you define the schema for that data. By building on the Object Role Modeling (ORM) in Chapter 2, "Decompose Specifications for Developers," you will build a database schema in which to store that data.

> **After this lesson, you will be able to:**
> - Define data requirements from ORM.
> - Recommend a data schema.
> - Identify correct use of stored procedures.
>
> **Estimated lesson time: 20 minutes**

Database Design Basics

Designing databases is easy to do but more difficult to do well. The difficulty of designing databases lies in the apparent simplicity of slapping together tables in a database designer. The problems with bad database design are more obvious in the longer term. Databases are rarely seen as problematic when they are initially created. But the longer a database is in use, the more it can tend to exhibit problems such as poor performance, lack of data consistency, and difficulty evolving the data model.

To create a good database design, design the database to be normalized to at least the third normal form (3NF). The third normal form simply states that the data has adhered to a level of consistency and was designed with the principles detailed in Table 8-1.

Table 8-1 Database Design Principles

Name	Description
Atomicity	Each entity in a database should be indivisible and consist of a single logical entity.
Primary Key Dependence	The primary key for an entity should be solely required to identify an entity. For cases in which the primary key is a single column, this is not a problem. For multiple-part keys, the entire key should relate to the entire entity.
Attribute Independence	Every attribute should be part of the entity and only of the entity. This means that every attribute for an entity should belong to the entity and only to the entity.

In general, normalizing your database design simply ensures that each of the entities in the database will be independent of each other. These design principles are meant to ensure that your database design can mature and adapt to different requirements over time. These princi-ples also make certain that the data in your database is as clean and consistent as possible.

MORE INFO   Normalization

Examining normalization in detail is outside the scope of this lesson. For more information on data-base design and normalization schemes, please reference the book *The Art of SQL* by Stephane Faroult with Peter Robson (O'Reilly Media, 2006) and the "Database Normalization" article on the Wikipedia Web site at *http://en.wikipedia.org/wiki/Database_normalization*.

Data Entities

In Chapter 2, you reviewed requirements for determining which objects your Web project requires. In this review, you created an ORM to determine what sorts of entities the system needed. Now you need to examine the ORM to determine what data entities you need to store in the database.

Data entities define containers for data that you need to store in the database. Typically, a data entity is represented in the database in a single table. There are exceptions, however, in which a single entity is better represented by multiple tables.

For example, the model shown in Figure 8-1 describes a simple project that will manage cus-tomers, sales people, and orders.

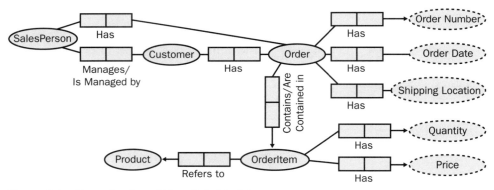

Figure 8-1   Example of an Object Role Model

By reviewing this model, you can confidently take each of the defined entities and create a sim-ple database design (as shown in an Entity Relationship Diagram in Figure 8-2).

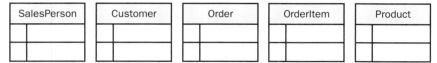

Figure 8-2   Initial database design

In this first pass of the database design, it is important to focus on the entities to be stored. You will have time to delve into the attributes of each entity as you complete the database design.

Figure 8-2 is a good first attempt at a database design, but do not accept the ORM diagrams as the final arbiter of what the database needs to look like. For example, if you look at Figure 8-1, you will see that it defines a shipping location for an order. It is obvious that you need a shipping location for an order but, taking the long-term view of the design, you have to ask yourself whether there will be other types of locations required as the product matures. In other words, should you normalize locations throughout the database schema into a single table?

For example, will the customer have a location (for example, his or her company address) for billing? Additionally, the sales person might need a location associated with a particular office in which they are working. You could certainly embed this information in the *Customer* and *SalesPerson* entities, but wouldn't it be better to abstract the idea of a location and store all locations as a single entity in your system? However, it might be simpler to just embed this information into each of your entities because the retrieval of the entities will be faster and, typically, it will be easier to write queries.

So how do you decide how much normalization is the right amount? Normalizing all of your entities to at least the third normal form is almost always the right approach. But be aware that breaking out every type of common data and creating a new entity will invariably cause problems in your database. There is a middle ground between overuse and underuse of reusable entities.

Real World

Shawn Wildermuth

I have seen both sides of the data normalization problem. In some projects I have seen, no formal normalization has occurred, and every table was created with a notion of keys or segmentation of data. Alternatively, I have also actually seen over-zealous use of abstracting in database designs. One example of this was a database designed to abstract out the notion of a date in the system into a single entity. Because of this, every table in the system had a foreign key constraint to this table. Writing even the most basic of queries was a nightmare. You can find more information on this example at *http://thedailywtf.com/forums/thread/75982.aspx*.

In this case, the right answer is to abstract out the location because that is a sizable entity that will likely appear in different places throughout the schema. Making this change in the schema will likely also necessitate a change in the ORM diagram. Figure 8-3 shows an updated ORM diagram based on the abstraction of the location entity.

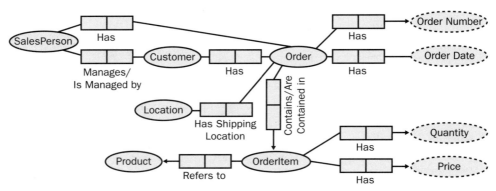

Figure 8-3   Updated Object Role Model

Note that I changed the *ShippingLocation* attribute to a *Location* entity. The new diagram does not define locations for customers and sales people because there is no requirement to do so. If a new requirement for locations for either of those entities surfaces, the database design will make that change simple, but do not include relationships in your database design for requirements that do not exist. Figure 8-4 shows the addition of this new *Location* entity.

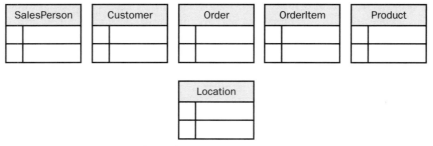

Figure 8-4   Updated database design

Now that you have identified your database entities, determine how to identify each of the entities.

Primary Keys

Once you have defined entities to be stored in the database, the next step is to define how to uniquely identify entities within each database table. Inside the database, this identifier is referred to as a *primary key*. Every table within your database design needs to have a defined primary key. Being able to distinguish a specific row within a table inside the database is crucial to practically all database operations; therefore, it is critically important to define a primary key for every table.

Whereas there are several rules of thought about entity identity, it is important to create an identity that is not only unique for each row in a table but one that will not change over time. For example, it might be tempting to use a salesperson number for the primary key. This is fine, except that if this salesperson number is visible to users within the resulting system, there will inevitably be a need to change that numbering system. Therefore, I recommend that you always use a primary key that is not directly exposed to users. In the case of a salesperson number, I would store that as an attribute in the database table but make the primary key a different, machine-generated number. For example, if you take the earlier table layout for your entities and add primary keys, they would look like Figure 8-5, which follows.

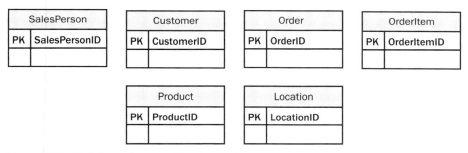

Figure 8-5   Database design with primary keys

In this example, I have used a simple integer to specify a special number associated with each of the entities to specify their primary key. In general, using numbers is preferable to other types of primary keys because doing so will reduce index fragmentation. Depending on your specific need, you can choose non-numeric primary keys as long as you understand that performance and maintenance issues might result.

Quick Check
1. Should you always use the same types of primary keys for different entities?
2. Do you need primary keys in all entities?

Quick Check Answers
1. Although there are exceptions to this rule, in general, you should always use the same kinds of primary keys for different entities. If you use an auto-incrementing number for the primary key of your "Customers" table, you should also use an auto-incrementing number for the other entities in the data model.
2. While there may be some real-world exceptions, it is exceptionally rare to have an entity without a primary key.

To create identifiers for each entity in your database design, perform the following steps:

1. Start with any entity in the ORM diagram.
2. Create a new column (or more than one column if you determine you need a multipart key) in the database design to hold the identifier for that entity.
3. Ensure that the identifier is marked both as required and as part of the primary key for that table.
4. Move on to the next entity in the ORM diagram and return to Step 2 for that new entity.

Data Warehousing and Primary Keys

One consideration when defining your primary keys is how your data will be used in large systems. In the case of data warehousing, it might be useful to create truly unique keys. For example, assume you are creating an e-commerce application for which you expect to deploy separate databases for each customer that buys your e-commerce application. A particularly big customer that buys several instances of your application might need to merge or warehouse data in each of these instances. If you use a simple numeric primary key, multiple databases will have the same key value that points to different logical entities.

In those cases, you have two options: remapping primary keys or using universally unique keys. Remapping primary keys is the process of reassigning keys as you merge databases together. This can be labor-intensive and processor-intensive but can often be the right decision in cases where performance of the original system is more important than the processing time during merging, though this is rarely the case. Alternatively, you can use universally unique keys (for example, globally unique identifier [GUID]). The problem with using universally unique keys is that they generally do not perform as well as simple unique keys do.

The rule of thumb is to remap primary keys by default and use universally unique keys only when you know that merging or data warehousing across databases will likely occur.

A mapping entity is a special type of entity that deserves attention. A mapping entity is used to create a many-to-many relationship in some schema designs. More often than not, you can define the primary key for these entities as a multipart key made up of the primary keys of each of the entities. For example, assume that you need a vendor table in your design to know who to buy your products from, but because you might buy products from more than one vendor, you need a way to "map" vendors to products. Your resulting table will be similar to Figure 8-6.

Figure 8-6   Mapping entity example

Once you have settled on your identity fields, you can move on to determining how the different entities are related.

Entity Relationships

When defining your database schema, it is important to define those relationships between entities so that the database can ensure that the data stored in the database is consistent and integral. To identify these relationships, you will go back to the ORM diagram for the first indication of what relationships are required. If you look at Figure 8-3, you will see that specific entities have relationships to other entities. For example, the *Salesperson* entity shows two relationships: to the *Customer* entity and to the *Order* entity.

A good first step is to use the ORM diagram as your guide to determining these relationships. Be cautious not to treat the ORM diagram as a final arbiter, though. There might be relationships that are implied in the ORM diagram and not obvious or are simply missing.

The ORM diagram is also where you will determine parentage of a relationship. In general, one of the entities needs to be the parent of the relationship. This can be determined by looking at the description of the relationship in the ORM diagram. For example, because *Salesperson* manages *Customers* in the ORM diagram, you can assume that *Salesperson* is the parent in the relationship. When one entity is the parent in a relationship, it means that the child will need to store the key of its parent. To extend the parent-child example, add an attribute to the *Customers* entity to hold onto the *Salesperson* identifier so that you can determine which *Salesperson* entity is the parent of this particular *Customer* entity.

Relationships are defined in database schema as foreign-key constraints. The term *foreign-key constraint* indicates that a column in a table uses a key that was defined elsewhere (that is, it is foreign). Therefore, to create a relationship in the schema, you need two things: a new attribute (or several for multipart keys) in a table and a foreign-key constraint to ensure the integrity of the relationship. For example, if you create the relationship between the *Salesperson* and *Customer* entities as discussed, you will need to not only add a SalesPersonID column to the Customer table but also to create a foreign key to make sure that only *Salesperson* entities currently in the Salesperson table can be used as a Customer's Salesperson. Figure 8-7 shows the foreign-key and new attribute.

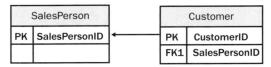

Figure 8-7 *Foreign-key* and *relationship* attribute

To identify all the entity relationships, perform the following steps:

1. Start with any entity in the ORM diagram.
2. Look for relationships from that entity to another entity. You can ignore relationships to attributes at this point.
3. Determine who the owner of the relationship is by looking at the relationship type (for example, unary, binary, ternary, and so on) and description.
4. Create attributes in the child of the relationship to hold the key of the parent.
5. Create a foreign-key constraint from the child table to the parent table on the new attribute(s) in the child table.
6. If you have more relationships in the ORM to review, pick a relationship and go back to Step 3 for that new relationship.

Using these steps, you can add the relationships to your schema to come up with the schema seen in Figure 8-8.

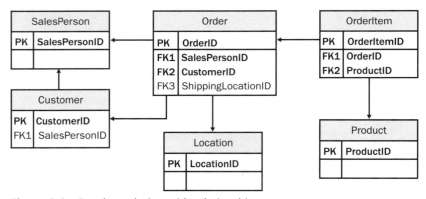

Figure 8-8 Database design with relationships

Typically, when you create relationships, you will also need to determine how you want to propagate changes down a relationship. For example, if an order is deleted, should all *Order-Items* associated with that order also be deleted? In most cases, the answer is yes, because you think of an order and its *OrderItems* as a logical unit. However, if an *OrderItem* is deleted, should the product that was in the *OrderItem* also be deleted?

When you create a foreign-key, you have the opportunity to specify how to propagate that change. Foreign keys allow you to specify a referential action on both the delete and the update of the parent entity. For example, you could specify that when an order is deleted, the child is also deleted. But alternatively, you could specify that if the primary key of a product is changed, the change will propagate down to the *OrderItem*. In most database engines, the referential actions that are detailed in Table 8-2 are supported for both deletes and updates.

Table 8-2   **Referential Actions**

Name	Description
No action	Nothing is changed in the child.
Cascade	Changes are propagated to the child. For deletes, that means the child is also deleted; for updates, the change is propagated to the child.
Set NULL	When the parent changes or is deleted, the child's foreign key is set to NULL.
Set Default	When the parent changes or is deleted, the child's foreign key is replaced with the column's default value.

Now that you have created entities, identifiers, and relationships, all that is left to do is add the rest of the attributes to your entities.

Entity Attributes

Usually, the ultimate goal for defining data is to store it. Once you have defined your entities and their keys, you can go through the process of determining the required data for a particular project. The ORM diagrams can indicate data that is required for each entity, but it will likely not include every piece of information you will need.

In your ORM diagram (Figure 8-3), several entities actually have associated attributes. The *Order* entity has *Order Number* and *Order Date* attributes. In addition, other entities do not have any nonrelationship attributes defined. For example, the *Salesperson* entity has relationships only to *Order* and *Customer* entities. This ORM diagram is indicative of a common problem in ORM diagrams: lack of complete detail on entity attributes. Your role is to determine the real data requirements for each entity.

The task of gathering attribute information about your entities is a fact-finding mission. It is part common sense and part detective work. It is your job to determine which attributes belong, but it is also important not to attempt to add every piece of data you think you might one day need.

To outline the task of gathering this attribute information, look at the *Order* entity. Currently, the ORM diagram dictates that you have an *Order Number* and an *Order Date.* In addition, you have *Shipping Location*, *Salesperson*, and *Customer*. Although these are foreign keys, they are also attributes. It is likely that an order is a common e-commerce application that will need more attributes about it. Using common sense, you can assume that there is a need for some more information. For example, you will want to store information about when an order was filled, when it shipped, and perhaps even a tracking number. You could also talk with the people responsible for fulfilling, shipping, and receiving payment for orders, to see what other information they will need. After discussing it with them, you might find that you need to store payment information as part of an order as well. This process might not only determine what attributes are necessary, but might also highlight new entities. You might find that after discussing orders with the accounting people, you will want to store payment information as a separate entity entirely.

When defining attributes, you must also determine whether you should support the notion of *null* for each attribute. Using *null* in the database indicates that there is no value for a particular attribute. In general, supporting *null* is a recommended practice because it will reduce your database storage requirements and make indexing more efficient.

In addition to specifying the attributes for each entity, you must also determine what kind of data a particular attribute can store. Depending on the particular database engine you are using, you will want to make informed decisions about how to store each type of data within the database. There are four main types of data that you need to determine how to store in your specific schema: strings, numeric values, date/time values, and Boolean values.

Strings

There are usually three decisions here: whether to use fixed-length strings, what length to allow, and whether to use Unicode versions. Each of these decisions has implications for the database design.

Whether or not you use fixed-length strings affects how the database server stores the strings. If you use fixed-length strings (for example, *CHAR* or *NCHAR*), the size of the fixed-length string will be taken up regardless of how big the actual string is. So if you have a *CHAR(10)*, but store "Hi" in it, it will still be taking ten characters of memory in the database. Variable-length strings store only the actual string length in them. In that case, a *VARCHAR(10)* with "Hi" stored in it takes the memory of only two characters instead of ten. In general, if your data is fixed length (for example, a two-character status field), use fixed-length strings. If your data will vary (such as an address), use variable length.

There are different approaches to determining the right length for strings in the database. It is usually the wrong approach to just make all the strings as long as possible. Limitations to the size of a row (which is different for different database engines) will likely not allow you to just make all strings huge. Discussing the requirements with the invested parties will almost always yield the right decision about string length. When you think about string sizes, consider strings in a database to be no longer than 250 or so characters in length. Anything longer should go into a special type of string that can store huge strings. These are referred to as Large Object Blocks. In Microsoft SQL Server 2005, you would refer to this large string data type as *VARCHAR(MAX)* or *NVARCHAR(MAX)*. Other databases may refer to these large strings as

CLOB (Character Large OBject) or Memo fields. These special types of strings are not stored at the row level, so they can store huge strings (some up to several gigabytes in size). They are a good solution for large, unbounded fields.

You also must determine whether to use Unicode strings in your database. Because Unicode strings can store extended character sets to deal with globalized data, it is usually the right decision to use Unicode strings by default. Unicode strings take two bytes per character, so choosing all Unicode strings will make all your strings take twice as much memory as non-Unicode strings take. The only time when you would not use Unicode strings is when you run into row size issues. For example, a row in SQL Server 2005 can be only 8,000 bytes in size. If you start to run into row size issues, moving back to non-Unicode strings is an option.

Numbers

Storing numeric values in the database is simpler than using strings. The decision you have to make in this case is what kind of numbers to store. For whole numbers only, using an integer-based number is an obvious choice. But when storing numbers like money values, percentages, or large scientific numeric values, you will need to consider carefully the types of data you want to store.

In your schema, you need to store several types of numbers. In the *OrderItem* entity, you will need quantity and price attributes. Because you do not know what kind of sales items your product needs, using a floating point value for the quantity makes more sense. This allows for non-whole numbers; for example, you could sell items per pound. Also in *OrderItem*, you need to store a price. Some databases have a data type called *Money* to specify that you are dealing with a monetary value. If you do not have a *Money* data type, you can specify either a floating point number or, more commonly, a fixed point number (such as NUMERIC[10,2] to mean a ten-digit number with two decimal places).

Date and Time Values

In general, most database engines have specific data types associated with dates and times, such as *DATETIME*, that will store both a date and a time. If you store just dates or just times in a *DATETIME* value, you will need to ignore the other part of that value manually.

Boolean Values

Storing Boolean (that is, *True* or *False*) values directly in your schema is a common approach. Because standard SQL does not support Boolean values, some databases do not have specific Boolean data types. For example, SQL Server does not have a Boolean data type but instead has a *BIT* data type that is essentially the same. A *BIT* is not a true *False* indicator but rather a numeric value that can store only zero or one. Generally, zero indicates *False*, and one indicates *True*. If your database engine does not support Boolean values as a data type, use a small numeric data type (*BIT*, *BYTE*, and so on) to indicate the true or false data you require.

Many times, you will find that you do not actually need to store a Boolean value in the database if other data implies that value. For example, in the *Order* entity, you could have a Boolean value for *HasShipped* as well as for *ShippedDate*. But the existence of *ShippedDate* effectively indicates that an order shipped, even without having a second field (*HasShipped*) that can get out of sync with the *ShippedDate* field. In cases like this, do not create the Boolean attribute if it can be discerned by other data in the entity.

Putting It Together

With this newly gathered information, you can fill in the attributes and new entities in your database design. Your new schema might look something like Figure 8-9.

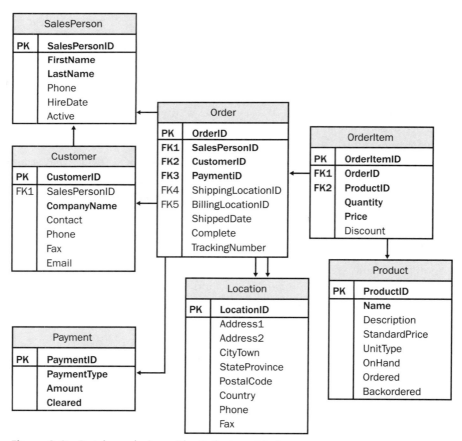

Figure 8-9   Database design with attributes added

Recommend a Data Schema

Now you have defined all your attributes, but there are still a couple of tasks left before you can recommend your schema for use in a project. These tasks include defining secondary indexes, adding data constraints, and determining an effective concurrency management strategy.

Secondary Indexing

Secondary indexing is simply the task of determining which other indexes to add to a database to make queries more efficient. It is called secondary indexing because when you defined the identifiers earlier in this chapter, every table in your schema received a primary key index to make searching by primary key very efficient. There is a cost for indexing: As new values are added to your tables, the indexes must be updated with any new values on which they are indexed. With this in mind, create as few indexes per table as possible, but, where necessary, add indexes judiciously.

You are probably responsible for making sure this is correct when you recommend a data schema. That does not mean that you cannot elicit advice. If your company employs database administrators, talk with them to help make smart indexing decisions.

When you want to determine which secondary indexes you need, look at what types of data in the schema will likely cause searches that do not use the primary key. For example, you might choose to add an index on the Order table's *OrderNumber* field so that searching for an order by its order number is a fast search.

Data Consistency

You need your database to help you make your data better. Other parts of the schema recommendation should be any constraints that are necessary to keep your data clean and consistent. For example, you might choose to make the e-mail address in your Customer table uniquely constrained to ensure that the same customer is not entered twice. You might also find that adding check constraints ensures that data that violates perceived consistency cannot be added to the database. For example, the *OrderItem* table's *Discount* column should probably have a check clause to ensure that you cannot add a discount greater than 100 percent.

Concurrency Management

When you design a database schema for an application, you will be forced to think a bit about the actual day-to-day use of the data in the database. In general, .NET database access uses disconnected concurrency to deal with sharing data in the database. This means that there must be a way to ensure that data in a particular row has not changed since the data was retrieved.

There are several approaches to dealing with concurrency, but most of them do not require changes to the schema recommendation. If you are using a non–SQL Server platform, you will need to do a data comparison to execute the disconnected concurrency. These types of data comparison techniques do not require that you change your database schema.

Alternatively, if you are using SQL Server, there is a common methodology that is highly efficient: timestamps. In SQL Server, you can use a timestamp field to support concurrency. A SQL Server timestamp field is not a time field at all, but an eight-byte number that is automatically updated every time the row is updated. You cannot change this number directly, but every update to a row will increase the value of a timestamp field. This means you can use the timestamp to ensure that the row is still in the same state as it was when you first retrieved the data. If you are using SQL Server as your database platform, it is suggested that you use timestamp fields to allow this concurrency management. This means adding a timestamp field to each of the schema tables, as seen in Figure 8-10.

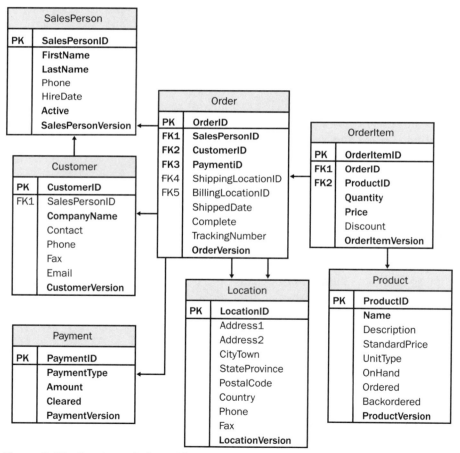

Figure 8-10   Database design with concurrency fields

Identify Data Procedures

The last step in finalizing your schema design is to identify procedural code that will be required by the schema. Procedural codes are simply stored procedures that perform most tasks that the database requires. Although stored procedures typically are created to perform many common database tasks, for the purpose of the schema design, you should be concerned only with the Create, Read, Update, and Delete (CRUD) operations. This usually means creating a stored procedure for each one of the CRUD operations, such as in the following examples:

- spCreateCustomer: Stored procedure to create a new customer
- spGetCustomer: Stored procedure to read a customer from the database
- spUpdateCustomer: Stored procedure to update a customer
- spDeleteCustomer: Stored procedure to delete a customer from the database

You should create stored procedures for each of these operations as part of your database design.

Exam Tip   On the exam, be sure to note that stored procedures are expected for most, if not all, database operations. Whereas in the real world, it is often a mix of parameterized queries and stored procedures, in the exam's simplified examples, you should suggest using stored procedures.

Lab: Defining Entity Relationships

In this lab, you will review an ORM diagram and identify what relationships are required between the entities.

▶ **Exercise: Defining Entity Relationships**

In this exercise, you will review an ORM diagram for relationships and then identify them.

1. Open ORM.pdf from Chapter 08 folder to view the ORM diagram.
2. Open an instance of SQL Server Management Studio.
3. This database file and its log are located in the Chapter 08\Exercise 1\Before directory.
4. Open the newly attached instance of the database and look at the "Lesson 8-1" database diagram.
5. Review the ORM diagram to determine what relationships are required, and add them to the database diagram.
6. Save the new diagram to ensure that it is correct. Your resulting diagram should look something like Figure 8-11, shown here:

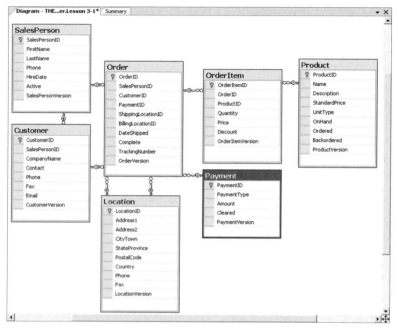

Figure 8-11   Database diagram after adding relationships

Lesson Summary

- You can use the ORM diagram to determine the entity requirements for a database schema.
- The ORM diagram is a good starting place to determine data requirements, but reviewing with stakeholders and discerning the requirements using common sense are both useful for fulfilling real requirements.
- Every data entity in a database schema must have a unique primary key associated with it.
- Relationships between entities can be identified by referring to the data requirements.
- Finalizing a database schema includes adding obvious indexing, ensuring data consistency with constraints, adding concurrency columns if necessary, and identifying stored procedures for use with the schema.

Lesson Review

You can use the following questions to test your knowledge of the information in Lesson 1, "Database Design." The questions are also available on the companion CD if you prefer to review them in electronic form.

NOTE Answers

Answers to these questions and explanations of why each answer choice is right or wrong are located in the "Answers" section at the end of the book.

1. Foreign keys provide which functionality? (Choose all that apply.)
   A. To provide unique identifiers for each row in a table
   B. To provide a relationship between two entities in the database
   C. To create consistency in data by ensuring that parent-child relationships are valid
   D. To provide a mechanism for propagating changes between related entities

2. At a minimum, what kinds of stored procedures should exist for every entity in a database?
   A. Create, Read, and Delete
   B. Create, Read, Update, and Delete
   C. Create, Update, and Delete
   D. Create, Read, Update, Delete, and Copy

3. Relationships in the ORM should become what in the database design?
   A. Primary keys
   B. Indexes
   C. Foreign keys
   D. Stored procedures

Lesson 2: Designing a Component

Designing each component of your Web-based application correctly requires that you think about the basic use of the component, keeping in mind both its current use and future use.

After this lesson, you will be able to:
- Determine the correct characteristics for a component.
- Create a high-level design of a component.

Estimated lesson time: 20 minutes

Component Characteristics

For each component that you need to design for your Web-based application, you will have to review the requirements to plan for the component's requirements. This process involves several decisions: how to package the component, where to host the component, and what type of component to build.

Packaging

When reviewing the component you need to build, it is important to determine how the component will be packaged. In many cases, creating a single component is the right decision, but as part of your design criteria, you need to evaluate whether the new component is a single discrete component or a series of related components. For example, an Invoice component might involve creating components for an Invoice or for an *Invoice* collection as well as other components for parts of invoices (for example, Line Items or Payment information).

When determining how many components are necessary, make sure each component is not trying to be too many things to too many people. Typically, this means a component should contain a single logical facility.

In addition, determine how the actual containers for your components will need to be handled. In .NET, components are contained within assemblies. Determining the exact packaging of your components into assemblies has a lot to do with how you want to reuse and deploy your code. You might choose to use a single assembly with most of your components because deploying a single assembly is simpler, and you do not have many applications on a single machine that use the code. On the other hand, you might choose a more granular methodology because you have a larger number of applications, each of which uses only a subset of the total number of components.

For example, if you know you need to build a component to store your customer information in the database, you could start by assuming that you need a single Customer component.

This component will be responsible for reading and writing data to the database for a customer. To start out, you can assume a single component, as shown in Figure 8-12.

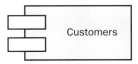

Figure 8-12 Customers component

Your customer might have related components to deal with different objects that they own (such as Invoices, Payments, and so on). In this case, however, a single Customers component is useful. But if the requirement was to store customers' data and their invoices, you would have to assume that you really need two separate components, as shown in Figure 8-13.

Figure 8-13 Customers and invoices components

Both of these components could have their own assembly (or package), but because they are so interrelated, it is probably more useful for them to live in a single package. Instead of thinking about what assemblies to create as you design your components, it is more useful to think of packaging throughout an application. This means developing logical assemblies for different types of code. For example, in a simple Web application, your packaging may be as straightforward as a Web application (for the user interface), a security package, a data package, and the database. Figure 8-14 shows an example of this structure.

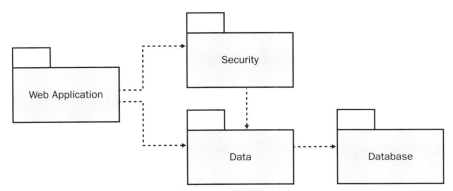

Figure 8-14 Packaging throughout the application

You might find more packages more effective, but in general, separating your user interface from the data is expected in all but the most primitive Web applications. Now that you have an idea of general packaging throughout your application, you can see clearly that your Customers and Invoices components belong in the Data package, as shown in Figure 8-15.

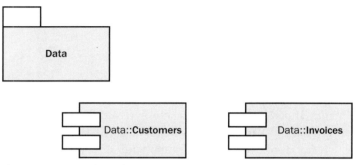

Figure 8-15   Packaged components

Location

When determining the characteristics of your component, you will also need to decide where a component belongs in the architecture. Whether you have designed your architecture to have a physical middle (or data) tier, it should have a logical middle tier to contain data components. So when developing components, it is important to determine where in the logical tier the components belong—for example, your Customers and Invoices components belong in the middle tier.

On the other hand, you might have a component that performs other tasks, such as a security component for a Web site. That component will more than likely belong in the user interface tier. Determining that location will help you determine the correct high-level design and what a component interface should look like. This is because if components are to be used across an architecture tier, this will probably affect the design and interface of a component.

Type

As the designer of a component, you will be challenged with how to capture the functionality of the component while making it accessible to other parts of the application. Your component could be a library of code, a custom Web control, or even a custom Web part. Deciding how to share the functionality with the clients of the component requires you to know how it is going to be used. For example, if your component is going to be used to show the name of the current user, then creating a custom ASP.NET control makes the most sense. On the other hand, if your component's job is to store information about a specific customer in the database, a custom library makes a lot more sense.

There are no rules about how to determine the right type of component to create, but there are some rough guidelines:

■ If the component is going to show a user interface, it should be a custom control or user control.

- If your component needs to be used in a Web site that supports personalization or on a Microsoft SharePoint site, it should be a custom Web Part Page.
- If your code does not have any user interface, it probably should be a library for consumers of the component to use.

High-Level Design

Once you have the characteristics of your component, you are ready to design the component. The process of doing the high-level design is not about writing code but about providing the parameters around which code will be created. High-level design requires you to look at your component's role in the bigger picture of the architecture. Doing the high-level design requires looking at the component with consistency, life cycle, and design patterns in mind.

Life Cycle

The life cycle of a component is simply taking into account the construction, lifespan, and destruction of the functionality you need. Some components are created and live for long durations, and others perform functional tasks that have very short lifespans. Determining the component's life cycle is critical to its design.

For example, in a simple Web request, you might create an instance of a component and have it do some work, as shown in Figure 8-16.

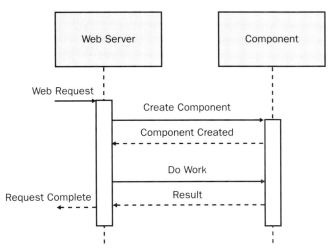

Figure 8-16 A simple component's life cycle

In this case, the life cycle is very well-defined: You create it, you have it do some work, and then you release it for garbage collection. The .NET Framework's garbage collector manages the allocation and release of memory for your application. In this case, your class skeleton might look something like this:

```vb
' VB
Public Class SomeComponent
  Public Sub New()
  End Sub

  Public Function DoWork() As Integer
    Return -1
  End Function
End Class
```

```csharp
// C#
public class SomeComponent
{
  public SomeComponent()
  {
  }

  public int DoWork()
  {
    return -1;
  }
}
```

Depending on the construction and any state that the component has, this might be excessive. If you need a component that is stateless and contains functionality that simply processes inputs and returns some sort of data, then a static (or shared, in Visual Basic) method might be a better solution. The sequence diagram of that life cycle is more basic, as seen in Figure 8-17:

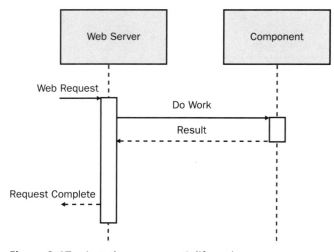

Figure 8-17   A static component's life cycle

When you create a skeleton of the code, it might look something like this:

```
' VB
Public Class SomeComponent
  ' Prevent Creation
  Private Sub New()
  End Sub

  Public Shared Function DoWork() As Integer
    Return -1
  End Function
End Class

// C#
public class SomeComponent
{
  // Prevent Creation
  private SomeComponent() {}

  static public int DoWork()
  {
    return -1;
  }
}
```

You might find that you need a more complex life cycle. In the world of Web application development, component life cycle can be complex. Instead of having a long-running process (like a Windows Forms or Service project), Web applications live only during a Web request. This is very efficient in allowing a single Web server to do lots of work for lots of clients, but it does mean that you need to think about life cycle in a very different way.

Instead of just keeping instances of classes around, think about where to store data that you need to access across Web requests. For example, in an e-commerce application in which you sell items directly on a Web site, your customers will want to browse items and add them to a shopping basket of some kind. Determining the right type of storage for this data is crucial to a good component design.

Web applications have a number of other types of life cycles that you have to take into account, as shown in Table 8-3.

Table 8-3   Life Cycle Descriptions

Life Cycle Type	Description
Application	Instances of components that are created when an application is created and kept around for the days, weeks, or sometimes months during which an application is running on a Web server.

Table 8-3 **Life Cycle Descriptions**

Life Cycle Type	Description
Session	Instances of components that live for the duration of a single user's visit to a Web site. This life cycle should not be confused with storing objects in "Session." The life cycle is for the length of a session but may be stored with different mechanisms.
User	Instances of components that live for a specific user and may be stored for longer than a session is, but are usually specific to a user.
Cache	Instances of components that live for a wildly varying lifespan that is dependent on how volatile the data is. These components are typically not user-specific.

When designing a component, attempt to determine which type of life cycle the component will need. Whereas each of these life cycles will likely look the same as the class design, it is important to design the class with the knowledge that it might need to be serialized into a longer-term storage (such as session state, cookies, database caches, and so on) or used as a remote object via Remoting.

The only caveat in designing your component for a particular Web application need (especially as it relates to Web application life cycles) is that you might find it too limiting. Your component might be useful in non-Web applications, and tying it to a specific life cycle might make it unusable in anything but a Web application. In general, allowing a component to be used in these Web scenarios without limiting them to only Web scenarios means making the component serializable. To make the component as reusable as possible, it usually means not storing the component in long-term storage itself.

Quick Check

■ If you are writing a component to be used in a Web application, should you always write it so it works in a non-Web environment?

Quick Check Answer

■ No, only do this if you think there is a reasonable chance it will be used in a non-Web environment. For example, if you have a component that processes a Web control in some way, then developing it for non-Web use does not make any sense.

Design Patterns

Rarely do we, as developers, run into problems that are completely unique to programming. This is where design patterns come in. In short, they are frameworks for solving common problems in software development. Design patterns are usually structural solutions for object-oriented concepts.

While designing your component, it is important to take advantage of design patterns as common solutions to your component structure. For example, one of the most common design patterns is the singleton. In some instances, you will need to design a class in which only a single instance of the class is appropriate. This is a classic place to use the singleton pattern; it provides a framework for creating a singleton. For example, a skeleton class using the singleton design pattern would look like this:

```vb
' VB
Public Class Singleton
  ' Prevent Construction outside the class
  Private Sub New()
  End Sub

  ' The single Instance
  Private Shared theSingleton As Singleton = Nothing

  ' The static property to get the instance
  Public Shared Function Instance() As Singleton

    If theSingleton Is Nothing Then
      theSingleton = New Singleton()
    End If

    Return theSingleton
  End Function
End Class
```

```csharp
// C#
public class Singleton
{
  // Prevent Construction outside the class
  private Singleton() {}

  // The single Instance
  private static Singleton theSingleton = null;

  // The static property to get the instance
  public static Singleton Instance()
  {
    if (theSingleton == null)
    {
      theSingleton = new Singleton();
    }

    return theSingleton;
  }
}
```

This pattern of creating a class that exposes a single instance is a tried-and-true method that has been around for years. Using this pattern will help you solve common design problems.

There are many design patterns you can use to design your component. You could spend hours combing through books, Web sites, and blogs to find the right pattern every time you are designing a component. In general, it is a best practice to start with the "Gang of Four" design pattern as outlined in the book *Design Patterns: Elements of Reusable Object-Oriented Software* by Erich Gamma, Richard Helm, Ralph Johnson, and John M. Vlissides. (The "Gang of Four" refers to the four writers of that book.)

MORE INFO   Design patterns

For more information, and other useful links about design patterns, see *Design Patterns: Elements of Reusable Object-Oriented Software*, by Gamma, Helm, Johnson, and Vlissides (Addison Wesley, 1995) and "Design Patterns: Solidify Your C# Application Architecture with Design Patterns" at *http://msdn.microsoft.com/msdnmag/issues/01/07/patterns/*.

To Prototype or Not to Prototype

At this point, you should have a good idea of what the design of your component might look like, even if it's only in your head. You now have an important decision to make: "Do I need to prototype the design?"

The decision about whether to prototype comes down to an assessment of the risks of not prototyping. You will need to look at the technological risks to help you make a decision about whether to prototype or not. If the component you are developing is particularly unusual or is using unproved or unfamiliar technology, you will do better to create a prototype to test your design.

Prototyping a component is also needed when the component design must be seen before the system design is complete. This can include a requirement that the project's proof of concept might need a prototype of your component to ensure that the project is feasible. There also might be situations in which it is more expedient to have a prototype of the component to satisfy eventual clients.

Real World

Shawn Wildermuth

During design of a component, I might write out several quick pieces of code to prove my technical assumptions about a component, but I do not generally consider this a real prototype. As a rule of thumb, if you are just testing out a technical idea and you do not expect anyone else to see the code, you cannot expect that to be a prototype. A component prototype is a partially or completely functioning attempt at the component and can be tested with other components.

Expressing the Design

Once you have an idea of what your component design will be, you must be able to capture that design in a way that can be communicated to others. This includes creating activity, sequence, and class diagrams of your component as well as, possibly, pseudocode to represent examples of how the component will be used.

For example, document the design of a fictional component called ProductFactory whose job it is to get information about a specific product from the database and cache the data for faster retrieval. You can document your new component in a number of UML diagrams. First, you can create a simple activity diagram like the one in Figure 8-18 to show the primary flow of the component.

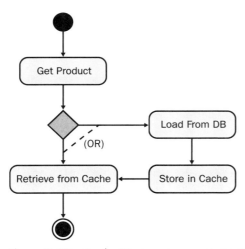

Figure 8-18 ProductFactory component activity diagram

Next, create a sequence diagram to show how you expect clients to use the component. The sequence will show not only the timeline and workflow but the interaction between different components. In Figure 8-19, you can see that your ProductFactory component is using the database to get product information.

Finally, you need a class diagram to show the data and operations of your component. In the case of the UML diagrams, using Visio to create your diagrams is required because Visual Studio 2005 cannot do your activity and sequence diagrams, but the Visual Studio 2005 class diagram is a richer tool for creating real class diagrams. For example, you can use Visual Studio 2005 to create a *ProductFactory* class diagram to show the basics of your new class, as seen in Figure 8-20.

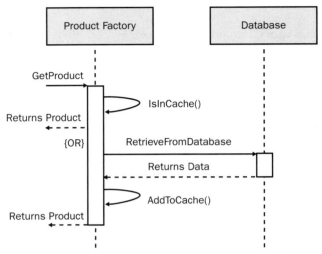

Figure 8-19   ProductFactory component sequence diagram

Figure 8-20   ProductFactory component class diagram

MORE INFO   Creating class diagrams

For more information about creating class diagrams in Visual Studio 2005, see the Microsoft Developer Network (MSDN) documentation on the Microsoft Web site at *http://msdn2.microsoft.com/en-us/library/ms304194.aspx*

BEST PRACTICES   Reviewing the design

Design is a very iterative process. As soon as you document your design, it is a good idea to review it to make sure you have made the best decisions possible for your component. This "design–document–review" iteration cycle is important for creating the right design. Reviewing a design might take the form of a self-analysis or something more formal, such as a peer review. No matter how long you have designed software or how smart you think you are, the more people who critique the design, the better that design is apt to become.

Design Tradeoffs

There is no such thing as a perfect design. If there were always a single "best" way to do something, you would not need to design your components; but as you design any component, you are going to have to make design tradeoffs. This means deciding how to prioritize performance, security, and maintainability. Depending on the scenario, any of these priorities might be most important to you. For example, if your application has no e-commerce features, but is expected to handle very large loads (for example, a news Web site), performance is likely the most important in your design decision. This does not mean that security and maintainability are not important; it simply means that they take a backseat to performance.

In the example of a news Web site, you might choose to have more back-end data in an unencrypted form to improve the performance of serving pages. But this might mean that if a hacker breaks into your data center, he or she might have more opportunity to change your content. Because you are a news Web site, not an e-commerce application, the damage done by that hacker may be limited to a possibly embarrassing episode.

In contrast, if you were designing an e-commerce application, you would want to keep much of the data encrypted and use strong authentication to ensure that the personal data of your customers was well protected. In this case, you would probably make security the highest priority, even at the expense of performance or maintainability.

There are no hard and fast rules about which factor is the most important for a particular component. Only your experience and domain-specific knowledge about the project you are designing will allow you to make design trade-off decisions.

Lab: Design a Logging Component

In this lab, you will design a component for logging information to a file.

▶ **Exercise: Design a Logging Component**

In this exercise, you will receive requirements for a logging component and then design the component.

1. You are given the following requirements for a logging component:
   ❑ The component allows clients to write textual information to a log file.
   ❑ The component should include information on when the information was logged.
   ❑ The component should work regardless of the type of project in which it is used.

2. In reviewing these requirements, you will need to determine the right packaging for the component. The packaging most likely is a simple .NET in-process component (for instance, an assembly).

3. In addition, you would probably determine that the component can be a simple .NET class that exposes the functionality of logging through a method call that allows log entries to be added to a file.

4. You might decide that the singleton design pattern would be useful for the component, so you would add that to your design.

5. Finally, you decide that the component is a fairly trivial one, so prototyping will not be necessary. Your resulting component's class diagram might look something like Figure 8-21:

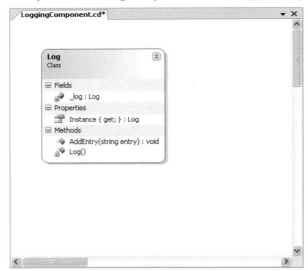

Figure 8-21 Log component class diagram

Lesson Summary

■ When designing a component, it is crucial to determine the component's initial characteristics, including packaging, location, and component type.

■ While designing a component, following styles of other components in the system as well as understanding its life cycle is crucial to getting a solid design.

- Most designs can be furthered by reviewing common design patterns to see whether the component can use an established software solution instead of inventing something completely new.
- Determining whether to prototype a component depends on the component's complexity, the client's requirements, and any technological risk factors.
- Using UML to express your design will allow you to communicate the design to a larger audience.
- Reviewing your design tradeoffs will allow you to ensure that decisions made in the design are in agreement with the overall goals of the project.

Lesson Review

You can use the following questions to test your knowledge of the information in Lesson 2, "Designing a Component." The questions are also available on the companion CD if you prefer to review them in electronic form.

NOTE Answers

Answers to these questions and explanations of why each answer choice is right or wrong are located in the "Answers" section at the end of the book.

---

1. What are good reasons to create a prototype for a component that you are designing? (Choose all that apply.)
   - **A.** Technological risks (such as new technology or a new application of an old technology)
   - **B.** Client request for a prototype
   - **C.** To get agreement on the component interface
   - **D.** Required to complete a proof of concept for the project
2. If you are creating a component that stores and retrieves data from the database, to which tier of the architecture does it belong?
   - **A.** User interface tier
   - **B.** Data tier
   - **C.** Database tier

Lesson 3: Component Interface

Designing the component entails more than determining what the component looks like; it also requires you to define how the component is called. In this lesson, you will learn how to design the interface to the component.

> **After this lesson, you will be able to:**
> - Develop component interfaces.
> - Determine the correct features for a component.
> - Understand the decisions made with respect to working with unmanaged resources.
>
> **Estimated lesson time: 20 minutes**

Component Interfaces

Working with components is simply a conversation between two objects inside the .NET Framework Common Language Runtime (CLR), also called the .NET runtime. For components to have a conversation, a common language must be decided on. That language is the component interface. In other words, the interface for a component includes the constructor, methods, properties, and events of a component. These are the ways that a conversation can take place between a client and a component.

The interface for a component is not necessarily an interface in the .NET sense. It may be a simple .NET class or it may be complicated, using interfaces, abstract (or *MustInherit* in Visual Basic classes), or even a Web service.

Consumers of the Component

Before you design the interface to your component, it is crucial to understand the consumer of your component. The code that will consume your component should provide you with key information about what kind of interface you will need. Consumers of the component might expect to use the component as a simple class, in which case, a simple class interface makes the most sense.

In contrast, you might have clients who use the component through Remoting. If your component will be accessed as a remote object, you will need to take that into account when defining the interface for your component. Why does remoting a component affect its interface? Remoting assumes that the actual object is across some expensive transport (for example, not in the current AppDomain). Because of this, you will want to allow the consumer to do as many of the operations of the component as possible, without lots of traffic across the transport. In other words, if you expect your object to be remoted, you will want to define the interface to avoid being chatty.

In addition, you might be developing a component that you expect to be called through a Web service. If you expect your component to be exposed as a Web service, it is important that your interface be as atomic and stateless as possible. Web services are more than just another transport layer; they are a disconnected transport. In general, the best practice for using Web services in your components is to make the interface to the component message-based. In other words, a single operation should be able to take a payload that allows as much of the job as possible to be done in a single call. Trying to expose an object across Web services can be a nightmare if you have a stateful, chatty component.

You must also consider that, because you are writing components for a Web project, your component might take the form of a control, Web Part, or other user interface–exposing component. When you consider who will consume your component, you should try to create components that are easily consumed. This means you might need to create wrappers for special needs, or in the case of creating controls and Web Parts, you will likely need to create design-time features such as a preview of the control's ultimate user interface (UI) output.

Component Lifetime Interface

One of the first decisions you will need to make is how the interface will handle the lifetime of the component. This includes both the construction and garbage collection of your component.

When deciding how to handle construction of your object, there are several options. If your component does not have any state but, instead, will perform some specific task, you might want to consider using a static class (or a singleton design pattern). This pattern means that, generally, no one will create an instance of your class but, instead, one will just call methods on your type. Although this is a powerful pattern, it is useful in only a very narrow use case.

For most components, you will need to decide how to create your objects. In general, asking for initialization data in the constructor is perfectly acceptable. Two-phase construction (for instance, empty constructors plus an "initialization" method) is not considered a best practice. There are always exceptions to this best practice, but in general, accepting initialization data in the constructor is the right thing to do. For example, here is an example of the one-phase versus two-phase interface design:

```vb
' VB
' Prefer single phase construction
' over two phase construction
Public Class OnePhase
  Public Sub New(ByVal someInit As String, ByVal moreInit As Integer)
    ' ...
  End Sub

  ' ...
End Class

' Don't use two phase construction unless you have a
```

```
' compelling reason to use it
Public Class TwoPhase
  Public Sub New()
  End Sub

  Public Sub Initialize(ByVal someInit As String, _
                        ByVal moreInit As Integer)
    ' ...
  End Sub

  ' ...
End Class
```

```
// C#
// Prefer single phase construction
// over two phase construction
public class OnePhase
{
  public OnePhase(string someInit, int moreInit)
  {
    // ...
  }

  // ...
}

// Don't use two phase construction unless you have a
// compelling reason to use it
public class TwoPhase
{
  public TwoPhase()
  {
  }

  public void Initialize(string someInit, int moreInit)
  {
    // ...
  }

  // ...
}
```

Passing initialization data in the constructor prevents confusion for the users of the component. There is a single way to initialize your new component, and that should provide clarity of interface. Passing the initialization data in the constructor also prevents unexpected side effects of users calling the initialization code twice.

Once you determine what you are going to do with a constructor, you have to look at how you are going to handle the end of a component's life. There are three different ways of dealing with this, as shown in Table 8-4.

Table 8-4   Handling the End of a Component's Life

Life Cycle Type	Description
Stack-based object	Value types are stored on the stack and are not garbage collected because they are destroyed when the stack is destroyed. This life cycle is very fast and should be used for lightweight objects that are not kept around for longer than a method call.
Heap-based object	Objects are garbage collected. Garbage collection occurs when the system is not under load. Most components will fall into this category.
Objects with Unmanaged Resources	When you need to determine when an object is released, you can implement the *IDisposable* interface. This is for resources that are not garbage collected (such as database connections, IO completion ports, and so on).

In general, you should not use Finalizers in your component designs at all. Finalizers allow you to perform clean-up code just before garbage collection occurs. Objects with Finalizers are slower to garbage collect and, in almost every case, you should be using the *IDisposable* interface if you need control over your cleanup code instead of creating a Finalizer.

Quick Check

1. Should you implement *IDisposable* on all components?
2. How is memory released if you implement *IDisposable*?
3. What is the implication of implementing a Finalizer?

Quick Check Answers

1. No. *IDisposable* should be reserved for only components that require cleanup of unmanaged resources.
2. Memory is still managed by the .NET Runtime (CLR). The *IDisposable* interface allows you to released unmanaged resources (for example, database connections and file handles), not memory.
3. Creating a Finalizer forces the garbage collector to wait a generation before releasing your object's memory because it releases the memory. Because the Finalizer indicates that there is code to call, the garbage collector will defer the releasing of the object's memory so it can free the memory of objects that are quicker to release. Only implement a Finalizer if you have a compelling reason to do so.

Design the Interface

Once you understand the life cycle of your component, all that is left is to actually design the methods, properties, and events. Not only must you look at how your component will fulfill its duties, but also at how homogeneous the component is as it relates to the rest of the project. Homogeny is important because consistency in how components work will make the development of client components or applications easier for developers.

In this case, homogeny means similarity of interface, naming, and workflow. For example, if the style of the interface of other components in your system is to have overloads for different types of operations, then yours should as well. For example, you might have this *Log* class in your system already:

```vb
' VB
Public Class Log
Public Sub Write(ByVal message As String)
    ' ...
  End Sub

  Public Sub Write(ByVal message As String, _
              ByVal ex As Exception)
    ' ...
  End Sub

  Public Sub Write(ByVal message As String, _
              ByVal ParamArray args As Object())
    ' ...
  End Sub
End Class
```

```csharp
// C#
public class Log
{
  public void Write(string message)
  {
    // ...
  }

  public void Write(string message, Exception ex)
  {
    // ...
  }

  public void Write(string message, params object[] args)
  {
    // ...
  }
}
```

Because this other class creates overloads for different types of messages, you might consider creating multiple methods that take different overloads to follow this stylistic pattern.

Lab: Determine the Component Interface

In this lab, you will decide how to implement the features of a new component. If you encounter a problem completing an exercise, the completed projects are available on the companion CD.

▶ **Exercise: Determine the Right Interface for a New Component**

In this exercise, you will review the requirements of a component that will take a name and allow access to different parts of a full name.

1. You are given the following requirements for a component that will be responsible for handling a person's full name:

   ❑ The component should accept a full name or a name in its separate parts when the component is created.

   ❑ The component should allow access to any part of the name separately (for example, FirstName, LastName, MiddleName, and so on).

   ❑ The component should allow retrieval of the full name as a single string.

2. In reviewing these requirements, you would determine that you need a simple class that derives from only the *Object* class as the best approach because this might be used anywhere in the system.

3. You would define two constructors based on the requirements: one to take the full name and one that takes each of the component parts of the name separately.

4. You would define properties for each of the separate parts of the name (for instance, FirstName, LastName, and so on).

5. You could determine that the best way to expose getting the formatted full name is to override the *ToString* method of the base *Object* class.

6. With these decisions made, your resulting class diagram might look something like Figure 8-22.

Figure 8-22   FullName component class diagram

Lesson Summary

■ Determining a component's interface is a matter of understanding the consumers of a component, what kind of lifetime the component has, and the style of interface on other components in the system.

■ Determining how to implement features of a component depends on what functionality is needed. Choosing between extending an existing component, composing a new component by mixing other components, or writing a component from scratch are the three options.

Lesson Review

You can use the following questions to test your knowledge of the information in Lesson 3, "Component Interface." The questions are also available on the companion CD if you prefer to review them in electronic form.

NOTE Answers

Answers to these questions and explanations of why each answer choice is right or wrong are located in the "Answers" section at the end of the book.

1. How should initialization data be passed to a component?
   A. In the constructor during construction of an instance of the component
   B. In an initialization method after construction of the component
   C. Using properties after construction of a component
   D. Does not matter

2. If your component has unmanaged resources, how should you change the way you implement the component?
   A. None, unmanaged resources will be handled by the garbage collector.
   B. Implement the *IDisposable* interface to allow for the client code to handle the unmanaged resources.
   C. Implement a Finalizer to handle the unmanaged resources when the object is collected by the garbage collector.
   D. Expose the unmanaged resources as public fields to allow the client to deal with the unmanaged resources.

Chapter Review

To further practice and reinforce the skills you learned in this chapter, you can complete the following tasks:

- Review the chapter summary.
- Review the list of key terms introduced in this chapter.
- Complete the case scenarios. These scenarios set up real-world situations involving the topics of this chapter and ask you to create a solution.
- Complete the suggested practices.
- Take a practice test.

Chapter Summary

- Designing a component requires you to understand both the environment in which a component will be used as well as where the component fits into the architecture.
- A high-level design of your component is the first step to completing that design.
- Reviewing how potential design patterns might be used will help your design be that much better in the end.
- Expressing your design in UML diagrams before communicating it to stakeholders and peers for review will help ensure your design meets their needs.
- Designing a well-thought-out interface requires you to understand who will use the component, what kind of lifetime it will have, and the stylistic preference for interfaces within the entire architecture.

Key Terms

Do you know what these key terms mean? You can check your answers by looking up the terms in the glossary at the end of the book.

- consumer
- database schema
- design patterns
- foreign key
- primary key
- UML

Case Scenarios

In the following case scenarios, you will apply what you've learned about how to design components. You can find answers to these questions in the "Answers" section at the end of this book.

Case Scenario 1: Design a Tax Calculation Component

You work for a small company that has an e-commerce application. You need to calculate taxes for online purchases that occur in any states in which your company has a location.

Interview

The statement made by the company's engineering manager follows:

Engineering Manager   Our Web developer, who is responsible for our e-commerce site, found out that we are not collecting taxes from customers who live in states where we have offices, which is required by law. Please create a component that will do that calculation for them.

Questions

Answer the following questions for the e-commerce Web developer.

1. I can pass you the state of the customer who is trying to make a purchase. Do you need to know any other information about the customer?
2. How will you give me the tax?

Case Scenario 2: Design a Timing Component

You work for a large company that has a large number of Web-based projects. Some of these projects are having performance problems of different sorts.

Interviews

The statement made by the company's engineering manager follows:

Engineering Manager   Different members of our teams are trying to isolate performance bottlenecks in our application. We need you to write a component that will be used in many different applications and that measures and records the amount of time some discrete piece of code ran.

Questions

Answer the following questions for your manager.

1. How would you package this so we can use it in a variety of scenarios?
2. What kind of lifetime management do you expect for the component to ensure that it is as lightweight as possible (so as not to skew the timing results)?

Case Scenario 3: Design a Database for an E-Commerce Application

You work for a small company that has an e-commerce application. You will need to create a database that can hold common e-commerce data such as customers, sales people, orders, and products.

Interviews

The statement made by the company's engineering manager follows:

Engineering Manager   We will be creating a new Web e-commerce application. Our design team has created an Object Role Modeling diagram that describes the different elements of the data design. We need you to create a data model for us, using Microsoft SQL Server 2005 as the database.

Questions

Answer the following questions for the design team.

1. What will you use for the primary key for the tables in the data design?
2. How are you handling concurrency in the database?

Case Scenario 4: Design a Database for a Company Blog

You are working for a large technology company. They have decided to allow their employees to have blogs, but they want to host them on their own site.

Interviews

The statement made by the company's engineering manager follows:

Engineering Manager   We need a database design for a simple blog engine. Each employee can have his or her own blogs with his or her own blog entries.

Questions

Answer the following questions for the developer working on the Web application code.

1. How many tables do you expect to have?
2. How are the tables related?

Suggested Practices

To successfully master the objectives covered in this chapter, complete the following tasks.

Establish the Required Characteristics of a Component

For this task, you should complete at least Practice 1. You can do Practice 2 for a more in-depth understanding of component characteristics.

- **Practice 1** Determine the characteristics of a component that will be used in a typical Web application.
- **Practice 2** Determine the characteristics of a component that will be used in a typical Web service.

Create a Database Schema

For this task, you should complete at least Practices 1 and 2. You can do Practice 3 for a more in-depth understanding of data design.

- **Practice 1** Create a database design for a simple membership Web site. Include information about when each user logs on as well as authentication information such as username, password, and so on.
- **Practice 2** Create constraints to ensure that the same user is not added to the database twice and that the name of the user is unique.
- **Practice 3** Add indexes on a commonly used column, such as username, to see how adding indexes can improve performance of queries.

Create the High-Level Design of a Component

For this task, you should complete at least Practices 1 and 2. You can do Practice 3 for a more in-depth understanding of component design.

- **Practice 1** Design a component that will show the date and time in separate user interface controls. Make up minimum requirements for the simple component.

- **Practice 2** Review the design with peers to see whether the design meets minimum requirements.
- **Practice 3** Implement the design to ensure that it still meets the requirements.

Develop the Public API of a Component

For this task, you should complete at least Practices 1 and 2. You can do Practice 3 for a more in-depth understanding of interface design.

- **Practice 1** Design the public interface of a component to provide authentication for a Web application.
- **Practice 2** Change the interface to meet requirements of Web service authentication.
- **Practice 3** Change the interface to meet requirements when it is used in a Remoted component.

Take a Practice Test

The practice tests on this book's companion CD offer many options. For example, you can test yourself on just one exam objective, or you can test yourself on all the 70-547 certification exam content. You can set up the test so that it closely simulates the experience of taking a certification exam, or you can set it up in study mode so that you can look at the correct answers and explanations after you answer each question.

MORE INFO Practice tests

For details about all the practice test options available, see the "How to Use the Practice Tests" section in this book's Introduction.

Chapter 9
Component Development

In Chapter 8, "Component Design," you learned to design a component. Now you will develop that component. Development of a component requires many different decisions. You need to determine exactly how you are going to implement the features, how to handle data in your components, and, finally, how to add any common component infrastructure. This chapter will walk you through those three parts of component development.

Exam objectives in this chapter:

- Develop the features of a component.
    - Decide whether existing functionality can be implemented or inherited.
    - Decide how to handle unmanaged and managed resources.
    - Decide which extensibility features are required.
    - Decide whether a component must be stateful or stateless.
    - Decide whether a component must be multithreaded.
    - Decide which functions to implement in the base class, abstract class, or sealed class.
- Develop the data access and data handling features of a component.
    - Analyze data relationships.
    - Analyze the data handling requirements of a component.
- Develop an exception handling mechanism.
    - Decide when it is appropriate to raise an exception.
    - Decide how a component will handle exceptions. Considerations include catching and throwing a new exception; catching, wrapping, and throwing the wrapped exception; catching and terminating, and so on.
- Develop a component to include profiling requirements.
    - Identify potential issues, such as resource leaks and performance gaps, by profiling a component.
    - Decide when to stop profiling on a component.
    - Decide whether to redesign a component after analyzing the profiling results.

Lessons in this chapter:

Before You Begin

To complete the lessons in this chapter, you should be familiar with Microsoft Visual Basic or C#

Real World

Shawn Wildermuth

While working on a variety of projects, I have been tasked with developing components ranging from simple, one-off components to complex, multifaceted components. In each case, I had to straddle the line between reusing other code and allowing my code to be used by other projects. With the reality of time pressures in all projects, developing your component within the time allotted and without making shortcuts that cost you more time later is the difficult job of the developer.

Lesson 1: Implementing Component Features

Once the design for a specific component is complete, you will need to determine how to implement the features of a component.

After this lesson, you will be able to:

■ Determine whether you need to extend, compose, or implement your component's specific features.

■ Understand the reasons to make a component stateful or stateless.

■ Make decisions about supporting multithreaded environments.

■ Know how to deal with unmanaged resources in components.

Estimated lesson time: 30 minutes

Extend, Compose, or Implement?

Before you can implement your component, review the requirements for the component and determine how you are going to fulfill its feature requirements. You need to determine what needs to be written and what can be built upon. Whether you use the expansive Microsoft .NET Framework 2.0, third-party controls, or even other in-house development, you must decide what features need to be built and what features can be reused from other components. There are three real choices here for any component: extend, compose, or implement.

You might find that a particular class or control is close to what you need, but needs customization to meet your needs. In this case, you should extend the class or control by inheriting from it and adding your customization. For example, you might find that the best way to create a logging component is to extend a *FileStream* class instead of writing the files yourself. In that case, you can use the same interface as the *FileStream* class but extend it to do the specific logging that you need. It is important to think of the new component as a type of the class or control from which you are deriving. In this example, you really want a *LogStream*, not just a log class. Because you want a stream that will write to only a text log, extending the *FileStream* is the right approach. Your *LogStream* class would have a class diagram that looks something like Figure 9-1.

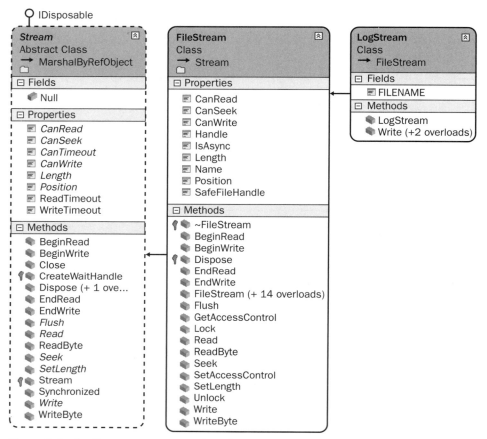

Figure 9-1 *LogStream* component class diagram

You might find that your component needs functionality from a number of different classes or controls. In this case, you should choose to compose a new component that includes the functionality of all the different classes or controls. The world of controls offers a very visual way of thinking about this. You might decide that you need a control that allows users to enter a date and a time as separate pieces of data. You might find that creating a component that is composed of a calendar control and a textbox is the best solution. The new component is not necessarily a calendar control or a textbox, but a new type of component that includes both. That is the essence of composition.

Finally, you might find that neither extending nor composing from existing components will work for your component's features. For example, you might have a component that needs to perform some calculations that are specific to your project. In this case, the only real option is implementing this logic in your own code.

Component implementations will always lean on other code, even if that code is just the *Object* class. But choosing the right approach to extending, composing, or implementing functionality is crucial to a well-designed and well-implemented component.

Building Class Hierarchies

There are times when you decide that you need a hierarchy of classes that make up a component. You might use a class hierarchy so that common functionality is shared by a variety of different types of components. This common functionality class is referred to as a base class. The *Stream* class in the .NET Framework is a classic example of this design. The *Stream* class itself is a base class that not only exemplifies the interface that the derived classes will follow but also supports basic functionality that all *Stream*-derived classes will share. Derived classes will specialize the stream for specific purposes. For example, the *FileStream* class is a *Stream* class that writes to a file. There are a number of different streams that are specialized versions of the *Stream* class, including *FileStream*, *MemoryStream*, and *DeflateStream*.

These *Stream* classes exemplify another decision that you must make: Do you need the base class to be abstract? Abstract classes (also referred to as a *MustInherit* class in Visual Basic) are classes that cannot be created. Specifically, only classes that inherit from the abstract class can be instantiated. For example, you might have an *Animal* base class from which a *Cat* class and a *Dog* class inherit. Although *Cats* and *Dogs* are both *Animals*, you cannot create an instance of the *Animal* class itself. All instances of the *Animal* class are actually specializations of the *Animal* class. For example, an instance of the *Cat* class is an *Animal*, but you cannot create an instance of the *Animal* class itself, only its specializations. That is the canonical example of the abstract class. In that case, the *Animal* class would be abstract.

The core concepts of abstract classes and interfaces can be seen as very similar, but they are actually different. An abstract class is used to share not only interface and implementation but also identity. An abstract class is an "is-a" relationship. A *Cat* is an *Animal*. A *Dog* is an *Animal*. Interfaces, on the other hand, define a calling convention or behavior. You might have an *IFeed* interface that defines that you can feed an object. That interface would probably exist on an *Animal* class. But that same interface could also exist on a *ParkingMeter* class. Although you feed an animal and a parking meter very differently, the interface in this fictitious *IFeed* interface might define that they both need to be fed.

Component State

One of the most important decisions you will make in developing a component is whether it will be stateful or stateless. Making this determination is simply a matter of establishing whether your component needs to maintain data across multiple calls to itself. In this context, "state" usually refers to any data that is not consumed during a single method call in a component. The decision about whether a component should be stateful or stateless is not about whether your component needs data to accomplish its task but about where that data is going to exist.

The general rule of thumb is that stateless components will scale out better but at the cost of working without local state. For example, assume that you need a component to create an e-mail for a customer to remind him or her of a payment that is due. You might have a stateful component that contains all the data for a customer (as is common with data access layers). You could decide to add the functionality to the existing customer component, which is stateful. When you issue a request for one of these e-mails, you need to get the customer's component and then ask that the e-mail be sent. As your customer base expands, you might find that reading so many customers out of the database just to send them a routine e-mail is slow because of all the user objects that are being created. That is, it does not scale out well. Instead, you should create a stateless component that uses the customer identifier to issue the e-mail. Internally, this e-mailing component might use data (such as the identifier you passed to it and the data it retrieved from the database) during the completion of the operation, but it could scale out faster because it could be reused for different customers. The additional scaling out of the component is accomplished in two ways. No extraneous data is being loaded that the component does not need, and you are avoiding any construction-destruction cycles for every e-mail creation. You can usually tell when a component takes state: It either has a constructor that takes data, or it includes a secondary initialization method (for instance, *Create* or *Init*).

Creating stateful components is not a bad idea. Most created components are stateful. Generally, you can develop stateful components more quickly, and they are required for many components that you will need in your development. However, isolating key components to make them stateless for the purposes of scaling out can be a real boon to most development projects.

Multithreading

Multithreading is using threads in your component to improve your throughput. When working with multithreading in your component, you will need to deal with two issues: thread safety and using multithreading in your component. Thread safety is determining whether your component will be called from multiple threads simultaneously.

Thread Safety

Assuming that your component will be stateful, you will need to determine whether the component will need to support thread safety. Thread safety is simply protection of data within a component from simultaneous access by multiple threads. But thread safety comes at a cost, regardless of which locking scheme you pick to protect your data from multithreaded access. This cost is in development time, performance of the component, and testing of the component, as well as in debugging difficulties.

It is important that any stateful component that you create knows whether it is valid to use in a multithreaded environment. If it is valid to call the component from multiple threads, you must protect that data. There are components that never need to be thread-safe because they are always used from a single thread. Typically, you should add thread safety only if your component specifically needs it.

Using Threads

As you implement your component's features, you will need to determine whether to use threads. Introducing threading can dramatically improve the performance of a component by allowing multiple threads to do work at once. At the same time, introducing threading will increase the complexity of your component, both in implementation and in debugging.

So how do you decide whether to use threading? You should introduce threading only when you need it. Not every type of operation will benefit from multithreaded code. Usually, multithreading can help a component when it has an operation that spends much of its time waiting. For example, you might have a component that uses a Web service to retrieve stock prices. Because the retrieval of that information over the Internet might take some time, your component might be waiting just for the results to return. Introducing threading to that component enables you to fire off several threads to retrieve different stock results all at the same time so that requests to the Web service are being made while other requests are pending.

The benefit of adding threading must outweigh the additional complexity. This is a black-and-white rule against which you can measure this decision. You will have to rely on your experience to understand the risk-versus-reward decision.

MORE INFO   Multithreaded access

For more information about multithreading, please refer to the chapter entitled "Threading" in *MCTS Self-Paced Training Kit (Exam 70-536): Microsoft .NET Framework 2.0–Application Development Foundation* by Tony Northrup, Shawn Wildermuth, and Bill Ryan (Microsoft Press, 2006).

Handling Unmanaged Resources

The Common Language Runtime (CLR) is an environment in which the memory is managed; that is, reference objects are garbage collected. The garbage collector manages memory. Once out of scope, reference objects are eligible to be reclaimed by the system when the garbage collector cleans up the environment. Other resources, however, are unmanaged. For example, database connections are an unmanaged resource. Even though the local memory associated with a database collection is managed by the CLR, the actual connection is not. If you open a database connection and wait until the garbage collection fires on the connection to close it, the database will end up with many unclosed database connections, which will impede basic performance of the database.

In the .NET Framework, the *IDisposable* interface was created to support unmanaged resources. If you write a component that has unmanaged resources, you must allow for those resources to be cleaned up by the users. You do this by supporting the *IDisposable* interface.

In addition, if you use objects that implement the *IDisposable* interface, you must call the object's *IDisposable.Dispose()* method to clean up their unmanaged resources. This means that if you use an object that supports *IDisposable* within a single call, you should wrap it with a using statement to call the *IDisposable* interface. If you hold on to an object that supports *IDisposable* for longer than a single call (which, for instance, is a member of your component), you must support the *IDisposable* interface so that, in your implementation of the *IDisposable.Dispose()* method, you call your member's *IDisposable* implementation.

In addition to working with members that support *IDisposable*, you should also be aware of other unmanaged resources. Typically, this is when you are holding on to resources that are outside the .NET Framework. For example, you might be using an external dynamic-link library (DLL) through interop. If the external DLL is being used through interop, the DLL is not a .NET component and is, therefore, unmanaged. You will need to release any resources you use from that DLL and, by supporting the *IDisposable* interface, you will end up with a well-defined pattern to clean up any resources.

Quick Check

1. How should you handle unmanaged resources in your own classes?
2. How should you handle classes that have unmanaged resources that you use within your own code?

Quick Check Answers

1. If your class has unmanaged resources, you should implement the *IDisposable* interface.
2. If you are using classes that have unmanaged resources (and therefore implement *IDisposable*), you will need to call the *IDisposable.Dispose* method to ensure that all resources are released.

Lab: Add Handling of Unmanaged Resources

In this lab, you will add support to handle unmanaged resources in an existing component. If you encounter a problem completing an exercise, the completed projects can be installed from the Code folder on the companion CD.

▶ **Exercise 1: Add Support for Unmanaged Resources**

In this exercise, you will take a partially completed class and add support for handling unmanaged resources.

1. Open the \Chapter 09\Lesson 1\Exercise 1\Before project in your preferred language. (C# and Visual Basic are included.)
2. In Microsoft Visual Studio, click File | Open | Project/Solution, and then navigate to \Chapter 09\Lesson 1\Exercise 1\Before.
3. Open the *Logging* class code file.
4. Identify the unmanaged resources (the *FileStream* and *StreamWriter* members).
5. Add the *IDisposable* interface to the *Logging* class.
6. Add the *Dispose* method of *IDisposable* to the *Logging* class.
7. Inside the *Dispose* method, call the *Dispose* methods of *FileStream* and *StreamWriter*.
8. The new *Logging* class might look like the following. Changes from the Before project are in bold. You can view the completed solution in the After folder.

```vb
' VB
Imports System
Imports System.Collections.Generic
Imports System.Text
Imports System.IO

''' <summary>
''' A class for writing information to a
''' standard log file.
''' </summary>
Public Class Logger
  Implements IDisposable

  Private Const logFileName As String = "logfile.txt"
  Private logFile As FileStream = Nothing
  Private writer As StreamWriter = Nothing

  ''' <summary>
  ''' Initializes a new instance of
  ''' the <see cref="T:Logger"/> class.
  ''' </summary>
  Public Sub New()
    MyBase.New()
    logFile = File.Open(logFileName, _
                        FileMode.OpenOrCreate, _
                        FileAccess.Write, _
                        FileShare.ReadWrite)
    writer = New StreamWriter(logFile)
  End Sub

  ''' <summary>
  ''' Adds the specified message.
  ''' </summary>
  ''' <param name="message">The message.</param>
  Public Overloads Sub Add(ByVal message As String)
    writer.WriteLine(message)
  End Sub
```

```
''' <summary>
''' Adds the specified message.
''' </summary>
''' <param name="message">The message.</param>
''' <param name="args">The args.</param>
Public Overloads Sub Add(ByVal message As String, _
                         ByVal ParamArray args() As Object)
    writer.WriteLine(message, args)
End Sub

''' <summary>
''' Performs application-defined tasks associated
''' with freeing, releasing, or
''' resetting unmanaged resources.
''' Implements the Dispose() method of the
''' IDisposable interface
''' </summary>
Public Sub Dispose() Implements IDisposable.Dispose
    writer.Dispose()
    logFile.Dispose()
End Sub

End Class

// C#
using System;
using System.Collections.Generic;
using System.Text;
using System.IO;

/// <summary>
/// A class for writing information to a
/// standard log file.
/// </summary>
public class Logger : IDisposable
{
    const string logFileName = "logfile.txt";
    FileStream logFile = null;
    StreamWriter writer = null;

    /// <summary> `ws 65
    /// Initializes a new instance of
    /// the <see cref="T:Logger"/> class.
    /// </summary>
    public Logger()
    {
        logFile = File.Open(logFileName,
                            FileMode.OpenOrCreate,
                            FileAccess.Write,
                            FileShare.ReadWrite);
        writer = new StreamWriter(logFile);
    }
```

```
/// <summary>
/// Adds the specified message.
/// </summary>
/// <param name="message">The message.</param>
public void Add(string message)
{
  writer.WriteLine(message);
}

/// <summary>
/// Adds the specified message.
/// </summary>
/// <param name="message">The message.</param>
/// <param name="args">The args.</param>
public void Add(string message,
               params object[] args)
{
  writer.WriteLine(message, args);
}

/// <summary>
/// Performs application-defined tasks associated
/// with freeing, releasing, or
/// resetting unmanaged resources.
/// Implements the Dispose() method of the
/// IDisposable interface
/// </summary>
public void Dispose()
{
  writer.Dispose();
  logFile.Dispose();
}
}
```

9. Open the *Program* class in the project.

10. Modify the code that creates the instance of the *Logging* class and uses it to support automatic calling of the *IDisposable* interface. The *Program* class might look like the following.

```
' VB
Class Program

  Public Overloads Shared Sub Main()

    Using theLog As New Logger()
      theLog.Add("Hello Mom")
    End Using

  End Sub

End Class
```

```
// C#
class Program
{
  static void Main(string[] args)
  {
    using (Logger theLog = new Logger())
    {
      theLog.Add("Hello Mom");
    }
  }
}
```

11. Compile the program and fix any coding errors you find. Run the program and, once complete, find the logfile.txt file in the same directory as the executable to ensure that the code worked as expected.

Lesson Summary

- By reviewing existing classes both inside and outside the .NET Framework, you can determine whether to extend an existing class, compose an existing class, or implement an entirely new class to meet your functional needs.
- You can determine whether to make the component stateful or stateless by reviewing its requirements.
- Weigh whether supporting the thread safety of your component's data is required.
- You must support the *IDisposable* interface if any of the data in your component is not managed.

Lesson Review

You can use the following questions to test your knowledge of the information in Lesson 1, "Implementing Component Features." The questions are also available on the companion CD if you prefer to review them in electronic form.

NOTE Answers

Answers to these questions and explanations of why each answer choice is right or wrong are located in the "Answers" section at the end of the book.

---

1. In what cases must you implement the *IDisposable* interface? (Choose all that apply.)
   A. Any time you have a stateful component
   B. If any of the component's data support the *IDisposable* interface
   C. If the component has any unmanaged resources
   D. If the component is stateless

2. What is a base class used for? (Choose all that apply.)
   A. To specify a naming convention
   B. To define a common interface for specialized classes
   C. To hide implementation details from inheritors
   D. To define common functionality to be shared by inherited classes

3. When should you make your component thread-safe?
   A. Always
   B. Never
   C. Only when the component is going to be used in a multithreaded environment

Lesson 2: Data Access in Components

Data access is central to almost every Web project that is developed today. Whether you are working with a small Microsoft SQL Server Express Edition database or with a data center full of SQL Server, Oracle, DB2, and other database servers, you will need to know how to create components that can consume that data.

After this lesson, you will be able to:

■ Review project requirements to determine the correct data access methodology.

■ Add business logic to your components.

Estimated lesson time: 10 minutes

Data Access

As you trudge through the development of your Web application, you will likely run into situations in which you need components that must consume, create, or change database data. Data access is the code that allows you to communicate with the database. Data access consists of four operations: create, read, update, and delete. These four operations are often referred to as CRUD operations. Adding any (or all) of these operations to a component makes it a data access component.

Implementing data access in your own components involves reviewing several methods to pick the correct one. These include typed DataSets, untyped DataSets, and *DataReader* objects, as well as Web services.

Real World

Shawn Wildermuth

This lesson explains data access using the .NET Framework alone, but data access in the real world is a very different animal. Depending on the requirements of your project, the skill sets of your team, and other factors, you will find that there are many tools to help you accomplish data access. These tools range from simple object-relational mapping products to complex frameworks for building your business objects. As you decide on a strategy for your Web applications, become familiar with solutions (both Microsoft and others) and how they match up to your requirements.

When you build components that consume data, the most basic approach is to access the data using ActiveX Data Object (ADO).NET to implement CRUD functionality. Typically, this means using *DataReader* to get data from the database and using *Command* when you insert, update, or delete. This approach can be very efficient (assuming your SQL code is efficient).

The *DataReader* class is essentially a forward-only fire hose of data to fill in your component data so that they get data from the database very quickly. Additionally, using *Command* (in conjunction with stored procedures) to make changes works very efficiently because you are working with the database at a very basic level.

Exam Tip   If performance is the most important requirement, then using *DataReader* classes in conjunction with *Command* is the methodology of choice.

Using *DataReader* and *Command* is very efficient at run time but at a cost of development time. For example, assume that you have a simple business object that can do all the CRUD functions for contacts. Coding your component using *DataReader* and *Command* might result in a class design like Figure 9-2.

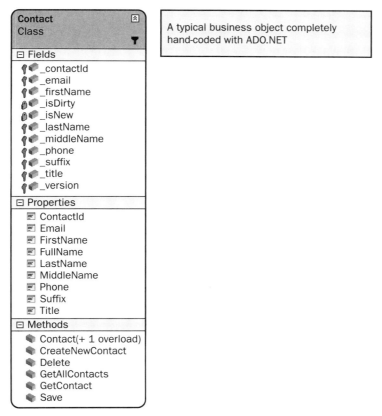

Figure 9-2   Contact component

Much of this class's interface is composed of constructors and methods to get, create, save, and delete a contact (or a list of contacts). The component contains fields to manage if a contact is new (_isNew) and if the contact has changes that need to be saved (_isDirty). Implementing this class means writing ADO.NET code in each of the data methods (for instance, *GetContact*, *Save*, and *Delete*). Although this is not difficult, it is labor-intensive. For example, here is the *GetContact* method:

```vb
' VB
Public Shared Function GetContact(ByVal contactID As Integer) _
  As Contact

  ' Get the connection from configuration
  Dim connInfo As ConnectionStringSettings = _
    ConfigurationManager.ConnectionStrings("AdventureWorks")
  Dim factory As DbProviderFactory = _
    DbProviderFactories.GetFactory(connInfo.ProviderName)

  ' Create the ADO.NET Objects
  Using conn As DbConnection = factory.CreateConnection
    Using cmd As DbCommand = conn.CreateCommand

      ' Setup command to use a stored procedure to
      ' get all the customers data
      cmd.CommandText = "Person.uspGetContact"
      cmd.CommandType = CommandType.StoredProcedure

      ' Add the input parameter
      Dim idParam As DbParameter = factory.CreateParameter
      idParam.ParameterName = "contactID"
      idParam.DbType = DbType.Int32
      idParam.Direction = ParameterDirection.Input
      idParam.Value = contactID
      cmd.Parameters.Add(idParam)
      Try

        ' Open the connection
        conn.ConnectionString = connInfo.ConnectionString
        conn.Open()

        ' Get the data
        Using reader As DbDataReader = _
          cmd.ExecuteReader(CommandBehavior.CloseConnection)

          ' Assuming only one record.
          ' If multiple are returned they are ignored
          If reader.Read Then
            Return New Contact(reader)
          End If

        End Using

      Finally

        If (conn.State <> ConnectionState.Closed) Then
```

```
          conn.Close()
        End If

      End Try

    End Using
  End Using

  ' Contact was not found, we return null
  Return Nothing

End Function
```

```csharp
// C#
public static Contact GetContact(int contactID)
{
  // Get the connection from configuration
  ConnectionStringSettings connInfo =
    ConfigurationManager.ConnectionStrings["AdventureWorks"];
  DbProviderFactory factory =
    DbProviderFactories.GetFactory(connInfo.ProviderName);

  // Create the ADO.NET Objects
  using (DbConnection conn = factory.CreateConnection())
  using (DbCommand cmd = conn.CreateCommand())
  {
    // Setup command to use a stored procedure to
    // get all the customers data
    cmd.CommandText = "Person.uspGetContact";
    cmd.CommandType = CommandType.StoredProcedure;

    // Add the input parameter
    DbParameter idParam = factory.CreateParameter();
    idParam.ParameterName = "contactID";
    idParam.DbType = DbType.Int32;
    idParam.Direction = ParameterDirection.Input;
    idParam.Value = contactID;
    cmd.Parameters.Add(idParam);

    try
    {
      // Open the connection
      conn.ConnectionString = connInfo.ConnectionString;
      conn.Open();

      // Get the data
      using (DbDataReader reader =
            cmd.ExecuteReader(CommandBehavior.CloseConnection))
      {
        // Assuming only one record.
        // If multiple are returned they are ignored
        if (reader.Read())
        {
```

```
        return new Contact(reader);
      }
    }

  }
  finally
  {
    if (conn.State != ConnectionState.Closed)
    {
      conn.Close();
    }
  }
}

// Contact was not found, we return null
return null;
}
```

In addition to the simple component that just needs to load itself up with data, you will need related entities. For example, if you had an Order component that had related Order Items, you would want an efficient way to just load up an order, and all related data in the database would be loaded at the same time. It is not intuitive to expect users of the Order component to then load all the Order Items when they need them. Understanding these relationships and modeling them in your components and the database is crucial to creating smart data access components. You can do this by writing related classes that compose the relationships, but this requires even more hand-coded ADO.NET to load related data in an efficient way.

As you scale out your solution, you can safely remote these objects (or refactor the factory methods into remoteable objects), so there is a clear upgrade path as your Web application needs additional scalability. This method of handcrafting your data access components is preferable when run-time performance and maintainability are high on the list of requirements for your components.

Another solution for performing your data access is to use *DataSet* classes. The *DataSet* class is a container for related data. The *DataSet* has an advantage over raw ADO.NET code in that some of the common data access functionality that you require is built into the *DataSet*. This functionality includes support for related entities, data-binding support in ASP.NET, standard mechanisms for change handling, and support for database-type schema to ensure validation of data before going to the database. In developing your data access components, you can compose your components using a *DataSet* internally to use built-in functionality instead of having to invent it all yourself. In addition, using *DataAdapter* can both simplify retrieval of multiple entity types and offer efficient ways to update *DataSet* data. However, the disadvantage of using *DataSet data* is that they are not as efficient as handcrafted ADO.NET solutions and are not as agile in evolving into solutions involving remoting.

In addition to using *DataSet* in your code, Visual Studio includes support for using typed DataSets. Essentially, typed DataSets are a tool-based solution for generating compile-time, type-safe wrappers around *DataSet*. Typed DataSets in themselves can help you create data access layers very quickly. Instead of using *DataAdapter* to actually perform the data access, *DataSet* uses a set of created classes called *TableAdapter*. In some cases, you can use *DataSet* as your components themselves. The Dataset Designer supports a partial class solution for adding your own functionality to the generated classes.

Although the *DataSet* solution takes the least time to develop, there are major problems with an upgrade path for *DataSet*. If you need to move from *DataSet* into real data access components, that will result in throwing away the *DataSet* code and starting from scratch.

Each of these solutions has its own pros and cons. How do you pick which one meets your requirements? Table 9-1 outlines general guidelines for which solution to pick and when.

Table 9-1   Data Access Methodologies

Data Access Method	Requirements
DataReader and *Command*	Where performance and scalability are most important, and development cost is least important.
DataSet	For good mix of scalability and development cost with some loss of run-time performance.
DataSet	For rapid application design (RAD) or prototyping. There is no good, clear upgrade path from *TableAdapter* to other data access methodologies.

Business Logic

Inside your components, you will need to handle working with the validation and rules that are associated with almost any application. This data-related logic is called business logic, and can include anything from ensuring that strings are not too big to fit into the database to more complex interactions such as not allowing new order creation if no credit is available for a particular customer.

Adding this logic to your components requires understanding both the explicit requirements as well as the implicit requirements. Explicit requirements include logic that is required to implement specific business processes. For example, your requirements might state that when an invoice is finalized, you must calculate the sales tax only for customers who are in certain states. Implicit requirements are more technical in nature, such as validating that data can be stored within the constraints of the database schema and that relationships are maintained. When implementing your data components, you must include functionality for both types of requirements.

Depending on the data access methodology, you will need to determine the correct way to add your business logic. For example, if you are using *DataSet* inside your component, you could use *DataSet* to validate the data against the schema (for example, field length validation, foreign key validation) and custom code in your component to perform the more complex business rules.

Lab: Picking a Data Access Methodology

In this lab, you will review the requirements of a particular Web project and suggest a data access methodology that fulfills the requirements.

▶ **Exercise 1: Choose a Data Access Methodology**

In this exercise, you will review the requirements for a Web project and suggest a data access methodology that fulfills those requirements.

- This project must be delivered by the first of August to meet the contractual obligation to the customer.

- This project must handle a large number of users because this new customer expects more than 1,000 concurrent users and needs room to grow to at least 10,000 concurrent users.

- The data the project must deal with is a complex relational database, and the component should be created with the expectation that the data structures will change over time.

1. Based on these requirements, you compare using ADO.NET with *DataReader* and *Command*, using the *DataSet* class and using typed DataSets.

2. Based on the need to deliver the project quickly, but with an eye to scaling up, you choose to use *DataSet* inside your components.

Lesson Summary

- Depending on the performance, development cost, and maintainability requirements of your particular project, you should be able to pick a suitable data access methodology among *DataReader*, *DataSet*, and typed DataSets.

- By using the data access methodology, you can add business logic to your components in the appropriate way.

Lesson Review

You can use the following questions to test your knowledge of the information in Lesson 2, "Data Access in Components." The questions are also available on the companion CD if you prefer to review them in electronic form.

NOTE Answers

Answers to these questions and explanations of why each answer choice is right or wrong are located in the "Answers" section at the end of the book.

1. Which of the following data access methodologies will perform best?
    A. *DataReader* and *Command*.
    B. *DataSet*.
    C. Typed DataSets.
    D. All work equally well.

2. How should you add business logic and data validation if you are using typed DataSets?
    A. Write custom code in the generated code.
    B. Write custom code in partial class.
    C. Use *DataSet* schema.
    D. Both B and C.

3. What type of data access methodology should you choose for quickly prototyping a component?
    A. *DataReader* and *Command*.
    B. *DataSet*.
    C. Typed DataSet.
    D. None, you should never prototype projects.

Lesson 3: Component Infrastructure

Unfortunately, developing your component's base features is often not enough for real-world systems. There are common infrastructure requirements that most components should include. These requirements include exception handling and profiling support. In this lesson, you will learn how to plan for this infrastructure.

> **After this lesson, you will be able to:**
> - Develop an exception handling mechanism.
> - Support profiling in your component.
>
> **Estimated lesson time: 10 minutes**

Exceptions

As you develop your component, you will need to plan for the unexpected. Your component needs to deal with exceptions. You need to determine when it is appropriate to throw an exception as well as what the right course of action is if an exception is thrown during your component's execution. You will deal with these two decisions separately in the following lesson.

Throwing Exceptions

Exceptions are about exceptional events. Ask yourself the question, "Is this an exceptional case?" It might be perfectly valid for your component to return a value that is indicative of failure without it being an exceptional case. For example, assume you have a Customer component that enables you to retrieve a customer based on the company name. If, when you attempt to find the customer, there is no customer with the specified name, should you throw an exception to indicate that the customer was not found? No, you should return a null (or nothing, in Visual Basic) to indicate that the customer was not found.

Avoid using exceptions for process flow. Exceptions are too heavy for process flow. For example, avoid this sort of code:

```
' VB
Try
  yourComponent.SubmitInvoice()
Catch re As InvoiceRejectedException
  ' ...
Catch ae As InvoiceApprovedException
  ' ...
Catch pe As InvoicePendingException
  ' ...
End Try

// C#
try
```

```
{
  yourComponent.SubmitInvoice();
}
catch (InvoiceRejectedException re)
{
  // ...}
catch (InvoiceApprovedException ae)
{
  // ...}
catch (InvoicePendingException pe)
{
  // ...}
```

Instead, create a return value that you can use to indicate the results, as follows:

```
' VB
Enum SubmissionResult
  Approved
  Rejected
  Pending
End Enum
```

```
// C#
enum SubmissionResult
{
  Approved,
  Rejected,
  Pending
}
```

Then you can use the return value to perform the same process flow without using exceptions:

```
' VB
Dim result As SubmissionResult = yourComponent.SubmitInvoice()

Select Case result
  Case SubmissionResult.Approved
    ' ...
    break
  Case SubmissionResult.Rejected
    ' ...
    break
  Case SubmissionResult.Pending
    ' ...
    break
End Select
```

```
// C#
SubmissionResult result = yourComponent.SubmitInvoice();

switch (result)
{
  case SubmissionResult.Approved:
```

```
{
  // ...
  break;
}
case SubmissionResult.Rejected:
{
  // ...
  break;
}
case SubmissionResult.Pending:
{
  // ...
  break;
}
}
```

MORE INFO   Scaling your application

For more information about scalability, refer to *Improving .NET Application Performance and Scalability* by J.D. Meier, Srinath Vasireddy, Ashish Babbar, and Alex Mackman (Microsoft Press, 2004).

When should you throw an exception? You should throw an exception only when something exceptional occurs, and you should throw your own exceptions whenever something happens in your code that is unexpected. For example, if you attempt to submit an invoice and find that the invoice is invalid in an unexpected way, you should throw an exception. If there is a .NET Framework exception that is indicative of the problem (for example, *ArgumentException*), you should throw that exception. If one does not exist, you should create your own exception class that derives from *System.Exception*.

BEST PRACTICES   Deriving custom exceptions

Prior to the .NET Framework 2.0, it was commonly recommended that all application exceptions derive from *System.ApplicationException*, but that provided a level of isolation with no real purpose. Deriving your own exceptions from *System.Exception* is now the accepted best practice.

Handling Exceptions

When the code inside your component causes an exception to be thrown (that is, not an exception you have explicitly thrown), you must determine whether to allow the exception to propagate or attempt to recover from the exceptional case. Consider the previous example of the Customer component. What happens if the database is not available? The ADO.NET managed provider will throw a *DbException* informing you that it could not locate the database server. At this point, you have two choices: Propagate the exception up the call stack or attempt to recover from the error.

When propagating an exception to the caller, you might find it useful to include contextual information about when the error happened. This is most often done by throwing a new exception and including the current exception as the inner exception. For example:

```vb
' VB
Try
  Dim result As InvoiceResult = yourComponent.SubmitInvoice()
  ' ...
Catch ex As Exception
  Throw New _
    InvoiceException("Exception thrown while submitting invoice.", ex)
End Try
```

```csharp
// C#
try
{
  InvoiceResult result = yourComponent.SubmitInvoice();
  // ...
}
catch (Exception ex)
{
  throw new
    InvoiceException("Exception thrown while submitting invoice.", ex);
}
```

If you cannot provide any additional information to help determine the source of the exception, you can choose not to catch the exception at all and simply let it flow up to the caller. Often, this is the right approach for exceptions over which you have no control (for instance, *OutOfMemoryException*).

Instead of propagating the exception, you have the choice of attempting to recover from the exception or exiting gracefully. In the case of the database not being available, you might attempt recovery by retrying the database after a small delay. If the recovery fails, you can either propagate the exception to the caller or attempt to exit gracefully. Both are valid options in different circumstances.

Exam Tip   Avoid deriving your own exceptions from *ApplicationException*; instead, derive them from the *Exception* class. This recommendation has changed from .NET Framework 1.x to .NET Framework 2.0.

Profiling Components

As part of the requirements for any component you develop, you should expect to profile that component to identify performance issues and resource leaks. Profiling a component entails using one of a number of profiling tools to test the effectiveness of the component. These tools are detailed in Table 9-2.

Table 9-2   **Profiling Tools**

Tool	Description
Visual Studio Performance Wizard	Monitors the run-time behavior of your component to report on the effective performance of code. Allows for either sampling or instrumentation. Sampling is useful for testing the effectiveness of a whole system. Instrumentation enables you to test the performance of individual components.
CLR Profiler	Enables you to create memory allocation scenarios under which to test your component or application. Enables you to see how well your application works in a variety of scenarios.
SQL Profiler	Enables you to profile operations inside SQL Server. Can help identify inefficient queries, stored procedure compilation issues, and deadlocks.

Before you can use the data in a profile, you must understand the requirements for your component:

- Do you have performance metrics for your component?
- What resource usage is acceptable for your component?
- Under what load scenarios do you need to test the component?

Quick Check
- What is profiling used for?

Quick Check Answer
- Profiling is used to test performance of a component against requirements and to isolate resource leaks.

Simply profiling your component to see how well it behaves will tell you only how it is working, not whether it's working well enough to meet the requirements. Understanding these requirements (or creating them) is crucial to profiling your component.

Lab: Propagating an Exception with Context

In this lab, you will create a new exception class and then use it to wrap an exception that occurs with context.

▶ **Exercise 1: Propagating the Exception**

In this exercise, you will create a new exception class and use it to propagate context with your exception.

1. In Visual Studio, click File | Open | Project/Solution, and then navigate to \Chapter 09 \Lesson 3\Exercise 1\Before.

2. Run the project as it is. You will notice that an exception is thrown when the invoice is submitted.

3. Next, add a new class called *InvoiceException* to the project. You will use this class to propagate the context information.

4. Derive this new class from the *System.Exception* class and create a constructor that takes a string for the message and an exception.

5. In the new constructor, call the base class's constructor with the string and exception arguments. The new *InvoiceException* class might look something like this:

```VB
' VB
Public Class InvoiceException
  Inherits Exception

  Public Sub New(ByVal message As String, _
                 ByVal innerException As Exception)
    MyBase.New(message, innerException)
  End Sub

End Class
```

```C#
// C#
public class InvoiceException : Exception
{
  public InvoiceException(string message, Exception innerException)
    : base(message, innerException)
  {
  }
}
```

6. Next, go to the *Submit* method of the *Invoice* class and create a *Try/Catch* block around the method body.

7. In the catch portion of the *Try/Catch* block, catch an Exception type of exception and throw your new *InvoiceException*, passing in an informative message and the caught exception. Changes from the Before project are in bold. The completed solution can be viewed in the After folder.

The method might look something like this:

```VB
' VB
Public Function Submit() As SubmissionResult
  Try
    Dim s As String = Nothing

    ' Exception will be thrown here
    Dim length As Integer = s.Length

    Return SubmissionResult.Success
```

```
  Catch ex As Exception
    Throw New InvoiceException("Failure during Invoice Submission.", ex)
  End Try

End Function

// C#
public SubmissionResult Submit()
{
  try
  {
    string s = null;

    // Exception will be thrown here
    int length = s.Length;

    return SubmissionResult.Success;
  }
  catch (Exception ex)
  {
    throw new InvoiceException("Failure during Invoice Submission.", ex);
  }
}
```

8. Compile the program and fix any coding errors that you find. Run the program under the debugger and, when the exception happens, notice the new exception with the informative message. Also look at the inner exception of the new exception to find the original one that was thrown.

Lesson Summary

- You should throw exceptions only in exceptional cases; do not use exceptions for program flow.
- When you propagate exceptions, include contextual information by wrapping them with a more descriptive exception.
- All components should be profiled to isolate performance problems and resource leaks.

Lesson Review

You can use the following questions to test your knowledge of the information in Lesson 3, "Component Infrastructure." The questions are also available on the companion CD if you prefer to review them in electronic form.

NOTE Answers

Answers to these questions and explanations of why each answer choice is right or wrong are located in the "Answers" section at the end of the book.

---

1. In which of the following examples should you throw an exception from a component? (Choose all that apply.)
   A. An invalid argument is sent to a method.
   B. While searching for a particular piece of data, it returns with no results.
   C. The system runs out of memory.
   D. The database is not available.

2. If you propagate an exception to the caller of a method, you should always wrap that exception to include context.
   A. True
   B. False

3. What are the goals of profiling a component? (Choose all that apply.)
   A. To ensure that the component meets all functional requirements
   B. To measure the performance of the component against any performance requirements
   C. To isolate resource leaks
   D. To ensure that the component will compile

Chapter Review

To further practice and reinforce the skills you learned in this chapter, you can complete the following tasks:

- Review the chapter summary.
- Review the list of key terms introduced in this chapter.
- Complete the case scenarios. These scenarios set up real-world situations involving the topics of this chapter and ask you to create solutions.
- Complete the suggested practices.
- Take a practice test.

Chapter Summary

- Implementing component features includes deciding how to create the desired functionality, including whether to extend, compose, or implement the functionality; whether to build a stateless or stateful component; where and how to use threads in the component; and how to deal with unmanaged resources.
- Creating data access components requires an understanding of which data access methodology to pick for your component.
- Adding business logic to a data access component can be accomplished in a number of ways based on the data access methodology chosen for the component.
- Dealing with component infrastructure includes deciding when and how to deal with exceptions.
- All components should be profiled to ensure that they meet performance metrics as well as to isolate any resource leaks.

Key Terms

Do you know what these key terms mean? You can check your answers by looking up the terms in the glossary at the end of the book.

- business logic
- profiling
- stateless
- thread-safe

Case Scenarios

In the following case scenarios, you will apply what you've learned about how to design components. You can find answers to these questions in the "Answers" section at the end of this book.

Case Scenario 1: Choose a Data Access Methodology

Your company needs data access components to be created for a new Web application.

Interviews

Following is the company engineering manager's interview statement:

- **Engineering manager**   We have a new Web application that needs to be brought up to allow employees of the company to request vacation time. The accounting department expected this to be completed already, so we have a severe time constraint on completing this to make them happy.

Questions

Answer the following questions for the Web developer:

1. Which methodology do we need?
2. How can I add the business logic needed to ensure that each employee has only one request pending at a time?

Case Scenario 2: Locate a Resource Leak

The e-commerce company for which you work released an application about five days ago. There is a problem with the application because it is consuming lots of memory. Your manager needs your help in locating the problem.

Interviews

Following is the manager's interview statement:

- **Your manager**   We are under the gun. The system was not profiled before it went live, and now the system is performing badly and just eating memory. We need you to find out why it is consuming so much memory.

Questions

Answer the following questions for your manager:

1. How do you propose to find the memory issues?
2. Can you isolate the problems to expose which components are causing the problems?

Suggested Practices

To help you successfully master the exam objectives presented in this chapter, complete the following tasks.

Create a New Logging Component

For this task, you should complete at least Practices 1 and 2. You can do Practice 3 for a more in-depth understanding of implementing component features.

- **Practice 1**   Create a new component to do the logging for a system. You will need to determine how to implement the component by deciding whether to extend, compose, or implement the features for a component that will log data.
- **Practice 2**   Decide whether you can create the component as stateless or stateful.
- **Practice 3**   Make the component thread-safe.

Create a Data Access Component

For this task, you should complete at least Practices 1 and 2. You can do Practices 3 and 4 for a more in-depth understanding of data access components.

- **Practice 1**   Create a new class that exposes data from a database table.
- **Practice 2**   Implement the features using a typed DataSet.
- **Practice 3**   Re-engineer the component to use a *DataSet* and *DataAdapter*.
- **Practice 4**   Re-engineer the component to use *DataReader* and *Command*.

Take a Practice Test

The practice tests on this book's companion CD offer many options. For example, you can test yourself on just one exam objective, or you can test yourself on all the 70-547 certification exam content. You can set up the test so that it closely simulates the experience of taking a certification exam, or you can set it up in study mode so that you can look at the correct answers and explanations after you answer each question.

MORE INFO   **Practice tests**

For details about all the practice test options available, see the "How to Use the Practice Tests" section in this book's Introduction.

Chapter 10
Reusable Software Components

Reusability has been the holy grail of software development for decades. It seems that when new technologies arise, a resurgence of interest in reusability comes with it. The dream of software factories that build and integrate components on demand has not been realized. In fact, quite the opposite is true. Organizations have traditionally done a poor job of reusing software. The past few years, however, have been different. The trend now seems to be toward more pragmatic reuse. Instead of spending excess time and money building the most generic, extensible, and reusable software possible, organizations focus more on constructing software to solve the current need while being *considerate* of future needs. That is, because it is cost prohibitive to try to anticipate all possible future uses, developers build software that can be extended if needed, although this might require additional development.

The Microsoft .NET Framework offers an excellent balance between building generic software and constructing modular, extensible components. In this chapter, you will examine some techniques for identifying reusable components and extending or restricting those components. You will also learn about testing and deploying reusable software components. These topics will provide you with the knowledge necessary to identify and extend reusable components in your software development efforts. Refer to Chapter 8, "Component Design," for information about designing reusable components.

MORE INFO   *Component* class and *IComponent* interface

Component is the default implementation of *IComponent*. The *Component* class is also the base class for all components in the common language runtime (CLR). For more information about the *IComponent* interface, visit *http://msdn.microsoft.com/library/default.asp?url=/library/en-us /cpref/html/frlrfsystemcomponentmodelicomponentclasstopic.asp*. For more information about the *Component* class, go to *http://msdn.microsoft.com/library/default.asp?url=/library/en-us/cpref /html/frlrfsystemcomponentmodelcomponentclasstopic.asp*.

Exam objectives in this chapter:
- Consume a reusable software component.
  - ❏ Identify a reusable software component from available components to meet the requirements.
  - ❏ Identify whether the reusable software component needs to be extended.
  - ❏ Identify whether the reusable software component needs to be wrapped.
  - ❏ Identify whether any existing functionality needs to be hidden.
  - ❏ Test the identified component that is based on the requirements.

Lessons in this chapter:

Before You Begin

To complete the lesson in this chapter, you should be familiar with Microsoft Visual Basic or C# and be comfortable with the following tasks:

■ Creating a ASP.NET Web page in Microsoft Visual Studio 2005

■ Creating class libraries in Visual Studio 2005

■ Working with object-oriented programming techniques and terms

---

Real World

Brian C. Lanham

Soon after college, while working as a programmer at a financial services organization, I earned the nickname "Captain Generic." (As an aside, I sort of ignored the "Generic" part and let myself believe people were calling me "Captain.") The reason for this nickname was because I worked constantly to improve the generalities in my software systems. It became my white whale, so to speak. I was convinced that I could construct a framework for the organization that would allow new systems to be constructed with little more effort than modifying a configuration file.

An older and wiser developer took me aside and taught me why I was there. He said that the bank was in the business of making money. This really stuck with me, and even today I remember that lesson. Basically, there is a fundamental reason that your organization is in business. Even software development companies such as Microsoft Corporation have to make money. That means we don't have all the time and resources in the world to build the quintessential, completely reusable, and interchangeable componentized system.

As a result of my epiphany, I worked to become more practical with software design. Before that, I would spend hours and hours trying to anticipate what *might* happen and how the business *might* be able to use this or that. Afterward, however, I focused my efforts differently. I started by ensuring that I solved the problem at hand. Then I determined whether I could modularize the design better to make some aspects more reusable. Then I stopped. I still use this technique, and it works really well for me. I hope to share some of this approach with you throughout the chapter.

Lesson 1: Consuming Reusable Software Components

This lesson is segmented into three distinct sections. The first section reviews some techniques for identifying reusable components. You will also learn how to avoid wasting time trying to force reusability. The second section covers the steps appropriate for extending or restricting reusable components. This topic will show you how to control and manage reusability. The final topic addresses testing and deploying your extensions and wrappers for reusable components.

After this lesson, you will be able to:

- Identify reusable components from existing components.
- Determine how to reuse components, including extending components to add new capabilities or wrapping components to hide existing capabilities.
- Test reusable components as well as components that use them.

Estimated lesson time: 90 minutes

Identifying Reusable Components

One of the most important realizations regarding reusability is that not everything is appropriate or available for reuse. Some things are truly singular of purpose and apply in only one situation. If you do not realize this, you might waste time trying to force reuse where none is possible.

Whether you are dealing with custom components or third-party software, there are some common factors to consider when looking for reusability.

Evaluating How a Component Might Be Reused

It is generally more important to ask yourself how, instead of why, a component can be reused. The answer to why a component can be reused is unchanging and consists of adages such as "Don't reinvent the wheel" and catchphrases such as "Object-oriented programming is all about reuse." Whether these are true is irrelevant. What is relevant is how a component can be reused in your organization. You can probably think of how someone, somewhere, at some time can reuse a component. But try to be practical and focus on your current organization within the scope of the strategic technology plan (which is generally three to five years in length).

Businesses are ever-changing. In some cases, changes are anticipated and even planned. It is in these situations that you can determine how a component can be reused. For example, suppose some new legislation regarding taxation rates will become effective within a few months. Your organization has several product offerings including a payroll product and a tax-filing product. You can easily see how both products can take advantage of a common component providing taxation business logic. Anticipating this, you can reuse the business logic in each product. As another example, consider mergers and acquisitions. A financial services company might plan to expand and include brokerage services within a year. Anticipating this, you can begin preparing now for system integration opportunities and common financial services business logic. Specifically, the trust and brokerage divisions of your organization perform very similar work. They differ in legislation aspects; however, for simplicity, they share common fee structures. You can see that there is opportunity for reuse in this environment. The business processes associated with handling both brokerage and trust transactions are similar, as is the fee structure of both. Even in these scenarios, it is unlikely that you will think of everything. However, you have some boundaries within which you can work to focus your reuse efforts.

Unfortunately, when a reusable component surfaces, there are no fireworks, no marching bands, and no announcements. In fact, reusable components are sneaky. They often hide until you tightly couple them with some other component. Then, without warning, they appear, clear and shiny. There are some standard guidelines that you can follow to identify reusable components. The following list describes some of the most useful steps for determining whether an available component is reusable.

- **Look for an immediate business need** Talk with your colleagues about their projects. It is possible that they are working on a system that has similar functionality or involves the same business units as yours. These are good opportunities for reuse. You might be able to share recipes for consuming third-party components and define a common set of classes to extend and restrict those components.

- **Build abstraction layers for existing systems** When using a third-party or custom system, it is likely that you will not have that system forever. Even if you have the same product for a while, you will almost certainly change versions. Most cases involving commercial, off-the-shelf applications are good scenarios for building your own components, which provide indirect access through an abstraction layer to an underlying component in the commercial application (a technique called "wrapping"). Doing this loosely couples any future applications with the existing system. This allows the existing system to change while minimizing the impact on applications that use it. For example, if you are building a system that uses a human resources (HR) system for retrieving employee information, you can build a set of classes around the HR system that your application and future applications can use.

- **Review the strategic plan** Take a look at upcoming projects and the business units that they affect. Also, look for planned changes in legislation and company policies. These can present appropriate opportunities to consider reuse in your systems. By anticipating future needs, you can design systems to reuse existing components better and allow more flexibility. For example, suppose you are using a third-party logging component for a particular application to provide audit trails. If you see an upcoming requirement to provide similar audit trails in other systems, you can wrap common logging features and make them readily available for other systems.

- **Inspect access levels** Not every component can be extended or wrapped. Also, even if a component is visible publicly, some of its members might not be. You need to inspect the component to determine what is available for wrapping.

Reuse Pitfalls

The quest for reusable components can suck you into a long and drawn-out search for a perfect design. Here are some common pitfalls to avoid when considering reusability in your design.

- **Do not fabricate a reuse scenario** It can be easy to create a could-happen scenario. The problem with this is two-fold. First, there might be many possible scenarios, and it is probably cost-prohibitive to try to account for all of them. Second, you are going to spend a lot of effort on scenarios that might occur but in reality will probably never occur.
- **Avoid wrapping an entire system** It might be tempting to create an abstraction layer for the entire functionality of an existing system. For example, if you are building a wrapper to access functionality from the HR system, you might be tempted to wrap the entire HR system. You should avoid this and instead focus on wrapping only the needed functionality. You can always wrap more features later.

Extending and Restricting Reusable Components

Once you've identified a reusable component, you can reuse it as it is, but you will likely need to extend it or restrict it in some fashion. In this section, you will look at forms of reuse, techniques for reuse, and ways of extending and restricting the functionality of existing components.

Choosing Appropriate Reuse Techniques

Almost all reuse opportunities come in one of three rudimentary forms. *Code blocks* are blocks of code that are copied and pasted among systems. Perhaps you have a string parsing routine that your colleague finds useful. You can give her the code (in an e-mail or a text file, for example) and she can embed that method in her system. *Recipes*, which are extensions of blocks, describe how to reproduce some behavior in terms of consuming an existing component. For example, if your colleague writes a data access component, she can give you a recipe for how to reference it in your system and how to write code to consume that component. Finally, you can reuse the *binaries*, including executables (files with an .exe extension) and dynamic-link libraries (files with a .dll extension) distributed on local or remote systems without distributing them with each project.

Within the three rudimentary forms, there are two basic ways to reuse software. You can use the component, without changing it, in multiple systems. Using components without changing them generally falls under the recipes category and should be straightforward. Second, you can extend or restrict functionality of the component for individual systems. The next sections will cover extending and restricting components.

Extending Components

One often thinks of reusing software in terms of either using components without changing them or of extending them. This section will discuss ways to extend components. This discussion assumes that you are extending a binary component. Even if the source code is available, modifications to the source are not the topic of this section. Instead, it will cover how to use inheritance and polymorphism to add your own custom attributes and behaviors to existing software.

Inheriting   The .NET Framework 2.0 supports single *inheritance*. That means a class can inherit from only one class. Inheriting from a class is called implementation inheritance because the child or derived class is inheriting the actual implementation or functionality in the parent or base class. The following code samples show how to inherit in Visual Basic and C#.

```
' VB
Public Class ChildClass
Inherits ParentClass
End Class
```

```
// C#
public class childClass : parentClass
{
}
```

There are some special rules you must follow regarding *constructors*–procedures used to create instances of objects–and *destructors*–procedures used to destroy instances–in the context of inheritance. Following are some specific constructor rules.

- **Derived class constructors in Visual Basic**   The first line of each constructor in the derived class must be a call to the constructor of the base class unless the base class has a constructor with no arguments *and* is accessible to the derived class.
- **Derived class constructors in C#**   If a base-class constructor is not explicitly called by a constructor in a derived class, then the default constructor is called implicitly. If there is no default constructor, the derived class must call a constructor in the base class.

MORE INFO   **Constructors and destructors**

For more information on constructors and destructors in Visual Basic .NET, see "Using Constructors and Destructors" in the MSDN Library at *http://msdn.microsoft.com/library/default.asp?url= /library/en-us/vbcn7/html/vaconusingconstructorsdestructors.asp*. For more information on C#, see the C# Programming Guide at *http://msdn2.microsoft.com/en-us/library/ace5hbzh.aspx* for constructors and at *http://msdn2.microsoft.com/en-us/library/66x5fx1b.aspx* for destructors.

Remember that not every property and method in the parent class is available to the child class, and this includes constructors and destructors. Access modifiers are keywords added to code element declarations to indicate the visibility of individual elements. The following list of keywords describes the visibility adornments available in the .NET Framework and how each affects inheritance.

Public (Visual Basic) / public (C#)	Members declared as public have unrestricted visibility and are available to any code that can see them, including external and derived classes. Public classes are also unrestricted in visibility, and other classes can inherit from them.
Private (Visual Basic) / private (C#)	Private members are available only to the class in which they are defined. Private classes *must* be nested within other classes. All classes declared at the namespace level must be public.
Protected (Visual Basic) / protected (C#)	Protected members behave like private members in that they are visible only within the class in which they are defined. However, protected members are also visible to derived classes of the class in which they are defined. Classes declared as protected must be within another class. All classes declared at the namespace level must be public.
Friend (Visual Basic) / internal (C#)	Friend and internal members are visible within the current assembly. Types outside the assembly in which friend and internal members are defined cannot see the friend and internal members. Classes declared as friend must be within another class. All classes declared at the namespace level must be public.

MORE INFO   **Access levels in Visual Basic**

Access to an element of a component is determined according to how the element is declared *and* how the container of the element is declared. More information about which access levels can be used on each element type (classes, properties, interfaces, and so on), and the effect of the access level, can be found in the MSDN Library at *http://msdn2.microsoft.com/en-us/library/76453kax.aspx*.

Access modifiers can be applied at varying scopes such as at class, module, property, method, and variable definitions. One of the most common class-level access modifier combinations is Protected Friend (Visual Basic) / protected internal (C#). Using this combination of modifiers allows you to hide members to all but derived classes and other classes in the same assembly. Other combinations do not make much sense. For example, combining Friend with Public or Private is illogical.

Exam Tip   Access levels (Public, Protected, and Friend) are important in determining whether component features, including the entire component, can be extended, which features can be extended, and how. This pertains to the class definition and to member definitions (properties, methods, and events).

In addition to using access levels to restrict member visibility in classes, you can also control inheritance. By adorning a class with NotInheritable (Visual Basic) / sealed (C#), you prevent derivations of that class. By adorning a class with MustInherit (Visual Basic) / abstract (C#), you require a derived class to be created. The following code samples demonstrate these techniques.

```
' VB
' The base class cannot be used as is and must be derived.
Public MustInherit Class MyBaseClass

    Public MustOverride Function CalculateInterest(ByVal LoanAmount As Decimal, ByVal Term As
Integer) As Decimal

End Class

' The derived class cannot, in turn, have another derived class.
Public NotInheritable Class MySubClass
    Inherits MyBaseClass

    Public Overrides Function CalculateInterest(ByVal LoanAmount As Decimal, ByVal Term As
Integer) As Decimal
        ' Do some work.
    End Function

End Class
```

```
// C#
// The base class cannot be used as is and must be derived.
public abstract class MyBaseClass
    {
        public abstract decimal calculateInterest(decimal loanAmount, int term);
    }

// The derived class cannot, in turn, have another derived class.
    public sealed class MySubClass : MyBaseClass
    {
```

```
    public override decimal calculateInterest (decimal loanAmount, int term)
    {
        // Do some work.
    }
}
```

Quick Check

Inheritance is a technique whereby one class can be derived from another (the base class), taking advantage of the functionality of the base class. List the modifiers that can be added to a class declaration with respect to inheritance.

Quick Check Answer

- NotInheritable (Visual Basic) / sealed (C#) prevents a class from being used as a base class.
- MustInherit (Visual Basic) / abstract (C#) prevents a class from being created. This class can be used only as a base class for a derived class. This is sometimes referred to as an *abstract class*.

Overriding and Overloading You do not need to accept the implementation of a base class as it is. You can extend the existing implementation by defining new implementations of existing methods. The .NET Framework provides support for overriding and overloading members.

Overriding is replacing a base class member with a derived class member of the same name. The *ToString()* method is an often overridden method. Instead of accepting the default implementation of *ToString*, you can override the implementations in the base class. In Visual Basic and C#, you use the *Overrides* keyword (although it is not capitalized in C#) to indicate that a member is overriding another member of the same name in the base class.

Classes can require overriding for some members. Adorning Visual Basic members with the *MustOverride* keyword requires that the implementation for that member is provided by a derived class. In C#, members are declared as abstract to accomplish the same behavior. In Visual Basic, you must also adorn the class with the *MustInherit* keyword if a member is declared as *MustOverride*. In C#, the class containing the abstract member must also be abstract. The following code samples demonstrate this.

```
' VB
Public MustInherit Class MyBaseClass

    Public MustOverride Function CalculateInterest(ByVal LoanAmount As Decimal, ByVal Term As
Integer) As Decimal

End Class
```

```
Public Class MySubClass
    Inherits MyBaseClass

    Public Overrides Function CalculateInterest(ByVal LoanAmount As Decimal, ByVal Term As
Integer) As Decimal
            Return 15.5
    End Function

End Class
```

```
// C#
    public abstract class MyBaseClass
    {
        public abstract decimal calculateInterest(decimal loanAmount, int term);
    }

    public class MySubClass : MyBaseClass
    {
        public override decimal calculateInterest (decimal loanAmount, int term)
        {
            return 15.5M;
        }
    }
```

The .NET Framework 2.0 adds a new exception type to give you additional flexibility when inheriting from classes that require overriding. Use the *NotImplementedException* when you do not want to provide an implementation. Using this exception allows you to uphold the interface contract associated with inheritance without requiring you to implement features that aren't appropriate. The following code samples demonstrate this.

```
' VB
Public Class MySubClass
    Inherits MyBaseClass

    Public Overrides Function CalculateInterest(ByVal LoanAmount As Decimal, ByVal Term As
Integer) As Decimal
Throw New NotImplementedException
    End Function

End Class
```

```
// C#
    public class MySubClass : MyBaseClass
    {
        public override decimal calculateInterest (decimal loanAmount, int term)
        {
            throw new NotImplementedException ();
        }
    }
```

Overloading differs from overriding in that it allows you to provide multiple implementations of the same members. Suppose, for example, that you have an HR system that defines several types of employees in an inheritance chain. In this system, the base class *Employee* is derived by *ExemptEmployee* and *NonExemptEmployee* classes. Further, suppose that there is a component in the system that calculates the amount of vacation time available to the employee. The calculation is, however, different for exempt and non-exempt employees.

Clearly, you can write one method and use conditional logic (an if statement) to determine which calculation to perform. However, if a new type of employee is added to the system, you must modify the conditional logic everywhere it occurs. (Suppose, for example, that an employee type called "intern" is added and is defined by the human resources department as a non-exempt employee.) Not only that, but the code becomes unwieldy and difficult to maintain. Instead of using conditional logic, you can use overloading and polymorphism.

Polymorphism literally means "many forms." In the context of object-oriented programming, it is a powerful technique for customizing functionality based on particular types. In the preceding scenario, you can use polymorphism to minimize the amount of conditional logic that must be maintained. The following code samples show how to use polymorphism and method overloading in this scenario.

```vb
' VB
Public Class Employee
    Public ReadOnly Property HoursWorked() As Decimal
        Get
            ' Fetch the hours worked from the database.
        End Get
    End Property
End Class

Public Class ExemptEmployee
    Inherits Employee
End Class

Public Class NonExemptEmployee
    Inherits Employee
End Class

Public Class VacationCalculator
    Public Overloads Function GetAvailableVacationHours(ByVal forEmployee As ExemptEmployee)
As Decimal
        ' Compute
    End Function

    Public Overloads Function GetAvailableVacationHours(ByVal forEmployee As
NonExemptEmployee) As Decimal
        ' Compute
    End Function
End Class
```

```
// C#
   public class Employee
   {
       public decimal HoursWorked
       {
           get
           {
               // Fetch the hours worked from the database.
           }
       }

   }

   public class ExemptEmployee : Employee {}
   public class NonExemptEmployee : Employee {}

   public class VacationCalculator
   {
       public decimal GetAvailableVacationHours (ExemptEmployee forEmployee)
       {//Compute}
       public decimal GetAvailableVacationHours (NonExemptEmployee forEmployee)
       {//Compute}
   }
```

These code samples show how you can use overloading to replace conditional logic. Overloading is a powerful tool that greatly improves both extensibility and maintainability in your applications. The following code demonstrates how to use the overloaded members polymorphically.

```
' VB
Dim exEmp As ExemptEmployee = New ExemptEmployee
Dim nonexEmp As NonExemptEmployee = New NonExemptEmployee
Dim vc As VacationCalculator = New VacationCalculator

vc.GetAvailableVacationHours(exEmp)
vc.GetAvailableVacationHours(nonexEmp)

// C#
ExemptEmployee exEmp = new ExemptEmployee ();
NonExemptEmployee nonexEmp = new NonExemptEmployee();

VacationCalculator vc = new VacationCalculator();

// The runtime "knows" which overloaded definition
// to call based on the method signature.
vc.GetAvailableVacationHours(exEmp);
vc.GetAvailableVacationHours(nonexEmp);
```

> ## Quick Check
>
> 1. Overriding is a technique by which a derived class can refine the behavior of the base class. List the modifiers that can be added to a method or property of a class with respect to overriding.
> 2. Which of these modifiers can be used within the base class?
> 3. Which of these modifiers can be used within the derived class?
>
> ### Quick Check Answers
>
> 1. There are four modifiers pertaining to overriding. They are:
>   - ❏ *Overridable* Allows a property or method in a class to be overridden in a derived class.
>   - ❏ *Overrides* Overrides an *Overridable* property or method defined in the base class.
>   - ❏ *NotOverridable* Prevents a property or method from being overridden in an inheriting class.
>   - ❏ *MustOverride* Requires that a derived class override the property or method.
> 2. The base class can use *NotOverridable*, *MustOverride*, and *Overridable* to allow or restrict enhancement of the base-class functionality by a derived class. The base class can also be a derived class. As a derived class, the base class may use the *Overrides* modifier.
> 3. The derived class must use *Overrides* if the base class has used *MustOverride* on any methods.

When inheriting, there are times when you want to reference the members of the base class explicitly. Suppose, for example, that you want to override a method in the base class to add new functionality, but you do not want to lose the existing functionality. You can reference the method in the base class directly by using the keyword *MyBase* (Visual Basic) / *base* (C#).

Continuing with the employee time management scenario, suppose you have a component to compute overtime pay. The business logic is the same for all employees. However, in addition to the base logic, non-exempt employees are to receive an additional hourly payout if the over-time work is between midnight and the beginning of the work day. You can accomplish this by truly extending the functionality in the base class, as the following code samples demonstrate.

```vb
' VB
Public Class Employee
    Public ReadOnly Property HoursWorked() As Decimal
        Get
            ' Fetch the hours worked from the database.
```

```
        End Get
    End Property
End Class

Public Class ExemptEmployee
    Inherits Employee
End Class

Public Class NonExemptEmployee
    Inherits Employee
End Class

Public Class OvertimeCalculator

    Public Overridable Overloads Function GetOvertimePay(ByVal forEmployee As ExemptEmployee)
As Decimal

    End Function

    Public Overridable Overloads Function GetOvertimePay(ByVal forEmployee As
NonExemptEmployee) As Decimal

    End Function

End Class

Public Class MyOvertimeCalculator
    Inherits OvertimeCalculator

    Public Overrides Function GetOvertimePay(ByVal forEmployee As NonExemptEmployee) As
Decimal
        Dim basePay As Decimal
        basePay = MyBase.GetOvertimePay(forEmployee)
        ' Perform custom logic to adjust base pay and return adjusted amount.
    End Function

End Class

Public Class OvertimeTester
    Public Sub Test()
        Dim exEmp As ExemptEmployee = New ExemptEmployee
        Dim nonexEmp As NonExemptEmployee = New NonExemptEmployee
        Dim otc As MyOvertimeCalculator = New MyOvertimeCalculator

        ' This call actually calls the method in the base class.
        otc.GetOvertimePay(exEmp)

        ' This call uses the method in the derived class which,
        ' in turn uses the method in the base class.
        otc.GetOvertimePay(nonexEmp)

    End Sub
End Class
```

```csharp
// C#
public class Employee
{
    public decimal HoursWorked
    {
        get
        {
            // Fetch the hours worked from the database.
        }
    }

}

public class ExemptEmployee : Employee {}
public class NonExemptEmployee : Employee {}

public class VacationCalculator
{
    public decimal GetAvailableVacationHours (ExemptEmployee forEmployee)
    {}
    public decimal GetAvailableVacationHours (NonExemptEmployee forEmployee)
    {}
}

public class OvertimeCalculator
{
    public decimal getOvertimePay(ExemptEmployee forEmployee)
    { }
    public decimal getOvertimePay(NonExemptEmployee forEmployee)
    { }
}

public class MyOvertimeCalculator:OvertimeCalculator
{
    public override decimal getOvertimePay(NonExemptEmployee forEmployee)
    {
        decimal basePay;
        basePay = base.getOvertimePay(forEmployee);
        // Perform custom logic to adjust base pay and return adjusted amount.
    }
}

public class OvertimeTester
{
    public void Test ()
    {
        ExemptEmployee exEmp = new ExemptEmployee ();
        NonExemptEmployee nonexEmp = new NonExemptEmployee();

        MyOvertimeCalculator otc = new MyOvertimeCalculator ();

        // This call actually calls the method in the base class.
        otc.getOvertimePay (exEmp);
```

```
        // This call uses the method in the derived class which,
        // in turn uses the method in the base class.
        otc.GetOvertimePay(nonexEmp)
    }
}
```

Pitfalls of Extending Components   Extending is a powerful and useful tool. However, there are some potential issues with extending reusable components, especially if doing so with inheritance. The following list highlights some important pitfalls to avoid.

- **Deep inheritance chains**   As with most good things, too much inheritance can be bad. The deeper the inheritance chain, the more fragile the super base class becomes. Any change, no matter how small, can have an impact on inherited classes down the line. Avoid creating deep inheritance chains. Consider, instead, refactoring your wrapping classes to include the additionally needed functionality.

- **Excessive overriding**   In some situations, it is appropriate to override functionality in a base class. However, if you override excessively, you are fundamentally changing the class definition. This means that, although the derived class is of the same type as the base class, it truly is not like the base class. Instead of trying to force a derived class to be a base class, simply create a new class.

- **Ignoring security**   If there is security in the base class, it is there for a reason. You should not wrap an existing component for the purpose of bypassing its security mechanism.

Restricting Components

Developers consider restricting components less often than they consider extending them. Restricting, however, is just as appropriate and valid as extending. Some reasons for restricting functionality include licensing compliance, security, and data protection. In this section, you will review some techniques for restricting the functionality available in reusable components.

Exam Tip   When using a component that must be modified to meet requirements, remember the following:

- To inherit is to derive a new component from the original component to extend functionality.

- To wrap is to create an instance of the original component within the new component to restrict functionality.

Creating Wrappers   When extending components, you can inherit from a base class and add your own functionality as needed. Although some restricting can be accomplished with inheritance, restricting functionality typically requires a slightly different technique. Instead of inheriting from a base class, you can create a wrapper class. The wrapper class is a stand-alone class that contains an instance of the reusable class and exposes the limited functionality of that class. It is important to note that because the wrapper class is responsible for instantiating the component, it is also responsible for disposing of the component. Also, the wrapper class is responsible for any threading safety required.

Restricting members is a straightforward technique. You can create the wrapper class so that within the wrapped class only the members that you specify are exposed. For example, suppose the existing component has an overloaded method to perform some operation, and you want to force only one of the several overloaded options. You can simply wrap the component and provide only one way to call the overloaded methods. In this manner, users of your wrapper are forced to follow the constraints you establish. The concept of housing an instance of one class within an instance of another is called *aggregation*. The following code samples demonstrate wrapping a component.

```vb
' VB
Public Class ReusableComponent
    Public Overloads Function PerformCalculation(ByVal count As Integer) As Decimal
    End Function

    Public Overloads Function PerformCalculation(ByVal count As Integer, ByVal weightfactor As
Decimal) As Decimal
    End Function

    Public Overloads Function PerformCalculation(ByVal count As Integer, ByVal weightfactor As
Decimal, ByVal bonus As Decimal) As Decimal
    End Function
End Class

Public Class Wrapper
    Private _ru As ReusableComponent

    Public Sub New()
        _ru = New ReusableComponent
    End Sub

    Public Function PerformCalculation(ByVal count As Integer, ByVal weightfactor As Decimal)
As Decimal
        ' This forces the use of only one overloaded member.
        _ru.PerformCalculation(count, weightfactor)
    End Function

End Class
```

```csharp
// C#
    public class ReusableComponent
    {
        public decimal PerformCalculation(int count)
        { }
        public decimal PerformCalculation(int count, decimal weightfactor)
        { }
        public decimal PerformCalculation (int count, decimal weightfactor, decimal bonus)
        { }
```

```
    }

    public class Wrapper
    {
        private ReusableComponent _ru;

        public Wrapper()
        {
            _ru = new ReusableComponent();
        }

        public decimal PerformCalculation(int count, decimal weightfactor)
        {
            // This forces the use of only one overloaded member.
            _ru.PerformCalculation(count, weightfactor);
        }
    }
```

If you do want to restrict members with inheritance, there are techniques for that as well. Suppose, for example, that you want to restrict a single item in your base class from being exposed through your derived class. You can suppress the member in question by using a concept called *hiding by name*. This is implemented in Visual Basic with the *Shadows* keyword and in C# by redeclaring the method as *private*. The following code samples demonstrate hiding by name.

```
' VB
Public Class ReusableComponent
    Public Function PerformCalculation(ByVal count As Integer) As Decimal
        ' Do some work.
    End Function
End Class

Public Class Wrapper
    Inherits ReusableComponent

    ' This member hides the member of the same name in the base class.
    Private Shadows Function performcalculation(ByVal count As Integer) As Decimal
        MyBase.PerformCalculation(count)
    End Function

End Class

// C#
public class ReusableComponent
{
    public decimal PerformCalculation(int count)
    { // Do some work. }
}

}
```

```
public class Wrapper : ReusableComponent
{
    // This member hides the member of the same name in the base class.
    private decimal PerformCalculation(int count)
    {
        base.PerformCalculation(count);
    }
}
```

Testing and Deploying Components

Wrapping components and extending or restricting their functionality is only the first step. The components as well as their wrappers must be introduced into the production environment. Do not assume that existing components have been properly tested or tested at all. Consider performing some black-box testing on reusable components before deploying them. Black-box testing is called that because you cannot see inside the box you are testing. Just as with existing components, you cannot see the code that is performing the work. You have access to only the public (and possibly the protected) interface.

To some degree, you can perform unit testing on the component by writing tests to use each member available. This can be useful if you receive regular updates from the component vendor and want to ensure that the component continues to behave as expected between releases. There are several robust testing frameworks, such as NUnit, to help you create and maintain libraries of tests for reusable components.

MORE INFO **NUnit and test-driven development**

You can learn more about NUnit and test-driven development (TDD), and download NUnit for free, at *http://www.nunit.org/*.

In addition to unit testing, you must perform integration testing on reusable components. You cannot assume that, once integrated, the component will behave as expected. There are many factors affecting the operations of reusable components. Scalability, performance, and concurrency, among others, can all be affected by integrated components competing for common resources. Integration testing is beyond the scope of this chapter; however, you must, be aware of the risks associated with integrating reusable components and of some of the factors affecting successful integration.

When deploying reusable components, you must consider the scope of reuse. For example, if a component is going to be used only within a single application, it can be deployed with that application. However, if it is going to be used by several applications, you might need to deploy it with each application, distribute it to an application server, or register the component with the global assembly cache (GAC) for reuse on a single machine. Also, you must be cognizant of the deployment scenarios so that future deployments do not interrupt service or inadvertently break other applications.

Lab: Consume a Reusable Software Component

In this lab, you will create a reusable component that you can extend and restrict. In Exercise 1, you will create the component. Exercises 2 and 3 will demonstrate extending and restricting the component, respectively. If you encounter a problem completing the exercises, the completed files can be installed from the Code folder on the companion CD.

▶ **Exercise 1: Creating the Reusable Component**

In this exercise, you will create a component for use in the remaining exercises.

1. Start Visual Studio 2005. Create a class library project called **ReusableComponent**.

2. Add a class called **TimeCalculator** to the project, with the following declaration.

```vb
' VB
Public Class TimeCalculator

    Public Function CalculatePaidTimeOff(ByVal EmployeeType As Short) As Double

        Select Case EmployeeType
            Case 1I ' Exempt
                Return 60D
            Case Else
                Return 20D
        End Select

    End Function

    Public Function CalculateVacation(ByVal EmployeeType As Short) As Double

        Select Case EmployeeType
            Case 1I ' Exempt
                Return 60D
            Case Else
                Return 20D
        End Select

    End Function

    Public Function CalculateHolidays(ByVal EmployeeType As Short) As Double

        Select Case EmployeeType
            Case 1I ' Exempt
                Return 80D
            Case Else
                Return 40D
        End Select

    End Function

    Public Function CalculateSickTime(ByVal EmployeeType As Short) As Double
```

```
        Select Case EmployeeType
            Case 1I ' Exempt
                Return 12D
            Case Else
                Return 6D
        End Select

    End Function

End Class

// C#
    public class TimeCalculator
    {
        public double CalculatePaidTimeOff(int EmployeeType)
        {
            switch (EmployeeType)
            {
                case 1: // Exempt
                    return 60;
                default:
                    return 20;
            }

        }

        public double CalculateVacation(int EmployeeType)
        {
            switch (EmployeeType)
            {
                case 1: // Exempt
                    return 60;
                default:
                    return 20;
            }
        }

        public double CalculateHolidays(int EmployeeType)
        {
            switch (EmployeeType)
            {
                case 1: // Exempt
                    return 80;
                default:
                    return 40;
            }
        }

        public virtual double CalculateSickTime(int EmployeeType)
        {
            switch (EmployeeType)
            {
                case 1: // Exempt
```

```
                        return 12;
                default:
                        return 6;
            }
        }
    }
```

3. Add a class called **BenefitsCalculator** to the project, with the following declaration.

```vb
' VB
Public MustInherit Class BenefitsCalculator

    Public Function CalculateSTD(ByVal EmployeeType As Short) As Double

        Select Case EmployeeType
            Case 1I ' Exempt
                Return 240D
            Case Else
                Return 120D
        End Select

    End Function

    Public MustOverride Function CalculateRetirement(ByVal EmployeeType As Short) As
Double

End Class
```

```csharp
// C#
    public abstract class BenefitsCalculator
    {
        public double CalculateSTD(int EmployeeType)
        {
            switch (EmployeeType)
            {
                case 1: // Exempt
                    return 240;
                default:
                    return 120;
            }
        }

        public abstract double CalculateRetirement(int EmployeeType);
    }
```

▶ Exercise 2: Extending the Component

This exercise demonstrates extending the functionality of the class created in Exercise 1.

1. Add a class library project called **ExtendingRestrictingComponent**.
2. Extend the existing *BenefitsCalculator* class. Add a class to the project called **MyBene-fitsCalculator**, which inherits from *BenefitsCalculator*. Implement the *CalculateRetirement* method to perform a calculation appropriate to your business. Assume that in

your organization, only exempt employees are offered a retirement option. Also assume that your organization is a nonprofit organization licensed in the United States. The following definition shows the implementation.

```vb
' VB
Public Class MyBenefitsCalculator
    Inherits BenefitsCalculator

    Public Overrides Function CalculateRetirement(ByVal EmployeeType As Short) As Double

        ' "My" company is a non-profit licensed in the United States.
        ' Therefore, use 403B.
        Select Case EmployeeType
            Case 1I ' Exempt
                Return 403D
            Case Else
                Return 0D
        End Select

    End Function

End Class
```

```csharp
// C#
    public class MyBenefitsCalculator : BenefitsCalculator
    {
        public override double CalculateRetirement(int EmployeeType)
        {
            // "My" company is a non-profit licensed in the United States.
            // Therefore, use 403B.

            switch (EmployeeType)
            {
                case 1: // Exempt
                    return 403;
                default:
                    return 0;
            }

        }
    }
```

▶ Exercise 3: Restricting the Component

This exercise demonstrates restricting the functionality of the class created in Exercise 1, using the project created in Exercise 2.

1. Add a class to the project called **RestrictedSubClass**.

2. Restrict the existing *TimeCalculator* class. Add to the project a class called **MyTimeCalculator,** which inherits from *TimeCalculator*. Assume that your organization does not separate vacation time from sick time. Therefore, you need to prevent the sick

time calculation from producing any time. Shadow the *CalculateSickTime()* method with the following definition.

```vb
' VB
Public Class MyTimeCalculator
    Inherits TimeCalculator

    ' "My" company does not provide separate sick time.
    ' Instead, it is all vacation time.  Therefore, the
    ' sick time calculation is superfluous.
    Public Shadows Function CalculateSickTime() As Double
        Return 0D
    End Function

End Class
```

```csharp
// C#
    public class MyTimeCalculator : TimeCalculator
    {
        public new double CalculateSickTime(int EmployeeType)
        {
            return 0;
        }
    }
```

Lesson Summary

- Inheritance is the ability to extend existing functionality by defining a new class that inherits functionality from an existing class and then adds to it.

- You can control inheritance by forcing or preventing it. You can control access to some members in base classes by using access modifiers such as *Public*, *Private*, and *Protected*.

- Overloading enables you to create multiple definitions of the same member with differing signatures. Overriding allows you to redefine members that are in a base class to provide a custom implementation using the same name.

- Shadowing is a technique that allows you to hide a base class member in a derived class.

Lesson Review

You can use the following questions to test your knowledge of the information in Lesson 1, "Consuming Reusable Software Components." The questions are also available on the companion CD if you prefer to review them in electronic form.

NOTE Answers

Answers to these questions and explanations of why each answer choice is right or wrong are located in the "Answers" section at the end of the book.

1. You have found a third-party component that provides much of the functionality you need, but not all of it. You decide to create your own component and inherit the third-party component. The third-party component declaration is:

```
Friend Class AcmeCalculator
```

You want your new component to be accessible to other assemblies. Which of the following declarations would meet this requirement for your class?

   A. ```
      Friend Class MyClass
          Inherits AcmeCalculator
      ```

   B. ```
      Private Class MyClass
          Inherits AcmeCalculator
      ```

   C. ```
      Public Class MyClass
          Inherits AcmeCalculator
      ```

   D. The requirement cannot be met.

2. You have been given access to three components. The declarations of the components are as follows:

```
Class ComponentA
```

```
MustInherit Class ComponentB
```

```
NotInheritable Class ComponentC
```

You decide to derive your own component to extend the functionality and use some of the components as they are. Which of the following are valid code samples?

   A. Class MyComponent

      ```
      Inherits ComponentA

      Inherits ComponentB

      Dim c as ComponentC
      ```

   B. Class MyComponent

      ```
      Inherits ComponentA

      Dim b as ComponentB

      Dim c as ComponentC
      ```
      ```

    C.   Class MyComponent

```
Inherits ComponentB

Dim a as ComponentA

Dim c as ComponentC
```

    D.   Class MyComponent

```
Inherits ComponentC

Dim a as ComponentA

Dim b as ComponentB
```

3. Which of the following statements are true regarding overriding? (Choose all that apply.)

    A. Private methods are *NotOverridable* by default.

    B. Public methods are *Overridable* by default.

    C. *MustOverride* methods can be contained only in a class declared as *MustInherit*.

    D. *MustOverride* methods can not contain code statements.

Chapter Review

To further practice and reinforce the skills you learned in this chapter, you can complete the following tasks:

- Review the chapter summary.
- Review the list of key terms introduced in this chapter.
- Complete the case scenarios. These scenarios set up real-world situations involving the topics of this chapter and ask you to create a solution.
- Complete the suggested practices.
- Take a practice test.

Chapter Summary

- You can reuse blocks of code, techniques for implementing existing components (called *recipes*), and components outright without changing them. You can also change existing components by extending or restricting their features.

Key Terms

Do you know what these key terms mean? You can check your answers by looking up the terms in the glossary at the end of the book.

- abstract class
- aggregation
- component
- control
- inheritance
- polymorphism
- shadow

Case Scenarios

In the following case scenarios, you will apply what you've learned about reusable components. You can find answers to these questions in the "Answers" section at the end of this book.

Case Scenario 1: Extending a Reusable Component

You have been asked to introduce a third-party loan management application into your organization and to integrate the application into several existing custom systems in your technology portfolio. You have also been asked to make the function that calculates interest accept custom interest parameters for theoretical loan calculations. The third-party system's function accepts no parameters and uses system configuration settings.

1. Which of the three forms of reuse (code samples, recipes, and distributed binaries) might be appropriate for this scenario?
2. Describe how you will meet the requirement regarding the interest calculation.

Case Scenario 2: Restricting a Reusable Component

Your manager requires you to implement a new human resources package in your organization. You must integrate the new package with existing systems such as payroll and accounting systems. The third-party application implements features that the business does not support.

1. Describe how you can hide the functionality that the business does not support.
2. While wrapping one of the third-party classes, you realize that it cannot be instantiated and must be inherited. How do you inherit from this class while still restricting access to members that must be overridden?

Suggested Practices

To help you successfully master the exam objectives presented in this chapter, complete the following tasks.

Consume a Reusable Software Component

Complete these tasks to learn more about consuming a reusable component. You should complete all practices.

■ **Practice 1**   Modify the Lesson 1 lab to include a new class in the ReusableComponent project in Exercise 1. Make the new class require inheriting to access its functionality. Use the *MustInherit* and *MustOverride* combination in Visual Basic and the *abstract* keyword in C#.

Inherit from the new class with two separate classes. In one class, implement the overridden members. In the other class, throw the new NotImplementedException.

■ **Practice 2**   Practice inheritance chains by creating a new class that inherits from a derived class created in Exercise 2 of the Lesson 1 lab.

Create a new public member in the super base class and see how that new member is available in the new derived class.

Take a Practice Test

The practice tests on this book's companion CD offer many options. For example, you can test yourself on just one exam objective, or you can test yourself on all the 70-547 certification exam content. You can set up the test so that it closely simulates the experience of taking a certification exam, or you can set it up in study mode so that you can look at the correct answers and explanations after you answer each question.

MORE INFO   **Practice tests**

For details about all the practice test options available, see the "How to Use the Practice Tests" section in this book's Introduction.

Chapter 11
Application Logic Layer

What is *application logic* or the *application logic layer*? The application logic layer, or *business logic layer*, as it is often referred to, is the part of an application that performs the required data processing. It refers to the routines that perform the data entry, update, query and report processing, and, more specifically, the processing that takes place behind the scenes, as opposed to the presentation logic required to display the information on the screen. An application is made up of a user interface (UI) and application logic. The UI and the application logic do not necessarily need to be running on the same computer. If the UI and application logic are separated, developers often speak of a client and application server. To complicate things further, in the case of a Web application, the Web server takes on the role of the client. A single Web project that contains both the UI and the application logic is called a single-tier Web application.

Thinking about how and where to implement application logic is probably one of the most complicated parts of developing an application. In the previous chapter, you saw how to create reusable components. When implementing application logic, you will need to consider a number of factors, such as the application architecture, data and state management, deployment model, and, of course, security implications. This chapter will explain the impact of these factors on your application logic and help you choose an appropriate approach for implementing it. Design patterns will play an important part in solving the challenges that arise.

Exam objectives in this chapter:

- Choose an appropriate implementation approach for the application design logic.
    - Choose an appropriate data storage mechanism.
    - Choose an appropriate data flow structure.
    - Choose an appropriate decision flow structure.
- Choose an appropriate exception handling mechanism.
    - Evaluate the current exception handling mechanism.
    - Design a new exception handling technique.

Lessons in this chapter:

Before You Begin

To complete the lessons in this chapter, you must have:

- A computer that meets or exceeds the minimum hardware requirements listed in the Introduction at the beginning of this book.
- Read and completed the labs from Chapter 1, "Application Requirements and Design," regarding the creation of documents such as the design diagram and class diagram.
- Read and completed the labs from Chapter 3, "Design Evaluation," regarding evaluating the logical and physical design.
- Read and completed the labs from Chapter 6, "Data Validation," regarding validating data and basic exception handling.
- Read and completed the labs from Chapter 8, "Component Design," regarding designing a component.
- Experience creating and viewing Universal Modeling Language (UML) diagrams in Micrsoft Office Visio 2003 or later.
- A basic understanding of what a design pattern is and how to apply one in code.

Real World

Mark Blomsma

Deciding how and where to implement application logic is not a trivial matter. Not too long ago, I was called in on a project that tried to implement some basic workflow scenarios using a Microsoft ASP.NET 2.0 application. The developer used all the drag-and-drop controls that come with ASP.NET and quickly built a large part of the application—typing virtually no code! A success story, you think? Not quite. When it came to test, it became obvious that somehow the updates that were fired toward the database didn't have the correct parameters. After a couple of hours of trial and error in trying to locate the cause of the problem, we became so frustrated that we decided to change the application by adding a layer, effectively implementing the layered application pattern. The Web pages were no longer allowed to access the database directly, and instead had to use multiple *ObjectDataSource* controls. This allowed us to set breakpoints at crucial points within the code and debug our data access code. The problem was discovered in no time.

Implementing application logic is not just about creating an application for the end user; it is also about creating an application in which you, the developer, can find your way around and easily adjust behavior and locate errors, if needed.

In this particular case, the next step was to convince the customer to start writing unit tests to check the quality of the business layer, allowing easy regression testing.

Lesson 1: Designing the Application Logic

In this lesson, you'll look at factors such as application architecture, data and state management, deployment models, and security, all of which will be considered when implementing data storage, data flow structure, and decision flow structure. You'll use design patterns as much as possible to implement said items. Design patterns are standard solutions to common but specific problems. By applying one or more design patterns when designing your application, your design will be more readable to someone who is not familiar with your application domain but who knows about design patterns. To illustrate the choices you need to make, you'll assume throughout this chapter that you're building a Web application for an online store selling CDs.

MORE INFO   Design patterns

When it comes to design patterns, recommended reading materials are *Patterns of Enterprise Application Architecture* by Martin Fowler (Addison-Wesley Professional, 2002) and *Design Patterns* by Erich Gamma, Richard Helm, Ralph Johnson, and John Vlissides (Addison-Wesley Professional, 1995).

After this lesson, you will be able to:
- Organize your code.
- Apply design patterns.
- Choose an appropriate implementation approach for the application design logic.
   - Choose an appropriate data storage mechanism.
   - Choose an appropriate data flow structure.
   - Choose an appropriate decision flow structure.

Estimated lesson time: 30 minutes

Organizing Application Logic

The first step in designing application logic is to organize it. In organizing code, you lay down a set of rules that will help you create a blueprint of the application. Having a clear blueprint will help in designing the application logic because code will be in an appropriate place. If developers and designers follow the rules of the blueprint, maintenance, debugging, and fixing errors will go much more smoothly because code is located in a logical place.

Layers

First, consider logical layers (as opposed to tiers).

NOTE Layers vs. tiers
Layers are about creating boundaries in your code. The top layer may have references to code in lower layers, but a layer may never have a reference to code in a higher layer. Tiers are about physically distributing layers across multiple computers.

Layering is about assigning responsibilities to specific areas of code. The three basic layers are shown in Figure 11-1.

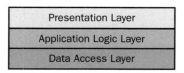

Figure 11-1 Basic three-layer organization

Layering is about level of abstraction. The layering shown in Figure 11-1 is representative of how layering exists in most applications. They are also referred to as the "three principal layers" and may go by various other names. As a rule, code in the presentation layer may call on services in the application logic layer, but the application logic layer should not be calling methods in the presentation layer. The presentation layer should never directly call on the Data Access Layer (DAL) because doing so would bypass the responsibilities implemented by the application logic layer. The DAL should never call the application logic layer.

Each layer has its responsibilities, some that might not be evidenced by the name, as shown in Table 11-1.

Table 11-1   The Three Principal Layers

Layer	Responsibilities
Presentation	Display of information, collection of user input, command-line input, interfaces to external systems
Application logic	Processing data, managing transactions
Data access	Interaction with data store, messaging systems, remote system access

Layers are just an abstraction; creating folders in your project and adding code to the appropriate folder is probably the easiest way to implement the layering. A more useful approach would be to place each layer in a separate project, thus creating separate assemblies. The advantage of placing the application logic in a library assembly is that it enables you to create unit tests, using Microsoft Visual Studio Team Systems or NUnit, to test the logic. It also gives you flexibility in choosing where to deploy each layer.

MORE INFO   NUnit

NUnit is an open-source unit-testing framework for all .NET languages. It is discussed in Chapter 14, "Define and Evaluate a Testing Strategy." For more information, go to *http://www.nunit.org*.

Physical Layers

In a Web application, the presentation layer will sit on your Web server. The application logic and Data Access Layers are usually deployed together and can either sit on the Web server or be deployed to a separate computer, the application server. If they are deployed to an application server, you will have to choose whether to access the application server using Microsoft .NET Framework remoting or Web services. See Chapter 3 for more information about making this choice. In either case, you will add some code to the presentation layer to access the remote services easily. If you're using Web services to access the services on your application server, Visual Studio 2005 will do the work for you and generate proxy code, automatically providing an implementation of the *remote proxy pattern*.

MORE INFO   Patterns and Practices

Design patterns can be of great help in organizing your application logic. This chapter has covered a couple, but there are many more out there, and new patterns are discovered regularly. Keep up to date! The Microsoft Patterns and Practices group regularly publishes new material. To learn more about the Microsoft Patterns and Practices group, visit *http://msdn.microsoft.com/practices/*.

Adding Patterns to Layers

The three basic layers provide a high-level overview. Now add a couple of structural patterns to create a robust enterprise architecture. Figure 11-2 shows what this would look like.

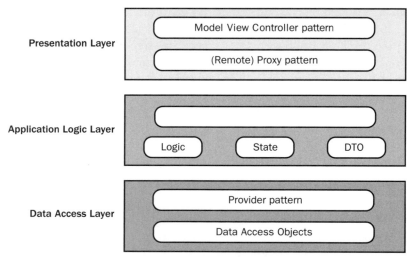

Figure 11-2 Combining patterns and layers to make a robust blueprint

In Chapters 4 through 7, you learned how to design and implement the UI, so now you can focus on the application logic.

Quick Check
- Is a three-layer application the same as a three-tier application?

Quick Check Answer
- No, tiers relate to physical distribution of the application. Layers indicate logical separation of code, assigning responsibility per layer.

The Application Logic Layer

Figure 11-2 shows that the application logic layer uses a *façade pattern* to access the actual logic. A façade is an object that provides a simplified interface to a larger body of code such as a class library. A façade can reduce dependencies of outside code on the inner workings of a library because most code uses the façade, thus allowing more flexibility in developing the system. To do so, the façade will provide a "coarse-grained" interface to a collection of "fine-grained" objects.

Exam Tip Remember the façade pattern and three principal–layer pattern. These two patterns will come back in almost any solution.

Figure 11-2 also shows that the application logic consists of managing state and logic. The following design issues need to be addressed when designing the state and logic of the application layer:

- Security
- Error logging
- Transaction management
- Data validation
- State management
- Data flow

Here's a look at each of these in more detail.

Security

Security is about authentication and authorization. *Authentication* is the process of attempting to verify the digital identity of the sender of a request. This lesson will talk about the sender as "the user," but keep in mind that the user, or sender, may be a person using a computer, a computer itself, or a computer program. Your code is running in the application logic layer and will always be accessed by the presentation layer. Thus, you have no direct contact with the original sender of a request. Authentication will have to be implemented in the presentation layer, and the identity of the sender will have to be communicated to the logic layer. The logic layer will have to trust that the presentation layer will do a good job.

There are several ways of communicating the identity of the original sender:

- When using Web services, use Integrated Windows Authentication in Microsoft Internet Information Services (IIS) to allow only domain users to access the Web services.
- When using .NET remoting, add information about a user to a remoting call, using a custom *ClientChannelSink*.
- Pass the identity of the user as a parameter of the service call.

Authorization is about allowing methods to be accessed only by those users that have been granted permission to them. The default mechanism in .NET is that of role base security. It is based on placing a *principal* on the thread running the current request. The principal contains both the *identity* and a list of roles that have been assigned to the user. A user may, for instance, be assigned the role of both Guest and Author, allowing him or her to access functionality designed for both those roles.

To authenticate a user, the application server must rely on the presentation layer. To authorize a user, a choice must be made. Does the presentation layer implement authorization to allow the user access to only authorized screens, reports, batches, and services? If so, do you trust the presentation layer enough that you do not wish to repeat an authorization check in the application layer? It's considered a best practice to have the application logic layer minimize its

dependencies on the outside world and not rely on the UI to do the right thing. All authorization checks should be performed again at the application server. The façade is a great place to
use attributes to check authorization. The following code shows an example of using the *Prin-
cipalPermissionAttribute* to specify that only users with the role *RegisteredUsers* are allowed to
submit an order.

```vb
' VB
Imports System.Security.Permissions

Namespace MSLearning.TK547.Chapter11.Samples
    '/ <summary>
    '/ BookStoreFacade offers coarse grained access
    '/ to the application domain.
    '/ </summary>
    Public Class BookStoreFacade
        '/ <summary>
        '/ Submit an order for processing.
        '/ </summary>
        '/ <param name="order">The order to be processed.</param>
        <PrincipalPermission(SecurityAction.Demand,
                            Role="RegisteredUser")> _
        Public Sub SubmitOrder(ByVal order As Order)
        End Sub
    End Class
End Namespace
```

```csharp
// C#
using System;
using System.Security.Permissions;

namespace MSLearning.TK547.Chapter11.Samples
{
    /// <summary>
    /// BookStoreFacade offers coarse grained access
    /// to the application domain.
    /// </summary>
    public class BookStoreFacade
    {
        /// <summary>
        /// Submit an order for processing.
        /// </summary>
        /// <param name="order">The order to be processed.</param>
        [PrincipalPermission(SecurityAction.Demand,
                            Role="RegisteredUser")]
        public void SubmitOrder(Order order)
        {
        }
    }
}
```

Implementing security as shown in this code is extremely secure in that the common language runtime (CLR) will check the roles of the user before executing *SubmitOrder* and will throw a security *exception* if the user is not authorized. So you're checking authorization as soon as possible. An exception represents an error that occurs during application execution, indicating that the regular program flow has been aborted. In this case, the method call is aborted before it starts.

Data-driven authorization is a special scenario. Say you have a business rule that only users with an *Employee* role are allowed to submit orders of more than $1,000. You'll need to write some application logic to check this. Where do you implement this? You could start adding code to your façade method, but just like layers in the overall architecture, each class in your application logic should have responsibilities. So what are the responsibilities of the façade? The façade has two assigned responsibilities: security checks and error logging. Everything else is handled by a secondary class, in this case, the *OrderManager*. The following code shows the result.

```
' VB
Imports System.Security.Permissions
Imports System.Threading
Imports System.Security

Namespace MSLearning.TK547.Chapter11.Samples
    '/ <summary>
    '/ BookStoreService is the facade to the
    '/ BookStoreComponent
    '/ </summary>
    Public Class BookStoreService
        '/ <summary>
        '/ Submit an order for processing.
        '/ </summary>
        '/ <param name="order">The order to be processed.</param>
        <PrincipalPermission(SecurityAction.Demand, Role = "Employee")> _
        <PrincipalPermission(SecurityAction.Demand, Role = "RegisteredUser")> _
        Public  Sub SubmitOrder(ByVal order As Order)
            Try
                If if(order.TotalExcludingTax > 1000 And Then
                    Throw New SecurityException(
                            "Insufficient privileges to submit
                             an order over $1000.00.")
                End If

                ' delegate processing to order manager
                Dim mgr As OrderManager =  New OrderManager()
                mgr.ProcessOrder(order)
            Catch exception As SecurityException
                ' no need to log security exceptions
                throw
            Catch exception As Exception
                ' log error
            End Try
        End Sub
```

```
      End Class
End Namespace

// C#
using System;
using System.Security.Permissions;
using System.Threading;
using System.Security;

namespace MSLearning.TK547.Chapter11.Samples
{
    /// <summary>
    /// BookStoreService is the facade to the
    /// BookStoreComponent
    /// </summary>
    public class BookStoreService
    {
        /// <summary>
        /// Submit an order for processing.
        /// </summary>
        /// <param name="order">The order to be processed.</param>
        [PrincipalPermission(SecurityAction.Demand, Role = "Employee")]
        [PrincipalPermission(SecurityAction.Demand, Role = "RegisteredUser")]
        public void SubmitOrder(Order order)
        {
            try
            {
                if (order.TotalExcludingTax > 1000 &&
                    Thread.CurrentPrincipal.IsInRole("Employee") == false)
                {
                    throw new SecurityException(
                            "Insufficient privileges to submit
                             an order over $1000.00.");
                }

                // delegate processing to order manager
                OrderManager mgr = new OrderManager();
                mgr.ProcessOrder(order);
            }
            catch (SecurityException exception)
            {
                // no need to log security exceptions
                throw;
            }
            catch (Exception exception)
            {
                // log error
            }
        }
    }
}
```

Note that, instead of handling the check for *Insufficient privileges to submit an order over $1,000.00* as a security exception, you can also choose to implement this as a domain exception. Lesson 2, "Implementing Exception Handling," will talk more about domain exceptions and general exception handling.

Error Logging

If you wish to deploy your application as a Web server and application server, the façade implements the boundary between these two, and it becomes essential to at least log any technical error that occurs on the computer. As noted, the place to implement this is the façade. All that is required is a simple *try/catch* around code that performs the processing.

Transaction Management

Some might consider transaction management to be the domain of the Data Access Layer. This is wrong. The DAL needs to be able to take part in transactions and, preferably, support transactions, but deciding the scope of a transaction and determining when to commit or roll back a transaction is very much a behavior that belongs in the domain of application logic. For Web applications, the best approach to managing concurrency is to implement optimistic locking. This chapter will discuss more about optimistic locking later, when you learn about data storage mechanisms. For now, it's sufficient to know that optimistic locking allows you to avoid unnecessary locking of data in the database and to perform all the necessary reads before starting a transaction.

Data Validation

The application logic layer is responsible for enforcing data validation. The presentation layer may choose to implement data validation redundantly to provide the user with a richer user experience, but remember that this can never replace validation in the application logic layer. However, there are two exceptions to this rule.

First, it is good practice to make the services on your application logic layer as strongly typed as possible. The following code shows a poor method signature and a much better method. By forcing the presentation layer to provide data in the correct format, you can avoid implementing a lot of trivial parsing and clutter in the application logic. In most cases, this works out fine anyway because if a user uses an incorrect date format, you will most likely have a *Compare-Validator* control linked to the date field to inform the user of his or her mistake.

```
' VB
'/ <summary>
'/ Poor method signature for application logic layer.
'/ </summary>
Public  Sub ChangeDeliveryDate(ByVal date As String)
    ' Have to implement string parsing and
```

```
        ' checks for the 'date' parameter.
End Sub

'/ <summary>
'/ Much better method.
'/ </summary>
Public  Sub ChangeDeliveryDate(ByVal date As DateTime)
    ' Just work with the date.
End Sub
```

```csharp
// C#
/// <summary>
/// Poor method signature for application logic layer.
/// </summary>
public void ChangeDeliveryDate(string date)
{
    // Have to implement string parsing and
    // checks for the 'date' parameter.
}

/// <summary>
/// Much better method.
/// </summary>
public void ChangeDeliveryDate(DateTime date)
{
    // Just work with the date.
}
```

The second exception would be if the UI has performed a number of validations and is able to communicate these to the application logic. You could, for instance, create a class that has a *Validate()* method and an *IsValid* property. The *IsValid* property would be set to *False* the instant the state of the object changes, requiring new validation. The application logic layer can check the *IsValid* property and decide whether to revalidate the information in the class. There are some caveats when implementing this solution, the most important being that the application logic layer needs to be able to trust the presentation layer to supply correct information. Also, the validation performed by the presentation layer typically will be limited due to the amount of information to which it has access at the time of validation. More complex validations, which might require more data, will still need to be performed by the application logic layer. This might result in some confusing situations when the presentation layer claims that an object is valid, but the application logic marks the object as invalid.

State Management

A choice needs to be made about statefulness of the application logic layer. The options are simple: The layer as a whole is either stateless or stateful. This design choice is very significant if the application logic layer is deployed to a dedicated application server.

What is the main difference? A stateful server remembers client data (state) from one request to the next. A stateless server, on the other hand, keeps no state information between requests.

The application logic layer in a Web application needs to be stateless. Advantages of a stateless application server are that the server is much more robust and scalable. When an application server is stateless, it doesn't need to have any prior knowledge of a client when handling a request. Thus it becomes possible to scale out by adding more servers and load balancing requests across multiple servers. When the application server is stateful, then, after the initial request, you need to ensure that each request from the same client is directed to the same application server. Another drawback is that the application server is using resources after the client is already gone.

Data Flow

The last choice to be made is about data transformation and data carriers, in effect designing the data flow through your application. This will be covered in more detail later in this lesson. First, look at choosing a data storage mechanism.

Choosing a Data Storage Mechanism

When designing your Web application, you will undoubtedly have to design some sort of data store. The following stores and forms of data storage are available:

- Registry
- Web.config
- XML files
- Plaintext files
- SQL database
- HTML files
- Message queuing

Each store has its own unique characteristics and may be suitable to specific requirements.

Registry

Your Web application should never write data to the registry. Access to the registry is restricted from an ASP.NET application and, unless the security settings on your computer have been altered for the worse, you'll get a security exception when trying to do so.

A Web application can, however, read from the registry. This is useful in that your application might want to store some very sensitive information, such as a decryption key. The key can be written to the registry when installing the Web application.

The .NET Framework 2.0 offers the possibility of encrypting the content of your web.config file, making it extremely rare for you to need to write anything in the registry, although the option is available.

NOTE   Reading from the registry

The registry is an invisible place to store a setting. A good strategy is to implement a fallback when reading from the registry. If the setting is not present in the registry, attempt to read the setting from the web.config file. This is particularly useful when developing in a team in which a configuration file can be easily retrieved from source control but a registry setting cannot be.

Web.config

The web.config file is a simple text file containing easily understandable XML. It can contain application-wide data such as database connection strings, custom error messages, and culture settings. Being an XML file, the web.config file can consist of any valid XML tags, but the root element should always be *<configuration>*. Nested within this tag, you can include various other tags to describe your settings.

▶ **Add a configuration file to a Web site**

1. In Visual Studio 2005, right-click the project in the Solution Explorer.
2. Choose Add New Item, and then choose Web Configuration File. The filename needs to be web.config. A file will be added to your Web site, containing the following XML:

```xml
<?xml version="1.0"?>
<!--
    Note: As an alternative to hand editing this file you can use the
    web admin tool to configure settings for your application. Use
    the Website->Asp.Net Configuration option in Visual Studio.
    A full list of settings and comments can be found in
    machine.config.comments usually located in
    \Windows\Microsoft.Net\Framework\v2.x\Config
-->
<configuration>
    <appSettings/>
    <connectionStrings/>
    <system.web>
        <!--
            Set compilation debug="true" to insert debugging
            symbols into the compiled page. Because this
            affects performance, set this value to true only
            during development.
        -->
        <compilation debug="false" />
        <!--
            The <authentication> section enables configuration
            of the security authentication mode used by
            ASP.NET to identify an incoming user.
```

```
        -->
        <authentication mode="Windows" />
        <!--
            The <customErrors> section enables configuration
            of what to do if/when an unhandled error occurs
            during the execution of a request. Specifically,
            it enables developers to configure html error pages
            to be displayed in place of a error stack trace.

        <customErrors mode="RemoteOnly" defaultRedirect="GenericErrorPage.htm">
            <error statusCode="403" redirect="NoAccess.htm" />
            <error statusCode="404" redirect="FileNotFound.htm" />
        </customErrors>
        -->
    </system.web>
</configuration>
```

You can add settings by adding to the *appSettings* node or by defining a new configuration section and placing settings in the newly created section.

Your application should not attempt to write to the web.config. The web.config is monitored by the ASP.NET worker process, and any change to the .config file will lead to the worker process being recycled (restarting the Web application).

XML Files

Your application might choose to store data in XML files. Any file in the Data folder of your Web application will be protected from browsing, so any data files you place there will be safe. Reading and writing to this directory are possible. The limitations are those of the file systems in terms of the number of files per directory and, of course, locking issues. If you have one file with, say, all customers, then only one person can lock the file at a time.

XML files are good for storing data that is changed by only a small number of users. If the files are very frequently retrieved, write some code to cache them.

Plain Text Files

Instead of using XML files for storage, you can choose to use a comma-separated file or even fixed American Standard Code for Information Interchange (ASCII) files. XML is a more popular format because the .NET Framework Class Library has rich support for XML files and XML manipulation (located in *System.Xml*).

Database

A database is the data store of choice when having to store either a large amount of data or having to service a large number of users.

When choosing a database as the data store for your Web site, you'll also need to consider availability. If you let the Web site connect to your enterprise database, your Web site will be down whenever the database is down for maintenance. You can choose to implement a dedicated Web site database, which contains enough data to keep your Web site running even when the main database is unavailable. Security considerations might be another reason for not letting the Web site write data to your main database.

HTML Files

HTML files are read-only storage for information. Data that is changed infrequently but is retrieved often may be retrieved by a daily batch and used to generate static HTML, which can be served up quickly with minimum performance impact on the Web server.

Message Queuing

Microsoft Message Queuing, also known as MSMQ, is a unique data store in that messages are posted to a queue and stored in the queue only until they are processed by a different process. Message queuing can be used to increase the availability of your Web application. Your Web application can post messages into the queue requesting updates to your enterprise database while the database itself may be down for maintenance.

Quick Check

- Should your application write data in the web.config file?

Quick Check Answer

- No, changes in the web.config file will lead to a recycling of the ASP.NET worker process, restarting the Web application and disconnecting any active user sessions.

Designing the Data Flow

As discussed, your application is divided into three layers, and if you also take the database (or other data store) into consideration, data is going through the following:

- Storage
- Retrieved/updates (by the DAL)
- Being processed (by logic)
- Presentation/modification

For each of these stages, it might or might not be optimal for the data to be accessible in a format most suited for that stage.

Stored data has a format propriety to the data store. Microsoft SQL Server, for example, will store data in tables inside an .mdf file.

Retrieving data using .NET will most likely involve Microsoft ActiveX Data Objects (ADO).NET classes, and data will be collected using *DataSet*, *DataTable*, and *DataRow* objects.

Processing data may be done using *DataSet*, *DataTable*, and *DataRow* objects. Alternatively, your application might use object relational mapping and transform data from *DataRow* objects to business objects, also referred to as domain objects, when retrieving data. The application then transforms the data back to *DataRow* objects when updating data to the data layer. When using an object relational mapping solution, you'll find that a layer is often added between the DAL and the application logic layer, or the DAL is replaced by the object relational mapping layer.

The presentation layer wants to present and modify data. It needs to retrieve data—fitted to a specific action—and will submit data for processing to the application logic.

Consider two scenarios. In the first, you will use ADO.NET classes to act as your data carriers through all layers of your application. In the second, you will have a somewhat more complex scenario and will transform data per layer.

Data Flow Using ADO.NET

The Microsoft .NET Framework Class Library offers an extensive application programming interface (API) for handling data in managed code. Referred to as ADO.NET, the API can be found in the *System.Data* namespace. An important design feature of ADO.NET is the complete separation of data carriers and data stores. Classes such as *DataSet*, *DataTable*, and *DataRow* are designed to hold data but retain no knowledge of where the data came from. They are considered "data source–agnostic." A separate set of classes, such as *SqlConnection*, *SqlDataAdapter*, and *SqlCommand*, take care of connecting to a data source, retrieving data, and populating the *DataSet*, *DataTable*, and *DataRow*. These classes are located in sub-namespaces such as *System.Data.Sql*, *System.Data.OleDB*, *System.Data.Oracle*, and so on. Depending on the data source to which you want to connect, you can use the classes in the correct namespace and, depending on the completeness of the product you're using, you'll find that these classes offer more or less functionality.

Back to *DataSet*. Because the *DataSet* is not connected to the data source, it can be used quite successfully for managing the data flow in an application. Figure 11-3 shows the flow of data when doing so.

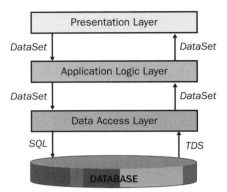

Figure 11-3 The *DataSet* as the center of your data flow

Now go step by step through this design by imagining that someone has logged on to your bookstore's Web site and ordered three books. The presentation layer has managed the state of the shopping cart. The customer is ready to order and has provided all necessary data. He clicks Submit Order. The Web page transforms all data into a *DataSet* holding two *DataTable* objects, one for the order and one for the order lines. It inserts one *DataRow* for the order and three *DataRow* objects for the order lines. The Web page then displays this data back to the user one more time, data-binding controls against the *DataSet*, and asks, "Are you sure?" The user confirms the order, and the order is submitted to the application logic layer. The application logic layer checks *DataSet* to see that all mandatory fields have a value and checks whether the user has more than $1,000 in outstanding bills. If the user passes the check, the *DataSet* is passed on to the DAL, which connects to the database and generates *insert* statements from the information in the *DataSet*.

Using the *DataSet* in the illustrated manner is a fast and efficient way of building an application, using the power of the .NET Framework Class Library and the ability of ASP.NET to data-bind various controls, such as the *GridView*, against a *DataSet*. Instead of using plain *DataSet* objects, you can use *Typed DataSet* objects and improve the coding experience when implementing code in both the presentation layer and the application logic layer. The advantage of this approach is also the disadvantage. Small changes in the data model do not necessarily lead to a lot of methods having to change their signatures. So, in terms of maintenance, this works quite well. Remember, the presentation layer is not necessarily a UI; it can just as well be a Web service. If you modify the definition of the *DataSet*, perhaps because you're renaming a field in the database, then, in effect, you're modifying the contract that underwrites the Web service. As you can imagine, this can lead to some significant problems, so this scenario works well if the presentation layer is just a UI. But for interfaces to external systems or components, you will want to hide the inner workings of your application and transform data to something other than a copy of your data model. You will want to create data transfer objects (DTOs). You will learn more about DTOs later in this chapter.

NOTE *DataSet* objects vs. *DataTable* objects vs. *DataRow* objects

The previous scenario describes the *DataSet* as the data carrier. If the application you're writing requires inserts or updates to only one table, you can substitute the *DataSet* for the *DataTable*. Similarly, if the presentation layer is interested in only one row of data, you may use a *DataRow* as the data carrier.

NOTE Table Module pattern

The Table Module pattern is a good way to organize code when using *DataSet* objects as the choice for implementing data flow. When using the Table Module pattern, you implement one class per table to handle all application logic for all rows in a table. These classes can interact with each other to implement complex logic.

Data Flow Using Object Relational Mapping

Using ADO.NET to manage data flow is a very data-centric approach. Data and logic are discrete. At the other end of the spectrum, you can take an object-oriented approach. In an object-oriented approach, classes are created to bundle data and behavior. The aim is to define classes that mimic data and behavior found in the business domain for which the application is created. The result is often referred to as a business object. The collection of business objects that make up the application is called the *domain model*. Some people claim that a rich domain model is better for designing more complex logic. It's hard to actually prove or disprove any such claim. Just know that you have a choice, and it is up to you to make it.

Figure 11-4 shows a data flow similar to that in Figure 11-3, except that now you've added the object relational mapping layer and substituted the *DataSet* objects for different data carriers.

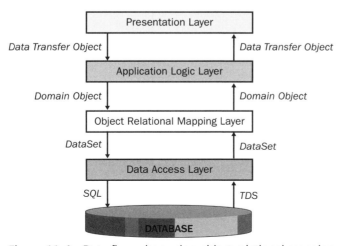

Figure 11-4   Data flow when using object relational mapping

Complete the same exercise that you did before and imagine that someone has logged on to your bookstore and ordered three books. The presentation layer has managed the state of the shopping cart. The customer is ready to order and has provided all necessary data. The customer clicks Submit Order and the Web page transforms all data into a *data transfer object*. The data transfer object is actually an aggregation of objects, holding one object for the order plus three objects for the order lines. The Web page then displays this data back to the user one more time, data-binding controls against the data transfer object using the *ObjectDataSource* in ASP.NET 2.0, and asks whether the user is sure. The user confirms, and the data transfer object is submitted to the application logic layer. The application logic layer transforms it into a business object of type *Order*, the order having a property for holding three *OrderLine* objects. The *Order.Validate()* method is called to validate the order and check that all mandatory fields have a value, and a check is performed to see whether the user has more than $1,000 in outstanding bills. To do this, the order will call *Order.Customer.GetOutstanding-Bills()*. If all is fine, the *Order.Save()* method is called. The order will submit itself to the object relational mapping layer. Here, the order and order lines are mapped to a *DataTable* in a *DataSet*, and the *DataSet* is passed to the DAL, which connects to the database and generates *insert* statements from the information in the *DataSet*. There are, of course, many ways in which object relational mapping can take place. Not all mappings will include transformation to a *DataSet*; some will create the *insert* statements directly but still use the DAL to execute that statement.

As you can see, quite a few transformations take place. The use of DTOs is necessary because a business object implements behavior, and behavior is subject to change. To minimize the impact of these changes on the presentation layer, transform the data, take it out of the business object, and put it in a data transfer object. In Java, the data transfer object is normally referred to as a *value object*.

A big advantage of working with business objects is that it really helps in organizing your code. And, if you look back at a piece of complex logic, it is usually very readable because there is very little "plumbing" code. The disadvantage of working with business objects is that the majority of data stores are still relational, and the mapping of business objects to relational data can become quite complex.

Data Flow Alternatives

You have just seen two opposite ways of managing data flow. Many variations are possible. You will often see a dataset used as the basic data carrier from UI to data store whereas separate schemas (DTOs) are used for Web services that are called from other systems.

Of course, you can use business objects in the Web application and skip the DTO transformation, but this usually works well only if the application logic is deployed together with the Web application. Remember that to call *Order.Save()*, you'll need a database connection. You and probably your chief security officer should assess whether this is desirable.

Designing the Decision Flow

You've now looked at choosing a data storage mechanism, which, for most enterprise Web applications, will be an enterprise database. You've looked at designing the data flow, which will be either data-centric or object-oriented. Now it's time to look at the decision flow. Decision flow is all about how you design the methods on the façade of your application logic layer. There are two approaches to organizing your decision flow:

- Action-driven
- State-driven

Action-Driven Decision

When basing the organization of the application logic on the actions of the user, you will essentially be implementing application logic by offering services in which each service handles a specific request from the presentation layer. This is also known as the Transaction Script pattern. This approach is popular because it is simple and feels very natural. Examples of methods that follow this approach are *BookStoreService.AddNewOrder(Order order)* and *BookStoreService.CancelOrder(int orderId)*.

The logic needed to perform the action is implemented sequentially with the method, making it easy to read but difficult to reuse the code. Using other design patterns, such as the Table Module pattern, can help solve that.

State-Driven Decision

Alternatively, you can implement the decision flow of the application in a much more state-driven fashion. The services offered by the application server are more generic in nature—*BookStoreService.SaveOrder(Order order)*, for example. This method will now look at the state of the order and decide whether to add a new order or cancel an existing order.

Lab: Designing the Application Logic

This lab will walk you through the steps of conceptualizing and designing the application logic for a specific Web application according to specific business needs.

If you encounter a problem completing an exercise, the completed projects can be installed from the Code folder on the companion CD.

▶ **Exercise: Layering, Data Flow, and Data Stores**

Imagine you're working for a music store and you're charged with building a Web application that will allow a customer to reserve, for 24 hours, a CD that is in stock. The MOD (manager of the day) needs to be notified by e-mail of any reservation so he can pull the CD and set it aside in the back of the store. The Web application can use the inventory database of the store to retrieve inventory information. Your IT manager is not sure he wants to give the Web write access to this database and wants you to consider alternatives.

Let's look at the steps involved in arriving at a proper solution to this challenge.

1. First think of the application architecture from a thousand-mile overhead view and then pencil in some details to verify you're on the right path; draw a picture.

   One option is to throw a couple of Web pages together quickly and call it good. The other option is to design your solution and consider that you'll probably be expanding the functionality of the Web site over the coming months, including adding features. Think of the layers and the data stores. Think also about deployment and the hardware needed to run the Web site.

2. Open Visio and draw a picture of what you think the data flow and data storage in the Web application should look like. Add the classes you'd expect to find.

3. Organize the application into the three principal layers. This will allow you to deploy the application logic to a separate server if that becomes necessary.

4. Use two data stores: an inventory database that is read-only and a site database to which you can write your reservations. In this database, you'll also be storing account and user information.

5. Use *Typed DataSet* objects for retrieving data from the inventory database. This is read-only data, and very limited logic is needed. You also use *Typed DataSet* objects when reading from the site database.

6. Pencil in some of the classes that you expect to find in each layer:

   ❑ **InventoryDB**   Used to read data from the inventory database.

   ❑ **SiteDB**   Used to read and write data to the site database.

   ❑ **EmailGateway**   Used to send e-mail.

   ❑ **CompactDiscService**   The façade that offers services to the presentation layer in an action-type interface.

   ❑ **InventoryManager**   Used to determine how much inventory is available. This needs to be determined by subtracting the reservations from the current stock.

   ❑ **ReservationManager**   Used to make a reservation, call on the *InventoryManager* to check availability, and then claim a CD and send an e-mail.

The presentation layer has a number of Web pages. This number will most likely grow as the site takes shape and form.

7. After performing steps 1 through 6, your final diagram will resemble Figure 11-5.

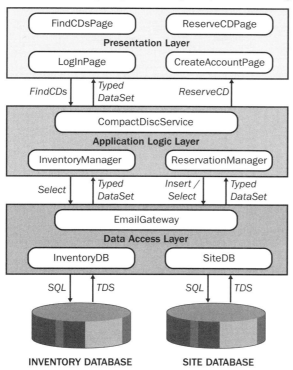

Figure 11-5 Overview of layering, data flow, and data stores

You now have a good basic idea of our solution. It's time to create a UML design of what you intend to build.

8. Open Visio and start a new diagram. Use the UML Model Diagram template.

9. Rename the initial diagram **Packages**.

10. Add three packages to the diagram; call them **StoreWeb**, **StoreServices**, and **StoreDAL** and add the correct dependencies. Your screen should look like Figure 11-6.

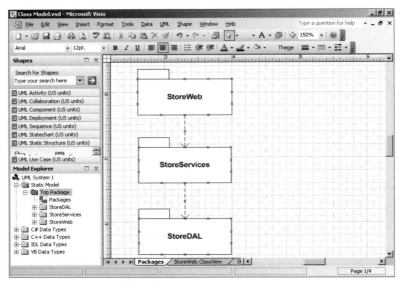

Figure 11-6   UML representation of layers

11. Next, add the correct classes to each package, create a new diagram called **Class Overview**, drag each class to the diagram, and draw the links between the classes. Figure 11-7 shows what your screen should resemble now. Notice the added *Asp-NetSqlMembershipProvider*. Because the account creation and logon is all handled by standard .NET Framework functionality, it is good to show that dependency.

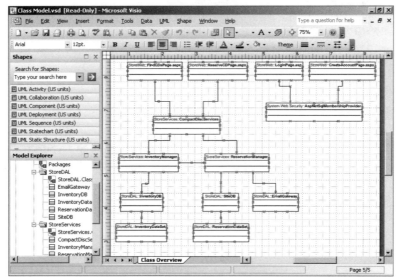

Figure 11-7   Class Overview diagram

MORE INFO   Complete Visio diagram on the CD

The complete Visio diagram can be installed from the Code folder on the companion CD. The file is named Class Model.vsd and is located in the Chapter 11\Lesson 1\Diagrams folder.

Lesson Summary

- Deciding on a data store mechanism is the first step in organizing the application logic. One or multiple stores might be needed, depending on security and availability considerations. Some data may be stored in read-only stores such as the registry or the web.config file.

- Layering your application allows for flexibility and maintainability of your code. It makes your code scalable by design and can be valuable when testing and debugging your application. Initially, it requires more effort, so the tradeoff is "invest now or pay later."

- Data flow can be data-centric, object-oriented, or a mixture of the two. The .NET Framework offers a rich API when using *Typed DataSet* objects to manage data flow. Object orientation allows for great flexibility in creating complex code but requires some effort when it comes to mapping your business objects to a relational database.

- Decision flow can be either action-driven or state-driven.

Lesson Review

You can use the following questions to test your knowledge of the information in Lesson 1, "Designing the Application Logic." The questions are also available on the companion CD if you prefer to review them in electronic form.

NOTE   Answers

Answers to these questions and explanations of why each answer choice is right or wrong are located in the "Answers" section at the end of the book.

---

1. Which of the following statements are correct? (Choose all that apply.)
    A. Application logic should never run on the Web server.
    B. Application logic should be designed stateless.
    C. Application logic should be strongly typed as much as possible.
    D. Application logic should always be object-oriented.

2. When implementing application logic using a façade, you can choose to make the interface of your façade action-driven or state-driven.

    A.   True

    B.   False

3. You've designed a method that has a signature that looks like *void Save(Order order)* in C# or *sub Save(order as Order)* in Microsoft Visual Basic on the façade of your application logic. Which statement is correct?

    A.   This method is designed in a state-driven fashion.

    B.   This method is designed in an action-driven fashion.

    C.   This method is both action-driven and state-driven.

    D.   This method is neither action-driven nor state-driven.

Lesson 2: Implementing Exception Handling

An important part of implementing application logic is thinking about what can go wrong. When can a condition occur that is not part of the regular flow of your program but that you want to recover from without telling your user to call the system administrator? In this lesson, you'll look at evaluating exceptions and how to design an exception-handling approach.

After this lesson, you will be able to:

■ Choose an appropriate exception handling mechanism.

❑ Evaluate the current exception handling mechanism.

❑ Design a new exception handling technique.

Estimated lesson time: 30 minutes

Choosing an Appropriate Exception Handling Technique

Look at the .NET Framework Class Library. All .NET Framework operations indicate failure by throwing exceptions. Exceptions are the standard mechanism for reporting errors. As an extension of this practice, applications and libraries should not use return codes to communicate errors but should throw exceptions when applicable.

Using exceptions to report errors creates consistent behavior in line with the .NET Framework that is the basis of your application. It also allows methods that already have a return type or members that do not have a return type, like constructors or set operations, to generate error reporting. A failure will never go unnoticed because the exception will abort the regular flow, ensuring that invalid values for parameters and such are not passed along any further.

Throwing an Exception

When throwing an exception, consider that the information in the exception should be useful to the piece of code that is catching it. The exception should be specific and should tell the user the following three things:

■ **When did processing fail?**   The timestamp of the exception might be crucial if more than one piece of code is failing.

■ **Where did processing fail?**   Where in the code did the processing fail? The stack trace provides vital information about where the exception originated.

■ **What went wrong?**   The exception needs to be clear about why processing failed. There are two pieces of relevant information here. The first is the exception type, for instance, an *ArgumentOutOfRangeException*. The exception type gives a clear indication of what went wrong. In this case, a method received a parameter that was outside the range of expected values. The other piece of information in the exception message should then be specific; for instance, it should specify which argument was out of range.

Catching an Exception

The caller of the member needs to determine whether to handle an exception or let the exception bubble up to the presentation layer. If unhandled, an exception will lead to a page being displayed to the user, informing him or her of an unhandled exception. On a developer computer, the developer might see some additional information, but the basic text is "An unhandled exception occurred during the execution of the current Web request. Please review the stack trace for more information about the error and where it originated in the code." The program flow has been terminated at that point.

NOTE Exception bubbling

Exception bubbling derives from the term "event bubbling," first used when describing the event mechanism in Microsoft Internet Explorer. Exception bubbling refers to the process of an exception traveling up through the call stack until a *try/catch* block handles the exception.

When designing your application, think about when to catch exceptions and what to do with them. The façade is an important place to catch and log exceptions. It might or might not be a machine boundary, and system administrators will need to know by looking at the event log whether your application is healthy. This does not apply to technical errors only. More functional messages, which are useful to the end user, are rarely interesting to see in the event log and will only clutter your system administrator's view of the application.

Handling Exceptions

In the .NET Framework, exceptions can be handled by placing *try/catch* blocks around a piece of code, as shown here:

```vb
' VB
Try
    File.WriteAllText("c:\test.txt", "hello")
Catch ioException As System.IO.IOException
    ' handle error or
    ' log and throw
    Throw New BookStoreException("Unable to store order", innerException)
Catch exception As Exception
    ' handle error or
    ' log and throw
    Throw
Finally
    ' clean up code
End Try
```

```csharp
// C#
try
{
    File.WriteAllText("c:\test.txt", "hello");
}
catch (System.IO.IOException ioException)
{
    // handle error or
    // log and throw
    throw new BookStoreException("Unable to store order", innerException);
}
catch (Exception exception)
{
    // handle error or
    // log and throw
    throw;
}
finally
{
    // clean up code
}
```

The preceding code shows that you're trying to execute some file-related code. You anticipate that an *IOException* might occur, and you would like to handle that in a specific manner. You also want to log any other exception that occurs, and the sample shows that the .NET Framework also allows for a piece of code to be executed, regardless of an exception occurring. This piece of code needs to be placed in the *finally* block.

Chapter 12, "Logging and Monitoring," covers logging of exceptions and choosing an appropriate event-logging method.

Notice also in the preceding sample that you can use the *throw* statement in a *try/catch* block to re-throw the exception. This is better than using *throw exception* because using just *throw* will preserve the stack trace of the exception.

When handling exceptions in the UI, you should be able to distinguish between technical errors and functional errors. Functional exceptions should, therefore, have a different type than technical exceptions do. Part of designing the application logic is deciding which exception the user can correct. Normally, if a user can correct the problem, the exception is not technical but, rather, functional. Making the distinction can be tricky. For example, in the application logic, you have a service that creates a file with financial information. The user is allowed to enter the filename, which is passed to the service. The service attempts to create a new file, but a file already exists. The DAL will throw an *IOException*. A *try/catch* block in the application logic should catch the error, wrap the exception in a custom functional exception, and change the message to "A file with this name already exists; please provide a new name."

Handling Unhandled Exceptions

You can use web.config to redirect the user to a custom page, informing him or her of the error, or you can choose to handle any unhandled errors in the *ApplicationError* event handler, which can be added to your Web application by adding a global application class, the Global.asax, and adding code to the *Application_Error* method, as shown in the following sample code:

```vb
' VB
 Private  Sub Application_Error(ByVal sender As Object, ByVal e As EventArgs)
    ' Code that runs when an unhandled error occurs
    Response.Write("Hello, an error occurred.")
    Response.End()
End Sub
```

```csharp
// C#
void Application_Error(object sender, EventArgs e)
{
    // Code that runs when an unhandled error occurs
    Response.Write("Hello, an error occurred.");
    Response.End();
}
```

The settings in web.config that manage redirection are found in the *customErrors* section, which is created and commented out by default by Visual Studio 2005 when adding web.config to the Web site.

```xml
<customErrors defaultRedirect="GenericErrorPage.htm">
  <error statusCode="403" redirect="NoAccess.htm" />
  <error statusCode="404" redirect="FileNotFound.htm" />
  <error statusCode="500" redirect="InternalError.htm" />
</customErrors>
```

Considerations When Designing Exceptions

The .NET Framework Class Library may throw a variety of exceptions at you and, as seen in the previous paragraphs, your own code should be doing its part to throw exceptions when things go wrong. Thinking of how and when to throw an exception requires some thought, though.

Here's an example. A customer has signed on to your Web store and is creating an account. He saves the information, calling *AddNewCustomer* on the façade of your application logic layer, where, upon receiving the *CustomerRow*, you are now validating the *CustomerRow*. Do you want to throw an exception if, when validating the customer ZIP code, you discover it is invalid? You could, but this would terminate the application flow and report to the presentation layer that the customer's information could not be saved because the ZIP code is invalid. The user corrects the ZIP code and clicks Save again. This time, the validation of the ZIP code passes, and next, the phone number is checked. Oops, the phone format is invalid;

let's throw an exception. As you can see, this would not be a great way to provide feedback to your customer. It would be better to perform all validations and then throw one exception for all problems.

Lesson learned? A method should throw an exception only if the expected end result cannot be reached. You could choose to catch and collect all of these exceptions, but there is significant overhead in the run time of *try/catch* statements. Use them when you need to, but consider alternatives. In this case, design Boolean validations to determine as many errors as possible, and then combine the result in one exception. For example, implement a *void Validate(CustomerRow customer)* method, which in turn calls *bool IsZIPCodeValid(..)*, *bool IsPhoneNumberValid(..)*, and so on.

Exceptions and Traceability

Exceptions need to tell the user where the exception originated. A *System.IO.IOException* should originate only from a piece of code that is part of the *System.IO* namespace. You should avoid using this exception yourself. The only exceptions that are generic and can be used in your application logic or application framework are the exceptions in the root namespace. Even then, most of the exceptions will not make sense to use in your application logic. The most frequently used exception in application logic is the *System.ArgumentException* and the exceptions derived from this class. To make your own exceptions more traceable, create a unique exception per assembly or, at the very least, a unique exception per significant namespace. By defining an exception with internal constructors only, you will know that your exception is unique to your code. Create your exception by implementing a class that inherits from *System.Exception*. Note that sometimes you'll want to inherit from a different class. For instance, if you're implementing a custom *AspNetMembershipProvider*, it will make sense to make your exception inherit from *ProviderException*.

Quick Check
- What is the most common class from which to inherit when implementing a custom exception?

Quick Check Answer
- System.Exception

Exam Tip   Remember how to create a custom exception.

Implementing the Chosen Technique

You want to implement at least one custom exception per namespace and, because each layer on your application will have its own namespace, you'll implement one for the application logic layer as well as for the DAL.

The following code shows how to define an exception specific to the DAL of your bookstore application. You create a number of internal constructors, matching with the standard constructors of the standard *System.Exception*.

```vb
' VB
Namespace MSLearning.TK547.Chapter11.Samples.DAL
    Public Class BookStoreDALException
        Inherits Exception

        Friend Sub New()
            MyBase.New()
        End Sub

        Friend Sub New(ByVal message As String)
            MyBase.New(message)
        End Sub

        Friend Sub New(ByVal message As String, innerException as Exception)
            MyBase.New(message, innerException)
        End Sub

    End Class

End Namespace
```

```csharp
// C#
using System;

namespace MSLearning.TK547.Chapter11.Samples.DAL
{
    public class BookStoreDALException : Exception
    {
        internal BookStoreDALException()
            : base()
        {
        }

        internal BookStoreDALException(string message)
            : base(message)
        {
        }

        internal BookStoreDALException(string message,
                                       Exception innerException)
```

```
            : base(message, innerException)
        {
        }
    }
}
```

An alternative approach is to take matters a step further: mark the constructors as private, implement the factory pattern on the exception, and create a unique factory method for each exception. This allows you to throw exceptions with the same message from multiple places. It also helps with solving problems. If someone comes to you and says that he or she received a particular error, check the exception type, go to the corresponding factory method, right-click, and choose Show All References. The code for this approach looks like the following code.

```vb
' VB
Public Class BookstoreValidationException
    Inherits Exception
    Private Sub New(String message)
        MyBase(message)
    End Sub

    Friend Property BookstoreValidationException() As static
        Get
            Return New BookstoreValidationException("Quantity is mandatory and
                                           cannot be empty.");
        End Get
    End Property
End Class
```

```csharp
// C#
using System;

public class BookstoreValidationException : Exception
{
    private BookstoreValidationException(string message)
        : base(message)
    {
    }

    internal static BookstoreValidationException
                GetQuantityIsMandatoryException()
    {
        get
        {
            return new BookstoreValidationException("Quantity is mandatory and
                                           cannot be empty.");
        }
        set
        }
```

Throwing the exception will look like this:

```
' VB
If order.Quantity = 0 Then
    Throw BookstoreValidationException.GetQuantityIsMandatoryException()
End If
```

```
// C#
if (order.Quantity == 0)
{
    throw BookstoreValidationException.GetQuantityIsMandatoryException();
}
```

As you can see in this code, there are now two exceptions in the *BookStore* namespace. A *BookStoreException* should, therefore, be implemented, and the two exceptions should inherit from this instead of from *System.Exception*.

Using the Error Fields

A frequently seen alternative to throwing exceptions is using the error fields in the *DataRow*—*DataRow.RowError* and *DataRow.SetColumnError*—to add error information. The *DataRow* is passed back to the UI, where the UI will pick up on the errors and display them to the user. This is more useful in a WinForm application than in an ASP.NET application, in which the *GridView* will not display the errors, but a *DataGrid* in a WinForm will. Note that an exception is still required to abort the regular flow and inform the client of the interrupted flow of your application.

Lab: Implement Exception Handling

This lab will walk you through the steps of creating and implementing a custom exception. After creating the exception, you'll throw your custom exception from a façade class.

If you encounter a problem completing an exercise, the completed projects are available on the companion CD in the Code folder.

▶ Exercise 1: Implementing a Custom Exception

In this exercise, you will create a class that you'll then turn into a custom exception by inheriting from *System.Exception*.

1. Open Visual Studio 2005 and create a blank solution named **MSLearning.Exercises**.
2. Add a new C# or Visual Basic Class Library project.
3. Name the project **BookStoreServices**.
4. In Solution Explorer, right-click the project and click Properties. In the Default Namespace or Root Namespace text box (depending on what language you've chosen), on the Application tab, type **MSLearning.Chapter11.BookStoreServices**.
5. Delete the Class1 file shown in Solution Explorer.

6. From the Visual Studio Project menu, click Add New Item.

7. From the Add New Item dialog box, select Class and name the class **BookStoreServices-Exception.** Click Add and define it as illustrated in the following code example:

```vb
' VB
Namespace MSLearning.Chapter11.BookStoreServices

    Public Class BookStoreServicesException

    End Class

End Namespace
```

```csharp
//C#
using System;

namespace MSLearning.Chapter12.BookStoreServices
{
    public class BookStoreServicesException
    {
    }
}
```

8. Make your class inherit from *System.Exception* and add three constructors to match the constructors of *System.Exception*. Your code should look like the following:

```vb
' VB
Namespace MSLearning.Chapter11.BookStoreServices
    Public Class BookStoreServicesException
        Inherits Exception

        Friend Sub New()
            MyBase.New()
        End Sub

        Friend Sub New(ByVal message As String)
            MyBase.New(message)
        End Sub

        Friend Sub New(ByVal message As String, innerException as Exception)
            MyBase.New(message, innerException)
        End Sub

    End Class

End Namespace
```

```csharp
// C#
using System;

namespace MSLearning.Chapter11.BookStoreServices
{
    public class BookStoreServicesException : Exception
```

```
        {
            internal BookStoreServicesException()
                : base()
            {
            }

            internal BookStoreServicesException(string message)
                : base(message)
            {
            }

            internal BookStoreServicesException(string message,
                                                Exception innerException)
                : base(message, innerException)
            {
            }
        }
    }
```

▶ **Exercise 2: Throwing and Catching a Custom Exception**

Continuing where you left off in Exercise 1, you'll now catch the custom *BookStoreServices-Exception.*

1. If you do not have the solution opened already, open Visual Studio 2005 and then open the solution named MSLearning.Exercises.

2. On the Visual Studio Project menu, click Add New Item.

3. In the Add New Item dialog box, select Class, name the class **BookStoreService**, and define it as illustrated in the following code example:

```
' VB
Imports System.Collections.Generic
Imports System.Text

Namespace MSLearning.Chapter11.BookStoreServices
    Public Class BookStoreService

    End Class
End Namespace

// C#
using System;
using System.Collections.Generic;
using System.Text;

namespace MSLearning.Chapter11.BookStoreServices
{
    public class BookStoreService
    {

    }
}
```

4. Add a public method named **AddCustomer**. Add one parameter, a string called **name**, and make the method throw an exception if the name is fewer than four characters long.

5. Add a *try/catch* block to catch an exception if it is of type *BookStoreServicesException*, and then re-throw the exception, or log the exception in the event log and then re-throw the exception. Note that, because logging is not covered until Chapter 12, just adding comments with a TODO will suffice. Your code should look like this:

```vb
' VB
Namespace MSLearning.Chapter11.BookStoreServices
    Public Class BookStoreService
        Public Sub AddCustomer(ByVal name As String)
            Try
                If name.Length < 4 Then
                    Throw New BookStoreServicesException("Customer name is too short.")
                End If
            Catch bookStoreException As BookStoreServicesException
                ' do nothing but preserve stack trace
                Throw
            Catch exception As Exception
                ' TODO: log error
                Throw
            End Try
        End Sub
    End Class
End Namespace
```

```csharp
// C#
using System;

namespace MSLearning.Chapter11.BookStoreServices
{
    public class BookStoreService
    {
        public AddCustomer( string name)
        {
            try{
            if ( name.Length < 4 )
            {
                throw new BookStoreServicesException(
                            "Customer name is too short.");
            }
            }
            catch(BookStoreServicesException bookStoreException)
            {
                // do nothing but preserve stack trace
                throw;
            }
            catch(Exception exception)
            {
                // TODO: log error
                throw;
```

```
                    }
                }
            }
        }
```

Lesson Summary

- Separate validations and exceptions in your code.
- A validation does not fail but returns information about the validity of current state.
- An exception informs the caller of the code that regular program flow has been aborted.
- An exception needs to inform the caller of when, where, and why program flow has been aborted.
- A custom exception can be created by implementing a class that inherits from *System.Exception* either directly or indirectly.
- Each namespace should have its own base exception.

Lesson Review

You can use the following questions to test your knowledge of the information in Lesson 2, "Implementing Exception Handling." The questions are also available on the companion CD if you prefer to review them in electronic form.

NOTE Answers

Answers to these questions and explanations of why each answer choice is right or wrong are located in the "Answers" section at the end of the book.

---

1. An exception informs the caller of the code that regular program flow has been aborted.
   A. True
   B. False
2. You're implementing a service that will run a dedicated application server. The logic is very simple, and no validation logic is present. Do you need to implement a *try/catch* block?
   A. Yes
   B. No

3. Assume you're implementing some application logic that needs to check whether an order total is more than $1,000. If the order total is more than $1,000, the order needs to be flagged as special and stored in the database. If the order total is less than $1,000, the order just needs to be stored. Analysis has shown that 95 percent of the order total is less than $1,000. Should you use an exception when validating the order?

   A. Yes

   B. No

4. Which of the following is true? (Choose all that apply.)

   A. An exception should always have a timestamp.

   B. An exception should tell you why the application flow aborted.

   C. An exception should tell you where the application aborted.

   D. An exception should always tell you the Web page where the error occurred.

5. You're creating a custom exception for a piece of code that performs a calculation. The code will fail with a *DivisionByZero* exception. You want to catch the exception, add more detailed information, and then throw a custom exception. Which of the following names would be a good name for the custom exception?

   A. *CalculationFailedException*;

   B. *ParameterOutOfRangeException*;

   C. *GeneralFailureException*;

Chapter Review

To further practice and reinforce the skills you learned in this chapter, you can complete the following tasks:

- Review the chapter summary.
- Review the list of key terms introduced in this chapter.
- Complete the case scenarios. These scenarios set up real-world situations involving the topics of this chapter and ask you to create a solution.
- Complete the suggested practices.
- Take a practice test.

Chapter Summary

- Using patterns to organize your code will improve maintainability.
- Organizing your application by using, for instance, the three principal layers pattern will help make your code robust against future changes and demands.
- Choose an interface style, action-driven or state-driven, and use it to be consistent in your service layer design.
- An exception informs you of an aborted action; do not use exceptions if you do not mean to abort your code.
- Exceptions should inform you of what, where, and when the regular flow of your application was aborted.

Key Terms

Do you know what these key terms mean? You can check your answers by looking up the terms in the glossary at the end of the book.

- ADO.NET
- design pattern
- exception
- exception bubbling

Case Scenarios

In the following case scenarios, you will apply what you've learned about designing application logic, organizing code, and creating, catching and logging exceptions. You can find answers to these questions in the "Answers" section at the end of this book.

Case Scenario 1: Catching and Logging Technical Exceptions

Your company sells books and runs an online store. Recently, customers have called customer service and claimed that they have ordered books but haven't received their orders. Queries on the database show that the orders were never entered into the database. Your manager is upset and wants answers to the following questions.

1. If something goes wrong with the application server, how do we know?
2. Will every exception be logged in the event log?
3. Can the system administrator view the functional errors?

Case Scenario 2: Scaling Out

Technical choices and business requirements do not always match. The end user in your business sees opportunities to make money or to save money by improving his or her process. Your technical expertise is required, but applying the soundest solution in a timeframe that satisfies the end user can be quite a challenge. The following scenario shows that more than one person in your organization needs to be satisfied, even when time pressure is high.

Interviews

Following is a list of company personnel interviewed and their statements.

- **IT Manager**   "We're building a Web application because the finance department wants to interview the employees electronically. They claim it is a one-time project, but I want the basics of the application to be reusable because I've heard rumors that marketing wants something similar for interviewing visitors of our Web site."
- **Finance Department Manager**   "We need this intranet application in two weeks. Our department is financing this application, so it needs to be implemented quickly and cheaply."

Question

How would you design a solution that meets the requirements of both managers?

Suggested Practices

To help you successfully master the exam objectives presented in this chapter, complete the following tasks.

Designing the Application Logic

To further your skills in designing the application logic, it is recommended that you complete at least Practice 1. Practice 2 is optional.

- **Practice 1**   Create a solution with four projects: a Web site, a Web service, a class library for the application logic, and a class library for data access. Retrieve the customer from the *AdventureWorks* database, which comes as an optional install with Microsoft SQL Server 2005, but can also be downloaded from *http://www.microsoft.com/downloads /details.aspx?FamilyID=E719ECF7-9F46-4312-AF89-6AD8702E4E6E&displaylang=en*, and write an application logic to total his or her orders. Return the data through a Web service and display it on your Web site using a *GridView*.

- **Practice 2**   Expand on the solution created in Practice 1 and implement a Web page for adding a customer, add a Web service to add a customer, and store the customer in the *AdventureWorks* database. Use a *Typed DataSet* as parameters for the services.

Practice Implementing Exception Handling

The following two practices will help you implement exception handling without the aid of a step-by-step tutorial. Test yourself on how well you've understood the material.

- **Practice 1**   Create a solution with four projects: a Web site, a Web service, a class library for application logic, and a class library for data access. Implement a Web page for adding a customer, add a Web service to add a customer, and store the customer in the *AdventureWorks* database. Use a *Typed DataSet* as parameters for the services. Implement three validations on the customer: Name is mandatory, address is mandatory, and name needs to be more that three characters. Create a custom exception to throw these exceptions if the customer makes a mistake. Adjust the UI to display these functional exceptions in a user-friendly manner, allowing the user to correct the mistakes.

- **Practice 2**   Adjust Practice 1 so that, if more than one error occurs, the user will get two or more error messages at once.

Take a Practice Test

The practice tests on this book's companion CD offer many options. For example, you can test yourself on just one exam objective, or you can test yourself on all the 70-547 certification exam content. You can set up the test so that it closely simulates the experience of taking a certification exam, or you can set it up in study mode so that you can look at the correct answers and explanations after you answer each question.

MORE INFO   **Practice tests**

For details about all the practice test options available, see the "How to Use the Practice Tests" section in this book's Introduction.

Chapter 12
Logging and Monitoring

Web applications are expected to operate without constant supervision. They run on servers sitting in darkened rooms where the presence of people is occasional at most. Therefore, from an operational standpoint, Web applications need a way to let the outside world know how they're doing. What kinds of requests are being processed? What types of errors are being encountered? Moreover, along with simply detecting these conditions, the Web application needs to be able to pass this information along, whether it's in the form of a log file for later review or on a real-time monitor. This chapter discusses the techniques that allow Web applications to meet this very important operational requirement.

Exam objectives in this chapter:

- Choose an appropriate event logging method for the application.
    - Decide whether to log data. Considerations include policies, security, requirements, and debugging.
    - Choose a storage mechanism for logged events. For example, database, flat file, event log, or XML file.
    - Choose a system-wide event logging mechanism—for example, centralized logging, distributed logging, and so on.
    - Decide logging levels based on severity and priority.
- Monitor specific characteristics or aspects of the application.
    - Decide whether to monitor data. Considerations include administration, auditing, and application support.
    - Decide which characteristics to monitor—for example, application performance, memory consumption, security auditing, usability metrics, and possible bugs.
    - Choose event monitoring mechanisms, such as System Monitor and logs.
    - Decide monitoring levels based on requirements.
    - Choose a system-wide monitoring method from the available monitoring mechanisms.

Lessons in this chapter:

Before You Begin

To complete the lessons in this chapter, you must have:

- A computer that meets or exceeds the minimum hardware requirements listed in the "About This Book" section
- Microsoft Visual Studio 2005 installed on the computer, with either Microsoft Visual Basic or C# installed

---

Real World

Bruce Johnson

In the world of logging and monitoring, a Web application is a different beast for most developers. If you're used to working with a user interface (UI), such as a Windows Form, getting at what happens during a page request is more challenging than one would hope. Of course, you can step through the processing while debugging with Visual Studio. But what can you do once the application goes live? How do you find out what steps have been performed so you can more easily identify the source of any problem?

But beyond the debugging requirements, Web applications differ from Windows Forms applications in their audience. Frequently, the people who access the Web application are not operating inside the corporate security boundary. As a result, keeping track of the requests and responses is as much an auditing function as it is a debugging function. And don't even talk about the marketing people who want to know which Web pages were hit and for how long. All of these subjects fall into the realm of Web application logging, and this lesson covers some of the techniques that you can use.

Lesson 1: Logging Application Events

There is a great deal of similarity between the questions that need to be answered in logging and the questions that need to be answered in monitoring. That said, the audiences for logging and monitoring tend to be different, and that drives which technology is used to implement each function. This lesson focuses on logging, with the attendant audiences of developers, auditors, and a few select others.

After this lesson, you will be able to:
- Identify the expected audience for logging data, including the different requirements that those audiences might have.
- Understand available options for storing logging data.
- Decide whether a logging framework is appropriate for your Web application.

Estimated lesson time: 40 minutes

Who Needs Logging?

Decisions about logging emanate from the question of who is interested in the data. Each audience needs different types of data generated at different levels of granularity, and they want to get at the data by using different methods. So let's consider the interested parties.

- **Developers**   Contrary to popular opinion, developers don't normally spend their evenings reading log files. And yet, on occasion, it is necessary to delve through reams of text files looking for that one clue to understanding why every hundredth user isn't getting the expected results. Although the debugging tools available in Visual Studio are wonderful, they can't help in situations like this. It is possible to debug the Web application by attaching to the appropriate process; however, this has a negative impact on the Web site as a whole. In this situation, the developer wants to see the equivalent of checkpoints in the log, an indication of which path was taken in processing the request, and any values that are important to the decisions.

- **Marketing teams**   The logged information for a Web site is not limited to the values that the application can write out. You can configure Microsoft Internet Information Services (IIS) to generate log files that can then be processed into a number of useful reports. The collected information includes the source of the request (by Internet Protocol (IP) address or domain), the initial page, the path taken through the Web site, and even just the requested pages. There are third-party applications that can process these log files and generate colorful reports that a number of groups, including marketing teams, can use. Marketing teams will care about the path taken, the raw activity, and, perhaps, the last page viewed on the site.

- **Auditors**   In certain situations, all the details of a particular transaction need to be persisted. Financial transactions, such as transfers between bank accounts, are a canonical example, but by no means is the need to audit transactions limited to the financial world.

Laws such as the Health Insurance Portability and Accountability Act (HIPAA) and the Sarbanes-Oxley Act mandate auditing of certain types of transactions. Although these laws apply only to the United States, your organization might need to comply if you plan on doing business in the United States. The result of all this interest is that auditors have, quite recently, become one of the more demanding audiences for logging information.

■ **Security**   A common requirement is to log any requests that were made to access secured resources, whether successful or not. The audience interested in the security aspect of logging is a little different from the other two groups mentioned. Just tracking which requests have succeeded or failed is one thing, but the operational side of many Web sites would also like to be notified of failure patterns. That way, they can react more quickly to attempts to breach security. For this reason, both this lesson and the lesson on monitoring cover the security audience.

The idea of successful resource access brings up an interesting point that you must consider when determining which data to log and who will be able to see it. Any logged data has the potential to violate the privacy of some person. Logging successes creates a trail that can be used to determine a person's actions. Placing certain types of information into the log file can create a huge hole in security. Logging a customer's credit card information is a clear example, but hackers can even use phone numbers and addresses. And, whereas the database administrator might make certain that only the appropriate people have access to the customer list, a developer can easily write this "secured" information to a plaintext log file that can be viewed by anyone who knows where to look.

You also need to be aware of the potential for violating privacy laws. The web of privacy laws is quite complex, especially once national boundaries have been crossed. Although it's doubtful that your company expects you to be an international privacy expert, upper management needs to be aware of the type of information that is being collected so that they can make the appropriate policy decisions.

Real World

Bruce Johnson

To get an idea of the possible impact logging can have on privacy, consider the case of Google and the U.S. government. Late in 2005, the U.S. government sued Google to attempt to make the company turn over logs related to user searches on objectionable words. As it turns out, detailed logs were available because that sort of information is invaluable to Google in terms of both generating revenue and improving search result criteria. But, because the detailed logs were available, the government was able to go to a judge and request that they be turned over. This is an instance in which, if Google maintained less-detailed logs, the government's ability to learn about users' searches would have been severely curtailed.

What Data Is Required?

Once the audience for the data has been identified, the question of what data needs to be captured becomes a lot easier to answer. However, there are still a few issues that need to be ironed out.

Granularity

The *granularity* of logged data is broken down into two categories based on the amount of data that is stored.

- **Coarsely grained**   Coarsely grained data is a high-level, general type of data. The data does not include details about individual transactions but, instead, aggregates the details to reduce the volume of collected data. The lower volume makes it easier for people to process the data and, in many cases, the patterns of usage are more important than the details.

- **Finely grained**   Finely grained data is pretty much the opposite of coarsely grained. The data is detailed, transaction-level information taken down to the lowest level. The volume of logged data at this level has the potential to be quite large. For this reason, the processing of finely grained data is normally automated.

As you might expect, there are times when both coarsely grained and finely grained data are required. More interesting, they are not mutually exclusive. Much of the management performed by the operations staff is done "by exception." That is to say, in the big picture, coarsely grained information is adequate right up to the moment when something exceptional happens. As soon as the application detects the exception, finely grained logging is suddenly more useful. This could be true whether the exception is a security breach or an exception being raised within the application. In this type of situation, the need to switch logging levels in real time can be critical in quickly identifying the underlying issue.

Logging Levels

This apparently contradictory requirement for both finely grained and coarsely grained logs leads to the idea of levels. A *log level* indicates the importance of logging a particular piece of information. Although the names of log levels are arbitrary, the *Windows Event Log* includes the following levels.

- **Error**   This is a significant problem with the application. This level usually indicates a loss of data or functionality that needs to be addressed immediately.

- **Warning**   This is a less significant problem than Error. Although there is no immediate concern, warnings could be an indication of impending problems.

- **Information**   This type of entry indicates that an operation of interest has occurred.

- **Failure Audit** This is an audit entry for a failed attempt to access a secured resource.
- **Success Audit** This is an audit entry for a successful attempt to access a secured resource.

Given that each statement used to log information now has an associated severity level, the other piece of the puzzle is for the Web application itself to specify which level of logging takes place. For example, a setting might be added to web.config that determines whether only Errors and Failure Audits are logged or if even the informational data should be persisted. The logging mechanism that your application uses evaluates the configuration setting and determines whether to persist a particular piece of information.

Changing Log Levels

The need to switch from coarsely grained to finely grained logging implies that a mechanism is required to adjust the configuration setting and detect the change within the Web application. Prior to Microsoft .NET Framework 2.0, this would have been problematic. Whereas changing the value in web.config requires little more than a text editor, when web.config is updated, ASP.NET starts a new process to handle incoming requests. If there was any state information at the root of the problem being investigated, it could be lost by this restarting of the virtual directory. Fortunately, .NET Framework 2.0 introduced a couple of attributes to eliminate this problem.

But don't get any hopes up about keeping the configuration information in the web.config file. Any changes to web.config still result in a restart of the virtual directory. Although the *RestartOnExternalChanges* and *ConfigSource* attributes allow configuration to be placed in an external file, configuration values can still be accessed from within the code as if the values were physically in web.config.

The first step is to move the configuration information to a separate file. As an example, a file called logging.config could be created with contents like the following.

```
<?xml version="1.0"?>
<appSettings>
   <add key="LoggingLevel" value="warning" />
</AppSettings>
```

Notice that, with the exception of the <?xml> declarative, contents of the file look like the corresponding section in the web.config file.

After the configuration settings have been moved out of web.config, a small change needs to be made to a section in web.config to reference the external file. For the *AppSettings* example, the web.config would look like the following.

```
<AppSettings configSource="logging.config"
   RestartOnExternalChange="false">
</AppSettings>
```

In the interests of full disclosure, because the section referenced is *AppSettings*, the *RestartOn-ExternalChange* attribute is, in all likelihood, not required. In the machine.config file, the *App-Settings* section already defines *RestartOnExternalChange* to be false, and web.config inherits this value. As a result, it isn't necessary to include it here. Moreover, if you define your own configuration section, the section definition needs to include the *RestartOnExternalChanges* attribute. The section definition would look something like the following.

```
<section name="MyAppSettings"
   type="System.Configuration.AppSettingsSection, System.Configuration,
   Version=2.0.0.0, Culture=neutral, PublicKeyToken=b03f5f7f11d50a3a"
RestartOnExternalChanges="false" />
```

The Interesting Data

Finally, going back to the original problem, what data should be captured in the log? As mentioned, the audience plays a big role in this determination. Based on the focus, the data usually falls into the following categories.

- **General application health**   Is the Web site available? Are the external resources (databases, files, external Web services, and so on) required to satisfy available requests successfully? What exceptions (expected or unexpected) have been thrown?
- **Performance**   How many requests per second are being processed? How long does each request take?
- **Security auditing**   What failed attempts to access a secured resource took place? Where did the request come from? How many failed attempts have occurred recently?

Regardless of the areas on which logging focuses, the audience is key. You must strike a balance between overwhelming the audience with too broad a set of data, which doesn't provide useful information, and too narrow an approach. Making the correct choices requires a holistic view of the audience requirements and the available data to match them up appropriately.

Data Storage Choices

Both logging and monitoring have the same choices for data storage. However, certain types of storage are more likely to be used for logging or for monitoring. This section focuses on the persistence choices that are much more likely to be used in a logging scenario. For each option, the characteristics will be considered within the context of logging and how the gathered information might be used.

Flat Files

For too many developers, "log file" is just another name for "flat file." The structure of a flat file is simple, but its strength is in its simplicity. Each line in a log file contains the information for one event. The information for an event includes one or more fields related to the event (date, time, description, source, and so on). The structure of each line generally falls into one of the following categories.

- **Comma-delimited** Each field is separated by a comma. This is a common enough file format that Microsoft Office Excel can open it without conversion. The biggest drawback is the restriction placed on the content by the use of a comma as a delimiter. The result is that the field values can't contain a comma without surrounding the value with quotes. Once the value is surrounded by quotes, it can't contain a quote. Yes, there are solutions, but other available options avoid this issue altogether.

- **Tab-delimited** Conceptually, a tab-delimited file is the same as a comma-delimited file, but the separator is a tab character, not a comma. The idea is that field values are much less likely to contain a tab than a comma. And it's true enough that problems with tab-delimited files are rarely even seen in the real world.

- **Fixed-length** Rather than use a delimiter to separate fields, this format limits the size of each field value. The number of characters in each field is fixed, regardless of the field value being stored. This means that the need for field delimiters is removed, along with the single/double quote question. This is a relatively old format that is used mostly because of compatibility with existing systems. It can result in some information being lost (if the field value is too long for the allocated space) or the generation of overly large log files (because field values are padded with spaces to fit).

One of the drawbacks to using a flat file as a logging mechanism is that, in general, the file is local to the process performing the logging. That's not to say that you can't place a log file onto a remote machine, only that it's rare because, if the remote machine is unavailable, nothing will be logged. Also, in the particular case of Web applications, the user under which the request is being processed (keeping in mind that best practices say it should be a low-privileged user) won't have access to the network.

Exam Tip Keep in mind the negative side of flat files when considering questions related to the data storage options for logging.

Event Logs

The other common location for logging events is the appropriately named event log. There are two main differences between the flat file and the event log. Whereas the schema for the flat file is completely up to the developer, the event log has only a fixed set of fields that can be assigned values. On the other hand, you can use the Windows Event Viewer application to view logs either on the local machine or on a remote one. Table 12-1 contains some of the fields that are populated in the event log.

Table 12-1 Event Log Fields

Field Name	Description
Source	The name of the application that is the source for the event log. It must be registered on the computer before it can be used.
Description	The string that is the message for the log entry.
Type	The type of log entry. It must be one of the *EventLogEntryType* values.
Event ID	An application-specific identifier for the event.
Category	An application-specific subcategory associated with the log entry.
Raw Data	A set of binary data associated with the log entry.

"Event log" is actually a bit of a misnomer. There is actually more than one log available for the insertion of event information. By default, three logs— Application, Security, and System—are created. In general, the System log contains entries associated with the operating system and its related processes. The Security log contains successful and failed resource-access events. The Application log contains entries associated with other non-operating system applications. The Application log is the most likely target for developers. The purpose of these logs is to assemble related information, making it easier for the audience to find the desired information.

Using the *CreateEventSource* method on the *System.Diagnostic.EventLog* class, as shown in the following example, it is also possible to programmatically add logs other than the three default ones.

```
' VB
EventLog.CreateEventSource("Source Name", "Log Name")
```

```
// C#
EventLog.CreateEventSource("Source Name", "Log Name");
```

This statement creates a new event log called Log Name as well as adding a potential source, called Source Name, for events. Although this is a simple way to add an event log, a permission limitation restricts when the statement can be used.

The permissions associated with both creating event logs and writing to them mean that the developer needs to be aware of code access security within ASP.NET. First, it requires administrator rights to be able to create an event log, so someone with elevated privileges must run the *CreateEventSource* method shown previously. Unless your systems administrator is not paying attention, the ASP.NET user is not granted administrator privileges. This means that waiting until the first request to create the event source is not normally a successful strategy. Therefore, because creating event sources requires administrative privileges, they should be created during the installation of the Web application, when it's easier to require that the installer has the necessary permissions.

Even writing to the event log requires permissions that are not normally granted to the default ASP.NET user. However, there are techniques that can be used to allow ASP.NET applications to add events to the event log.

As a best practice, the ASP.NET user should be granted only a low privilege level. With ASP.NET, the suggested level is known as *medium trust*. By default, medium trust can't add events to the event log. The solution is to create a custom policy based on medium trust that includes access to the event log. Once the custom policy file is present, it can be referenced by modifying the trust in web.config. Adding the following element to web.config accomplishes this, as shown here:

```
<system.web>
   <securityPolicy>
     <trustLevel name="Custom"
                 policyFile="web_customtrust.config" />
   </securityPolicy>
   <trust level="Custom" originUrl="" />
 </system.web>
```

Note that the *<trust>* element references the Custom level, and the *<trustLevel>* named custom points to a physical file, which is the policy file.

In the policy file, there is a *<SecurityClasses>* element. Within this element, a reference to the *EventLogPermission* class needs to be added. You can accomplish this by adding the following element within *<SecurityClasses>*.

```
<SecurityClass Name="EventLogPermission"
   Description="System.Diagnostics.EventLogPermission,
   System, Version=2.0.0.0, Culture=neutral,
   PublicKeyToken=b77a5c561934e089" />
```

Finally, *EventLogPermission* needs to be added to the ASP.NET named permission set. The following XML element would be added to the policy file.

```
<PermissionSet class="NamedPermissionSet" version="1"
   Name="ASP.Net">
   <IPermission class="EventLogPermission" version="1">
     <Machine name="." access="Write"/>
   </IPermission>
</PermissionSet>
```

Once the policy file has been changed, you should restart the virtual directory so it will pick up the changes. (If you had just changed the web.config file to reference the custom policy, the restart would have occurred when web.config was saved.)

MORE INFO   **Running ASP.NET in a medium trust environment**

For more information about how to run ASP.NET in a medium trust environment, check out the Microsoft Developer Network (MSDN) Library article "How To: Use Medium Trust in ASP.NET 2.0" at *http://msdn.microsoft.com/library/default.asp?url=/library/en-us/dnpag2/html/PAGHT000020.asp.*

Adding an entry to an event log is fairly straightforward. The *System.Diagnostics.EventLog* class contains a static method called *WriteEntry*. By passing a string parameter, that value is used as the description portion of a log entry in the Application log with an entry type of Information, as shown here.

```
' VB
System.Diagnostics.EventLog.WriteEntry("This is the log message")
```

```
// C#
System.Diagnostics.EventLog.WriteEntry("This is the log message");
```

In more complicated overloads, you can specify additional information, including the log to which the event will be written (Application, System, Security, or your own log), the event log type, the event identifier, the event category, and an array of bytes (the *RawData* field) to be included with the entry.

Exam Tip   The permission requirement for writing to the event log is a commonly forgotten requirement, which makes it more likely to appear on the exam.

Using the event log solves some of the problems associated with a flat file. Although it is not technically a centralized location, the event log allows the information to be easily accessed remotely, and the common format in which events are recorded means that third-party applications can be employed to monitor and report on the entries.

However, the cost of this centralization is decreased flexibility. With a flat file, the developer can define whatever fields he or she wants in whatever order is desired. The event log has a set list of fields. The only areas where anything goes are the *Message* and *RawData* fields.

There is also the potential for a poorly configured event log to cause a Web application to become unavailable. One of the configuration settings on the event log indicates the maximum size for the log and what should happen when the log file becomes full. The default behavior is to not allow additional entries once the log is full. Unfortunately (from a logging perspective), this setting, combined with a full log file, causes an exception to be raised when the *WriteEntry* method is invoked. But having a logging statement throw an exception is quite unexpected and will probably result in the Web application not working as expected.

There are two possible solutions. The first involves designing the application so that exceptions thrown during logging do not stop the application from functioning. This requires some forethought or the use of the framework to centralize the changes. In some cases, not logging information could be an undesirable result, depending on exactly what is being logged.

The second solution involves changing the configuration of the event log. Increasing the size of the event log only postpones the inevitable; however, you can set the event log so that old events are overwritten as needed. In that way, if the event log does unexpectedly become full, old log entries will be deleted, and the application continues to function.

Databases

Whereas the first two data store types are adequate for many situations, neither of them address the issues of centralized accessibility, not to mention that flat files and the event log are useful when it comes to generating reports. (Yes, flat files can be used as the input to some reporting engines, but they are not optimal and, in fact, depend on a consistency of event information that is frequently absent.) If your audience requires these centralized storage or reports, then using a database is quite possibly the solution for which you're looking.

Database tables have the same fixed field layout as the event log. However, unlike in the event log, the developer is able to define the fields that are stored, which the programming staff appreciates. In addition, the limits of what can be stored increase from whatever settings are in the event log to whatever is the maximum size of a database table.

As for the reporting, there can be little argument that a database is a step or two up from a flat file. Not only are databases designed to facilitate reporting, but there are tools available for reporting. If Microsoft SQL Server 2000 or SQL Server 2005 is the database in use, then SQL Reporting Services can not only generate professional-looking reports, but can also automate delivering and retaining them. In other words, using a database makes it easy to retain, analyze, report on, and manage logging information.

There are two main disadvantages to using a database. One is the need for a database server. The flat file and event log storage types are provided by default with Microsoft Windows. If the data store is on the local computer, there is no way that a flat file or the event log will be unavailable unless the logging application doesn't have permissions.

The second issue is that the database needs to be running to act as a data store. Assuming that the database is not stored on the Web server, the network needs to be up. So using the database as a logging mechanism introduces one additional point of failure to the Web application. More important, this potential point of failure might cause important information to be unavailable. For example, assume the database used for logging is the same database that the application uses. If the database is unavailable, then the application will try to log that event. However, because the database is unavailable, it won't be able to. So the application will fail without any pertinent logging information being stored.

The mechanics of placing data, logging or otherwise, into a database are familiar. For an ASP.NET application, this means that ADO.NET is likely to be involved. Given that most developers understand ADO.NET well and that detailed coverage is outside of the scope of this book, the sample code will be simplistic.

```vb
' VB
Dim cn As New SqlConnection(connectionString)
Dim cmd As New SqlCommand( _
   String.Format("INSERT INTO LogTable VALUES" & _
   "(GetDate(), '{0}', '{1}')", logType, logMessage))
cmd.CommandType = CommandType.Text
cn.Open()
cmd.ExecuteNonQuery()
cn.Close()
```

```csharp
// C#
SqlConnection cn = new SqlConnection(connectionString)
SqlCommand cmd = new SqlCommand(
   String.Format("INSERT INTO LogTable VALUES" +
   "(GetDate(), '{0}', '{1}')", logType, logMessage));
cmd.CommandType = CommandType.Text;
cn.Open();
cmd.ExecuteNonQuery();
cn.Close();
```

Quick Check

1. Which data storage option is most appropriate if significant reporting on the logged information is required?
2. Which data storage option is more appropriate if the log needs to be viewable using standard third-party tools?
3. Which data storage option is more appropriate if the information being logged can change format from event to event?

Quick Check Answers

1. From a reporting perspective, using a database as the data store provides the most reporting functionality. Although a flat file can be reported on (even by SQL Reporting Services), that presupposes that the format of every record in the flat file has the same schema. If that's true, then the flat file is also a possibility.
2. The event log is the format that is most likely to be accessed by third-party tools. The event log has the benefit of a known format that can be processed without additional configuration or mappings.
3. Both the event log and a database suffer from the inflexibility of a set schema. Even though the database table is freely defined by a developer, each record in the table has to have the same structure. A flat file, on the other hand, can take on the format and structure required by the application.

System-Wide Logging

Logging is a mildly schizophrenic function. The type and location of the logging that needs to take place depends greatly on the audience. The result tends to be that logging statements are scattered all over the application—both in places where they should be as well as in places where log entries *could* be needed in the future.

The result, for most applications, is that a single method might have two or three or more logging statements in it, each targeted at a different audience and each going to a different data store. In the majority of cases, the "logging statement" in question can be more than one line of source code: perhaps a test to see whether the log entry is required, followed by collection of the logging information and sending it to the log. When you consider that, it's no wonder that "avoiding code clutter" is a frequent reason for not including logging in an application.

The solution to this problem is to provide a central location for logging to take place—for example, a single method that takes all the required details as parameters and generates the necessary log entry. This has the potential to reduce the code clutter in that only one line is needed to perform logging.

 However, the logging requirements for an application can become even more complicated. What if, for example, the logs that were placed into the event log now must be sent to a file? Or the file format must be modified? Certainly, the centralized method can be modified, but the updated assembly will need to be moved into production, which will force a restart of the virtual directory. For a Web site for which availability is a concern, restarting the application might not be appropriate (not to mention that, even with a minimal change to the assembly, thorough testing will be required).

The solution, it appears, is to use configuration information to control the logging function. By defining the appropriate settings within the web.config file, you can change the destination for a log entry from a flat file to the event log. You could even go so far as to detect the source of the log entry (that is, which assembly or method made the call) and change the destination accordingly. You could also arrange for the log entry to have more than one destination.

Whereas skilled developers, such as the reader, could probably whip out a centralized logging mechanism in mere minutes, for most of the rest of the population, creating a logging method that is this flexible is a significant undertaking. For this reason, using a third-party logging mechanism becomes quite appealing. In the .NET world, there are a number of available options. One popular option is the Logging Application Block, which is part of the Enterprise Library, produced by the Prescriptive Architecture Group at Microsoft. Another is Log4Net, an open-source logging framework based on the Log4j framework. Both of these frameworks are surprisingly full-featured and extensible, and both provide source code to handle any situations that haven't already been considered.

The difference between a framework and a centralized logging mechanism might seem purely semantic. Frameworks tend to be more generic and, as a result, are usually designed upfront for these features. Centralized logging grows in the direction, and at the speed, required by the corporation in which they are used. The real difference comes down to the configuration element. Because of the flexibility in the design, frameworks usually require a great deal of configuration. Centralized methods usually support only the features that are required and are, therefore, simpler to deal with from a developer perspective.

A common question is whether the friction of framework configuration outweighs the benefits. The answer comes down to which types of functionality are needed and how flexible the logging needs to be. In the Enterprise Library, the *Write* method can be configured to route messages to multiple data stores under different conditions, such as the severity level and the message source. Each message can be sent to more than one destination. The destination for each message can be modified in the moment and changes can be detected immediately. It is truly (as the name suggests) enterprise-level in terms of functionality. If that is or even might be a requirement, then consider using the Logging Application Block. Even if it seems slightly excessive, it's probably still worth it. After all, the framework includes code that has already been tested by others. That in itself could make the framework worthwhile.

Lab: Common Logging Issues

In this lab, you will look at some of the issues associated with adding logging to a Web application, specifically, changing log levels in real time and setting permissions to allow access to update the event log.

▶ **Exercise 1: Changing Log Levels in Real Time**

The purpose of this exercise is to demonstrate a simple technique to allow for modification of log levels in a Web application without forcing the virtual directory to be restarted. To demonstrate this, you're going to use the fact that the default storage location for session information is in process. Therefore, when the virtual directory is restarted, all of the session information will be lost.

The starting point for this lab is a Web page that displays some session information: the date/time of the initial request. As the Web page is refreshed, the session information stays the same, so the date/time is constant. But when web.config is edited, the next refresh gets a new date/time. When the log level information is implemented appropriately, however, changing the log level will not affect the session values.

1. Launch Visual Studio 2005.
2. Click File | Open | Web Site to open a solution.
3. Navigate to the Chapter12\Lesson1\Lab1\<*language*>\Before\WebConfigChange directory. Click Open.
4. In the Solution Explorer, double-click the web.config file. You won't do anything with this file yet except prepare for the initial display of the change behavior.

5. Press F5 to launch the application. Notice that a page similar to the one shown in Figure 12-1 is displayed.

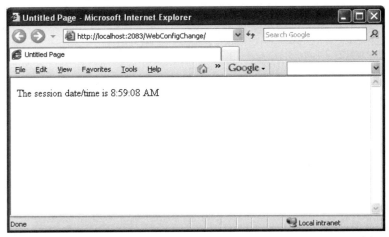

Figure 12-1   The initial Web page for the Web Application Restart lab

6. In Microsoft Internet Explorer, click the Refresh button or press F5 to refresh the page. Notice that the displayed date and time don't change.

7. In the web.config file that you opened in step 4, change the value of the *logLevel* key in *appSettings* to **warning**. Save the change.

```
[code]<add key="LogLevel" value="warning" />[/code]
```

8. In Internet Explorer, click the Refresh button (or press F5) to refresh the page. Notice that the displayed date and time have been updated to reflect the current time.

9. Close Internet Explorer. This terminates the debug session for the project.

10. In Solution Explorer, add another .config file to the project by right-clicking the project and selecting Add New Item.... Select the Web Configuration File as the template and name it **external.config**. Click Add.

11. In the newly created external.config file, replace with the following all of the contents that were added by default. Note how this section closely resembles the *appSettings* section in the web.config file.

```
<?xml version="1.0"?>
<appSettings>
<add key="LogLevel" value="information" />
</appSettings>
```

12. In the web.config file, locate the *appSettings* section. Replace the *appSettings* tag with the following so that it references the external.config file, as shown.

```
<appSettings configSource="external.config" />
```

13. Run the application by pressing F5. Note the time in the displayed Web page.

14. In external.config, change the value of the *logLevel* key to **warning**. Save the change.

15. Refresh the Web page by clicking the Refresh button or pressing F5. Note that the time in the displayed Web page is unchanged.

▶ **Exercise 2: Writing to the Event Log**

The purpose of this exercise is to demonstrate a simple technique to allow log levels in a Web application to be modified without forcing the virtual directory to be restarted. To demonstrate this, remember that the default storage location for session information is in process, so when the virtual directory is restarted, all of the session information is lost.

The starting point for this lab is a Web page that displays some session information: the date/time of the initial request. As the Web page is refreshed, the session information stays the same, so the date/time is constant. But when web.config is edited, the next refresh gets a new date/time. When the log level information is implemented appropriately, however, changing the log level will not affect the session values.

Before starting this exercise, "before" and "after" directories for each language need to be configured as virtual directories in IIS. To do this, launch the setup.cmd file in the Chapter12\Lesson1\Lab2 directory from the Visual Studio 2005 Command Prompt window.

1. Launch Visual Studio 2005.

2. Click File | Open | Web Site to open a solution.

3. Navigate to the Chapter12/Lesson1/Lab2/*<language>*/Before/EventLogPermission directory. Click Open.

4. In Solution Explorer, right-click the Default.aspx file and select View Code from the menu.

5. In the *Page_Load* method, add the following line of code to add an entry to the event log.

```
' VB
EventLog.WriteEntry("ASP.NET 2.0.50727.0", "This is a test entry")
```

```
// C#
EventLog.WriteEntry("ASP.NET 2.0.50727.0", "This is a test entry");
```

6. In Solution Explorer, right-click Default.aspx and select Set As Start Page.

7. Press Ctrl+F5 to launch the Web page. This starts the application without debugging, a scenario that will be important later on. Notice that the Web page displays a security exception error. Close the browser to terminate the execution.

8. In Solution Explorer, double-click web.config.

9. At the bottom of the *<system.web>* section, add the following code to create a reference to a custom policy file.

```
<securityPolicy>
    <trustLevel name="Custom" policyFile="web_customtrust.config"/>
</securityPolicy>
<trust level="Custom" originUrl=""/>
```

10. In Solution Explorer, double-click web_customtrust.config.

11. Locate the bottom of the *SecurityClasses* elements. Add the following *SecurityClasses* element to create a reference to the *EventLogPermission* class.

```
<SecurityClass Name="EventLogPermission"
    Description="System.Diagnostics.EventLogPermission, System,
        Version=2.0.0.0, Culture=neutral, PublicKeyToken=b77a5c561934e089" />
```

12. Still in the web_customtrust.config file, locate the *PermissionSet* with a name attribute of ASP.NET. There are already a number of *IPermission* elements. Add the following *IPermission* element, which defines the access allowed to *EventLogPermission*.

```
<IPermission class="EventLogPermission" version="1">
    <Machine name="." access="Write"/>
</IPermission>
```

13. Launch the application by pressing Ctrl+F5 to run without debugging. Although running without debugging was not required in step 7, it is required now. The medium trust setting does not provide sufficient permissions for debugging. Once the Default.aspx page appears, open the Event Viewer to see the newly added event log entry.

14. Once you have finished working with this exercise, the virtual directories that were created can be removed. To do this, run the cleanup.cmd file in the Chapter12\Lesson1\Lab2 directory from the Visual Studio 2005 Command Prompt window.

Lesson Summary

■ Logging is useful from both a debugging and an auditing perspective.

■ Consider the audience for the logging output when determining the granularity of the messages.

■ The ability to change logging levels in real time is important when the logging is being used for debugging purposes.

■ The need for a framework grows as the logging requirements for a Web application increase. As the logging goes from simply placing text into a file to configuring multiple destinations based on the severity or source of the logging event, frameworks become more likely to make sense.

Lesson Review

You can use the following questions to test your knowledge of the information in Lesson 1, "Logging Application Events." The questions are also available on the companion CD if you prefer to review them in electronic form.

NOTE Answers

Answers to these questions and explanations of why each answer choice is right or wrong are located in the "Answers" section at the end of the book.

1. Your company's applications need to run 24 hours a day. To help notify the operations group of problems, you will be instrumenting your application, but the operations group doesn't want to be notified of all monitoring messages. For which of the Windows Event Log levels should operations look?

     A. Error

     B. Warning

     C. Information

     D. SuccessAudit

     E. FailureAudit

2. Your company's Web application is running on a server hosted by a third-party provider. The database that the application uses resides within your internal corporate network. Connection is provided through a Virtual Private Network (VPN) connection with only the ports used by SQL Server kept open. To help ensure reliability, only the third-party provider's staff deploys updates to the Web application. None of your developers have access to the Web server. You would like to create a logging mechanism that gives you and your fellow developers access to the work being performed by the Web applications. What data storage type should you use?

     A. Flat file

     B. Event log

     C. Trace listeners

     D. Database

3. You have created a Web application that is sold to other clients and deployed on their servers. You have run into the problem that when an attempt is made to create an event log entry, an exception is thrown. Further investigation reveals that the exception is caused because the event source (which didn't exist previously) cannot be created. What is the best way to address this issue?

     A. Configure the Web site to use impersonation.

     B. Create the event sources when the Web application is installed.

     C. Configure the Web site to use Windows authentication.

     D. Create the event sources when the first Web request is received.

Lesson 2: Monitoring the Application

When it comes to the interesting data, the differences between logging and monitoring are minimal, relating to how immediately the data is required. When an application is monitored, the people doing the monitoring typically require quick notification of important events. This element of timeliness has the greatest impact on where and how the event is routed.

Monitoring also includes the idea that the application has an ongoing status, which is available for review. It could be a running count of the transactions, a heartbeat that indicates the health of the application, or a graph of the CPU cycles being consumed. But regardless of how the information is visualized, there is real-time (or near real-time) feedback on the status and events associated with the Web application.

The purpose of this lesson is to describe the techniques that you can apply to monitor ASP.NET applications, from both a status and an exceptional event perspective.

After this lesson, you will be able to:
- Identify the expected audience for the monitoring information (the information generated through the monitoring process).
- Decide which delivery mechanism is most appropriate for the monitoring data.
- Determine whether a system-wide approach to monitoring makes sense based on the classes available to ASP.NET.

Estimated lesson time: 35 minutes

Who Needs Monitoring?

This lesson begins with the same kind of question that began Lesson 1, "Logging Application Events." Again, each audience for monitoring information requires different data and notifications. So this starting point, in which you review the interested parties, is still quite reasonable, even if the list of suspects has changed.

Operations

The operations staff is responsible for ensuring the continued functioning of the corporate infrastructure. And beyond just functioning, elements of performance and uptime are usually part of the operations charter. For this reason, monitoring is critical to the operations group. They need to know what is going on and, more importantly, what is going wrong, quickly.

The proactive side to operations monitoring is determining the health of a Web site. Whereas receiving events as they happen is good, being able to detect that something is going wrong prior to a failure is even more useful. For this reason, the operations group likes to see the checks for server status as well as for the external resources on which the Web site depends.

Security

The security group (which sometimes falls into the same group as operations) also has an interest in monitoring Web applications. In fact, they are really the only group that benefits from both logging and monitoring.

As noted in Lesson 1, security logs are of interest to anyone trying to identify systematic failures indicating that someone is trying to see where the holes in your Web site might be. But security groups also want to know when the attack is going on, so not only should security failures be logged, but also a notification should be sent immediately to the interested person. In this way, the attack can be monitored while in progress, providing the potential for a closer look at the technique being used.

As with logging, the monitoring of security-related events must also address a separate security issue: the event needs to avoid exposing private information. It's easy for a developer to know not to place private details into an accessible log file, but there is a tendency to ignore that same edict for a security event. The problem with this is that the process that raises the event doesn't know what or who is on the receiving end, and, even if the credentials are exposed for a moment, it is possible that they can be captured and preserved in an unexpected (and undesirable) way.

Exam Tip   Keep in mind which groups of users require logging and which require monitoring. Specifically, operations and security will be interested in the immediacy of monitoring, while auditors, developers, and administrative personnel will be happy with logs.

Data Storage

The need for timely monitoring of information places a couple of demands on the storage options. First, the method of event notification is different from that in logging. Whereas logging could easily be placed into a file for future observation, monitoring can't wait for someone to look at the file.

E-mail

As many of you are probably aware (and curse about regularly), e-mail can be sent and received almost anywhere and at any time—almost certainly more often than many of us want. Our inability to get away from our inboxes is what makes e-mail good for those events that are of critical importance. When an event requires immediate attention, sending notification via e-mail is more likely to be noticed than waiting for someone to check a flat file.

E-mail also has the capability to send notifications beyond the boundary of the corporate infrastructure. The "e-mail everywhere" idea is embodied in cell phones and personal digital assistants (PDAs), that are so prevalent in the corporate world. For database, flat files, and the event log, you need to have access to the company network to access the information.

The greatest problem with using e-mail as a data store is that it really doesn't store data. Some of you might disagree because you have an inbox larger than some databases, but that doesn't count. E-mail notifications are really a one-time notification. If the information in the event needs to be included in any future reporting or review process, then the event should be logged to a different data store such as a database.

There is one additional design choice that using e-mail affects: the granularity of events. As was mentioned in Lesson 1, in terms of frequency and volume of information, events can be either finely grained or coarsely grained. E-mail, in many cases, is interruptive technology. If you're online, you get visual and audio signals indicating that a new message has arrived. If you're on a mobile device, physical signals as well as audio ones are possible. In both cases, something happens to get your attention. That's one of the reasons e-mail works in the monitoring scenario.

However, if notification e-mails arrive with unimportant information, or they occur too frequently, the effect can decline. The recipient can be numbed to the messages to the point where those messages don't have the necessary impact. To avoid this situation, the developer needs to ensure that only critical events trigger an e-mail message.

A new class named *System.Net.Mail.SmtpClient* was introduced with .NET Framework 2.0 to assist with sending e-mail messages. There are two steps involved. The first involves the creation of a new *System.Net.Mail.MailMessage* object. The *MailMessage* contains the subject, the body, and the From and To addresses for the message. The second step uses the *SmtpClient* class to send the message to the mail server. After identifying the mail server by name, the *Send* method submits the *MailMessage* for processing.

Although this process is simple, it doesn't handle one of the most common requirements for sending e-mails: authentication. Most mail servers require that you specify a user name and password before you can send an e-mail message. To do this, the *NetworkCredential* class is used in conjunction with the *Credentials* property on the *SmtpClient* object.

The *NetworkCredential* class is part of the *System.Net* namespace. A new *NetworkCredential* object is created with the necessary user name and password. The object is then assigned to the *Credentials* property. To avoid transmitting the current user's Windows identity, the *SmtpClient* needs to be told that the default credentials should not be sent. The following code sends an e-mail message to an authenticated mail server:

```
' VB
Dim message As New MailMessage(fromAddress, toAddress, _
    subject, messageBody)
Dim emailClient As New SmtpClient(mailServerName)
Dim smtpUserInfo = New _
    System.Net.NetworkCredential(txtSMTPUser.Text, txtSMTPPass.Text)
```

```
emailClient.UseDefaultCredentials = False
emailClient.Credentials = smtpUserInfo
emailClient.Send(message)

// C#
MailMessage message = new MailMessage(fromAddress, toAddress,
    subject, messageBody);
SmtpClient emailClient = new SmtpClient(mailServerName);
System.Net.NetworkCredential smtpUserInfo = new
    System.Net.NetworkCredential(txtSMTPUser.Text, txtSMTPPass.Text);
emailClient.UseDefaultCredentials = false;
emailClient.Credentials = smtpUserInfo;
emailClient.Send(message);
```

Performance Monitor

E-mail messages are quite useful as a monitoring notification device. However, as was already noted, email messages are not a good repository for data, nor can they be used to track the health of a Web site in any sort of proactive manner. E-mail messages are sent after something important has happened; they can't be used to view the ebb and flow of a Web site's status. Flat files, the event log, and databases have the same problem, albeit for different reasons.

The performance monitor, also called the system monitor, provides a nice compromise between the two data stores. The performance monitor can be used to track a large amount of information from different areas and applications throughout the operating system. The information, provided in the form of counters, can be retrieved on a recurring basis and displayed in a graphical manner. Figure 12-2 shows the performance monitor with the standard counters included.

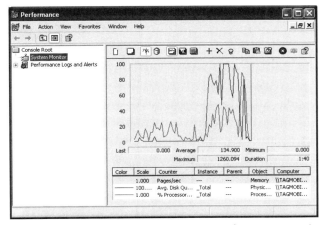

Figure 12-2 A sample display for the performance monitor

The performance monitor includes a large variety of counters associated with various aspects of the operating system, and applications installed on the system have the ability to add their own counters. This includes the custom applications that your company is creating. Regardless of how the counters are installed, any of them are capable of being captured and viewed using the same interface shown in Figure 12-2.

The main benefit of using the performance monitor is the ability to observe the moment-to-moment status of an application. In a monitoring situation, this allows for a dashboard view of the Web site's status. And when custom information is included, the operations staff can see information that is specific to the health and performance of your own application.

Still, there are some drawbacks to using the performance monitor. A performance counter, unlike all the techniques described so far, does not allow for an arbitrary message to be sent. It is a numerical value that can only be incremented or decremented. Therefore, the performance monitor is good for keeping track of the health and progress of an application but not good for capturing information that could be used to help solve a problem. For this, more persistent data stores (flat file, database, and so on) are necessary.

Following are the five types of performance counters.

- **Average**   Measures the counter value over a period of time. The displayed value is the average of the last two measurements. An average is actually a combination of two counters: a base counter that tracks the number of samples and a regular counter that tracks the values.
- **Difference**   Displays the difference between two successive measurements. This particular counter cannot be negative, so if the second measurement is less than the first, a value of zero is displayed.
- **Instantaneous**   The displayed value at that point in time.
- **Percentage**   The displayed value as a percentage. This is different from instantaneous only in the way it is displayed.
- **Rate**   The displayed value as the change in counter value divided by the change in time—in other words, the rate of change of the counter over time.

New performance counters can be created either programmatically or directly through the Server Explorer in Visual Studio 2005. Because the counters are more likely to be created programmatically, that's the technique that this lesson will demonstrate.

The first step is to create the category. The *PerformanceCounterCategory* class has a static method named *Exists*. This method is used to determine whether a particular category has already been defined. If it has not been, the *Create* method can be used to create the category.

The *Create* method can also be used to add counters to the new category. This is an important point because it turns out that this is the only way to add counters programmatically. You cannot add counters to existing categories. Instead, you would have to delete the category and then re-create it with the appropriate counters.

The creation of a counter involves two classes. The first, named *CounterCreationData*, is used to define the information about an individual counter. The second, named *CounterCreation-DataCollection*, is a collection of *CounterCreationData* objects that gets passed into one of the overloads of the *Create* method.

```vb
' VB
Dim CounterDatas As New CounterCreationDataCollection()
Dim cntr1 As New CounterCreationData()
Dim cntr2 As New CounterCreationData()

cntr1.CounterName = "DemoCounter1"
cntr1.CounterHelp = "A description of DemoCounter1"
cntr1.CounterType = PerformanceCounterType.NumberOfItems64
cntr2.CounterName = "DemoCounter2"
cntr2.CounterHelp = "A description of DemoCounter2"
cntr2.CounterType = PerformanceCounterType.NumberOfItems64

CounterDatas.Add(cntr1)
CounterDatas.Add(cntr2)

PerformanceCounterCategory.Create("Demo Category", _
    "A help message for the category", _
    PerformanceCounterCategoryType.SingleInstance, _
    CounterDatas)
```

```csharp
// C#
System.Diagnostics.CounterCreationDataCollection CounterDatas =
    new System.Diagnostics.CounterCreationDataCollection();

System.Diagnostics.CounterCreationData cntr1 =
    new System.Diagnostics.CounterCreationData();
System.Diagnostics.CounterCreationData cntr2 =
    new System.Diagnostics.CounterCreationData();

cntr1.CounterName = "DemoCounter1";
cntr1.CounterHelp = "A description of DemoCounter1";
cntr1.CounterType = PerformanceCounterType.NumberOfItems64;
cntr2.CounterName = "DemoCounter2";
cntr2.CounterHelp = "A description of DemoCounter2";
cntr2.CounterType = PerformanceCounterType.NumberOfItems64;
```

```
CounterDatas.Add(cntr1);
CounterDatas.Add(cntr2);

PerformanceCounterCategory.Create("Demo Category", _
    "A help message for the category", _
    PerformanceCounterCategoryType.SingleInstance, _
    CounterDatas);
```

MORE INFO   *PerformanceCounter* and permissions

Although most accounts can read and update performance counters, the creation of a performance counter category and the counters themselves require a higher level of permissions. The
only default groups that have the ability to create categories and counters are Administrators and
Power Users. For ASP.NET applications, this means that the code to add categories and counters to
performance monitors should be included in the installation of the Web application, not in the
code that is executed while servicing a request.

When it comes to updating the numeric value associated with a performance counter, the *PerformanceCounter* class contains all of the necessary methods and properties. You create a *PerformanceCounter* instance by specifying the category and counter name in the constructor, as
follows.

```vb
' VB
Dim pc as New PerformanceCounter("Category", "CounterName")
```

```csharp
// C#
PerformanceCounter pc = new
    PerformanceCounter("Category", "CounterName");
```

Once instantiated, the counter can be updated using one of the methods shown in Table 12-2.

Table 12-2 *PerformanceCounter* Update Methods

Method/Property	Description
Decrement	Reduces the value of the counter by one
Increment	Increases the value of the counter by one
IncrementBy	Increases the value of the counter by the specified amount
RawValue	Sets the value directly through a simple assignment

Quick Check

■ If you are a member of the operations staff tasked with ensuring that the transactions-per-second performance of an application stays above a certain level, which data storage mechanisms are you most likely to need?

Quick Check Answer

■ You could use either the performance monitor or e-mail in this situation. The correct answer will depend greatly on the type of operations infrastructure that is currently in place in your company. If there is already an operations staff that is watching the Web application by using the Performance snap-in of the Microsoft Management Console (MMC), then performance counters are the most likely to be appropriate. However, if there isn't an operations staff, or if the staff doesn't pay attention to performance counter information, then delivering notifications through e-mails is a better choice.

System-Wide Monitoring

When it comes to choosing a system-wide mechanism, the monitor function has some of the same requirements and options that logging has. This is to say that much of the discussion about the Logging Application Block also applies to monitoring. Specifically, the Logging Application Block can be configured so that e-mails are transmitted or performance counters updated in response to logged events from within the application. This provides the same level of configurability as logging, including monitoring levels, multiple destinations, and changing in real time.

However, when it comes to monitoring Web applications, there is one area that neither logging nor the Logging Application Block addresses: health monitoring. The idea behind health monitoring is to keep track of the availability of a Web site. "Availability" means not only whether the server on which the application is running is active, but also whether any of the underlying resources used to satisfy any request are active. After all, if the Web server is running, but a necessary database server is down, the Web application is not "live."

ASP.NET 2.0 provides a namespace that includes classes to monitor the health of deployed Web applications easily. The classes in this namespace implement the provider pattern that is so prevalent in .NET 2.0. Web health; monitoring events (also known as Web events) are raised during the course of normal processing. The events are consumed by listeners (the providers in the pattern) that examine the information and record it appropriately. The steps involved in configuring and implementing health monitoring are as follows.

1. The Web application raises a Web event.
2. ASP.NET detects the raising of the event.

3.   ASP.NET checks the configuration settings for registered providers and events.

4.   When a match is found between the raised event and a corresponding provider, the appropriate method on the provider is invoked.

Here's how to put these steps into practice.

Raising a Web Event

The base class for a Web event is the *WebBaseEvent* class. In this class, there are two methods used to raise a Web event. A shared/status *Raise* method takes an instance of a *WebBaseEvent* object (or an instance of a class derived from *WebBaseEvent*). An instance-level *Raise* method also raises the current event.

As the name suggests, *WebBaseEvent* is simply the base class for a hierarchy of classes that describe various Web events. Included with the *System.Web.Management* namespace are a number of classes (shown in the list in Table 12-3) that use *WebBaseEvent* as the base class.

Table 12-3   Web Event Classes in *System.Web.Management*

Class Name	Description
WebApplicationLifetimeEvent	Represents a significant event in the lifetime of an ASP.NET application. Possible events that qualify include application startup and shutdown.
WebAuditEvent	Serves as the base class for all ASP.NET health-monitoring audit events.
WebAuthenticationFailureAuditEvent	Contains information about ASP.NET authentication failures.
WebAuthenticationSuccessAuditEvent	Contains information about successful authentication events.
WebBaseErrorEvent	Serves as the base class for all the health-monitoring error events.
WebBaseEvent	Serves as the base class for the ASP.NET health-monitoring events.
WebErrorEvent	Contains information about errors that occur within the ASP.NET application.
WebFailureAuditEvent	Provides information about failed security events. This is distinct from the authentication events because, at the time this event is raised, the user has been authenticated. The event indicates that an attempt to access a secured resource failed, based on the user's current credentials.

Table 12-3   Web Event Classes in *System.Web.Management*

Class Name	Description
WebHeartbeatEvent	Acts as a timer for the ASP.NET health-monitoring system. *WebHeartbeatEvent* events are raised at an interval defined by the *heartbeatInterval* attribute of the *healthMonitoring* configuration section.
WebManagementEvent	Serves as the base class for events that carry application and process information.
WebRequestErrorEvent	Contains information associated with Web requests that failed.
WebRequestEvent	Serves as the base class for events associated with Web requests.
WebSuccessAuditEvent	Provides information about successful security events.
WebViewStateFailureAuditEvent	Contains information associated with failures surrounding the retrieval and processing of the view state.

As evidenced by the liberal inclusion of base classes in Table 12-3, you have the ability to create your own custom Web event class if the need arises. If you create such a class, the main method to override is *FormatCustomEventDetails*, which is used to customize the information included with the event.

As an example, the code to create and raise a *WebErrorEvent* is as follows.

```vb
' VB
If HealthMonitoringManager.Enabled Then
  WebBaseEvent.Raise(New WebErrorEvent("Error message", Nothing, _
      5000, Nothing))
End If
```

```csharp
// C#
if (HealthMonitoringManager.Enabled)
  WebBaseEvent.Raise(New WebErrorEvent("Error message", null, _
      5000, null));
```

Configuring Web Event Processing

As expected, the configuration for health monitoring is done within the web.config file, specifically, within the *healthMonitoring* element of web.config. At a top level, the *healthMonitoring* element contains two attributes. An *Enabled* attribute indicates whether health monitoring is active, and a *heartbeatInterval* attribute defines how often the *WebHeartbeatEvent* should be raised.

Within *healthMonitoring*, there are five possible elements.

- **bufferModes**   Defines how Web events are buffered within the monitoring mechanism. Because ASP.NET is a multithreaded environment, it's possible that a Web event can be fired before the previous one has finished processing. By defining the buffer mode, the administrator can create a queue of events, each of which is processed in turn. However, to avoid getting overrun with events, thresholds can be defined so that if events are queued beyond that threshold, they are flushed without further processing.

- **eventMappings**   Maps Web event data types to more friendly names. These names then are used in other places within the health-monitoring configuration.

- **profiles**   Defines a profile with which a number of values are associated, specifically, the number of occurrences before an actual event is fired, the number of occurrences before firing will no longer take place, and the minimum time interval between two event firings.

- **providers**   Defines a provider that will be used to process the Web events when they occur. A number of attributes associated with this element may or may not be required. There is, however, a *bufferMode* attribute that can contain a name related to the same named element in the *bufferMode* section.

- **rule**   This element is used to tie the other elements together. The *rule* element relates the name of the event (as defined in *eventMappings*) to a provider (as defined in *providers*), as well as to a profile (as defined in *profiles*).

The core of the listeners is found in the providers that are available. The .NET Framework 2.0 includes a number of providers that can be used out of the box. Table 12-4 contains the list of providers.

Table 12-4   Web Event Providers Included with .NET Framework 2.0

Provider Class	Description
SimpleMailEventProvider	Sends an e-mail message in response to a Web event
TemplatedMailWebEventProvider	Uses templates to create the e-mail message that the provider sends
TraceWebEventProvider	Sends the Web event information using trace messages
EventLogEventProvider	Places the Web event information into the event log
SqlWebEventProvider	Stores the Web event information in a database
WmiWebEventProvider	Maps the Web event information to a Windows Management Instrumentation (WMI) event

To put together an example, work from the bottom (the provider), and then fill in the related pieces. Start with the *providers* element. The following provider will route Web event information to a SQL Server database. Specifically, it will be the one found in the *connectionStrings* section named *LoggingConnectionString*.

```
<providers>
   <add name="SqlWebEventProvider"
      type="System.Web.Management.SqlWebEventProvider, System.Web,
         Version=2.0.0.0,Culture=neutral,PublicKeyToken=b03f5f7f11d50a3a"
      connectionStringName="LoggingConnectionString"
      maxEventDetailsLength="1073741823"
      buffer="true"
      bufferMode="Normal"/>
</providers>
```

The provider definition refers to a *bufferMode* element named *Normal*. As a result, the following *bufferModes* definition is required.

```
<bufferModes>
    <add name="Normal"
         maxBufferSize="1000"
         maxFlushSize="100"
         urgentFlushThreshold="100"
         regularFlushInterval="00:05:00"
         urgentFlushInterval="00:01:00"
         maxBufferThreads="1"/>
</bufferModes>
```

This definition limits the number of waiting events to 1,000. Every five minutes, the queue is checked and, if there are more than 1,000 events waiting, the oldest 100 are flushed. The *urgentFlushInterval* defines the minimum amount of time that must pass between flushes.

The *rules* element is used to link particular Web events with a provider and profile. The following element creates a relationship between the All Errors event mapping and the *SqlWebEvent-Provider* that was already defined. In addition, there is a reference to a profile with a name of Default Profile.

```
<rules>
   <add name="All Errors Rule"
        eventName="All Errors"
        provider="SqlWebEventProvider"
        profile="Default Profile"
        minInterval="00:00:30"/>
</rules>
```

After the rules element has been added, what remains is to define the event mapping with a name of All Errors and a profile with a name of Default Profile. The *eventMapping* section looks like the following.

```
<eventMappings>
   <add name="All Errors"
      type="System.Web.Management.WebBaseErrorEvent, System.Web
      Version=1.0.1573.21549, Culture=neutral,
      PublicKeyToken=2a0b23915ac7352b"/>
</eventMappings>
```

This element maps the *WebBaseErrorEvent* type onto the event names All Errors. Now whenever a Web event is derived from *WebBaseErrorEvent*, it will be processed by the All Errors Rule rule. This means that the *SqlWebEventProvider* will be invoked.

The final piece is the *profiles* element.

```
<profiles>
    <add name="Default Profile" minInstances="1" maxLimit="Infinite"
  minInterval="00:10:00"/>
</profiles>
```

The name of the profile matches the *profiles* attribute in the *rules* *<add>* element. It also includes the default values for the number of occurrences of the same type of event before the actual event is processed (the *minInstances* attribute), the maximum number of times the event is raised (the *maxLimit* attribute), and the minimum time between raised events (the *minInterval* attribute). Of course, these values can be overridden in the *rules* element (as is already done with the *minInterval* attribute).

Lab: Monitoring a Web Application

This lab demonstrates how to use the health monitoring functionality in ASP.NET 2.0 to keep track of the health of a Web application.

▶ **Exercise 1: Configuring the Heartbeat**

In this lab, you will demonstrate the technique used to turn on the heartbeat event for a Web application. When the application is first launched, the heartbeat starts. You will configure the application to place an entry in the Event Log for each heartbeat, with an interval of 10 seconds on the heartbeat.

1. Launch Visual Studio 2005.
2. Click File | Open | Web Site to open a solution.
3. Navigate to the Chapter12\Lesson2\Lab1*<language>*\Before\HeartbeatEvent directory. Click Open.
4. In the Solution Explorer, double-click the web.config file. At the bottom of the *<system.web>* element, add the health-monitoring element. The enabled attribute is set to *True* to turn health monitoring on, while the *heartbeatInterval* element is set to 10 so that the heartbeat event is triggered every 10 seconds, as follows.

   ```
   healthMonitoring enabled="true" heartbeatInterval="10">
   </healthMonitoring>
   ```

5. In the *healthMonitoring* element, add an *eventMappings* element for the *WebHeartbeatEvent* class, as shown here.

   ```
   <eventMappings>
       <add name="ImAlive" type="System.Web.Management.WebHeartbeatEvent"/>
   </eventMappings>
   ```

6. Below the *eventMappings* element but still in the *healthMonitoring* element, add a rule. This rule takes the event named *ImAlive* (which has already been mapped to the *WebHeartbeatEvent*) and invokes the *EventLogProvider* when it is raised, as shown here.

```
<rules>
    <add name="Demo Rule" eventName="ImAlive"
        provider="EventLogProvider" minInterval="00:00:01"/>
</rules>
```

7. Press Ctrl+F5 to launch the application.

8. Open the Windows Event Viewer and, on the left-hand pane of the viewer, click Application to display the entries in the Application log. Notice that you probably already have some recent events with a source of ASP.NET 2.0.50727.0. Double-click one of the events.

   Notice that the second line of the message indicates that the entry is related to an Application heartbeat.

   If you close the browser that launched when the application started, notice that the heartbeat does not stop.

9. Click Action | Refresh in the Event Viewer, and you will notice that an entry is still being recorded every 10 seconds.

10. To stop the heartbeat, the virtual directory needs to be restarted. To do this, go back to Visual Studio and open the web.config file. Then press Ctrl+S to save the file. This marks the web.config as being changed (even though it really hasn't changed), which causes the virtual directory to shut down.

Lesson Summary

- The term *data store* is not really appropriate for monitoring. Instead, monitoring is really more concerned with how event information can be delivered to the intended audience.

- Web application health monitoring requires a more immediate feedback mechanism than, for example, application debugging requires.

- In many cases, the monitoring event needs to be paired with a logging mechanism. This is because the delivery of an event to a monitoring listener doesn't mean that the data is then available for future review and reporting. E-mail delivery is a good example in that, without an additional logging element, there is no easy way to see what events have transpired.

Lesson Review

The following questions are intended to reinforce key information presented in Lesson 2, "Monitoring the Application." The questions are also available on the companion CD if you prefer to review them in electronic form.

NOTE Answers

Answers to these questions and explanations of why each answer choice is right or wrong are located in the "Answers" section at the end of the book.

1. The company store Web application that is about to be deployed contains logging statements in a number of areas within the code. You need to determine which of the following areas should be treated as monitoring information (meaning the operations team should be notified), as opposed to those areas that should simply be logged for future review. Which of the following areas should be monitored? (Choose all that apply.)

   A. Successful logons

   B. Failed logons

   C. Database access

   D. Invalid page requests

   E. Completed sales transactions

Chapter Review

To further practice and reinforce the skills you learned in this chapter, you can complete the following tasks:

- Review the chapter summary.
- Review the list of key terms introduced in this chapter.
- Complete the case scenarios. These scenarios set up real-world situations involving the topics of this chapter and ask you to create a solution.
- Complete the suggested practices.
- Take a practice test.

Chapter Summary

- The audience for the logging or monitoring information needs to be considered when determining all of the other factors associated with recording the information. It is important to provide the correct level of detail to ensure that valuable information isn't missed or overlooked.
- Data stores are available to support all of the most common logging and monitoring requirements. How the information is pushed into the store means that if a particular requirement isn't supported "out of the box," creating the necessary store should be pretty easy.
- There are a number of frameworks that make it easy to implement the vast majority of logging scenarios without requiring coding of a centralized logging mechanism. Where appropriate, lean toward using a framework instead of taking a do-it-yourself approach.

Key Terms

Do you know what these key terms mean? You can check your answers by looking up the terms in the glossary at the end of the book.

- flat file
- granularity
- instrumentation
- log level
- logging
- medium trust
- monitoring
- Windows Performance Monitor
- Windows Event Log

Case Scenarios

In the following case scenarios, you will apply what you've learned about logging and monitoring. You can find answers to these questions in the "Answers" section at the end of this book.

Case Scenario 1: Instrumenting a Web Application for Monitoring

You are a corporate developer creating a Web application that will be available to users on the Internet. The application will be deployed on a Web farm with a central state server used to manage sessions across multiple requests from the same source. The operations group within your company needs to be able to watch the ongoing performance of the application to identify usage patterns as well as to address performance issues as soon as they are noticed.

Your challenge is to determine which instrumentation technique should be used to address this situation. Answer the following questions for your manager.

1. Where should the information used to determine usage patterns be stored? What criteria should be used to identify the most appropriate location?
2. Where should the information about the current health of the Web application be stored?

Case Scenario 2: Instrumenting a Web Application for Logging

You are a corporate developer creating a Web application that will be available to users on the Internet. The application will be deployed on a Web farm with a central state server used to manage sessions across multiple requests from the same source. To help with the occasional debugging problems, you would like to place a tracing message at strategic points within the code.

Your challenge is to determine which instrumentation technique should be used to address this situation. Answer the following questions for your manager.

1. Where should the tracing information be stored?
2. What technique should be used to modify the log level?

Suggested Practices

To help you successfully master the objectives covered in this chapter, complete the following tasks.

Logging Application Events

For this task, you should complete both practices. The first practice focuses on creating an unhandled event handler, something that every self-respecting Web application should have.

The second practice deals with the process of using an enterprise-level framework to provide the code that instruments a Web application for logging.

- **Practice 1**   Create an application error event handler for an existing Web application. In the event handler, make an entry in the event log for every unhandled exception that occurs within the Web application.

- **Practice 2**   In an existing Web application, add support for the Logging Application Block. Along with adding the logging code in the appropriate places, add the necessary configuration steps to web.config. Create an external logging configuration file so that the logging level can be modified in real time.

Monitoring the Application

For this task, you should complete both practices. The first practice focuses on performance counters, quite a common task for Web developers. The second practice, on the other hand, is a little less practical. Because the heartbeat event is new in ASP.NET 2.0, the infrastructure might not be in place for every application to take advantage of it.

- **Practice 1**   For an existing Web application, add a performance counter category for the application. Also, add a counter representing the number of requests processed. Update the counter every time a successful page request is complete.

- **Practice 2**   For an existing Web application, configure the application to raise a *Web-HeartbeatEvent* every five minutes. Use the *SqlWebEventProvider* class to make an entry in a database for as long as the Web application is running.

Take a Practice Test

The practice tests on this book's companion CD offer many options. For example, you can test yourself on just one exam objective, or you can test yourself on all the 70-547 certification exam content. You can set up the test so that it closely simulates the experience of taking a certification exam, or you can set it up in study mode so that you can look at the correct answers and explanations after you answer each question.

MORE INFO   **Practice tests**

For details about all the practice test options available, see the "How to Use the Practice Tests" section in this book's Introduction.

Chapter 13
Application Configuration

This chapter explains how to manage application configuration information in Microsoft ASP.NET 2.0. You will learn how the structure of application configuration files has changed and which classes are used to access configuration information. You will also learn about new tools that simplify the administration of configuration files.

Exam objectives in this chapter:
- Evaluate the application configuration architecture.
  - Decide which configuration attributes to store.
  - Choose the physical storage location for the configuration attributes.
  - Decide in which format to store the configuration attributes.
  - Choose when to use ASP.NET administrative tools.

Lessons in this chapter:

Before You Begin

To complete the lessons in this chapter, you should be familiar with developing Web-based applications with Microsoft Visual Studio 2005, using Microsoft Visual Basic or C#. In addition, you should have:

- A computer that meets or exceeds the minimum hardware requirements listed in the introduction at the beginning of this book
- Visual Studio 2005 and the Microsoft .NET Framework 2.0 installed on your computer.
- Familiarity with XML
- Microsoft SQL Server 2005 Express Edition installed on your computer (recommended)

Real World

Shannon Horn

I recently created an ASP.NET 2.0 Web application for a nonprofit client. The application consists of an interactive Web presence, including e-commerce, where the client sells a small amount of promotional material. The site is fully data-driven and includes a public interface as well as a private and secured administrative interface. The client requested that the application be created using the latest .NET Framework technologies. To keep expenses at a minimum, most of the data used to drive the application is stored in XML files. Furthermore, the administrative interface is designed to accommodate an unlimited number of users with, potentially, an unlimited number of permissions.

I was able to manage all users and permissions for the application easily, using the web.config file for the application and the classes in the *System.Web.Configuration* namespace. All user credentials were hashed prior to being stored in the web.config file, and connections to clients are secured using Secure Sockets Layer (SSL). Other configuration settings are also stored in the web.config file, including the name and location of the simple mail transfer protocol (SMTP) server and an optional list of recipients to be notified via e-mail when an error occurs in the application. Additional data are stored in custom XML files and managed using the classes in the *System.Xml* namespace.

Lesson 1: Maintaining Application Configuration Information

This lesson describes the preferred method for storing configuration information for ASP.NET Web applications. It also describes storing information in the web.config file, storing information in custom XML files, when to encrypt configuration information, and how to use the ASP.NET administrative tools.

After this lesson, you will be able to:
- Identify where configuration information should be stored.
- Review the structure of the ASP.NET web.config file.
- Determine whether configuration information should be stored in the web.config file or in a custom XML configuration file.
- Manually store configuration information in the web.config file.
- Determine when configuration information should be encrypted.
- Use the ASP.NET administrative tool to manage configuration information automatically.

Estimated lesson time: 60 minutes

Identifying Configuration Information and Storage Options

The first step in discussing configuration information is to define it. Configuration information is any data used to define the behavior of an application, particularly data that might need to be adjusted in the future to refine the behavior of that application. A common example of configuration information is a database connection string, which defines how an application should connect to a database, including the name of the server, the name of the database, security credentials, and, optionally, other connection options. The information that composes the database connection string is volatile, and it could require modification at any time. It is common for database security to be adjusted or databases to be moved or scaled to more servers as a business grows. A change in any facet of a database could require a modification to the connection string. You must think carefully about how an application will manage a database connection string and similar configuration information.

Configuration information differs from application data. Application data is managed by an application. An example of application data is the data that defines a customer and the orders associated with that customer.

When you design an application, you will encounter many pieces of information that are used to define the behavior of the application. It might seem obvious that some pieces of information, such as the database connection string discussed previously, might require future modification. However, you should be constantly aware of any data that is being used to define the behavior of an application and treat it as configuration information. Rest assured that if you assume that the data used to define a particular application behavior will never need to be modified, it will need modification at some future point and, more than likely, it will need modification when the application goes into beta testing.

The next thing to consider when determining how to manage application configuration information is where to store it. While application configuration information can be stored internally or externally to the application, storing it externally is the preferred and standard method. Application configuration information that is stored internally must be stored directly in the application's source code. This is typically more secure because the information is compiled into the application. However, the downside of compiling configuration information into the application is that it is not easy to modify. To modify the configuration information, the application source code would need to be recompiled and redeployed.

Application configuration information that is stored externally to the application source code is typically easy to modify but might be less secure unless you take precautions to secure it. When configuration information is stored externally, it is stored in a file or in the Microsoft Windows registry. Traditionally, Windows initialization (.ini) files were used to store application configuration information. However, .ini files were text files that did not use a standardized format and could be difficult to navigate, manage, and read. Furthermore, a primary goal of the .NET Framework is to enable creation of applications that are not tightly coupled to Windows. The registry is proprietary to Windows. With that in mind, .NET Framework applications could not rely on the Windows registry for storing configuration information.

When the .NET Framework was introduced, application configuration information was stored in files that had a .config extension and were composed using XML. Occasionally, if you require a custom format for your configuration information file, a .config file might not be adequate, and you'll need to store your configuration information in a standard XML file.

ASP.NET web.config File

Microsoft considered application configuration early on when the .NET Framework was created, and a configuration hierarchy was provided for storing configuration information for .NET applications. When you install a version of the .NET Framework, the default installation directory is located at *%SystemRoot%*\Microsoft.NET\Framework. For instance, when.NET Framework 2.0 is installed, the default installation path to the framework files is *%SystemRoot%*\\Microsoft.NET\Framework\v2.0.50727. A subdirectory named Config is created under the installation directory. The Config directory contains a file named machine.config as well as various other configuration files.

The machine.config file is a very large XML file that contains the default configuration settings for all .NET Framework applications on the local computer. The machine.config file is analogous to a registry for the .NET Framework. As any .NET Framework application is started, configuration information is read from the machine.config file. Not all settings in the machine.config file will apply to every application.

However, what if you need to customize configuration information for an application? Microsoft provided a solution for this as well. You can use local configuration files to customize the behavior of a particular application. Local configuration files are also created using XML but contain only a subset of the settings contained in the machine.config file. With most .NET Framework applications, the local configuration file is named app.config. With ASP.NET applications, the local configuration file is named web.config.

After reading configuration information from the machine.config file, the .NET Framework reads any configuration settings in the local configuration file. Settings contained in the local configuration file override settings read from the machine.config file. By default, a web.config file resides in the root directory of an ASP.NET application created using Visual Studio 2005. However, an ASP.NET application might contain multiple web.config files. When a web.config file is encountered, the settings contained in it apply to all resources in the directory where it resides and resources in all subdirectories. Using this strategy, you can design ASP.NET applications in which resources contained in a subdirectory are more secure than are resources contained in higher-level directories.

Following is an example of an ASP.NET web.config file.

ASP.NET web.config File

```
<?xml version="1.0"?>
<configuration xmlns="http://schemas.microsoft.com/.NetConfiguration/v2.0">
    <appSettings>
        <add key="errorRecipientList" value="shannonhorn@msn.com "/>
    </appSettings>
    <connectionStrings/>
    <system.web>
        <pages theme="Default"/>
        <compilation debug="true">
            <assemblies>
                <add assembly="System.Configuration.Install, Version=2.0.0.0,
Culture=neutral, PublicKeyToken=B03F5F7F11D50A3A"/></assemblies></compilation>
        <authentication mode="Windows"/>
        <customErrors mode="RemoteOnly" defaultRedirect="GenericErrorPage.htm">
            <error statusCode="403" redirect="NoAccess.htm" />
            <error statusCode="404" redirect="FileNotFound.htm" />
        </customErrors>
    </system.web>
    <system.net>
    <mailSettings>
            <smtp from="website@website.com">
                    <network host="mail.website.com" password="" userName=""/>
            </smtp>
        </mailSettings>
    </system.net>
</configuration>
```

Structure of the web.config File

The ASP.NET web.config file is an XML file that uses a nested hierarchy of custom XML tags and attributes that specify the configuration settings for most facets of an ASP.NET application. Most of the ASP.NET-specific configuration settings are included as child elements of the *<system.web>* element that correlates to the *System.Web* namespace. Table 13-1 lists some of the most commonly used elements in the web.config file.

Table 13-1   Commonly Used Elements in the ASP.NET web.config File

Element	Description
<authentication>	This element is used to identify how ASP.NET should authenticate, or identify, users. The authentication element has a single attribute, *mode*, which identifies how authentication should be handled. Possible values for the *mode* attribute are *Windows*, *Forms*, *Passport*, and *None*. *Windows* is the default value and indicates that Internet Information Server (IIS) will handle authentication. *Forms* indicates that ASP.NET should handle authentication. *Passport* indicates that Microsoft Passport services will handle authentication. *None* indicates that no authentication will be performed. The authentication element may contain one of two child elements, *forms* or *passport*, which, as their names suggest, provide control over forms authentication and passport authentication.
<authorization>	This element is used to allow or deny access to users, roles, and Hypertext Transfer Protocol (HTTP) verbs. The authorization element may contain one of two child elements, *allow* and *deny*, which, as their names suggest, respectively provide control over granting and denying access. Typically, the authorization element is used in conjunction with forms authentication to allow or deny users and groups identified in the *forms* element.
<compilation>	This element is used to configure compilation settings. The *compilation* element has several attributes, including *debug*, *defaultLanguage*, *batch*, and *tempDirectory*. The *compilation* element may contain one of two child elements, *compilers* and *assemblies*, used respectively to define one or more compilers to be used and one or more assemblies to reference during compilation.
<customErrors>	This element is used to define how to handle errors that an ASP.NET application encounters. The *customErrors* element includes two attributes, *mode* and *defaultRedirect*, used respectively to configure how errors are handled and to define that a generic error page appear to a user when an error is encountered. The *customErrors* element may contain a single child element, *error*, which accommodates a custom redirect action for each error identified.

Table 13-1   Commonly Used Elements in the ASP.NET web.config File

Element	Description
\<pages\>	This element is used to configure page-level settings. The *pages* element may contain several attributes, including *buffer*, *enableSessionState*, *enableViewState*, *smartNavigation*, and *theme*.
\<sessionState\>	This element is used to configure ASP.NET session state. The *sessionState* element may contain several attributes, including *mode*, *cookieless*, and *timeout*. The *mode* attribute may be assigned one of four values: *Off*, *InProc*, *StateServer*, or *SQLServer*. The *Off* value disables session state. The *InProc* value configures session state to be managed using the IIS default. The *StateServer* value, typically used in a Web farm environment, configures session state to be managed by a central Web server. The *SQLServer* value configures session state to be managed using a SQL Server database and preserves session state best.

MORE INFO   ASP.NET Configuration

For more information on the structure of the ASP.NET web.config file, see the topic entitled "ASP.NET Configuration Overview" located at *http://msdn2.microsoft.com/en-us/library/ms178683.aspx*.

connectionStrings Section

The *connectionStrings* section is new in the web.config file for ASP.NET 2.0. Earlier in this lesson, a database connection string was used as an example of a piece of configuration information commonly requiring frequent changes. As a standard, prior to ASP.NET 2.0, connection strings were stored in the web.config file due to the possibility of required changes. Microsoft recommended this practice and, to reinforce it, they added the *connectionStrings* section to the web.config file. The *connectionStrings* section may contain one of three child elements: *add*, *remove*, or *clear*. The *add* element is used to add connection string configuration information to what has already been read into memory. The *remove* element is used to remove connection string configuration information already read into memory. The *clear* element is used to clear all connection string configuration information already read into memory. Following is an excerpt of a web.config file that illustrates the *connectionStrings* section.

ASP.NET web.config *connectionStrings* Section

```
<configuration>
<connectionStrings>
  <add name="Patients"
      providerName="System.Data.SqlClient"
      connectionString=
```

```
"server=medicalServer;database=medicalOfficeDB;uid=tryToUseWindowsIntegratedAuth;pwd=neverUs
eASimplePassword" />
</connectionStrings>
</configuration>
```

appSettings Section

What do you do if you exhaust all of the sections in the ASP.NET web.config file and do not find a section to accommodate your configuration information? Microsoft has provided in the web.config file an optional section called *appSettings*, used to store custom configuration information. The *appSettings* section may contain one of three child elements: *add*, *remove*, or *clear*. Typically, you will use *add* child elements of the *appSettings* element to define simple custom configuration information. Each *add* element may contain two attributes: *key* and *value*. Following is an excerpted example of the *appSettings* section.

ASP.NET web.config *appSettings* Section

```
<configuration>
    <appSettings>
        <add key="errorRecipientList" value="shannonhorn@msn.com "/>
    </appSettings>
</configuration>
```

Other Namespace Sections

As mentioned, the configuration settings that are stored in the web.config file and affect ASP.NET are contained in the *<system.web>* element. The web.config file may contain configuration information that uses functionality from other namespaces as well. Typically, if functionality from additional namespaces is included in the web.config file, the namespace functionality will be contained in an element that bears the name of the namespace and is a sibling element to the *<system.web>* element. For instance, in the following excerpt, functionality from the *System.Net* namespace is used to identify and configure the SMTP server.

ASP.NET web.config Additional Namespace Functionality

```
<configuration>
    <system.net>
        <mailSettings>
            <smtp from="website@website.com">
                <network host="mail.website.com" password="" userName=""/>
            </smtp>
        </mailSettings>
    </system.net>
</configuration>
```

Custom Sections

The schema and behavior of the web.config file are defined by .NET Framework 2.0, using the *configSections* element, which can also be used to further define custom sections within the web.config file. The *configSections* element may contain one or more of four child elements: *clear*, *remove*, *section*, or *sectionGroup*. The *section* element is used to define a single custom element that appears in the web.config file. The *sectionGroup* element is used to define a group of custom elements that appear in the web.config file. The *sectionGroup* element may contain one or more *section* elements to define custom elements in the custom group.

The following excerpt illustrates creating a custom section in the web.config file named whereWeAre.

ASP.NET web.config *configSections* Element

```
<configuration>
   <configSections>
      <section name="whereWeAre"
               type="System.Configuration.SingleTagSectionHandler" />
   </configSections>

   <whereWeAre addressLine1="123 Main Street"
               addressLine2=""
               cityStateZip="Peoria, AZ  85345"
               phone="(623) 555-1212" />
</configuration>
```

Custom XML Files

Although you have the *appSettings* section at your disposal for storing simple custom values, and you have the *configSections* element for defining custom sections and section groups, your configuration information might require a more elaborate schema than the web.config file is capable of accommodating. In this scenario, you must store your configuration information in a custom XML file or other data store such as a database. If you use a custom XML file for storing your configuration information, you must manage your configuration information using the XML classes in the *System.Xml* namespace.

Accessing Configuration Information

After storing your configuration information in the web.config file, how do you access it? Prior to .NET Framework 2.0, access to configuration information for all types of .NET applications was obtained using the classes in the *System.Configuration* namespace. Since the introduction of ASP.NET 2.0, configuration information in the web.config file has been accessed using classes in the *System.Web.Configuration* namespace. The most commonly used class in the *System.Web.Configuration* namespace is the *WebConfigurationManager* class.

The *WebConfigurationManager* class contains the *GetSection* method used to retrieve a section from the web.config file by name. When a section is retrieved, it is retrieved as an XML node list and can be cast to an object that represents the section. The *System.Web.Configuration* namespace includes classes to represent sections in the web.config file. Other namespaces in the .NET Framework include classes that represent configuration sections associated with classes in each namespace. For example, in the following code excerpt, the *WebConfiguration-Manager.GetSection* method is used to retrieve the system.net/mailSettings section and cast it to a *MailSettingsSectionGroup* object. The *MailSettingsSectionGroup* object can then be used to access information about the SMTP server when building the e-mail to report an error.

ASP.NET *WebConfigurationManager* Class

```vb
' VB
Imports System
Imports System.Data
Imports System.Configuration
Imports System.Net.Configuration
Imports System.Net.Mail
Imports System.Web
Imports System.Web.Configuration
Imports System.Web.Security
Imports System.Web.UI
Imports System.Web.UI.WebControls
Imports System.Web.UI.WebControls.WebParts
Imports System.Web.UI.HtmlControls

Partial Public Class _Default
    Inherits System.Web.UI.Page

    ' Class level data members.
    Dim mailSettings As MailSettingsSectionGroup =
CType(WebConfigurationManager.GetSection("system.net/mailSettings"),
System.Net.Configuration.MailSettingsSectionGroup)

    Protected Sub Page_Load(ByVal sender As Object, ByVal e As EventArgs)

        ' Email if something goes wrong...
        Dim errorMessage As MailMessage = New MailMessage(mailSettings.Smtp.From,
WebConfigurationManager.AppSettings("errorRecipientList"), "An error occurred loading the
home page data file for service times.", "")
        errorMessage.Priority = MailPriority.High
        Dim smtp As SmtpClient = New SmtpClient(mailSettings.Smtp.Network.Host)
        smtp.Send(errorMessage)
    End Sub
End Class


// C#
using System;
using System.Data;
using System.Configuration;
using System.Net.Configuration;
```

```
using System.Net.Mail;
using System.Web;
using System.Web.Configuration;
using System.Web.Security;
using System.Web.UI;
using System.Web.UI.WebControls;
using System.Web.UI.WebControls.WebParts;
using System.Web.UI.HtmlControls;

public partial class _Default : System.Web.UI.Page
{

    // Class level data members.
    MailSettingsSectionGroup mailSettings = WebConfigurationManager.GetSection("system.net/
mailSettings") as MailSettingsSectionGroup;

    protected void Page_Load(object sender, EventArgs e)
    {

        // Email if something goes wrong...
        MailMessage message = new MailMessage(mailSettings.Smtp.From,
WebConfigurationManager.AppSettings["errorRecipientList"], "An error occurred loading the
home page data file for service times.", "");
        message.Priority = MailPriority.High;
        SmtpClient smtp = new SmtpClient(mailSettings.Smtp.Network.Host);
        smtp.Send(message);
    }
}
```

Using the ASP.NET Web Site Administration Tool

If you are using Visual Studio 2005 to create ASP.NET Web applications, you can use the ASP.NET Web Site Administration Tool to automate the management of configuration information stored in the web.config file. To access the administration tool, select ASP.NET Configuration from the Website menu when an ASP.NET Web application project is open, as shown in Figure 13-1.

The administration tool will appear in a new instance of Microsoft Internet Explorer, and you will be presented with the home page shown in Figure 13-2. The home page is the welcome page and includes options for help and for navigating to the Security, Application, and Provider pages of the tool.

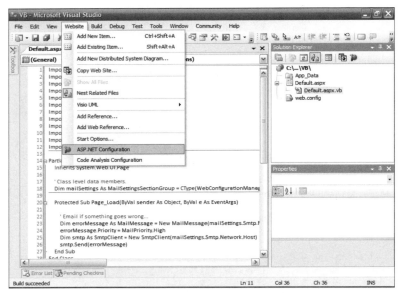

Figure 13-1   The Visual Studio 2005 Web site menu with the ASP.NET Configuration option highlighted

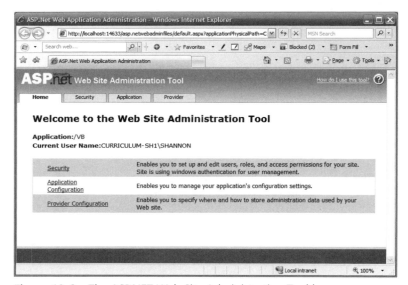

Figure 13-2   The ASP.NET Web Site Administration Tool home page

The administration tool automates security and application configuration information. Application configuration settings are stored in the web.config file. However, security configuration settings are stored in a data store. ASP.NET uses data classes, known as data providers, to access the data store where security settings are stored. A data provider is similar to a data access object that is typically used in an application. AspNetSqlProvider, the default data provider used by ASP.NET, is the provider for SQL Server 2005. If you have SQL Server 2005 Express Edition installed when initially running the administration tool, Visual Studio 2005 will automatically create a new SQL Server Express database in the App_Data directory for the current project. The database created will include a schema ready for security configuration settings to be stored.

If you do not have SQL Server 2005 Express Edition installed when you initially run the administration tool, you must provide the administration tool with a connection string to a database. If you opt to use another edition of SQL Server 2005 for storing security configuration information, you must first prepare the database by running aspnet_regsql.exe from the Visual Studio 2005 Command Prompt utility to create the security schema. You can also create custom data providers to access custom data stores.

To review the data provider the administration tool is using, or to configure the data provider, select the Provider tab in the administration tool. If a data provider is already in use, the name of the provider will appear. Additional links on the Provider tab enable you to modify the data provider being used. The administration tool Provider tab is shown in Figure 13-3.

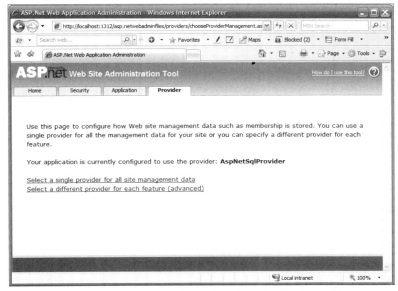

Figure 13-3   The ASP.NET Web Site Administration Tool Provider page

To configure security configuration information using the administration tool, navigate to the Security tab. The Security tab offers options for configuring security settings manually or with the Security Setup Wizard. The options for manual configuration enable you to manage users, roles, and access rules. Figure 13-4 shows the administration tool Security tab.

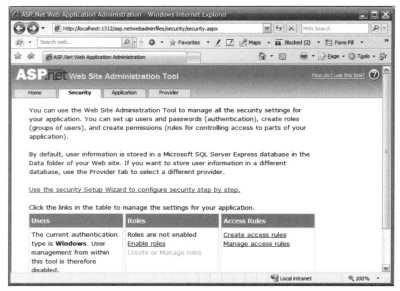

Figure 13-4   The ASP.NET Web Site Administration Tool Security page

You can use the Security Setup Wizard to configure security configuration information easily for your ASP.NET Web application. The Security Setup Wizard includes an introduction and options for selecting users' methods for accessing your Web application; selecting your application's data store; and defining roles, users, and access rules. The Create User page of the wizard is shown in Figure 13-5 with the Create User form displayed.

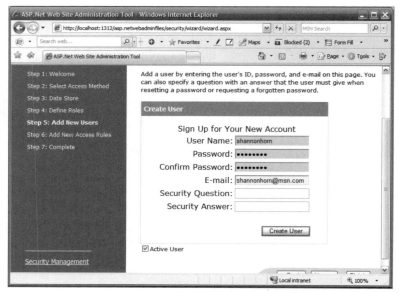

Figure 13-5   The ASP.NET Web Site Administration Tool Security Setup Wizard Create User page

You create access rules to grant and deny resource access to users and roles. In Figure 13-6, the Data Modifiers group has been granted access to the MyApplicationData directory whereas all anonymous users have been denied access to this directory.

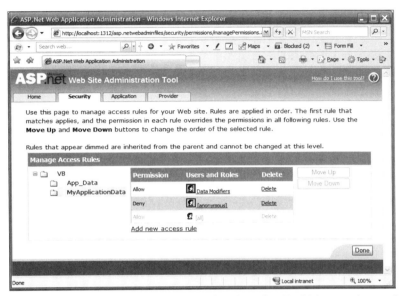

Figure 13-6 The ASP.NET Web Site Administration Tool Manage Access Rules page

The final tab of the administration tool, the Application tab, is used to configure general Web application settings, including SMTP server settings, application status, debugging, tracing, and user-defined settings stored in the *appSettings* section. Figure 13-7 shows the administration tool Application tab.

Once configuration within the administration tool is complete and the tool is closed, you can review the web.config file for changes that the tool made to the file. In the previous example, the *<roleManager enabled="true" />* element was added to the web.config file to enable the role manager. In addition, as mentioned earlier, if you had SQL Server 2005 Express Edition installed and elected to use the data provider to connect to Express Edition, you will notice a new Express database named ASPNETDB.MDF in the App_Data directory.

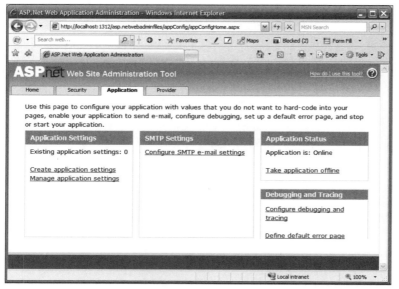

Figure 13-7   The ASP.NET Web Site Administration Tool Application tab

Quick Check

1. What is the recommended method for storing application configuration information in ASP.NET Web applications?
2. In what section of the web.config file should database connection information be stored?
3. How should configuration information stored in the web.config file be accessed from code?
4. How can you easily manage user authentication information using Visual Studio 2005?

Quick Check Answers

1. ASP.NET application configuration information should be stored in the web.config file.
2. Database connection information should be stored in the *<connectionStrings>* element section of the web.config file.
3. Configuration information stored in the web.config file should be accessed using the *WebConfigurationManager* and other classes in the *System.Web.Configuration* namespace.
4. User credential information can be managed easily in Visual Studio 2005 by using the ASP.NET Web Site Administration Tool.

Lab 1: Configuring an ASP.NET Web Application

In this lab, create a new ASP.NET Web project, add resources to the project, and adjust the security settings to determine the impact of modifying configuration information. If you encounter a problem completing this lab, the completed projects in both Visual Basic and C# can be installed from the Code folder on the companion CD.

For easy completion of this lab, be sure that SQL Server 2005 Express Edition is successfully installed prior to beginning the lab.

▶ **Exercise 1: Creating an ASP.NET Web Project**

In this exercise, you create a simple new ASP.NET Web application that functions correctly. However, the new application will include simulated content that must be secured.

1. Start Visual Studio 2005 and select File | New | Web Site.
2. Select ASP.NET Web Site, and then click OK.
3. From the Location drop-down menu, select File System.
4. Select your language of choice from the Language drop-down menu.
5. Click Browse to create the new Web site in the Exercise subdirectory for Lesson 1, "Logging Application Events," of Chapter 12, "Logging and Monitoring," or in another location that doesn't overwrite another Web site.
6. Click OK.
7. Add a Web form that must be secured.
   a. Right-click the project in the Solution Explorer and select Add Existing Item.
   b. Navigate to the Solution subdirectory for Lesson 1 of Chapter 13 and select Default.aspx.
   c. Click Add. You should be prompted twice to confirm overwriting an existing file. Click Yes both times.
   d. Right-click Default.aspx in Solution Explorer and select Set As Start Page.
8. Enable debugging and execute the Web application.
   a. Press F5 or click the Start Debugging button on the Standard or Debug toolbar. You should be prompted to enable debugging. Click Cancel.
   b. Double-click web.config in the Solution Explorer to open the file. Examine the file. The *debug* attribute of the *<compilation>* element should be set to *False*. Modify the value of the attribute manually to be *True*.
   c. Close the web.config file and save the changes you made.
   d. Press F5 or click the Start Debugging button on the toolbar. This time, the Web form should display successfully, as shown in Figure 13-8.

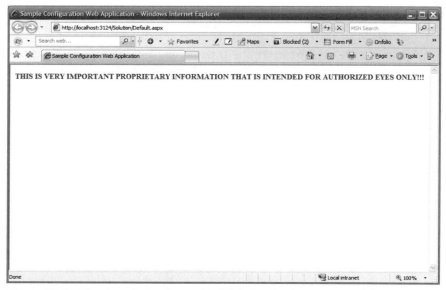

Figure 13-8 The Sample Configuration Web Application unsecured form

Manually modifying the configuration information in the web.config file permitted the Web form to display successfully in debug mode. However, as the Web form illustrates, it is a sample form that displays proprietary information for authorized eyes only.

▶ **Exercise 2: Securing an ASP.NET Web Form Using the ASP.NET Web Site Administration Tool**

Your next task is to secure this Web form so that user authorization is possible. Currently, all users who can navigate to the page can view its contents.

1. Create an ASP.NET Web form to authenticate users.
    a. Right-click the project in the Solution Explorer and select Add New Item. In the Add New Item dialog box, select Web Form.
    b. Name the Web form Login.aspx or something similar.
    c. Select your language of choice from the Language drop-down menu.
    d. Click Add.
2. Create the login Web form.
    a. From the Login section of the Toolbox, drag a *Login* control to the new Login Web form. While in Source view, place the new *Login* control between the opening and closing <div> tags on the new Login Web form.
    b. Switch to Design view. The *Login* control should work successfully and automatically use the default data provider. The Login Web form in the designer should resemble Figure 13-9.

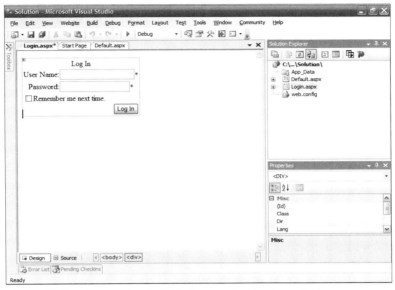

Figure 13-9   The new Login Web form with a *Login* control

3. Configure the default data provider using the ASP.NET Web Site Administration Tool.

   a. Start the ASP.NET Web Site Administration Tool by selecting ASP.NET Configuration from the Website menu.

   b. From the Security tab, select the Use The Security Setup Wizard To Configure Security Step-by-Step link to start the Security Setup Wizard.

   c. Click Next to navigate to Step 2 of the wizard. Select From The Internet to indicate that users should be authenticated using ASP.NET Forms authentication and click Next.

   d. Click Next to accept the default data provider and navigate to Step 4 of the wizard.

   e. Select the Enable Roles For This Web Site check box and click Next to define roles. Just as with Windows authentication, you can manage security at the user level; however, it is more efficient to manage security at the role level.

   f. Type **GeneralUsers** (or something similar) and click Add Role to create a general user role.

   g. Type **AdministrativeUsers** (or something similar) and click Add Role to create an administrative user role.

   h. Click Next to navigate to Step 5 of the wizard.

   i. Create at least two user profiles in Step 5 and click Next to navigate to Step 6 of the wizard.

    j. In Step 6, select the root folder of the project and the AdministrativeUsers role, and then click the Allow radio button. Click Add This Rule.

    k. Select the GeneralUsers role and the Deny radio button, and then click Add This Rule.

    l. Select Anonymous Users and Deny, and then click Add This Rule.

    m. Click Finish.

4. Assign roles to users.

    a. On the Security tab, select the Manage Users link.

    b. Select Edit Roles for at least one user and add the user to the AdministrativeUser role.

    c. Select Edit Roles for at least one user not in the AdministrativeUser role and add the user to the GeneralUsers role.

    d. Close the administration tool.

5. Press F5 or click the Start Debugging button on the toolbar. The Login.aspx Web form should be displayed to authenticate users.

6. Attempt to log on to the Web application, using a user in the GeneralUsers role. Your logon attempt should be unsuccessful. You could make the example more elaborate by redirecting the user or displaying a message.

7. Attempt to log on to the Web application, using a user in the AdministrativeUsers role. Your logon attempt should be successful.

Lesson Summary

- Configuration information is any data that is used to define the behavior of an application.
- The .config file used for ASP.NET Web applications is the web.config file.
- All .NET applications read configuration information from the machine.config file first and then read configuration information from local configuration files. Local configuration information overrides configuration information read from the machine.config file.
- The *connectionStrings* section of the web.config file is used to store database connection strings.
- The *appSettings* section of the web.config file is used to store user-defined key and value pairs.
- Configuration information stored in the web.config file is easily accessible by using the *GetSection* method of the *System.Web.Configuration.WebConfigurationManager* class.
- The ASP.NET Web Site Administration Tool is used to automate management of most Web application configuration information.

Lesson Review

You can use the following questions to test your knowledge of the information in Lesson 1, "Maintaining Application Configuration Information." The questions are also available on the companion CD if you prefer to review them in electronic form.

NOTE Answers

Answers to these questions and explanations of why each answer choice is right or wrong are located in the "Answers" section at the end of the book.

---

1. Where should database connection information be stored?
   - A. The *appSettings* section of the web.config file
   - B. The *connectionStrings* section of the web.config file
   - C. The databases section of the web.config file
   - D. The *configSections* section of the web.config file
2. Which namespace contains the classes used to access the configuration information in the web.config file?
   - A. *System.Web*
   - B. *System.Net.Configuration*
   - C. *System.Configuration*
   - D. *System.Web.Configuration*
3. What is the default data provider used by the administration tool?
   - A. SQL Server 2005 Professional Edition data provider
   - B. SQL Server 2005 Express Edition data provider
   - C. XML data provider
   - D. Oracle data provider

Chapter Review

To further practice and reinforce the skills you learned in this chapter, you can complete the following tasks:

- Review the chapter summary.
- Review the list of key terms introduced in this chapter.
- Complete the case scenarios. These scenarios set up real-world situations involving the topics of this chapter and ask you to create a solution.
- Complete the suggested practices.
- Take a practice test.

Chapter Summary

- Configuration information is any data used to define the behavior of an application, particularly information that might need adjustment in the future to refine the behavior of the application with which it is associated.
- The web.config file is used to store configuration information for ASP.NET Web applications.
- Configuration information stored in the web.config file is accessible using the classes in the *System.Web.Configuration* namespace.
- The ASP.NET Web Site Administration Tool includes a wizard called the Security Setup Wizard for easily configuring security settings.

Key Terms

Do you know what these key terms mean? You can check your answers by looking up the terms in the glossary at the end of the book.

- access rule
- connection string
- Extensible Markup Language
- machine.config file
- role
- user
- web.config file
- XML

Case Scenarios

In the following case scenarios, you will apply what you've learned about how to manage configuration information for ASP.NET Web applications. You can find answers to these questions in the "Answers" section at the end of this book.

Case Scenario 1: Storing Custom Application Configuration Information

You are developing an ASP.NET 2.0 Web application for a client. Your application includes data-driven pages that display a calendar of upcoming events and a complete profile for each employee. The Web application uses a secured administrative interface to allow employees to maintain their profile information. Each employee has access to the administrative interface, using security credentials that grant the employee access to only his or her profile. Your client has mandated that all employee profile and security credential information be stored in a single table named Employees.

Questions

1. How should employee security and profile information be stored?
2. Can you use the ASP.NET Web Site Administration Tool to maintain employee security information for the application?

Case Scenario 2: Specifying Default Application Configuration Settings

You are configuring Web servers for Proseware, Inc., a company that develops and hosts ASP.NET Web applications for clients. Proseware has developed a custom framework for ASP.NET applications and would like to modify the default values of several ASP.NET configuration settings for all hosted applications. Proseware also needs to add some custom configuration settings to all hosted applications. All ASP.NET applications hosted on Proseware Web servers will require the modified configuration settings.

Questions

1. How should the default values of existing ASP.NET configuration settings be modified for all applications?
2. How should custom configuration settings be applied to all applications?

Suggested Practices

To help you successfully master the exam objectives presented in this chapter, complete the following tasks.

Evaluate the Application Configuration Architecture

To help you master this objective, complete the following tasks.

- **Practice 1** Treat any data used to define the behavior of an application as configuration information.
- **Practice 2** Store configuration information externally to an application in the web.config file.
- **Practice 3** Define application configuration information using the web.config file and rarely modify the machine.config file.
- **Practice 4** Manage permissions at the role level, if possible, instead of at the user level.
- **Practice 5** Use the ASP.NET Web Site Administration Tool to set up the security for a Web application quickly. However, remember that some of the more advanced configuration settings cannot be configured using the administration tool.

Take a Practice Test

The practice tests on this book's companion CD offer many options. For example, you can test yourself on just one exam objective, or you can test yourself on all the 70-547 certification exam content. You can set up the test so that it closely simulates the experience of taking a certification exam, or you can set it up in study mode so that you can look at the correct answers and explanations after you answer each question.

MORE INFO   **Practice tests**

For details about all the practice test options available, see the "How to Use the Practice Tests" section in this book's Introduction.

Chapter 14
Define and Evaluate a Testing Strategy

The quality of your application's released code often directly relates to the quality of your testing strategy. A well-defined and thorough testing strategy will lead to a solid, issue-free user experience, whereas relying on the team to define their strategy as they create their tests will often lead to software that is poorly tested and riddled with issues upon initial release. A good testing strategy, along with good testing and tracking tools, will help you avoid releasing bad software.

This chapter covers creating and evaluating testing strategies that measure the quality of your application. You will look first at creating an effective unit testing strategy. This strategy is typically owned and created by developers. You will then learn how, as a developer, you can evaluate and provide input into the stress and performance testing plans created by the test team. Finally, you will explore the feedback provided by a Web developer relative to the test lab hardware, software, and data used for testing.

Each of these testing strategies—unit, stress, and performance—measures an application from a specific angle. For example, *unit tests* measure the quality of the code (objects and their methods) that defines the behavior of your application in terms of business rules and data interaction. Load tests, or stress tests, indicate how your application will scale and respond to increased or fluctuating demand. Performance tests determine whether your application meets the benchmarks set forth for the project and help you identify any gaps. Taking a disciplined, planned approach to testing your application from each of these angles will ensure that you always release a high-quality software product.

Exam objectives in this chapter:
- ■ Evaluate the testing strategy.
  - ❑ Create the unit testing strategy.
  - ❑ Evaluate the integration testing strategy.
  - ❑ Evaluate the stress testing strategy.
  - ❑ Evaluate the performance testing strategy.
  - ❑ Evaluate the test environment specification.

Lessons in this chapter:

Before You Begin

To complete the lessons in this chapter, you should be familiar with Microsoft Visual Basic or C# and be comfortable with the following tasks:

- Creating an ASP.NET Web page
- Developing a business object (class) that contains domain-specific properties and methods

---

Real World

Mike Snell

Testing takes time and costs money. However, that time and money spent always seem worthwhile if you deliver quality software to your users; customers never forget buggy, difficult-to-use software—no matter how cheap it was or how many days ahead of schedule you delivered.

I have spent nearly my entire career as a consultant or in managing consultants, and I have learned this lesson firsthand. I have had many customers who wanted my team to compromise quality for schedule or costs. I can think of a number of cases in which projects ran long and management made suggestions to pull the time out of testing. Of course, that never worked. Imagine being a tester whose test window keeps shrinking.

These days, we define this up front: quality software comes at a cost. If customers want us to compromise on this, we have to walk away. (Typically, they want the same thing that we want; they just need to understand it.) Thankfully, we can now use a number of automated testing strategies to help us deliver quality. Taking actions like performing unit testing, Web testing, load testing, and performance testing all help to keep quality high and costs reasonable.

Lesson 1: Creating a Unit Testing Strategy

An effective unit testing strategy can lead to higher-quality code, increased productivity, and easier maintenance. This lesson examines what goes into creating an effective unit testing strategy by first looking at an overview of developer unit testing. Then it will discuss defining an approach for managing and creating unit tests. Finally, it will cover the best practices that surround a good unit testing strategy.

MORE INFO   Creating unit tests

This lesson focuses squarely on defining a unit testing strategy. For information on creating a unit test, see Lesson 1 in Chapter 15, "Create Development Tests."

> **After this lesson, you will be able to:**
> - Determine where, in your solution, to manage unit tests.
> - Determine an approach for creating unit tests.
> - Determine the conditions that should be tested as part of a unit test.
> - Understand best practices for defining a unit test.
> - Establish metrics for unit test code coverage.
>
> **Estimated lesson time: 30 minutes**

Unit Testing Overview

Developers are responsible for testing their code prior to its alpha or beta release. Traditionally, this has meant that they walked through their code, line by line, inside a debugger. To do so, they often created a crude user interface (UI, or test harness) that could be used to simulate standard user interaction, edge cases, and error conditions. This approach was problematic for a number of reasons. First, it relied on the developer to re-execute tests after each change. Along the same lines, it was not automated and repeatable by other developers or testers. Last, it relied on the developer to confirm that all code was tested. The end result of following this approach was a lower-quality product released to the test team.

A more formal process for developer testing was needed, and the concept of a unit test evolved. A *unit test* isolates a portion of your application and tests all conditions of that unit. Unit tests can be manual or automated. A manual unit test is typically one that is documented and then executed by a developer. Manual unit tests have many of the same problems mentioned previously. However, automated unit tests seek to solve these problems.

An automated unit test is a piece of test code that you write to exercise a portion of your application code. These automated unit tests exist inside a unit test framework that is responsible for running the tests and communicating the results. The first testing framework to work with the Microsoft .NET Framework was NUnit. With NUnit, you can create unit tests that can be automatically run inside of Visual Studio and then reported on. A similar unit testing framework is now built into the .NET Framework version 2.0.

MORE INFO   NUnit

NUnit was originally ported from JUnit (for Java). It is an open-source project that works with all versions and languages of the .NET Framework. It became very popular for the .NET Framework versions 1.0 and 1.1. It is currently maintained and updated at *http://www.nunit.org/*.

Benefits of Automated Unit Testing

The principal benefit of defining an automated unit test is that you can create a complete, repeatable test for a given unit of your code. This test ensures that the unit of code works as developed. Once created, it can be run repeatedly to make sure the code continues to operate as designed. In addition, new conditions can be added to the test as they arise (or are thought of). In this way, the tests grow stronger over time. This seemingly simple goal of creating a repeatable test for a unit of code has a number of additional, ancillary benefits as well. Let's take a look.

Confirm That Code Is Tested   The unit testing framework in .NET tracks which code is tested by the unit tests and which code is not. It then reports this information. In this way, you get real metrics on exactly what code (and what percentage of code) is tested. A developer can use this information to make changes that increase the unit test *code coverage*.

Build a Set of Regression Tests   You create unit tests one at a time. However, as you continue to build unit tests, the result is that you accumulate a set of tests that exercise a major portion (if not all) of your application. This set of tests often becomes a large portion of your regression test. A regression test (also called a smoke test) is a baseline to exercise the entire application. Typically, a regression test is known to have worked at one time and can, therefore, be used after changes are made to determine whether things still work.

Make Changes with Confidence   Having a set of unit tests allows you to make changes to an existing application more confidently. This can be great if you are a new developer and wish to change someone else's code. In addition, if you are doing a code review and wish to refactor some portion of the code late in the cycle, you can do so with a higher degree of confidence. The unit tests can be run after the change and should then identify any problems that resulted from the change.

Aid in Understanding   Developers can use unit tests to walk through and understand the intention of existing code. The unit tests serve as a sort of documentation of what should and shouldn't be possible for a given method or property. By reading this code and watching it execute, a developer can understand more quickly the intent behind the code.

Unit Testing Limits

Unit testing is just one piece of the testing puzzle. It helps developers ensure that each unit of their code works as intended. However, testers still need to do their part. Unit testing does not cover integration, Web user interface, load, or performance testing. Testers still need to execute these types of tests to ensure that the application is tested from all angles.

Quick Check

1. What is the definition of a unit test?
2. What is the primary purpose of a unit test?
3. What are the benefits of coding a set of unit tests using a unit test framework?

Quick Check Answers

1. Strictly speaking, a unit test isolates a portion of code and tests it for expected behavior and outputs based on a certain set of inputs. An automated unit test in Visual Studio 2005 is a piece of code that is written to call an isolated segment of the application (usually a single method or property). The unit test asserts a set of truths about the expected results after the application code has been called. This automated unit test is then run by the unit test framework built into Visual Studio.

2. The primary purpose of a unit test is to help the developer ensure that the code works as intended. The unit test isolates the code and tests it for a specific condition. A single piece of application code may be tested for many conditions using many unit tests.

3. Writing automated unit tests as part of a unit test framework has all of the following benefits: it builds up a set of regression tests for the application, confirms that each method works as intended, helps identify dependency issues between bits of code when there are changes made to the application, and aids in understanding the intent of a given piece of code.

Managing and Storing Unit Tests

You have a number of options available for storing and managing the unit tests you create for your application. It is helpful to define a single strategy in this regard, communicate it, and stick to it. In doing so, it is important to remember that unit tests are the domain of the developer. Developers create them initially and run them the most often. Testers may use them, but developers must take ownership. You want to make sure they have the best experience when working with these tests. Therefore, it is advisable that you not embed your unit tests in the middle of a large testing project that contains the many additional tests of the test team. Your developers will, most likely, be running a version of Visual Studio that does not have access to these other tests. In addition, these other tests might get in the way of the development team and the testers. Therefore, segment your unit tests into a separate test project. You have a number of options for doing so, including both of the following strategies:

- **Create a single test project within your solution**   This strategy involves defining a single unit testing project inside your solution. Developers will add their unit tests to this project. The result is a centralized store for all unit tests on the project. When you run the unit tests, you typically run all tests in the project. This approach can, therefore, be good if you wish each developer to run the full set of tests each time.

- **Create one test project per application project**   With this strategy you define a one-to-one relationship between class library or project and unit test project. This can be helpful if you wish your developers to focus on a single piece of the application at one time. It is also great if you are developing reusable components because the component and component's tests are discrete. However, it can become difficult to run the full set of unit tests for the entire solution using this method.

Naming Unit Test Files

It is advisable to have a single unit testing file for each code file you intend to unit test. This creates a one-to-one relationship between items in your application and your tests. For example, if you have both *Product.cs* and *Order.cs* class files, you should also have two separate unit test files (one for each class file). In addition, name your unit test files according to the class they test. In the previous example, you would create the files *ProductTest.cs* and *OrderTest.cs*.

Defining an Approach to Creating Unit Tests

There are two primary methods for creating unit tests for your project: automatically generating them and manually crafting them. Each method has its advantages, given a particular situation. It is important to make a decision about how you will employ one of these methods in a disciplined approach. This will ensure that your team builds a full set of tests for your application. Let's take a look at each option.

Manually Create Unit Tests

You can create your unit tests from a standard class file without any help from Visual Studio. Typically, you employ this strategy in test-first, or *test-driven development*. This approach is conceptually different from the typical development process of writing code and then testing it. Test-driven development demands the opposite approach. You create your tests first; you then write application code to satisfy those tests. The reason is that you want to see a test fail before you write code. In fact, if you add a new feature to your application, you start by defining that feature's tests. You then write the code around those tests.

A test-driven approach can help you ensure two things. First, only enough code to pass the tests will be written. Developers should not write more code than is needed to pass the tests.

Second, your unit tests should end up high-caliber with high code and condition coverage. This is a result of coding (and thinking about) the tests before writing the application code.

A test-driven strategy requires a switch in mindset for most developers. It is just not how developers have been trained to work or think. In addition, to be effective, it requires total buy-in from the team and a very disciplined approach. It is also not always practical. Many applications exist today with little or no unit tests. It would not be practical to try to rewrite these applications test-first.

Generate Unit Tests

Visual Studio 2005 allows you to generate a set of unit tests from existing code. You can run the Unit Test Wizard and select the classes, and their members, for which you want unit tests generated. Visual Studio will then create a test file that contains a number of partially-implemented unit tests that are stubbed out and, in many cases, have the beginning of your unit test.

This strategy can be very effective when working with an existing class or library that does not already have unit tests defined. You can generate the unit tests and begin to fill in the details around them. This offers more productivity than does creating a unit test by hand. In addition, many developers who are accustomed to creating code and then doing their testing will find this approach more in line with their experience. In this way, they can code a class or set of features and then work to write appropriate unit tests, but with a head start provided by Visual Studio.

Quick Check

1. What is test-driven development?
2. In what ways can you define a unit test?

Quick Check Answers

1. Test-driven development demands that you write tests before you write application code. You write application code only to satisfy broken tests. This ensures that your tests and code stay in full synch. It also makes sure you do not write a lot of extra code. However, it requires a different discipline and approach for most developers.
2. You can create a unit test using a test project and a class file. You can also select an existing set of application code (class) and have Visual Studio generate your unit tests for you.

Defining What Needs to Be Unit Tested

A good unit testing strategy defines exactly what in the application will be unit tested and exactly how it should be unit tested. This ensures that developers understand where and when to employ various unit test types and also that they test for all conditions. This section looks at the various types of unit tests and the many conditions that should be tested.

Unit Test Types

Unit tests are created mostly to test class libraries. They work best when they call the members of a given class, pass a set of parameters, and make assertions based on the results. They are typically not written to exercise a user interface or validate the structure and content of a database. There are other tests that can be employed to do these things. Unit tests are focused on testing developer code.

That said, .NET defines a few subtypes of unit tests. You will want to understand when to employ these tests as part of your overall strategy. The following list describes each type of unit test and indicates when it is best to use each.

- **Class (or standard)** You create a unit test to test the methods and properties for a given class. This is the standard unit test that you create most often. In fact, the following unit tests defined here are simply derivatives of this type.
- **Data-driven** A data-driven unit test is bound to a data source. The test is typically run once for each row in the data source. You will want to create data-driven unit tests for methods that take a wide variety of input. In these cases, instead of writing a number of separate but common unit tests or creating a looping structure, you can define one test and bind it to a data source.
- **ASP.NET** An ASP.NET unit test is created to test the classes (or business logic) inside an ASP.NET application. This strategy is not meant for testing Web forms. It is meant for testing the class files that make up a Web application. ASP.NET unit tests are run in the context of a Web server. Therefore, you get access to ASP.NET objects (such as the *Page* object) inside your test.
- **Web services** You can create unit tests that call Web services. You define these unit tests as you would other unit tests. The difference is that you must define a Web reference to the service from your unit test project. You can then call the Web service and make assertions relative to the results.

Unit Test Conditions

A good unit test should single out a piece of code (method or property) in your application and test a single condition. You might need to make multiple assertions in the test, but the overall test should be focused on a given condition such as a success condition, error condition, null values, and so on. The condition should either fail or pass. You do not want to test multiple conditions in a single unit test. The following represent some of the conditions and scenarios for which you will want to write tests:

- **Success baseline**   Start by defining a unit test that represents a common, successful path through your code. This test should represent the most likely scenario for executing your code.

- **Parameter mix**   Create a unit test that provides a varied mixture of parameters for a given method. This will ensure that more than just the success path works effectively. Consider creating this scenario as a data-driven unit test.

- **Bounds checking**   Create one or more unit tests that test the upper and lower limits of your code. That is, if your method takes a numeric value, you will want to test that method with values that represent both the upper and lower range of the data type.

- **Null values**   Make sure your unit tests measure what happens when null values are passed to a given method or property.

- **Error conditions**   Create unit tests that trigger error conditions in your code. You can tell the unit test that you expect a certain error as a result. If that error is not thrown, then the test will fail.

- **Code coverage scenarios**   Make sure that all the code in your method is called by one or more unit tests. You do not want untested code sitting inside of conditional statements. If this happens, write tests that hit those conditions inside your application code.

Defining Code Coverage Metrics

Your unit testing strategy should define a metric for code coverage. *Code coverage* refers to the percent of code that is exercised by the unit tests. Prior to Visual Studio 2005, this metric was difficult to obtain. Now, this information is readily available from the tool. This gives you a measurable understanding of what portion of your code is tested. The measurement is based on the code executed by the tests relative to the total logic in the application.

Typically, strive for 70 percent code coverage or better. You can use this metric to measure the effectiveness of your unit tests and the quality of a given build. For example, it means something completely different if a given build has all unit tests pass but has a unit test code coverage of only 20 percent versus a build with 90 percent coverage.

Developers can also use code coverage analysis to identify code that is not covered by unit tests. They can turn on code coverage for a given library from the .testrunconfig file. They can then view test results and see low-coverage areas in their code. The results window will allow them to jump straight to those areas and then create tests to increase their coverage.

NOTE   **Prevent source control check-in for poorly covered code**
You can create a build rule that prevents code check-in that does not meet your standard for unit test code coverage.

Quick Check

1. What are some common unit test types or scenarios in which unit tests work well?
2. What conditions should you make sure to examine with your unit tests?

Quick Check Answers

1. You can write standard unit tests that test methods and properties of your objects. You can also use unit tests for binding data to test methods that take a wide variety of input. You can create ASP.NET unit tests when you need access to the ASP.NET objects. Web services can also be tested with unit tests.

2. There are many conditions that can be tested with unit tests. Start by ensuring that you test the common, successful scenario. Then make sure your application behaves appropriately under error conditions. Check your inputs with null values and values that verify the upper and lower bounds of a given data type. Finally, make sure your unit tests cover all the lines of code in your application.

Unit Testing Best Practices

The more you do something, the better you become. The same is true for use cases. As you create more, you start to see patterns and best practices emerge. Your unit testing strategy should take into account these best practices. The following represent some of the best practices that have been established for writing effective unit tests:

- **Write one test for each scenario**   You should test each outcome or scenario independently. If your method has a number of expected outcomes, write a test for each scenario.

- **Create atomic unit tests**   Your unit tests should not require others tests (or a sequence of tests) to be run prior to their execution or as part of their execution.

- **Cover all conditions**   Your unit tests should cover all cases. An effective set of unit tests covers every possible condition for a given method, including bounds checks, null values, exceptions, and conditional logic.

- **Run without configuration**   Your unit tests should be easy to run (and rerun). They should not require setup or configuration. You do not want to define tests that require a specific environment every time you run your tests (or they will not be run). If setup is required, code that into a test-initialize script.

■ **Test a common application state**   Your unit tests should be run against a common, standard, good state. For example, if your application works with data, this data should be set to common state prior to the execution of each unit test. This ensures that one test is not causing an error in another test.

Lab: Define a Unit Testing Strategy

The best way to ensure your understanding of this material is to create an actual unit testing strategy. You can use this practice section as an aid to define a unit testing strategy for your organization or your next project.

▶ **Exercise 1: Document Your Unit Testing Strategy**

In this exercise, you will define and document a unit testing strategy. You will want to apply the guidance provided in this chapter to your real-world conditions. Each of the following steps represents a section that you should define for your strategy.

1. Determine where you intend unit tests to be stored and managed in your application. Document your reasoning relative to your specific project, process, or situation.

2. Define and document how you intend to create unit tests on your project. Consider the tradeoff between test-first development and the ability to generate tests from existing code.

3. Indicate what, in your application, will be unit tested. Set boundaries between the various elements of the application and unit tests. Define when you intend to use data-driven and ASP.NET unit tests.

4. Document the conditions you expect to see for each unit test in your application. You might also define the bounds for each data type (such as a date range) as an aid for developers.

5. Indicate an acceptable metric for unit test code coverage.

6. Consider creating a reference implementation of a set of unit tests for a given class. This reference implementation should follow your standards. It will serve as an example for developers when they implement their own tests.

7. Finally, present your strategy to your organization or project team. Get their feedback and understand their acceptance criteria for your strategy. This will not only refine your strategy but should also serve to solidify these concepts for you.

Lesson Summary

■ Unit tests are the responsibility of developers (not testers). Therefore, the unit testing strategy should come from the technical lead or a senior developer on the team. The strategy should be documented and reviewed by the team.

- An automated unit test is a piece of code you write that isolates a specific method or property in your application and executes it for a given condition. Your unit tests should not require configuration; they should be atomic in nature, and they should test a common application state. Your unit tests should examine all conditions for a given unit. This includes both success and error conditions. They should also include bounds checking on various parameters.

- You add unit tests to a test project in Visual Studio. You can create a single, centralized unit test project or solution. Alternatively, you can define a single unit test project per application project. Visual Studio also lets you automatically generate unit tests for your project. This is useful for existing code that has no unit tests already developed.

- Unit tests have their limits. They are best used for testing class libraries. They do not work well for ensuring the user interface, doing integration testing, testing an application for load, or for performance testing.

- You can bind a unit test to a database or data source. This is useful for calling the test for each item in the data source. In this way, you can feed the test with multiple sets of parameters.

- Visual Studio can provide you with statistics on what code was tested by your unit tests. These statistics are referred to as code coverage analysis. You can get a percentage of code that is covered and uncovered. You can also jump straight to uncovered code in the IDE.

Lesson Review

You can use the following questions to test your knowledge of the information in Lesson 1, "Creating a Unit Testing Strategy." The questions are also available on the companion CD if you prefer to review them in electronic form.

NOTE   Answers

Answers to these questions and explanations of why each answer choice is right or wrong are located in the "Answers" section at the end of the book.

---

1. You want to define a strategy that ensures that the entire set of unit tests for your application can be run as a group. What action should you take?
    - **A.** Define separate unit testing projects for each project in your application.
    - **B.** Create a single class file inside the App_Code directory. Mark the class file as a test class. Define all your tests within this class file.
    - **C.** Add a class to each project in your application. Mark each of these classes as a test class. Define the tests for the given project inside of each class file.
    - **D.** Create a single test project for your application. Add classes to this project. Mark each class as a test class.

2. Which of the following are characteristics of unit tests? (Choose all that apply.)
   A. A full set of unit tests results in the ability to do smoke (or regression) testing.
   B. Unit tests are useful for determining performance issues with your code.
   C. Unit tests help to document your code.
   D. Unit tests help to confirm the execution of your user interface.

3. As part of your unit testing strategy, you need to define the items that you intend to test using unit testing. Which of the following items are good candidates for testing with unit tests? (Choose all that apply.)
   A. A business object
   B. ASP.NET Web service
   C. Database access code
   D. Database table relationships

4. You have just delivered a new build of your application. Nearly all of the unit tests pass. You need to decide if the build is of a high enough quality to pass to the test team. What action should you take?
   A. Check the ratio of passing tests to failed tests. If this ratio is high, then pass the build to the test team.
   B. Check the ratio of code tested to total logic. If this ratio is high, then pass the build to the test team.
   C. Check the ratio of new code relative to existing code. If this ratio is low, then pass the build to the test team.
   D. Check the ratio of code churn relative to stabilized code. If this ratio is low, then pass the build to the test team.

5. You have a method that takes a date for a parameter. This method should work with all dates from January 2004 onward. You define a unit test that passes the dates January 1, 2004, and December 31, 2027, as parameters. This is an example of what type of test?
   A. Regression test
   B. Boundary check
   C. Manual unit test
   D. Code coverage analysis

Real World

Mike Snell

Early on in my career, I worked on a number of projects in which developers were responsible for communicating their level of unit testing. As you might imagine, there were mixed results. Project managers would always ask the developer if he or she had physically seen every line of code execute in the debugger. The answer was always "yes." The better project managers would also confirm the existence of at least some crude test harness to call the code.

Things invariably slipped through the cracks. Many times, these bugs ended up in production. The application would run along smoothly sometimes for weeks and then there would come a call. These calls always seemed to happen at night or on a Saturday. I personally debugged some of these items only to find some very simple, stupid mistake inside a conditional statement or error handler. I have even seen these errors surrounded by comments like, "The code should never reach this spot."

These errors were always easy to fix. The point is that they could have just as easily been avoided if the developer had executed those lines. Now, with code coverage analysis, I am able to make sure all lines of the application are touched by some test prior to the code reaching production.

Lesson 2: Evaluating the Integration, Stress, and Performance Test Strategies

Once you have completed your unit tests and are satisfied with your code coverage, it is time to turn the code over to the test team. At this point, the testers should verify that all the components work as a cohesive system, determine the amount of stress that can be applied to the system before it breaks, and measure the application's performance. These test types fall inside the domain of testers. However, given their proximity to the application, developers and architects should provide their input into these test plans. You should help define how these tests are created and what to expect in terms of results.

This lesson examines the input developers should provide to an application's testing strategy. First, take a look at how to aid with integration testing input. Then look at both stress testing and performance testing.

After this lesson, you will be able to:

- Define developer responsibilities relative to the integration testing strategy.
- Provide feedback and guidance concerning the appropriate stress levels for your application.
- Define key performance metrics that should be monitored during performance testing.
- Provide feedback on the test lab setup used for load testing your application.

Estimated lesson time: 25 minutes

Developer Responsibilities for Integration Testing

The primary goal of *integration testing* is to find and fix issues that are discovered when individual components are brought together to form a single, cohesive solution. Typically, each module or component is developed by one or more developers who write their component, unit test it, and rely on the overall application design to know they are building toward a cohesive application. It is only when their component is integrated with the other components that this design will be fully tested and confirmed.

Exam Tip

The exam focuses on the responsibility of the developer (and not the tester). You need to be aware of this delineation of roles and focus your study efforts proportionately. This means spending more time on unit testing. Be aware of developer inputs to load, performance, stress, and integration testing.

When to Perform Integration Testing

Integration testing happens after unit testing is considered complete or nearly complete. Many testing methodologies suggest that integration testing, like unit testing, should be a continuous process. Application components should be integrated as they are developed and unit tested. This is referred to as *continuous integration*.

An integration testing strategy that stresses continuous integration helps find bugs related to integration early in the software development life cycle. Integration tests found early in the process are easier (and cheaper) to fix. You invite big surprises into your project when you wait until the end to begin integration testing. These surprises cause schedule overruns and extra costs. In addition, with early testing, you are less likely to repeat the root causes that are behind the integration problems. All bugs, especially integration-related bugs, tend to cluster in specific areas of the application. They also tend to look alike. For example, if you find a bug related to calling a specific Web service, chances are good that this bug can be found repeatedly in the application—that is, unless this issue is found early and communicated to the development team. This allows the team to take corrective action and prevent repetition of the same issue. This has the effect of reducing costs and increasing overall quality.

NOTE   **Integration tests should always call real code (not stubs)**

A unit test may call a method stub (or a simple interface). This allows a developer to continue working on the code while another developer finishes the interface stub. This is acceptable for unit testing. However, integration tests should always call the real code being tested via integration.

Integration testing leads to system testing. These two types of tests are often combined as the same, or similar, tests. The difference is that with continuous integration, each block or module of the application gets added to the overall system test. In this way, you end up testing the system as you build it. You add new modules or components to the already-tested and verified system. Once you are finished coding the system, or code-complete, you should then have a full set of unit tests and a complete set of integration tests. These integration tests can be run as a group to verify the entire system (system testing).

IMPORTANT   **System test against a production environment**

Your final system test should be a comprehensive integration test that is performed in a testing environment that is identical to your production environment. In addition, once your code has been moved to the production environment, it is wise to perform this same test again (if possible) to ensure that the deployment was complete and successful.

> **Quick Check**
> 1. What is the definition and purpose of integration testing?
> 2. When should you perform integration testing?
>
> **Quick Check Answers**
> 1. Integration testing is the process of testing various application elements together as a single solution that performs a business function. The purpose of integration testing is to ensure that the individual units of an application work together to form a complete solution.
> 2. Integration testing should be done on a continuous basis. As units are made ready by developers, they should be integrated into the build and tested with the other application elements.

Black Box Testing

Integration testing is considered functional, or *black box*, testing. That is, testers write *test cases* that indicate a given input into the application. Based on this input, they make assumptions about the output of the application. The testers then execute these integration tests as a black box. That is, they do not care about what happens inside the box (the code); they simply care that they get the expected results based on the given input.

Developers typically help the test team understand the expected black box behavior of their code. They do so by reviewing the test cases and providing example input and output. As an example, a test case might indicate that if a user executes a credit card transaction that fails, the user should be visually notified of the failure. When a developer reviews this test case, he or she may add to the test case so that failed transactions get logged by the system. The tester may then add to the test case to verify this logging behavior.

NOTE White box vs. black box testing

White box testing refers to testing that works with the application's internals (or code). White box (or glass box) testing is typically done by developers using the IDE, debugger, and unit tests. Testers usually interact with the application through black box testing. They provide input to the box (through the application interfaces) and verify the output.

Defining an Integration Test Plan

The integration *test plan* is typically the responsibility of the test team. They work to understand the system as a sum of its constituent parts and then define test cases that will verify each of these parts as they are brought together to form progressively bigger portions of the overall application. A *test case* represents a series of steps that a tester can execute (through manual or automated testing) to verify the proper application response based on input. Test cases work to verify the integration of components as well as the requirements of the system.

Developers play a role in the creation of the integration test plan. Specifically, they should help verify the test cases. They should make sure that the test cases cover the many possible integration points, that they test the application on multiple levels, and that they consider all aspects of the application. Finally, developers should provide details on the expected metrics and outputs of the various test cases. The following checklist should be applied to the test cases during developer review.

- Verify that the test cases include scenarios that test application communications. This includes communication from the user interface to the server or Web services, communication from one application to another (application integration), communication between processes, database communication, and so on.

- Ensure that the test cases define a series of inputs to the application interfaces along with expected outputs. This includes inputs and expected results for the user interface, the public Web services, and any component or programming layers.

- Verify that expected performance levels relative to application output responses are set. This is not performance testing. Rather, it is meant to help testers understand when they encounter areas of the application that are not performing to anticipated metrics. These metrics might indicate a response time for a Web request or the amount of time it takes to receive confirmation of an order, for example.

- Check that the test cases will be run multiple times to verify that the results are always consistent. This helps test for reliability.

- Verify that the test cases define specific bounds testing relative to integration. The test cases should cover a common or normal scenario. However, they should also define inputs that are at or just outside the boundaries of the expected input. It has been proven that errors often happen at these boundary levels.

- Verify that the plan is to test the components in a simulated production environment. Most unit tests are executed on a developer's machine. An integration test should run the application on real servers that mimic the production environment.

NOTE Finding similar integration defects

Developers should work closely with the test team, especially when defects are found. When an integration issue is identified, developers can research a fix for the issue. They can also often search the rest of the code for similar defects. It is very likely that, if you find one integration defect, the same or very similar defect will be found in other places in the code.

Developer Responsibilities for Load, Stress, and Performance Testing

Load, stress, and performance testing are all interrelated. In fact, they are often all grouped together under the term *load testing*. This is because they each are meant to exercise a system through the simulation of user load. Stress and performance testing are derivatives of load testing. The goal of a load test is to ensure that your application behaves as required given the anticipated load. *Stress testing* tries to find the application's breaking point by applying additional load or stress until the application no longer behaves as intended. Performance, of course, is a key indicator in each of these tests. However, the primary goal of performance testing is to find the areas in the application that do not perform according to the required standards. This includes verifying your performance under normal load and during stress conditions.

The test team is responsible for conducting these tests. They define the application's test plan (including the load, stress, and performance test strategy) at the onset of the project. They then work to define test cases that simulate user interaction with the system. These test cases can be used to represent virtual users applying load to the system.

Developers and architects help review the load test strategy and provide proper guidance. Some of this guidance is provided during requirement definition and system specification. For example, developers should be involved with defining what is reasonable with respect to performance metrics for the application. Developers should also verify that the test plans realistically simulate the actual user load for the application.

Testers should begin executing load tests as soon as complete modules of the application are available. In a Web application, this usually means that a screen in the user interface is working as expected (connects to the middle tier, writes data to the database, and so on). This ensures continuous load testing as the application builds. The tests should be run in an environment that approximates the production infrastructure. The tests should again be performed as a group once the application reaches a release point such as beta release. Visual Studio 2005 Team Test lets you automate these tests so they can be easily run repeatedly as the application evolves.

Load Testing

The goal of load testing is to make sure your application works under the expected, concurrent user load. This expected load is typically defined at the beginning of the project. For example, your Web application might be required to support up to 100 concurrent users. The test team needs to verify that the code deployed into the environment meets this requirement.

Testers can create automated load tests for the application. They typically start this process by defining a Web test. A *Web test* is a recorded set of user requests to your application. A tester starts recording a Web test and then begins walking through the various screens that make up the application as if he or she was a user. This means executing predefined test cases. Once complete, he or she stops recording and is able to work with the requests that define the Web test.

Here's an example. Suppose a page in your application allows a user to view a product in your e-commerce catalog. The request might be sent to the Web page by appending the product's identification number to the query string in the URL. A tester might have recorded a single request to access a single product. However, the tester can bind that request to the many products in your catalog. He or she does so by adding a data source to the Web test. The tester then connects the query string parameter to a field in the data source and edits the .testrunconfig file to indicate that the request should be run once for every row in the database. This type of Web test helps verify what happens in the application when varied data is loaded. It also serves as a basis for defining load tests.

Load tests usually are built from one or more Web tests that represent the application's test cases. The load tests define which test cases will be examined, what data will be used for testing, and how the user load will be simulated. They simulate multiple users opening a connection to your server and making multiple HTTP requests. Developers should review the load tests and provide their feedback. When reviewing a load test, consider all of the following:

- Make sure the load tests use test cases that simulate user load—that is, they access the application through its intended user interfaces (and not through unit tests or otherwise). These test cases might be seeded with random data from a data source.

- The standard load test should be set to approximate the required number of concurrent users. It should not step up the user load. A stepped load adds progressively more users to the application over time. This is great for stress testing. However, the standard load test should verify that the application works with the required user load.

- Ensure that the test cases are distributed to various sections of the application based on real user behavior. For example, if your users log 20 calls to get one order, define a Web test for logging a call and another for taking an order. Then set the test distribution ratio of the log call test to 95 percent and set the take order distribution to 5 percent.

- Verify that the load tests assume a standard set of think times. *Think times* represent the time a user spends thinking between requests. You can use recorded think times or a standard set. However, you do not want to turn off think times because load tests will then not approximate real user load.

- It is important to distribute the load across the connection types that will be used by users accessing the application. For example, if 60 percent of your users are expected to access your application over a cable modem and 40 percent over 56k dial-up, indicate this mix.

- Make sure that validation rules and extractions are turned off for Web tests. These items do not represent actual application behavior. Instead, they are used during Web testing to check the application's response. They can artificially degrade your load test results. Therefore, they should be turned off by the load test.

NOTE **Use load tests for performance and stress testing**

Load tests can also be used to determine the performance and stress of the components that make up your application. You can do so by defining a load test using your unit tests (and not your Web tests). Unit tests can also be seeded with data. In this way, you can load test sections of code, such as your data-access routines, specifically.

Stress Testing

The goal of stress testing is to discover the breaking point of your application in its current environment. Load testing confirms that the application meets the required safe working load. Stress testing pushes the application beyond this safe load and determines where and when it might fall down.

NOTE **Stress testing for peak load**

Stress testing can also be used to make sure your application can perform at a peak load. This is typically set to 1.5 times the expected load. Therefore, if you expect to support up to 1,000 concurrent users, you should stress test for a peak load of 1,500 concurrent users. The application should not break under this peak load. It might behave slightly more poorly than expected, but it should continue to operate.

Stress testing should be performed by the test team. Load tests are used for this purpose. A tester may simply copy a load test and apply a different concurrent load to simulate additional stress. When you review the stress tests, follow the guidelines outlined in the load test section. In addition, developers should also consider how user load is stepped.

User load should be stepped up throughout the stress test. That is, the tests should start with a set of concurrent users. As time progresses, additional concurrent users should be added in steps. Each step should be run for a realistic duration (enough time for each user in the step to get through their activities at least once). Additional stress is applied to the application as load is stepped. It stands to reason that, at some point, the application will be stressed to its maximum capacity and will either break or begin to respond in unacceptable time frames. This breaking point may be defined as a combination of the number of rejected requests, the threshold for response times, a threshold for processor usage on the server, and so on.

Once you become aware of your application's stress levels, you can work to either modify the software or hardware to increase your capacity or simply publish these levels to the support team. The support team should then monitor the application to make sure that they take appropriate action if the load begins to trend up toward the breaking point.

Performance Testing

Performance testing is meant to verify that the application performs to the metrics defined during the requirements phase. For example, your application might be required to respond to all user requests in under four seconds. The performance testing can verify this metric and report on pages in the site that do not meet the requirement.

Testers execute the performance testing strategy. They do so again through the load tests. There are typically three levels of performance testing: single user performance, performance under normal load, and performance at peak stress points. The first step allows the tester to ensure that the application behaves correctly for an individual user. Testers should expect this test to have the best performance. They then must verify that the application still performs as expected under normal load conditions. Finally, they should record how the application performs under a spike in load (usually 1.5 times the normal load). It might be acceptable to be 20 percent outside the bounds of the expected performance metrics under these peak conditions.

Developers should help the testers understand which performance indicators to monitor and what is the acceptable range of results. In most Web applications, you will want to monitor the number of requests per second, the average response time, and the maximum response time. Testers should also look at the individual pages in the test to find any that do not perform as required.

NOTE   **Define notification thresholds**

The Visual Studio tools allow a tester to define thresholds and receive warnings and errors when the application nears or surpasses these thresholds. This can save testers the eyestrain of looking over the many performance indicators on the output graphs.

Quick Check

- Explain the differences between load, stress, and performance testing.

Quick Check Answer

- Load testing verifies that an application works as expected based on a target, concurrent user load pattern. Stress testing increases user load to find where, when, and how an application breaks under extreme stress. Performance testing verifies performance metrics for the application in terms of execution and response times.

Evaluate the Test Lab Hardware and Software

When executing your load, stress, and performance tests, it is important to configure a proper testing lab so you don't interrupt normal business and to ensure the validity of your tests. Ideally, your tests should be executed on a quit network and on hardware identical to the production environment. A *quit network* is one that is dedicated to the test lab only. Business users don't rely on it, nor does it transmit their traffic (and, thus, potentially skew your test results). This lab needs to be instrumented to output the proper metrics. You also need a machine to execute the tests and a machine to capture and report on the collected data.

The test lab setup should be the responsibility of the infrastructure team. Both the test team and the developers should provide input into the setup of this test lab. You should have a general understanding of how this lab should be set up so that you can provide proper feedback into the plan.

Agents, Clients, Servers, and Controllers

A load test that requires the simulation of a large number of concurrent users requires a more complex setup. This is generally the case for Web-based applications. You can use Visual Studio Team Test to accomplish the setup and execution of large load scenarios.

In these scenarios, there are four types of machines: clients, servers, agents, and a controller. These items are collectively known as the *rig* or *test rig*. You set up this rig in the test environment and use it to manage the load testing of your application. The following provides details on each of the machine types in the rig:

- **Clients** Represent the machine of one or more testers. The client is used by testers to create and edit tests and view published test results.
- **Servers** Represent the test environment in which your application is deployed. This environment might include one or more Web servers, a database server, a load balancer, and so on.
- **Agents** Computers that run your tests. Agents listen for commands from the controller. They then execute the intended test and pass their results back to the controller. Each agent can have only one controller at a given time. Agents execute load tests on multiple threads concurrently. Each thread represents a user. In addition, a typical load test will use multiple agents.
- **The controller** A single, central computer that administers the agents and collects their results. The test lab typically has one controller. The controller passes the test to the agents for execution. It then tells them when to start and stop. The controller can apply a weight to various agents to help distribute the load. Agents with more horsepower should have a higher weight because they can handle more load.

Test Lab Data

Most Web sites these days connect to one or more data sources. It is important for you to consider these data sources when testing your application. For example, your performance results will vary if you run your tests against a test database with just a few thousand rows when you expect millions of rows in production. It is, therefore, imperative that you test your application using a realistic version of your production data. This can present a challenge to the test team. Consider all of the following related to test lab data when reviewing the test lab setup:

- Tests should be run against a test version of the database. They should not be run against your production database servers.

- Your test data should be of the same nature and size as the data in your production server. This includes tables, their relationships, their indexes, and their data. If, for example, you have a table with millions of rows, it is important to test your application against a similar table with the same number of rows.

- You should test a steady state of the database. This ensures that tests are testing against a stationary target. They may run and change this steady state, but when they are rerun, they should be rerun against the initial state of the database. This also helps you compare results between tests.

- You should create an automated means to initialize your test database. Your tests should be easily executed and reexecuted. Having this automation ensures that tests can easily set up and reinitialize the database as required.

- Test data typically should not be an exact copy of your production data. Most databases store some sort of personal or confidential data such as credit card information, user names and addresses, social security numbers, and so on. Write a data extraction algorithm that either replaces this data with scrambled versions or removes that data. There are tools available that can help you with this process.

Lab: Create a Test Plan

Testers are responsible for creating the test plan. However, if you really want to understand what should go into the test plan, it can be beneficial to create one yourself. Alternatively, you can work with the test manager on your team to create a test plan. You can use this lab section as an aid to define a test plan that takes into account the many black box tests: integration, Web, load, stress, and performance.

▶ Exercise 1: Define Your Project's Test Plan

In this exercise, you will define and document a black box test plan. You will want to apply the guidance provided in this chapter to an actual project with which you are working. Each of the following steps represents an action you should take to define the test plan.

1. Determine how your project will be integration tested. Make sure you consider testing the communication between components and any third-party systems. Also, define a plan that includes continuous integration. This plan should define a process by which developers pass their complete, unit-tested components to the test team on a daily basis.

2. Help write one or more test cases. When writing a test case, consider the requirements of the application. If you have previously defined use cases (or user scenarios), these will help greatly. With a user scenario, you can define a test that takes a common path

through the system to enable a common user activity. You then define the input and expected output from executing the test. The test cases should also define alternate scenarios such as those that should generate errors.

3. Determine and document the expected load for the application in terms of concurrent users. If your application typically has peak load times, use the figure that represents the concurrent users that you expect during these spikes.

4. Define a load test plan for the application. This load test plan should indicate test case, think time, network, and browser distributions. These distributions should simulate the anticipated load.

5. Define a stress test plan that uses the load tests to determine a breaking point in your application. Define a stepped user load that can be applied to the application in chunks of time. You should also define a threshold by which you determine the application to be broken (for instance, the average page response time exceeds seven seconds).

6. Define an acceptable set of performance metrics for the application under load. For example, you might indicate that most page requests return in under four seconds. You might also point out the transactions in the system that are allowed to take a little longer, such as processing an order or retrieving a report.

7. Define the test lab that should be used for load testing. This lab should identify hardware that approximates production. In addition, plan for a dedicated machine as a test controller. Finally, plan to install test agents on multiple computers that can be used to simulate load.

8. Present the test plan to the project team. Get their feedback on your testing strategy. Presenting the strategy will really help to solidify these concepts in your mind.

Lesson Summary

- Integration, load, stress, and performance tests are the responsibility of the test team. Developers should understand how these tests are performed and should be expected to provide feedback on and input into the tests.

- Integration tests verify that the application's parts work together as a cohesive solution. Load testing verifies that the application works as expected when the target concurrent user load is applied. Stress testing uses the load tests to find the application's breaking point in terms of concurrent users. Performance tests are used to find any performance problems with the application under the expected load.

- Integration, load, stress, and performance tests should be done continuously throughout the project as modules become available. This reduces costs and surprises that cause schedule overruns.

- Integration, load, stress, and performance tests are built from the test cases. The full set of integration tests often suffices to form the final system test.

- Integration, load, stress, and performance tests are all examples of black box testing. Test cases are run and the output is verified. Testers do not look inside the application (the box).

- Integration, load, stress, and performance tests should be performed in a test environment that approximates the production environment. They should also be done on a quit network, using hardware that simulates the production environment.

Lesson Review

You can use the following questions to test your knowledge of the information in Lesson 2, "Evaluating the Integration, Stress, and Performance Test Strategies." The questions are also available on the companion CD if you prefer to review them in electronic form.

NOTE   Answers

Answers to these questions and explanations of why each answer choice is right or wrong are located in the "Answers" section at the end of the book.

---

1. You want to determine the number of simultaneous users your Web site can support before it becomes unusable. This is an example of what type of testing?
    - A. Web testing
    - B. Load testing
    - C. Performance testing
    - D. Stress testing

2. Which of the following are true statements about integration testing? (Choose all that apply.)
    - A. Integration tests, like unit tests, are white box tests and, thus, the responsibility of developers.
    - B. Integration tests should define a series of inputs and expected outputs for each test case.
    - C. Testers are advised to wait until all code for the application is complete before executing integration testing. This ensures that the entire system can be integration tested as a unit.
    - D. Each integration test should succeed multiple times before the test is considered as passed.

3. You determine that your application must support approximately 1,000 concurrent users. This user base primarily accesses your application via a Microsoft Internet Explorer browser. Approximately 800 of the users come in through the local area network (LAN) and 200 through a dial-up network. In addition, you process one order for

every 10 shoppers. Which of the following represents how you should configure your load test? (Choose all that apply.)

A. Define a load test that steps users in increments of 100 to a maximum of 1,500 users (or 1.5 times your expected load).

B. Set your network distribution to 80 percent LAN and 20 percent dial-up.

C. Create two Web tests, one for processing orders and one that represents a shopper. Configure your load test distribution to be 90 percent for the shopper test and 10 percent for the load test.

D. Create one Web test that mimics a shopper browsing for 10 products before placing an order. Configure your load test to use this Web test.

4. Your testers plan to conduct performance testing of your Web application. They wish to make sure that each of the Web pages in the site returns with the expected performance metrics. Which performance indicator should be monitored?

A. Web server processor use

B. Web server memory use

C. Number of requests per second

D. Request response time

5. Your test lab includes clients, servers, agents, and a controller. Which of the following are the responsibility of the test controller? (Choose all that apply.)

A. The test controller executes multiple tests on multiple threads.

B. The test controller provides test data to agents.

C. Agents provide performance data to the test controller.

D. Testers use the test controller to author and edit tests.

Chapter Review

To further practice and reinforce the skills you learned in this chapter, you can complete the following tasks:

- Review the chapter summary.
- Review the list of key terms introduced in this chapter.
- Complete the case scenario. This scenario sets up real-world situations involving the topics of this chapter and asks you to create a solution.
- Complete the suggested practices.
- Take a practice test.

Chapter Summary

- Developers create unit tests to automate the testing of an isolated unit (method or property) in an application. Good unit tests should not require configuration; they should be atomic in nature; they should test a common application state; and they should test all method conditions, including errors, null values, and boundary checks. You can verify the percentage of code that is covered by your unit tests. Target at least 70 percent coverage for your unit tests.
- Integration, Web, load, stress, and performance testing are all black box tests performed by the test team. Developers need to be aware of how these tests should be performed, so they can provide feedback on testing their code to the test team. Integration tests verify that components work together to create a complete solution. Load tests are used to verify the application's performance under load. You can use load tests to stress test and performance test your application.

Key Terms

Do you know what these key terms mean? You can check your answers by looking up the terms in the glossary at the end of the book.

- agent
- black box testing
- bounds check
- code coverage
- continuous integration
- controller
- integration test
- load test

- performance test
- quit network
- rig
- stress test
- test case
- test-driven development
- test plan
- think times
- unit test
- Web test
- white box testing

Case Scenario

In the following case scenario, you will apply what you've learned about definining and evaluating a testing strategy. You can find answers to these questions in the "Answers" section at the end of this book.

Case Scenario: Evaluating a Testing Strategy

You have been assigned the lead developer for your company's new Web-based employee performance portal. Your company sells canned goods to supermarkets. This application will provide employees and managers scorecard information on key employee performance metrics. Employees will use the application to understand better their performance relative to their goals. Managers will use the application to assess overall employee performance and to set individual goals. The executive management team will look at employee performance by product line, department, division, and as a summary of the company's overall well-being.

Interviews

You attend a meeting to discuss testing scenarios with the project stakeholders. This meeting is facilitated by the test manager. The following is a list of the project stakeholders interviewed and their statements.

- **IT Manager**   "We will need to create separate components for extracting data from multiple data sources. Some of the data will come from our time-tracking system, some from the production management system, some from our quality analysis application, and some from the job scheduling application. Some of these components are already available as Web services; others will have to be created as file-based extracts."

"The final application will be using hundreds of thousands of rows—maybe millions. This data needs to be aggregated for the reports, but users should still be able to drill into it."

- **Project Manager** "We need to report on the quality of the application in the weekly reports throughout the development phase. We need to report on which tests are passing and which are failing."

- **Development Manager** "The development team will be made up of developers from various departments and groups. Therefore, each developer will work on his or her piece of the system in isolation. These pieces will need to be integrated when they are completed."

  "The architect has already stubbed out the integration interfaces. This will allow the developers to code against these dummy interfaces and get a response."

  "It would be nice if developers were forced to have 75 percent or greater code coverage for their unit tests prior to checking in their code."

- **Department Manager** "Supervisors must be able to enter employee goals and edit actual employee performance indicators. These are busy people. The site should allow them to get in and enter this data with response times under three seconds."

  "There are approximately 25 department managers, and each manages up to 10 supervisors. Each supervisor has up to 10 direct reports. These employees won't access the application directly. Instead, they will rely on the posted reports around the work place."

  "We have over 20 vice presidents who will be looking at this report on a weekly basis. Some will add it to their corporate dashboards. They need very fast, very accurate information."

- **Test Manager** "We are able to assign only one full-time resource to help test the project. This resource has been working with the business analysts to define test cases for the application. In addition, this resource was recently given Team Test training."

- **Application Support Manager** "Right now, we get a lot of support calls on Monday mornings when the other report updates come out. These support calls indicate a major slowdown in all network traffic. I am sure that management will want to see this data first thing Monday as well."

  "We also have users coming in from home. Some of these users have a dial-up connection, some have digital subscriber lines (DSL), and some have cable modems. I would say that 95 percent of the users are on the LAN and 5 percent are connected via other means."

Test Plan

After the test planning meeting, the test manager sends you a draft copy of the test plan. You are supposed to provide your input and feedback. The following is a high-level overview (or summary) of the test plan's content:

- **Unit testing** Each developer will be responsible for unit testing his or her code. We will ask developers in the weekly status meeting what percentage of their code is covered by unit tests. We plan to create a single, central project for managing developer unit tests.

- **Integration testing**   We will take advantage of the use cases to define our test cases for integration. These use cases cover how a user successfully interacts with the application. An integration test should be considered successful if no error conditions are thrown.
- **Web testing**   The test team will create a single Web test that covers a manager entering employee goals as well as each role accessing his or her versions of the report and then drilling into these reports. We will then bind this Web test to the data table that represents users and report types and a set of employees and goal data.
- **Load testing**   We will create a load test that runs a steady load of users for one hour. We will set the networking of these users to the LAN. We will use standard think times.
- **Stress testing**   The application will be stress tested using the load test defined in the load test plan. The stress test will be set to run overnight for four hours.
- **Performance testing**   We intend to verify that users can enter employee goals and metric data with request and response times under three seconds. To verify this information, we intend to monitor the average response time and the response time for individual requests on specific pages. We will use the standard Web test to verify this information.
- **Test lab**   We intend to build the test lab on a quit network. We are going to use the test team's PC for running test agents. These agents should run only early in the morning, at lunch, or at night. We will put the test controller on a separate PC. We will build out the database schema on a test database server. We will not be able to use real data until nearly the end of the project. Therefore, the tester will add at least 20 rows of data to each table. Once this initial data is loaded into the database, the testers and developers will be able to manipulate as they need to.

Questions

1. What changes would you suggest to the unit test plan?
2. How many concurrent users should the test team target for load testing? For stress testing?
3. What are the advantages and disadvantages of the tester defining a single Web test for the application?
4. How should the load test strategy be modified to better test the actual way in which users will use the application?
5. What thresholds should you suggest for testers when monitoring the server during load testing?
6. What improvements would you suggest relative to the integration test plan?
7. How would you suggest improving the test lab definition to simulate your actual environment better?

Suggested Practices

To help you successfully master the exam objectives presented in this chapter, complete the following tasks.

Creating a Unit Testing Strategy

If you have never written unit tests before, you should execute the tasks in the first practice. This will help you better master this objective. If you have spent some time writing unit tests but want to make sure you understand them, try Practice 2. If you have the option to demonstrate unit testing to another developer, you should be focusing on this objective when it comes to the test.

- **Practice 1**   Find some old code. You can use any code whose language you are familiar with. The important thing is that you are not currently familiar with this code. Examine the methods in the code. Try to design unit tests as pseudocode for these old methods. Think about what tests you will want to create and how you will segment these tests.
- **Practice 2**   Convince a manager or another team member to consider unit testing. He or she will have questions and wonder why unit testing is important. Sometimes, explaining this to another person out loud helps you solidify these concepts in your mind. The adage, "If you want to really learn something, try teaching it to someone else" applies here.

Evaluation Integration, Stress, and Performance Testing Strategies

Most developers do not spend a lot of time testing. However, to become a professional developer, it is important that you understand this key aspect of the software development life cycle. The following tasks will help you master this objective.

- **Practice 1**   Spend an hour with a tester for your application. Watch him or her work; understand his or her process. This can help you understand better how to deliver input into the testing of your code.
- **Practice 2**   Create a set of Web tests for your application, using Visual Studio 2005 Team Test. (You can download a trial version from the Microsoft Download Center if you do not own it. You can also download Team Test demos.)
- **Practice 3**   Use the Web tests you created during Practice 2 to define load, stress, and performance tests. Evaluate the results. Watch the tests perform against your application.

Take a Practice Test

The practice tests on this book's companion CD offer many options. For example, you can test yourself on just one exam objective, or you can test yourself on all the 70-547 certification exam content. You can set up the test so that it closely simulates the experience of taking a certification exam, or you can set it up in study mode so that you can look at the correct answers and explanations after you answer each question.

MORE INFO   Practice tests

For details about all the practice test options available, see the "How to Use the Practice Tests" section in this book's Introduction.

Chapter 15
Creating Development Tests

Developers are an integral part of the testing process, although they might not always agree on this point. The quality of the product that a developer delivers to the test team has a direct, positive impact on overall quality, schedule, and cost. A better product equates to less rework, fewer builds, and reduced verification of rework. In addition, it is often much more difficult and costly for a tester to find a bug in your code than it is for you to root it out during development. This is because the development process (and experience) is unique to the developer; no one will ever be as close to the operation of the code as the original developer during the initial development. It is for this reason that developers are perceived as being so close to the code that, given the proper training and tools, they should be able to squash the vast majority of bugs before (or as) they happen. Therefore, developers are, and for the foreseeable future will be, given their fair share of the testing process—whether they want it or not.

This chapter is the second and final chapter on testing and stabilizing an application. The first, Chapter 14, "Define and Evaluate a Testing Strategy," dealt primarily with the creation and analysis of testing strategies and plans. This chapter covers the tasks that developers, not testers, undertake to create and perform development-specific tests. You will first examine how you design and implement good unit testing. You will then take a look at the process of doing a code review. Next, you will walk through how to perform integration testing of components. Finally, you will end the chapter by looking at how you should approach troubleshooting, evaluating, and fixing bugs in your application.

Each of these tasks—creating unit tests, carrying out code reviews, performing integration testing, and troubleshooting bugs—is usually the responsibility of the professional developer. You are certain to deliver higher-quality code once you have a better understanding of how you can perform these tasks in your everyday development work. Higher-quality code translates into higher-quality software, reduced cost, and greater success—both for the project and for you as a developer.

Exam objectives in this chapter:
- Design a unit test.
  - ❏ Describe the testing scenarios.
  - ❏ Decide coverage requirements.
  - ❏ Evaluate when to use boundary condition testing.
  - ❏ Decide the type of assertions to conduct.

- Perform integration testing.
    - ❏ Determine if the component works as intended in the target environment.
    - ❏ Identify component interactions and dependencies.
    - ❏ Verify results.
- Resolve a bug.
    - ❏ Investigate a reported bug.
    - ❏ Reproduce a bug.
    - ❏ Evaluate the affect of the bug and the associated cost and timeline for fixing the bug.
    - ❏ Fix a bug.

Lessons in this chapter:

Before You Begin

To complete the lessons in this chapter, you should be familiar with developing Web-based applications with Microsoft Visual Studio 2005 using Microsoft Visual Basic or C#. In addition, you should be comfortable with all of the following tasks:

- Creating an ASP.NET Web page and working with the ASP.NET controls
- Using object-oriented development concepts
- Reading and working with class diagrams
- Developing a business object (class) that contains domain-specific properties and methods
- Working with attributes in your development
- Working with the unit testing framework in Visual Studio 2005 Team Edition to write and execute tests

---

IMPORTANT   To complete the practice exercises for Lesson 1, you will need to have Microsoft Visual Studio 2005 Team Edition for Software Developers installed on your computer. This is available as part of Visual Studio 2005 Team Suite. You can download a free 180-day trial version of Visual Studio 2005 Team Suite from *http://www.microsoft.com/downloads/details.aspx?FamilyId=5677DDC4-5035-401F-95C3-CC6F46F6D8F7&displaylang=en*. You will need to uninstall Visual Studio 2005 Professional to install Visual Studio Team Suite on the same computer.

Real World

Mike Snell

I have heard the statements, "Developers should not test their own code," and "Developers do not make good testers," many times throughout my career. In fact, this seems to be generally accepted as software development wisdom or fact. I admit there can be some truth to these statements. I am sure they have their origins in projects that lacked dedicated testing personnel and tools. I can certainly sympathize with that. However, I have often seen these statements used as excuses for delivering bad code or for not meeting a schedule.

I recall challenging a developer on just what he delivered to the test team, only to be given one of these apologies. It seemed that the developer was under the impression that quality was someone else's job; he was paid to create.

This is a very shortsighted view of things. Quality is noticed and rewarded. If you pass off the responsibility of quality to someone else, you will be noticed for all the wrong reasons. Indeed, many developers might not make good testers; however, they must understand how to deliver quality. They must incorporate some level of testing into their coding process. Thankfully, these days, it seems that most developers understand this fact. Or, perhaps I have simply surrounded myself with—that is, hired—this type of developer.

Lesson 1: Creating Effective Unit Tests

The unit test framework built into Visual Studio 2005 Team Edition enables you to define tests for your code as you write your application (or before you build it, in the case of the test-driven approach). The namespace *Microsoft.VisualStudio.TestTools.UnitTesting* provides the classes and features that make this possible. This lesson examines those features. It starts by reviewing the basic structure of a unit test. You will then look at some best practices for creating a unit test using test cases, requirements, and the unit test plan. (See Chapter 14 for more details on unit test plans.) You will also examine the developer's role in integration testing. You will finish the lesson by walking through a detailed lab in which you create a set of unit tests and verify key integration points for your code.

> **After this lesson, you will be able to:**
> - Understand how to read a use case to write better test cases.
> - Understand the elements of a test case and why test cases help developers.
> - Review and refine your unit tests based on the unit test plan and the test cases.
> - Determine which unit test assertions to make.
> - Write an effective set of unit tests for key methods in your application.
> - Understand the developer's role with regard to integration testing.
>
> **Estimated lesson time: 60 minutes**

The Basic Structure of a Unit Test

It makes sense to start by looking at an existing simple unit test. This will help you recall the makeup and structure of a unit test. Recall that a unit test is code that you write to call the methods and properties of your application. Inside the unit test, you first make a call to a method or property; you then execute a number of assertions to confirm the results of your call. For example, you might assert that the return value of a given method is true based on the parameters you pass into the method. If this assertion fails, the unit test fails. Let's examine how this example looks as code.

A Sample Application

In this chapter, you will create an application that enables travelers to book guide service for their vacation. Call this application *The Booking Manager*. It will help you illustrate your testing examples. The sample application has a few straightforward classes that make up the domain model. Figure 15-1 illustrates these classes. The principal class here is *Booking*. It represents a reservation for a guided trip or excursion. Notice that this class exposes the customer who is doing the booking as well as the guide that is being booked.

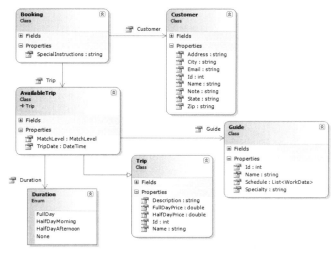

Figure 15-1   The sample business objects

Now that you have established the domain model, you must create some actions to support customers booking their guide services. These actions will be contained in a separate, static class called *BookingMethods*. Figure 15-2 shows this class and its methods. You have defined methods for both booking and retrieving the details of a given trip, and created a few methods that allow customers to check the availability of either a date they are considering or the availability of a certain guide. Again, you will use these methods and the domain model to illustrate example tests throughout this chapter.

Figure 15-2   The *BookingMethods* class

A Sample Unit Test

Let's start by looking at a simple example. This will help you recall the basic structure of unit tests. In this example, you are testing the *GetBooking* method of the *BookingMethods* class. The following code shows your example test.

```
' VB
<TestMethod()> _
Public Sub GetBookingTest()
  Dim bookingId As Integer = 987456
  Dim target As Booking = BookingMethods.GetBooking(bookingId)
  Assert.AreEqual(target.Id, bookingId)
End Sub
```

```
// C#
[TestMethod()]
public void GetBookingTest() {
  int bookingId = 987456;
  Booking target = BookingMethods.GetBooking(bookingId);
  Assert.AreEqual(bookingId, target.Id);
}
```

Notice that the test is decorated with the *TestMethod* attribute class. This indicates to the unit test framework that this method is a test, and it should be executed during a test run. Inside the actual test, you simply retrieve a known booking. You then use the *Assert* class to make sure the *Booking* instance that is returned is what you requested. If this assertion and the test method succeed, the test succeeds. If anything fails, the test is considered failed. Of course, this is a basic example. You might add a few more assertions to round out the test. You might also create a few additional tests for the *GetBooking* method. However, you should now have a basic review of a unit test. You will build on this in the coming sections as you examine a few approaches to writing more effective unit tests.

A Primer on the Unit Test Framework

The classes and methods in the unit test framework can be found in the *Microsoft.VisualStudio.TestTools.UnitTesting* namespace. This includes key attribute classes that are used to decorate classes and methods for execution by the framework. Table 15-1 lists the common attribute classes you need for unit testing.

Table 15-1   Attribute Classes in the *UnitTesting* Namespace

Attribute Class	Description
TestClass	Use this class to decorate an entire class as containing unit tests.
TestMethod	Use this class to indicate that a given method is a unit test. A test method must not return a value and cannot take parameters. However, you may bind data to a test method.

Table 15-1 Attribute Classes in the *UnitTesting* Namespace

Attribute Class	Description
TestInitialize	Use this class to indicate that the decorated method should be run by the framework prior to each unit test. This is useful if you need to reset the database between each test, for instance.
TestCleanup	Use this class to indicate that the decorated method should be run after each test.
ClassInitialize	Use this class to indicate that the decorated method should be run once prior to running any tests.
ClassCleanup	Use this class to indicate that the decorated method should be run once after all tests have been executed.
ExpectedException	Use this class to indicate that the decorated method should expect a certain exception as the result.

The *Assert* class inside the *UnitTesting* namespace is another class that is used in nearly all your unit tests. This class contains a number of methods that enable you to evaluate given conditions for true and false values. If the result of any assertion in your test is false, your unit test is considered to have failed. Table 15-2 lists the key assertion methods, which are all static, for unit testing.

Table 15-2 Assertion Methods of the *Assert* Class

Attribute Class	Description
AreEqual / AreNotEqual	Tests whether two values are equal to one another
AreSame / AreNotSame	Tests whether two objects are the same object
IsInstanceOfType / IsNotInstanceOfType	Tests whether an object is of a specified type (or class)
IsNull / IsNotNull	Tests whether an object contains a null reference
IsTrue / IsFalse	Tests whether a condition is true

Create Test Cases

Your unit tests will be more effective at finding issues with your code if they are thought out and planned in the context of actual requirements and usage scenarios. In Chapter 14, you worked to define the unit test strategy. It is helpful to think of the unit testing strategy as the guideline for how your company writes unit tests. What is not defined by this guideline is a method for ensuring that your unit tests cover the actual usage patterns of the application. That is the domain of the test case. In this chapter, you will look at creating effective unit tests based both on that strategy and on the requirements of the application. This is accomplished by writing test cases that help drive effective unit tests.

Determine Methods and Properties That Warrant More Testing

Most developers create a set of unit tests for each method and property in their application. This task is made easy by the Generate Unit Test feature of Visual Studio 2005. With this feature, you can quickly set up tests to make sure that in your property, the "gets" and "sets" methods operate correctly. You also get a one-for-one set of test methods to application methods. This offers a simple, straightforward approach to creating unit tests. It ensures that most of your code is run, creates a good regression (or smoke) test, and helps you meet your code-coverage requirements.

However, every application has a set of methods that really defines the functionality of the application. These principal methods typically result in the most bugs, the highest percentage of coding effort, and the most reworking. Therefore, it is important to identify them and plan additional testing around them. In addition, you need to understand how other developers might use them. You also need to explore how users will work with them to accomplish their tasks. This additional planning, focused on a key set of methods, will result in a big benefit to the overall quality of the application.

Thankfully, these methods are typically easy to recognize in your application. They are usually the methods that do the principal work of the application, such as executing transactions and saving data. The following list presents an ordered overview of which methods to look for when identifying principal methods that require additional unit test focus (ordered from highest importance to lowest).

1. Methods that execute transactions on behalf of the user or the system. These methods often have the most business logic built into them and can therefore be very complex. Some examples are methods that update inventory, process an order, and debit a credit card.

2. Methods that save or update data. Examples are methods that save a customer's profile or update product information in your system. Again, these methods are usually full of business logic.

3. Methods that check, verify, and validate data. Often this logic is embedded in the methods mentioned previously. However, it is sometimes pulled out to allow many methods to access the same set of checks. Examples might be verifying a customer's credit limit or checking inventory on hand.

4. Methods that delete data or cancel a transaction. Examples are deleting a customer's shipping address or canceling his or her order.

5. Methods that execute a search-and-retrieve-data function. These methods have less business logic but can require special attention to make sure that the right data is refined based on many, often varied, parameters. Some examples are methods that retrieve orders based on a set of criteria or find a set of customers with similar buying behaviors.

6. Other methods that retrieve data based on a set of parameters. Some examples are methods that get a customer's order, find his or her profile, or return his or her transaction history.

7. Methods that set and get specific properties or methods that do very simple tasks. These are less critical than those previously mentioned. Some examples are methods that set a customer's name, update his or her password, or calculate the tax on a given order.

You can use this list to help score the methods in your application. Methods that fall in the top three or four categories should be identified and targeted for additional unit testing based on usage scenarios.

For example, if you were to apply this list to the *BookingManager* class in the example in Figure 15-2, you should be able to identify the methods that require the most focus in terms of developing unit test cases. The methods would be categorized as follows (parentheses indicate the category number from the previous list): *BookTrip* (1), *CheckDateAvailability* (3), *CheckGuideAvailability* (3), *CancelTrip* (4), *GetBooking* (6), *GetBookings* (6), *GetCustomer* (6). From this information, you can then determine that *BookTrip*, *CheckDateAvailability*, and *CheckGuideAvailability* warrant additional focus in terms of unit testing and test case development. The other methods should still be tested. However, the unit tests to do so will most likely be straightforward and should not require as much attention. Using this method allows you to concentrate your efforts where they will generate the most results.

Understand How Your Code Will Be Consumed

In deciding how to develop test cases for your unit tests, you also need to consider the many ways in which other developers might consume your code. For example, you might be writing a library or base class that other users will rely on for their development. You might also be writing methods that will be called by other components out-of-process or over the Web. You must understand these and similar cases so that you can factor them into your test cases and thereby add tests to ensure functionality under these conditions.

Review or Create Use Case Scenarios

Other inputs into your test case are the use cases or user scenarios. A *use case* is a description of tasks centered on a common user goal. The use cases and related requirements directly influence the code you write. Use cases are often developed to support the requirements before code is written. They are typically created by a business analyst and reviewed by the user community or the community's representatives. An application designer or architect then works with this information to design the system. Developers then code to this design.

It is important for your unit testing to loop back to the original set of user scenarios to make sure the code meets the goals set forth by the user community. In addition, these use cases often describe how a bit of code will be used and therefore tested. You can often drive your test cases directly from the use cases.

A Sample Use Case Scenario

Let's take a look at a use case to help you better understand how use cases can provide input into your test cases. In your Booking Manager application, there is a use case that defines a standard user scenario for booking an excursion. This use case might look like the following.

1. User navigates to the home page of the resort's Web site.
2. User logs on to the site as a registered customer. (See Logon use case.)
3. Registered customer selects the option to "Book a Guided Excursion."
4. System presents a list of trip types and related pricing to the registered customer. Trip types might include fishing, kayaking, hiking, snorkeling, rafting, and bird-watching.
5. System asks the registered customer to select a date for his or her guided excursion, along with his or her duration preference.
6. Registered customer selects an excursion type, duration, and potential date for the trip. Once complete, the registered customer selects the Check Availability option.
7. System searches the guide schedules for guides that are available for the given trip type, duration, and date combination. System displays matching combinations as well as alternate options, such as different duration or date, for the same trip type to the registered customer.
8. Registered customer reviews the information and selects a trip.
9. Registered customer indicates he or she would like to book the trip.
10. System asks the user to make a deposit to reserve the booking.
11. Registered customer enters payment details for the deposit and indicates to the system to finish the booking.
12. System reserves the excursion (guide, duration, date) for the registered customer.

By examining this use case, you can determine just how users will be working with your code. This will give you a better understanding of how you should approach defining your test cases and related unit tests. For example, you can see from this use case that users might execute a number of varied checks against trip availability prior to selecting their trip. For this reason, you might create a unit test for checking trip availability and then decide to bind this unit test to a series of data that represents a number of potential date, duration, and trip-type combinations. In addition, you want to write test cases that verify searching for trips and booking them according to this use case. You will look at writing the test cases in a moment.

Edge Cases

A good use case defines the standard path to the common user goal. It then defines a number of alternate paths or what are commonly called *edge cases*. Edge cases are alternate paths that users might take to reach the same goal, tasks they might perform that are out of the ordinary success path, options they might have, and so on. A good use case writer (and a good tester, coincidentally) knows how to look for and find edge cases. It is here, within these edge cases, where your unit tests can really benefit. The edge cases will define additional tests you might not have considered. Let's look at an example.

In the previous use case, a user has searched for available trips and then selected a trip to book. However, it is very possible that during the time it takes to book the trip, a different customer has already reserved it. The use case should account for this alternative path. Typically, alternate use cases might look like the following examples, which refer back to the preceding use case example steps.

▶ **Alternate Case: Selected Trip Already Booked**

1. Use case follows the standard path through to step 11 from the preceding sample use case list.

2. System verifies trip availability prior to executing the booking.

3. If the trip is no longer available, the system cancels the transaction. (No deposit should be made, and no guide should be scheduled.)

4. System does another search for the user, as indicated in step 7 of the preceding use case list.

5. System indicates to the user that the trip is no longer available and presents the user with additional options (search results). The use case then continues with the steps following step 7.

You can see that this alternate path is a good edge case to think about as a developer and as a tester. A developer wants to plan for this occurrence; a tester wants to confirm how the system will react under this edge case. If one or both don't do their jobs, it will be the user who eventually discovers the consequences of a double booking. Therefore, you will want to be sure to write a unit test that simulates this edge case to confirm that you have accounted for it.

Let's look at another alternate case. This edge case examines what should happen if the system fails to finish the booking between steps 11 and 12. Recall that the user was asked for a deposit. You want to make sure that the deposit is transactional; that is, it should go through only if the booking succeeds. The same is true for the booking: It should succeed only if the deposit succeeds. Imagine that, as in most systems, the deposit transaction represents a call to another system such as a credit card processor. You will want to look for or write these important edge cases as well. The following is an example.

▶ **Alternate Case: Deposit or Booking Transaction Fails**

1. Use case follows the standard path through to step 11. (See also "Alternate Case: Selected Trip Already Booked.")

2. System reserves booking.

3. System debits the credit card for the booking deposit amount (20 percent).

4. If the deposit fails, the system cancels, or rolls back, the booking transaction.

5. If the deposit succeeds, the system writes the deposit transaction ID back to the booking.

6. If the system fails to write the transaction ID back to the booking, the system must cancel (refund) the deposit.

7. System indicates the details of any failure to the user.

When you write these edge cases, it is important to remember that you are writing a use case and not a design specification. You can see from this last alternate use case that the author is trying to think through possible conditions that might arise and how they might be handled. The system could fail in the booking, the deposit, or when writing the deposit ID back to the booking. You will want to write test cases to simulate each of these scenarios. This will ensure that you know exactly how your code will behave when these edge cases are encountered.

It can often be helpful to have your testers review the use cases to help develop error cases. Testers will think up many potential error scenarios with your code. Of course, it is often not practical to define a use case for every potential error condition. In fact, your users might not see the benefits of reviewing, refining, and signing off on all of these use cases; they might only be confused by the many additions to the standard path. In this event, you might opt to draw a line between real user scenarios and these alternate error cases. You can then save the latter for the test cases. You will now look at just how use cases and test cases can work together to drive higher quality.

Distinguish Test Cases from Use Case Scenarios

Test cases and use cases are very similar, so you can usually derive one from the other. Use cases are written first, so it makes sense that you typically move from a use case to a test case. Recall that a use case describes a set of tasks focused on a common user goal. A test case typically is also focused on a common user goal. However, a *test case* describes a set of tasks (and related data) that a tester can execute to verify a use case, requirement, or feature of the system.

BEST PRACTICES   Using test cases

Testers write test cases. However, developers should use these test cases to help them write better unit tests. For this reason, developers should review the test cases and provide input into them. Developers should also consume them and use them to enhance the quality of the code.

The Structure of a Test Case

A test case typically has many elements. It can define the state of the system prior to the beginning of the test case. It can also describe the inputs and expected outputs for the test case. A good test case includes explicit instructions about how to work with the system, what data to enter, and what to expect as the result. Following are potential elements of a test case.

- **Name**   This represents the name of the test case. This is usually in relation to the use case or feature that is being tested by the test case, for example, "Book an Excursion" or "Check Guide Availability."

- **Description of functionality tested**   Describe which features or use cases you intend to verify with the test case. You can use a reference here to an existing definition of requirements or use cases.

- **System state / dependency**   Describe the system state prior to the test being run. For instance, if you need to reset the test data in the database prior to running the test, you would indicate that here. You can also define dependencies for the given test case (such as that another test case must execute first). Try to minimize dependencies because they often block test cases from being executed.

- **Test case / steps**   Describe the detailed steps for executing the test case. Indicate to the user which URL to access, which navigation button to click, the text boxes into which to type input, and so on. You will also want to link these steps to the data input definitions.

- **Data input**   Define the data that should be used for the test. Define data that is relevant to your test. If you are defining a success-path test, define common data as input. Alternatively, if you are writing a bounds-check test case, enter data at and outside the bounds of the expected.

- **Expected result**   This is your hypothesis or goal for the test to succeed. For example, you might expect that no errors are thrown and that you can verify that the data has been entered, changed, or deleted. You might also have negative tests in which the expected result is that a user cannot complete an action such as logging on or accessing secure data.

You might wish to define a standard successful test case as you would with a use case; you can then define derivatives for each edge test case. These variants can use the same tasks as listed in the test case but require different data. They also typically reset the definition of your expected result.

A test case should also include execution information. The execution information should represent a running log of who ran the test case and what the results were. Of course, Visual Studio Team Foundation Server and Team Test provide this type of functionality. You can also keep a log in a Microsoft Office Excel spreadsheet.

<hr>

Quick Check

1. What attribute class indicates to the testing framework that a given method is a unit test?
2. What is the purpose of the *Assert* class in the unit testing framework?
3. On what type of methods should you focus most of your unit test efforts?
4. What is a use case, and why is it important to unit testing?

Quick Check Answers

1. The *TestMethod* attribute class is used to decorate methods as unit tests.
2. The *Assert* class exposes a number of static methods that are used to verify whether conditions evaluate to true or false (success or failure) for a unit test.
3. Be sure to perform a number of varied unit tests on methods that execute important transactions on behalf of users. Consider also those methods that save and update data.
4. A use case describes a series of actions a user may take to achieve a common goal. Use cases feed test cases. Test cases can be used to write better unit tests.

<hr>

A Sample Test Case

Let's look at a sample test case. You will use the use case defined previously for booking an excursion as the basis for the test case. Recall that the test case will describe how the user interacts with the system to verify the use case and requirements. This means that some design, and possibly some code, has been created between use case and test case. For now, assume this design, but please don't think that you are overlooking this important task. Rather, you are focusing on just the test case here. The Book an Excursion test case might resemble the following example.

- **Name**   Book an Excursion
- **Description of functionality tested**   This test case verifies the requirements associated with a user booking an excursion through the online interface. This includes the Book an Excursion use case and the associated set of requirements.
- **System state / dependency**   The database should be loaded with only the standard test data prior to test execution. The test data includes registered customer, guides, guide schedules, and excursion details.

  This test case is also dependent on the Logon test case, which should be executed prior to executing the Book an Excursion test case.
- **Test case / steps**   Following are the steps required to execute this test case.

- **Precondition** The tester has logged on to the system as a registered customer.
  1. Select the Book Excursion option on the main navigation menu.
  2. Verify that you are now on the Define Excursion page and that this page lists the following excursions for selection: Fishing, Kayaking, Hiking, Snorkeling, Rafting, and Bird Watching.
  3. Select Fishing as the value for the Your Excursion field.
  4. Enter a requested excursion date that is two weeks from the current date in the Excursion Date field.
  5. Select Full day from the drop-down list as your excursion duration.
  6. Click the Check Availability button.
  7. Verify that you are now on the Select an Excursion page, that it displays only Fishing Excursion to match your request, and that it offers additional durations within two (2) days on either side of your requested date.
  8. Select one of the trips on display and click the Book button.
  9. Verify that you are now on the Make a Deposit page and that you are being asked to deposit 20 percent of the cost of the selected trip.
  10. Type the name on your credit card, the test credit card number (xxxx-xxxxxx-xxxxx), and the expiration date.
  11. Click the Finish Booking button.
  12. Verify that you are now on the Booking Receipt page, and your booking details are listed accordingly.
  13. Try to execute another booking with the same details. Verify that the same booking on the same date with the same guide is not available. Also verify that the system indicates a scheduling conflict with your current booking and asks if you'd like to cancel.
- **Data input** The success path test data can be found inside the Book Excursion Test Data.xls file. This data contains a variety of possible customers, excursions, dates, durations, and deposit details to try to execute.
- **Expected result** This test case should execute without error. Each row listed in the test data should result in a successful booking, but only one time.

Edge Test Cases

This test case example defines the standard path to test booking an excursion transaction. The tester also needs to consider alternate paths, or edge cases, that do not have such successful results. These alternate paths should have a different set of expectations to pass. The alternate paths might derive from the alternate paths defined for the use cases or might originate as error cases here in the test case. You will use your earlier use case definition to create your alternate test cases. Following are examples of alternate test cases to the previous sample test case:

- **Alternate case**   Selected Trip Already Booked
- **Description of functionality tested**   This tests that users cannot book a trip that is already booked even if they can select it.
- **System state / dependency**   The system should be initialized to the testing data prior to execution.
- **Test case / steps**   Following are the steps required to execute this test case.
    1. Begin booking a trip as defined in the prior test case. Stop before finishing the booking.
    2. In another browser, start to book exactly the same trip. Again, stop before finishing the booking.
    3. Return to the first booking and finish the booking. It should succeed.
    4. Navigate to the second booking that you have in progress. Attempt to finish the booking.
    5. Verify that the booking did not succeed. This information should be indicated on the page. You should also be presented with alternate bookings on the Select an Excursion page.
    6. Navigate to the Guide Schedule page. Verify that the guide is not double- booked.
    7. Navigate to the credit card transaction log. Verify that the second booking did not execute a credit card transaction.
- **Data input**   You can use the success path test data as defined in the main test case.
- **Expected result**   This test case should execute as described. The second booking should not succeed, the guide should not be double-booked, and no credit card transaction should take place.

Let's define another alternate test case. The second edge case from the use cases examined what would happen if the system failed to finish its booking after it made the deposit or made a deposit but failed to write the deposit ID to the booking. The point is to make sure that the deposit and booking is a transactional unit. This needs to be accounted for and tested. The following is a sample test case around this scenario.

- **Alternate case**   The Deposit or Booking Transaction fails
- **Description of functionality tested**   This confirms that the deposit and booking are transactional.
- **System state / dependency**   The system should be initialized to the testing data prior to execution.

- **Test case / steps**   Following are the steps required to execute this test case.
    1. Begin booking a trip as defined in the prior test case.
    2. When entering the deposit information, use the bad credit card details for the credit card number field.
    3. Finish the booking.
    4. Verify that the booking failed based on a credit card–declined error.
    5. Navigate to the Guide Schedule page. Verify that the booking did not succeed. Check this on the My Schedule page also.
    6. Navigate to the credit card transaction log. Verify that a failed credit card transaction is in the log for the appropriate booking attempt.
- **Data input**   Use a success path data row but type the bad credit card number.
- **Expected result**   This test case should execute as described. No booking should result, and a credit card–declined record should be written in the log.

You will use this test case and its alternates in the lab. You will build actual unit tests for a portion of the sample application. This will show you how use cases fuel test cases and how good test cases make your unit tests strong and your code of higher quality.

Perform Integration Testing

Before you start the lab, look at the developer's role in integration testing. As discussed in Chapter 14, integration testing is not the responsibility of developers. Developers should write their code, write their unit tests, perform code reviews, and fix bugs. All other tasks in the testing process are the primary responsibility of the test team. However, as you've seen with other parts of the testing process, some integration testing will fall to developers. The question is, "Where do you draw the line between developer integration testing and the role of the tester?" The following tasks will help you draw that line. Each defines an integration test task that falls to the developer.

- **Verify your application programming interface (API)**   Developers need to verify that code they write that is intended for the consumption of other developers has an appropriate public API. This API will be used for communication and integration with other components in the system. Therefore, check your API against the published specification. If this is a new version or upgrade, you should verify that you have not broken compatibility with prior versions.
- **Verify deployment**   Developers need to make sure the components they release to the build will operate as intended in the target environment. If, for instance, you write your code against Microsoft .NET Framework 2.0 and the target environment is running .NET Framework 1.1, you have a problem. The same holds true for other settings such as the Web server's meta-base. A good configuration management plan will help you define the target environment. You might then create a virtual computer (using Microsoft Virtual

PC or a similar program) that mimics this target. This will allow the developers to test deployment in the target environment to prevent breaking a build.

■ **Identify dependencies** Developers need to check their code for dependent items. This includes items that might be used at the integration level as well as dependent libraries running on the development computer. Your goal is to release your software to the build without breaking the build or another developer's code. Therefore, if your public interface requires an object you wrote that is not part of the test build, you cannot release your code. In addition, if you are dependent on a third-party component, you need to make the build manager aware of this before releasing your code.

Developers should strive to run their code in a development environment that is similar to the testing and production environments. This will help confirm integration at the production environment level. Once they verify the results, they can hand their code off to the test team for the full integration test. Taking this extra step will result in fewer broken builds and less rework for the team.

Exam Tip   The exam deals mostly with the developer's role regarding integration testing. It is not designed to test knowledge of the tester's process. In addition, when studying for the exam, you should focus mostly on integration tests that verify calls to external libraries.

Lab: Translating the Test Case into Unit Tests

The test case as described sounds like a set of manual tests to be executed by a tester sitting at a computer. If that tester has test tools, he or she might record these steps to build out a Web test; he or she might then bind the test to a data source. That is the principal intent behind a test case: to define a test for a tester. However, as you look through the test case with the eye of a developer intending to write unit tests, you see that the test case leads to unit tests that you should write. In this lab, you will walk through each step of the test case and examine how the test case might influence the unit tests you write. If you encounter a problem completing this lab, the completed projects in both Visual Basic and C# can be installed from the Code folder on the companion CD.

IMPORTANT   **Beyond simple unit tests**

The tests you write in this lab go beyond the standard tests you should write for each class and method in your application. You still need to write those. However, this lab assumes that those tests have been written and that you are now reviewing the test case for additional input into your unit tests.

Lab Setup

This lab builds a set of unit tests from exercise to exercise. Start with Exercise 1 and move through each exercise in sequence. You can perform the following steps to set up the lab on your computer.

1. Use Windows Explorer to copy either the C# or Visual Basic version of this lab to your computer. The lab can be found in the following path: Chapter 15\Lesson1\.

2. You will need Microsoft SQL Server 2005 Express Edition running on your computer for this lab. (This can be installed as part of Visual Studio.) The lab contains a file-based SQL Server Express Edition database called *BookingManager.mdf*. This file is inside the LessonDatabaseFiles folder. Note the path on your machine where you copied this file. You will use this path to update the connection strings used by the projects in this application.

3. You need to reset the connection string in the testing project to point to the database file on your computer. You can do so by opening the App.config file in the *BookingManagerTests* project. This class contains a configuration element called *BookingManagerConnectionString*. Set the attribute *connectionString* to point to your copy of the database. This configuration element appears as follows.

    ```
    <connectionStrings>
      <add name="BookingManagerConnectionString"
        connectionString= "DataSource=.\SQLEXPRESS;AttachDbFilename=
        '<PathToFile>\BookingManager.mdf';
        Integrated Security=True;User Instance=True" />
    </connectionStrings>
    ```

4. You need to replace the <PathToFile> in the prior example with the actual path to the file on your computer.

5. Follow the same procedure as outlined in steps 3 and 4 for the App.config file in the SetupProjectTrackingDb project. Point this configuration to the TestData.mdf file.

6. If you are using any of the completed projects—not just walking through the exercise—then you will also have to modify another connection string. At the top of the Exercise 3 App.config code is an attribute to bind the test to data. Modify the connection string in this attribute to point to the same database file, TestData.mdf.

▶ **Exercise 1: Create a *ClassInitialize* Method to Load the Test Data**

In the System state / dependency section of the test case, notice that the test case requires the database to have standard test data loaded prior to execution. Consider doing the same thing prior to executing your unit tests. This will ensure that you are always running tests against the same standard view of the data. In this exercise, you will write a method to reset the test database when the test class is initialized by the unit test framework.

1. Navigate to the test class called *BookingManagerTest.cs*. This file contains the unit tests for the methods in the *BookingManager* class.

2. Create a static method called *ClassInit*. This will serve as your class initializing method.

3. Add code to the *ClassInit* method to reset the *BookingManager* database. A static method inside of the *ResetTestData.cs* class has been created to do so. This method parses the database script file *ResetDbScript.sql* and executes this script against the database. If you have never written a test file like this, you might want to peruse this code. The call to this method is as follows.

```
TestDatabaseSetup.ResetTestData.ResetTestDatabase()
```

4. Add the *ClassInitialize* attribute class to the *ClassInit* method. This will tell the testing framework to run this method prior to executing and tests. Your method should now look as follows.

```
' VB
<ClassInitialize()> _
Public Shared Sub ClassInit(ByVal testContext As TestContext)
  TestDatabaseSetup.ResetTestData.ResetTestDatabase()
End Sub
```

```
// C#
[ClassInitialize()]
public static void ClassInit(TestContext testContext) {
  TestDatabaseSetup.ResetTestData.ResetTestDatabase();
}
```

5. Run the test class a couple of times and verify the database to make sure everything is working as expected. You will have to create an empty test to ensure that the initialize routine runs. You can use the following code to do so.

```
' VB
<TestMethod()> _
Public Sub SomeTest()
End Sub
```

```
// C#
[TestMethod()]
public void SomeTest() {
}
```

▶ **Exercise 2: Create a Unit Test to Verify Excursion Types**

In step 2 of the test case, the tester is being asked to verify the excursion types available for selection. You should consider a unit test to do the same. In this exercise, you will write a unit test to call the method that returns the excursion types, and then you will test the return data values.

1. Navigate to the test class called *BookingManagerTest.cs*. This file contains the unit tests for the methods in the *BookingManager* class.

2. Create a new test method called **VerifyTripTypesTest** as follows.

```
' VB
<TestMethod()> _
```

```vb
  Public Sub VerifyTripTypesTest()
End Sub
```

```
// C#
[TestMethod()]
public void VerifyTripTypesTest() {
}
```

3. Add code to your unit test to call the *GetTrips* method of the *BookingMethods* class. This method returns a collection of *Trip* objects. The code to call this method should resemble the following.

```vb
' VB
Dim trips As List(Of Trip)
trips = BookingMethods.GetTrips()
```

```
// C#
List<Trip> trips;
trips = BookingMethods.GetTrips();
```

4. You now need to add additional code to the test method to verify the results of the call. This requires you to set up the known excursion types and then search through the results to verify what was returned. This will require a number of assertions and data validations. You need to check for blank items, too many items, duplicate items, and so on. The following is a complete example of this unit test.

```vb
' VB
<TestMethod()> _
Public Sub VerifyTripTypesTest()

  Dim tripTypes As String() = New String() _
    {"Fishing", "Hiking", "Kayaking", _
    "Bird Watching", "Snorkeling", "Rafting"}

  'get trips
  Dim trips As List(Of Trip)
  trips = BookingMethods.GetTrips()

  'should only be 6 trip types in the database
  Assert.IsTrue(trips.Count = tripTypes.GetUpperBound(0) + 1, _
    "Wrong number of trip types")

  Dim match As Boolean

  For Each t As Trip In trips

    'verify trip object and trip name
    Assert.IsNotNull(t, "Trip cannot be null")
    Assert.IsNotNull(t.Name, "Trip name cannot be null")
    Assert.IsTrue(t.Name <> "", "Trip name cannot be blank")

    match = False
    Dim i As Integer
```

```
      For i = 0 To tripTypes.GetUpperBound(0)
        If t.Name = tripTypes(i) Then
          match = True
          'clear the trip type so it cannot be used again
          tripTypes(i) = ""
          Exit For
        End If
      Next
      Assert.IsTrue(match, "Invalid trip type: " + t.Name)
    Next
  End Sub

  // C#
  [TestMethod()]
  public void VerifyTripTypesTest() {

    string[] tripTypes = new string[]
      { "Fishing", "Hiking", "Kayaking", "Bird Watching",
        "Snorkeling", "Rafting" };

    //get trips
    List<Trip> trips;
    trips = BookingMethods.GetTrips();

    //should only be 6 trip types in the database
    Assert.IsTrue(trips.Count == tripTypes.GetUpperBound(0)+1,
      "Wrong number of trip types");

    bool match;
    foreach (Trip t in trips) {

      //verify trip object and trip name
      Assert.IsNotNull(t, "Trip cannot be null");
      Assert.IsNotNull(t.Name, "Trip name cannot be null");
      Assert.IsTrue(t.Name != "", "Trip name cannot be blank");

      match = false;
      for (int i = 0; i <= tripTypes.GetUpperBound(0); i++) {
        if (t.Name == tripTypes[i]) {
          match = true;
          //clear the trip type so it cannot be used again
          tripTypes[i] = "";
          break;
        }
      }
      Assert.IsTrue(match, "Invalid trip type: " + t.Name);
    }
  }
```

5. Run the test and verify that it passes. You can try to change a trip type in the database. Try also to add a new one. This should cause the test to fail. Remember to do so using the database reset script and not the database itself. This test validates both code and data.

▶ **Exercise 3: Bind Data to a Unit Test**

Steps 3 through 7 of the test case, in this exercise, define a set of parameters that should be used to find a booking. Use these steps as guidance for writing a unit test for the *Check-DateAvailability* method. In fact, it is clear from both the use case and the test case that this method will be called a number of times with varying parameters. Therefore, you should bind this unit test to a set of data. In this exercise, you will create a unit test method for *CheckDateAvailability* and bind it to a data source. In addition, you will verify that this test data includes bounds-check data for each parameter.

1. Navigate to the test class called *BookingManagerTest.cs*.

2. Create a new test method called **CheckTripAvailability** as follows.

```vb
' VB
<TestMethod()> _
Public Sub CheckTripAvailability()
End Sub
```

```csharp
// C#
[TestMethod()]
public void CheckTripAvailability() {
}
```

3. Define assertions based on the results of a call to the *CheckDateAvailability* method inside the *BookingMethods* class. The test case defines a number of evaluations of the data. Make sure that matching trips are returned and that the alternative trips returned are within the defined range. The following provides an example.

```vb
' VB
<TestMethod()> _
Public Sub CheckTripAvailability()
  'define parameters
  Dim tripType As Integer = 1
  Dim tripName As String = "Fishing"
  Dim duration As Duration = duration.FullDay
  Dim checkDate As DateTime = New DateTime(2007, 2, 5)

  'check for trips in the parameter range
  Dim trips As List(Of AvailableTrip)
  trips = BookingMethods.CheckDateAvailability( _
    tripType, duration, checkDate)

  'based on test data, params should return results
  Assert.IsTrue(trips.Count > 0)

  'verify results against expectations
  For Each avt As AvailableTrip In trips
    'check date of returned data
    Assert.IsTrue(avt.TripDate >= checkDate.AddDays(-2) _
      AndAlso avt.TripDate <= checkDate.AddDays(2))
```

```
      'check trip type returned
      Assert.IsTrue(avt.Id = tripType)
      Assert.IsTrue(avt.Guide.Specialty = tripName)

      'verify match level
      If avt.TripDate = checkDate Then
        Assert.IsTrue(avt.MatchLevel = MatchLevel.Match)
      Else
        Assert.IsTrue(avt.MatchLevel = MatchLevel.Close)
      End If
    Next
  End Sub

  // C#
  [TestMethod()]
  public void CheckTripAvailability() {

    //define parameters
    int tripType = 1;
    string tripName = "Fishing";
    Duration duration = Duration.FullDay;
    DateTime checkDate = new DateTime(2007, 2, 5);

    //check for trips in the parameter range
    List<AvailableTrip> trips;
    trips = BookingMethods.CheckDateAvailability(
      tripType, duration, checkDate);

    //based on test data, params should return results
    Assert.IsTrue(trips.Count > 0);

    //verify results against expectations
    foreach (AvailableTrip avt in trips) {

      //check date of returned data
      Assert.IsTrue(avt.TripDate >= checkDate.AddDays(-2)
        && avt.TripDate <= checkDate.AddDays(2));

      //check trip type returned
      Assert.IsTrue(avt.Id == tripType);
      Assert.IsTrue(avt.Guide.Specialty == tripName);

      //verify match level
      if (avt.TripDate == checkDate) {
        Assert.IsTrue(avt.MatchLevel == MatchLevel.Match);
      } else {
        Assert.IsTrue(avt.MatchLevel == MatchLevel.Close);
      }
    }
  }
```

4. Run the test and view the results. The tests should pass.

5. Recall that the test case talked about verifying multiple options. Now use the test case you have defined and bind it to a set of test data. You can view the test data that has been defined by connecting to the *TestData.mdf* SQL Server Express Edition database file. This file contains the *check_availability* table, which contains data for checking trip availability and verifying the expected results. Open the file and review its contents. Figure 15-3 provides an overview of the test data.

trip_type	duration	check_date	trip_name	expect_trips
1	1	2/1/2007 …	Fishing	True
1	2	2/12/200…	Fishing	False
2	3	2/2/2007 …	Hiking	True
2	1	2/5/2007 …	Hiking	True
3	2	2/7/2007 …	Kayaking	True
3	3	1/29/200…	Kayaking	False
4	1	1/31/200…	Snorkeling	True
4	2	3/1/2007 …	Snorkeling	False
5	3	2/6/2007 …	Rafting	True
5	1	2/9/2007 …	Rafting	True
6	3	2/10/200…	Bird Watching	False
6	2	2/7/2007 …	Bird Watching	True
NULL	NULL	NULL	NULL	NULL

Figure 15-3   TestData.mdf

6. Now, modify your unit test definition to use this test data as a data source. You do so by using the *DataSource* attribute class of the unit testing framework. This class takes a provider, connection string, default table, and access method. You will want to set the provider to *System.Data.SqlClient*, the connection string to the *TestData.mdf* file, the table name to *check_availability*, and the access method to *DataAccessMethod.Random*. The following is an example of this code.

```vb
' VB
<TestMethod(), DataSource("System.Data.SqlClient", _
"Data Source=.\SQLEXPRESS;AttachDbFilename=
  '<PathToFile>\TestData.mdf';
  Integrated Security=True;User Instance=True", _
  "check_availability", DataAccessMethod.Random)> _
Public Sub CheckTripAvailability()
```

```csharp
// C#
[TestMethod()]
[DataSource("System.Data.SqlClient",
  @"Data Source=.\SQLEXPRESS;AttachDbFilename=
  '<PathToFile>\TestData.mdf';
  Integrated Security=True;User Instance=True",
  "check_availability", DataAccessMethod.Random)]
public void CheckTripAvailability() {
```

7. Now, connect the parameters of your unit test to the bound data. You can do so through the *DataRow* method of the *TestContext* object. The following block of code binds variables to the data source elements.

```vb
' VB
Dim tripType As Integer = _
  CInt(TestContext.DataRow("trip_type").ToString())
Dim tripName As String = _
  TestContext.DataRow("trip_name").ToString()
Dim duration As Duration = _
  CType(CInt(TestContext.DataRow("duration").ToString()), Duration)
Dim checkDate As DateTime = _
  DateTime.Parse(TestContext.DataRow("check_date").ToString())
Dim expectTrips As Boolean = _
  CBool(TestContext.DataRow("expect_trips").ToString())
```

```csharp
// C#
int tripType = int.Parse(TestContext.DataRow["trip_type"].ToString());
string tripName = TestContext.DataRow["trip_name"].ToString();
Duration duration =
  (Duration)int.Parse(TestContext.DataRow["duration"].ToString());
DateTime checkDate =
  DateTime.Parse(TestContext.DataRow["check_date"].ToString());
bool expectTrips =
  bool.Parse(TestContext.DataRow["expect_trips"].ToString());
```

8. Finally, rework your assertions slightly to use this new data. In addition, it is a good idea to add messages to each assertion so that you now have more data when a test fails. Your unit test should resemble the following.

```vb
' VB
<TestMethod(), DataSource("System.Data.SqlClient", _
"Data Source=.\SQLEXPRESS;AttachDbFilename=
  '<PathToFile>\TestData.mdf';
  Integrated Security=True;User Instance=True", _
  "check_availability", DataAccessMethod.Random)> _
Public Sub CheckTripAvailability()
  'define parameters
  Dim tripType As Integer = _
    CInt(TestContext.DataRow("trip_type").ToString())
  Dim tripName As String = _
    TestContext.DataRow("trip_name").ToString()
  Dim duration As Duration = _
    CType(CInt(TestContext.DataRow("duration").ToString()), Duration)
  Dim checkDate As DateTime = _
    DateTime.Parse(TestContext.DataRow("check_date").ToString())
  Dim expectTrips As Boolean = _
    CBool(TestContext.DataRow("expect_trips").ToString())

  'check for trips in the parameter range
  Dim trips As List(Of AvailableTrip)
```

```vb
    trips = BookingMethods.CheckDateAvailability( _
      tripType, duration, checkDate)

    'based on test data, params should return results
    If expectTrips Then
      Assert.IsTrue(trips.Count > 0, _
        "Expected trips but no trips returned")
    ElseIf Not expectTrips Then
      Assert.IsTrue(trips.Count = 0, _
        "Did not expect trips, but trips returned. CheckDate: {0}", _
        checkDate.ToShortDateString())
    End If

    'verify results against expectations
    For Each avt As AvailableTrip In trips
      'check date of returned data
      Assert.IsTrue(avt.TripDate >= checkDate.AddDays(-2) _
        AndAlso avt.TripDate <= checkDate.AddDays(2), _
        "Trip date out of range")

      'check trip type returned
      Assert.IsTrue(avt.Id = tripType, _
        "Wrong trip type returned")
        Assert.IsTrue(avt.Guide.Specialty = tripName, _
        "Invalid trip name")

      'verify match level
      If avt.TripDate = checkDate Then
        Assert.IsTrue(avt.MatchLevel = MatchLevel.Match, _
          "Expected trip to match")
      Else
        Assert.IsTrue(avt.MatchLevel = MatchLevel.Close, _
          "Expected trip to be close to a match")
      End If
    Next
End Sub
```

```csharp
// C#
[TestMethod()]
[DataSource("System.Data.SqlClient",
  @"Data Source=.\SQLEXPRESS;AttachDbFilename=
  '<PathToFile>\TestData.mdf';
  Integrated Security=True;User Instance=True",
  "check_availability", DataAccessMethod.Random)]
public void CheckTripAvailability() {

  //define parameters
  int tripType = int.Parse(TestContext.DataRow["trip_type"].ToString());
  string tripName = TestContext.DataRow["trip_name"].ToString();
  Duration duration =
    (Duration)int.Parse(TestContext.DataRow["duration"].ToString());
```

```
DateTime checkDate =
  DateTime.Parse(TestContext.DataRow["check_date"].ToString());
bool expectTrips =
  bool.Parse(TestContext.DataRow["expect_trips"].ToString());

//check for trips in the parameter range
List<AvailableTrip> trips;
trips = BookingMethods.CheckDateAvailability(tripType,
  duration, checkDate);

//based on test data, params should return results
if (expectTrips) {
  Assert.IsTrue(trips.Count > 0, "Expected trips but no trips returned");
} else if (!expectTrips) {
  Assert.IsTrue(trips.Count == 0,
    "Did not expect trips, but trips returned. CheckDate: {0}",
    checkDate.ToShortDateString());
}

//verify results against expectations
foreach (AvailableTrip avt in trips) {
  //check date of returned data
  Assert.IsTrue(avt.TripDate >= checkDate.AddDays(-2) &&
    avt.TripDate <= checkDate.AddDays(2), "Trip date out of range");

  //check trip type returned
  Assert.IsTrue(avt.Id == tripType, "Wrong trip type returned");
  Assert.IsTrue(avt.Guide.Specialty == tripName, "Invalid trip name");

  //verify match level
  if (avt.TripDate == checkDate) {
    Assert.IsTrue(avt.MatchLevel == MatchLevel.Match,
      "Expected trip to match");
  } else {
    Assert.IsTrue(avt.MatchLevel == MatchLevel.Close,
      "Expected trip to be close to a match");
  }
}
}
```

9. Run the unit test and view the results. The test should pass. You can view the details of the passed test to see how each bound data row behaved. Figure 15-4 shows an example of the test results.

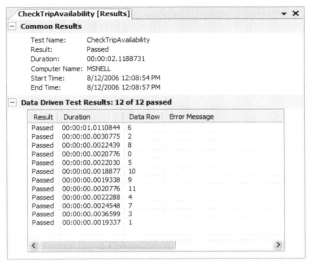

Figure 15-4   Data-bound unit test results

▶ **Exercise 4: Verify the Booking Process**

In this exercise, steps 8 through 11 of the test case represent the actual booking process. This process requires a deposit and should execute as a transaction. In this exercise, you will write a unit test to verify that the standard booking process works without exception and returns a booking confirmation number.

1. Navigate to the test class called *BookingManagerTest.cs*.

2. Create a new test method called **BookTripTest** as follows.

```vb
' VB
<TestMethod()> _
Public Sub BookTripTest()
End Sub
```

```csharp
// C#
[TestMethod()]
public void BookTripTest() {
}
```

3. Write a unit test to book an available trip and verify the results through assertions. Your unit test might resemble the following.

```vb
' VB
<TestMethod()> _
Public Sub BookTripTest()
```

```
  Dim booking As New Booking()
  Dim card As String = "xxxx-xxxxxx-xxxxx"

  'get a customer to book
  booking.Customer = BookingMethods.GetCustomer( _
    "lauren41@adventure-works.com")
  booking.SpecialInstructions = "We will see you there!"

  'get an available trip
  Dim trips As List(Of AvailableTrip)
  trips = BookingMethods.CheckDateAvailability( _
    1, Duration.FullDay, New DateTime(2007, 2, 1))

  'set to first available trip
  booking.Trip = trips(0)

  Dim confirmation As Integer = _
    BookingMethods.BookTrip(booking, card)

  Assert.IsNotNull(confirmation)
  Assert.IsTrue(confirmation.ToString().Length > 0)

End Sub

// C#
[TestMethod()]
public void BookTripTest() {

  Booking booking = new Booking();
  string card = "xxxx-xxxxxx-xxxxx";

  //get a customer to book
  booking.Customer = BookingMethods.GetCustomer(
    "lauren41@adventure-works.com");
  booking.SpecialInstructions = "We will see you there!";

  //get an available trip
  List<AvailableTrip> trips;
  trips = BookingMethods.CheckDateAvailability(
    1, Duration.FullDay, new DateTime(2007, 2, 1));

  //set to first available trip
  booking.Trip = trips[0];

  int confirmation = BookingMethods.BookTrip(booking, card);

  Assert.IsNotNull(confirmation);
  Assert.IsTrue(confirmation.ToString().Length > 0);

}
```

4. Run the unit test. The test should pass. You will build on this test in the next exercise.

▶ **Exercise 5: Check for a Bad Credit Card**

In this exercise, you will write a unit test similar to the one you wrote in Exercise 4. However, here you will pass a bad credit card number for the deposit. This test is part unit test and part integration test. You are testing the *BookTrip* method, but you are making sure that its call to the external Web service that makes deposits works as expected.

1. Navigate to the test class called *BookingManagerTest.cs*.
2. Copy and paste the *BookTripTest*.
3. Rename this test to **BookTripTestBadDeposit**.
4. Modify the credit card variable to pass a bad credit card. The following is an example.

```
' VB
Dim card As String = "BADx-xxxxxx-xxxxx"
```

```
// C#
string card = "BADx-xxxxxx-xxxxx";
```

5. When you run this test, it fails. However, it is doing what it is supposed to do—returning an exception. You can tag the test method as expecting the exception. This will cause the test to pass. The following is an example.

```
' VB
<TestMethod(), ExpectedException(GetType(ApplicationException))> _
Public Sub BookTripTestBadDeposit()
```

```
// C#
[TestMethod()]
[ExpectedException(typeof(ApplicationException))]
public void BookTripTestBadDeposit() {
```

▶ **Exercise 6: Book the Trip Again**

Step 13 of the test case describes a situation in which users might try to book themselves redundantly for the same trip. Chances are good that you probably wouldn't have considered this case in your unit tests. In this exercise, you will write a unit test that verifies that the trip just booked by a user is no longer available.

1. Navigate to the test class called *BookingManagerTest.cs*.
2. Copy and paste the *BookTripTest*.
3. Rename this test to **BookTripTwice**.
4. Modify this test to book the same trip twice. Also, set the *ExpectedException* attribute for the test method. The following code is an example.

```
' VB
<TestMethod(), ExpectedException(GetType(ApplicationException))> _
Public Sub BookTripTwice()
  Dim booking As Booking = New Booking()
  Dim card As String = "xxxx-xxxxxx-xxxxx"
```

```vb
    'get a customer to book
    booking.Customer = BookingMethods.GetCustomer( _
      "lauren41@adventure-works.com")
    booking.SpecialInstructions = "We will see you there!"

    'get an available trip
    Dim trips As List(Of AvailableTrip)
    trips = BookingMethods.CheckDateAvailability( _
      1, Duration.FullDay, New DateTime(2007, 2, 1))

    'set to first available trip
    booking.Trip = trips(0)

    'book once
    Dim confirmation1 As Integer = _
      BookingMethods.BookTrip(booking, card)

    'try to book again
    Dim confirmation2 As Integer = _
      BookingMethods.BookTrip(booking, card)

End Sub

// C#
[TestMethod()]
[ExpectedException(typeof(ApplicationException))]
public void BookTripTwice() {

  Booking booking = new Booking();
  string card = "xxxx-xxxxxx-xxxxx";

  //get a customer to book
  booking.Customer = BookingMethods.GetCustomer(
    "lauren41@adventure-works.com");
  booking.SpecialInstructions = "We will see you there!";

  //get an available trip
  List<AvailableTrip> trips;
  trips = BookingMethods.CheckDateAvailability(1, Duration.FullDay,
    new DateTime(2007, 2, 1));

  //set to first available trip
  booking.Trip = trips[0];

  //book once
  int confirmation1 = BookingMethods.BookTrip(booking, card);

  //try to book again
  int confirmation2 = BookingMethods.BookTrip(booking, card);

}
```

5. Run the test. *Notice that it fails.* It does not return an exception. This means you have not trapped for this condition in the code. You would now have to consider adding code to check for this condition as well as setting a unique constraint in the database to prevent this occurrence. Figure 15-5 shows the failed test results.

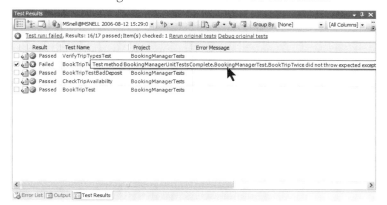

Figure 15-5 Failed test results

NOTE Two users booking the same trip

You now need to consider the edge cases inside the test case. Recall that the first edge case deals with two different users trying to book the same trip. Clearly, one will succeed before the other. This test would look just like the test you wrote for this exercise. The only change would be to modify the customer on the second call to *BookTrip*. In fact, these tests are so similar that they are functionally equivalent, and therefore, you need only write one or the other.

▶ **Exercise 7: Verify Booking Process Integration**

The second alternate test case requires verification of the booking process as a transactional unit. You need to make sure that the booking is set, the deposit is made, the deposit ID is written back to the booking, and a booking confirmation is generated. If one step fails, they all should fail. This test case is part unit test and part integration test. For this exercise, you will focus on the developer's role in the integration test part. Recall that it is the tester's responsibility to verify that everything actually executes. It is the developer's responsibility to verify that the code integrates with the credit card processing interface as required.

The credit card processing interface in your example is a Web service. The first step a developer should take is to write unit tests to call the Web service interface. This unit test should verify that you have rights to call the interface and that you get the expected results. You will assume these unit tests were written. Your focus will be on testing the *BookTrip* method to ensure that it behaves properly in a transaction.

1. Navigate to the test class called *BookingManagerTest.cs.*

2. Copy and paste the test you created in Exercise 5, BookTripTestBadDeposit. You will use this test as the basis for your new test.

3. Rename this test to **BookTripTestBadDepositTrx**. Also, remove the expected exception. In this test, you will expect an exception, but you will handle it.

4. Next, modify the test to handle the exception. Create an assertion to verify that the exception was thrown. Inside the exception handler, make a call to verify that the deposit was not actually made. Use the *AreNotEqual* assertion to do so. This method takes a generic type for verification. Your new test should resemble the following.

```vb
' VB
<TestMethod()> _
Public Sub BookTripTestBadDepositTrx()
  Dim booking As Booking = New Booking()
  Dim card As String = "BADx-xxxxxx-xxxxx"

  'get a customer to book
  booking.Customer = BookingMethods.GetCustomer( _
    "lauren41@adventure-works.com")
    booking.SpecialInstructions = "We will see you there!"

  'get an available trip
  Dim trips As List(Of AvailableTrip)
  trips = BookingMethods.CheckDateAvailability( _
    1, Duration.FullDay, New DateTime(2007, 2, 1))

  'set to first available trip
  booking.Trip = trips(0)

  'we expect an exception, it must be there and we need to 'eat' it
  Dim expectedException As Boolean = False
  Try
    Dim confirmation As Integer = _
      BookingMethods.BookTrip(booking, card)
  Catch appEx As ApplicationException
    expectedException = True
    'check that the deposit was not made
    Dim status As String = _
      BookingMethods.CheckDepositStatus(card)
    Assert.AreNotEqual(Of String)("CONFIRMED", status, _
      "Transaction succeeded. Expected failure.")
  End Try

  'verify the exception was thrown
  Assert.IsTrue(expectedException, _
  "Expected exception was not thrown")
End Sub

// C#
[TestMethod()]
```

```
public void BookTripTestBadDepositTrx() {

  Booking booking = new Booking();
  string card = "BADx-xxxxxx-xxxxx";

  //get a customer to book
  booking.Customer = BookingMethods.GetCustomer(
    "lauren41@adventure-works.com");
  booking.SpecialInstructions = "We will see you there!";

  //get an available trip
  List<AvailableTrip> trips;
  trips = BookingMethods.CheckDateAvailability(1, Duration.FullDay,
    new DateTime(2007, 2, 1));

  //set to first available trip
  booking.Trip = trips[0];

  //we expect an exception, it must be there and we need to 'eat' it
  bool expectedException = false;
  try {
    int confirmation = BookingMethods.BookTrip(booking, card);
  } catch (ApplicationException appEx) {
    expectedException = true;

    // check that the deposit was not made
    string status = BookingMethods.CheckDepositStatus(card);
    Assert.AreNotEqual<string>("CONFIRMED", status,
      "Transaction succeeded. Expected failure.");
  }

  //verify the exception was thrown
  Assert.IsTrue(expectedException, "Expected exception was not thrown");
}
```

5. Run the test. It should pass. The exception will be thrown, and you can verify that the deposit transaction did not complete.

Lesson Summary

- Visual Studio 2005 ships with the unit testing framework, *Microsoft.VisualStudio.TestTools.UnitTesting*, which you use to create unit test methods. You define such a method by marking a method with the *TestMethod* attribute class. You can also use the *ClassInitialize* attribute to create a method that executes prior to your unit tests, and you can create a method to run between each unit test by using the *TestInitialize* method.

- You use the static methods of the *Assert* class to determine success or failure of your unit test. This class has assertions for checking Boolean values (*IsTrue*, *IsFalse*), null values (*IsNull*, *IsNotNull*), whether objects are the same (*AreSame*, *AreNotSame*), and more.

- You should write one or more unit tests for every method and property in your application. However, for methods that are key transactions of the system, spend time reviewing the use cases and test cases. Then use this information to write additional unit tests for these methods.

- Integration testing is the responsibility of testers. However, developers should verify their applications' APIs, define the dependencies, and identify component interactions. They should run their code in a test environment. Once they have verified the results, they can hand off the application to the test team.

Lesson Review

You can use the following questions to test your knowledge of the information in Lesson 1, "Creating Effective Unit Tests." The questions are also available on the companion CD if you prefer to review them in electronic form.

NOTE   Answers

Answers to these questions and explanations of why each answer choice is right or wrong are located in the "Answers" section at the end of the book.

---

1. You want to make sure that code you wrote to reset the database is run before each unit test is executed. What action should you take?

    A. Add the *TestCleanup* attribute to the database reset method.

    B. Add the *TestInitialize* attribute to the database reset method.

    C. Add the *ClassCleanup* attribute to the database reset method.

    D. Add the *ClassInitialize* attribute to the database reset method.

2. You need to write an assertion to verify that two objects are identical. Which of the following code segments should you choose?

    A. `Assert.AreEqual(obj1, obj2)`

    B. `Assert.IsTrue(obj1, obj2.TosString())`

    C. `Assert.IsInstanceOfType(obj1, typeof(obj2))`

    D. `Assert.AreSame(obj1, obj2)`

3. You have been given an extra couple of days to write some additional unit tests. Which of the following methods should you consider for additional unit test work? (Choose all that apply.)

    A. A method to return the descriptive details of a product

    B. A method that updates inventory data after an order has been processed

    C. A set of properties that allows you to access configuration information for your application

    D. A method that is used by multiple applications to calculate the estimated shipping date and price for an order

4. Which of the following statements describe a test case? (Choose all that apply.)

    A. A test case is written to flush out the requirements of the system. It does so by describing a set of steps centered on a common user goal.

    B. A test case is typically written by a tester and derived from a use case.

    C. A test case is written to aid developers in writing unit tests.

    D. A test case includes steps, data, and expected results.

5. For which of the following integration testing tasks are developers responsible? (Choose all that apply.)

    A. Execute a test case to verify that all components work together as an integrated solution.

    B. Confirm that calls to external libraries work as intended.

    C. Verify that component deployment works in the test environment.

    D. Identify component dependencies against the configuration management plan.

Lesson 2: Performing a Code Review

Code reviews are another tool that developers can use to improve the quality of their code. Typically, code reviews are done on a peer-to-peer basis or by an application architect or technical lead. Code reviews should be performed before code is released into the test build. This lesson looks at how developers can help one another through the code review process.

After this lesson, you will be able to:

- Understand the process for performing a code review.
- Identify issues to look for when reviewing code.
- Understand the automated code review tools available to you.
- Propose improvements to help developers fix their code.

Estimated lesson time: 20 minutes

Real World

Mike Snell

There is no substitute for a second set of eyes on your code. Early in my career, I had a development manager who insisted on code reviews. In fact, he felt code reviews should happen in a meeting room and without a computer. His plan was to make a developer explain his or her code to another developer, using nothing but a printout of the code. The developer would indicate that the code was complete. At this time, he or she was told to schedule a code review. He or she would meet with another developer in a conference room and come equipped with two copies of the code.

This process seemed very strange at first. I had never before even considered printing out code. However, when you sit with another person and another pair of eyes and have to explain the choices that you made, you soon realize that this is part peer-review and part self-review. Taking the computer and compiler out of the mix forces you to think about your code from a different perspective. You look at it for its structure, its readability, its adherence to standards, and its design.

This process also helped stratify the team. It was a very large team with high turnover. Good developers found themselves discovering their own issues during the review. They got better and better and became strong architects. Poor developers were quickly found out when they could barely understand how their own code worked. Instead, many had cobbled some copied-and-pasted code together. The review showed this, and these developers were then sent to training.

The distribution of teams and the new tools have changed the code review process. Now code is partly reviewed and partly refactored. Getting team members together is very difficult because they are spread across offices and time zones. However, if I find a developer who is becoming perplexed by a piece of the system, I might ask him or her to print two copies of the code and meet me in my office or via the video conference.

The Code Review Process

A *code review* is simply the process of checking code to improve its quality and help ensure that the development team follows best practices. There are many code review processes that help reach this goal. Many development teams follow a peer-to-peer review process in which each developer checks the other developer's code and suggests improvements.

Other teams have a more formal process in which code reviews are made mandatory and tracked closely. For example, you might have a code review checklist and form. An architect or technical lead might review a portion of code and then fill out the checklist and online form. The issues listed on the form must be resolved before the code moves to testing or production.

There are even code reviews that are done by third parties. You might, for instance, have your code reviewed by a company that acts as a testing center or certification house. You might even have your code audited by another company for compliance with security measures.

Each of these processes has a common set of steps for reviewing code and identifying issues. The following list represents some of the standard steps involved in doing a code review.

- Define standards.
- Identify adherence to standards.
- Propose resolution and improvements.
- Refactor code.

This list is the beginning of a code review checklist. You can see that you start with standards. You then review the code against these standards. You can also verify the code with respect to best practices for such things as error handling, security, and performance. Let's take a closer look at each of these code review steps.

Define Standards

It is impossible to review code without a baseline for standards. You need to know what the target is for the system before you can indicate that the code does not hit the target. For example, if your standard is to use the Microsoft Enterprise Library for .NET Framework for writing errors to the error log, you need to define that for the development team. There are naming standards, coding standards, architecture standards, and best practice standards. It is a good idea to get these standards on paper and make sure the team understands them. The following list shows a definition of each type of standard.

- **Naming standards**   You need to define how you name classes, variables, methods, and properties. Naming standards are important to make sure the system is maintainable and readable. Today, most .NET applications follow the naming standards set forth by Microsoft for the .NET Framework. This is always a good place to start.

- **Coding standards**   Coding standards guide developers on how they should and shouldn't write their code. These standards typically define things such as the use of switch (C#) or select case (Visual Basic) statements, how to exit loops properly, how to handle exceptions and log errors, the use of reference parameters, the proper way to comment and document your code, and more.

- **Architecture standards**   You should create a solution architecture document for your application. This document is meant solely to define the application's overall architecture. It should cover things such as application layers, state management, frameworks, the use of application blocks and third party libraries, and more. In addition, a reference implementation of this architecture is helpful to both solidify the architecture and serve as a model for developers.

- **Best practice standards**   These standards represent generally accepted best practices for building .NET applications. They help with performance, maintainability, security, and many more considerations. The standards are available in the .NET documentation, white papers, and the patterns-and-practices documentation. Senior developers and architects need to be aware of these standards to review code against them.

Identify Adherence to Standards

Once you define the standards by which your application should be reviewed, you can then review it for compliance to these standards. Most naming and coding standards and some best practices standards can be verified automatically by using the Code Analysis features of Visual

Studio 2005. (See the Automated Code Reviews section of this chapter.) Of course, you can still read through the code and check it for these things, if you like.

Architecture standards are more difficult to verify. This requires a careful review. For example, if your architecture dictates that you put no user interface (UI) logic or validation into the actual UI forms but instead put it in a UI layer, you must go through the UI form code to verify that your code conforms to this requirement.

NOTE Use templates to enforce standards

Visual Studio 2005 provides a number of tools that you can use to help enforce compliance with standards. You can write your own project templates that set up the project using your standards. You can also create your own item templates that you set up with your standards and your guidance.

Propose Resolution and Improvements

The next step in the process is to log the issue for tracking and provide guidance on resolving it and improving the code base. This task is typically the responsibility of the reviewer. However, there are some environments in which each developer logs his or her own issues.

It is often best to log the issue in terms of the library, class, and line number. You then need to label the issue. The label might be related to the standard that is out of compliance. Then either point to the standard or write a brief paragraph that describes how the developer might resolve the issue. The following is an example of a logged issue in a formal review.

- Reviewer: <name of reviewer>, <date of review>
- Build: <build number or build date>
- Library: MyApplicationLibrary
- Class / Method: SomeClass.SomeMethod
- Line Number(s): 456-461
- Issue Name: Reliability Issue. Does not use *Dispose*.
- Issue Description: You need to dispose of objects before the application loses scope. Notice that the code potentially exits the method inside the *if* block without calling *Dispose*.
- Proposed Resolution: Suggest you use the *using* statement to ensure the object is disposed.
- Resolved by: <developer name>, <date of resolution>
- Resolution: <description of how resolved>

NOTE Use Microsoft Team Foundation Server

You can use Microsoft Team System and Team Foundation Server to log and track code review issues. You create a new work as defined previously. Developers can then be assigned these items, attach progress notes, and connect the issue with the code that resolves it.

Refactor Code

The final step in the code review process is to resolve any issues found during the code review. Visual Studio 2005 now provides a number of tools to aid in making these changes. These tools are referred to as refactoring tools. They are available to C# developers via the Refactor menu.

MORE INFO Refactoring with Visual Basic

Visual Basic developers can download a version of these tools from a third party. See *http://msdn.microsoft.com/vbasic/downloads/tools/refactor/* for details.

The tools use the compiler to make sure your changes don't break other code in the system. This was always the worst part of code reviews. Just when things are working, you have to go back and make changes that start breaking things. Thankfully, these tools help decrease this risk. In addition, a proper set of unit tests will help you find any areas affected by code review changes. Table 15-3 presents the refactoring tools inside of Visual Studio 2005.

Table 15-3   Refactoring Tools Inside of Visual Studio 2005 (C#)

Tool	Description
Rename	Used to rename fields, properties, methods, and variables
Extract Method	Used to create a new method, using existing code within a different method or routine
Promote Local to Parameter	Used to move a local member of a method to a parameter of the method
Reorder Parameters	Used to change the order of parameters for a given method
Remove Parameters	Used to remove a parameter from a method
Encapsulate Field	Used to create a property quickly from an existing field
Extract Interface	Used to create an interface from an existing class or structure

> ### Quick Check
>
> 1. Describe the purpose of a code review.
> 2. What are three types of code review processes?
> 3. What are the types of standards you should define for your application?
>
> ### Quick Check Answers
>
> 1. The purpose of a code review is to improve the quality of the application and help developers follow coding standards and best practices.
> 2. Code review processes include peer-to-peer, formal, and third-party reviews.
> 3. You should define naming standards (for classes, methods, and properties), coding standards (for exception handling, conditional statements, and so on), and architectural standards.

Automated Code Reviews

It is getting increasingly difficult and costly to review and check by hand all code in an application. Code reviews can add weeks to development schedules. Visual Studio 2005 Team Edition has provided an automated Code Analysis tool to help.

The Code Analysis tool is based on its precursor, FxCop. FxCop was a command-line tool that shipped with earlier versions of the .NET Framework. It checked code against a common set of rules. The new tool, called Code Analysis, has a common set of rules, standards, and best practices built into it. You can turn these rules on and off. You then run them against your code base and receive warning wherever a rule is broken.

Figure 15-6 shows the Code Analysis tool in Visual Studio. You access this tool through the property pages of your application. You then select the Code Analysis tab along the left side. If you are working with a Web site, you can access a similar dialog box from the Web site menu item, Code Analysis Configuration. You must enable Code Analysis for it to run. You can do so with the check box titled Enable Code Analysis.

Notice that rules are grouped by category. There are rules for naming conventions, globalization, security, and so on. If you expand a group, you see a set of individual rules. Each rule has a description. You can turn various rules on and off for your application.

Each Code Analysis rule has an identification that starts with the letters CA. You can use this identification to look up the details of the rule inside the Microsoft Visual Studio 2005 Documentation. Each rule is documented in terms of cause, description, and how to fix.

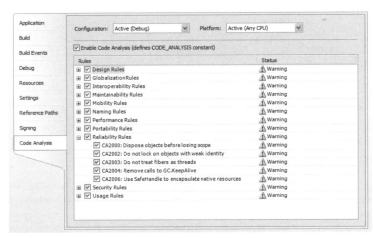

Figure 15-6   Code Analysis settings

Lab: Perform a Code Review

If you have not worked on a team that does code reviews, give them a try. Code reviews can lead to better quality throughout your application. You can use this practice section to help you get started.

▶ **Exercise 1: Define Standards and Review Code**

In this exercise, you will define your coding standards and execute a code review. Each of the following steps represents input into your code review process.

1. Define your coding standards for your application. You might already be able to point to a set of standards. You should at least be able to point to your solution architecture. As an alternative, you can adopt the .NET naming standards and use the Code Analysis rules as your standards.

2. Create a code review checklist. This checklist should define the items that should be verified during the code review. The checklist is meant to provide mental triggers to the reviewer to prevent missing anything during the review.

3. Create a formal code review form or work item. This step is optional. However, if you are just getting started with code reviews, it can be helpful to document the first few rounds formally. If you use Team System and Microsoft Solutions Framework (MSF) for Capability Maturity Model Integration (CMMI), there is already a Review work item. If you are using MSF Agile, consider creating a code review work item.

4. Ask another developer to review your code. Sit with another developer, or group of developers, and have your code reviewed against the standards.

5. Review the code of another developer.

6. Document the issues and propose resolutions. Document any issue you find during the code review. In addition, try to propose the resolution for each item.

7. Use the refactoring tools and unit tests to make changes to your code. The refactoring tools will make the changes easier. Your unit tests should confirm that things still work as intended.

▶ **Exercise 2: Run the Code Analysis Tool**

In this exercise, you will use the Code Analysis tool to check your code against known rules.

1. Open some existing code inside of Visual Studio 2005. If you do not have code available, select a code file from the lab in Lesson 1.

2. If you are analyzing a class library or executable, right-click the project and choose Properties. On the Property page, select the Code Analysis tab. If you are analyzing a Web site, choose Code Analysis Configuration from the Website menu to open a similar dialog box.

3. Select Enable Code Analysis to turn on code analysis. Review the rules. Turn off any rules that you do not think apply to your situation.

4. Right-click your class library or executable and choose Run Code Analysis. If you are checking a Web site, right-click it in Solution Explorer and choose Run Code Analysis On Website.

5. Review the results. Right-click a warning and get additional help about the warning item.

6. Fix the issues that make sense to fix. Turn the other issues off for future Code Analysis.

Lesson Summary

■ A good code review process should improve the quality of the application and help developers follow coding standards and best practices.

■ Consider implementing either a peer-to-peer or formal code review process. Some applications require third-party reviews and audits.

■ To be successful, a code review should start with a definition of standards. Define naming standards (for classes, methods, and properties), coding standards (for exception handling, conditional statements, and so on), and architectural standards.

■ Track issues identified in the code review process. Give each issue a name, description, and proposed resolution.

■ You can use the refactoring tools inside of Visual Studio 2005 to help you make changes identified during code reviews.

■ Visual Studio provides an automated static code analyzer called Code Analysis. This tool reviews code for known issues concerning security, globalization, performance, naming, and more.

Lesson Review

You can use the following questions to test your knowledge of the information in Lesson 2, "Performing a Code Review." The questions are also available on the companion CD if you prefer to review them in electronic form.

NOTE Answers

Answers to these questions and explanations of why each answer choice is right or wrong are located in the "Answers" section at the end of the book.

1. Which of the following are steps in the code review process? (Choose all that apply.)
    A. Define standards.
    B. Write a test case.
    C. Identify adherence to standards.
    D. Propose a resolution and improvements to code.

2. Which of the following items represent a coding standard? (Choose all that apply.)
    A. Data access methods should not trap exceptions. Rather, these exceptions should be raised up to the layers of the application at which they will be dealt with by the central error handling mechanism.
    B. Developers should not put data access code inside of their business objects.
    C. Developers should avoid switch statements in their code.
    D. All variables should be camel case, as in *someVariable*.

3. Which of the following is a refactoring operation that enables you to define a new method from a portion of the code inside an existing method?
    A. Extract Interface
    B. Encapsulate Field
    C. Promote Local Variable to Parameter
    D. Extract Method

4. Which of the following statements are true about the Code Analysis tool? (Choose all that apply.)
    A. The Code Analysis tool reviews executing code in-process.
    B. You must run all the Code Analysis rules against your code.
    C. Issues found by using the Code Analysis tool are treated as warnings in your code.
    D. Each issue found by Code Analysis has an associated how-to-fix section.

Lesson 3: Evaluating and Fixing a Bug

When you test software, you will end up creating bugs. That is the goal of testing: to find and fix as many bugs as possible. Developers do their best to ensure that their code has been properly unit tested and integrated into the build. However, issues will still arise during the testing phase. When they do, you need to be ready to investigate, reproduce, analyze, and fix these bugs.

This lesson describes how you should go about investigating bugs and fixing them. You will also look at how to evaluate the impact of a bug and analyze tradeoffs of potential actions.

After this lesson, you will be able to:
- Investigate the cause of a bug.
- Understand how the environment can be responsible for the bug.
- Work with testers to reproduce a bug.
- Evaluate the impact of a bug and analyze possible tradeoffs.
- Understand the process for fixing a bug.

Estimated lesson time: 20 minutes

Investigate a Reported Bug

Testers report bugs. These bugs are typically triaged by a lead developer or project manager. During triage, the bug is analyzed; its impact is assessed; and a decision is made to fix the bug, defer it to a later phase, or escalate it to the project stakeholders. Developers are assigned to fix bugs; they are also assigned to assess a bug's impact so a decision can be made.

Evaluate the Impact of the Bug

The triage process typically involves some assessment of the bug. It identifies its impact, sets the priority, categorizes it, and assigns a developer. Often, the person doing the triage work will assign the bug to a developer for further investigation. In fact, the workflow for the bug-work item inside of Team System supports this step. Developers are often asked to assess the impact of a given bug. This assessment helps the person doing the triage make a decision on how to proceed. When assessing the impact of a bug, consider all of the following.

- **Time to fix**   Estimate the number of hours it will take to fix the bug.
- **Resources to fix**   Determine who can fix the bug. Understand how their schedule might be affected by the bug.

- **Bug risk**   Identify the risk the bug poses to the integrity of the application. This can be difficult to assess. It helps to think of this in terms of "What would be the risk of not fixing the bug?"
- **Impacts**   Identify the components, people, and other resources that are affected by the bug. Are your trading partners, for instance, affected by this bug? Will the marketing department be affected? Those affected most should help determine how to proceed with the bug.

Pass this information back to the person doing the triage work to help him or her make a decision. Ultimately, he or she will have to decide whether to proceed with fixing the bug, to defer it, or to escalate the bug to project stakeholders and key decision makers.

Prioritize a Bug

You need to be able to triage a bug relative to the other bugs in the system. This is an important step in making sure the right resources are applied to the right issues during testing. Priorities help developers know which items they need to fix first. A list of priorities might comprise critical, high, medium, and low levels. Critical usually means that the bug breaks the build or is preventing testers from completing a test case. On the other end, low means the bug is more of an annoyance than anything else. Expect to fix all bugs that are of critical and high priority. These bugs typically also take the longest to troubleshoot and fix. Bugs lower on the priority scale can be assigned in batches to a junior developer. They typically involve making text changes or making similar adjustments. Of course, the longer you test an application, the higher up the scale these bugs move. In the early days of development of an application, only critical bugs are marked as such. When you are near the release date and have eliminated all the critical issues, bugs that would have previously seemed less than critical tend to move up the scale. This is understandable. A little issue becomes magnified when there are so few issues and you are nearly ready for release.

Like priority levels, bug categories are important to help the team members understand where to focus their efforts. Change, bug, enhancement, user interface, data, and validation might constitute a typical set of bug categories. Bugs that are marked as enhancement or change might be pushed into the next release. Of course, bugs that are marked as a bug need to be fixed. The other categories help determine whether a given bug is a UI issue, an issue with the data, or an issue with validation and business rules. Categorizing bugs also helps you report on quality metrics in the system. It is one thing to report 50 bugs in your application and another to indicate that you have 10 bugs, 30 UI issues, five data issues, and five validation issues.

> **Quick Check**
> 1. Which role in the development process should be responsible for triaging bugs?
> 2. Which role should be responsible for assessing the impact of a bug?
>
> **Quick Check Answers**
> 1. The lead developer or a strong project manager is often the best choice for triaging bugs.
> 2. Developers should determine the impact of a bug in terms of schedule, resources, and risk.

Reproduce and Fix a Bug

When you are assigned a bug, try first to reproduce it. Hopefully, the tester has indicated the steps to reproduce the bug. You should try these steps in your environment with your version of the source code. If you see the bug the tester has described, begin stepping through the code and identifying possible fixes. If you cannot reproduce the bug, sit with the tester and walk through the steps that produce the issue. Often, you see the application through someone else's eyes and realize they are using it differently than you had anticipated. This can be a good learning experience. At other times, you determine that the bug is happening in only the test environment. In this case, you need to re-create the bug environment.

Re-Create the Bug Environment

First, look for differences between the environments. You might have a good configuration management plan, but it might not have been followed. There might be differences among your development environment, the staging (preproduction) environment, and the production environment. Some of the typical differences include security (authorization, authentication), Microsoft Internet Information Services (IIS) settings such as session persistence, the operating system, the framework, third-party tools, hardware configuration, and so on. If you can identify the difference, you can usually either fix the bug by updating the test environment or re-create the bug by changing your environment.

Additional things to look for are the data and the code version. It is possible that the data the tester is using is something you did not predict. Getting a load of this data or pointing your code to the test database can help here. Of course, make sure your code matches what is deployed in the test environment. It is possible that the bug was fixed and the fix has not yet been deployed. In this case, you need to return to the branch of code that is in the test environment to verify the issue and the resolution.

Fix a Bug

All developers are familiar with the task of fixing a bug. They do it all the time. Sometimes it is in response to unit tests or debugging efforts. At other times, fixing a bug is a more formal process in response to a bug that has been assigned. Team System, for example, makes the process of fixing a bug very structured. This structure should be used for all professional development, whether or not you use Team System. The common structure for fixing a bug is as follows.

1. The developer receives some notification that a bug has been assigned. This is typically communicated through an e-mail.

2. The developer might check out the given bug work item. This indicates that he or she is working to resolve the bug.

3. The developer should then try to reproduce the bug.

4. Once identified, the developer should check out the code associated with the bug.

5. The developer should then work to fix the bug and update the unit test. The developer needs to verify the fix by running the code.

6. The developer should then check the code back into source control and comment on it with respect to the bug information. If you are using Team System, associate the change set with the bug work item.

7. The developer should then add his or her fix information to the deployment plan and release notes. This ensures that the code will be deployed with the next build. It also tracks which bugs were fixed in the given build. (Team System can do this for you.)

8. Finally, the developer should update the bug tracking software to mark the bug as resolved. The developer cannot close the bug; that is the role of the tester after he or she has verified the fix.

Lab: Assess and Triage Bugs

It is possible that you have never had the opportunity to triage bugs before. This process involves making decisions about which bugs should be fixed, by whom, and when. It is an important step to becoming a professional developer. You can use this practice section to understand the process better.

▶ **Exercise: Define Standards and Review Code**

In this exercise, you will be presented with a number of bugs. Your task is to evaluate each bug and determine how you would triage it. You should evaluate the bug as follows.

- **Impact**   Indicate whether the bug requires no additional impact assessment, requires an impact assessment, or requires escalation to stakeholder consideration.
- **Risk**   Define the risks associated with not fixing the bug.

- **Priority**   Define the bug's priority as critical, high, medium, or low.
- **Category**   Determine a category for the bug, such as bug, enhancement, specification change, user interface, data, or validation.

The following are the bug descriptions for your evaluation.

1. When testing the View Product page, I noticed that products are being displayed with the wrong product information. The image looks right, the price is correct, and the product name and number seem right, but the product description does not match the product being shown.

2. When testing the lease application process, I get to step three out of the six, and the system returns me to the first page in the step. I have tried with multiple customers and get the same results.

3. Marketing has requested that we modify the application's theme based on the new company colors and logo, but the current version of the application is using the older color scheme.

4. I was testing the system's globalization and noticed that a number of labels (over 100) on many different pages were not picking up the alternate language translation. I know this build will not be distributed to other cultures, but we did intend to prepare for a future build that supports multiple languages.

5. I was reviewing the application with the engineering team members, and they have decided that they would like to include a product configuration option. This feature should allow users to select the options they would like to receive on their ordered products.

Lesson Summary

- Testers find and document bugs. These bugs are typically triaged by a lead developer on the team. Then they are sometimes assigned to a developer who will assess the impact of the bugs so the team can make a decision about how to proceed.

- Developers should assess the impact of a bug in terms of hours to fix, resources required, the risk of not fixing the bug, and the impact the bug will have on the system and the users.

- Bugs should be prioritized based on their criticality. The most critical bugs are those that stop the testing from proceeding or that break the build.

- Bugs should be categorized into groups such as enhancement, specification change, user interface, data, validation, and bug. This categorization helps the developer understand the nature of the items that are being logged by the test team.

■ To fix a bug, you must be able to re-create it. Code often works in one environment and not in another. If this is the case, you need to review the environment and find the differences.

■ It is important for developers to follow a structured process for fixing a bug. This includes updating code, updating unit tests, verifying the fix, updating the build plan, and updating the bug as fixed.

Lesson Review

You can use the following questions to test your knowledge of the information in Lesson 3, "Evaluating and Fixing a Bug." The questions are also available on the companion CD if you prefer to review them in electronic form.

NOTE   Answers

Answers to these questions and explanations of why each answer choice is right or wrong are located in the "Answers" section at the end of the book.

---

1. You are late in the stabilizing phase of your application. You are code-complete and nearing a release. Based on the following bug synopses, which makes the most sense to escalate to project stakeholders prior to fixing?

   A. Marketing has asked to redesign the layout of the product search results page. The page is working right now. The development team has looked at the layout and indicated that it will take about two hours to accommodate the request.

   B. The administrative console application is crashing when users try to save new products to the database. The development team believes this is an issue with the code, and it will take about four hours to fix.

   C. The order management team members indicated that their request for an order tracking feature was not delivered in the current build. Upon further investigation, it seems their requirements were never included in the specifications. The development team has indicated that this feature will take more than 80 hours to code and unit test.

   D. The system is not validating user e-mail addresses. Instead, it allows any text to pass through. Developers have looked at the code and indicated that it is a bug. It should take about one hour to fix.

2. You are assigned a bug. You cannot reproduce the bug in your environment. Which of the following should you look at to determine the reason? (Choose all that apply).
   A. Version of the code between your environment and the test environment
   B. Operating system and Microsoft .NET Framework version
   C. User credentials for the executing code
   D. The data in the test environment
3. Once you've fixed a bug and verified your fix, what additional steps should you take? (Choose all that apply.)
   A. Branch your code to create a new build that isolates your fix.
   B. Update the deployment plan and release notes to include your fix.
   C. Update the bug item and mark it as fixed.
   D. Add a comment to your code to associate it with the bug tracking system.

Chapter Review

To further practice and reinforce the skills you learned in this chapter, you can complete the following tasks:

- Review the chapter summary.
- Review the list of key terms introduced in this chapter.
- Complete the case scenarios. These scenarios set up real-world situations involving the topics of this chapter and ask you to create a solution.
- Complete the suggested practices.
- Take a practice test.

Chapter Summary

- The unit testing framework is built into Visual Studio 2005. The namespace, *Microsoft.VisualStudio.TestTools.UnitTesting*, provides the classes and methods that make up this framework. This includes attribute classes such as *TestMethod*, *ClassInitialize*, and *ExpectedException*. The *TestMethod* class is used to mark a method as a unit test. The *ClassInitialize* class enables you to create a method to execute prior to executing your unit tests. The *ExpectedException* class indicates that a given unit test expects an exception to be raised as its result. In addition, the namespace includes the *Assert* class to help you determine whether a unit test succeeded or failed. This class has assertions for checking Boolean values (*IsTrue*, *IsFalse*), checking for null values (*IsNull*, *IsNotNull*), verifying whether objects are the same (*AreSame*, *AreNotSame*), and so on.

- Certain methods in your application are vital to its success and, therefore, warrant additional unit tests. You need to identify these methods as system transactions and work with the use cases and test cases to determine what additional tests you should consider.

- Test cases are written by testers to help validate that the system meets the requirements. They are typically derived from the user scenarios (or use cases). A test case includes the steps a tester should take to validate a feature, the data he or she should enter, and the expected results. You should pay special attention to alternate (or edge) cases; these typically represent good test opportunities that are not always obvious.

- Testers are responsible for integration testing. Developers need to play a part, however. Developers should verify their API, define their dependencies, and identify component interactions. They should run their code in a test environment. Once they have verified the results, they can hand off their code to the test team.

- Code reviews should start with a definition of standards. Define naming standards (for classes, methods, and properties), coding standards (for exception handling, conditional statements, and so on), and architectural standards. Once these standards are in place, implement peer-to-peer or formal code reviews. The intent is to improve the quality of the application and help developers follow best practices.

- You can use Visual Studio 2005 Team Edition to help you with your code reviews. Its Code Analysis tool, for managed code, checks code for known issues concerning security, globalization, performance, naming standards, and so on.

- Senior developers and project managers typically review bugs logged by the test team. This process is called a triage. Bugs are triaged as accepted, deferred, or requiring more information. If a bug is accepted, it typically is given a priority and category and then is assigned to a developer. Deferred bugs use enhancements, change requests, or items that are too risky to fix. Bugs that require more information are assigned to a developer to do an impact assessment.

- Developers should follow a structured process for fixing a bug. First, you need to be able to re-create the bug. Code often works in one environment and not in another. If this is the case, you must review the environment and find the differences. Once you have identified the issue as a bug, update your code, update your unit tests, verify your fix, update the build plan, and update the bug as fixed in the tracking log.

Key Terms

Do you know what these key terms mean? You can check your answers by looking up the terms in the glossary at the end of the book.

- Code Analysis
- code review
- edge case
- test case
- use case

Case Scenarios

In the following case scenarios, you will apply what you've learned about the developer's responsibilities for creating tests. You can find answers to these questions in the "Answers" section at the end of this book.

Case Scenario 1: Defining Unit Tests from a Test Case

You are a developer at a company that manages event registration. You are working on a new release of the software. Your code covers the event registration module. You have written this code to specification and developed one basic unit test for every property and every method in the application. You've just been given the event registration test case for your review.

Test Case

The following represents the event registration test case.

- **Name**   Event Registration
- **Description of functionality tested**   This test case verifies the requirements associated with a user registering for an event. The user works with the online interface to select an event, enter his or her details, and receive confirmation. This test case references the use case with the same name.
- **System state / dependency**   This test case requires that both the test event and the customer data be loaded into the test database.

  This test case requires connectivity to the hotel registration system and the payment processing engine.
- **Test case / steps**
  1. Navigate to the event management system.
  2. Select the given test event and choose View Details.
  3. Select the option to register for the event.
  4. Verify that you are now on step 1 of 5 for registering an event. This step should be to log on.
  5. Use the registrant test credentials (name and password) to log on to the site.
  6. Verify that you are now on the confirm attendee information page (step 2 of 5).
  7. Enter the registrant test details for name, name on badge, company information, address information, and demographic data.
  8. Select Next to continue the registration process.
  9. Verify that you are now on the Enter Social Networking data page (step 3 of 5).
  10. Select a random set of topics for the registrant in the Most Interested In section. Do the same for the section titled Vendors That Should Contact Me.
  11. Select Next to continue the registration process.
  12. Verify that you are now on the Book A Hotel page (step 4 of 5).
  13. Select a hotel from the list. Verify the hotel pricing against the expected data. Verify the hotel's availability. Verify that you can link to the hotel's Web site for additional information. Select one of the hotels on the list.
  14. Select Next to continue the registration process.
  15. Verify that you are now on the Finish Registration page (step 5 of 5).
  16. Enter the test payment details to book the registration.
  17. Select Finish to complete the registration process.
  18. Verify you are on the confirmation page and that all data reflects your input.

- **Data input**   Use a mix of data to properly test this application. The test data can be found in an Office Excel spread sheet titled EventRegistrationTestData.xls. This test data includes registrant information, social networking data, hotel options, payment processing, and a set of expected results.

- **Expected result**   Look at each row in the EventRegistrationTestData.xls spreadsheet to confirm the results of each instance of this test.

Alternate Case 1

- **Name**   User Not Registered

- **Description of functionality tested**   This case tests the process that a user follows when he or she is not registered in the system.

- **Test case / steps**

    1. Follow the registration process. However, upon logon, choose the New Registrant link.
    2. Verify that you are on the Define Registrant Details page.
    3. Enter the test registrant details. This includes choosing an e-mail address and password for logging on to the site.
    4. Press the Next button to continue.
    5. Verify that you have returned to the registration process at step 2.

- **Data input**   See the Non-users tab in the EventRegistrationTestData.xls spreadsheet for a list of non-registered customer data.

- **Expected result**   Each row in the Non-users worksheet in the EventRegistrationTest-Data.xls spreadsheet lists the expected results. This data includes successful tests, bounds checks, bad passwords, and so on.

Alternate Case 2

- **Name**   Hotel Unavailable

- **Description of functionality tested**   This case tests how the system behaves when the selected hotel is no longer available.

- **Test case / steps**

    1. Follow the registration process. However, select a bad hotel from the choices that follow.
    2. Verify that the booking fails and that the user is properly notified.
    3. Verify that the system returns the user to the Book A Hotel page.
    4. Select a good hotel from the list. Click the Next button to continue.
    5. Verify that the transaction completes and that the confirmation page is accurate.

- **Data input**   See the Bad Hotels tab in the EventRegistrationTestData.xls spreadsheet for a list of hotel bookings that will fail.
- **Expected result**   Each use of a Bad Hotels choice should fail. Subsequent bookings with a good hotel should succeed without incident.

Alternate Case 3

- **Name**   Transaction Denied
- **Description of functionality tested**   This case tests how the system behaves when the payment transaction fails.
- **Test case / steps**
    1. Follow the registration process. However, upon entering payment details, type the bad credit card numbers from the choices that follow.
    2. Verify that the booking fails and that the user is properly notified.
    3. Verify that the system returns the user to the Deposit page.
    4. Type the good test credit card number. Click the Next button to continue.
    5. Verify that the transaction completes and that the confirmation page is accurate.
- **Data input**   See the Bad Payment Details worksheet in the EventRegistrationTest-Data.xls spreadsheet for a list of payment details that will fail. The list includes bad credit numbers, bad expiration dates, bad confirmation codes, and bad billing ZIP codes.
- **Expected result**   Each use of a bad payment detail should fail. Subsequent bookings with good payment details should succeed without incident.

Questions

While thinking about your unit tests and the preceding test cases, answer the following questions.

1. What modifications might you make to your test cases based on the System state / dependency section of the use case?
2. What additional unit test might you consider for verifying the navigation of the system through the event registration wizard from page to page?
3. What additional unit test might you consider after reading the entire test case?
4. What changes might you make to your RegisterEvent unit test based on the Data Input and Expected Results sections of the test case?
5. What additional unit tests might you consider based on the three alternate test cases?

Case Scenario 2: Performing a Code Review

You are a senior developer hired to work at a consulting company. The last couple of projects this company did had a number of quality issues that seemed to stem from the code being unnecessarily complex and disjointed. In addition, the development team is composed of a number of new developers with very little experience. Your company cannot afford another quality issue and needs to track quality closely.

The development manager sets up a meeting with you to discuss this issue. During the meeting, he mentions that they have very little in terms of documented coding process and standards. He then starts asking you questions about doing code reviews.

Questions

Answer the following questions for your development manager.

1. We want to set up a process for doing code reviews. Where should we start?
2. Who should do the code reviews? Should this be a peer-to-peer process?
3. How will code reviews help us improve quality?
4. How can we report on the effectiveness of the code reviews?

Suggested Practices

To help you successfully master the exam objectives presented in this chapter, complete the following tasks.

Creating Effective Unit Tests

If you have just started creating unit tests, consider completing both of the following tasks. These will help you think through how you do more than just create simple unit tests. They will help you write effective unit tests that will make a significant improvement in quality.

- **Practice 1** If you are currently working on a project, you can use it for a basis. If not, find some old code that you wrote or download someone else's code. Think of this code from the users' perspective. Document the scenario to describe their steps for working with the feature. Use this information to create an effective test case. Think through the edge cases you would write to make sure the feature is sufficiently tested. If you have a tester on the team, ask him or her to review your test case and provide feedback.

- **Practice 2** Use the test case you created in Practice 1 to define a set of unit tests. Think about which methods will require the most unit tests. Think about how you can improve your unit tests to satisfy the test case and edge cases. If you already have unit tests for this code, compare them to what you concluded. Document the gaps. If you do not have unit tests, consider writing them. This will be good practice.

Performing a Code Review

To help master this objective, complete the following tasks. If you already do code reviews, you might wish to skip this practice section.

- **Practice 1**   Talk to your development manager about defining a set of standards. This does not need to be a big process. Just work as a team to brainstorm ideas. Document them and post them in a central area. As the team writes code, have them add to the standards.
- **Practice 2**   Create a code review checklist. You can use the standards document from Practice 1 for a guide. Consider also your architecture document and some of the items inside the Code Analysis tools as input. Review this checklist with the team members and get their input.
- **Practice 3**   Perform peer-to-peer code reviews. You can start by working with another team member to spot-check each other's code. You might consider working with your development manager to formalize a code review process.

Evaluating and Fixing a Bug

To help master this objective, complete both of the following tasks.

- **Practice 1**   The next time you are assigned a bug, think about it from an impact perspective. It might make sense to document the bug's impact in terms of estimated time to complete, risk of not fixing it, priority, and so on. This will help you understand the importance and cost of quality.
- **Practice 2**   If you do not have a formal bug management system, consider creating something in Excel to log and track these items. You can create simple graphs that report on the quality of the system. Use these graphs to help provide a window into the testing process and the current state of the application.

Take a Practice Test

The practice tests on this book's companion CD offer many options. For example, you can test yourself on just the content covered in this chapter, or you can test yourself on all the 70-547 certification exam content. You can set up the test so that it closely simulates the experience of taking a certification exam, or you can set it up in study mode so that you can look at the correct answers and explanations after you answer each question.

MORE INFO   **Practice tests**

For details about all the practice test options available, see the section titled "How to Use the Practice Tests" in this book's Introduction.

Chapter 16
Deploying an Application

By the time you deploy an application, the application architecture should be well established. Even though the information presented in earlier chapters will have influenced how you deploy your application, there are still many things to consider before you simply copy files up to a production server.

The first lesson in this chapter will show you how to create an application flow-logic diagram. This kind of diagram helps identify the major components of your application. It will be just one document used to evaluate your deployment plan. The second lesson will focus on validating the production configuration environment. This, too, will be useful when it is time to devise and evaluate the deployment plan. The last lesson will analyze not only the application flow-logic diagram, but also other documents created in earlier chapters.

Exam objectives in this chapter:
- Create an application flow-logic diagram.
  - ❑ Evaluate the complexity of components.
  - ❑ Evaluate the complexity of interactions with other components.
- Validate the production configuration environment. Considerations include load balancing, Web farms, and Web gardens.
  - ❑ Verify networking settings.
  - ❑ Verify the deployment environment.
- Evaluate the deployment plan.
  - ❑ Identify component-level deployment dependencies.
  - ❑ Identify scripting requirements for deployment.

Lessons in this chapter:

Before You Begin

To complete the lessons in this chapter, you should have:

- A computer that meets or exceeds the minimum hardware requirements listed in the Introduction at the beginning of this book

- Read and completed the labs from Chapter 2, "Decompose Specifications for Developers," regarding the creation of documents such as the design diagram and class diagram
- Read and completed the labs from Chapter 3, "Design Evaluation," regarding evaluating the logical and physical design
- Read and completed the labs from Chapter 8, "Component Design," regarding designing a component
- Read and completed the labs from Chapter 14, "Define and Evaluate a Testing Strategy," regarding defining an integration test plan
- Experience creating and viewing Unified Modeling Language (UML) diagrams in Microsoft Office Visio 2003 or later

---

Real World

Sara Morgan

When I first started doing application development 13 years ago, a typical server had only 64 megabytes (MB) of random access memory (RAM), applications were mostly self-contained, and although Distributed Component Object Model (DCOM) existed, people generally tried to avoid it. There were no Web applications at that time, so all applications were based on the client/server model. The biggest issues involving deployment involved the client. Because the client application had to be installed on each computer, deployment could be very tedious when dealing with hundreds or thousands of clients. There was also the dreaded "DLL hell," in which the application could be broken if someone changed the version of a dependency DLL (dynamic-link library).

Fast-forward to today, and everything is very different. For starters, there are Web-based applications, which are the focus of this book. These applications can be distributed across multiple platforms, they can easily serve thousands of concurrent users, and DLL hell is no longer a problem. Also, Web applications have resolved many deployment issues because the client does not require an installation to access the application. However, there are still many things to consider when planning a deployment.

Typical Web-based applications designed with the Microsoft .NET Framework 2.0 are composed of multiple projects joined together to form a solution. In many cases, a distributed component is used to further the capabilities of the application. This can introduce many issues surrounding configuration. In addition, you have many options regarding the network settings for server(s) to which you deploy.

Deployment planning should be considered an important step in the development of Web-based applications. Do not wait until the eve of your deployment to consider how this will be handled.

Lesson 1: Creating an Application Flow-Logic Diagram

At this point in your application development, the application architecture has been well established, and you already have a good idea of all the pieces that fit together to form your Web application. This lesson will identify a fictional Web application that customers use to access order information. You will design an application flow-logic diagram to represent the major components of this application. This diagram will eventually be used in Lesson 2, "Validating the Production Configuration Environment," to help plan the fictional application's deployment.

After this lesson, you will be able to:

- Determine and evaluate the complexity and interaction of your application's components.
- Identify the major components of your application and use Office Visio to create an application flow-logic diagram.

Estimated lesson time: 45 minutes

What Is an Application Flow-Logic Diagram?

An application flow-logic diagram is a UML diagram used to represent the major components of your application. To identify what the major components are, you will need to evaluate the interaction of all components. The purpose of this exercise is to help identify how components are related so that you can later determine the best way to package them together for deployment.

NOTE **What is UML?**

As introduced in Chapter 2, UML provides a standard way of describing objects used in an application. This is done by using a diagram to represent an object such as a class, which is drawn as a box. You can also use UML to represent other objects, such as a package and a component.

Using a Customer Order Web Application

To properly execute the process of creating an application flow-logic diagram, you will need a Web application with which to work. For this lesson and the rest of the chapter, you will refer to a fictional Web application that is used by customers to access information about orders they have placed.

Customers will be asked to log on by providing their customer number and a password that they select. If the customer has not already registered, he or she can do so at this time. Once validated, the customer will be redirected to a Web page that lists his or her current orders.

Links to each order allow the customer to drill down into the order details. He or she will also be able to search the database for orders that have already been shipped.

Even though the application will be contained within a single solution file, it will actually consist of multiple projects. The following is a breakdown of the five projects that comprise this solution:

- **Business access project**   Contains the classes used to represent the major components of this application. This includes the *Customer*, *Order*, and *Security* classes, and the overall project represents the *Business Access Layer (BAL)*. The BAL can be represented as a separate project or a folder within a project. It will have one or more class files that contain the business logic used to manipulate data returned from the database.

- **Data access project**   Contains a class file named *DataAccess*, which represents the *Data Access Layer* (DAL). Like the BAL, the DAL can be a separate project or folder that contains one or more class files. Any connections to the database should be made here and then data will be passed to the BAL.

- **Database project**   Contains SQL scripts used to create and alter the Microsoft SQL Server database. This project will be especially important when you get to the deployment stage.

- **Web service project**   Used to call functions and methods from the BAL. The Web service project is a distributed technology that, in this case, is another layer between the interface and the business logic and data access layers.

- **Web site project**   Represents the interface used by the customer to access his or her order information over the Internet. It will call Web methods exposed by the Web service project. This is known as the presentation layer.

Quick Check

- What is the application flow-logic diagram, and what is it used for?

Quick Check Answer

- The application flow-logic diagram is a UML-based diagram that is used to diagram the major components of your application. This is useful when forming the deployment plan and identifying which components need to be deployed.

Identifying Application Components

As you learned in Chapter 8, separating functionality into different components is critical for Web applications. Typically, you are going to separate your user interface from the data and the business logic. This is just a standard practice for all but the most basic of Web applications.

Therefore, you will likely have a data component used to access data from a database. This is typically known as the DAL. For the Web application that applies to this lesson, the DAL is contained within a separate project.

Components will be created to group functionality related to similar entities such as a customer or an order. The functionality for these components will typically reside within classes, and data will be exposed through properties and attributes. For the Web application in this lesson, a *Customer* class and an *Order* class will exist within the Business Access project. This will represent the BAL.

Because this application deals with a customer's order information, security is a primary concern. In this case, you will have a security component that handles authentication. It will contain methods and functions used to verify that the customer is valid and, therefore, the only one able to access his or her customer and order data.

A Web service will be used in the Web application for this lesson. You may also have additional components that are implemented via other distributed technologies. These distributed technologies allow for remote accessibility, efficient processing, and queued access, and include some of the following:

- **Web services** Used to expose data and functionality over the Internet using a communications protocol such as Simple Object Access Protocol (SOAP). The Web services are highly interoperable and can be accessed by almost any platform.
- **Remoting** Allows you to call objects from different processes and, potentially, different computers, just as if the objects resided within the same application. This requires special configuration, but it can offer a significant performance advantage with respect to remote access.
- **Enterprise services** Provide a method of building component-based applications using COM+ services. They can take advantage of services such as transactions and object pooling.
- **Microsoft Message Queue services (MSMQ)** Used to communicate asynchronously using a message queue. This is very useful when working with disconnected clients because any requests will be queued until the application is available again.

It is important to identify your distributed components because they will be deployed separately from the Web application and, typically, require special configuration. This will be important when you get to Lesson 2, "Validating the Production Configuration Environment." For the fictional Web application identified in this lesson, a Web service will be used to call methods and functions from the Customer and Order components, which, in turn, call methods and functions from the Data component. The Data component then executes stored procedures residing on the database server.

MORE INFO Distributed application development

For more information about distributed application development, refer to *MCTS Self-Paced Training Kit (Exam 70-529): Microsoft .NET Framework 2.0 Distributed Application Development* (Microsoft Press, 2006). More information is available on the Microsoft Learning Web site at *http://www.microsoft.com /learning/default.mspx*.

Your Web application may also use one or more third-party components. Typically, these components are used by Web applications to extend the interface. For example, a third-party component could be used to render a specially formatted tree view or a menu bar. Your application might also use a third-party component to perform some complex back-end function such as transferring files via the File Transfer Protocol (FTP). Each component may require special deployment steps, but at this point, you need to be concerned only with the identification of these components.

Designing an Application Flow-Logic Diagram

You will create your application flow-logic diagram using Office Visio. Using Office Visio for Enterprise Architects, available through a Microsoft Developers Network (MSDN) Premium subscription, enables you to create UML diagrams using the UML Model Diagram template.

MORE INFO MSDN premium subscription

The MSDN premium subscription can be purchased for one of five different Microsoft Visual Studio 2005 products. You can access more information about the subscription at *http:// msdn.microsoft.com/vstudio/products/subscriptions/premium/*.

The basic purpose of this diagram is to identify the components that make up your application so that you can plan your deployment. You will focus on major components only. You want to make sure each project is represented because each will produce a separate assembly that will need to be deployed. You also want to make sure that any third-party components are represented. Typically, the inclusion of third-party components will result in an additional .dll file being added to the deployment process.

The UML template contains several shapes that can be added to your diagram. Shapes are grouped into stencils that can be accessed in the left-hand pane. Refer to Figure 16-1 to see what a blank UML diagram looks like.

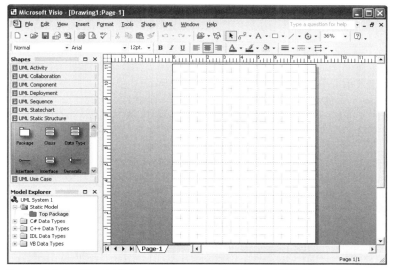

Figure 16-1 Blank UML diagram created with the UML Model Diagram template in Office Visio for Enterprise Architects

It doesn't matter which shapes you select for the diagram, but you might want to consider some of the following to build your diagrams:

- **Initial State (UML Activity stencil)** Represents the beginning of the customer ordering process.
- **Interface (Gene Sarson stencil)** Represents the interface to the customer, which is typically a Web application or Web service.
- **Component (UML Deployment stencil)** Represents each major component in the customer ordering process. Each component included will be considered for deployment.
- **Data Store (Gene Sarson stencil)** Represents the data source, which is typically a database.
- **Data Flow (Gene Sarson stencil)** Connector that represents the flow of data between the data source and a component or interface.
- **Dependency (UML Static Structure stencil)** Connector that represents a dependency between two objects.
- **Control Flow (UML Activity stencil)** Connector that represents the passing of control from one component to another.

The most important requirement is that you represent all the major components of your application. Ask yourself whether the component in question will need to be part of the deployment procedures. In the case of the fictional Web application described earlier, the following components will need to be included because each will require a step in the deployment procedures.

- Web site application
- Web Service project

- Business Access project
- Data Access project
- Database

NOTE   A note about selecting components

Keep in mind that you do not need to identify the steps involved in deployment at this time. This diagram is simply a tool that will be used later when designing the deployment plan. For this reason, although a single component might require multiple steps for deployment, these steps will not be reflected on the diagram.

Exam Tip   When doing the labs and suggested practices for this chapter, try to work with a production or near-production application. If possible, locate an application that contains multiple tiers and third-party components. Also, take the time to identify all the network requirements for your organization; do not assume that you know what all of them are. You might need to talk with network and database administrators to identify all the unique issues within your company's network.

Lab: Creating an Application Flow-Logic Diagram

This lab will walk you through the steps for creating an application flow-logic diagram when you are given a specific application architecture. If you encounter a problem completing an exercise, the completed Office Visio diagram is available in the \Chapter 16\Lesson 1\Exercise 1 folder on the companion CD.

▶ **Exercise 1: Create an Application Flow-Logic Diagram**

You are given the following requirements for a Web application that you need to deploy:

- You need to design a Web application that allows customers to add and modify orders. The solution you design will contain several projects that separate the presentation layer from the data access and business logic layers. These components will be called directly from the Web application.

- The Web application uses a special third-party component to provide calendar scheduling capabilities. This will allow customers to easily select order and shipping dates.

- The Business Access Layer will not access the database directly. Instead, it will make calls to the Data Access Layer.

- The Data Access Layer will communicate directly with the database.

In reviewing the requirements listed, create an application flow-logic diagram that will be used to plan the applications deployment.

1. Open Office Visio and create a new drawing by going to File | New | Software | UML Model Diagram.

2. To begin the diagram, you can add an *InitialState* object from the UML Activity stencil. Stencils should be available from the left-hand window. If the UML Activity stencil is not visible, you can select File | Stencils | Software | UML Activity.

3. The next object to add is an *Interface* object from the Gene Sarson stencil. You can right-click the object and select properties to add a name for this object. In this case, name the object *CustomerOrderWebSite*. You can use a *ControlFlow* object to draw an arrow between the initial state and the customer order Web site.

4. Next, you will add a *Component* object from the UML Deployment stencil that represents the third-party scheduling component. You can use a *Dependency* object to draw a link between the component and the customer order Web site.

5. You will also need to add a *Component* object from the UML Deployment stencil that will represent the Web service project, and you can use an *Interface* object to create a connection between the customer order Web site and the Web service. You will continue to add objects representing the BAL and the DAL with interface objects connecting the components.

6. The last object to be added is a *DataStore* to represent the database. You can add this object from the Gene Sarson activity stencil. You can use *DataFlow* objects to indicate that data flows back and forth from the database.

7. The resulting diagram might resemble Figure 16-2.

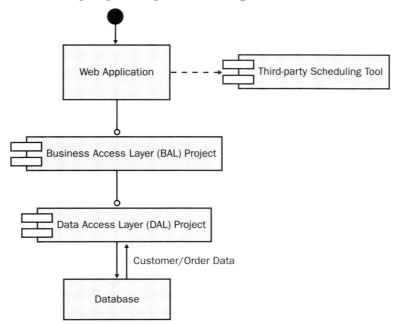

Figure 16-2   Visio diagram representing the application flow-logic diagram for the application described in this lab

Lesson Summary

- An application flow-logic diagram is a UML-based diagram that represents all the major components of your application. This will be useful when you begin planning the deployment.

- Typically, your Web application will include multiple projects, and the data access and business logic will be separated from the presentation layer. The application may also use distributed components such as Web services, remoteable objects, Enterprise services, or Message Queue Server.

- The application flow-logic diagram can be created using Office Visio for Enterprise Architects. Stencil objects can be used to represent each of the application's major components.

Lesson Review

You can use the following questions to test your knowledge of the information in Lesson 1, "Creating an Application Flow-Logic Diagram." The questions are also available on the companion CD if you prefer to review them in electronic form.

NOTE Answers

Answers to these questions and explanations of why each answer choice is right or wrong are located in the "Answers" section at the end of the book.

---

1. What is the primary purpose of an application flow-logic diagram?
   - **A.** To represent the way data flows through the application
   - **B.** To verify the validity of the initial application design
   - **C.** To represent the major components of your application
   - **D.** To identify gaps in the logic before a deployment is attempted

2. Which components would typically be included in an application flow-logic diagram? (Choose all that apply.)
   - **A.** Classes that comprise the Data Access Layer
   - **B.** Classes that comprise the Business Access Layer
   - **C.** Distributed components such as Web services, remoteable objects, enterprise services, or message queue services
   - **D.** A Web application that represents the presentation layer

Lesson 2: Validating the Production Configuration Environment

Because the process of deployment involves moving your application to another computer, it is necessary for you to know the network settings associated with the target server(s). The operational requirements of your application will determine whether more than one server needs to be involved and how each server will be configured. Identification of the deployment environment is necessary, so you can configure the application properly.

After this lesson, you will be able to:
- Verify network settings.
- Verify the deployment environment.

Estimated lesson time: 45 minutes

Analyzing Operational Requirements

Decisions regarding the operational requirements for your application should have been firmly established at this point. Most of this analysis would have been done in Chapter 3 when you were evaluating the logical and physical design. These decisions would have affected design decisions such as whether the application uses MSMQ messaging, distributed technologies, or caching. It is possible that some of the requirements established in Chapter 3 might have changed when you got to the point of performing integration tests. It is important to know what the operational requirements are so you can verify that the deployment environment satisfies those requirements.

To determine the operational requirements of your application, list out any issues specific to your application as they relate to the following categories:

- Performance
- Scalability
- Availability and recoverability
- Security

Verify Network Settings

Once you have identified the operational requirements specific to your applications, it is time to verify the network settings that will be needed to support this application. In most cases, the network settings will not be under the control of the development staff. Typically, the settings discussed in this section are controlled very tightly by your company's IT staff. This section will review the various network settings that you need to consider before planning your deployment.

Web Farms

A Web farm is a set of servers that are configured identically. Their purpose is to share the workload for a single application or a set of applications. Web farms are commonly used by Web applications that anticipate a high number of concurrent users. Because the load is distributed over multiple servers, these applications tend to scale better than applications residing on a single server. If one server starts to get too swamped, the requests are forwarded to another server. You can deploy .NET Framework applications to a Web farm using Microsoft Application Center.

Server Cluster

Server cluster refers to a set of servers that typically perform a specific function such as sharing the load for a data server. Software such as Microsoft Cluster Server can be used to create and manage the cluster. Server clusters are not only useful for sharing the load, but they can be used to provide high availability. When one of the servers in the cluster fails or is taken offline, requests are automatically directed to the available servers, and the users experience only a momentary delay. Only Microsoft Windows Server 2003 Enterprise Edition allows you to create a server cluster.

Firewalls

Firewalls come in two basic styles: software and hardware. Most companies will use one or more hardware firewalls in an effort to protect the network from security violations. The firewall sits between the Internet and your internal network servers. Depending on the firewall filters put in place by your company's IT staff, you might have issues running your application. For this reason, work closely with the IT staff to let them know where and when you plan on deploying your application.

Perimeter Network

A perimeter network represents an area of your company's network that sits between the Internet and your internal network servers. Just like a firewall, the purpose of a perimeter network is to protect the internal network, and, in many cases, it is used in conjunction with a firewall. Intruders trying to connect to servers in this area will not be able to access resources on the internal network. Typically, you will place one or more Web servers inside the perimeter network, but then your database and application servers would reside behind it.

SECURITY   Do not try to bypass network security. It is critical that you do not ignore or try to bypass the firewalls and perimeter networks implemented on your company's network. The best security system in the world will not protect you if it is not used.

User Authentication

A Web application exposed on the Internet does not always require user authentication. In this case, the *virtual directory,* which is the Web folder to which users will browse, will be configured to use anonymous authentication. This means that no user name and password is required.

User authentication is necessary when there is a need to protect the content exposed by the application. You can use a Windows or custom authentication method. If using Windows authentication, you will need to create a Windows account that uses one of the following for each user:

- **Basic**   User name and password are encoded but not encrypted (transmitted in clear text), so they can be intercepted.
- **Basic over Secure Sockets Layer (SSL)**   Uses SSL to send the user name and password, which makes it more secure than basic, but requires an SSL certificate.
- **Integrated Windows**   Uses a challenge-response mechanism for authentication, which is generally considered the most secure method.

Typically, forms-based authentication is used when the application is exposed to the general public through the Internet. It offers a secure way of protecting content without the need to create a Windows account for each user.

Quick Check

- What typical methods are used to protect a company's network from intruders?

Quick Check Answer

- Software or hardware firewalls are commonly used by even the smallest of networks, including those in your home. Companies with sensitive information might also wish to implement a perimeter network to further protect the data inside their network.

Verify the Deployment Environment

Typically, the development environment, and possibly even the staging environment, will be different than the actual deployment environment. The differences generally involve the number of servers as well as the specifications of those computers. Ideally, these environments would mirror the production environment, but not all companies can afford to dedicate that many servers to the development process. For this reason alone, you need to determine exactly what the deployment environment will consist of before you can plan the deployment.

Usually, there will be multiple servers involved in your deployment. You will have at least one Web server to host your Microsoft ASP.NET Web application. The database will reside on a back-end server that is usually protected behind a firewall. Remote components may reside on separate application servers and may also be placed behind the firewall.

Server Requirements

To ensure that your application performs appropriately, it will need to be installed on a computer with one of the following operating systems:

- Windows 2000 Server with Service Pack 2
- Windows 2000 Advanced Server with Service Pack 2
- Windows Server 2003 Web Edition with Service Pack 1
- Windows Server 2003 Standard Edition with Service Pack 1
- Windows Server 2003 Enterprise Edition with Service Pack 1
- Windows Server 2003 Standard Edition R2
- Windows Server 2003 Enterprise Edition R2

MORE INFO   **Comparing operating system versions**

For a detailed breakdown of the differences among Windows 2003 versions, refer to *http://www.microsoft.com/windowsserver2003/evaluation/features/comparefeatures.mspx#64Web%20 and%20Application%20Services*.

Depending on the needs of your application, such as whether you need server clusters, one version may be eliminated from consideration.

If your application accesses a SQL Server database, you will need to make sure the server that hosts the DAL has the correct edition of the Microsoft Data Access Components (MDAC) installed.

MORE INFO   **How to obtain the latest version of MDAC**

You can go to *http://msdn.microsoft.com/data/ref/mdac/downloads* to download the latest version of MDAC.

Servers that will run ASP.NET applications will need to have Microsoft Internet Information Services (IIS) 5.0 or later installed. IIS 6.0 is installed by default with Windows Server 2003.

The processor and memory requirements will depend on the operating system installed, but typically, install as much memory as possible and use a fast multiprocessor computer.

.NET Framework 2.0

Any servers that execute .NET Framework assemblies will need to have the .NET Framework 2.0 installed. It is possible that the .NET Framework is already installed if this is a server computer, but it might be the .NET Framework 1.1 and not the 2.0 version. You will need to verify that the correct version is installed on the servers that will host your ASP.NET application.

If the server to which you are deploying to both the .NET Framework 1.1 and 2.0 installed on it, you will need to verify that your application is configured to use the 2.0 version. Do this through the IIS properties for your application's virtual directory, as shown in Figure 16-3.

Figure 16-3 View of the ASP.NET tab used to select the version of the .NET Framework used by the virtual directory

Application Integration

It is likely that the target server has other applications already installed on it. You need to be aware of the potential impact your application will have on other applications. It is possible that the Web server or the database server will need to be taken offline for a period of time.

It is also possible that your application will need to seamlessly integrate with another Web application. For instance, the Web application described in Lesson 1, "Creating an Application Flow-Logic Diagram," was a customer order Web application. If the company already has a public Web site, you would want customers to think that the order Web site was just part of the existing Web site.

If the customer order Web site uses an interface similar to that used by the public Web site, it is not necessary for the two to exist as a single assembly. In fact, they do not even need to exist on the same server. The only step that might be necessary to integrate the two applications is to change the public Web site so that it links to Web pages in the new application. Inversely, you might need to add to the customer order Web site navigation buttons that link back to the public Web site.

Lab: Identifying Server Requirements

In this lab, you will identify the server requirements for a Web application that will be deployed on the Internet.

▶ **Exercise 1: List Server Requirements**

1. You are given the following requirements for a Web application that you need to deploy:
    - ❑ The Web application solution will contain several projects used to separate the presentation layer from the data access and business logic layers. No remote components will be used.
    - ❑ The Web application will be deployed on the Internet but will not require special security because the content is not customer-specific.
    - ❑ The most important requirements for this application are that it scale for a large number of concurrent users and perform well under peak load times.
    - ❑ Using the latest version of MDAC, the Web application will access a SQL Server database.

2. In reviewing the requirements listed in Step 1, you need to determine what the server requirements for this application should be.
    - ❑ To implement a server cluster, the servers will need Windows Server 2003 Enterprise Edition SP1 or R2. The server cluster will help the application maintain good performance under peak load times. By using this version of Windows Server, IIS 6.0 will be installed by default.
    - ❑ The server that contains the DAL will need MDAC version 2.8 installed.
    - ❑ The Web application can be configured with anonymous authentication, as shown in Figure 16-4.

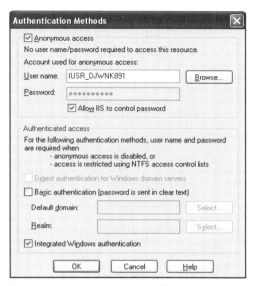

Figure 16-4   View of the Authentication Methods dialog box, which is available on the Directory Security tab for the virtual directories IIS properties

Lesson Summary

- Use the following categories when listing the operational requirements for your application: performance, scalability, availability and recoverability, and security.
- Web farms and server clusters can be used to distribute the load of an application over multiple servers.
- Firewalls and perimeter networks can be used to protect your internal network from intrusions. You should determine where servers will be placed in relation to the perimeter network before deployment.
- Web applications can be configured to use one of the following authentication methods: anonymous, Windows, custom, or forms-based.
- Typically, more than one server will be involved in the deployment. Which version of the operating system is used depends on the operational requirements of the application.
- You will need to verify that the .NET Framework 2.0 is installed on the Web server. If the application needs to be integrated with an existing application, you might need to make changes to the existing application.

Lesson Review

You can use the following questions to test your knowledge of the information in Lesson 2, "Validating the Production Configuration Environment." The questions are also available on the companion CD if you prefer to review them in electronic form.

NOTE **Answers**

Answers to these questions and explanations of why each answer choice is right or wrong are located in the "Answers" section at the end of the book.

---

1. Which operational requirement does a Web farm typically address?

    A. Security

    B. Scalability

    C. Extensibility

    D. Data integrity

2. In a multiserver deployment of an ASP.NET application, which types of entities are involved? (Choose all that apply.)

    A. Application server

    B. Back-end server

    C. End-user application

    D. Web servers

3. Which authentication method is typically used when the Web application is exposed to the public over the Internet?

    A. Forms-based

    B. Anonymous

    C. Windows - Basic

    D. Windows - Integrated

Lesson 3: Evaluating the Deployment Plan

Deployment is the process of taking a production-ready application and moving it to another computer. In some cases, this might involve using one or more setup programs to automate the steps required. This lesson will evaluate the different options available for deployment. Based on the requirements discussed in the first two lessons and on documents created in earlier chapters, you will generate a deployment plan.

After this lesson, you will be able to:
- Identify component-level dependencies.
- Identify scripting requirements for deployment.

Estimated lesson time: 45 minutes

Real World

Sara Morgan

I recently worked for a company that produced software for city legislatures. We followed very strict methodologies regarding design and development. But, when it came to deployment, we tended to get a little lazy. According to the rules we had established, all deployments were supposed to be done using setup programs. The problem was that we always seemed to be running up against a deadline and, because copying the files was the fastest option, that was typically what was done. In many cases, a developer would copy over just the files that had been changed, using the drag-and-drop feature of Windows Explorer.

The problem was that there were times when a copy of files did not result in a clean deployment. Either certain dependency files were not included or some scripting step was left out. The biggest issue was that there was no archive of the deployment versions. By using setup programs that were named according to the version deployed, we were able to keep an archive of each version. Even though we had Microsoft Visual Source Safe (VSS) to use for versioning control, it was helpful to have a setup file that could quickly be run and did not require us to roll back to a previous code version.

The moral of this story is that deployment is just as important as any of the other development steps. If your deployment is not done properly, your application might not run correctly, and all that hard work you did during development will have been for nothing.

Review Design Documents

Before you begin planning your deployment, review some of the documents created earlier, such as the application flow-logic diagram created in Lesson 1. These documents will help you to identify all the component-level dependencies and identify any scripting opportunities. By doing this, you will be prepared to create a project plan outline that lists the steps needed for deployment.

In addition to the application flow-logic diagram, consider the following documents created in earlier chapters:

- **Component Diagram from Lesson 3, "Create Application (Physical) Models for Developers," in Chapter 2**   This is a UML-based diagram that represents all the components of a .NET application. It is more detailed than the application flow-logic diagram, which was used to represent the high-level components. This diagram will get into more detail and might help identify anything that was missed in the application flow-logic diagram.

- **Class Diagram from Lesson 3 in Chapter 2**   This is a UML-based diagram that provides a basic overview of your application. It describes the objects in your application, which are usually represented as classes. Just like with the component diagram, this should help identify any component dependencies for your application that might have been previously overlooked.

- **Integration Test Plan from Lesson 2, "Evaluating the Integration, Stress, and Performance Test Strategies," in Chapter 14**   Unit testing involves testing the individual pieces of your application that might have been created by separate developers. Integration testing involves the testing of all these pieces operating as a whole. It gives you a big picture and sometimes uncovers problems that you would not see by testing just individual components. You would have created a test plan for this type of testing in Chapter 14, and this would be useful in identifying any areas that might need to be deployed.

Create a Project Plan Outline

It is a good practice to create a project plan outline for your deployment. The outline document will simply list the steps needed for a successful deployment. It will take into account configuration requirements and any other special steps needed to deploy your applications. In many cases, the steps will include the execution of setup projects or the creation of backups. Additional steps might include the notification of key people affected by the deployment. The tool used to create the document is not important, although I would suggest a tool such as Microsoft Office Word.

Define a Timeline

Include a timeline for deployment that includes a target deployment date and estimates how long the deployment will take to complete. Remember to expect the unexpected. Whatever can go wrong usually does. It is better to add buffer room to your time estimates than to end up in a bad situation.

Typically, schedule your deployment during a time when users will not be on the network, such as in the evening. For companies that operate 24 hours a day, seven days a week, this is not possible. Most companies will need to schedule the downtime of their Web applications, particularly if they are available on the Internet. Again, select a time when the lowest number of users will be accessing the system. You can review IIS log files to determine when this time period is. And do not forget to give yourself plenty of time to handle the unexpected delays.

Determine Resource Requirements

Typically, a deployment will involve more than just a single developer. Make a list of these resources including what time period during the deployment they are needed. This will also include any preparation prior to the actual deployment. Depending on the complexity of your application, you might have all or some of the following resources involved:

- Development lead
- Development team
- Quality assurance representative/tester
- Decision maker/manager
- Windows administrator
- Network administrator
- Database administrator
- End user (if the application is used internally by your company)

Schedule a Deployment Pilot

It is important to allow for a test run of your deployment. At this point, you will quickly discover whether your deployment plan is feasible. The pilot should involve executing all steps listed in the deployment plan.

More than likely, you will not be able to deploy to the production environment until the day of deployment, but you can still schedule a pilot run. If your staging environment closely resembles the production environment, you can practice by deploying or redeploying to these servers.

NOTE Redeploying an existing application

When updating an application that is already in production, use a setup program and, when it is executed, specify that the files will be copied to a new directory. You can then change the virtual directory to point to the new directory. You could also create a new virtual directory and verify that the deployment was successful before reconfiguring the original virtual directory.

Specify a Back-out Plan

Always include a back-out section in your project plan. This should provide detailed steps for how you will reverse everything that has been done. It is not enough to simply reverse the deployment steps.

To complete a back-out plan, go through each deployment step and determine what would need to be done if you backed out at that point. Make sure you include a step for notification of the appropriate people.

Deployment Options

The .NET Framework provides the following three methods for deploying your application:

- **XCOPY Deployment**   A simple process of just copying your files from one location to another using a command-line tool called XCOPY, File Transfer Protocol (FTP), or Windows Explorer. This method does not allow for automation opportunities through the use of scripts.

  IMPORTANT   **Restarting the application**

  One thing to keep in mind when doing an XCOPY deployment is that when you replace the web.config in an application, ASP.NET automatically performs an application restart. Depending on the complexity of your application, this can cause problems with the way it performs.

- **Copy Web Site**   Web sites can be copied using the Copy Web Site dialog box (see Figure 16-5), which is available from the Visual Studio Website menu item. Just like XCOPY deployment, this is a simple process that copies the files from only one location to another. It should be used only for simple deployment scenarios.

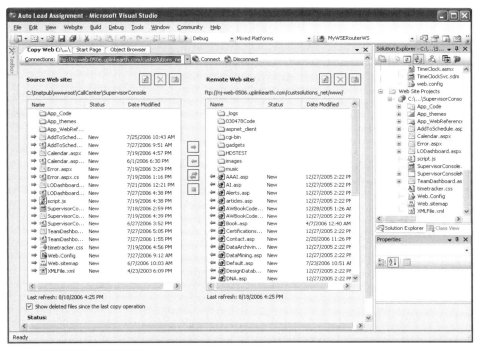

Figure 16-5 View of the Copy Web Site dialog box, which is used to copy a Web site from the local computer to a remote host

■ **Web Setup Projects** Web setup projects package all the files needed to deploy a Web application into a single Microsoft installer file. These files have a .msi file extension, and they allow you to automate certain tasks such as the creation and configuration of a virtual directory. They also allow you to roll back the installation in case of failure and initiate an uninstall if necessary. For these reasons, setup projects are generally the preferred method of deployment.

MORE INFO **About deployment**

The Microsoft .NET Framework Developer Center provides a .NET Deployment Guide that would be useful to candidates preparing for this exam. You can access this document at *http://msdn.microsoft.com/netframework/technologyinfo/infrastructure/deployment/default.aspx*.

Lab: Create a Web Setup Project

In this lab, you will create a Web setup project using a test Web application. If you do not have a test application available, you can download and install the Time Tracker ASP.NET Starter Kit from MSDN. You can access this starter kit at *http://msdn.microsoft.com/vstudio/*

express/vwd/starterkit/default.aspx#timetracker. Exercise 1 shows the steps required to download and use the Time Tracker Starter Kit. If you have an application available, you may skip to Exercise 2.

NOTE   Install SQL Server Express and the Time Tracker Starter Kit

You will need to have SQL Server Express installed on your computer to execute the application. You will also need to download and install the Time Tracker Starter Kit from *http://msdn.microsoft.com /vstudio/express/vwd/starterkit/default.aspx# timetracker.*

▶ **Exercise 1: Download and Install the Time Tracker Starter Kit**

In this exercise, you will download and install the ASP.NET Time Tracker Starter Kit from MSDN.

1. Browse to *http://msdn.microsoft.com/vstudio/express/vwd/starterkit/default.aspx#time tracker* and click the Download the Kit link.

2. Download the time.vsi file to your local computer and execute this file. This will start the installer, and you can accept the defaults to install the template on your local development computer.

3. Open Microsoft Visual Studio 2005.

4. Select File | New | Web Site.

5. Select Time Tracker Starter Kit from My Templates and enter the name and location of a project. Then select the language you wish to use (Microsoft Visual Basic or Visual C#), and then click OK. This will create a new project by using the installed starter kit template.

6. Press Ctrl+F5 to start the application without debugging. The application should open to the logon page inside your Web browser.

7. Click Create New User, enter the required information, and click Create User.

8. Using the user logon you just created, you can now execute pages within the Time Tracker application.

▶ **Exercise 2: Add a Web Setup Project**

In this exercise, you will add a Web setup project to an existing Web application solution. This project can be used to deploy the application to a remote server.

1. Open Visual Studio 2005 and open either an existing Web application solution or the Time Tracker application created in Exercise 1.

2. Select File | Add | New Project.

3. Expand the *Other Project Types* node, select Setup and Deployment, and then select Web Setup Project as the template.

4. Accept the default name and location for the project file and click OK. A new deployment project will be added to the solution.

5. Click the WebSetup project and then, in the Properties pane, locate the *RemovePreviousVersions* property. Change this to a value of *True*, which tells the installer to remove previous versions of the application before beginning the new install.

6. From the Properties pane for the Web project, change the *Title* property to **My Web Setup Project** and the *ProductName* property to **Web Application**.

7. Click the Web Application Folder on the left and locate the *VirtualDirectory* property. Change this to a value of **TestWebApplication**. This will be the name of the virtual directory created on the target computer.

8. Right-click the project file and select Build. Ensure that the bottom-left taskbar displays Build Succeeded.

9. Locate the WebSetup.msi file on your development computer. It should be in a debug folder for the WebSetup project. Copy this file to a new computer that has IIS installed on it.

10. Execute the WebSetup.msi file on the target computer and note the appearance of the title and product name fields that you entered as properties.

11. You can go back through the Web setup project and change other property values. Then rebuild the project and execute the WebSetup.msi file again. Note any changes you made and see how they affected the installation.

Lesson Summary

■ The first step in creating a deployment plan is to review some of the design documents. These documents include the application flow-logic diagram, component diagram, class diagram, and integration test plan.

■ A deployment project plan should include all the steps necessary for deployment. This will serve as a checklist during the deployment.

■ The project plan should include a timeline that allows for unanticipated issues. It should also include a listing of the resources required before, during, and after deployment.

■ The project plan should also include a pilot plan and a back-out plan. The pilot plan will quickly identify potential problems, and the back-out plan can be implemented in case of emergencies.

■ The .NET Framework provides the following three methods for deployment: XCOPY deployment, Copy Web Site, and the creation of Web setup projects.

Lesson Review

You can use the following questions to test your knowledge of the information in Lesson 3, "Evaluating the Deployment Plan." The questions are also available on the companion CD if you prefer to review them in electronic form.

NOTE   Answers

Answers to these questions and explanations of why each answer choice is right or wrong are located in the "Answers" section at the end of the book.

---

1. Identify the resources that may be specified in the resource requirements section of your deployment project plan. (Choose all that apply.)

    A. Development lead

    B. Manager

    C. End user

    D. Network administrator

2. Which deployment method provides a way of rolling back an installation?

    A. Copy Web Site

    B. Web setup project

    C. XCOPY deployment

    D. Both A and B

Chapter Review

To further practice and reinforce the skills you learned in this chapter, you can complete the following tasks:

- Review the chapter summary.
- Review the list of key terms introduced in this chapter.
- Complete the case scenarios. These scenarios set up real-world situations involving the topics of this chapter and ask you to create a solution.
- Complete the suggested practices.
- Take a practice test.

Chapter Summary

- As part of the deployment planning process, it is useful to create an application flow-logic diagram. This UML-based diagram is used to identify the major components that comprise your application.
- The application flow-logic diagram can be created using Visio for Enterprise Architects.
- Several factors will go into determining the operational requirements for your application. Many of these will be determined through the initial design, but some factors will be determined based on the restrictions of your company's network. Some of these factors will include the use of Web farms or server clusters. You might also have to work with existing firewalls and perimeter networks.
- A deployment project plan should be created prior to deployment. It should include the following: detailed steps to complete deployment, a timeline, resource requirements, a pilot plan, and a back-out plan.
- The following types of deployment may be performed with the .NET Framework: XCOPY deployment, use of the Copy Web Site dialog box, and creation of a Web setup project.

Key Terms

Do you know what these key terms mean? You can check your answers by looking up the terms in the glossary at the end of the book.

- Business Access Layer (BAL)
- Data Access Layer (DAL)
- enterprise services

- Microsoft Message Queue services (MSMQ)
- Remoting
- Unified Modeling Language (UML)
- virtual directory
- Web services

Case Scenarios

In the following case scenarios, you will apply what you've learned about deploying an application. You can find answers to these questions in the "Answers" section at the end of this book.

Case Scenario 1: Designing a Plan

You work for an insurance company that has spent months developing a complex ASP.NET application. The Web application will be used by the company's customers to access insurance quotes and then apply for insurance coverage.

The application is near completion, and you were just told by the applications manager that the team plans to deploy it into production at the end of the month. You ask to see the deployment plan, and the manager tells you one does not exist. What do you suggest?

Case Scenario 2: Using a Web Setup Project

You have just completed development of a small ASP.NET application that will be used by your company to track employees' time. The application is designed to use a tiered structure, and it also uses third-party components.

You expect that once the application is deployed, employees in the company will request changes, so this application will constantly be enhanced. Your manager has asked how you plan to deploy the project to production. What do you tell him?

Suggested Practices

To help you successfully master the exam objectives presented in this chapter, complete the following tasks.

Create an Application Flow-Logic Diagram

To perform these practices, you will need a production-ready application. If you do not have one in your organization, download and install the latest version of the Time Tracker ASP.NET Starter Kit, available at *http://msdn.microsoft.com/vstudio/express/vwd/starterkit /default.aspx#timetracker*.

- **Practice 1** List all the high-level components involved with your application. Determine how they relate to each other to see whether there are any dependencies.
- **Practice 2** Create an Office Visio diagram that identifies all the major components of your application. This type of diagram was used in Lesson 3 to evaluate the deployment plan.

Validate the Production Configuration Environment

To perform these practices, you will need to identify the configuration environment for your company. This will likely involve speaking to other people in your organization, such as development leads and/or network administrators.

- **Practice 1** List all the settings in your network that will affect how the application will be deployed. This will include things such as whether there is a firewall or a perimeter network. You also need to determine whether scalability and performance tools such as Web farms and server clusters are needed.
- **Practice 2** List all the settings that are specific to your deployment environment. This includes identifying the number of servers needed for deployment along with the server requirements for those servers.

Evaluate the Deployment Plan

To perform these practices, try to locate a production-ready application used in your organization. If one is not available, you can download and install the latest version of the Time Tracker ASP.NET Starter Kit from MSDN at the following URL: *http://msdn.microsoft.com/vstudio/express /vwd/starterkit/default.aspx#timetracker*.

- **Practice 1** Based on the information collected from the first two practices, create a deployment project plan. Think about all the things that would be required to deploy the application in your company's production environment. You might have to speak with IT staff and members of other groups to get a handle on the necessary steps.
- **Practice 2** Create a Web setup project using the Web application. Execute the resulting .msi file to install the Web application on a test server or development computer.

Take a Practice Test

The practice tests on this book's companion CD offer many options. For example, you can test yourself on just one exam objective, or you can test yourself on all the 70-547 certification exam content. You can set up the test so that it closely simulates the experience of taking a certification exam, or you can set it up in study mode so that you can look at the correct answers and explanations after you answer each question.

MORE INFO   Practice tests

For details about all the practice test options available, see the "How to Use the Practice Tests" section in this book's Introduction.

Chapter 17
Supporting an Application

Once you deploy your application to production, the next thing to consider is support. An application is a living thing in that it often needs maintenance to perform optimally.

Lesson 1, "Monitoring Application Performance," will show you how to evaluate the performance of your application based on certain key indicators. You will learn how to identify performance spikes, analyze performance trends, and track response times and logon times. Collection and analysis of this data will enable you to identify any problem areas of your application.

Lesson 2, "Analyzing Performance Data," will focus on analyzing the data retrieved in Lesson 1. You will learn which system monitor counters are optimal for monitoring how well your application is performing. You will also learn how to use the Health Monitoring application programming interface (API) available with the Microsoft .NET Framework 2.0.

Exam objectives in this chapter:
- Evaluate the performance of an application that is based on the performance analysis strategy.
    - ❑ Identify performance spikes.
    - ❑ Analyze performance trends.
    - ❑ Track page response times.
    - ❑ Track logon times.
- Analyze the data received when monitoring an application.
    - ❑ Monitor and analyze resource usage.
    - ❑ Monitor and analyze security aspects.
    - ❑ Track bugs that result from customer activity.
    - ❑ Choose when to use ASP.NET 2.0 Health Monitoring APIs.

Lessons in this chapter:

Before You Begin

To complete the lessons in this chapter, you must be familiar with the Microsoft Windows Performance console and have:

- A computer that meets or exceeds the minimum hardware requirements listed in the Introduction at the beginning of this book.
- Microsoft Visual Studio 2005 and the .NET Framework 2.0 installed on your computer.
- Microsoft SQL Server 2005 Express Edition installed on your computer.

Real World

Sara Morgan

Unfortunately, not all application problems can be uncovered before deployment. Very often, issues with an application are not discovered until "real" users start using the system. Up until that point, you do not truly know how the application will behave.

Don't get me wrong. This does not mean that I think unit and integration testing should not be done. I think preliminary testing is absolutely necessary and should be done in all cases. However, in my experience, some application problems will not arise until after the application has been deployed into production.

For example, I once deployed into production an ASP.NET application that did not experience problems until three months after deployment. All of a sudden, the application would periodically lock up the application server. Initially, the problem did not seem to be caused by any one action, but after two weeks, I discovered that the problem was triggered by one user who performed a particular sequence of actions. In the initial testing, the faulty sequence was never tested, so the problem was not uncovered until after deployment.

This chapter covers what you should do once the application has been deployed. With proper monitoring, you might be able to catch problems before the user is even aware of them. There is no better feeling than to head off a problem before it becomes a disaster.

Lesson 1: Monitoring Application Performance

This lesson will focus on using Windows System Monitor or the Performance Monitor tool to monitor the performance of your application. You will learn how to use objects and counters to track the progress of certain key counters. By seeing the results displayed graphically, you can quickly locate spikes and trends in the data.

After this lesson, you will be able to:
- Use System Monitor to identify performance spikes and performance trends.
- Use System Monitor to track page response times and look at data specific to the .NET Common Language Runtime (CLR).

Estimated lesson time: 60 minutes

Using Windows System Monitor

System Monitor (also known as perfmon) is a utility tool that can be used to track the performance of an application in real time. You can start System Monitor by clicking Start | Settings | Control Panel | Administrative Tools | Performance. Alternatively, you can click Start | Run and type **perfmon.msc**. Doing so will open the Performance console (see Figure 17-1) and, by default, System Monitor will already be monitoring certain key counters for the current computer.

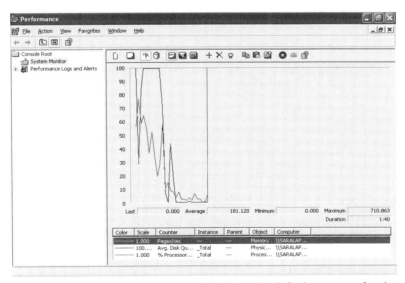

Figure 17-1 System Monitor tool displaying the default counters for the current computer

System Monitor allows you to log the data collected by the tool. This is important because it is not likely that you will have someone available to continually watch the graph as it displays activity. Logging allows you to save this data and review it later. Data can be saved to a log file or a database table.

You can create alerts that apply to specific *performance counters*. The counter represents the measurement of a specific performance object or system component. *Alerts* will be triggered when the value of a counter is over or under some predetermined threshold. The counter and the capabilities of the application server determine what the value of this threshold should be. You can configure the alert to log an entry to the application event log, send a network message to a certain network account, write an entry to a log file, or execute a specific program when triggered.

MORE INFO   How to obtain the Performance Monitor Wizard

You can download the Performance Monitor Wizard, which will take you through the steps necessary to create a performance monitor log. Not only will it help you select the settings for configuration, but the standard perfmon log will select which counters are best. The free download is available from *http://www.microsoft.com/downloads/details.aspx?FamilyID=31fccd98-c3a1-4644-9622 -faa046d69214&displaylang=en&Hash=7YTJ6NC.*

To add counters, you can click the Add button (plus sign) on the toolbar or right-click inside the graph and select Add Counters. The Add Counters dialog box (see Figure 17-2) allows you to add one or more counters to the current graph. By default, it will point to the current computer. You have the option to provide the name of a remote computer as long as your network account has permission.

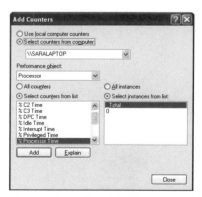

Figure 17-2   The Add Counters dialog box, which is used to add performance counters to the current graph

---

NOTE **Permissions needed to add counters**

To add counters to a performance log, your Microsoft Windows account must be a member of the local Administrator group or Performance Log Users group. Alternatively, your Windows account can belong to the Domain Admins group for the network.

You also need to specify the object, counter, and instance. The *performance object* refers to the subsystem you are monitoring. For instance, if you want to monitor data specifically related to the memory on the server, you will select the memory object. The objects that appear in the Performance Object drop-down list depend on what is installed on the computer. For instance, if SQL Server 2005 is installed, you will see several objects that begin with the SQLServer prefix.

Once the object is selected, the counters list box will contain a list of counters specific to that object. To see the description for a counter, select the counter and click the Explain button. Values displayed in the instance list box are also specific to the object selected. This is necessary because some objects, such as *Processor*, might have more than one instance associated with them, but not all objects will have the ability to select an instance. Once the counter and instance are selected, the Add button is used to add an instance of that counter to the current graph.

Through the View Report button located on the toolbar, System Monitor provides a quick view of the counters that have been selected thus far. By selecting this button, you will see the counter results displayed as text (see Figure 17-3) rather than in a graphical format.

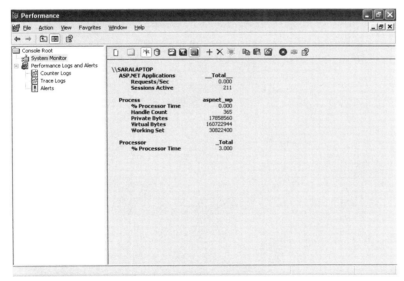

Figure 17-3   The Peformance console displaying a report for currently added counters

Identifying Performance Spikes

A *performance spike* is an anomaly that would likely go undetected if performance was not being tracked and logged. It represents a temporary rise in activity, which might not be handled gracefully by the application. If spikes happen too often, it could be an indication that the server hosting the application is overloaded. In certain situations, it might be necessary to make a change to the application or the application environment.

Not all performance spikes indicate a problem that needs to be corrected. Very often, you need to evaluate multiple counters over a period of time before you can draw a conclusion about the effect of the performance spike. Performance spikes are important in that they are sometimes the first indication of a problem.

Analyzing Performance Trends

Performance spikes represent a temporary and dramatic rise in the value of a performance counter. This might or might not indicate a problem with the application. Rather than looking for spikes in the data, it might be better to analyze performance trends. A trend represents a consistent rise or fall in the value of a performance counter over a specified period of time.

One method for identifying whether a trend is significant is to compare it to a baseline. A *performance baseline* represents a measurement of certain performance counters under normal circumstances. By comparing data collected from the baseline against the data during the performance trend, you can see whether the trend was significant. Figure 17-4 shows a baseline for a simple ASP.NET application.

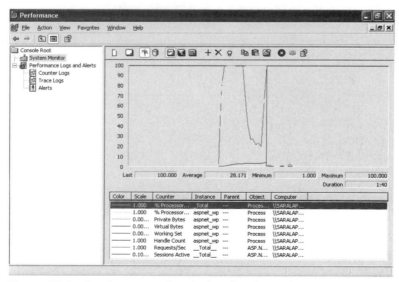

Figure 17-4   Graph representing the baseline for an ASP.NET application

Quick Check

- Describe the difference between performance trends and performance spikes.

Quick Check Answer

- Performance spikes represent a sudden escalation in the value of a performance monitor. They might or might not indicate a problem with the application and, by themselves, are generally not indicative of a problem. Performance trends are more useful in identifying application problems because they involve comparing the results of multiple counters against a baseline. The baseline represents a period of time when the application was performing satisfactorily.

MORE INFO Referencing the ASP.NET worker process instance

Some performance counters require you to specify an instance. For performance objects such as the *Process* object, you will want to specify the aspnet_wp instance when monitoring ASP.NET applications. (Note that wp stands for "worker process.") It is important to note that the aspnet_wp instance will not appear in the drop-down box unless it has been initiated on the computer being monitored. The aspnet worker process is initiated the first time that an ASP.NET Web page is requested.

The Microsoft Developer Network (MSDN) identifies the counters listed in Table 17-1 as key system monitor counters. These are but a few of the many objects and counters available to you. Exactly which counters are needed is something you will determine through experience and practice.

Table 17-1 Key Performance Counters for ASP.NET Applications

Object	Counter	Instance	Description
Processor	% Processor Time	_Total	Indicates the amount of processor activity by displaying the percentage of busy time.
Process	% Processor Time	aspnet_wp	Indicates the percentage of elapsed time that was used to execute instructions for the current request. Because you picked the aspnet_wp instance, it specifically relates to your ASP.NET application.
Process	Private Bytes	aspnet_wp	Current size, in bytes, of memory that cannot be shared with another process.
Process	Virtual Bytes	aspnet_wp	Current size, in bytes, of virtual space dedicated to the aspnet worker process.
Process	Handle Count	aspnet_wp	Total number of threads open for the application.

Table 17-1   Key Performance Counters for ASP.NET Applications

Object	Counter	Instance	Description
Process	Working Set	aspnet_wp	Current size, in bytes, of the memory dedicated to the aspnet worker process.
ASP.NET Applications	Requests/Sec	_Total_	Number of requests executed per second.
ASP.NET Applications	Sessions Active	_Total_	Number of sessions currently active.
ASP.NET	Application Restarts	—	Number of times the application has been restarted.
ASP.NET	Requests Rejected	—	Number of requests rejected because the queue was full.
ASP.NET	State Server Sessions Active	—	Current number of sessions active, if you are using a State server to store your session state.
ASP.NET	Request Execution Time	—	Number of milliseconds to execute the current request.
Memory	Available Mbytes	—	Amount of physical memory in Mb available on the server.
Web Service	Current Connections	_Total	Number of connections currently established.
Web Service	ISAPI Extension Requests/sec	_Total	Rate of Internet Server Application Programming Interface (ISAPI) extension requests currently being processed.

Once you have determined which counters to add, you can create a log that records the data collected for a specified period of time. The log file will represent your performance baseline and can be compared against data collected in the future. The important thing here is to ensure that your baseline was recorded at a time when the application was performing satisfactorily—in other words, no errors were experienced, and the response to users was fast and consistent.

Exam Tip   There are hundreds of performance counters available on most servers. Do not try to memorize all the available counters and objects. Just focus on those specifically listed in the tables of this chapter.

Tracking Page Response Times

Page response time is one of the most important factors in determining the success of your Web site. If users are forced to wait several seconds for a Web page to be fully rendered, they will quickly become frustrated. Therefore, it is important for you to keep an eye on how fast your Web application renders Web pages.

To measure the page response time, you need to take into account several factors, such as the time it takes for both the server and the client to process the request. When analyzing the page response time for your Web site, you want to look at Web pages that you expect will take the longest to render. Typically, these will be search pages or those Web pages that require heavy processor-intensive database requests. Consider also those pages that are accessed most frequently. If you are not sure which pages are accessed the most, check your Microsoft Internet Information Services (IIS) log files. Consider calls to a Web service and distributed transactions also.

Once you have identified the Web pages to measure, you will need to use a tool such as the Microsoft Web Application Stress Tool (available as a free download from MSDN at *http://www.microsoft.com/downloads/details.aspx?familyid=E2C0585A-062A-439E-A67D -75A89AA36495&displaylang=en*) to simulate the load. This tool can be used to simulate multiple requests to the same Web page through a recorded script. At the same time, you will use System Monitor to measure certain counters related to page response time, such as requests per second.

NOTE Determine whether an NLB cluster is used

Because a Network Load Balancing (NLB) cluster (also known as a Web cluster) is used to distribute the load of Web requests over multiple servers, you need to use special settings with the Web Application Stress Tool to account for this situation. Refer to the documentation that accompanies the stress tool for more information regarding which settings should be altered.

Another tool that you can use to simulate user requests (specifically, dynamic requests that use variables) is Microsoft Application Center Test (ACT), which comes bundled with Microsoft Visual Studio Enterprise Edition. This tool offers several helpful features and can be considered an advanced tool for analyzing your applications performance.

System Monitor allows you to store collected data in a log file or a Microsoft SQL Server database. By doing this, you can maintain a log of data that is analyzed periodically. You can access the log properties by clicking the the View Log Data button on the Performance console toolbar or by pressing Ctrl+L. To log the data to a SQL Server database, you will need to specify a system data source name (DSN) along with a time range.

NOTE **Consider using data mining to analyze log data**

SQL Server Analysis Services 2005 features the ability to generate data-mining models. Mining models can be used to form predictions based on historical data. If you store in a database data collected from System Monitor, you can then build a mining model against that data. You will then have access to a rich set of charts and graphs that can help you identify trends within your data.

Tracking Logon Times

You can use performance counters to track user and connection activity. This type of monitoring can be useful for determining the number of users accessing your application. It can also help identify problems with the application keeping too many connections open. Table 17-2 lists some of the counters available with the Web Service performance object.

Table 17-2 Performance Counters to Track User and Connection Activity

Counter	Description
Connection Attempts/sec	The rate per second at which connections are made
Current Connections	The number of current connections
Logon Attempts/sec	The rate per second at which logons are established
Total Connection Attempts	Total number of connections attempted
Total Logon Attempts	Total number of logons attempted

You might also wish to track the specific logon times for users of your application. This type of information can be useful not only as an auditing tool but might indicate trends such as users from one department accessing the system more than users from another department.

It can also be useful to track logon failures and either write these failures to the server's application event log or alert a server administrator. You can create a new alert by executing the following steps.

1. From System Monitor, expand the *Performance Logs* and *Alerts* node and select the node named *Alerts*.
2. Right-click the *Alerts* node and select New Alert Settings. Enter a name for your alert.
3. From the General tab, specify a description and add one or more performance counters. (See Figure 17-5.)
4. Specify threshold values for the counter by selecting a value from the Alert when the value is drop-down box. The alert can be generated when a value falls under or over some predetermined limit.
5. On the Action tab, specify an action that will be performed such as sending an e-mail, writing an entry to the event log, or executing some program.

Figure 17-5   Dialog box used to specify counters for a Performance Alerts

Lab: Monitoring Application Performance

In this lab, you will download and install the ASP.NET Time Tracker starter kit. You can then create and execute your own ASP.NET application based on the starter kit template. While you are executing the application, you can use System Monitor to observe some of the key performance monitor counters. If you encounter a problem completing an exercise, the completed projects can be installed from the Code folder on the companion CD.

▶ **Exercise 1: Download and Install the Time Tracker Starter Kit**

In this exercise, you will download and install the ASP.NET Time Tracker starter kit from MSDN. Note: You will need to have SQL Server Express Edition installed on your computer to execute the application.

1. Browse to *http://msdn.microsoft.com/vstudio/express/vwd/starterkit/default.aspx#timetracker* and then click the Download The Kit link.

2. Download the time.vsi file to your local computer and execute this file. Accept the defaults to install the template on your local development computer.

3. Open Visual Studio 2005.

4. Select File | New | Web Site.

5. Select Time Tracker Starter Kit from My Templates, and enter the name and location of a project. Then select the language that you wish to use (either Microsoft Visual Basic or C#). This will create a new project, using the installed starter kit template.

6. Press Ctrl+F5 to start the application without debugging. The application should open to the logon page inside your Web browser.

7. Click Create New User, enter the required information, and click Create User.

8. You can now execute pages within the Time Tracker application, using the user logon that you just created.

▶ **Exercise 2: Monitor Time Tracker by Using System Monitor**

In this exercise, you will use System Monitor to track key performance counters while executing the Time Tracker application.

1. On the Windows Start menu, select Run.
2. Type **perfmon.msc** and press Enter.
3. On the toolbar, click the Add button, or press Ctrl+I.
4. Select *Processor* object as the performance object and % Processor Time as the counter, and then click Add.
5. Select *Process* object as the performance object, and then select the following counters (instances):
    - ❑ % Processor Time (aspnet_wp)
    - ❑ Virtual Bytes (aspnet_wp)
    - ❑ Private Bytes (aspnet_wp)
    - ❑ Handle Count (aspnet_wp)
    - ❑ Working Set (aspnet_wp)
6. Select the *ASP.NET* object as the performance object, and then select the following counters:
    - ❑ State Server Sessions Active
    - ❑ Application Restarts
    - ❑ Requests Rejected
7. Select the *ASP.NET Applications* object as the performance object, and then select the following counters:
    - ❑ Requests/sec
    - ❑ Sessions Active
    - ❑ State Server Sessions Active
    - ❑ Request Execution Time
8. Select the *Memory* object as the performance object, and then select the following counter:
    - ❑ Available Mbytes
9. Select the *Web Service* object as the performance object, and then select the following counters:
    - ❑ Current Connections
    - ❑ ISAPI Extension Requests/sec

10. Go back to the Time Tracker application created in Exercise 1, "Download and Install the Time Tracker Starter Kit," and press Ctrl+F5 to run the application. When the logon page appears in the browser, log on as the user you created in Exercise 1. As you browse through the application, switch back to System Monitor and note how the counter values are changing.
11. Select each counter and note the values in the Last, Average, Minimum, Maximum, and Duration labels beneath the graph.

Lesson Summary

- System Monitor (or perfmon) is a utility tool that you can use to collect data about how your ASP.NET application is performing. You can add one or more counters to a real-time graph, and the data values can be saved to a database or log file.
- Performance spikes represent a temporary rise in the value of a counter. They might or might not indicate a problem with the application.
- Performance trends can be identified by comparing the values of several data counters against a baseline. The baseline represents the same set of counter data, recorded during a time when the application was performing well.
- User and connection properties can be tracked to indicate how many and what types of connections are being made.
- You can create alerts in which certain actions are performed when a performance counter exceeds or falls below a certain value.

Lesson Review

You can use the following questions to test your knowledge of the information in Lesson 1, "Monitoring Application Performance." The questions are also available on the companion CD if you prefer to review them in electronic form.

NOTE Answers

Answers to these questions and explanations of why each answer choice is right or wrong are located in the "Answers" section at the end of the book.

1. What does a performance spike typically represent?
    A. A serious architectural flaw in the design of your application.
    B. A temporary rise in activity that might or might not indicate a problem with the application.
    C. Not enough virtual memory is allocated to handling applications.
    D. A problem with the application having access to the database server.

2. What method typically is used to analyze performance trends?
   A. The collection and analysis of recent performance spikes
   B. The collection and analysis of performance spikes that occurred over the past year
   C. The collection and analysis of key performance counters over an extended period of time
   D. The collection and analysis of key performance counters that is compared to the same counters collected from a baseline

3. What is the quickest and easiest way to alert administrators of a logon failure in your application?
   A. Manually send them an e-mail notifying them of each incident.
   B. Create an Alert within System Monitor that sends an e-mail directly to the administrators.
   C. Create an Alert within System Monitor that executes a custom program for alerting administrators.
   D. Create an Alert within System Monitor that logs the alert to a database.

Lesson 2: Analyzing Performance Data

This lesson focuses on analyzing the data received from monitoring an application. In the previous lesson, you learned how System Monitor could be used to monitor critical information about your servers. This lesson will expand on that discussion and specifically look at monitoring resource usage and security aspects. It will also look at ways to track bugs generated from your application. Finally, it will take a look at the Health Monitoring API, which monitors applications and diagnoses problems within them.

> **After this lesson, you will be able to:**
> - Analyze performance counters concerning resource usage and security aspects.
> - Identify ways that bugs generated from your application can be tracked.
> - Understand ways the Health Monitoring API can be used to monitor and diagnose your deployed applications.
>
> **Estimated lesson time: 60 minutes**

Analyzing Resource Usage

Monitoring and analyzing the resource usage for your application means focusing on three main areas: processor use, disk activity, and memory use. This section covers which counters you should monitor to determine the performance of the server or servers hosting your application.

NOTE   Run System Monitor remotely

Using System Monitor to monitor your servers does consume resources. Therefore, it is best to monitor servers remotely to ensure unbiased results.

Processor Use

Processor use involves monitoring usage of the server's central processing unit (CPU). This is typically done using the % Processor Time counter for the *Processor* object. You might recall that this was identified as one of the key performance counters in Lesson 1. You do not want this value to exceed 85 percent consistently.

If the server has multiple processors, you will need to add counters for each instance. Alternatively, you can monitor the % Processor Time counter for the Total instance, which will account for all processors.

More than likely, your application will be deployed on more than one server. Web farms distribute the load of an application across multiple servers, and, therefore, you need to monitor them as you would a server with multiple processors.

Another consideration is that remote components might be deployed on a server other than that hosting your Web application. Also, the database will likely reside on a separate database server. Just keep in mind that your Web application will likely span multiple servers and that all of these servers affect application performance.

When considering CPU usage, think about processes waiting in the processor queue, too. This is represented by the Processor Queue Length counter for the *System* object. Typically, you do not want this to exceed a value of more than twice the number of processors for that server.

Real World

Sara Morgan

This lesson covers analyzing resource usage on your application servers. Although it is important for application developers to know and understand these topics, you might not have access to the production servers in your organization.

In just about all the companies I have worked for, each member of the IT staff had a very specific job, and there was little crossover between them. In many cases, network administrators were the only individuals with administrative access to the production servers. The developers had limited or no access at all, and we had to ask specific questions to find out how servers were configured.

To properly prepare for your certification exam, one approach might be to request special access to your organization's production servers. And do not be afraid to ask administrators how many processors each server has or whether they use a redundant array of independent disks (RAID) array. It is also helpful to ask them what performance counters they prefer to use. Their explanations might stick in your mind when you take your test.

Disk Activity

The measurement of disk use involves looking at how the physical disk handles read and write operations or system input/output (I/O). It also involves determining whether excessive paging is occurring. This can happen when too much memory is allocated to a certain application, or the server has an insufficient amount of physical memory.

When measuring disk I/O, two counters associated with the *Physical Disk* object that you might want to look at are:

- **% Disk Time**   Indicates the percentage of time that is spent handling read/write operations. If this value is consistently high (above 85 percent), check the value of the next counter.

■ **Avg Disk Queue Length**   Indicates the average number of requests waiting to be processed. This value should not exceed a value of twice the number of spindles for the disk. Note that RAID arrays will have more than one spindle (disk).

NOTE   Monitoring servers with RAID arrays

RAID is a disk system containing multiple physical disks that represent one or more logical volumes. Because of this, a RAID array can affect the value of the % Disk Time counter. The value for this counter could be over 100 percent, and it would not necessarily indicate a problem. For this reason, it is important to determine whether the server you are monitoring is using a RAID array.

Memory Use

Most servers these days are packed with plenty of memory, so memory use is becoming less of a problem. But it is still possible that your application could suffer the poor effects of a server that lacks enough memory. This is even more true for database servers, which tend to consume more memory than Web servers.

The three main counters associated with the *Memory* object and used to assess memory use are:

■ **Available Mbytes**   Displays the amount of available memory on the computer. On average, this value should be at least 20 percent of the available physical memory, but a higher value is preferable.

■ **Pages/sec**   Rate at which pages are written to the disk to resolve page faults. If this value is consistently above 20, it could indicate excessive paging problems.

■ **Working Set**   Indicates the amount of memory, in bytes, available for a particular process, depending on the instance selected. If this value is always lower than the minimum amount dedicated to that process, you might want to adjust the server memory options.

Quick Check
■ What three areas should you focus on when analyzing your application for resource usage?

Quick Check Answer
■ Processor use enables you to evaluate the server's CPU and determine whether it is being used too much.

■ Disk activity enables you to look at how the physical disk handles read and write operations and whether enough physical memory is allocated.

■ Memory use enables you to determine whether the application server has enough memory.

Analyzing Security Aspects

The CLR, which is the foundation for the .NET Framework, has its own set of performance counters. There are counters for categories such as exceptions, data, networking, and remoting. There is also a category that deals specifically with security. The counters for this object provide information about the security checks performed by the CLR.

The two main counters associated with the .NET CLR *Security* object are:

- **Total Runtime Checks**   Displays the total number of run-time checks since the application started. If the *Stack Walk Depth* counter is also consistently high, you might be experiencing a performance penalty when doing security checks.
- **Stack Walk Depth**   Displays the depth of the stack since the last security check was performed.

Bug Tracking

Although you would like to think that every application that you write will be free of bugs, this is typically not the case. *Bugs*, which represent any problem in an application, can range from exceptions to missing or incorrect functionality. It is important to establish a method for tracking these bugs. This will help you ensure that the appropriate resources are assigned to resolving them. The information collected can also be helpful to resources supporting the application.

Although there are plenty of third-party software vendors offering bug-tracking utilities, it is not always necessary to purchase one of these. At a minimum, you can record information about your bugs in a central spreadsheet. Another alternative is to record the information in a database table. What type of information is recorded depends on what type of bug is encountered.

Exception-Handling Logging

In Chapter 9, "Component Development," you learned about selecting an exception-handling mechanism. One of the methods for handling exceptions is to log information about the exception to a database. This can be helpful when it comes to assigning responsibility for resolving the exceptions. The information collected about the exception can be fed into a bug-tracking program or spreadsheet. Typically, information recorded about the exception includes the following.

- Exception description
- Date/time when exception occurred
- Exception number

- Assembly/class/method/line number where exception occurred
- Stack trace (a dump of all the information related to the exception)
- UserID (applicable for applications requiring a logon)

Bugs Reported by Users

Application problems reported by users might or might not be collected by an exception-handling mechanism. The problem might involve some piece of missing or incorrect functionality that does not result in an exception being thrown. You will need some method of recording this information to ensure that the issue is assigned to an appropriate resource. Information that can be collected includes the following.

- Problem description
- Category/subcategory
- Date/time the problem was reported
- Reported by (name/ID of person reporting the bug)
- Assigned to (name/ID of resource to resolve the bug)
- Resolution description
- Date/time the problem was resolved

Health Monitoring

ASP.NET 2.0 includes an API that can be used to monitor and diagnose problems with your ASP.NET applications. It works similarly to how the Exception Handling or Logging and Instrumentation Application Blocks work. Health Monitoring is helpful when monitoring your application because you can record details about events rather than just the values of specific data counters.

MORE INFO Application blocks

The Patterns and Practices groups provide several application blocks that are free to download and are available at *http://msdn.microsoft.com/practices/guidetype/AppBlocks/*. One of the blocks offered is for exception handling and logging and instrumentation.

Health Monitoring providers, which are responsible for handling ASP.NET events, are configured by adding entries to your application's web.config file. The entries are wrapped inside a *<healthMonitoring>* element. (See Table 17-3.) Each provider will execute a specific action such as writing to the event log or e-mailing an individual. Rules are used to tell the providers which events should be handled.

Table 17-3 Child Elements of the *<healthMonitoring>* Element

Element	Description
bufferModes	Used to specify the buffering capabilities for each provider specified.
eventMappings	Used to map friendly event names, such as "All Events," to specific event types such as *System.Web.Management.WebBaseEvent*.
Profiles	Used to specify a set of parameters used to configure events.
Providers	Used to specify the providers that handle events. You can use several built-in providers such as the *EventLogWebEventProvider*, *SqlWebEvent-Provider*, and *WmiWebEventProvider*.
Rules	Used to specify which events apply to a particular provider.

The events that you can track range from exceptions to the successful completion of application starts and stops. Following are the types of events that you can capture.

- **Application lifetime events** Includes events such as application starts and stops
- **Audit events** Involves security-related events
- **Error events** Includes any Web request errors
- **Authentication events** Tracks successes and failures
- **Request processing events** Involves Web request events
- **View state events** Tracks view state failures

The following is an example of what the *<healthMonitoring>* section of a web.config file might look like. In this case, the Web application will be configured to record all events to the event log.

```
<healthMonitoring enabled="true">
    <providers>
      <add
name="EventLogProvider"        type="System.Web.Management.EventLogWebEventProvider,
System.Web,Version=2.0.0.0,Culture=neutral,
PublicKeyToken=b03f5f7f11d50a3a" />
    </providers>
    <rules>
      <add name="LogAllEvent"
          eventName="All Events"
          provider="EventLogProvider"/>
    </rules>
  </healthMonitoring>
```

Lab: Logging Data with Health Monitoring

In this lab, you will use the Health Monitoring API to log all events to the application event log. You can use the application that you created in the Lesson 1 lab. By adding entries to the web.config file, you will be able to record event information in the event log for your development computer. If you do not have a production-ready ASP.NET application available, complete Exercise 1 of the Lesson 1 lab before continuing.

▶ **Exercise: Make a Change to web.config to Enable Health Monitoring**

1. Open Visual Studio 2005.
2. Select File | Open | Web Site.
3. Browse to the location of your production-ready ASP.NET application or to the location where you installed the Time Tracker application.
4. Double-click the web.config file from Solution Explorer to open the file editor.
5. Add the following code below the *<system.Web>* element:

```
<healthMonitoring enabled="true">
    <providers>
    <add name="EventLogProvider"
        type="System.Web.Management.EventLogWebEventProvider,
        _System.Web,Version=2.0.0.0,Culture=neutral,
        _PublicKeyToken=b03f5f7f11d50a3a" />
    </providers>
    <rules>
        <add name="LogAllEvent"
            eventName="All Events"
            provider="EventLogProvider"/>
    </rules>
</healthMonitoring>
```

6. Select File | Save to save your changes.
7. Press Ctrl+F5 to execute the application without debugging. If you are executing the Time Tracker application, the User Login page should appear.
8. Enter a user name and password that you know is not in the database, and then click Log In. The error message, "Your logon attempt was not successful. Please try again" should appear.
9. Navigate to Control Panel | Administrative Tools | Event Viewer.
10. Select the *Application* node. Near the top of this file, you should see an entry that looks similar to the message displayed in Figure 17-6.

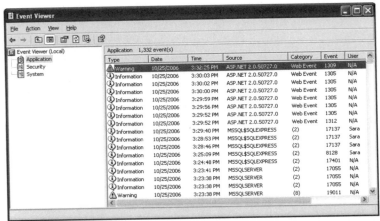

Figure 17-6   Event Viewer Application log listing a message about a Web event

Lesson Summary

- System Monitor can be used to analyze how your servers are handling resources. You can look at counters related to processor use, disk activity, and memory use.

- *Processor*: % Processor Time and *System*: Processor Queue Length counters can be monitored to determine whether the server's CPU is overloaded.

- *Physical Disk*: % Disk Time and *Physical Disk*: Avg Disk Queue Length counters can be monitored to measure the effects of read/write operations on your servers.

- Available Mbytes, Pages/sec, and Working Set counters from the *Memory* object can be used to monitor the memory use on your servers.

- Total Runtime Checks and Stack Walk Depth counters for the .NET CLR *Security* object can be used to monitor the CLR security activity on your servers.

- Bugs can show up in the form of exception errors or missing or incorrect functionality. Recording information about bugs in a database or spreadsheet can be useful when assigning responsibility for resolving the bugs.

- ASP.NET 2.0 includes a set of classes that you can use to perform Health Monitoring of, and diagnosis of problems with, your production servers.

Lesson Review

You can use the following questions to test your knowledge of the information in Lesson 2, "Analyzing Performance Data." The questions are also available on the companion CD if you prefer to review them in electronic form.

NOTE Answers

Answers to these questions and explanations of why each answer choice is right or wrong are located in the "Answers" section at the end of the book.

1. Which two counters are most helpful when determining whether a server's CPU is performing poorly? (Select all that apply. Answers are formatted as Object: Counter.)

    A. *System*: % Processor Time

    B. *Processor*: % Processor Time

    C. *System*: Processor Queue Length

    D. *Processor*: Processor Queue Length

2. Which object can be used to identify how well the CLR is handling security requests?

    A. *Security*

    B. .NET CLR

    C. .NET CLR *Logon*

    D. .NET CLR *Security*

3. Which Health Monitoring entity controls how ASP.NET events are handled by executing a specific action?

    A. *Provider*

    B. *Profile*

    C. *Rules*

    D. Actions

Chapter Review

To further practice and reinforce the skills you learned in this chapter, you can complete the following tasks:

- Review the chapter summary.
- Review the list of key terms introduced in this chapter.
- Complete the case scenarios. These scenarios set up real-world situations involving the topics of this chapter and ask you to create a solution.
- Complete the suggested practices.
- Take a practice test.

Chapter Summary

- The Performance Console System Monitor (or perfmon) utility enables system administrators to monitor several indicators used to diagnose the health of a server or application. Counters are specific to system objects and physical resources. The data related to counters, displayed in a real-time graph, can be logged and later analyzed to identify performance spikes and trends.

Key Terms

Do you know what these key terms mean? You can check your answers by looking up the terms in the glossary at the end of the book.

- alerts
- bugs
- performance baseline
- performance counter
- performance objects
- performance spike
- RAID

Case Scenarios

In the following case scenarios, you will apply what you've learned about how to support production applications. You can find answers to these questions in the "Answers" section at the end of this book.

Case Scenario 1: Diagnosing a Server Problem

You work for a company that has recently deployed a portal ASP.NET application for use by their external partners. Stress tests that were performed during the development phase indicated that the application could easily support over 1,000 concurrent users. In the past two days, the Web server hosting the application has experienced significant delays during certain periods of the day. You have been asked to assist the network administrator in determining the cause of the delays. What recommendations would you make?

Case Scenario 2: Implementing Bug Tracking

You are a developer for a financial company that has recently deployed an ASP.NET Web application for their internal employees. The program uses the Exception Handling Application Block to log all exceptions to an external database. The IT department operates a help desk that employees can call when they have computer problems.

Currently, there is no method for accessing the exception data, nor is there a way to log new issues with the application. When employees call the help desk concerning problems with the application, the help desk employee records their issue in an e-mail that is sent to the IT manager. The IT manager then forwards the e-mail to the appropriate developer and asks him or her to resolve the issue. You have been asked to design a better solution. What might you recommend?

Suggested Practices

To help you successfully master the objectives covered in this chapter, complete the following tasks.

Monitor Performance Data

For this task, you should complete at least Practice 1. You can do Practice 2 for a more in-depth understanding of performance monitoring.

- **Practice 1**   Download and install the Web Application Stress Test Tool from MSDN. Use the stress-testing tool to generate a script while executing any ASP.NET application. Run System Monitor on your local development computer, using the key counters from Table 17-1 while the script is being replayed. Notice the effect that executing the script has on the value of the counters displayed.
- **Practice 2**   Run System Monitor against a Web server at the same time that a production Web application is executing. Add the key counters listed in Table 17-1 to the graph and configure System Monitor to log this data to a SQL Server database.

Take a Practice Test

The practice tests on this book's companion CD offer many options. For example, you can test yourself on just one exam objective, or you can test yourself on all the 70-547 certification exam content. You can set up the test so that it closely simulates the experience of taking a certification exam, or you can set it up in study mode so that you can look at the correct answers and explanations after you answer each question.

MORE INFO   Practice tests

For details about all the practice test options available, see the "How to Use the Practice Tests" section in this book's Introduction.

Answers

Chapter 1: Lesson Review Answers

Lesson 1

1. **Correct Answer: B**
   - A. **Incorrect:** A business requirement defines an actionable, measurable feature for the system from the business perspective.
   - B. **Correct:** This requirement is talking about supportability. That is a quality-of-service requirement.
   - C. **Incorrect:** A user requirement defines a task the users need to be able to perform to meet the objectives of their jobs.
   - D. **Incorrect:** A functional requirement is a specification for a developer.

2. **Correct Answers: A, C, and D**
   - A. **Correct:** Testers can trace the application back to the agreed-on set of requirements.
   - B. **Incorrect:** The process by which a user accomplishes a given task is a use case (or scenario) and not a requirement.
   - C. **Correct:** The principal benefit of documenting requirements is gaining a consensus on the business problem that is to be solved.
   - D. **Correct:** The requirements should feed the technology recommendations.

3. **Correct Answer: B**
   - A. **Incorrect:** A standard browser-based client does not support the high interactivity required.
   - B. **Correct:** Using AJAX inside a browser will facilitate a good user experience and work with multiple browsers on multiple operating systems.
   - C. **Incorrect:** Users cannot connect outside of their corporate PC.
   - D. **Incorrect:** The Smart Client will not work on non-Windows operating systems.

4. **Correct Answer: C**
   - A. **Incorrect:** There is no justification for SQL Enterprise in this situation.
   - B. **Incorrect:** SQL Express would work. However, it takes up more hard drive space than SQL Everywhere. In addition, it does not synchronize as easily.
   - C. **Correct:** This offers a low-impact install with the ability to work while disconnected. Users have to get database updates only on a monthly basis.
   - D. **Incorrect:** This is too big and too costly to install on each user's computer or device.

Lesson 2

1. **Correct Answer: B**

   A. **Incorrect:** A vertical prototype covers a vertical slice of the entire application. These requirements consider only gaps in the understanding of the UI.

   B. **Correct:** A mockup prototype, also called a horizontal prototype, fills in the gaps that exist in the understanding of the UI.

   C. **Incorrect:** A proof-of-concept prototype validates the application's architecture and technology. These requirements consider only gaps in the understanding of the UI.

   D. **Incorrect:** A reference architecture is another term for a proof-of-concept prototype. These requirements consider only gaps in the understanding of the UI.

2. **Correct Answers: A, B, and C**

   A. **Correct:** A reference architecture will give you an understanding of the level of effort for the various layers in the system.

   B. **Correct:** You can help validate your estimates by getting an accurate picture of the screens, the screen types, and their complexities.

   C. **Correct:** A reference architecture takes a look across the layers. Look also at unique elements in the UI and elsewhere to confirm your scope and the effort that will be required.

   D. **Incorrect:** You should update your requirements. However, this does not help you validate your estimates.

3. **Correct Answers: A, B, C, and D**

   A. **Correct:** You need to confirm your authentication mechanism (forms or Windows).

   B. **Correct:** You need to verify your approach to how users will be authorized to access features and data.

   C. **Correct:** You should evaluate how key resources, such as files or connection strings, will be secured.

   D. **Correct:** You should work with the infrastructure team to determine whether your recommendations are feasible in terms of firewall rules and so on.

4. **Correct Answers: A and C**

   A. **Correct:** The intent of a prototype is to uncover gaps. You know you've done your job when you see this happen.

   B. **Incorrect:** This might be true; however, it does not indicate that the prototype was effective. It might indicate either that the prototype did not go far enough or that it was not warranted.

C. **Correct:** This is a good sign. You need to identify areas of high risk and work to reduce this risk.

D. **Incorrect:** This rarely happens with new technology. You need to make sure that the prototype went far enough. If it did, that's great. However, by itself, this fact does not indicate effectiveness.

Chapter 1: Case Scenario Answers

Case Scenario 1: Evaluate Requirements and Propose an Application Design

1. The high-level user requirements of the system might be documented as follows:

    ❑ Best-practice teams should be able to create a best-practices, collaborative area for documenting and discussing a best practice within the company.

    ❑ A best practice can be a process, document, template, form, instruction, or combination of these.

    ❑ Best-practice teams should be able to upload documents to the best-practices, collaborative area.

    ❑ Best-practice teams should be able to define tasks, supporting documents, and personnel related to a best practice.

    ❑ Best-practice teams should be able to participate in online discussions regarding a best practice.

    ❑ Best-practice teams should be able to publish a best practice to the users in the company. They should also be able to modify an existing best practice.

    ❑ The system should notify users when new content is available.

    ❑ Users should be able to subscribe to, and unsubscribe from, notification alerts.

    ❑ Department managers should be able to approve a best practice before it is distributed to the entire organization.

    ❑ Each corporate department should have a private (secured) area for storing and managing key corporate assets in terms of files, artwork, and so on.

    ❑ Corporate asset data should be categorized by client, creator, and data created.

    ❑ The history of corporate asset data should be tracked by the system.

    ❑ Users should be able to search the corporate asset data.

    ❑ Users of the system should be able to go to the application to retrieve consolidated and aggregated sales reports.

    ❑ Users should be able to create their own version of the sales reports (ad hoc reporting).

❑ Users of the system should be able to view corporate profiles, including report-to and direct-reports information.

❑ Users of the system should be able to update their own profiles.

2. The high-level business requirements of the system might be documented as follows:

❑ We need an application that helps the organization understand and distribute its best-practice knowledge.

❑ The application should reduce the overall re-work required to execute a given best practice.

❑ The application should reduce the training time for new hires.

❑ The application should help members of the organization recognize where they can turn for help and who is in charge of a given process.

3. The high-level QOS requirements of the system might be documented as follows:

❑ The application should respond to user requests in less than five seconds.

❑ The application should have a clean UI and be approachable and easy to use.

❑ The application should support up to 100 concurrent users.

❑ The application should expect to store the data from over 1,500 users.

4. The following are requirements from the interviews that are functional in nature.

❑ It must support Internet Explorer, Firefox, and Safari.

❑ The report data should be retrieved as XML from *http://contosco/reports /reportservic.asmx*. There are three Web service methods: *GetSalesEast()*, *GetSalesWest()*, and *GetInternationalSales()*.

5. The following high-level requirements are ambiguous and not very actionable:

❑ The application should have a clean UI and be approachable and easy to use.

❑ All of the business requirements are ambiguous. They read like goals, not requirements. You might decide to turn these into goals and then track the requirements that realize a given goal. Or you might rewrite these in an unambiguous manner.

6. Based on the requirements, you should recommend a standard, Web-based UI. This will allow you to support the multiple browsers. It will also allow your new developers to feel comfortable with the .NET Framework. You might decide to introduce some client-side JavaScript (AJAX) at some future point.

7. Your security model should leverage the fact that everyone is in Active Directory. You can, therefore, use Windows or integrated security.

8. The application requirements sound a lot like a company portal or intranet. You should, therefore, consider WSS or SharePoint Portal Server. You might decide to look at other portal solutions as well. In addition, the requirement for reports and ad hoc reporting should lead you to examine a reporting tool such as SQL Reporting Services.

9. You should recommend a standard edition of SQL Server. You have a large number of users, a sizable scale, and a lot of information you need to store and protect.

10. The requirements do not lend themselves to any one particular UI format. Therefore, you should create a mockup prototype to validate the requirements and define the inter-action a user will have with the system. In addition, your developers are new to the .NET Framework. Therefore, consider creating a reference architecture of key elements in the system. This includes Web pages, Web Parts, data objects, and database code (a vertical implementation).

Chapter 2: Lesson Review Answers

Lesson 1

1. **Correct Answer: C**

   A. **Incorrect:** These items represent only the primary objects. Others are missed.

   B. **Incorrect:** These items represent only a few of the objects.

   C. **Correct:** These are all objects from the statements. You can use these objects to begin building your ORM.

   D. **Incorrect:** These are not objects. They are actions.

2. **Correct Answer: B**

   A. **Incorrect:** There are three parts that make up the relationship (*Order*, *Customer*, and *Book*). Unary is a single object relationship to itself.

   B. **Correct:** An *Order* cannot exist with just a *Customer* or just a *Book*. Therefore, two binary relationships would not be sufficient.

   C. **Incorrect:** A ternary relationship exists among *Order*, *Book*, and *Customer*.

   D. **Incorrect:** This is the inverse of B. An *Order* cannot exist with just a *Customer* or just a *Book*. Therefore, two binary relationships would not be sufficient.

3. **Correct Answers: A and C**

   A. **Correct:** This is the left-to-right reading of the relationship fact.

   B. **Incorrect:** This does not model the fact as defined. It assumes a new object, *Reports*.

   C. **Correct:** This is the right-to-left reading of the relationship fact.

   D. **Incorrect:** This may be true, but it does not model either side of the fact.

4. **Correct Answer: A**

   A. **Correct:** A shipping slip must have a single ship-to address. Therefore, the shipping slip is mandatory to form the relationship. However, a ship-to address does not need a shipping slip. So the inverse part of the relationship is not mandatory (a ship-to address defines zero or more shipping slips). The arrow over the left side (Shipping Slip) indicates a many-to-one relationship. That is, each ship-to address can define many shipping slips.

   B. **Incorrect:** This indicates that the ship-to address is mandatory to form this relationship. However, the relationship does not exist without a shipping slip. The arrow on the right indicates a one-to-many relationship. This would be true only if a shipping slip were allowed to ship to multiple locations.

   C. **Incorrect:** No circle indicates that neither item is required for the relationship. This is not true. A shipping slip is required to form this relationship. The two arrows indicate a one-to-one relationship. That would be true only if the ship-to address could exist on only a single shipping slip. That is, an address could receive only a single shipment.

   D. **Incorrect:** The mandatory part of the relationship is correct. However, the single long arrow indicates a many-to-many relationship. This would be true if the shipping slip allowed multiple ship-to addresses. However, this would confuse the shipper.

Lesson 2

1. **Correct Answers: A, B, and D**

   A. **Correct:** Creating layers can increase reuse. A layer for just the business logic, for example, may allow other systems to access this information. A database abstraction class or application services code can be used by other applications.

   B. **Correct:** Layers provide a logical understanding to developers of where their code should be written and what code is accessible (referenced) from that code. Layers provide guidelines and structure to the code base.

   C. **Incorrect:** Layers are logical. They do not dictate the physical packaging or deployment. The layers might influence some of your decisions, but they are not a primary benefit.

   D. **Correct:** By encapsulating code into layers, you can more easily change individual pieces without affecting other code elements.

2. **Correct Answers: A and C**
   A. **Correct:** The presentation layer abstracts the UI layout code from the code to make it execute. Therefore, XHTML markup would fit the definition of presentation.
   B. **Incorrect:** The presentation and developer code is being separated as part of your design. A single-file model couples these two elements together.
   C. **Correct:** The code-behind model abstracts the presentation from the development code. These are two separate files.
   D. **Incorrect:** The code-behind files themselves are not presentation code. They are part of the UI, but they are responsible for making the UI work, not for affecting the layout of the presentation.

3. **Correct Answer: C**
   A. **Incorrect:** Having this many layers is excessive based on the constraints. The application is simple and small. The layers should be few in number.
   B. **Incorrect:** Separating the application into even three layers is not warranted based on the constraints. The simple business layer code can be embedded in the UI.
   C. **Correct:** The application is a throwaway, has a tight time frame, a small number of users, is simple, and will be deployed on a single server. Therefore, the fastest solution here will be a two-tier ASP.NET application.
   D. **Incorrect:** There is nothing in the constraints that indicates the use (or need) for application services.

Lesson 3

1. **Correct Answer: D**
   A. **Incorrect:** The component diagram shows the logical grouping of classes. It is not a specification that can be implemented.
   B. **Incorrect:** A collaboration diagram shows how objects work together through message calls. It does not define the specification for those objects.
   C. **Incorrect:** Pseudocode illustrates a complex method using code-like terms.
   D. **Correct:** A class diagram is a static view of your classes and their relationships, properties, and methods. Developers can use this model to implement code. They use the other models to help understand how the code works as a solution.

2. **Correct Answers: B, C, and D**
   A. **Incorrect:** Both sequence and collaboration diagrams can show asynchronous messaging.
   B. **Correct:** A sequence diagram is read left-to-right, top-to-bottom. You must follow the numbers on the messages to read a collaboration diagram's order.

C. **Correct:** A collaboration diagram does not show when objects are created and destroyed. This is left up to interpretation.

D. **Correct:** A collaboration diagram can be useful when you want to see objects laid out in a different manner.

3. **Correct Answers: B, C, and D**

A. **Incorrect:** Class interactions are best defined through sequence diagrams. Class groupings are defined through component diagrams.

B. **Correct:** An activity diagram is good for modeling the steps inside complex algorithms.

C. **Correct:** An activity diagram allows you to indicate activities both in sequence and in parallel. It also shows where things fork and where they come back together (or join). Therefore, it is very good at showing workflow. This is not often a physical model but it can be useful, nonetheless.

D. **Correct:** An activity diagram can show actions in parallel. For this reason, it is often used to model multithreaded methods.

4. **Correct Answers: A, B, C, and D**

A. **Correct:** A node in a component diagram illustrates where components will be deployed. This is typically a server or piece of hardware.

B. **Correct:** You can define a dependency between nodes. You can label this node with a communication protocol.

C. **Correct:** You can group your components into UML packages. These packages can be defined to represent your layers. Your component model will then show which components are part of which layer.

D. **Correct:** The dependencies between components on the diagram illustrate references between objects.

Chapter 2: Case Scenario Answers

Case Scenario: Evaluate User Inputs and Create Physical Models

1. The following figure presents a possible ORM diagram for the use case listed here. This ORM model was created by defining the objects in the system and their relationships from the use case.

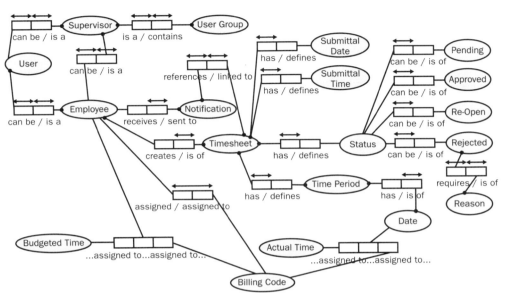

2. The following figure presents a possible application layers diagram based on the afore-mentioned design goals. The presentation tier should be made separate, given the number of devices supported. The business objects should be their own layer, given that the business services will be reused across different user experiences. Define an application layer for the enterprise library services. The database access code should go on its own layer, given that the Web server cannot connect to the database directly.

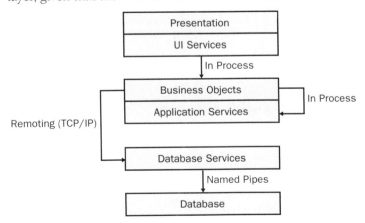

3. The following figure presents a possible object model for the solution. This model does not show the security model for the application or the additional details (properties and methods) not indicated by the use case. It also does not consider the UI.

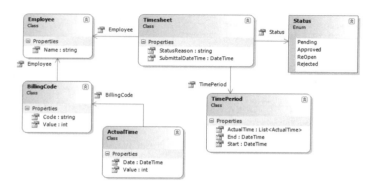

4. The following figure presents a possible sequence diagram for the preceding use case. This use case assumes the application layers defined as part of the model. The call to *ActualTime()* is illustrating the calls to return the properties of the *TimeSheet* for display to the user (via *ApproveTimeSheetUI*).

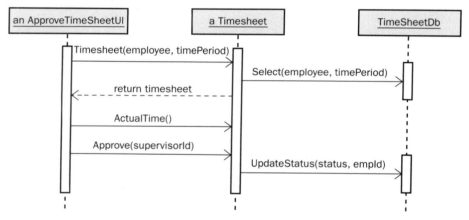

Chapter 3: Lesson Review Answers

Lesson 1

1. **Correct Answer: B**
    A. **Incorrect:** There is no need to expose Windows authentication for Web sites that do not have any login functionality.
    B. **Correct:** Because users will already have Windows logins, using their Windows identities to allow them access to Web applications is perfectly acceptable.
    C. **Incorrect:** Using Windows authentication for publicly available Web applications does not work well. Windows security does not scale up to a large number of users,

and giving each user a Windows identity is a security risk; you inadvertently give them access to internal resources.

    D. **Incorrect:** Using Windows authentication without a VPN, even for users within your enterprise, unnecessarily exposes your enterprise's network to authentication break-ins such as brute force hacking of passwords or user names.

2. **Correct Answers: B and C**

    A. **Incorrect:** Dynamically created SQL statements are prone to SQL injection attacks.

    B. **Correct:** Stored procedures protect against SQL injection attacks.

    C. **Correct:** Parameterized queries protect against SQL injection attacks.

    D. **Incorrect:** Dynamically created SQL statements, even with error checking, are still prone to SQL injection attacks because your error checking is not likely to check every possible type of SQL injection attack.

3. **Correct Answer: A**

    A. **Correct:** A component in the logical design should be part of one, and only one, of the logical tiers.

    B. **Incorrect:** If a component exists in more than one tier, the maintainability and reuse of the code is severely reduced.

    C. **Incorrect:** Components should exist in one, and only one, tier of development. Separating out functionality into tiers ensures that code is maintainable and reusable.

    D. **Incorrect:** Components are tied to logical tiers to better separate the types of functionality into different jobs. By tying a component to a specific tier, you can better determine what type of work that specific component should be doing.

Lesson 2

1. **Correct Answers: A, C, and D**

    A. **Correct:** *ViewState* affects the size of the generated page that is delivered to clients.

    B. **Incorrect:** Although a large number of controls on a page can affect its size, the number of controls is not directly related to the size of the generated page.

    C. **Correct:** The size of images that are served does affect the size of the generated page and should be reviewed.

    D. **Correct:** Although the size of the delivered page is not affected by the use of session state, accessing session state on a page or control can affect the performance of serving that page.

2. **Correct Answers: B and C**

   A. **Incorrect:** The user interface should not be required to enforce data integrity. Allowing the data tier and the database to enforce the integrity ensures that the data is safe from any code.

   B. **Correct:** Enforcing the integrity in the data tier will reduce the need to go to the database with inconsistent data.

   C. **Correct:** Enforcing the integrity in the database ensures that the data is consistent no matter where the data is changed (in your application, or by direct change to the data by other tools).

   D. **Incorrect:** XML Schema is not intended to enforce the types of data integrity that are necessary for database data. Allowing the data tier and the database to enforce the integrity ensures that the data is safe from any code.

3. **Correct Answer: A**

   A. **Correct:** Strongly naming your assemblies can prevent intruders from replacing your assemblies with new versions of the code.

   B. **Incorrect:** By failing to strongly name your assemblies in a publicly available Web site, you allow your assemblies to be replaced by intruders who could inject malicious code into them.

Chapter 3: Case Scenario Answers

Case Scenario 1: Review the Logical Design for a CRM Application

1. By reviewing the original requirements, I will compare them to the logical design to ensure that there are no gaps.

2. By ensuring that the design has kept the user interface and business logic tiers separate, I can ensure that the maintainability of the system is adequate for our needs.

Case Scenario 2: Review the Physical Design for a CRM Application

1. By reviewing the physical design to determine what kind of security is going to be used, we can evaluate the security model of the physical design.

2. The location of shared components and controls needs to be evaluated to make sure that updating individual shared elements will positively affect other projects using those same controls.

Chapter 4: Lesson Review Answers

Lesson 1

1. **Correct Answer: B**

   A. **Incorrect:** The Web.config file is used to hold configuration data for the Web application.

   B. **Correct:** The XMLSiteMapProvider used by the *SiteMapPath* control expects a file of this name located in the root of the virtual directory.

   C. **Incorrect:** The XMLSiteMapProvider is specifically looking for an extension of .sitemap.

   D. **Incorrect:** The XMLSiteMapProvider is specifically looking for an extension of .sitemap.

2. **Correct Answer: D**

   A. **Incorrect:** The *VirtualPath* attribute specifies the path to the file that generates the type. However, *TypeName* can also be used.

   B. **Incorrect:** The *TypeName* attribute specifies the data type, which is the class name of the acceptable previous page. However, *VirtualPath* can also be used.

   C. **Incorrect:** If you use both attributes at the same time, the directive fails.

   D. **Correct:** You can force the recipient page to accept postings from only specified pages by using the @ *PreviousPageType* directive. This directive defines two mutually exclusive attributes: *TypeName* and *VirtualPath*.

3. **Correct Answer: C**

   A. **Incorrect:** The ASP.NET *Menu* control allows you to develop both statically and dynamically displayed menus for your ASP.NET Web pages. You can configure the contents of the *Menu* control directly in the control, or you can specify the contents by binding the control to a data source.

   B. **Incorrect:** The *SiteMapPath* displays a navigation path (which is also known as a breadcrumb) that shows the user the current page location and displays links as a path back to the home page.

   C. **Correct:** *Panel* is a placeholder control used to contain other controls. As such, it provides no explicit UI.

   D. **Incorrect:** The *TreeView* Web server control is used to display hierarchical data, such as a table of contents or file directory, in a tree structure. This also works well for navigating a Web site when bound to hierarchical data representing the Web site layout.

Lesson 2

1. **Correct Answer: D**
   A. **Incorrect:** Web Part pages provide the user with the ability to personalize a page by choosing controls and the location of controls on the page.
   B. **Incorrect:** CSS can be used for page layout by use of <DIV> tags. However, the use of master pages is done within ASP.NET and is, therefore, easier for the developer who might not be familiar with CSS.
   C. **Incorrect:** Themes provide a consistent appearance and behavior for a Web application but do not provide a consistent layout.
   D. **Correct:** Master pages provide a template with a predefined layout. Content pages then reference the master page through the *MasterPageFile* attribute of the @ *Page* directive.

2. **Correct Answer: A**
   A. **Correct:** Content placeholders refer to regions of a master page wherein data, controls, and other output specific to the content page are placed.
   B. **Incorrect:** If a .css file is placed in the theme directory, the style sheet is applied automatically as part of the theme.
   C. **Incorrect:** Themes can include graphics and other resources such as script files or sound files.
   D. **Incorrect:** A skin file contains one or more control properties that define how the control should look. Skin files are part of ASP.NET themes.

3. **Correct Answer: A**
   A. **Correct:** A theme contains skin files. Skin files in turn contain one or more control properties that define how the control should look. Use the *Theme* property of the page to assign the theme for all controls on the page.
   B. **Incorrect:** A named skin is a control skin with a *SkinID* property set. Named skins do not automatically apply to controls by type. Instead, you explicitly apply a named skin to a control by setting the control's *SkinID* property. Creating named skins allows you to set different skins for different instances of the same control in an application. This solution would require setting the *SkinID* property of each *GridView* control on the page.
   C. **Incorrect:** *RowStyle* and *AlternatingRowStyle* set the appearance of the data rows and alternating rows in a *GridView* control. This option requires these two properties to be set on every *GridView* control in the system.

D. **Incorrect:** The *CssClass* property specifies the *CSS* class to render on the client for the Web server control. This option requires this property to be set on every *Grid-View* control in the system.

4. **Correct Answer: A**

A. **Correct:** The *PreInit* is fired before the controls are loaded; the theme must be set before the controls are loaded. Note that this prevents directly allowing users to set the theme on the page and have the theme applied immediately.

B. **Incorrect:** The *Init* event is used to read and initialize control properties.

C. **Incorrect:** The *Load* event is used to read and update control properties.

D. **Incorrect:** The *PreRender* event is used to make final changes to the contents of the page.

Chapter 4: Case Scenario Answers

Case Scenario 1: Build an Intranet Application

1. Master pages are the best way to provide a consistent layout for all pages in the application. Using a master page, you can create a banner, main menu, and footer that are available by default to all content pages created using the master page.

2. The *SiteMapPath* control provides the ability to display portions of a site map in a breadcrumbs-style format. This provides users with immediate feedback about their current location with respect to the root page of the application. You can also provide a link to a site map. The site map can use the *SiteMap* control to show the entire application's hierarchy of pages.

3. You can use themes to satisfy this requirement. Specifically, create a separate theme for each department represented in the application. Based on the user's membership, you can set the appropriate theme for the pages at run time.

Case Scenario 2: Provide Personalized Experiences

1. Web Parts and their respective ASP.NET 2.0 components are designed specifically to allow users to customize the functionality available to them as well as the layout of that functionality on the page.

2. Again, you can use themes to satisfy this requirement. Specifically, create a set of themes and allow users to choose a theme that fits their current mood.

Chapter 5: Lesson Review Answers

Lesson 1

1. **Correct Answer: B**

   A. **Incorrect:** A Web Part control is a control that can be included and moved to different locations on a Web Part page by the user at run time. Web Parts, however, might not be part of the architecture of each application. Therefore, although you could use a Web Part to contain a control to provide the needed functionality, the Web Part itself might not be usable across your organization.

   B. **Correct:** Custom Web controls are compiled and then need only to be referenced by the application.

   C. **Incorrect:** User controls require the source code to be located in each application. Because this control will be used by multiple applications, it is not the best choice.

   D. **Incorrect:** Web Part controls, custom Web controls, and user controls are all server controls, as are many intrinsic controls contained in the toolbox. Specifically using a custom Web control, however, is the best answer.

2. **Correct Answer: A**

   A. **Correct:** The *@Register* directive is required only once, regardless of the number of times the user control is used on the page.

   B. **Incorrect:** The *@ Register* directive for a user control contains a *TagPrefix* attribute, which associates a prefix with the user control. This prefix will be included in the opening tag of the user control element. It also contains a *TagName* attribute, which associates a name with the user control. This name will be included in the opening tag of the user control element. An *Src* attribute defines the virtual path to the user control file that you are including.

   C. **Incorrect:** The source code for a user control is included in the solution as an .ascx file.

   D. **Incorrect:** In Design View, you can drag and drop the user control directly onto the page. Visual Studio 2005 creates the correct *@ Register* directive and supplies the user control declaration. The *@ Register* directive is created only once, even if you place multiple instances of the user control on your page.

3. **Correct Answer: C**

   A. **Incorrect:** The source for user controls is stored in the project in an .ascx file. Custom Web controls are compiled assemblies, and a reference is set to the control.

   B. **Incorrect:** User controls can be dragged onto a page by dragging the .ascx file onto the page. Custom Web controls can be added to the toolbox and then dragged onto the page.

C. **Correct:** This statement is not true. Custom Web controls can be extended by creating a control that inherits the custom Web control and then adding additional properties and methods.

D. **Incorrect:** Custom Web controls are compiled assemblies and may be signed with a strong name and stored in the GAC.

Lesson 2

1. **Correct Answer: C**

   A. **Incorrect:** Some controls display hierarchical data whereas others display only relational data. This must be considered.

   B. **Incorrect:** The data could be requested once a day, as in sales totals for yesterday, or many times a day, such as for remaining inventory.

   C. **Correct:** Who is requesting the data should not be considered. This would be an authorization concern, not a consideration for choosing a UI control.

   D. **Incorrect:** If there is a large amount of data, pagination, sorting, and filtering might be required, and this would affect the choice of the control.

2. **Correct Answers: A, B, C, and D**

   A. **Correct:** Dozens of intrinsic controls are included in the toolbox in the Visual Studio IDE.

   B. **Correct:** A custom Web control is a control derived from the *System.Web.UI.Control* class and provides a means of creating additional controls for a Web page.

   C. **Correct:** Any HTML element on a page can be converted to an HTML server control by adding the attribute *runat="server."*

   D. **Correct:** You create user controls by combining intrinsic controls and saving them as an .ascx file.

3. **Correct Answer: C**

   A. **Incorrect:** Globalization is the process of designing and developing an application that supports localized UIs and regional data for users in multiple cultures.

   B. **Incorrect:** Localization is the process of translating an application's resources into localized versions for each culture that the application will support.

   C. **Correct:** The *CurrentCulture* property is a per-thread setting that determines the default formats for dates, times, currency, and numbers, and the sorting order of text, string comparisons, and casing.

   D. **Incorrect:** The *CurrentUICulture* property is a per-thread setting that returns the current UI culture. This property is used by the *ResourceManager* class to look up culture-specific resources at run time. This is used for setting UI elements such as strings, error messages, dialog boxes, menus, and embedded object resources.

4. **Correct Answer: A**

   A. **Correct:** *Table* is the best choice. The table has a *TableHeaderRow*. The *TableHeader-Row* class represents a heading row in a *Table* control. This class supports displaying tables on devices with a limited screen size. On these devices, a table with many columns and rows must be rendered across multiple pages. Adding a *Table-HeaderRow* to a *Table* control allows you to specify a heading row that is rendered as the first row on each page that displays a view of the table.

   B. **Incorrect:** The *GridView* control is new to the .NET Framework 2.0. The *GridView* displays the values of a data source in a table in which each column represents a field, and each row represents a record. The *GridView* control allows you to select, sort, and edit these items.

   C. **Incorrect:** The *DataGrid* control renders a tabular, data-bound grid. Although the *GridView* is the preferred multirecord data in ASP.NET 2.0, the *DataGrid* control is still supported in ASP.NET 2.0 for backward compatibility.

   D. **Incorrect:** The *MultiView* and *View* Web server controls act as containers for other controls and markup and provide a way for you to present alternate views of information easily.

5. **Correct Answer: C**

   A. **Incorrect:** The *DataGrid* displays multiple records in a tabular format. Although the *DataGrid* is still supported for backward compatibility, the new *GridView* in ASP.NET 2.0 is a more robust control.

   B. **Incorrect:** The *GridView* is new to the .NET Framework 2.0. The *GridView* displays multiple records, not a single record.

   C. **Correct:** The *FormView* control is similar to the *DetailsView* in that it displays a single record. However, it provides the added functionality of using templates to create the display of the data, for example, the *EditItemTemplate*.

   D. **Incorrect:** The *DetailsView* control is used to display a single record from a data source in a table in which each field of the record is displayed in a row of the table. This control does not meet the requirement of combining three fields—city, state, and ZIP code—into a single row.

Chapter 5: Case Scenario Answers

Case Scenario 1: Choosing an Appropriate Control

1. Writing a Web user control is the most appropriate solution to this problem. This is because the scope of the control is within a single application, which will be part of the internal network.

2. The *MultiView* control is appropriate for providing users with the ability to navigate between multiple views.

3. The *DetailsView* or the *FormView* control is appropriate in this situation. Recall that the primary difference between them is that the *FormView* requires you to create the layout with templates whereas the *DetailsView* shows each field as a separate row.

Case Scenario 2: Expanding Your E-Commerce Site

1. The *CurrentCultureUI* control provides you with the capabilities necessary to expose localized text to users.

2. The *CurrentCulture* property enables you to configure programmatically how localized representations of dates, monetary units, and other culture-specific information is rendered.

Chapter 6: Lesson Review Answers

Lesson 1

1. **Correct Answers: A and D**

   A. **Correct:** The *RequiredFieldValidator* is the only validation control that ensures that a user entered a value. The other validation controls will pass validation when no value is present.

   B. **Incorrect:** Although the *RangeValidator* validates within an upper and a lower bound, it will not be sufficient for these requirements. The ISBN designation for the U.S. is a range of numbers; however, there are multiple ranges.

   C. **Incorrect:** The *CompareValidator* compares one control to another or to a constant. This does not help ensure valid input by the user in this instance.

   D. **Correct:** The *CustomValidator* control provides the developer with a structure to create custom client-side and custom server-side code. Due to the complexity of the validation rules surrounding the ISBN, this is an appropriate choice.

2. **Correct Answer: A**

   A. **Correct:** The *RequiredFieldValidator* control is used to ensure that data was entered in a particular input control. Because the library card number is required input, this control contributes to the validation requirements.

   B. **Incorrect:** The *RangeValidator* control validates that input is above a lower boundary, below an upper boundary, or both. There is no requirement listed stating an upper or lower boundary for the library card number; therefore, this control does not contribute to meeting the validation requirements.

   C. **Incorrect:** The *RegularExpressionValidator* control validates that an entry in an input control follows a predefined pattern (regular expression). There is no requirement listed stating a pattern for the library card number; therefore, this control does not contribute to meeting the validation requirements.

    D. **Incorrect:** The *CompareValidator* control compares the entered values against another control or a constant. This control does not contribute to meeting the validation requirements.

3. **Correct Answer: B**

    A. **Incorrect:** Exceptions are expensive regarding performance; therefore, they should not be used for anticipated activities. Invalid input by a user is considered an anticipated activity.

    B. **Correct:** This option provides the best scalability because it is the least expensive in terms of performance. If client-side scripting is available, capturing an error and providing feedback to the user all at the client side is the least expensive. If client-side scripting is not available, validating the user input at the server side and returning feedback is still less expensive than throwing an exception.

    C. **Incorrect:** Logging an error to the event log does not provide feedback to the user entering the data. In addition, the event log does not scale to systems using server farm architecture. Although this example did not mention server farms, it did mention scalability, and a server farm might be called for as the system usage grows.

    D. **Incorrect:** Raising an event requires the event handlers for the event. Also, raising an event does not capture the error at the earliest time possible and has a more expensive performance cost than other options.

Lesson 2

1. **Correct Answer: A**

    A. **Correct:** The *HeaderTemplate* property allows the developer to design a custom UI for the header row of the *Wizard* control.

    B. **Incorrect:** The *HeaderText* property is the caption displayed in the header area.

    C. **Incorrect:** If both the *HeaderText* and *HeaderTemplate* properties are defined, the *HeaderText* property has no effect.

    D. **Incorrect:** The *Wizard* control does not have a *Text* property.

2. **Correct Answer: C**

    A. **Incorrect:** Context-sensitive help provides assistance to the user based on the current state of the system for the user. Examples include tooltips and the *F1* key opening to a section of a help manual.

    B. **Incorrect:** Tooltips provide assistance to the user by displaying text, descriptive in nature, when the mouse hovers over a control. The *WebControl* class (*System.Web.UI.WebControls* namespace) has a *ToolTip* property. Therefore, all controls that inherit from this class also have a *ToolTip* property.

    C. **Correct:** The use of red text as feedback to a user does not meet user assistance standards. Users who are colorblind often cannot discern red text from other colors.

    D. **Incorrect:** JavaScript can be used to display information to the user in the Microsoft Internet Explorer status bar.

3. **Correct Answer: B**

    A. **Incorrect:** When both the *Text* property and the *ErrorMessage* property of a validation control are set, the *Text* property is displayed by the validation control, and the *ErrorMessage* is displayed by the *ValidationSummary* control.

    B. **Correct:** When both the *Text* property and the *ErrorMessage* property of a validation control are set, the *Text* property is displayed by the validation control, and the *ErrorMessage* is displayed by the *ValidationSummary* control.

    C. **Incorrect:** Setting the *Display* property of a validation control to *Dynamic* displays the *Text* property (or the *ErrorMessage* property if it has a value and no value was set for the *Text* property). The *ValidationSummary* control displays the value of the *ErrorMessage* property.

    D. **Incorrect:** Setting the *Display* property of a validation control to *Dynamic* displays the *Text* property (or the *ErrorMessage* property if it has a value and no value was set for the *Text* property). The *ValidationSummary* control displays the value of the *ErrorMessage* property.

Chapter 6: Case Scenario Answers

Case Scenario 1: Providing User Guidance

1. The new *Wizard* control is ideal for this situation.

2. Credit card numbers generally fall into specific formats in that they are all numeric and consist of four groups of four digits each. As such, a *RegularExpressionValidator* control is appropriate. Also, because the credit card number is required, a *RequiredFieldValidator* is necessary.

3. Because the list of options is predefined, a default option is specified, and this field cannot be blank. Therefore, no validation control is required.

Case Scenario 2: Performing User Input Validation

1. *RequiredFieldValidator* controls are clearly required for the password and password confirmation fields. Additionally, a *CompareValidator* control can be used to ensure that the data in both fields is identical. Finally, a *RegularExpression* validator can ensure that the password adheres to corporate security standards for password formatting.

2. The database supporting the application houses the existing user names. Therefore, you can use a *CustomValidator* control. However, you will need to set the *EnableClientScript* property to *False* because the client will not have access to the database. Instead, you must rely on server-side validation only for this field.

3. Phone extensions must be numeric, so a *RegularExpressionValidator* control is appropriate. In addition, you can use a *RangeValidator* control to ensure that the extension provided is valid in the company directory.

Chapter 7: Lesson Review Answers

Lesson 1

1. **Correct Answer: B**
   A. **Incorrect:** This technique allows the student to download the material, which is a direct violation of the requirements.
   B. **Correct:** This is an appropriate technique because the media is streamed to an embedded control. Embedding the control allows you to provide a custom UI, making it extremely difficult for the student to download the material.
   C. **Incorrect:** Even though the media is streamed, the external media player may provide capabilities for saving it. In addition, you don't have the control over the external player that you have over an embedded player.
   D. **Incorrect:** The physical location of the file is mostly irrelevant once it is streamed to the client. Therefore, this option does not change anything from the other options.

2. **Correct Answer: A**
   A. **Correct:** This is a streaming video format. Streaming formats allow playback to begin before the file is completely downloaded.
   B. **Incorrect:** This format is an audio format. Video is a requirement.
   C. **Incorrect:** This format is an audio format. Video is a requirement.
   D. **Incorrect:** This format is a nonstreaming format. Even though it is video, the student will have to download the entire file before playback begins.

3. **Correct Answers: A, C, and D**
   A. **Correct:** The Windows Media Player exposes a COM component as an *ActiveX* control that is actually invoked on the client; therefore, it must be installed on the client.
   B. **Incorrect:** The Windows Media Player is not a server control. The embedded player control is not intrinsically available in the Toolbox.

C. **Correct:** The *<OBJECT>* HTML element instructs the Web browser to invoke an *ActiveX* object. Because the Windows Media Player embedded control is an *ActiveX* object, an *<OBJECT>* element must be used.

D. **Correct:** The *CLASSID* attribute indicates the GUID of the COM class to instantiate. Therefore, it is required to instruct the browser about which class to create in the *ActiveX* control.

Chapter 7: Case Scenario Answers

Case Scenario: Add Instructional Videos to a Web Site

1. Truly, any combination is appropriate. However, in this case, site visitors might want to download the instructions for later use. Therefore, nonstreaming media played back through an external client is most appropriate.

2. Because you will be using Windows Media Player for playback, you can use many different formats. However, because you are using nonstreaming video playback, you should use the Audio Video Interleaved (.avi) format.

Chapter 8: Lesson Review Answers

Lesson 1

1. Correct Answers: B, C, and D

   A. **Incorrect:** Unique identification is the job of primary keys, not foreign keys.

   B. **Correct:** A foreign key indicates a relationship between entities.

   C. **Correct:** A foreign key constrains the use of an entity between parent and child tables in the database.

   D. **Correct:** A foreign key provides a way to specify how deletions and updates are propagated between entities.

2. Correct Answer: B

   A. **Incorrect:** Create, Read, and Delete are required, but Update is also required.

   B. **Correct:** Create, Read, Update, and Delete are required.

   C. **Incorrect:** Create, Update, and Delete are required, but Read is also required.

   D. **Incorrect:** Create, Read, Update, and Delete are required, but Copy is not required.

3.   **Correct Answer: C**
   A.   **Incorrect:** Relationships between objects in the ORM should be foreign keys. Primary keys indicate unique identifiers within a single table.
   B.   **Incorrect:** Relationships between objects in the ORM should be foreign keys. Indexes are for improving performance of lookups in a table, not for defining relationships between tables.
   C.   **Correct:** Relationships between objects in the ORM should be foreign keys.
   D.   **Incorrect:** Relationships between objects in the ORM should be foreign keys. Stored procedures are functional code, not relationships between tables.

Lesson 2

1.   **Correct Answers: A, B, and D**
   A.   **Correct:** Technological risks can be lessened by a component prototype, which will ensure that assumptions made by the design can be achieved.
   B.   **Correct:** If a client requests a prototype, this is reason enough to have a prototype created. A client may be the user of the component or a stakeholder in the project.
   C.   **Incorrect:** You can get agreement on the component interface through the class diagram; a prototype is not required to get that agreement.
   D.   **Correct:** If a prototype of the component is needed to complete a project proof of concept, it is perfectly acceptable to create the prototype.

2.   **Correct Answer: B**
   A.   **Incorrect:** Components that facilitate data access do not belong in the user interface tier.
   B.   **Correct:** Components that facilitate data access should live in the data tier of the architecture.
   C.   **Incorrect:** Even though the component facilitates data access, it does not belong in the database. It belongs in the data tier.

Lesson 3

1.   **Correct Answer: A**
   A.   **Correct:** Initialization data should be passed as part of the construction of an object. There is no benefit in using a multi-phase construction.
   B.   **Incorrect:** Initialization data should be passed as part of the construction of an object. Single-phase construction prevents unexpected work flow patterns. For example, calling the initialization method more than once might produce unexpected results.

    C. **Incorrect:** Initialization data should be passed as part of the construction of an object. There is no benefit in deferring it to property calls after the object is constructed.

    D. **Incorrect:** The best practice is to pass initialization data in the constructor.

2. **Correct Answer: B**

    A. **Incorrect:** The garbage collector will not handle unmanaged resources and will likely leak these resources.

    B. **Correct:** The *IDisposable* interface handles unmanaged resources in a timely manner.

    C. **Incorrect:** Although a *Finalizer* will eventually clean up unmanaged resources, using the *IDisposable* interface is the correct way to handle unmanaged resources.

    D. **Incorrect:** Exposing your unmanaged resources for the client to deal with is not acceptable because not all clients will know how to free the unmanaged resources.

Chapter 8: Case Scenario Answers

Case Scenario 1: Design a Tax Calculation Component

1. Passing me the state is important, but I might need to know about cases in which the customer is outside the country to determine whether we need to calculate the tax.

2. I will give you the effective tax rate for the area in question. You will be responsible for calculating the tax rate against what they are purchasing.

Case Scenario 2: Design a Timing Component

1. I would package this as a simple library component that can be added to each project individually.

2. I would develop this component as a stack-based object (for instance, struct) to ensure that the component does not slow down the system during testing.

Case Scenario 3: Design a Database for an E-Commerce Application

1. The primary key for each table will be an auto-incremented integer value.

2. I will be including a *timestamp* field to make concurrency management easier.

Case Scenario 4: Design a Database for a Company Blog

1. There will be two tables, an Employee table and a BlogEntry table.

2. There will be a foreign key from the BlogEntry table into the Employee table.

Chapter 9: Lesson Review Answers

Lesson 1

1. **Correct Answers: B and C**
    A. **Incorrect:** If you have state in your component, but none of the state supports *IDisposable*, you do not have any unmanaged resources.
    B. **Correct:** The *IDisposable* interface is indicative of an unmanaged resource; therefore, you must release this unmanaged resource in your class.
    C. **Correct:** If you have any unmanaged resources (which could include unmanaged resources that are not wrapped in .NET classes), you should implement the *IDisposable* interface.
    D. **Incorrect:** If the component is stateless, you have no resources and, therefore, no unmanaged resources.

2. **Correct Answers: B and D**
    A. **Incorrect:** Base classes are not used to define naming conventions.
    B. **Correct:** A base class can be used to define a common interface for derived classes.
    C. **Incorrect:** Base classes are not used to hide implementation details from inherited classes.
    D. **Correct:** A base class can be used to create common functionality that is used by inherited classes.

3. **Correct Answer: C**
    A. **Incorrect:** Making all components thread-safe is unnecessary and a waste of effort, both in development time and in performance.
    B. **Incorrect:** Some components need to be thread-safe to allow them to be used safely in multithreaded code.
    C. **Correct:** Adding thread safety is crucial to components that will be used in multithreaded code, but the cost of thread safety is not worth it if the component will not be used from multiple threads.

Lesson 2

1. **Correct Answer: A**
    A. **Correct:** *DataReader* in combination with *Command* are the best performing of all the methodologies.
    B. **Incorrect:** No, *DataReader* in combination with *Command* are the best performing of all the methodologies.

    C. **Incorrect:** No, *DataReader* in combination with *Command* are the best performing of all the methodologies.

    D. **Incorrect:** No, *DataReader* in combination with *Command* are the best performing of all the methodologies.

2. **Correct Answer: D**

    A. **Incorrect:** You should never change the generated code in a typed *DataSet*.

    B. **Incorrect:** You can write custom code in the partial class to add business logic, but you should also use *DataSet* schema to do data validation.

    C. **Incorrect:** The *DataSet* schema is good for data validation, but the business logic should be added to the partial class.

    D. **Correct:** Using a mix of *DataSet* schema and custom code in the partial class will allow you to add business logic and data validation.

3. **Correct Answer: C**

    A. **Incorrect:** *DataReader* in combination with *Command* are the most labor-intensive; therefore, you should be using typed *DataSets* to prototype a project.

    B. **Incorrect:** No, typed *DataSets* will allow you to prototype your project the quickest.

    C. **Correct:** Typed *DataSets* are the quickest way to develop data access and, therefore, should be used for prototyping.

    D. **Incorrect:** Prototyping projects is perfectly acceptable, and using typed *DataSets* to accomplish prototyping is the quickest way to develop data access and, therefore, should be used when prototyping a project.

Lesson 3

1. **Correct Answers: A, C, and D**

    A. **Correct:** Sending a method an invalid argument is an exceptional case and should result in an exception being thrown.

    B. **Incorrect:** Executing a search and finding no results is not exceptional but is a valid result; therefore, you should not throw an exception.

    C. **Correct:** Running out of memory is exceptional and should result in an exception being thrown.

    D. **Correct:** The database not being available is exceptional and should result in an exception being thrown.

2. **Correct Answer: B**

    A. **Incorrect:** You should include contextual information only if it is helpful in correcting exceptional cases. For systemic issues (for instance, *OutOfMemoryException*), just allowing exceptions to propagate without context is acceptable.

      B. **Correct:** You should include contextual information only if it is helpful in correcting exceptional cases. For systemic issues (for instance, *OutOfMemoryException*), just allowing exceptions to propagate without context is acceptable.

  3. **Correct Answers: B and C**

      A. **Incorrect:** Profiling will not ensure that all functional requirements are met.

      B. **Correct:** Profiling can ensure that a component meets performance requirements.

      C. **Correct:** Profiling can be used to find resource leaks.

      D. **Incorrect:** Profiling will not ensure that a component compiles.

Chapter 9: Case Scenario Answers

Case Scenario 1: Choose a Data Access Methodology

1. We should use typed *DataSets* because we need to complete this project very fast, although it may mean that we have to re-engineer part of this project again later; time is the most important factor.

2. Put any business logic in the partial class that can be generated with the typed *DataSet*. Do not put any code in the generated classes.

Case Scenario 2: Locate a Resource Leak

1. We should profile the system in two phases. First, we should use the CLR Profiler to see which components are consuming the most memory. Second, we should instrument the targeted components to see why they are eating up the memory.

2. We can isolate the problem by using a variety of profiling tools, although the CLR Profiler and the Visual Studio Performance Wizard are probably the best tools for the job.

Chapter 10: Lesson Review Answers

Lesson 1

1. **Correct Answer: D**

      A. **Incorrect:** The Friend access type does not make your component accessible to other assemblies. Friend is accessible to the current component and derived components.

      B. **Incorrect:** The Private access type causes your component to be accessible only to the current assembly.

   C. **Incorrect:** You cannot use a less restrictive access modifier on a derived class. Public is less restrictive than the Friend modifier used on the declaration of AcmeCalculator and, therefore, cannot be used.

   D. **Correct:** The base class access level prevents other assemblies from accessing the class; therefore, any class derived from the base class cannot be accessed from other assemblies. The derived class cannot be less restrictive than the base class.

2. **Correct Answer: C**

   A. **Incorrect:** Visual Basic does not permit multiple inheritances. You can inherit from only one class. You can implement multiple interfaces, but all three of these were components, not interfaces.

   B. **Incorrect:** A class that is declared with the *MustInherit* modifier cannot be created; it can be used only as a base class for a derived class.

   C. **Correct:** Classes can inherit from other classes. Classes can also create instances of other classes as long as the appropriate references have been set.

   D. **Incorrect:** A component that has been declared with the *NotInheritable* modifier cannot be used as a base class.

3. **Correct Answer: C**

   A. **Incorrect:** Private methods are *Overridable* by default.

   B. **Incorrect:** Public methods are *NotOverridable* by default.

   C. **Correct:** If you are creating *MustOverride* methods or properties, the class must be inherited.

   D. **Incorrect:** *MustOverride* methods contain only the declaration statement for a Sub, Function, or Property. In addition, there is no *End Sub* or *End Function* statement for methods.

Chapter 10: Case Scenario Answers

Case Scenario 1: Extending a Reusable Component

1. Recipes might be appropriate. However, because there are multiple custom systems that will use the application, it is more appropriate to create a distributed binary component that provides centralized access to the features in the third-party application.

2. You can create a derived class of the class that calculates the interest and overload the interest-calculating method to provide a method signature that accepts appropriate parameters for computing the interest.

Case Scenario 2: Restricting a Reusable Component

1. You can shadow the methods and properties that are not supported. In the shadowed versions, you can throw an exception of type *NotImplementedException*.

2. You can create a class that inherits from the third-party class. You can override the members as required but instead of implementing functionality, you can throw an exception of type *NotImplementedException*.

Chapter 11: Lesson Review Answers

Lesson 1

1. **Correct Answers: B and C**

   A. **Incorrect:** Application logic should be designed in such a way that deploying it to a dedicated application server is a possibility, not a necessity.

   B. **Correct:** The stateless nature of Web applications means that your application logic will be most robust if implemented in a stateless fashion. Also, in Web application scenarios, it is unpredictable when you need to scale out. Designing stateless logic prepares your application for such a move.

   C. **Correct:** Transforming strings or objects to basic .NET types needs to be done in the presentation layer. The application logic layer operates in a strongly typed manner.

   D. **Incorrect:** Application logic can be data-centric or object-oriented.

2. **Correct Answer: A**

   A. **Correct:** Action-driven or state-driven are the two styles of design for your interface.

   B. **Incorrect:** There are only two basic styles: action-driven or state-driven.

3. **Correct Answer: A**

   A. **Correct:** State-driven interfaces have methods that are named very generically. The method will look at the state of the data it receives and choose an appropriate action. In this example, the order could be new or changed, requiring an insert action or a delete action. This is for the application logic to decide.

   B. **Incorrect:** In an action-driven design, there would be multiple methods, for instance, *AddNewOrder* and *UpdateOrder*.

   C. **Incorrect:** A method cannot be both action-driven and state driven.

   D. **Incorrect:** A method is always either state-driven or action-driven.

Lesson 2

1. **Correct Answer: A**
   A. **Correct:** The moment an exception is thrown, the regular program flow is aborted.
   B. **Incorrect:** Regular program flow has been aborted the moment the exception is thrown.

2. **Correct Answer: A**
   A. **Correct:** Even though it might seem that code will never fail, it still might. There are many things outside the scope of the developer that can cause an exception, low memory, insufficient privileges, and so on. When deploying a nonvisual application, always add *try/catch* blocks and log errors.
   B. **Incorrect:** Always anticipate that code might fail and, at the very minimum, log an error when crossing service boundaries.

3. **Correct Answer: B**
   A. **Incorrect:** You should *not* resort to using exceptions for managing the regular flow of your program. Even though only five percent of the orders will be more than $1,000, your program is expected to deal with the situation by design. An *if/else* block would be more suitable and create less performance overhead.
   B. **Correct:** The requirements clearly state that an action is required in either case. Aborting the *Save* method of your application by implementing an exception is not prudent.

4. **Correct Answers: A, B, and C**
   A. **Correct:** To re-create the timeline of when and where things went wrong, it is vital for an exception to have a timestamp.
   B. **Correct:** An exception should give you as much information as possible about why the program flow was aborted. This will help in solving the bug that caused the exception.
   C. **Correct:** The stack trace shows the application flow until the moment of the exception.
   D. **Incorrect:** If the exception occurred in a Web application, you might be able to log the Web page where the error occurred, but a service on the application server might not be privy to this information.

5. **Correct Answer: A**
   A. **Correct:** This name gives a good indication of what failed.
   B. **Incorrect:** This name matches a name already present in the .NET Framework and is, therefore, a poor choice as a name for your custom exception.
   C. **Correct:** This exception does not give any indication of what has failed and is, therefore, a poor choice as a name for your custom exception.

Chapter 11: Case Scenario Answers

Case Scenario 1: Catching and Logging Technical Exceptions

1. You've set up the façade of your service layer to log every technical exception that is being thrown. The event log shows all the exceptions, and this way, the event log shows almost every technical exception.

2. No, the more functional exceptions (functional meaning that it is within the capacity of the user to correct the problem) are recognized because they are of a different type and are not logged in the event log. It is the user, not the system administrator, who needs to deal with these exceptions.

3. No, but if you want to analyze the functional behavior of your application, you could add code to log the functional exception to the database. Make sure to coordinate this with your manager because you're moving into the gray area of logging end-user behavior, and the country that you're in might consider this an invasion of privacy. Be careful of what you do and do not log.

Case Scenario 2: Scaling Out

The best approach is to design your application in layers. The application logic and data access should be as independent of the UI as possible. You could implement this in a separate assembly but, at this point, aim at deploying everything to the Web server. For intranet purposes, that will suffice, and the customer needs it quickly.

When the marketing department begins their project, you'll be able to reuse the application logic and data access and just rewrite the UI. In this scenario, you might want to deploy your application logic on a server other than your Web server.

Chapter 12: Lesson Review Answers

Lesson 1

1. Correct Answers: A and E
   A. **Correct:** The Error level is intended for critical, application-threatening situations—certainly something that operations would like to see immediately.
   B. **Incorrect:** The Warning level is intended to be less critical than an error. Although operations might want to see warnings, they won't want to monitor for them because the number of false positive log entries might obscure serious problems.
   C. **Incorrect:** The Information level is purely for informational messages and should not be directed to the operations monitoring application.

   D. **Incorrect:** Accessing a resource successfully is not something to which operations should be alerted.

   E. **Correct:** If users attempt to access a resource to which they don't have permission, operations should be notified immediately.

2. **Correct Answer: D**

   A. **Incorrect:** The flat file log will be placed on the local (to the Web server) computer. This would make it inaccessible to the development staff, and the VPN restrictions mean that the log cannot be stored on a remote server inside the corporate network.

   B. **Incorrect:** The event log is a local mechanism, meaning that the data is stored locally. Although the Event Viewer does allow for viewing events on remote computers, the VPN doesn't allow the necessary ports to be open.

   C. **Incorrect:** Tracing runs into the same problems as the event log. It is really intended to be a local-only mechanism, and, without any listeners, the information will be of no use to developers.

   D. **Correct:** The database is the only data storage mechanism that works in this environment. The fact that the database is already available through the VPN is pretty much the clinching factor in the argument.

3. **Correct Answer: B**

   A. **Incorrect:** Although impersonation does allow the security context of the request to flow to the request, the creation of the event source requires administrator permissions. There is no guarantee that the first requestor will have administrator rights, which would still result in the exception being thrown.

   B. **Correct:** If you configure the installation process to create the event sources, you can place a requirement so that the installer must have administration rights. Then you can be sure that the event sources are successfully added, and no exceptions would be thrown in the Web application—at least not exceptions that are caused by the event sources being unavailable.

   C. **Incorrect:** Using Windows authentication on the Web site means that any user who accesses the application must be a valid Windows user. It does not mean that the user must have administration privileges, which is a requirement for creating the event sources.

   D. **Incorrect:** The database is the only data storage mechanism that works in this environment. The fact that the database is already available through the VPN is pretty much the conclusive factor in the argument.

Lesson 2

1. **Correct Answers: B and D**

    A. **Incorrect:** The normal path taken by a user involves a successful logon. Because this will be the common event, operations shouldn't be bothered with it and, therefore, it should not be monitored.

    B. **Correct:** Unlike the successful logon, a failed logon is of more interest to the operations staff. In a more sophisticated application, this type of event might not be raised until there have been multiple failed logon attempts from the same source or within a short period of time.

    C. **Incorrect:** In a data-driven application, database access will take place on a frequent basis. The operations group isn't likely to care unless the database access failed.

    D. **Correct:** Whether invalid page requests should be sent to operations depends heavily on how the operations group wants to handle potential security or denial-of-service attacks. For a well-designed system, the number of invalid page requests should be low enough that receiving one is indicative of a potential problem.

    E. **Incorrect:** Although the completion of a sales transaction is an event that someone within the company might want to know about, the operations group isn't that group. Also, using a monitoring infrastructure to provide business-level functionality is not a good idea. There are too many other options that will be better suited for sales completion notification.

Chapter 12: Case Scenario Answers

Case Scenario 1: Instrumenting a Web Application for Monitoring

1. The ability to process usage pattern information will hinge on how easy it is to visualize the large volume of data that could be generated. The conversion of data into a visual format (such as a report) is best accomplished by retrieving information from a data store designed for reporting, which means that the usage log messages should be stored in a database.

2. Still, even though the database might seem like an obvious choice, the "correct" answer is going to be contingent on the tool used to process the data. If performance counters are used, then the Performance snap-in for the MMC might be sufficient. Alternatively, the Microsoft Operations Manager (MOM) can use the same data source. So, when you're faced with this choice, the tools and the capabilities that they bring to the table will ultimately determine the "correct" answer.

The application status information should be made available through a number of counters in the performance monitor. This mechanism allows for monitoring applications (both Web and Windows) through a common repository. The fact that it's common means that third-party tools designed to hook into the performance counter system will be able to interact with the application you're creating in the same manner as does any Windows application.

Case Scenario 2: Instrumenting a Web Application for Logging

1. For tracing information, it might seem that a flat file is the most appropriate choice and, in many situations, it is. However, the application running on a Web farm makes flat files less practical, and multiple requests from the same user can be processed on different servers, making correlation between them difficult at best. Therefore, the tracing information should be stored in a central repository, which, in this case, would be a database.

2. With a Web application, the biggest challenge associated with changing log levels is whether the virtual directory in which the Web application runs is shut down. This happens automatically when the web.config file is saved. When the virtual directory stops running, there are at least two immediate consequences. The first is that any values cached in memory are lost. The second is that any sessions stored in memory are lost.

   To avoid restarting the virtual directory (and thus allow all of the session, caching, and so on to be maintained), the log level configuration element must be defined outside of the web.config file. Now the Web application may not use session variables or caching. Even in that situation, however, when restarting the virtual directory is a nonissue for the Web application, it's possible that the cause of the problem is "fixed" when the virtual directory starts running. So, from a debugging perspective, it's better to keep the log level configuration elements in a separate file.

Chapter 13: Lesson Review Answers

Lesson 1

1. **Correct Answer: B**

   A. **Incorrect**: Prior to ASP.NET 2.0, database connection strings were generally stored in the *appSettings* section, but in 2.0, they are now stored in their own dedicated section, the *connectionStrings* section.

   B. **Correct:** Database connection strings are stored in the *connectionStrings* section.

   C. **Incorrect:** The databases section is not a valid section of the web.config file.

   D. **Incorrect:** The *configSections* section of the web.config file is used to define custom sections.

2. **Correct Answer: D**

   A. **Incorrect:** The *System.Web* namespace does not contain configuration access classes.

   B. **Incorrect:** The *System.Net.Configuration* namespace contains network-related classes for casting types that are retrieved from the web.config file; however, the *System.Net.Configuration* namespace does not contain configuration access classes.

   C. **Incorrect:** The *System.Configuration* namespace contains classes that are largely obsolete in the .NET Framework 2.0.

   D. **Correct:** The *System.Web.Configuration* namespace includes classes for accessing the configuration information stored in the web.config file.

3. **Correct Answer: B**

   A. **Incorrect:** Although you can use SQL Server 2005 Professional Edition to store configuration information, the default provider is the SQL Server 2005 Express Edition data provider.

   B. **Correct:** The default provider is the SQL Server 2005 Express Edition data provider.

   C. **Incorrect:** Configuration information can be stored in XML files; however, you must create a custom provider.

   D. **Incorrect:** Configuration information can be stored in an Oracle database; however, you must create a custom provider.

Chapter 13: Case Scenario Answers

Case Scenario 1: Storing Custom Application Configuration Information

1. Employee security information is typically considered application configuration information and can be stored inside the web.config file. However, it is preferable, and more secure, to store employee security information in a SQL Server 2005 Express database. Furthermore, due to the stated requirement that all employee information be stored in a single table, the web.config file could not easily meet this need. In this scenario, employee security information should be stored in a custom XML file or in a SQL Server 2005 Express database.

2. To continue with the preceding answer, the options for storing employee security information are typically a custom XML file or a SQL Server 2005 Express database. The default ASP.NET 2.0 data provider is for SQL Server 2005; however, a data provider exists for custom XML files, and a custom data provider could always be created by extending the data provider base class. In addition, the table used by the ASP.NET Web

Site Administration Tool to maintain employee security information may contain addi-tional columns, but the base schema should adhere to the schema created by the tool.

Case Scenario 2: Specifying Default Application Configuration Settings

1. If configuration settings must be applied consistently to all ASP.NET applications, the configuration settings could be applied to each application individually in the web.con-fig file for each application. However, the machine.config file is read before the web.con-fig file, and all settings in the machine.config file are applied to all applications. Hence, if configuration settings must be applied to all ASP.NET applications on a computer, the easiest way to apply the settings is to modify the settings in the machine.config file.

2. Custom configuration information can be added to a configuration file using the *<con-figSections>* element. To apply the custom configuration settings to all ASP.NET applica-tions, add the custom sections to the machine.config file.

Chapter 14: Lesson Review Answers

Lesson 1

1. **Correct Answer: D**

   A. **Incorrect:** This approach creates a separate unit testing project for each project in your application. You can then run each test project only individually. This is a valid approach; however, it does not satisfy the ability to run all tests as a group.

   B. **Incorrect:** The .NET unit testing framework requires you to define a test project to house your unit tests. These tests would not be run by the framework.

   C. **Incorrect:** This approach is similar to answer B. The .NET unit testing framework requires that you define a test project to house your unit tests. These tests would not be run by the framework.

   D. **Correct:** This is the correct answer. If you create a single unit testing project for your application, you will be able to easily run all your tests as a group.

2. **Correct Answers: A and C**

   A. **Correct:** The existence of unit tests allows you to make changes to your code with confidence. You can execute the unit test as a smoke test (a quick validation) prior to checking in changes to a build.

   B. **Incorrect:** Unit tests examine units of functionality in your code. Unit tests either pass or fail. They do not simulate or report on performance or load.

    C. **Correct:** Unit tests are very useful to developers trying to work with unfamiliar code. The unit tests serve as code-based documentation on exactly how the code should both work and fail.

    D. **Incorrect:** Unit tests do not work well for the user interface. ASP.NET Web testing is better suited for exercising your Web-based user interface.

3. **Correct Answers: A, B, and C**

    A. **Correct:** Unit tests are primarily used to test middle-tier objects.

    B. **Correct:** You can write unit tests to test Web services in a way similar to how you would test any other method.

    C. **Correct:** Unit tests are great at testing code libraries. This includes libraries that access data.

    D. **Incorrect:** Unit tests are used to test application code. They are not used for testing things like SQL and database table structures or relationships.

4. **Correct Answer: B**

    A. **Incorrect:** A large number of passing tests is only one indication of quality. You must also ensure that those tests are covering the vast majority of the code in the application. For example, tests that pass but cover only 10 percent of the code do not provide an accurate picture of quality.

    B. **Correct:** You want to set a metric for code coverage (typically 70 percent or better). If the test cases for the given build meet or exceed this value, then you can pass the build on to the test team.

    C. **Incorrect:** This is an important statistic. A lot of new code late in a development cycle, for instance, can trigger an alarm. However, this is not an indication of the quality or coverage of your unit tests.

    D. **Incorrect:** This too is an important measure. You want to know how much code has changed from one build to the next. However, this does not indicate if that code has been covered by your unit tests.

5. **Correct Answer: B**

    A. **Incorrect:** A regression test is one that you create to test the entire application. You use regression tests for smoke testing an application after a change is made. The full set of unit tests for your application is the start of a regression test.

    B. **Correct:** This example uses both upper and lower bounds for the given data type (date). In this way, the test ensures that dates within this range should work. It also tests the outer extremes for potential problems. This type of test is called a *bounds check* or boundary testing.

C. **Incorrect:** A manual unit test is simply one that is documented and executed by a developer manually (typically with the debugger and some test harness).

D. **Incorrect:** Code coverage analysis refers to determining the percent of code that is covered by unit tests.

Lesson 2

1. **Correct Answer: D**

   A. **Incorrect:** Web testing is used to verify a Web-based user interface. You can use your Web tests as part of your stress test. However, by themselves, Web tests do not simulate user load or stress.

   B. **Incorrect:** Load testing should be used to understand if the application behaves relative to the target metrics given the intended load. It is not meant to find an application's breaking point by adding stress to the application in the form of additional users.

   C. **Incorrect:** Performance testing helps you find performance issues with your code. It also verifies that the application performs to the required metrics. It is not meant to stress your application to a breaking point.

   D. **Correct:** Stress testing is the process of progressively applying more concurrent users to the site until it no longer performs to expected metrics.

2. **Correct Answers: B and D**

   A. **Incorrect:** Integration testing should be done by testers after the code has been unit tested. Integration tests should also be black box tests.

   B. **Correct:** Integration testing is black box testing. As such, it should define a series of inputs and expected outputs for each test case.

   C. **Incorrect:** Testers should practice continuous integration testing. This reduces risk and cost for the application. After the application is complete, the integration tests should be run through again as a form of system testing.

   D. **Correct:** Integration tests help test the reliability of your application. This can be done through repeatedly executing these tests.

3. **Correct Answers: B and C**

   A. **Incorrect:** A load test should test for expected concurrent load. A stress test can be used to test for potential peaks or spikes in load. It is a good idea to use a stress test to make sure your application can withstand up to 1.5 times the normal load.

   B. **Correct:** You need to set your user access distribution to match the actual anticipated network access.

C. **Correct:** You want to define a test distribution that mimics user interaction with your application.

D. **Incorrect:** There is no distribution defined by a single test. You should define two tests to mimic the way users work with your system.

4. **Correct Answer: D**

A. **Incorrect:** You do not want your Web processors to be overtaxed. However, this metric should be monitored during stress testing and not performance testing.

B. **Incorrect:** The memory use metric is another stress indicator. It does not provide details about Web page performance.

C. **Incorrect:** The requests per second indicate how many requests are coming in to the server, not how pages are performing.

D. **Correct:** The response time represents the average response time for requests. You can drill into this data to determine actual page response times.

5. **Correct Answers: B and C**

A. **Incorrect:** Agents execute your tests. Controllers manage the agents.

B. **Correct:** The test controller tells the agents which tests to run and when to start and stop the tests.

C. **Correct:** Agents send their test data back to the controller. The controller is used to review the aggregated agent results.

D. **Incorrect:** Testers use clients to author and edit tests.

Chapter 14: Case Scenario Answers

Case Scenario 1: Evaluating a Testing Strategy

1. First, the developers will be working independently. Therefore, you should suggest creating a number of separate projects for storing unit tests. In addition, each developer is not concerned about the other developer's code; this is the responsibility of integration testing. Second, you should define a real metric for unit testing inside the test plan. It was suggested in the interviews that at least 75 percent code coverage be enforced. Finally, you should indicate that all unit test code coverage for a build be published to a central server for reporting. The project manager should not rely on word-of-mouth for this information. If you can't publish this data to a server, you need visual verification.

2. Your load test should be created to support at least 295 concurrent users during peak load. You arrive at that figure by multiplying the number of department managers (25) by the number of supervisors who report to them (10), and then adding the department

managers (25) and the VPs (20). Remember, employees will not access the site. This is also your peak load. It is likely that your actual load will never approach this peak. To arrive here, the entire management structure of the company would have to be accessing the site.

You should not define a hard target for stress testing. Rather, you should step the user load in perhaps 10 percent increments until you find a breaking point. You should also confirm that this breaking point exceeds 1.5 times the peak load. This will ensure that the application has some room to scale if new demands are placed on it.

3. The Web tests verify the Web user interface. From this perspective, the tester might prefer to create a single Web test, add to it, and modify it as needed. This gives him or her one test to verify that the entire UI works or doesn't work. However, these Web tests will most likely also be used for defining the load, stress, and performance tests. For these tests, it is important to simulate actual user load based on actual user behavior. In the case scenario, the supervisors work with the application at different levels than, say, the VPs. For example, the VPs would never modify supervisor goals. You should, therefore, suggest that testers create separate Web tests per test case or user activity. This will allow them to distribute these tests across the simulated user load.

4. First, you should suggest that the load test include network distribution as defined by the application support team (95 percent LAN, five percent dial-up and cable modem mix). Next, you ensure that the test team documents an actual user load pattern for the load tests. They need to segment the tests based on how users work. Last, it is important to define the number of concurrent users (see Question 2) and what is meant by concurrent users. For the load tests, concurrent users should be defined as the number of users working with the site. These users are working; they are not all making simultaneous requests. Therefore, you should use standard think times between requests.

5. The testers need to set performance thresholds that should not be exceeded to verify that the load tests succeeded. Some simple thresholds include no rejected requests and no errors. You should also define thresholds for processor and memory usage. For example, you might indicate that the load test should be considered as failed if the processor spikes above 80 percent for longer than 10 seconds. You would define a similar statement relative to memory usage.

6. First, the integration testing does not identify how the integration will be tested at the database level. There need to be tests that confirm that data extracted from multiple systems gets into the database and aggregated correctly. Second, the integration tests should define (or point to) actual test inputs and expected outputs. The tests should be considered as passed only after the results have been compared. Finally, the plan calls for building integration tests from use cases. This is okay; however, there needs to be more work done to identify communication issues and what happens when things fail.

7. First, you should suggest that the test team also flood this quit network with traffic patterns that exist in the real network. This is the only way you can determine how the application will behave on the production network. Second, the database requires more test data. You need to generate data that approximates the database as it will be in production. You should also suggest creating an automated means of initializing the data and cleaning it up before tests are run.

Chapter 15: Lesson Review Answers

Lesson 1

1. **Correct Answer: B**

    A. **Incorrect:** The *TestCleanup* attribute indicates that a method should be run after each test is executed.

    B. **Correct:** The *TestInitialize* attribute indicates that the decorated method should be run before each unit test is run.

    C. **Incorrect:** The *ClassCleanup* attribute indicates that a method should be run once after all tests are executed.

    D. **Incorrect:** The *ClassInitialize* attribute indicates that a method should be run once before all tests are executed.

2. **Correct Answer: D**

    A. **Incorrect:** The *AreEqual* method is used to determine whether two values, not two objects, are equal.

    B. **Incorrect:** The *IsTrue* method checks a Boolean value, not an object. The second parameter is used for writing a message to the test results upon failure.

    C. **Incorrect:** The *IsInstanceOfType* method checks to see whether an object is of a certain type.

    D. **Correct:** This is the correct answer. The *AreSame* method checks to verify that two objects are identical.

3. **Correct Answers: B and D**

    A. **Incorrect:** This method simply returns data from the database. Standard unit tests should cover this method.

    B. **Correct:** This method represents a key transaction in the system. It should, therefore, warrant additional testing.

    C. **Incorrect:** It should be sufficient to test these properties with standard unit tests.

    D. **Correct:** This method has a lot of business logic. In addition, it will be shared by multiple applications. Therefore, you should consider writing additional unit tests for this method.

4. **Correct Answers: B and D**

   A. **Incorrect:** Use cases are meant to flush out requirements. Test cases are typically derived from use cases.

   B. **Correct:** Testers write test cases from use cases.

   C. **Incorrect:** Test cases are written for testers to verify that the system meets the requirements. However, developers can take advantage of test cases to help them write better unit tests.

   D. **Correct:** Test cases are made up of the steps a tester should take, the data he or she should enter, and the results he or she should expect.

5. **Correct Answers: C and D**

   A. **Incorrect:** Test case execution and full integration testing are the responsibility of the test team.

   B. **Incorrect:** Developers need only to make sure their calls to external libraries do not break the interface. Developers should not spend time verifying that the calls actually do what is intended. This is the responsibility of the tester and the author of the external library.

   C. **Correct:** Developers should verify that their code works not just on their computer but also in a simulated version of the test and production environments.

   D. **Correct:** Developers need to identify their dependencies. This includes looking at third-party libraries they might be using and verifying these libraries against the configuration management plan.

Lesson 2

1. **Correct Answers: A, C, and D**

   A. **Correct:** You need to define standards before you can review code against them.

   B. **Incorrect:** You create a standards document and log code review issues. You can also follow a code review checklist.

   C. **Correct:** You need to review code for its adherence to the defined standards.

   D. **Correct:** When you find an issue, you should propose a resolution to fix the issue.

2. **Correct Answers: A and C**

   A. **Correct:** A coding standard defines how developers should structure their code and handle errors.

   B. **Incorrect:** This is an example of an architectural standard.

   C. **Correct:** This represents a coding standard or rule.

   D. **Incorrect:** This is a naming (not coding) standard.

3.   **Correct Answer: D**
   A.   **Incorrect:** You call Extract Interface to define an interface from an existing class.
   B.   **Incorrect:** You call Encapsulate Field to create a property from a field variable.
   C.   **Incorrect:** You call Promote Local Variable to Parameter to move a local variable to a method parameter.
   D.   **Correct:** The Extract Method operation uses the selected code to create a new method.

4.   **Correct Answers: C and D**
   A.   **Incorrect:** The Code Analysis tool analyzes static code only.
   B.   **Incorrect:** You can configure the set of rules you wish to enforce with the Code Analysis tool.
   C.   **Correct:** When you select Run Code Analysis from Visual Studio, the issues are shown as warnings.
   D.   **Correct:** When an issue is shown in the Error List, you can right-click the issue and choose Show Error Help to view a possible resolution for the item.

Lesson 3

1.   **Correct Answer: C**
   A.   **Incorrect:** This change can be either deferred or made. There should be no reason to escalate such a small item to the project stakeholders. In addition, if marketing is part of the decision, you should lean toward accepting this request.
   B.   **Incorrect:** This is a bug. It needs to be fixed. It is preventing testers from completing their test case, but it does not require a decision from the project stakeholders.
   C.   **Correct:** This was a major miss by the team. However, a change this big this late in the project will require a decision from the project stakeholders.
   D.   **Incorrect:** This is a bug with a simple fix. It should be accommodated.

2.   **Correct Answers: A, B, C, and D**
   A.   **Correct:** You should verify that both environments have the same versions of the deployed code.
   B.   **Correct:** You should verify the operating system, its configuration—especially Microsoft IIS—and the .NET Framework setup.
   C.   **Correct:** Security is often the cause of code not working in a different environment.
   D.   **Correct:** You should check that the data being tested against is the same in both environments.

3. **Correct Answers: B and C**

   A. **Incorrect:** You should not create an entire branch just for your fix. Instead, your fix should be released as part of the next planned build.

   B. **Correct:** You should update the deployment plan and release notes to indicate that the bug was fixed and is in the new build. This will help testers know what to expect. It will also help the build team get the right code on the test server.

   C. **Correct:** You need to mark the bug as fixed in the bug tracking software. You might also decide to associate your change set with the work item in Team System.

   D. **Incorrect:** There is no need to clutter the code comments with release and bug information.

Chapter 15: Case Scenario Answers

Case Scenario 1: Defining Unit Tests from a Test Case

1. Consider creating a *ClassInitialize* or *TestInitialize* method to reset the database to the test data prior to running your unit tests.

   The connectivity to the hotel and payment systems represents an integration test. You need to simply verify that you can connect to these interfaces.

2. You can create an ASP.NET unit test to test methods inside an ASP.NET Web site. This will allow you to configure a test for a specific URL. In addition, the test will run inside the ASP.NET host process. This will give you access to the ASP.NET context data.

3. Consider creating a *RegisterEvent* test case that mimics the entire event registration process from a user's perspective. This will enable you to test the entire process without the user interface. Alternatively, you can work with the tester to create a Web test that works the same way. However, this requires a user interface.

4. Consider binding your unit test to the test data. This includes the expected results and will enable you to make certain assertions based on the context of each row in the test data.

5. Add a row in the bound test data to include users who are not already registered in the system. This will cover the first alternate test case. When these users are encountered, verify how your *RegisterEvent* test performs.

   The second and third alternate test cases involve verifying how your code works when third-party systems raise an exception. This is integration testing. However, if you wrote the code to call those methods, you are responsible for making sure they work in all scenarios. Therefore, you should create unit tests for these conditions.

Case Scenario 2: Performing a Code Review

1. Start by defining development standards. You cannot measure code without a target, and developers cannot be held to an undefined standard. Get the team together and start defining what is acceptable. You should also create an architectural standard that describes how you implement database code, objects, services, user elements, and so on.

2. This should not be a peer-to-peer process. The developers are too inexperienced for that to work. Instead, the technical lead or senior developer—you—should handle the code reviews to get started.

3. The code reviews will immediately help by mentoring developers in terms of best practices. In addition, a code review will help find gaps in quality. Finally, code reviews create a no-place-to-hide environment. Code reviews will help identify developers who need additional training.

4. Create a formal code review process. This will help the company keep a close eye on the quality of the code. It will also foster a knowledge base of known issues. Developers can use this repository as a learning tool. Management can use it to certify that the code is being written to standards.

Chapter 16: Lesson Review Answers

Lesson 1

1. **Correct Answer: C**
   A. **Incorrect:** Even though the word flow is used in the diagram's name, this diagram is not intended to track how data flows through the application.
   B. **Incorrect:** At this point, the application design should be very well determined and should not need to be validated with this diagram.
   C. **Correct:** The primary purpose of this diagram is to represent the major components of the application to assist in the process of planning a deployment.
   D. **Incorrect:** Even though this diagram is used toward a deployment, it is not to identify gaps in the logic. That type of analysis should have been performed in earlier development phases.

2. **Correct Answers: A, B, C, and D**
   A. **Correct:** You would want to add the Data Access Layer to the diagram if it exists as a separate project and, thus, is a separate assembly.
   B. **Correct:** You would want to add the Business Access Layer to the diagram and not identify each class or object within the BAL unless there was a reason to install each object separately.

C. **Correct:** You would want to represent any distributed components used, because they will require separate deployment and configuration.

D. **Correct:** You would want to include the Web application in the diagram because it will require a step in the deployment process.

Lesson 2

1. **Correct Answer: B**

    A. **Incorrect:** A Web farm does nothing to help with security. Security is typically handled with firewalls, perimeter networks, and user authentication.

    B. **Correct:** Web farms can help Web applications scale better because, as the load increases, requests can be directed to other servers in the farm.

    C. **Incorrect:** This typically indicates a system that is configurable at run time and is usually handled though application design.

    D. **Incorrect:** This involves the identification of data inconsistency and is typically handled through database settings such as check constraints.

2. **Correct Answers: A, B, and D**

    A. **Correct:** You may have one or more application servers that host components of your application.

    B. **Correct:** Back-end servers are typically used to store databases.

    C. **Incorrect:** For a Web application, it is not necessary to configure an end-user application because the user accesses the application through his or her Web browser.

    D. **Correct:** You may have one or more Web servers to host the presentation layer of your application.

3. **Correct Answer: A**

    A. **Correct:** This method does not require the creation of a Windows account, but it still allows for a secure method of Internet authentication.

    B. **Incorrect:** This method allows any user to access the Web site.

    C. **Incorrect:** Basic authentication does require a user name and password, but it is not a very secure method because this information is not encrypted.

    D. **Incorrect:** This is a secure method of authentication but requires the creation of a Windows account, which can be a problem for a Web site exposed to the public.

Lesson 3

1. **Correct Answers: A, B, C, and D**

    A. **Correct:** Both the lead and members of the development team will need to be involved in the deployment.

      B. **Correct:** A manager or decision maker will need to be involved or available in case important decisions, such as when to back out, need to be made.

      C. **Correct:** In cases in which the application used is internal to your company, having an end user present to evaluate whether the deployment was successful can be helpful.

      D. **Correct:** A network administrator may be needed to allow certain restricted actions to take place.

  2. **Correct Answer: B**

      A. **Incorrect:** Similar to an FTP file copy, this two-paned dialog box just allows you to copy files from one server to another.

      B. **Correct:** A Web setup project provides a way to uninstall and thereby roll back an installation.

      C. **Incorrect:** An XCOPY deployment simply copies files from one location to another.

      D. **Incorrect:** A Web setup project is correct, but Copy Web Site is not.

Chapter 16: Case Scenario Answers

Case Scenario 1: Designing a Plan

You should suggest to your manager that you lead the creation of a deployment as soon as possible. Explain to him how important the deployment plan is to the success of the project.

Explain that you will need to start by gathering and reviewing the design documents used to create the application, and from there, you will create a high-level application component diagram. Once all the major components have been identified, you can determine any special requirements or restrictions that exist in your network environment. You will also identify any dependencies on third-party components. Explain that is important also to identify any special database considerations such as scripting that would need to be performed before or during the deployment.

The end result should be a detailed deployment plan that lists the specific steps needed for a successful deployment at the end of the month.

Case Scenario 2: Using a Web Setup Project

You tell the manager that you plan on creating a Web setup project that will encapsulate all the files needed for deployment. This will include all the tiered components that make up your application along with the .dll files needed to support the application's third-party components.

You also tell the manager that not only will the Web setup project complete all steps needed for deployment, such as creating a virtual directory, but it will also allow you to archive different versions. By archiving the versions, you can roll back to a previous version easily in the case of an unexpected problem.

Chapter 17: Lesson Review Answers

Lesson 1

1. **Correct Answer: B**
   A. **Incorrect:** Typically, a spike is a temporary condition that might happen periodically with all counters without indicating a serious problem.
   B. **Correct:** A performance spike is typically a temporary rise in activity, and it might not indicate a serious problem.
   C. **Incorrect:** Not having enough virtual memory is a condition related to a specific counter and does not apply to spikes for all counters.
   D. **Incorrect:** Access to the database server is a condition that would generally result in application errors and not something that would be detected through performance monitoring.

2. **Correct Answer: D**
   A. **Incorrect:** Performance spikes typically represent an anomaly and not a consistent trend.
   B. **Incorrect:** Even though the spikes were collected for a period of a year, they were not compared against a baseline to determine if they were meaningful.
   C. **Incorrect:** You do need to collect key performance counters over a period of time, but you also need to compare that data against a baseline to determine if it is meaningful.
   D. **Correct:** The collection of key performance monitors that is compared against a baseline is a good method for the analysis of performance trends.

3. **Correct Answer: B**
   A. **Incorrect:** Manually generating an e-mail upon a logon failure is certainly not a quick and easy way of reporting failures.
   B. **Correct:** You can create an alert that sends an e-mail when a certain counter threshold is exceeded or not reached.
   C. **Incorrect:** Although you can set up an alert to execute an executable, it would be easier to just send an e-mail directly, using the alert.

D. **Incorrect:** You can log the failure to a database, but then another process would need to be responsible for notifying the administrator, so this would not be the quickest or easiest option.

Lesson 2

1. **Correct Answers: B and C**

   A. **Incorrect:** You want to look at the % Processor Time related to the processor object, not to the system object.

   B. **Correct:** The % Processor Time counter indicates the percentage of time that the processor instance is spending on requests and can indicate if the CPU is too busy.

   C. **Correct:** The Processor Queue Length counter indicates the number of requests waiting to process, and a high value per processor can indicate a problem.

   D. **Incorrect:** The Processor Queue Length counter belongs to the system object and not to the processor object.

2. **Correct Answer: D**

   A. **Incorrect:** There is no security object.

   B. **Incorrect:** There is no .NET CLR object. There are several objects for the .NET CLR, but they are all named according to their system (that is, .NET CLR *Security*, .NET CLR *Remoting*, and so on).

   C. **Incorrect:** There is no .NET CLR *Logon* object.

   D. **Correct:** The .NET CLR *Security* object contains counters that indicate the level and amount of CLR security processing taking place.

3. **Correct Answer: A**

   A. **Correct:** *Providers* are configured to perform a specific action when an event occurs.

   B. **Incorrect:** *Profiles* are used to set parameters related to events.

   C. **Incorrect:** *Rules* specify which events should be monitored.

   D. **Incorrect:** There is no *Actions* element in the Health Monitoring collection.

Chapter 17: Case Scenario Answers

Case Scenario 1: Diagnosing a Server Problem

Because it is not clear what is causing the problem, it would be useful to begin by running System Monitor on the server(s) hosting the Web application. You can start by logging data for both the periods in which delays have occurred and in which no delays have occurred. The data will be collected for the key performance monitor counters identified in Lesson 1. By comparing the logged data charts for both periods, you should be able to identify discrepancies between the counter values. This will help you identify the root cause of the problem and make a suggestion for a resolution, such as adding more memory to the server.

Case Scenario 2: Implementing Bug Tracking

Because application problems are currently handled manually with e-mails, it would be wise to suggest a more automated method of tracking bugs and assigning responsibility for their resolution. There are several third-party tools that handle bug tracking, but you can also consider designing and implementing a custom application. The application would need to enable help desk employees to enter information about the problem, including the description, the date and time, and the name of the reporting employee. You would also need a way to tie into the database where application exceptions are recorded.

Ideally, it would be best to design a way for the application to route messages automatically to the responsible developers as well as log the information to a bug-tracking database. The developer would then be able to record information about the problem's resolution and use the application to notify the reporting employee of the outcome.

Glossary

abstract class   A class that can be used only as a base class for a derived class. An abstract class cannot be created. The NotInheritable identifier is used with this type of class.

access rule   The combination of a user or role and a permission that is granted or denied.

activity diagram   A diagram that is similar to a UML flow chart. It shows the actions that happen one after another, the decisions that are made to gate those actions, and which actions happen in parallel. An activity diagram is useful for modeling business workflow and complex algorithms.

ADO.NET   ADO (ActiveX Data Objects) refers to Component Services (COM)–era technology. ADO.NET is the natural evolution of this technology into managed code. It can be found in the *System.Data* namespace.

agent   A computer that runs a load, stress, or performance test. A single agent typically runs multiple threads. Each thread runs the full set of tests.

aggregation   An object-oriented concept wherein one object's members are exposed through a containing object.

alerts   The notification of particular events to certain systems and/or individuals.

application library   A set of components that you can use in your solution.

application server   The term for the server software that runs your server code (typically, ASP.NET and the .NET Framework). Internet Information Services (IIS) is an application server.

black box testing   Testing that involves a tester providing input into an application and then reviewing the application's output or behavior against what is expected for the given test. Integration tests and load tests are both examples of black box testing.

bounds check   A test that checks how a unit performs at its parameter's boundaries. A boundary is defined based on expected values for the parameter or by the parameter's data type. Errors often occur at, near, or beyond these boundaries.

buffering   The act of obtaining a predefined amount of a streaming media file before beginning playback. Buffering allows playback to occur more smoothly as future content is obtained while current content is playing.

bugs   Application problems that are seen in the form of errors or missing or incorrect functionality.

Business Access Layer (BAL)   One or more classes that contain all the business logic for the application. Separating the logic into its own set of classes is part of the process to separate the business logic and data access from the user interface.

business domain   A domain that represents the classes that are derived from your logical model or ORM. These classes solve the primary business functions of the application.

business logic   Any functionality added to data access components that aid the business case for a component.

business requirement   A requirement that defines the success factors from the perspective of project stakeholders. A business requirement represents what the business believes to be important for the success of the project.

class diagram   A static representation of the classes, enumerations, structs, and interfaces that make up your code. A class diagram shows associations and inheritance.

client   A technology choice about how an application will be presented to the users.

Clients include browser-based, Windows, console, Office, and others.

codec   An abbreviation for compression/decompression. Software or hardware used to compress and decompress digital media.

code analysis   A tool built into Visual Studio 2005 Team Edition that reviews your source code against a set of rules. These rules define commonly accepted best practices for characteristics such as maintainability, readability, globalization, and performance. Also called static code analysis.

code coverage   A metric that defines the percentage of code that is exercised by a given test (typically a unit test). Code coverage provides a measurable understanding of what portion of a given application's code has been tested.

code review   The process of walking through code to verify it against known standards and best practices. Code reviews are typically done on a peer-to-peer basis.

collaboration diagram   A diagram that illustrates how objects work together to realize a use case. The order of message interaction is shown via numbered messages.

component   This term has a .NET Framework–specific definition and a general-purpose conceptual definition. In the .NET Framework, a component is a class that implements the *System.Component-Model.IComponent* interface or that derives directly or indirectly from a class that implements *IComponent*. In general, a component is a class or object that is reusable and works with other classes or objects.

component diagram   A diagram that shows the components and their relationships (references). It may also show how those components are deployed onto nodes.

compression   A process for removing redundant data from a digital media file or stream to reduce its size or the bandwidth used.

connection string   A semicolon-delimited string composed of settings used to connect to a database.

consumer   Any piece of code or architecture that will consume a component.

content page   A Web page that is configured to be merged with a master page to create a complete page.

content placeholders   Placeholders that refer to regions of a master page wherein data, controls, and other output specific to the content page are placed. A content placeholder uses the *ContentPlaceHolder* control to house the contents. Multiple content placeholders may be applied to a single master page.

continuous integration   A testing strategy that executes test cases as various components are developed and made available. A continuous integration testing strategy will find bugs early in the process where they can be cheaper to fix.

control   A component that provides user interface features. Controls are broken into two classes: Web controls and Microsoft Windows controls.

controller   A computer that is used to control test agents. Controllers start and stop agents. They also aggregate the performance metrics for review.

custom Web server control   A server-side component that encapsulates the UI and related functionality. A custom Web server control is one that you create. Web server controls derive from the *System.Web.UI.Control* class.

Data Access Layer (DAL)   One or more classes that provide an interface to the database. Separating the logic into its own set of classes is part of the process to separate the business logic and data access from the user interface.

data storage   Represents how your application will store and provide access to its data.

database schema   The layout of related data in a database, including rules about how data is stored, related, and constrained.

design pattern A standard solution to a common but specific problem. By applying one or more design patterns when designing your application, your design will be more readable to someone who does not know the problems in your application domain but knows about design patterns.

edge case An alternate path a user might take during a given use case. This path is typically not the common, successful route. Edge cases are important because they represent actions for which you need to test. Also called an alternate use case.

enterprise services A method of building component-based applications using COM+ services. They can take advantage of services such as transactions and object pooling.

exception Represents an error that occurs during application execution.

exception bubbling A term derived from "event bubbling," first used when describing the event mechanism in Internet Explorer. Exception bubbling refers to the process of an exception traveling up through the call stack until a *try/catch* handles the exception.

Extensible Markup Language *See* XML.

flat file The name given to a text in which each line in the file is the equivalent of a record in a database.

foreign key A primary key value from a related table that is used to identify a relationship between the two tables.

framework A set of base classes and components that abstract much of the architectural "plumbing" away from the developer.

functional requirement A requirement that defines a feature from the perspective of a developer. A developer should be able to review the specification or requirement and implement to that specification.

functional specification *See* functional requirement.

granularity The level of detail at which information is required or described.

horizontal prototype *See* mockup.

inheritance The ability to define classes that contain implementations or interfaces that serve as the basis for other classes, called derived classes.

instrumentation Placing code strategically within an application so that information about the status, progress, and problems of the application can be reported to the appropriate audience.

integration test A test that examines individual application components as a single solution. It is meant to confirm that individual units work together as intended. An integration test is built from a test case. The test case defines inputs into the system and expected outputs.

layers The logical division of code in your application to satisfy design goals such as increased reusability. Layers include UI, middle tier, and database.

load test A test to confirm that the application works under the expected load. Load is defined as the simulated distribution of the actual work across a representative set of concurrent users.

log level An indication of the relative severity of the information that is being logged. The log level is frequently used to determine the routing for a log entry.

logging The process of placing information about the status, progress, and problems of anapplication into a persistent data store.

logical design The separation of individual discrete units of work into logical groups for the purpose of designing a system.

machine.config file The primary configuration information file used by the Microsoft .NET Framework 2.0. The machine.config file is analogous to the Microsoft Windows registry.

master pages Pages that define the layout for a set of pages. A master page can contain static text and controls that should appear on all pages. Master pages are merged at run time with content pages that define page-specific content.

medium trust   The set of permissions under which ASP.NET should run, as recommended by the Prescriptive Architecture Group at Microsoft. This level includes restrictions on registry and event log access (among others) and is intended to minimize any damage that might be caused by an intruder.

Microsoft Message Queue services (MSMQ) A set of services that allows applications to queue user requests and communicate asynchronously.

mockup   A set of UI screens that helps verify the application's navigation, requirements, and use cases (also called a UI mockup or horizontal prototype).

monitoring   The real-time (or near real-time) watching of information about the status, progress, and problems of an application.

multiplicity   The definition of the number of objects in a relationship. These can be one-to-one, one-to-many, or many-to-many.

node   A UML representation of a place of deployment. It typically represents a piece of hardware (like a server).

object role modeling (ORM)   The process of creating diagrams that represent real-world concepts and their relationships. An ORM diagram is a logical model of your software.

optimistic   A way of managing multiple changes of data without locking users out of individual pieces of data while the changes are being made. Ordinarily allows data changes to be saved if the data has not changed recently.

performance baseline   Data, gathered from a collection of key performance counters over a specified period of time, that can be compared against recently collected data to identify trends.

performance counter   The physical or software components of a system, such as processors and memory, along with system objects such as application processes and threads.

performance objects   Used to measure the values of specific components on the application server such as processors, disks, memory. Also used to measure system components related to specific software products such as SQL Server and Speech Server.

performance spike   Identified through performance counters, this represents a temporary rise in activity related to an application.

performance test   A test to verify that your site, and the pages in your site, meet the target performance requirements.

pessimistic concurrency   Managing data changes by locking data in a data store to prevent multiple users from changing the same piece of information, resulting in lost changes.

physical design   The separation of individual units of work into their actual real-world counterparts on separate machines, processes, or other design elements.

polymorphism   From Greek, meaning "many forms"; describes the ability to define classes that can be used interchangeably by client code at run time with identically named members having differing implementations.

primary key   A value that is used to uniquely identify a row in a database table.

profiling   Testing code for performance as well as for memory and resource usage.

proof-of-concept prototype   A complete implementation of a feature through the architecture of the system. It looks at the application across the entire stack (UI, services, business objects, and database). It is meant to confirm the technology recommendations and high-level design.

pseudocode   Code that shows a complex algorithm as code-like text. This can be useful for those accustomed to writing or reading code (and not models).

quality-of-service (QOS) requirement   A requirement that defines nonfunctional requirements for the system around things such as performance, scalability, and standards.

quit network   A network that has no additional traffic outside of the test lab traffic.

RAID   Redundant array of independent disks; that can be configured through software or that exists as a hardware device. They are intended to provide redundancy and increased I/O performance.

reference architecture   Similar to a proof-of-concept prototype. It provides a reference implementation across the vertical stack of the application for the development team. It gives the developers a model on just how they should implement their code.

regular expression   A pattern that describes the format of a string—for example, an e-mail address or a nine-digit ZIP code.

Remoting   Distributed technology that lets you efficiently call objects residing on different computers as if they belonged to the same application.

rig   The term applied to test-lab hardware (agents and controllers).

role   A method of grouping or categorizing users for the purpose of managing permissions.

sequence diagram   A diagram that illustrates the sequence of messages that collaborate between objects to realize a use case. A sequence diagram illustrates a message flow from left-to-right and top-down.

shadow   The ability to hide and replace an implementation in a base class with that of a derived class.

skin file   A file containing one or more control properties that define how the control should look. Skin files are part of ASP.NET themes.

state (or application state)   Represents the data for an application. State moves between the layers of your system (from the user to the database and back).

stateless   Being able to perform work without storing data at the component level.

streaming   A method of delivering digital media across a network in a continuous flow. The digital media is played by client software as it is received. Typically, streaming makes it unnecessary for users to download a file before playing it.

stress test   Testing to determine how an application behaves under extreme load. Stress testing can often find breaking points in your application.

test case   A test case is a set of tasks a tester executes to satisfy a user requirement or use case. The test case should define steps a tester should take, the input for the test, and the expected results. Test cases are written by testers and can usually be derived from the use cases. They are used for creating Web, load, and integration tests.

test-driven development   The process of creating tests prior to writing code. In test-driven development, developers write the tests first and then write code to satisfy those tests.

test plan   A document that defines the strategy and approach that will be used to verify the application from multiple angles. A test plan is created by the test manager and should include details on all aspects of software testing.

themes   In ASP.NET, a collection of control properties, style sheets, and images that can be applied as a unit to a page or Web site to define an overall appearance.

think times   The term "think times" represents the duration a user spends "thinking" between their application requests. Users have to read a screen, make decisions, and enter data. You want to simulate this time in order to simulate real user load during testing.

third-party control   A control that is not created or maintained by the project team. Developers use these controls to shorten the schedule length and reduce risk. A third-party control can be something embedded in the Visual Studio Toolbox and used on a Web form, or it could be an entire application such as Microsoft BizTalk Server or Commerce Server.

thread-safe   Being able to use data simultaneously from multiple threads without data corruption.

UML   Unified Modeling Language: an object-modeling and specification language used in software engineering.

Unified Modeling Language (UML)   The standard way of representing objects within diagrams.

unit test   A test that isolates a portion of an application and tests all conditions of that unit. Unit tests are most effective when written as code and automated via a unit test framework (such as the one built into Visual Studio 2005).

use case   A description of tasks centered on a common user goal. Use cases are typically written by a business analyst. An example of a use case might be the set of tasks a user follows to rent a video or buy a product. Also called a user scenario.

user   A defined profile for accessing resources.

user control   A composite control to which existing Web server controls are added for embedding as a whole in Web pages, where they act as a unit.

user requirements   A requirement that defines a task the users must be able to accomplish to meet the objectives of their jobs.

validation   Verification that input provided by the user meets certain requirements. Examples include numeric, field length, range of values, and valid dates.

vertical prototype   *See* proof-of-concept prototype.

virtual directory   A component of Internet Information Services, this is the name that appears in the browser URL window. The directory, where the actual files remain, does not have to be named the same.

web.config file   The configuration information file used to store configuration settings for ASP.NET Web applications.

Web Parts   A general term referring to all of the controls that work together to expose Web Parts functionality, providing customization and personalization.

Web services   Distributed technology that lets you expose data to remote clients over the Internet.

Web test   A test created to test the application's user interface. Visual Studio Team Test supports the recording of Web tests and the seeding of data into the Web test parameters.

white box testing   Tests that have visibility into the application's code. Developers do white box testing.

Windows Event Log   The name for the central repository of log entries as reported by the various system components and applications.

Windows Media file   A file that contains audio, video, or script data. The content of the file is encoded with one of the Windows Media codecs.

Windows Performance Monitor   The Windows application that is included with the operating system to allow for the monitoring of various counters about the system and the applications that are running.

wizard   A form of user assistance that automates a task through a dialog box with the user.

XML   A markup language used to define data and governed by the World Wide Web Consortium (W3C).

Index

Get Ready. Get Set.
Get Certified.

MeasureUp™ is your one-stop certification destination.

Get to the finish line with MeasureUp! You've experienced a portion of what MeasureUp practice test questions can do to help you get ready for your certification exam. **Take advantage of the full features of the practice test and you'll be ready, guaranteed!**

- Online MCSE hands-on performance-based simulations
- Objectives thoroughly covered in questions similar to the exam
- Study mode gives detailed answer explanations
- Certification mode prepares you for exam taking conditions

Start your race for certification. Purchase your complete practice test at www.measureup.com today!

Test Pass Guarantee:

MeasureUp practice tests are the closest you can get to the actual exam. Use our complete practice test to prepare and you'll pass. **We guarantee it!**

www.measureup.com

MeasureUp is a Dice Company. ©2006 MeasureUp, Inc.

Additional Resources for Web Developers
Published and Forthcoming Titles from Microsoft Press

Microsoft® Visual Web Developer™ 2005 Express Edition: Build a Web Site Now!
Jim Buyens • ISBN 0-7356-2212-4

With this lively, eye-opening, and hands-on book, all you need is a computer and the desire to learn how to create Web pages now using Visual Web Developer Express Edition! Featuring a full working edition of the software, this fun and highly visual guide walks you through a complete Web page project from set-up to launch. You'll get an introduction to the Microsoft Visual Studio® environment and learn how to put the light-weight, easy-to-use tools in Visual Web Developer Express to work right away—building your first, dynamic Web pages with Microsoft ASP.NET 2.0. You'll get expert tips, coaching, and visual examples at each step of the way, along with pointers to additional learning resources.

Microsoft ASP.NET 2.0 Programming
Step by Step
George Shepherd • ISBN 0-7356-2201-9

With dramatic improvements in performance, productivity, and security features, Visual Studio 2005 and ASP.NET 2.0 deliver a simplified, high-performance, and powerful Web development experience. ASP.NET 2.0 features a new set of controls and infrastructure that simplify Web-based data access and include functionality that facilitates code reuse, visual consistency, and aesthetic appeal. Now you can teach yourself the essentials of working with ASP.NET 2.0 in the Visual Studio environment—one step at a time. With *Step by Step*, you work at your own pace through hands-on, learn-by-doing exercises. Whether you're a beginning programmer or new to this version of the technology, you'll understand the core capabilities and fundamental techniques for ASP.NET 2.0. Each chapter puts you to work, showing you how, when, and why to use specific features of the ASP.NET 2.0 rapid application development environment and guiding you as you create actual components and working applications for the Web, including advanced features such as personalization.

Programming Microsoft ASP.NET 2.0
Core Reference
Dino Esposito • ISBN 0-7356-2176-4

Delve into the core topics for ASP.NET 2.0 programming, mastering the essential skills and capabilities needed to build high-performance Web applications successfully. Well-known ASP.NET author Dino Esposito deftly builds your expertise with Web forms, Visual Studio, core controls, master pages, data access, data binding, state management, security services, and other must-know topics—combining definitive reference with practical, hands-on programming instruction. Packed with expert guidance and pragmatic examples, this *Core Reference* delivers the key resources that you need to develop professional-level Web programming skills.

Programming Microsoft ASP.NET 2.0
Applications: *Advanced Topics*
Dino Esposito • ISBN 0-7356-2177-2

Master advanced topics in ASP.NET 2.0 programming—gaining the essential insights and in-depth understanding that you need to build sophisticated, highly functional Web applications successfully. Topics include Web forms, Visual Studio 2005, core controls, master pages, data access, data binding, state management, and security considerations. Developers often discover that the more they use ASP.NET, the more they need to know. With expert guidance from ASP.NET authority Dino Esposito, you get the in-depth, comprehensive information that leads to full mastery of the technology.

Programming Microsoft Windows® Forms
Charles Petzold • ISBN 0-7356-2153-5

Programming Microsoft Web Forms
Douglas J. Reilly • ISBN 0-7356-2179-9

CLR via C++
Jeffrey Richter with Stanley B. Lippman
ISBN 0-7356-2248-5

Debugging, Tuning, and Testing Microsoft .NET 2.0 Applications
John Robbins • ISBN 0-7356-2202-7

CLR via C#, Second Edition
Jeffrey Richter • ISBN 0-7356-2163-2

For more information about Microsoft Press® books and other learning products,
visit: **www.microsoft.com/books** *and* **www.microsoft.com/learning**

Microsoft Press products are available worldwide wherever quality computer books are sold. For more information, contact your book or computer retailer, software reseller, or local Microsoft Sales Office, or visit our Web site at **www.microsoft.com/mspress**. To locate your nearest source for Microsoft Press products, or to order directly, call 1-800-MSPRESS in the United States. (In Canada, call **1-800-268-2222**.)

Additional Resources for Developers: Advanced Topics and Best Practices
Published and Forthcoming Titles from Microsoft Press

Code Complete, Second Edition
Steve McConnell • ISBN 0-7356-1967-0

For more than a decade, Steve McConnell, one of the premier authors and voices in the software community, has helped change the way developers write code—and produce better software. Now his classic book, *Code Complete*, has been fully updated and revised with best practices in the art and science of constructing software. Topics include design, applying good techniques to construction, eliminating errors, planning, managing construction activities, and relating personal character to superior software. This new edition features fully updated information on programming techniques, including the emergence of Web-style programming, and integrated coverage of object-oriented design. You'll also find new code examples—both good and bad—in C++, Microsoft® Visual Basic®, C#, and Java, although the focus is squarely on techniques and practices.

More About Software Requirements: Thorny Issues and Practical Advice
Karl E. Wiegers • ISBN 0-7356-2267-1

Have you ever delivered software that satisfied all of the project specifications, but failed to meet any of the customers expectations? Without formal, verifiable requirements—and a system for managing them—the result is often a gap between what developers think they're supposed to build and what customers think they're going to get. Too often, lessons about software requirements engineering processes are formal or academic, and not of value to real-world, professional development teams. In this follow-up guide to *Software Requirements*, Second Edition, you will discover even more practical techniques for gathering and managing software requirements that help you deliver software that meets project and customer specifications. Succinct and immediately useful, this book is a must-have for developers and architects.

Software Estimation: Demystifying the Black Art
Steve McConnell • ISBN 0-7356-0535-1

Often referred to as the "black art" because of its complexity and uncertainty, software estimation is not as hard or mysterious as people think. However, the art of how to create effective cost and schedule estimates has not been very well publicized. *Software Estimation* provides a proven set of procedures and heuristics that software developers, technical leads, and project managers can apply to their projects. Instead of arcane treatises and rigid modeling techniques, award-winning author Steve McConnell gives practical guidance to help organizations achieve basic estimation proficiency and lay the groundwork to continue improving project cost estimates. This book does not avoid the more complex mathematical estimation approaches, but the non-mathematical reader will find plenty of useful guidelines without getting bogged down in complex formulas.

Debugging, Tuning, and Testing Microsoft .NET 2.0 Applications
John Robbins • ISBN 0-7356-2202-7

Making an application the best it can be has long been a time-consuming task best accomplished with specialized and costly tools. With Microsoft Visual Studio® 2005, developers have available a new range of built-in functionality that enables them to debug their code quickly and efficiently, tune it to optimum performance, and test applications to ensure compatibility and trouble-free operation. In this accessible and hands-on book, debugging expert John Robbins shows developers how to use the tools and functions in Visual Studio to their full advantage to ensure high-quality applications.

The Security Development Lifecycle
Michael Howard and Steve Lipner • ISBN 0-7356-2214-0

Adapted from Microsoft's standard development process, the Security Development Lifecycle (SDL) is a methodology that helps reduce the number of security defects in code at every stage of the development process, from design to release. This book details each stage of the SDL methodology and discusses its implementation across a range of Microsoft software, including Microsoft Windows Server™ 2003, Microsoft SQL Server™ 2000 Service Pack 3, and Microsoft Exchange Server 2003 Service Pack 1, to help measurably improve security features. You get direct access to insights from Microsoft's security team and lessons that are applicable to software development processes worldwide, whether on a small-scale or a large-scale. This book includes a CD featuring videos of developer training classes.

Software Requirements, Second Edition
Karl E. Wiegers • ISBN 0-7356-1879-8

Writing Secure Code, Second Edition
Michael Howard and David LeBlanc • ISBN 0-7356-1722-8

CLR via C#, Second Edition
Jeffrey Richter • ISBN 0-7356-2163-2

For more information about Microsoft Press® books and other learning products, visit: **www.microsoft.com/mspress** *and* **www.microsoft.com/learning**

Microsoft Press products are available worldwide wherever quality computer books are sold. For more information, contact your book or computer retailer, software reseller, or local Microsoft Sales Office, or visit our Web site at **www.microsoft.com/mspress**. To locate your nearest source for Microsoft Press products, or to order directly, call 1-800-MSPRESS in the United States. (In Canada, call **1-800-268-2222**.)

Additional SQL Server Resources for Developers

Published and Forthcoming Titles from Microsoft Press

Microsoft® SQL Server™ 2005 Express Edition
Step by Step
Jackie Goldstein • ISBN 0-7356-2184-5

Teach yourself how to get database projects up and running quickly with SQL Server Express Edition—a free, easy-to-use database product that is based on SQL Server 2005 technology. It's designed for building simple, dynamic applications, with all the rich functionality of the SQL Server database engine and using the same data access APIs, such as Microsoft ADO.NET, SQL Native Client, and T-SQL. Whether you're new to database programming or new to SQL Server, you'll learn how, when, and why to use specific features of this simple but powerful database development environment. Each chapter puts you to work, building your knowledge of core capabilities and guiding you as you create actual components and working applications.

Microsoft SQL Server 2005 Programming
Step by Step
Fernando Guerrero • ISBN 0-7356-2207-8

SQL Server 2005 is Microsoft's next-generation data management and analysis solution that delivers enhanced scalability, availability, and security features to enterprise data and analytical applications while making them easier to create, deploy, and manage. Now you can teach yourself how to design, build, test, deploy, and maintain SQL Server databases—one step at a time. Instead of merely focusing on describing new features, this book shows new database programmers and administrators how to use specific features within typical business scenarios. Each chapter provides a highly practical learning experience that demonstrates how to build database solutions to solve common business problems.

Microsoft SQL Server 2005 Analysis Services
Step by Step
Hitachi Consulting Services • ISBN 0-7356-2199-3

One of the key features of SQL Server 2005 is SQL Server Analysis Services—Microsoft's customizable analysis solution for business data modeling and interpretation. Just compare SQL Server Analysis Services to its competition to understand the great value of its enhanced features. One of the keys to harnessing the full functionality of SQL Server will be leveraging Analysis Services for the powerful tool that it is—including creating a cube, and deploying, customizing, and extending the basic calculations. This step-by-step tutorial discusses how to get started, how to build scalable analytical applications, and how to use and administer advanced features. Interactivity (enhanced in SQL Server 2005), data translation, and security are also covered in detail.

Microsoft SQL Server 2005 Reporting Services
Step by Step
Hitachi Consulting Services • ISBN 0-7356-2250-7

SQL Server Reporting Services (SRS) is Microsoft's customizable reporting solution for business data analysis. It is one of the key value features of SQL Server 2005: functionality more advanced and much less expensive than its competition. SRS is powerful, so an understanding of how to architect a report, as well as how to install and program SRS, is key to harnessing the full functionality of SQL Server. This procedural tutorial shows how to use the Report Project Wizard, how to think about and access data, and how to build queries. It also walks through the creation of charts and visual layouts for maximum visual understanding of data analysis. Interactivity (enhanced in SQL Server 2005) and security are also covered in detail.

Programming Microsoft SQL Server 2005
Andrew J. Brust, Stephen Forte, and William H. Zack
ISBN 0-7356-1923-9

This thorough, hands-on reference for developers and database administrators teaches the basics of programming custom applications with SQL Server 2005. You will learn the fundamentals of creating database applications—including coverage of T-SQL, Microsoft .NET Framework, and Microsoft ADO.NET. In addition to practical guidance on database architecture and design, application development, and reporting and data analysis, this essential reference guide covers performance, tuning, and availability of SQL Server 2005.

Inside Microsoft SQL Server 2005:
The Storage Engine
Kalen Delaney • ISBN 0-7356-2105-5

Inside Microsoft SQL Server 2005:
T-SQL Programming
Itzik Ben-Gan • ISBN 0-7356-2197-7

Inside Microsoft SQL Server 2005:
Query Processing and Optimization
Kalen Delaney • ISBN 0-7356-2196-9

Programming Microsoft ADO.NET 2.0 Core Reference
David Sceppa • ISBN 0-7356-2206-X

For more information about Microsoft Press® books and other learning products,
visit: **www.microsoft.com/mspress** *and* **www.microsoft.com/learning**

Microsoft
Press

Microsoft Press products are available worldwide wherever quality computer books are sold. For more information, contact your book or computer retailer, software reseller, or local Microsoft Sales Office, or visit our Web site at **www.microsoft.com/mspress**. To locate your nearest source for Microsoft Press products, or to order directly, call 1-800-MSPRESS in the United States. (In Canada, call **1-800-268-2222**.)

System Requirements

We recommend that you use a computer that is not your primary workstation to do the lab exercises in this book because you will make changes to the operating system and application configuration.

Hardware Requirements

The following hardware is required to complete the lab exercises:

- Computer with a 600-MHz or faster processor (1 GHz recommended)
- 192 MB of RAM or more (512 MB recommended)
- 2 GB of available hard disk space
- DVD-ROM drive
- 1,024 x 768 or higher resolution display with 256 colors
- Keyboard and Microsoft mouse or compatible pointing device

Software Requirements

The following software is required to complete the practice exercises:

- One of the following operating systems:
    - Microsoft Windows 2000 with Service Pack 4
    - Windows XP with Service Pack 2
    - Windows XP Professional, x64 Editions (WOW)
    - Windows Server 2003 with Service Pack 1
    - Windows Server 2003, x64 Editions (WOW)
    - Windows Server 2003 R2
    - Windows Server 2003 R2, x64 Editions (WOW)
    - Windows Vista
- Visual Studio 2005 (A 90-day evaluation edition of Visual Studio 2005 Professional Edition is included on DVD with this book.)
- Microsoft SQL Server 2005 Express Edition running on your computer. (This can be installed as part of Visual Studio.)

IMPORTANT Evaluation edition is not the full retail product

The 90-day evaluation edition of Microsoft Visual Studio 2005 Professional Edition provided with this training kit is not the full retail product and is provided only for the purposes of training and evaluation. Microsoft and Microsoft Technical Support do not support this evaluation edition.

Information about any issues relating to the use of this evaluation edition with this training kit is posted to the Support section of the Microsoft Press Web site (*www.microsoft.com/learning/support /books/*). For information about ordering the full version of any Microsoft software, please call Microsoft Sales at (800) 426-9400 or visit www.microsoft.com.

IMPORTANT Visual Studio Team Suite

To complete the lab exercises for Chapter 15, Lesson 1, you will need to have Microsoft Visual Studio 2005 Team Edition for Software Developers installed on your computer. This is available as part of Visual Studio 2005 Team Suite. You can download a free 180-day trial version of Visual Studio 2005 Team Suite from http://www.microsoft.com/downloads/details.aspx?FamilyId=5677DDC4-5035-401F-95C3-CC6F46F6D8F7&displaylang=en. You will need to uninstall Visual Studio 2005 Professional to install Visual Studio Team Suite on the same computer.

To complete the lab exercises for Chapter 15, Lesson 1, you will need:

- 256 MB of RAM or more
- 3.3 GB available disk space to download Visual Studio Team Suite
- 2 GB available disk space to install Visual Studio Team Suite
- One of the following operating systems:
    - Microsoft Windows 2000 with Service Pack 4
    - Windows XP with Service Pack 2
    - Windows Server 2003 with Service Pack 1
        - Microsoft Windows 2000 with Service Pack 4
        - Windows XP with Service Pack 2
        - Windows Server 2003 with Service Pack 1
        - Windows Vista

What do you think of this book?

We want to hear from you!

Do you have a few minutes to participate in a brief online survey?

Microsoft is interested in hearing your feedback so we can continually improve our books and learning resources for you.

To participate in our survey, please visit:

www.microsoft.com/learning/booksurvey/

...and enter this book's ISBN-10 number (appears above barcode on back cover*).
As a thank-you to survey participants in the United States and Canada, each month we'll randomly select five respondents to win one of five $100 gift certificates from a leading online merchant. At the conclusion of the survey, you can enter the drawing by providing your e-mail address, which will be used for prize notification only.

Thanks in advance for your input. Your opinion counts!

* Where to find the ISBN-10 on back cover

Example only. Each book has unique ISBN.

Microsoft
Press

No purchase necessary. Void where prohibited. Open only to residents of the 50 United States (includes District of Columbia) and Canada (void in Quebec). For official rules and entry dates see:

www.microsoft.com/learning/booksurvey/

Save 15%

on your Microsoft® Certification exam fee

Present this discount voucher to any of 5,000 testing centers worldwide for 15% off one Microsoft Certification exam fee. Or, use the discount code on the voucher to register online or via phone with the Microsoft Certified Exam Provider of your choice.

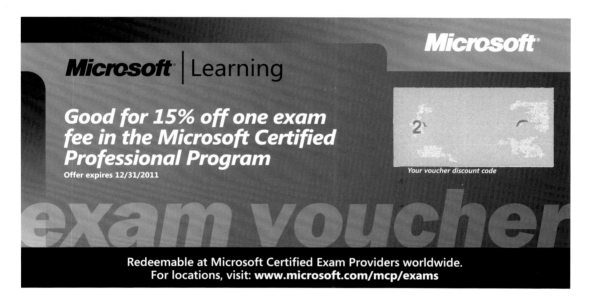

Microsoft | Learning

Good for 15% off one exam fee in the Microsoft Certified Professional Program
Offer expires 12/31/2011

Microsoft®

2

Your voucher discount code

exam voucher

Redeemable at Microsoft Certified Exam Providers worldwide.
For locations, visit: www.microsoft.com/mcp/exams

Promotion Terms and Conditions:

- Offer good for 15% off one exam fee in the Microsoft Certified Professional Program.
- Voucher code can be redeemed online or at Microsoft Certified Exam Providers worldwide.
- Exam purchased using this voucher code must be taken on or before December 31, 2011.
- Inform your Microsoft Certified Exam Provider that you want to use the voucher discount code at the time you register for the exam.

Voucher Terms and Conditions

- Expired vouchers will not be replaced.
- Each voucher code may only be used for one exam and must be presented at time of registration.
- This voucher may not be combined with other vouchers or discounts.
- This voucher is nontransferable and is void if altered or revised in any way.
- It may not be sold or redeemed for cash, credit, or refund.

© 2006 Microsoft Corporation. All rights reserved.
Microsoft is a registered trademark of Microsoft Corporation in the United States and/or other countries.

X12-41824